A History of
English Christianity
1920—1990

A HISTORY OF
ENGLISH
CHRISTIANITY

1920–1990

Adrian Hastings

SCM PRESS
London

This third edition first published 1991.
Previous editions were published under the title
A History of English Christianity 1920–1985
by William Collins and Sons, Ltd., London,
in 1986 and 1987.

SCM Press
9–17 St Albans Place
London N1 0NX

British Library Cataloguing in Publication Data

Hastings, Adrian
A history of English Christianity 1920–1990.
1. England. Christian church, history
I. Title   II. Hastings, Adrian. *History of English
Christianity 1920–1985*
274.2082

ISBN 0-334-02496-X

Third impression 1998

Printed and bound in Great Britain by
Mackays of Chatham PLC, Chatham, Kent

CONTENTS

ACKNOWLEDGEMENTS

The author and publisher acknowledge with
thanks material quoted in this volume, which
is acknowledged either in the text or in notes
at the end of the book.

For Ann
for Barbara
and for my mother

PREFACE

I have been writing this book for the last seven years. It began in Aberdeen. At times I have felt it was simply growing, like a tree almost independently of its planter, themes emerging of themselves while others never quite matured in the way I had anticipated. It provides in intention as objective a history as I could manage of what retains a wide public significance within the modern evolution of Christianity in England. The selection of 1920 as starting date was very deliberate. The end of the First World War appears by far the most appropriate point at which to commence a history of our own time, but the attempt to make that point a comprehensible one within ecclesiastical history forced me in the opening chapter so to sketch in the Edwardian background – and some earlier things too – as to make of the book effectively a history of the English Church in the twentieth century: some sort of sequel, if that is not too bold a claim, to Sir Owen Chadwick's *The Victorian Church*. Indeed the intention to provide such a sequel was part of the plan proposed to me from the start. The story closes at the date I ceased writing – June 1985 – but I have not attempted to portray or analyse developments of the 1980s in any detail or with great conviction. It is too early to do so.

It could appear that there has been something of a long standing conspiracy to over-secularize English history, the public character and sources of inspiration of society, to draw a veil of silence over the Church, at least from 1689. If it is remarkable how little historians of the 18th and 19th century mostly bother to say about the weight of religion, that of the Church of England especially, for the 20th century they have been almost wholly silent except for the occasional caricaturing aside. Neither Randall Davidson nor William Temple receive mention in Taylor's *English History 1914–1945* or Medlicott's *Contemporary England 1914–1964*.

This book is offered in part as a temperate piece of revisionism.

The enterprise has been necessarily conditioned by three very important factors. The first was a quantitative limitation – the desirability of restraining the length to that of a workable single volume. This has required a rather firm hand throughout and the exclusion of many fascinating things. The second is that the book is based overwhelmingly upon secondary material, on what has been published to date, and there are here many notable gaps which will, doubtless, be filled in coming years. The third is that the book depends unblushingly upon my own view of things – a personal judgment as to what really matters and why it matters. All good history must rise above the neutrality of unweighed objectivity in having behind it the largely unformulated standard of values of a particular historian. This book, whether good history or not, certainly has. The preferences are fairly clear. I trust that they are wide enough and defensible enough not to be mere prejudices. Furthermore I have become well aware of the problems inevitable in attempting so large an enterprise within contemporary history and – working for three of these years in Zimbabwe – I have told myself often enough of the folly of proceeding with it, a folly which others too have pointed out to me. But I am glad to have persevered and can now only offer it to a public, thousands of whose members must certainly know a great deal more about one side or another of the story than I do. I have to hope that, whatever the failings of some of the parts, the enterprise is justified precisely in its wholeness and that the book will be found sufficiently faithful to the infinitely more complex reality it attempts to portray, and sufficiently stimulating to its readers, to prove worth the sustained effort it has involved.

I would not have started it in the first place had it not been suggested in January 1978 by Canon David Edwards, then of Westminster Abbey, now Provost of Southwark Cathedral. To him my first word of thanks should go, and to Lady Collins who accepted the plan on his advice. Professor Donald and Lois MacKinnon read a first draft of Parts I and II several years ago. Their comments were immensely helpful. Later Ian Hamnett read the first three parts, Paul Gifford Part VI, Canon Martin and Ruth Reardon the whole book. I owe a great deal to the suggestions they have all made, and to discussion with colleagues both in Aberdeen and in Zimbabwe. Ann, my wife, has both typed various parts of the book and corrected much of its English. My mother retyped many sections some years ago and still this year, at the age of eighty-seven, has written in the final revisions upon the top copy in her incomparable hand. Without her hospitality and that of my sister Barbara in Oxford on visits from Zimbabwe and during six months of this year, the book would not now be complete. No printed word of thanks is remotely adequate for the help and care I have received at 186 Iffley Road.

Zimbabwe was a lovely place to live but it was not the best place in which to write this particular book. I wish to acknowledge most gratefully grants from the Research Board of the University of Zimbabwe both for visiting Britain and for typing. I am very grateful to my several typists, to Mrs Flora Angus in Aberdeen, Mrs Mafaidah Mwenye in Harare, Mrs Anne Robinson in Oxford, but especially to Mrs Mary-Ann Sheehy who retyped most of the book in 1984 in Gaberone. It is nice that one's book should be in some sense a common enterprise which could never have been completed without the encouragement and co-operation of many friends but, of course, its defects are all, and only, my own responsibility.

I have taken advantage of the publication of a paperback edition to correct a number of small errors and also to rewrite a couple of longer passages in Part VII. I am most grateful to all who have written to me pointing out mistakes, in particular Professor Sir Owen Chadwick, the Ven. Francis House, Mr Alistair Mason, the Revd Dr A. F. Munden, Bishop Lesslie Newbigin, Professor K. G. Robbins, Canon Eric Saxon, Bishop Oliver Tomkins, the Revd J. M. Turner, Dr Gavin White, Canon Alan Wilkinson, Dr R. W. Wilkinson and my sister Cecily Bennett.

21 July 1987   ADRIAN HASTINGS

PREFACE TO THE
THIRD EDITION

The first edition of this history was entitled '1920–1985' because I completed it in 1985 and could go no further. It was published by Collins in 1986. Some fairly small changes were included in the paperback edition of 1987. For this third edition, published by SCM Press and Trinity Press International, it has seemed right to add at the beginning a new chapter carrying the story on to 1990, which looks like a far better ending date than 1985. It has enabled me to consider the 1980s as a whole and even the entire period 1920–1990. I have otherwise, however, made no alterations to the text. It is too difficult to tamper effectively with one's judgements of five years ago.

17 October 1990   ADRIAN HASTINGS

Afterthoughts: The 1980s

When I completed writing the first edition of this *History* in the summer of 1985 it was still not entirely clear how significant Mrs Thatcher's coming to power in 1979 should be judged. She had already won a second term in 1983, largely as a fruit of the Falklands victory but also because of the extraordinarily ineffectual character of the Labour opposition, yet there was no majority in the country behind the government and some possibility remained that a reversal of policy might still be on the way. Nevertheless the confidence of the New Right, its growing entrenchment in the dominant and affluent south-east, the devastating defeat of the miners' strike, above all the intellectually threadbare condition of the Left, all this did seem to indicate that 1979 was likely to remain a fairly decisive date for British history: the end of the era of post-war semi-socialism and Welfare State ideology.

As I write at the end of 1990, over five years later, both the emphatic quality and the limitations of its decisiveness have become much clearer. The unitary character of the decade is remarkable. Never since Pitt and the 1790s has a whole decade seen a single Prime Minister. It was her third election victory in 1987 which ended all possibility of any sort of return to the political and ideological situation prior to 1979, ensured that the privatization programme would reshape the economic superstructure of the country irreversibly, but also at last convinced the Labour Party so to revise its character and programme as to relate it convincingly to the realities of a post-Thatcher Britain: the realities that denationalization could not be systematically reversed, that the expectations of the world of privatized affluence could not be safely scorned, but also that the problems of environmental destruction, the poverty of the most under-privileged, the crumbling condition of the nation's educational and medical services, the continuing poor economic performance of Britain were all growing more, not less, uncontrollable and alarming.

If Mrs Thatcher had not solved Britain's ailments, she had altered the agenda. At least, the cumulative pressure of the 1980s had altered the agenda. How far, in the last analysis, she was much more than a lucky figurehead for that cumulative pressure is another question. At least the way it was going was the way she wanted. That it left a great deal more for the churches and voluntary agencies to do neither surprised nor displeased her. However, while her agenda in 1979 was undoubtedly relevant to the nation's needs, its hardly changed form eleven years later had come to appear strangely irrelevant.

To make sense of the 1980s one needs to hold together the quite exceptional political stability of this decade with the stark reality that, while a single coherent set of remedies had been unflinchingly applied throughout and had knocked 1970s remedies into oblivion, they had not left a healthy patient. By 1990 nobody, except for Mrs Thatcher, cared much about how things had or had not been prior to 1979; what they did care about was a country and a world which more than ever needed a new therapy and that inevitably meant a therapy other than the one which had been applied so relentlessly for a full decade.

The stability of the 1980s was nothing unique to Britain. Ronald Reagan was President of the United States from 1980 to 1988 and was then succeeded by George Bush, his Vice-President. François Mitterand ruled France from 1981; Helmut Kohl Western Germany from 1982. John Paul II had been Pope since 1978. In Western politics it might almost seem as if nothing could happen any more. The power of those in power to manipulate the economic system to their own advantage had steadily grown. Where there was a basic harmony of view across the major states backed by the World Bank and a mass media more narrowly controlled internationally by a handful of politically-minded tycoons than ever before, it might appear exceedingly unlikely that anything much could change again. Americans, gulled by a popular historian, might even once more delude themselves that the end of history had arrived. Yet the implacable speed of change within modern society ensures of necessity that if the political superstructure hardens, it is sure to be quite quickly out of step with the underlying current of cultural consciousness.

Harold Macmillan's old claim 'You never had it so good' undoubtedly applied even more obviously to most English people in the 1980s. Yet if that was true of the 1980s over the 1970s, it had been true of the 1970s over the 1960s and the 1960s over the 1950s. Affluence has never ceased to spread in the post Second World War world, but it spread more evenly before 1980. In the 1980s home ownership above all multiplied. Foreign holidays multiplied. There were more costly gadgets in most people's homes, more cars on the roads, more motorways to carry the cars, more throw-away rubbish – the packaging of trivial affluence – by the road side. In fairly easily quantifiable terms the Thatcher recipe or – one might as truly say – the sheer onward surge of Western capitalist culture had undoubtedly 'worked' in the 1980s, in ways that would make a great many people vote for it again and again. But it had also manifestly left out a larger minority than had the recipes of earlier decades. It was a divisive influence.

What remains striking is the intellectual collapse of an earlier consensus which had carried Britain forward from the 1940s to the 1970s. Perhaps it collapsed simply because it had reigned, largely unchallenged, for so long that it had become elderly, slack, boring, and even verifiably wrong in some important sidelines of its achievement. It could now be derided as 'socialist', but its socialism had been of a very limited sort. It had, learning from Tawney, much stressed equality. It had enormously improved the condition of the poorer half of society. It had reduced the differential between very poor and very rich. It had, in all this, shared the common ideology of almost all of Western Europe – the ideology of Holland and France, Denmark and Germany. But it had also given Britain about the best educational and public health care system of any major state in the world. It had, nevertheless, become ossified within a welter of second-rate bureaucratic socialism, particularly at local government level. It had run out of imagination and in the 1980s its pundits, academic and political, had suddenly found themselves down-graded.

Nobody much cared any more what a Professor of Sociology at the University of Essex might have to say.

The government of the 1980s was at first immensely assisted by the frailty of opposition, but also by underlying currents of economic and intellectual life which were running in line with government policy. It was only from about the middle of the decade, and most noticeably from soon after the 1987 elections, that a new agenda – an agenda integrally related to both the achievements and the failings of the 1980s – really surfaced in social consciousness. In world-wide terms the gap between rich and poor had been growing for a long time. The economic and political decay of Africa in particular goes back at least to the early 1970s. Yet it undoubtedly grew more generally severe in the 1980s, and there was added to it in many countries, especially of eastern Africa, the prevalence of AIDS. British public concern for Africa, the government's concern most of all, no less steadily declined, apart from sudden surges of consciousness produced by an extra-special famine and the impact of Bandaid.

In Britain the poorest of all classes, the absolutely homeless, multiplied in the 1980s, partly as a direct consequence of government policies, a pinching of social services at almost every point, a great reduction in the amount of housing available for occupation but not for buying. The government did not intend, at least in the short run, to abolish the welfare state. What it did intend to do was to pinch its services so unpleasantly as to drive all who could afford it to turn to private medicine, private schooling, private insurance of every sort. It worked for yuppies at many levels, but it greatly impoverished the quality of what ordinary middle Britons received in regard to the things they needed most. The equipment, staff and morale of ordinary schools grievously deteriorated; the hospitals were under an often impossible strain; the social services were hugely understaffed. The universities of Britain, in reality hitherto the country's greatest working glory and almost certainly all in all the world's most effective university system, were profoundly damaged. It was not all damage. There was some logic and some achievement in government policy. Some institutions and people in every field, the most resilient or the most able to call on special private resources, could and did respond creatively. But in the larger number of cases this was simply impossible. Not only were people rubbished in consequence, but national resources were lost at a time when, for instance, the school system in most other West European countries was being greatly improved. British society manifestly suffered in relation to its European partners, whose governments were far less anti-interventionist than that of this country. Furthermore, the drive to reduce controls on economic activity, reduce government expenditure and laud 'enterprise' (undefined) also considerably added to the ecological crisis which in Britain, as elsewhere, was by the end of the 1980s becoming the most urgent of all public concerns. While Mrs Thatcher rendered ritual obeisance to the green cause and was solemnly filmed picking up three pieces of rubbish in a public park, she showed no intention of seriously modifying her policies to cope with the scale of the threat. Almost every proferred remedy was toned down to triviality.

The most startling change within the final phase of the decade was, however, very different and still less expected. It was the sudden transformation of Europe from 1989 onwards as the consequences of Gorbachev's *Perestroika* and *Glasnost* suddenly reached across the whole of Eastern Europe, Communist government after Communist government collapsed. Liberals and Christians soon ruled once more in Prague, Budapest, Warsaw and Berlin. The Soviet Union agreed to withdraw its troops entirely from Hungary and Czechoslovakia. Still more unthinkable, the Soviet Union itself trembled on the brink of dissolution as nationalist and non-Communist forces came to power in the Baltic republics and elsewhere. The official atheism which had been a central element in the policy of the state since 1917, pounding away at religious belief and practice year after year, seemed almost over. Keston College in Britain, established to monitor the anti-religious policies of the Soviet Union and its satellites, had practically to be disbanded – it had lost its function. For Britain all this might seem welcome news but very far off – far further than for Western Germany or even France. But the Channel Tunnel was now well under way and the unified Western European market was due to begin in 1992. But Western Europe, too, had lost defined meaning. One could no longer think about it as one had in 1987. At first Mrs Thatcher argued fiercely against the military reduction of NATO. It was soon, however, obvious enough that as NATO had been created to face a specific threat, produced by the Soviet domination of Eastern Europe, something which was now quickly ceasing to exist, it would be morally impossible for the forces of NATO not to be greatly and speedily reduced. But far beyond the structures of a military alliance were the mental and cultural implications for every European. Since the end of the Second World War we had lived within an extraordinarily sharply divided Europe. The 'Iron Curtain' was no meaningless reality. The consciousness of every post-war generation was dominated by it. Now it is no more. Prague, Warsaw and Budapest have become again European capitals akin to Vienna or Brussels. We cannot even stop at Warsaw. Not even at Vilnius. The essentially European character of Moscow may well be what should matter most to us all.

That all this should be happening contemporaneously with the preparation for the European open market of 1992 and the construction of the Channel Tunnel must force Britain to choose either suicide, both material and mental, or a commitment to Europeanization of an imaginativeness, educational, spiritual and structural, far beyond anything suggested by the recent past. Mrs Thatcher's commitment to Europe has been notoriously tepid. In this she has reflected faithfully enough a great deal of contemporary Britain and a great deal of our island history. But we have reached a point of no return just as England and Scotland came to it three hundred years ago.

It is indeed really rather extraordinary that a leader maintaining so considerable a measure of stability in policy as we have witnessed through the 1980s, with such apparent success in many areas in terms of the goals set, should so suddenly have passed from the centre to the circumference of the political agenda. This also makes it clear that 1979 will not be, in the long view of history, a really crucial turning point. In comparison with ten years later, it may well seem to matter little, the era of Mrs Thatcher appearing as but an epilogue to the post-1945 age, the age of Attlee, Macmillan and Wilson, the age before the environment became our most demanding concern and Europe as a whole the arena of our thought and political activity. As we move into the 1990s, regulations from Brussels or wherever are likely increasingly to undo the arrangements of the 1980s, but they will do it within a quite new context, no longer the context in which we have all of us lived hitherto, the context of a continent shaped by the outcome of Hitler's war. It will rather be the context of Charlemagne or of Napoleon. Britain belonged to the empire of neither. This time we will be part of it.

The churches in England for the most part have seen the present, the past and the future no clearer than the rest of mortals. They, too, in leadership have been remarkably stable and not wholly ungrateful to the Prime Minister's concern for religion – a concern vastly much greater than that of her two predecessors. Robert Runcie's appointment as Archbishop of Canterbury to succeed Donald Coggan was announced in the summer of 1979 – it was one of Margaret Thatcher's earliest duties – and he retired in January 1991. Basil Hume had been Archbishop of Westminster from 1976, Philip Morgan Secretary of the British Council of Churches from 1980. Between 1980 and 1990, then, the top ecclesiastical leadership at the national level changed no more than the political and, internationally, it related from first to last to the condition of Christendom as Pope John Paul II had made it and maintained it. Like it or not, he was its most decisive actor. The Church of England had entered deeply into the enterprise of reshaping its relations with Rome in the age of Pope John and Pope Paul. It could not now pull back even if it wanted to. Other issues, important as they were in themselves, such as the Covenant and the ordination of women priests, were to a very considerable extent controlled by this central project. At the archiepiscopal level the project was at the forefront of the concern of Michael Ramsay, Donald Coggan and Robert Runcie in turn; at the theological level ARCIC enjoyed a quite extraordinary prestige; at the local parochial level relations were no less decisively altered from the frigidity of the past, in a few places even churches being shared.

No one had done more for this than Runcie. From his first meeting with the Pope at Accra shortly after his enthronement, through the spectacular papal visit to Canterbury in 1982, to his own very extensive visit to Rome in 1989, Runcie steadily built up what can genuinely be described as a collegial relationship. In ten years he met the Pope on five different occasions. Such meetings had moved from symbolism to a working engagement, a semi-hierarchical communion, a necessary prelude – if it is ever to happen – to full communion. This is the more remarkable as it has gone on at a time when in general everyone has, not unreasonably, been lamenting a winter of ecumenism and Rome has, in many ways, moved away from the sort of behaviour which, twenty years earlier, excited Anglican and Protestant confidence. It is clear that with neo-conservatism dominant in Rome in what we may call the Ratzinger era, there is a limit to what can be achieved and no likelihood to expect further striking advances in the foreseeable future. What is remarkable is how effectively a debacle has been avoided, even over the issue of the ordination of women within the Anglican communion.

One remarkable consequence of the insistence upon taking Roman Catholics seriously in England has been the dissolution of the British Council of Churches after rather more than forty years of existence, and its replacement in 1990 by a different sort of ecumenical instrument to which Catholics belong. Despite the pleas of other churches, despite the fact that at local level Catholics had, by the end of the 1970s, joined a majority of councils of churches, despite the request of the Liverpool Pastoral Congress in 1980 to the Catholic bishops to reconsider their non-membership of the BCC, it was clear that the bishops, while genuinely embarrassed by remaining outside, were still reluctant to apply for membership. Perhaps they felt that the BCC had been shaped with other constituencies in mind and could not adapt itself sufficiently to Catholicism's special case. Perhaps they feared that the BCC would continue to come to resolutions of which they did not approve but would then not wish publicly to disapprove. The precise reasons are not now important. What matters is the consequence. Other churches became agreed that it was useless to continue with a national council of churches which left out Roman Catholics and so resolved that the BCC, for all the good it had done in its time, would have to be replaced by something different to which Roman Catholics could be fully committed from the word go. The crucial decisions upon both sides were taken at the *Not Strangers but Pilgrims* Conference, held at Swanwick in September 1987. Nothing illustrates better the new determination to ensure that Catholics are seen to be an absolutely integral part of the British Christian community, even if this involves actually unpicking some of the things achieved between Anglican and Free Churchmen a generation and more earlier. In its way the Covenant, a plan whereby the Church of England, the Methodists, the United Reformed Church and the Moravians would enter into a new kind of full but almost, at least at first, unstructured unity, represented the last phase of the old ecumenical strategy which sought to achieve 'Protestant' unity first. Its rejection by General Synod in July 1982, after very lukewarm commendation from Runcie, was the end of one road and the source of a good deal of immediate ecumenical near-despair. It helped lead, for better or worse, to the pursuit of another. Whether the replacement of the BCC by 'Churches Together' will turn out to be a case of something with limited effectiveness being replaced by something with none at all, only the future can tell. It has been a leap in faith and by both sides, so one can only hope that the willingness of the old BCC to die that new life might come will prove existentially sound in this case. It certainly represents the latest step in a process which goes back at least to Geoffrey Fisher's visit to Pope John in 1960 and which has had a very deep effect upon the whole ecclesiastical state of the country.

This continued advance of Roman Catholicism towards the centre remains in a way surprising when considered against a double background. On the one hand, there is Rome's own return under John Paul II to attitudes in some ways more akin to those of Pius XII than to those of either John or Paul. The movement towards unity sparked off by Pope John and the Vatican Council went with a whole range of other tendencies within Catholicism which may well be described collectively as 'Protestantizing', but which have since mostly fallen into disfavour in Rome. The age in which *Opus Dei* is as markedly favoured as it now is, in which theologians are silenced and bishops are selected by Rome with less and less local collaboration, in which centralization has actually increased, seems hardly one to favour the continued ecumenical advance, cautious as it may look, which we can detect in Britain. Yet it has continued to happen and it certainly owes a good deal to the sincere determination of a number of people on different sides – Basil Hume and Derek Worlock, Robert Runcie, John Habgood (who chaired all the discussions involved), Philip Morgan.

The other kind of 'background' is different but hardly less

paradoxical. It is that of the quite serious decline of Catholicism within England. To understand this aright we need to turn back a little. English religious history in the twentieth century began with the challenge provided to the established church by the Free Churches. It was, for a while, quite a fierce challenge, but by the 1920s it had begun to recede, just as the Liberal Party, with which the Free Churches had been so closely linked, faded into relative insignificance. Rivalry was giving way to collaboration. The more friendly, ecumenical and less privileged the Church of England began to appear, the less reason there was for not joining it. The interwar years saw a quite considerable movement of the young from Nonconformity to an Anglicanism led by William Temple, which seemed to answer most of the current insistences of the Free Church tradition but to offer something extra as well. The ecumenical spirit leads to local unity, and local unity in many parts of England seemed most naturally to mean worshipping in the old parish church. The foundation of the British Council of Churches in 1942 was something of a symbol of a marriage between the two traditions which brought Free Churchmen more into the mainstream of English church leadership but at the same time marked the end of any serious challenge to Anglican primacy.

Hardly had that happened than an alternative challenge, this time from Roman Catholicism, became increasingly evident. The Catholic Church had been growing pretty steadily in numbers when other churches were mostly declining, but it was only in the post-Second World War period that it started to appear a genuine rival to the Church of England in terms of the size of its active membership, the ability of its clergy, the distinction of many of its laity. If Anglican – Free Church relations provide the underlying thread of English ecclesiastical history 1900–1945, Anglican – Roman Catholic relations do so for the period 1945–1990, even if the other story obviously did not end in 1945.

The statistical peak for Roman Catholicism in England is to be found in the early 1960s. At that same moment the impact of the Second Vatican Council was bringing about a sudden change in Anglican–Catholic relations from rivalry to collaboration. The Church of England willingly entered yet again into the latter, but this time with a church which, unlike the Free Churches, had a structure similar to its own and, in some fields, greater resources.

The exciting vigour of world Catholicism in the 1960s, renewed by Vatican II, ensured that Anglicans were actually in some danger of being swallowed by a benign Catholicism rather more effectively than, hitherto, they had been outflanked by an aggressive Catholicism. It may well be that in the late 1970s Cardinal Hume came nearer to being the religious leader of the nation, in the eyes of the mutitude, than Archbishop Coggan. The more the two churches came together, the more the young might well feel drawn to the larger and more vigorous. If Roman Catholicism was now adequately reformed and adequately free, what real justification could there be for not being part of it?

The logic of that argument already came into trouble with the encyclical *Humanae Vitae* in 1968. Papal condemnation of all forms of artificial contraception, coupled with the increasingly clear refusal to open up the priestly ministry extensively to married men, even in areas of acute pastoral need, once more provided rational contemporary grounds for not moving in the Roman direction. Nevertheless a certain freedom of atmosphere in the Pauline era and the public diversity of views within the Catholic Church on such issues prevented the point from becoming quite self-evident. As the position of Rome hardened under John Paul II in the 1980s over a whole range of issues, the message became a great deal clearer for those in the middle ground. The matter of inter-communion was particularly important. The large majority of Roman Catholic marriages in England were now mixed marriages. In the accepted ecumenical atmosphere Catholics had come to recognize the Church of England, in Pope Paul's words, as a 'sister church', something very different from the gang of schismatical heretics, pretending to orders when they were really only laity, which was how their parents had mostly been taught to view the established church and its clergy. As these same Catholics were largely unconvinced by the papal line on contraception or for that matter by the refusal in most churches to allow non-Catholics to receive communion, the conclusion was a fairly obvious one: go Anglican. The liturgy is now almost identical in the two churches anyway. The flow of young middle-class Catholics into the Church of England in these years seems quite considerable. It is a flow created precisely by a combination of Roman ecumenism and Roman intransigance. It is even reflected in the clergy, where more priests than ever before have moved into the Anglican ministry, generally linking this with marriage. It is true that there has been a continuing flow in the other direction, too, mostly men of the high Anglo-Catholic tradition. But this counter-movement, while including a number of quite distinguished individuals as, for instance, in 1985 Peter Cornwell, the Vicar of St Mary's, the university church at Oxford, has not the same social significance or lay side to it.

The wider decline of the Catholic priesthood, diocesan and religious, in the twenty-five years from the end of the Council has been extremely severe. It has been coupled with a probably still larger decline in the orders of sisters and has not at all been matched in most dioceses by the ordination of permanent deacons. A considerable shortage of priests is now developing. There is no sign of the decline ending and the pastoral prospects of the church today are entirely different from those of a generation earlier. Many able men have left and the intellectual quality of the clergy is threatened as much as its quantity. While the situation, looked at coolly, in almost all dioceses is now a deeply depressing one – far more so than that in most Anglican dioceses – it is one out of which there seems little way of escape while the traditional model of priesthood is presented as the one and only acceptable norm, and the huge amount of thinking and writing that has gone into the development of a more diversified ministry since the Council is simply ignored by those in authority.

In its way all this is a repeat of history. The BCC has been rebuilt in order to achieve Catholic entry because a BCC without Catholics had come to be seen as an absurdity – which it was – yet the reality of Catholic pressure upon the former system had already begun to decline, just as that of Free Church pressure had already declined a little by 1942. Of course it was worthwhile establishing the BCC in 1942, and of course it was right to draw Catholics in with a new deal in 1990. Decline does not mean disappearance. The weight of English Catholicism, even in disarray, remains formidable. In terms of the quality of the younger leadership in the churches today, lay or clerical, there can sadly be little doubt – as there was much doubt twenty years ago – that the Roman Catholic is far excelled by the Anglican. Tragically, Catholicism shot itself in the foot. While Catholic policies remain as they are, it seems probable that the general religious drift will simply continue to erode Catholicism and slightly reinvigorate Anglicanism.

The Church of England's leadership has in fact been reaffirmed on its own account in the 1980s, and its strength may be noted here in regard to two areas. The first is that of the Anglican Communion. Archbishop Runcie has put more of his time into world travel than any of his predecessors. He has developed a regular pattern of meetings of the twenty-nine primates of the provinces of the Communion, including in this the Churches of South India, North India, Pakistan and Bangla Desh which had been excluded from the Communion at the time, after the Second World War, when they were constituted ecumenically from a range of local denominations uniting with Anglicans. He ensured that the Lambeth Conference of 1988, held at Canterbury as was that of 1978, was very well prepared and an undoubted success. The Anglican Communion has never been so clearly a world-wide federation of churches and, while it remains a very free federation, its bonds of unity have been enhanced in various ways. Canterbury is now in reality the centre of a vast patriarchate over 500 of whose bishops attended the 1988 Conference. There is, apart from Rome, nothing else quite like it in the world today, and the mounting international importance of the see of Canterbury is not something to be ignored at a time when the general international importance of Britain has continued to decline.

The second, local, side of Anglican leadership which requires noting is that of the report entitled *Faith in the City*, on the religious and secular needs of urban priority areas. Inner city riots, notably at Brixton, made it clear that both church and nation needed to take a quite new look at the most deprived areas at the heart of the larger cities, at the recent growth of poverty. In 1983 Runcie set up a very high-powered commission, mostly lay, chaired by Sir Richard O'Brien, formerly Chairman of the government's Manpower Commission, to examine the situation and make recommendations. The report was published in December 1985 and fiercely attacked by some Conservative politicians as a 'Marxist' document. In fact the Commission contained no Marxist and the report no Marxism. The government was unhappy to have attention drawn to a state of affairs about which it was at the time doing very little, but the report's analysis was in fact masterly. Most of its recommendations were directed to the church (a point its secular critics almost entirely overlooked: they attacked it as the work of a group of priests telling the government what to do. In fact it was far more a group of laity telling the church what to do). It led to the Church Urban Fund, to a new urban strategy and to a considerable improvement in morale among people working in this area. It provided a sense of direction, achievable goals and it generated a network of support, being followed by comparable local reports for Birmingham, Manchester and Leeds. It also almost certainly led to the government's greater concern for inner city areas as shown in the 1987 election, but it also showed that in regard to great human need at home as much as abroad the role of the church could still be of paramount importance if played with adequate competence. The ability to commission something of the quality of *Faith in the City* enhanced the authority of Canterbury.

It seems likely that in retrospect the two most significant events in English church history in the 1980s will be the Pope's visit to Canterbury and the publication of *Faith in the City*.

At the theological and spiritual level the direction of English Christianity seems no clearer in 1990 than in 1985. In France there is a quite considerable revival of monastic life. One hears of nothing comparable in this country. In theology there has been something of a more positive note, as also some slight closing of ranks between academic departments and the churches in contrast with previous decades in which the gap appeared to be growing wider and wider. If David Jenkins, Bishop of Durham and certainly the decade's best known theological name, has come under regular attack for unorthodoxy, for being a professor who should never have been given a bishopric, it is seldom noticed how deeply orthodox in intention a Christian theologian he really is. His public wrestling with the living reality and meaning of God and incarnation is both pastorally very serious and utterly different in effect from that of *The Myth of God Incarnate* of the previous decade.

It remains true, none the less, that not so much creative theology has been produced in Britain in these years. Attempts to dialogue with a decaying Marxism can still be intellectually demanding but have become culturally out of date and of quickly diminishing practical value; attempts to incorporate liberation theology may be socially appropriate but are often intellectually too simple; attempts to construct a convincing theology through the medium of story-telling or an explanation of contextualization and the relationship between gospel and culture are seldom sufficiently pressed to be quite satisfying either historically or theologically. None of this should be surprising. Society and the academic world as a whole have never enjoyed less of a sense of a shared convincing faith, ideology or philosophy. There is a great sense of suspended judgement about ultimates, including both the future and the meaning of the past. Theology could hardly be unaffected.

Within the church almost every possible movement seems to have been tried and found just a little wanting. A trouble with modern culture is the sheer speed with which it goes through things. Middle-aged Christians today can look back on the ecumenical and liturgical movements, upon Barthianism, Neo-Thomism and liberal theologies of various hues, upon Marxist theology and the charismatic movement, upon the hopes and fears which surfaced in and after the Second Vatican Council for a renewed Catholicism which would really have taken on board the values alike of the Reformation, the Enlightenment, the patristic age, biblical theology and Eastern Orthodoxy too – what a hope was that! Apart from various forms of feminist theology and the ordination of women (including, within the Church of England, ordination to the diaconate from 1987 but not yet to the priesthood), there are really no such movements today (apart from the commitment to Medjugorje), no comparable fresh large-scale networks seeking identifiable goals for a renewed church. There are not even any gurus to turn to with the charismatic, yet also intellectual, quality of an Yves Congar, a Teilhard de Chardin, a Michael Ramsey. Today's cultural condition seems to rule out almost anything of the sort. The church opening upon the 1990s may, quite possibly, so far as it still creatively exists, be in better heart for having no such 'movement' or pin-up figure upon which to focus devotion. What has happened, however, is that a residue of many of the movements of the last fifty years – very much including Christian feminism, which may be judged the most recent – has coalesced to form something of a new religious consciousness, increasingly taken for

granted by the young. In place of the long, decaying old denominational consciousnesses, sharply distinguished from one another,
one senses the development of an almost taken-for-granted
ecumenical consciousness, embracing liturgy and liberation theology, the ordination of women, a moderately positive attitude
towards an ecumenical papacy and a strongly negative attitude to
the papacy as it actually functions, a wider and more fluid
theological mix, more confident than that of a decade or two earlier
but hardly more hidebound. Against this the combative survival of
more monochrome consciousnesses, whether hard-line Roman,
Evangelical Fundamentalist, or charismatic, looks distinctly sectarian and marginal. Robert Runcie, who disclaims the skills of a
theologian but has grown as archbishop into a better theologian
than he admits, has stressed the absolute provisionality of all our
structures, movements and whatever. It is within the ordinary, not
the religiously extraordinary, that faith has to be found and
fostered. We have not to believe too utterly in any of the goals
before us. Faith in today's city means a long slog with very few
illusions or consolations.

Yet, as the 1990s embrace us, it is undoubtedly Eastern Europe
towards which the eyes of the more alert tend to turn. Like it or not,
post-war Europe has come to an end, but that cannot mean
returning to anything even remotely like the pre-1939 condition of
things in which Britain could still appear the world's central power
and Czechoslovakia a remote little state about which even our
Prime Minister knew and cared remarkably little. It will actually be
harder for us, far harder, to adjust to the new Europe than it was to
the Europe of the cold war. That still left us an offshore kingdom
with a national church not quite like anything else in Europe. We
have now to behave instead a good deal more like Dutchmen or
Danes. We may get by on our wits well enough, but no more on our
muscles and our past. The Falklands War was the last expression of
a form of national behaviour which may soon appear almost
medievally anachronistic. The new Europe will be under German
hegemony as was the Europe of the later nineteenth century. We
have no more reason to fear this than has a Belgian or a Czech. It is
simply a fact of European life, and Germany will remain quite
adequately balanced by a range of peoples to the East of it as well as
to the West.

Are our churches, any of them, even remotely prepared to share in this sort of society? Cardinal Hume is half-French and a natural European. Archbishop Runcie has been working very hard for years at continental connections, endeavouring to 'Europeanize' Canterbury, and the Church of England has recently made an important agreement, at Meissen, with the Evangelical Churches of Germany, for which he has much personal responsibility. But how far have most British Christians even an elementary knowledge of the ecclesiastical map of Europe, let alone any language but their own? We will have a long way to go.

1985 was not a particularly good date on which to end this book. It was simply the date on the calendar when I ceased writing. It had no lasting validity. 1990, on the other hand, the year of German reunification, is likely to be a pretty good one: not quite on its own, but flanked by 1989 and 1992, with a whole series of changes great and small, abroad and at home, including Mrs Thatcher's departure from Downing Street for a well-earned retirement, upheavals in the Soviet Union not yet achieved, even the beginning of Britain's new ecumenical instrument and a new Archbishop of Canterbury.

1920–1990 may well be seen by historians of the future as an era with a certain cohesion to it. While centred upon the disaster of Nazism, it had to live through the long working out, as far as the late 1980s, of the implications of the First World War, the Bolshevik Revolution in Russia, the terms of the Treaty of Versailles. All that may soon seem strangely far behind us. By the year 2000 we will be deep into a new age, but an age beginning now. This history will, I trust, retain some usefulness for many years, but it will truly be a history – the chronicle of a world that is past – and it would almost certainly not be appropriate to add to it any extension beyond this final review of the 1980s and of the longer story, culminating in the 1980s, of a land and its beliefs. It may seem rhetorical to say – yet one can be permitted a little romantic rhetoric in one's final paragraph – that this land was an island with the great strengths and the great weaknesses of an island but, in the way Shakespeare had John of Gaunt describe it and our ancestors defended and loved it, it is to be so no more. After all, in the words of one of the finest of our religious poets, no man is an island. Nor, really, should England be, nor can it be henceforth. From now on we shall indeed be Europeans, or we shall be nothing at all.

PART I

1920 *and Before*

I

Politics

The First World War – the war to end war – came to its end at
11 a.m. on 11 November 1918. It was entered into almost with
disbelief, quickly transformed into a transient crusading euphoria, but its lasting mood had been one of grim endurance, of the
most senseless carnage, mounting hatred of the enemy, an almost
complete incomprehension as to what it was all about. In intention it was the last of the old wars of dynastic Europe, a cavalry
war between emperors and old-fashioned patriotisms with a dose
of new technique thrown in for good measure. In fact it was an
infantry and conscript war, a mechanized war, a total war
involving the systematic destruction of human life by the million
and smashing the political structures that had produced it and
hoped to feed on it.

Before it the great empires of Europe – Germany, Austria,
Turkey and Russia – all went down. But in England strangely
little went down. David Lloyd George, the nation's inspired war
leader, scooped a massive victory in a hasty General Election in
December 1918 and looked forward to continuing for life as the
nation's peace leader. No British politician ever stood in greater
personal pre-eminence than the Welsh wizard at that moment, as
he set out for the peace conference in Paris.

1919 and 1920 were filled with conferences here and there,
with the founding of the League of Nations, with the chaos of
continued, rather incoherent, war in Russia, the Middle East and
Ireland. There was a certain post-war boom in some countries,
profound distress elsewhere as the great influenza epidemic, the
continued blockade of Germany, the moving (or massacre) of
minorities, and sheer political chaos in the wake of the collapse of
the old empires, all took their toll. In April 1919 at Amritsar 379

Indian demonstrators were shot dead on the orders of General Dyer. It was far too brutal and stupid an act to be in any way symbolic of British rule in India, but it was symbolic of the way things seemed to be falling apart across the globe. Yet for the British sphere it was – outside Ireland – more a symbol than a reality. In the realms of King George V the old order was not about to collapse.

These years quite undoubtedly represent the best beginning for what we can call, clearly if with inevitable ambiguity, 'the modern world'. The war and its immediate aftermath either effected, or coincided with, such a range of changes in every aspect of life, above all in Europe, as to signal quite unambiguously the beginning of a new era incredibly unlike anything that had gone before: an era of vast and growing uncertainties, of change on every side of life escalating with every decade, of the conquest of society by technology, of the diminution of Europe, of the political expansion of Marxism.

The war and the settlements that followed it precipitated and harnessed change. They did not necessarily cause it, rather they smashed some of the barriers that stood against it and then tried to erect new ones. It is curious to ponder what might have been the fate of the world if war had been avoided in 1914 and a lasting *modus vivendi* re-established between Britain and Germany: it could have happened and many things would have been vastly different if it had, but others would surely not. Indeed in the case of Britain itself, it would be mistaken to over-stress the effects of the war, bad or good. All in all, it made the changes already called for in pre-war society easier to bring about and once brought about they contributed to stabilize the situation rather than lead on to revolution. Only in Ireland, still a part of the United Kingdom, had the war effectively led to revolution and the consequent establishment of the Free State of southern Ireland, but here too, once accepted, the effect was counter-revolutionary – the removal from the United Kingdom of one of its major destabilizing elements.

The war, it may seem strange to say, had brought much good. Three-quarters of a million men from the United Kingdom had died in it – a terrible number, though far fewer than France, Germany or Russia had suffered. But in hard terms of the effect on the British population, it was far less significant than many imagine: emigration was proceeding at the rate of 300 thousand a year in the pre-war period. Perhaps if there had been no war the population would have been lower in 1920 than was the case, though the larger number of the permanently disabled must not be ignored. Losses had been far heavier among officers than men: it was the gentlemen of England, the young men of Oxford and Cambridge, who had volunteered with such enthusiasm in the early months to fight their opposite numbers of Germany, who were quite disproportionately swept away, but this may well have eased the path to a wider political readjustment and provided room for a useful upward social mobility in the post-war period.

The working class had shown little enthusiasm for the war: conscription indeed had been begun in 1915 because the workers could not be persuaded to volunteer in adequate numbers, as their social betters had done. But they benefited greatly. There was no more need to emigrate under pressure of near starvation. There was more money about. There was plenty of employment for women, so that Charles Masterman could find the women and children of the very poor far better fed and clothed at the end of the war than at its beginning.[1] There were 4,189,000 Trade Unionists in 1913 (and that was a big growth on a few years earlier), 8,081,000 in 1919. Fisher's Education Act of 1918 raised the school-leaving age to fourteen, and the same year women were for the first time given the vote, while the Unemployment Insurance Act of 1920 constituted an enormous advance on the first limited National Insurance Act of 1911. The first British D.Phil. emerged from Balliol in 1919 – harbinger of future technocracy. Women could now become Oxford graduates. Even the Church's Enabling Act passed by parliament in 1919, responding in part to the 'Life and Liberty' movement, represents something of this immediately post-war mood of emancipation and enlightenment. Somehow on all these fronts the war enabled the establishment, led now by the most skilful of opportunists – whose erstwhile image had been one of almost red revolution – to make some important reforms while damping down on the more revolutionary urges which had, for instance, raised the red flag over Glasgow in the strike of January 1919.

The mood of moderate but genuine reform was soon to pass, not so the enhanced expectations and sense of power in the common man, the demobbed serviceman. He had been uprooted as never before. His sense of deference to the local hierarchy, to squire, vicar and factory owner, to Tory or Liberal MP, had been gravely weakened by the sheer dreadfulness of what they had drummed him into in the trenches of Flanders. He now willingly joined one of the great new amalgamated unions, such as Ernest Bevin's Transport and General Workers' Union or the Amalgamated Engineering Union, both creations of these years (1920 and 1921), and he voted Labour. Fifty-nine Labour MPs were elected in 1918 where there had been thirty-nine in the previous parliament and – prior to the 1906 election – virtually none. And there would soon be far more.

Yet essentially all such changes were coming anyway. They can well be seen as a response to a long-developing revolutionary surge but as a response which, except in the case of Ireland, effectively nipped revolution in the bud. Without the war it might all have been much worse. Willingness to disobey the law had in fact been emerging in all sorts of apparently unlikely places: first of all, with Anglo-Catholic clergy who insisted on using illegal rituals or ornaments such as maniples and went bravely to prison, to the anguish of Archbishop Tait; then with the Nonconformists, Baptists especially, refusing to pay their rates because they disapproved of the Education Act of 1902 and the support it provided for Church schools. They went to prison or had their property seized equally nobly. Then came the suffragettes breaking the law to gain the vote. But in all these cases the defiance of parliament was basically symbolic and non-violent. It was a different matter when the leaders of the Conservative Party joined in the game in support of rebellion in Ulster. When Bonar Law, the party leader, declared in July 1912 at a great meeting at Blenheim Palace, 'I can imagine no length of resistance to which Ulster will go in which I shall not be ready to support them', and that at a moment when the Ulster Volunteers were being trained to resist in arms an Act of Parliament, a truly revolutionary situation had arrived. It is not wholly fanciful to suggest that the war rescued Asquith from the fate of being a British Allende, leading a government committed to a policy of social reform in

England, Home Rule in Ireland and Church Disestablishment in Wales, which had a parliamentary majority but was anathema to the governing class and the army. All this could conveniently be shelved with the coming of war which restored the unity of the British governing class, conveniently switched the threat of open revolution from Belfast to Dublin and made the sensibleness of women's suffrage at last obvious.

When Sinn Fein swept the constituencies of southern Ireland in the 1918 election, refused to sit at Westminster, constituted instead a Dail at the Mansion House in Dublin and on 21 January 1919 declared the Independence of Ireland, the British government had hardly the power any longer to say 'no'. Yet it had not the generosity to say 'yes' either nor – had it done so – could it have coped with Ulster. By an extraordinary somersault the 'Liberal' Lloyd George reneged on the whole Liberal policy of Home Rule which he now declared to be 'lunacy', and adopted instead the policy of Bonar Law. The result was to let loose the Black and Tans and two years of as appalling an Irish policy as Britain had ever attempted. All to no avail. The south could no longer be coerced, and in 1922 the union of the two countries – but also the unity of Ireland – came to an end. The point that needs making here is that without the Great War the same result would surely have come, but it might well have damaged England a great deal more than was in fact the case, discreditable as the immediate response of the coalition government to the Irish problem undoubtedly was. Willy nilly, a weakened Britain with a League of Nations in Geneva could no longer deny the Irish political will indefinitely. The attempt to rule Dublin from Westminster had at last to be abandoned. The consequences for English society and even for the prosecution of business in parliament were considerable, but they were stabilizing rather than revolutionary.

The Representation of the People Act of February 1918 turned Britain for the first time from an oligarchy of the more affluent into a parliamentary democracy: almost all adult men and many women would now have the vote – in all over twenty-one million in place of less than eight million in 1910: the poor man and the older woman were enfranchised together. The enfranchisement of women had become an almost revolutionary issue by 1914; it no longer seemed so in 1918 and at first sight might appear to have had small consequence, but that would be a short-sighted view. No woman was chosen for parliament in 1918 though Nancy Astor was very soon to be elected, but here what was crucial was far less any particular political effect – though Britain could now as a result for the first time be fairly termed a democracy. But the deeper consequences of the fact that in principle the most prestigious assembly and offices in national life were now open to women were rather socio-psychological. Hitherto the exclusion of women all across the board from the councils and professions of man had been the norm. Women had only been accorded a public role at the very top of the social scale – a Queen Victoria, a Baroness Burdett-Coutts – or at the bottom of the proletariat. In middle-class society their role was extremely private: wife, mother, mistress, maid. Their admission to any further role or institution had to be argued for. With their admission to parliament the victory had in principle been won. Doubtless the bastions of male privilege – segregated public schools and Oxbridge colleges and London clubs – were many and exceedingly powerful. Nevertheless from now on and increasingly the admission of women to every side of human activity would seem natural; their exclusion would require particular justification. Their needs would now be taken a lot more seriously. Perhaps symbolically, the first birth control clinic was opened in 1921.

A self-governing southern Ireland, parliamentary democracy, female suffrage, a powerful Labour Party, a vastly stronger Trade Union movement, a British Communist Party (founded in 1920), important further steps in education and insurance towards the welfare state: such were the not inconsiderable characteristics of the new post-war political order. But they were more than matched by a range of novelties destined to affect the life of everyman still more intimately. The car and the cinema had already made their appearance in Edwardian times – but rather as a lark for the rich than as a serious and constitutive factor in society. The war had been envisaged as a cavalry affair; it ended with a mass of lorries and cars. Horse-drawn traffic would very quickly fall before the motor car in the England of the 1920s. To the car was added the plane. The first air flight across the Atlantic was made in June 1919, the first from Britain to Australia in December of the same year. Doubtless the peacetime effect of this – except for increasing the rapidity of mail round the world – would for long be slight in the lives of most people. But the symbolic effect was great. The train was the great achievement in travel of the nineteenth century, the plane that of the twentieth: here would be the characteristic locus for the display of masculine 'magnificence'. But most practically important of all would be the radio: the BBC began to operate in 1922 and there were over a million licences by 1924. Relatively cheap, accessible, continuously influential, radio provided a whole new approach to the diffusion of reliable information (the BBC started life broadcasting the 1922 General Election results), the formation of popular culture and – in lands unblessed by the high-mindedness of J. C. W. Reith – the arts of propaganda. Probably the most important early effect of the BBC was the amount of music that it brought into ordinary homes.

Presiding, and not unfittingly, over this hasty and pragmatic mini-revolution in the ways of the nation – this tilting of the scales away from aristocracy and towards the satisfaction of more ordinary mortals of the lower classes, male and female – was Lloyd George. Stanley Baldwin, who loathed him and was resolved to be in every way his opposite, described Lloyd George as 'a great dynamic force . . . a very terrible thing'. He had only one partial parallel of a generation before, Joseph Chamberlain. Lloyd George was the supreme populist politician, the first man to occupy 10 Downing Street who was quite definitely not a gentleman. He had come to power on the wings of the great Nonconformist push of the first decade of the century and he could bewitch any good Protestant with Welsh hymns and a passion for sermons, but in his heart he cared not a fig for the preoccupations of the Nonconformist Conscience. If any man was the prime architect of the welfare state it was he. No socialist, he simply saw the need to rationalize and modernize, cutting down just a little the glaring inequalities of Edwardian society.

By far the most brilliant, dynamic and perceptive of twentieth-century politicians, his skill as a populist and as an achiever brought him unrivalled power at a time of national crisis, but that same brilliance made him a poor party man and an object of profound suspicion within a world of party politics. And people were right to be suspicious, for he was extremely untrustworthy, devious, a twister of words, and intensely self-seeking. Behind the histrionics and the constant appeal to high principle there was really no principle. It is not surprising that after 1922 he never returned to office, and that the Liberal Party never recovered from the dance he led it.

His immediate post-war record was typical of the man. The day after the armistice he spoke to his Liberal supporters, called to meet him in Downing Street, of a peace 'based on the fundamental principles of righteousness', and of the need to put away 'base, sordid, squalid ideas of vengeance and of avarice'. There was the voice of the prophet of the Nonconformist Conscience, but within three weeks – seeing which way the wind was blowing – he had promised instead to prosecute the Kaiser, punish German officers, expel or exclude Germans from Great Britain and 'exact the last penny we can get out of Germany up to the limits of her capacity'. John Maynard Keynes rightly described this appalling manifesto as a 'concoction of greed and sentiment, prejudice and deception'.[2] Lloyd George knew, of course, that it was all rubbish but it was what most of the press and his Conservative allies were braying for – and many of his opponents too. On the top of a bandwaggon he won a landslide victory. The Kaiser was neither tried nor hanged, and Lloyd George certainly worked hard in Paris to modify French and American demands for the humiliation of Germany, but the modifications were minor and the peace was appalling: the near-inevitable seed-bed of future war.

Lloyd George was very much more perceptive than most of his political rivals and vastly nearer to the mass of ordinary people, but no one debased the currency of political rhetoric more than he with religious and moral gush used for the pursuit of personal power, and modern Britain never came nearer to producing a Duce or a Führer. But the system was against him: his party was shattered, his Nonconformist power base dissolving, his allies thoroughly suspicious. He could bully the Cabinet but not the party system nor for long the nation.

Britain remained too stable a State to be long ruled by such a man – and too vast and traditional an empire. Never had the

Union Jack waved over wider territories. The administration of German colonies, most notably Tanganyika, had been taken over, together with Palestine and much of the Middle East. The British army's entry into Jerusalem in December 1917, the concurrent 'Balfour Declaration' upon which the whole development of Zionism and modern Israel has been grounded, and Britain's responsibility for the Holy City for the next thirty years, somehow symbolized the extraordinary scale, almost universality, of the empire in what was to be its final, autumnal phase. Moreover the vast African empire mostly acquired since 1890 was only just beginning to appear a profitable venture. Doubtless the power behind it all was declining together with the imperial urge; doubtless India under the influence of Gandhi was becoming increasingly ungovernable, but for the time being London was more the centre of the world than it had ever been, the capital of the only great empire to survive with a king and a court and a hereditary aristocracy and a still Established Church, the recipient of countless delegations and appeals, self-proclaimed standard bearer at one and the same time of democracy and of privilege.

Lloyd George could come and go, the Balfours, Curzons, Cecils, Baldwins of this land – blue-blooded aristocrats or suitably landed industrialists – would go on for ever: such might well seem to be the case, once the immediate shake-up of the aftermath of war had been overcome. But if change had been contained within Britain, apart from southern Ireland, the wider political effects of the war in the world could not conceivably be so minimized. From now on British politicians would have to relate to a very different world indeed from that which they and their fathers and grandfathers had known and understood: a world in which Paris, Berlin, Vienna, Petersburg and Constantinople had been almost all that mattered, a world dynastic, aristocratic and rather closely linked with the institutional Church. In the world that faced them now the governing British class would feel much less at home.

France, Belgium and Holland remained recognizably the same, but beyond that almost all seemed to change or be very open to change. New countries appeared or reappeared – notably Poland and Czechoslovakia – and all with a nominal commitment to democracy, so that the shape of eastern Europe in particular was entirely different from that of pre-war days. But still more important than the loss of old monarchies and the appearance of new frontiers was the psychological condition of Germany and the ideological condition of Russia: these would constitute the two decisive factors in world politics for the coming decades.

Germany had been the almost normative European nation of pre-war days, the war itself but the final military expression of Germanic hegemony. The preceding half-century had been indeed Germany's too abrupt age of political dominance during which, under Bismarck's prompting, her sheer power – in the spread of frontiers and colonies, her heavy industry, degree of centralization and military efficiency – had caught up with and then outpaced her earlier ascendancy in music, philosophy, science and theology. Because all this had come so quickly in comparison, say, with the English achievement, it had involved an extraordinary degree of seriousness, a particularly unselfcritical view of itself in the pride of Germanic nationhood, a view nevertheless which others had not wholly failed to agree with: the British deference to the Germanic in the late nineteenth century was profound. Hard as the war was for the allies, it finally confirmed their basic tenets; for Germany it was not only devastating in the loss of men, it was psychologically shattering. From being a lion, it had become a pariah, burdened with impossibly large reparations, excluded for years from the League of Nations, deprived of some of its most valuable regions and all its colonies, bound by all sorts of special regulations.

The Europe of the post-war years was effectively a continent deprived of its centrepiece, and when Germany could stand this no longer, it became instead a continent with its centrepiece recovering its power but in a mood of near insanity. That was not of course the consequence only of a too-severe peace treaty, it was the near inevitable consequence of collective hubris once it is broken, as – for the common good of Europe – it had to be. But not quite so ungenerously. In fact at the peace treaty Lloyd George had consistently argued to take German objections seriously and, on some points such as the fate of Upper Silesia, he had done so effectively. But all the victorious powers bore heavy responsibility for the subsequent development of Germany.

They had little responsibility for what happened in Russia – though they tried rather futilely to remedy this by dispatching troops to back the 'white' resisters to the Communist take-over. It is difficult today not to link 'Russia' and 'Communism' and to imagine a world in which Marxism had no governmental institutionalization whatsoever. The revolution of October 1917 whereby the Bolsheviks took possession of Russia and changed it with great violence into the USSR was, without doubt, the most absolutely decisive immediate consequence of the war and one which altered, not just Russia, but the outlook of the whole world. The strains of war everywhere had threatened the old essentially dynastic, aristocratic, non-nationalist structures of government, unleashing the pent-up forces of nationalism, socialism and sheer modernization. But nowhere had the old order been more anachronistic and inefficient than in Tsarist Russia, nowhere had the war done greater damage, and nowhere was the tide of revolution when it came more violent. Anarchy, revolution, civil war and famine were all mastered by Lenin to establish 'the dictatorship of the proletariat', effectively the dictatorship of a party committed to the ruthless implementation of a vision of society – godless, collectivist, egalitarian, one-party – which sent shivers of fear or hope around the rest of the world. Few people had any very clear understanding of what was really going on in Russia, good or bad, but the fact that it was there, that the Soviets existed, altered the dimensions of the possible for the working class and for revolutionary theorists everywhere. It identified Marxism as the most practically effective ideology, even neo-religion, of the twentieth century.

Most of the discussion hitherto has been about Europe, but what the war had finally demonstrated pretty emphatically was that the strongest country in the world was now the United States. Before the war America was still essentially provincial, after the war it was the world's greatest power. Without America the Allies would not have won, but while Britain and France had been enormously weakened by their exertions, the United States – entering the war only in 1917 – had not suffered significantly. Yet, psychologically, America remained provincial and quite unable to accept so suddenly its new international status. The consequence was isolationism. President Wilson had been the most influential figure at Versailles, the League of Nations was his pet idea, and yet in November 1919 the United States refused either to join the League or to ratify the Versailles Treaty. Congress had overruled President. This was not only a great and appalling betrayal of immediate responsibility, it also did more than almost anything else to ensure in the long run the incapacity of the League. In the background to the whole ineffectual history of international relations from Versailles to the Second World War lies American isolationism.

If the USA refused to join, the USSR was not invited to. Nor, for several years, was Germany allowed in. In the circumstances it is hardly surprising that the League as an international authority for the maintenance of peace was not a success. Its effective purpose came to seem little more than the maintenance of the Versailles status quo: not a very happy purpose at the best of times. Yet it would be a mistake simply to dismiss the League as an ass – which to some extent it surely was. Here after all was the beginning of a permanent international political order with institutions in principle independent of any particular government. With the League went the International Court of Justice at the Hague and the International Labour Organization (ILO). They were the start of world political institutions which have since grown enormously in scale and power. In the longer course of human history the formal start of the League of Nations on 13 January 1920 may well be seen as one of the most significant dates in our era.

One other 'power' excluded from the League of Nations, as it had been excluded from the Conference of Versailles, was the Vatican – much to the disappointment of Pope Benedict XV, one of the wisest of modern popes. During the war he had been too impartial to be popular with anyone and his peace proposals together with the sensible remark that the whole thing was a 'senseless massacre' had been bitterly condemned in the West, particularly by patriotic French Catholics. Moreover the distrust of the Catholic Church and its influence in the political field was enormous in the dominant class of western Europe, from which Catholics had been effectively excluded almost more in France or Italy than in England. But no one could feel much more dislike of the Catholic Church than Balfour or Asquith. The idea that a papal representative might be admitted to the League seemed to these gentlemen grotesque if not sinister. Not without reason they saw the Catholic Church as a particularly retrograde force, and yet they were just a little out of date. In fact the international revival of catholicism and of its political influence in Europe was already well under way, helped surely by the loss of the Papal States in 1870 and now by the loss of that rickety old bulwark of traditionalist catholicism, the Austro-Hungarian Empire.

In France the war had done much to reconcile Catholics with the Republic and it ended the hard anti-clericalism of the preceding period. Diplomatic relations between France and the Vatican were resumed in 1921 and St Joan was canonized. In Italy Catholics were at last free to enter politics with the rescinding by Pope Benedict in 1919 of the prohibition to do so (imposed after the seizure of the Papal States), thus enabling Don Sturzo to form his *Partito Popolare*. More widely the new political order brought three strongly Catholic States into existence – Poland, Lithuania and Ireland. All in all the Catholic community benefited greatly from the war and was at last widely adapting itself to a democratic rather than a monarchical milieu, and its influence would steadily grow in the coming years.

The full significance of many of these happenings could hardly have been evident even to a sharp-eyed observer in 1920. Yet the new order in these so many and varied ways was forming itself with great rapidity as the world settled into the uneasy peace of a new balance of social class and national state, a new technology, a new arena of ideological debate. And all these factors were to have their influence upon the churches of England as they too endeavoured to face bravely, if often uncomprehendingly, an uncertain future.

2

The Religion of England

'*Quod Ecclesia Anglicana libera sit*', 'That the Church in England should be free'. Such was one of the most fundamental provisions of the Great Charter, influenced by one of the wisest and ablest of medieval ecclesiastics, Cardinal Stephen Langton, Archbishop of Canterbury. The *Ecclesia Anglicana* of the Great Charter was the whole Christian community of England, led by the archbishops of Canterbury and York, in communion with and under the very real authority of the pope in Rome. A single Church, it was to be 'free', that is to say not dominated by the king and the aristocracy, its bishops to be chosen according to the canonical norms without royal intimidation or direction.

It was an ideal never fully realized, yet for a while in the thirteenth century achieved in part, under such great leaders as Langton himself, Grosseteste of Lincoln, St Edmund Rich. The maintenance of its freedom was a balancing act, between the pressures of a centralizing papacy upon the one hand, a nationalistic monarchy upon the other. In the sixteenth century the pressures proved too much and *Ecclesia Anglicana* in due course split three ways which have been with us ever since: the Established Church, the Roman Catholic Church, the Free Churches. If any man truly stood for *Ecclesia Anglicana* in the sixteenth century it was Thomas More, a layman, lawyer, philosopher, theologian, Speaker of the House of Commons, Lord Chancellor, martyr: 'The King's good servant but God's first'. He was a man often critical of the pope and of ecclesiastical abuse and by no means prepared to commit himself to a particular theology of the papacy, yet absolutely certain that it was unchristian and against all tradition for royal authority to take control of the Church and to sever it from the Roman jurisdiction and Catholic commun-

30

ion. But that is what happened. The large central section of English Christians accepted the royal *coup d'état* in its various ecclesiastical phases, justified Erastianism theoretically and held on to the buildings, the cathedrals and parish churches, while maintaining the ancient episcopal jurisdictions together with a vernacular liturgy which Cranmer had devised with exquisite skill from pre-sixteenth-century Catholic forms. The positive justification for this was, of course, not just a political or Erastian one but the 'reformation' of abuses, doctrinal and pastoral. The point was the renewal of gospel religion in place of the legalistic and seemingly 'mechanical' practices of the medieval Church. The reformers were committed and willing to die for a set of things, most of which Catholic reformers like Erasmus would also have liked to adopt and which almost every modern Christian takes for granted, but which the contemporary papacy was quite unwilling to admit. 'Be of good cheer, Master Ridley, and play the man. We shall this day light such a candle, by God's grace, in England, as I trust shall never be put out.' Bishop Latimer was right. The candle was lit and England became in its own lay understanding, without the slightest doubt, a Protestant country. What did that candle really consist in? Not, for the Established Church, a commitment to Calvinism or to any other system of doctrinal Protestantism, so much as to the rejection of papal power over a number of crucial, but practical matters: free use of the vernacular Bible, worship in the vernacular, communion of the cup for the laity, rejection of 'the multiplication of masses', the freedom of the clergy to marry. For such things did Latimer die and was papal authority rejected.

The small conservative minority within *Ecclesia Anglicana* which followed More in the radical refusal to break with Rome had necessarily to reject such reforms (except the vernacular Bible) and little by little re-shaped its ranks with little foreign help in personnel but through the building up of new institutional bases – seminaries, monasteries and convents – upon the Continent, at Douai, Rome and elsewhere. By the latter part of Elizabeth's reign it was clear that this Catholic group, led now by the Lancashire-born Cardinal William Allen, was growing rather than fading away and from then on, for a long while, it would suffer heavy, if intermittent, persecution.

The second decisive division within English Christianity only came to a head later, in the course of the seventeenth century. The issue here was: how Protestant was 'the Church of England' going to be? For out and out Protestants the Elizabethan Establishment was but a half-way house – 'reform' had still to go further, bishops to be abolished together with most of what Cranmer had preserved of pre-Reformation liturgy. Instead of thus going further the leaders of the Establishment were inclined, however, rather to pull back, to re-emphasize (particularly in the early seventeenth century) 'Catholic' rather than 'Protestant' elements, to reject Calvinism. The result, following the Civil War, the Commonwealth and the restoration of the monarchy, was the decisive separation between the 'Establishment' and the 'Free Churches' – Congregationalist, Baptist, Presbyterian, besides Quakers and Unitarians.

By 1662 English Christianity had achieved its characteristic shape: a large central mass and two dissident wings. The large central mass, 'the Church of England', was Erastian, episcopalian and rather undogmatic. It was overwhelmingly 'Protestant' in sentiment but uncommitted to Protestant dogmatisms. Intellectually one of the freest of Christian churches, socially it had become one of the most subservient, not only to the Crown and to parliament but to the whole gamut of the English class structure. Its relationship to the nation was essentially ambiguous. It claimed to be the 'National Church', included for long – if somewhat passively – the large majority of the nation, and its privileges provided for legal discrimination against all non-members. Yet in fact it was not the National Church – significant elements of the nation had firmly refused to be included within it – though the implications of that basic fact were too painful to be admitted by many Anglicans even into the twentieth century.

The Catholic minority had become a very small group by the late eighteenth century, chiefly to be found in south-west Lancashire and in some of the remoter parts of Yorkshire and Northumberland, but there were surviving pockets in almost every county, as well as in London. When the industrial revolution began Catholics spread naturally to the new towns, well before the wave of Irish immigrants appeared to flood their little churches with new members.[1] Catholicism remained a minority profoundly withdrawn from the general religious and political life of the nation, but less than has often been imagined from its wider social, economic and intellectual life.

Far more important numerically and in the public life of the country were the Free Churches, favoured above all by the lower middle class, shopkeepers and small tradespeople and industrial artisans. It is true that at no time did they fully recover from their defeat at the Restoration. England has never gone back on that basic national decision, political and religious, in contrast to America where at the same time the religious decision was taken – and equally by Englishmen – quite the other way. The Free Churches were however immensely reinforced from the eighteenth century by Methodism, strong especially in the north and in Cornwall, while the older churches – Congregationalists and Baptists – were strongest elsewhere throughout the south (except the home counties) and the Midlands. By the middle of the nineteenth century attendance at the Free Churches on a Sunday was higher than Anglican. This was largely because the Church of England had failed to respond to the shift and total growth in population produced by the industrial revolution, but it was also because its earlier hold on the rural working class was in many parts far more tenuous than might be imagined. The effect of the industrial revolution was both to emphasize the essential churchless character of a large proportion of the poorer classes, particularly in the north, and to provide great scope for more mobile, less class-ridden churches.

Sir Alec Douglas-Home once asked Harold Macmillan at what point 'the slide in values set in' and the latter replied 'when people stopped going to Church regularly on a Sunday morning'.[2] Perhaps by 'people' he meant only the upper classes. For the nation as a whole it is a fallacy to suppose that there was a time, at least since the seventeenth century, when nearly everyone went regularly to church. Certainly by the late eighteenth and early nineteenth centuries the proportion must have been decidedly small. Religion and irreligion are contemporaneous phenomena, both at home in almost every age, but both can take an endless variety of forms, greatly affected by the laws and wider mores of society. Patterns of secularization, just like patterns of revival,

are not terminal but cyclical. Law and social pressures of conformity with the powerful had indeed for long strongly backed
religion of a sort, but with the greater social freedom and
mobility of the early industrial age the appeal of established
religion to the common man was shown to be extremely weak,
while for the upper class it had been so domesticated as to appear
little more than the most easily entered of gentlemen's professions. The Church of Jane Austen was a profoundly secularized
one. That is where the nineteenth century began. 'The Church as
it now stands no human power can save', was Thomas Arnold's
judgment. In fact the next fifty years witnessed an amazing recovery of religion, both Established and dissenting. The
clergy, evangelical and tractarian, of the later nineteenth century
took its pastoral task with deep seriousness and mounting
efficiency. New church buildings went up by the thousand,
attendances steadily increased. England in the mid-Victorian
age – at least middle-class England – can be claimed
as one of the most consciously religious societies that ever
existed.

The apparent institutional and pastoral well-being of all the
main churches continued well into the Edwardian age.[3] The
Church of England itself was still advancing in clerical numbers
and, even more, clerical efficiency: the theological colleges, quite
recently founded, were just beginning to dint the general impression of gentlemanly amateurishness which characterized the
Anglican priest. Anglo-Catholics, in particular, equipped with an
army of curates were demonstrating in some big town parishes an
extremely disciplined pastoral professionalism. Think of Portsea,
that dockyard Portsmouth parish where Cosmo Lang and then
Cyril Garbett presided over a dozen or more unmarried, very
poorly paid, ever busy curates; or St Mary's, Bramall Lane,
Sheffield, where from 1893 R. H. Hammond was vicar for many
years: he had a Bible class of 270 women, and one for up to 700
men; 145 open-air services a year, 135 teachers in his Sunday
schools, while his Watch-Night service could pack the church
with over 2,500 people.[4] Parishes of that sort – even in parts of
England as truly missionary territory as Sheffield – were not
uncommon around 1900.

Late Victorian ecclesiastical prosperity was, nevertheless, deceptive. Anglican statistics for the thirty years before the First World War are susceptible to two contradictory interpretations. One is that the Established Church had never done so well, the other that the mid-Victorian boom was over and a heavy decline had set in. There is some truth in each.

The proportion of marriages solemnized in an Anglican church is probably as sure a guide as any from the mid-nineteenth century on (before that there was no effective freedom to be married elsewhere) to the size of the adult population which felt some degree of identity with the Established Church – though it did include some Nonconformists who liked the village church for marrying but were otherwise staunch chapel folk. Doubtless in the countryside it could still be pretty inconvenient in many places to be married anywhere else than the parish church, nevertheless it was possible. So the figures inflate the impression of Anglican commitment somewhat, but their general message is clear enough:

(per thousand marriages)

1874 – 747	1904 – 642
1884 – 707	1909 – 614
1894 – 686	1919 – 597

Of course the total size of the population was growing considerably in this period. Hence a percentage fall of this sort could be masked by an actual rise in the total number of marriages performed.

At the same time – between 1890 and the war – there is evidence too, some of which we shall see, for considerable decline in church attendance, at least in town areas. It cannot be doubted that there was a serious increase in these years in that part of the population which had lost all real sense of connection with the Church of England. The Church's penumbra, its larger and looser constituency, was steadily shrinking, and as it did so the Church itself was declining in national significance.

But something else was going on too: baptisms, confirmations, Easter communions, were all rising. Anglican baptisms per thousand live births were 623 in 1885; 641 in 1895; 678 in 1907; 705 in 1917. Confirmations rose absolutely from 176,783 in

35

1881, through 214,531 in 1891 to 244,030 by 1914.[5] Easter communions were as follows:

| 1881 – 1,225,000 | 1901 – 1,945,000 |
| 1891 – 1,490,000 | 1911 – 2,293,000 |

The explanation of these very considerable increases may be primarily in terms of the greater efficiency of the clergy, but the rise in Easter communions at least is manifestly also an index of growing lay participation. What seems to have been happening is a major alteration in the relationship of ordinary people to their parish church. Previously very many who went to church, even quite regularly, were never confirmed and so never received communion. Communion was, after all, not so common a service. They went happily to matins or evensong, most happily to a harvest festival. But that was altering for various reasons: an increased sacramentalism in the Church was putting more stress on confirmation and communion; an improved schools system (there were 3,722,317 children in Church schools in 1903, the vast majority of them in Church of England schools) was making it easier to provide the foundation for confirmation and communion. The clergy themselves saw this as their task to a far greater extent than previously.

Certainly there remained very many people who went to Anglican churches but never to communion, nevertheless the pattern that was already developing was of a considerably smaller total constituency, but of a higher sacramental commitment within the constituency. Less, one may say, of a loose National Church; more of a large, fairly vigorous denomination.

The Free Church pattern was different. Their membership had grown fairly steadily in absolute terms through the nineteenth century, but also steadily less fast – no longer in fact proportionately with the general population. It continued to grow until 1906, and particularly in the three years after 1902 (perhaps as a consequence of the fighting spirit generated in hostility to the Education Act of that year). There was no feeling of decline in Nonconformity in the early Edwardian age; on the contrary, the feeling was that the Free Churches had come to maturity, never so influential, so capable of making their institutional presence felt.

Their penumbra had enormously widened – in a way most unusual for free and minority churches of the 'gathered' type. Beyond formal membership their Sunday schools, organized leisure activities, newspapers and close links with the Liberal Party had given the Free Churches for a brief while a wider national constituency almost comparable with that of the Established Church. They might seem indeed, and half believed themselves, about to take over the central religious role within the life of the nation. Yet in fact the growth of their full membership no longer quite kept up with the growth of the nation, and it was now crucially dependent upon the vigour of the Sunday schools. Methodist churches alone had well over a million and a half children in Sunday school in the Edwardian years. It would, however, prove a risky foundation for the future, and one already beginning to be threatened by such rival attractions as the Scouts.

It is essential then not to underrate the pastoral vigour and congregational vitality to be found in churches throughout England at the beginning of this century. Nevertheless it is important also to be clear about their limitations, the fading away of the great religious leap forward which in many ways mid-Victorian England did represent, above all how many people it never did include. 1881 might represent as well as any date a high point of church going. A number of amateur religious censuses in that year showed that 40 per cent or more of the population attended church or chapel on a Sunday in Bristol, Portsmouth, Ipswich, Coventry, Gloucester, Hastings and Scarborough, but less than 25 per cent in Liverpool, Sheffield, Nottingham, Bolton, Burnley, Stockport, Warrington and Darlington (and of that 25 per cent not half was Anglican).[6] In many villages and small towns it will have been a lot higher than 40 per cent. But what these figures show indisputably is that at the best of times the large majority of the working-class town population, at least in the north, did not go to church. They had not gone earlier, they did not go later. The working-class urban population of England has never been, since the Industrial Revolution, a church-going population. Here and there that generalization has been dinted by the Primitive Methodists, the Baptists, or – for the Irish – by Roman Catholics, but it is basically true. The religious onslaught on urban disregard for religion, spear-headed by Anglo-Catholic clergy on one side, thousands of Nonconformist chapels on another, did splendid work in all sorts of ways but it never made any great overall difference. And by the beginning of the twentieth century, despite all the effort, the position was getting rather noticeably worse.

For London, which was admittedly a law unto itself, we have the very valuable religious census organized by the *Daily News* in 1903 under the directorship of Richard Mudie-Smith. There had been an earlier, less efficient religious census of London in 1886. The figures for the two are as follows:

	Anglicans (excluding missions)	Nonconformists
1886	535,715	369,349
1901	396,196	363,882

The Anglican decline in fifteen years is striking. In the poorer areas the failure was still more manifest; the Church of England had 60,086 attendances in east London, the Nonconformists 81,816 and the Roman Catholics 16,224. In west London, on the other hand, in the wealthier boroughs the position was quite reversed. Here the Church of England drew 12.6 per cent of the population, Nonconformity 5.8 per cent, Catholics 3.2 per cent. In upper-class Kensington practising Anglicans were three times as great as Nonconformists. Charles Masterman analysing the south London results compared adult church attendance in a very poor area, Walworth, with a section of suburbia:[7]

	Population	Adult Attendance			Percentage of Population
		C. of E.	Nonconformist	Total	
St Mary, Walworth	20,142	189	1,089	1,278	6
Five Dulwich and Sydenham parishes	21,373	3,320	2,858	6,178	29

Anglican weakness in Walworth, and the overall contrast between the two areas, are very striking. The Church of England might just claim to be the National Church in Kensington but it barely existed in Walworth. 'In all central south London,' Masterman remarked, 'I have only seen the poor in bulk collected at two places of religious worship – Mr Meakin's great hall in Bermondsey (Wesleyan), and St George's Roman Catholic Cathedral at Southwark'. This, of course, was just before the establishment of an Anglican diocese of Southwark, but that would not make a great difference. Cyril Garbett was bishop there for twelve years from 1919; and a more serious pastoral bishop it would be hard to find. At the end of his time he had this to say:

> Most of the churches on the riverside had minute congregations: the people did not even know where their parish church was. I very soon discovered that, when I went to take a confirmation, it was useless to ask the way to St ———'s; I had to find out beforehand from the incumbent the name of the nearest public house.[8]

It looks very much as if the pattern of south London was pretty similar to that of many of the larger urban areas of the Midlands and north. A survey of Merseyside from after the war calculated that in Liverpool both Anglican and Free Church attendance had diminished by over 14 per cent between 1902 and 1912, though Catholic attendance had increased by 8 per cent. But, all in all, not much more than 20 per cent of the population attended church and – again – the unskilled working class was hardly to be found anywhere except in Catholic churches.

In Tyneside in 1928 a religious census was taken in two areas – Wallsend and South Shields. In the former 20 per cent of the adult population went to church (7,698 out of 33,000): 15 per cent to the Church of England, 42 per cent Roman Catholic, 43 per cent Nonconformist. In South Shields the church-going proportion was lower, only 13 per cent, of which 30 per cent was Anglican, 22 Catholic, and 48 Nonconformist (mostly Methodist).[9] A group of mining villages in the Deerness valley, Co. Durham, produced the following rough religious affiliation for 1919: 40 per cent Methodist (two Primitive to one Wesleyan), 10 per cent Anglican, 10 per cent Catholic, 4 per cent Baptist, 35 per cent 'No religion'.[10] The 35 per cent 'No religion' would doubtless often be put down as 'Church of England' with less or more reason.

The weakness of religion, and above all of the Established Church, throughout the industrial north at the start of our period seems manifest.

All in all, for the country as a whole rather over 60 per cent were nominally Anglican: they were married by the Church of England and their children were baptized by the Church of England – Anglican commitment being higher in the rural south, far weaker in the industrial north. Roughly 15 per cent were Free Church and 5 per cent Catholic and both were stronger in the north. Probably about 15 per cent of the population were quite emphatically nothing, but in practice that rose to a good 50 per cent. In the larger towns almost nowhere was anything like 40 per cent of the population effectively church-going. Again, almost nowhere was the real urban unskilled working class to any large extent Anglican – though perhaps a bit more in Lancashire than elsewhere. In places it was Methodist or Baptist or Roman Catholic. Mostly it was nothing. The rural working class was Anglican or Free Church, more occasionally nothing. The upper class was largely Anglican, the middle classes Anglican or Free Church, the skilled working class Free Church, occasionally Anglican, most often nothing.

Ponder this reflection of an Anglican priest working in the twenties in a Tyneside parish: 'It interested me that in those days the Church of England willy-nilly raised people in the social scale whereas the Roman Church didn't seem to do so. I never knew whether to be glad or sorry.'[11] This is a perceptive comment and one could hazard an explanation at two levels, intentional and sociological. The intentional: Anglican clergy wanted to raise people from their slum conditions. Many slum priests were Anglo-Catholics with more than a touch of romantic socialism. They saw social reform, very properly, as part of their ministry. For Roman Catholic priests, in contrast, this hardly entered into their conscious intention. They might provide soup for the very hungry, their nuns would care for the dying, but few had much sense of social mission beyond that. They were conditioned, like their people, to acceptance of the status quo. Sociologically: anyone in a slum parish responding to Anglican ministry was in fact entering a social network whose obvious centre was a great deal higher up in the scale. By entering it, you were drawn upwards by your priest who was in most cases so very clearly a 'gentleman' who had come down to you at some personal cost. In the Catholic Church this was not so. The network was predominantly one of the poor and you were at home in the Church precisely by being poor. The Church could not, and did not, pull you upwards by the weight of its own membership. It provided instead a sort of spiritual solidarity of the poor, as the Free Churches also still did in some circumstances. This the Church of England could never do.

What was new in the Edwardian age was less the Church's loss of the working class because the poor had never really belonged to it, than the unmistakable decline in Christian belief of the middle class. That was Charles Masterman's verdict in his distinguished book, *The Condition of England*:

> It is the middle class which stand for England in most modern analyses. It is the middle class which is losing its religion; which is slowly or suddenly discovering that it no longer believes in the existence of the God of its fathers. . . . Among the middle classes – the centre and historical support of England's Protestant creed – the drift away is acknowledged by all to be conspicuous.[12]

Yet it is also true that the early years of the century marked the highest numbers that Baptists, Methodist and Congregationalists had ever reached: for them, cultivating for the most part a constituency rather lower in the social hierarchy than the Anglican, the decline had not yet set in so clearly. The pattern of irreligion in Edwardian England would appear to be one of a double movement – up from its old stronghold in the urban slum, down from the swelling scepticism of the upper class – while in between them, in the expanding lower middle class, the world of Mr Pooter, religion was still expanding too. The fifty Baptist churches, the forty Congregationalist churches, the twenty-nine Wesleyan churches of north London provided the real spiritual strength of that area: 'In every respect', the Mudie-Smith inquiry reported, '– in point of numbers, in strength of organization, in new adventure, in spiritual tone and vigour, and in influence upon the public conduct and conscience – they lead the way.'[13]

Religion in the Edwardian age was, as it has remained, a wider thing than church-going. 'If you follow the Book, you won't go wrong' was the core of working-class Protestant Christianity, and it remained alive for many people who for one reason or another did not favour regular attendance at any service. In the upper-class family prayers, grace and even 'the Book' were fading away, but church attendance might remain, while in the working class it could be the other way round: the institutional and social attachment was a good deal less, the religious attachment rather more, but for both 'one God, no devil, and twenty shillings in the pound' was a popular, and not unfair summary of what religion had come to mean for the generality of people by 1920, including many a churchgoer. The core religion of England had long been lay, Protestant, middle-class and scriptural: a simple biblical fundamentalism. That would no longer do. Evolution and historical criticism, by the Edwardian age, had punctured it quite irredeemably. While pockets of active resistance remained – Evangelical, Anglo-Catholic and Roman Catholic – the main stream of the bourgeoisie was now flowing uncontrollably towards an agnosticism surfaced over for some with soft undogmatic pieties nourished, for want of better, upon sunsets and daffodils.

If religion had a great deal to do with class, it also had a lot to do with sex. There are societies in which the men rather than the women attend religious rituals, and there are societies in which the contrary is the case. The Victorian boom in religion was at least as much a masculine as a feminine matter, and so was the continued Free Church boom in the early twentieth century, but decline, at least in the upper social strata, affected the men well before it affected the women, so that the Church of England in particular was becoming already noticeably a church of women. Female confirmations were far more numerous than male ones: 142,824 to 101,206 in 1911; the York 1901 religious census showed 65 women for 35 men among Anglicans, and the Merseyside surveys revealed much the same. It was true to some extent of all churches but most of all for Anglicans.

Yet in the practice of most churches, far more than now, there was a rather rigid distinction between the active and the passive, and with very rare exceptions indeed, all the active were men and all the women were passive. The odd churchwarden might be a woman but she remained decidedly odd and the Convocation of

Canterbury, despite a petition to the contrary, had in 1897 affirmed the necessity of every other member of a parish council being male.[14]

There were many women church workers of one sort and another, above all deaconesses and teachers. For the most part they were miserably paid, poorly educated and kept most firmly subordinate to male authority. A woman's voice might be heard in the bishop's bed but not in his council. It was on special occasions or in para-ecclesiastical institutions, or other new areas of growth, that there was most room for female initiative: in the mission field, in the Salvation Army, in convents, in the Student Christian Movement. In the Anglican Church Congress of 1913 twenty-one speeches were made by women. The Salvation Army was the first Christian body to accept full and effective female equality and nearly half its officers were women, including many of the ablest. The ecumenical Student Christian Movement was not so radical a body and edged forward more cautiously towards the admission of female initiative; here again class may have had much to do with it. The SCM was led by young men from Oxford and Cambridge, and the young upper-class male seemed particularly averse to admitting the female in public to shared activities other than the Commem. Ball. But the SCM did so, especially as it moved after 1908 from a more narrowly evangelistic to a wider social concern. By 1920 women were taking a full part in its leadership. People like Zoe Fairfield, Ruth Rouse, Winifred Sedgwick and Margaret Wrong were able to attain roles of national significance through the SCM in a way which would have been almost unthinkable in other sides of Christian life.

One side, however, in which it would not have been unthinkable was that of religious orders, Roman Catholic above all, though the same applied to Anglican religious communities which had grown considerably in the last fifty years.[15] It was, of course, a segregated segment of Church life; nevertheless it was an important one. It provided little scope for personal initiative among most ordinary nuns, but a good deal for Mothers Superior. The great growth in convent schools, responding to the newly sensed need for girls' education, was a characteristic of the period, and the best of them were remarkable. Mother Janet

43

Erskine Stuart ruled over more than six thousand Sacred Heart sisters from her headquarters in Brussels, as earlier Mother Digby had done in Paris; she toured not only Spain and Germany and Austria, but North and South America and Australia, inspected hundreds of schools, kept up a ceaseless correspondence across the world and wrote important books about the education of girls. It would be difficult to find any other woman in Edwardian England whose responsibilities could compare with those of Mother Stuart.[16]

'The scheme of the ladies who desire ordination has for a long time been familiar to me; I have never found occasion to do anything but laugh at it,' wrote Canon Lacey in the *Church Times* (18 August 1916). That was, and long remained, the prevalent Anglican point of view, but in the age of the suffragettes the Free Churches were already moving. Baptists and Congregationalists had accepted the ordination of women. In 1917 Constance Todd was ordained to be Dr Orchard's assistant at King's Weigh House. The national champion here was Maud Royden, an Anglican in her forties, who had distressed fellow Anglicans and earned episcopal rebuke by accepting a pastoral ministry at the City Temple, the most important Congregationalist church in the city of London, in which she had preached and even baptized three children. She was a member of the council of William Temple's Life and Liberty movement, but life and liberty should not really go so far as for women to baptize children or even preach (they had not been allowed to do so, even from the sanctuary steps, during the 'National Mission' of 1916), and when in October 1917 the council went into conference and retreat at Cuddesdon Theological College to plan its great forthcoming strategy Miss Royden was forbidden by J. B. Seaton, the college principal, to sleep on the premises: her presence by day was bad enough, at night it would be impossibly contaminating. Miss Royden resigned with dignity. What a very revealing incident! Years later Archbishop Garbett declared that Seaton of Cuddesdon and Cunningham of Westcott were the two men who had had most influence in the Church of England in his time, so in Seaton we are facing no old dodderer but one of the major opinion-formers in the Church. But the position of Temple is still more enlightening. He had just one woman upon his 'Liberty' committee yet was willing to lose her because neither he nor his committee of stalwart radicals was prepared to stand by her or stand up to the Principal of Cuddesdon. Temple's biographer – also a member of the committee – assured his readers that most of the council regarded Seaton's position as 'ludicrous', but his further comments upon Temple's acquiescence in such an absurdity are more revealing, perhaps, than he realized: 'There was no doubt where Temple's personal sympathies lay, and he was much distressed to lose so valuable a member from the Council; but he could not help remembering that they were the guests of the Principal . . .'[17]

How was England's religion affected by the war?[18] The extraordinary euphoria produced by the outbreak of war carried away the clergy as much as anyone. Not all of them: Archbishop Randall Davidson was as pondered and unhurried in his judgments and statements as ever, as moderate in his attempts to hold together different points of view, but – of course – at such a time it is not the person who keeps quiet or is a little evasive who steals the limelight, but the man who does not hesitate and says exactly what the papers want him to say. Such a one was Arthur Winnington-Ingram, Bishop of London, 'the Bayard of the Church of England, the *chevalier sans peur et sans reproche*'; the 'idol of the East End'. So his friend Archbishop Lang described him.[19] 'An intensely silly bishop', was Asquith's rather different opinion,[20] and Asquith was a fair judge of bishops. It was this good man, the master of gushing words suited to the immediate popular mood, who drummed the nation into the army: and who better to do it than the Bishop of London? His was a long campaign, from the first recruiting services, through his message to the *Guardian* (10 June 1915) on 'What the Church is to do. I answer, MOBILISE THE NATION FOR A HOLY WAR'; on to the famous Advent sermon of 1915 and the call in it 'to kill the good as well as the bad, to kill the young men as well as the old'. But he was not, of course, alone and Robertson Nicoll, the editor of the *British Weekly* and about the most powerful voice in Nonconformity, was just as violently bellicose. Few there were at first who had the sensitivity to stand back, to judge that it was not the role of a priest to be also a recruiting sergeant, but Davidson at least declined to instruct the clergy so to use their pulpits.

Clearly it was – to start with – a gentleman's war. The clergy of the established Church were gentlemen, so if they could not themselves take part, they could at least show their enthusiasm by urging on the lower orders to enlist. John Oman noted sadly how often in private gatherings 'the religious official is the most belligerent person present'.[21] Some, of course, wished themselves to enlist and Davidson fought a long battle in his endeavour to prevent them from doing so: chaplains, yes; fighting soldiers, no. But as the mood of the nation altered with the years – especially the mood of the troops themselves – and the war appeared less and less like a crusade, the fiery recruiting sermons did not exactly endear the clergy to the common man whose approach to the war became immeasurably cynical.

It was, admittedly, difficult to know what to do. A world war between Christian nations, justified upon both sides by distinguished ministers of religion, must constitute an impossible moral dilemma for the more sensitive. The defence of Belgium seemed the soundest and simplest of moral grounds for going to war, and not many could take the road of absolute pacifism. 'We need not trouble about the distribution of responsibility,' wrote J. H. Oldham to John Mott in August 1914, 'We need to get behind that to the fundamental fact that Christian Europe has departed so far from God and rejected so completely the role of Christ that a catastrophe of this kind is possible.'[22] Few could remain so mentally calm in those bewildering days. There was a small band of Christian Pacifists. The great majority of the 16,500 conscientious objectors were committed Christians, and the large majority of these were Free Churchmen. Many were linked by the Fellowship of Reconciliation, founded in December 1914 as a supporting but by no means a proselytizing body – and such the Fellowship has always remained. Its first president was Henry Hodgkin, a Quaker. Its secretaries during the war were Richard Roberts, a Presbyterian, and Leyton Richards, a Congregationalist. A number of its members, like William Paton, had found their pacifism through the Student Christian Movement. Many were Quakers, Christadelphians or Congregationalists. There were few Anglicans and still fewer Roman Catholics.[23] Absolute Pacifists were mostly (though not all) treated extremely badly. It was a slow struggle and most of their defence from some quite appalling ill-treatment came from Free Church circles[24] or humanists like Gilbert Murray. Nevertheless the recognition by the State, however grudging, that they did exist and had to be tolerated, the slow endeavour of the establishment – secular and ecclesiastical – to understand at least a little of what pacifism really signified, was one of the better gains of the war.

No one questioned the need for chaplains, though what they should actually do was a vastly more difficult matter: the best made themselves endlessly available, simple sacraments of humanity, the writers of letters home, the providers of cigarettes, the companions of the dying. A few, like 'Woodbine Willie' (G. A. Studdert-Kennedy) became almost mythical heroes. The objectivity of the sacraments as against preaching and exhortation was increasingly valued in the front line. Many, totally unprepared for a form of ministry so wholly different from that of the Edwardian vicarage, proved dreadfully ineffectual and were scathingly criticized in war memoirs such as Robert Graves's *Goodbye to All That*.[25] Unfair as much of the criticism probably was, the fact is that it was made. The Church, feeble enough at home, could appear still more futile in the trenches. What war chaplaining did do was to convince the more clear-minded of padres just how non-religious a nation England was. The war did not create irreligion so much as reveal it.

It was an Anglican war padre, David Railton, whose vision created the twentieth century's most moving symbol of national pride in and over war – the tomb of the Unknown Warrior. It was inaugurated by the King in Westminster Abbey on 11 November 1920 with vast solemnity, copied that very day in Paris and then throughout the world: one example of the way the religious mind could still produce the symbols needed by the contemporary world, even if the symbols were not really themselves religious.[26]

There was no genuine religious revival during the war nor after the war, nor was there a pastoral or theological revival – though these things were sought for, and even claimed to be coming, at the time. The war unleashed bewilderment and hate, and the churches had done very little to help with either. By the end of the war many were sorry enough for the simplistic clerical bellicosity of the early months. What in retrospect did it really matter? Christianity already appeared to have lost the intellectual battle well before the First World War began. What the war did was to shatter its social and political role as well: to unveil the truth to high and low alike of ecclesiastical near-irrelevance. When it was over the churches had simply to start again, from a weaker position and with next to no new resources or inspiration. As the war ended and pastoral activity began to resume its conventional pattern, let us look at just one intermediate scene which may stand in its way for many. 'I had a wonderful experience this morning,' wrote the Catholic priest at Letchworth in May 1919:

> I rode my bicycle a long way, to say Mass in a prisoners' camp. I did so in the attic of a granary, so badly lit that I could scarcely read the missal. The Catholic Germans had rigged up an altar of planks and thrown their blankets over it. They had made absurd bouquets of wild flowers, buttercups and dandelions and things, and put them in mugs. I heard their confessions, and said Mass, and preached, and gave them communion. . . . It was like the Catacombs – the low dark places, and the rows of those nice peasants, Bavarians, Westphalians, Rheinlanders, kneeling on the ground all round their rough altar . . . I was back in the days when I said Mass at Innsbruck and the morning light shone on the great white mountains. They sang the old hymns I have not heard for years – all day since the tune of '*Hier liegt vor deiner Majestät*' has been sounding in my head . . . I talked a bit to my prisoners and said I hoped they would soon be back in their own homes. So I came out into the bright sunlight and passed the barbed wire and the sentry – and I was in England again.[27]

The war was over and the churches which may at least have learnt from it with hindsight a certain restraint, a recognition of their own limitations, had now to return to the bright sunlight of ordinary day and pick up the threads as best they might.

3

Establishment[1]

'How *can* you go on believing in an Established Church?' asked
Bishop Gore crossly of Archbishop Lang in 1912.[2] The answer
we may offer was a simple one: not to do so was too awkward.
The dilemma, some might argue the tragedy, of the Church of
England throughout our period has been the *damnosa hereditas*
of an Establishment which had been historically inevitable and
fruitful too but was now making less and less clear sense. The
'establishment' of a church implies exclusivity or, at the very
least, privilege and was of course meant so to imply. Its inherent
obverse was the non-recognition of ecclesiastical alternatives for
Englishmen. The Church of England was 'established' because it
was the 'National Church', what William Temple – with that
smooth avoidance of the more awkward aspects of contemporary reality which at times characterized him – called 'the whole
people of England in its religious capacity'.[3] It wanted to be
national and claimed to be so, yet in hard fact it was not, because
a very considerable minority of the nation had long refused to
participate in it, however tolerant and comprehensive it tried to
be within its walls. At first their existence was denied but when,
by the early nineteenth century, this had become too manifestly
ridiculous and it was accepted that Englishmen could in fact be
non-Anglicans – Baptists, Roman Catholics, Jews, atheists or
whatever – then the anomaly grew still greater: in some areas of
life there was to be equality between Anglican and non-Anglican
and hence effectively between the organized religious efforts of
the two, in others there was not. The religio-political history of
the nineteenth century is from one point of view a history of the
whittling away of Anglican privilege in one little area after
another, inevitable because every example of privilege was an

example too of non-liberalism, an expression of discrimination against the non-Anglican Englishman.

Clearly the more the privileges went – the tie between the Established Church and the franchise, political office, university membership, marriage, the graveyards, the land itself (through tithes) – the more Free Church hostility to the Establishment declined: strong in the nineteenth century, it quickly faded in the twentieth. Once the Church in Nonconformist Wales had been disestablished there was relatively little left for the non-Anglican to complain about. But the same process began to make what remained irksome in the eyes of the Anglican. The complaints against 'Establishment' started to come instead from the faithful churchman – left, he felt, with all the defects but none of the advantages. 'We are finding ourselves disestablished almost everywhere except in the lunatic asylums,' declared Gore.[4] The privileges had gone and yet the Church remained, 'confined in every department of its constitutional existence within statutory bars which Parliament itself alone can break or reshape'.[5] Why not go the whole hog? Gore's fellow bishops did not agree – just enough privilege remained – and indeed nearly all, including Davidson, fought as hard as they could against Welsh disestablishment, despite the manifest fact that Anglicans were but a minority of the Welsh people whose majority had voted emphatically in parliamentary elections for disestablishment to go through.

Archbishop Davidson believed profoundly in Establishment, and he had his reasons and in this represented the vast majority of Anglicans. The whole nature of the Church of England, at its best as well as its worst, appeared to require establishment: the basic sense that you were here for everyone, that you represented in as non-partisan a form as possible the Protestant Christian religion, and that you did so by royal and parliamentary authority which was itself thereby committed to Christianity. It was a not too unreasonable model for a Christian institution, but it could only be acceptable if it more or less corresponded to the empirical facts, and in England by the twentieth century that was, too manifestly, no longer so (and in Wales, of course, still less so).

It was of the nature of Establishment in England (though not in Scotland) to be profoundly Erastian, and that meant at one and the same time to be lay controlled and to be politically controlled. It was the laity in parliament that formed the final judge. This might make sense, on some ecclesiologies, while parliament represented England alone. It made absolutely no logical sense when parliament had become British and the Church of England was in no way established in Scotland, Ireland or, finally, even in Wales. Necessary as it doubtless was in English terms it was also logically an anachronism from the Act of Union with Scotland in the eighteenth century, surviving on the English inability to distinguish between England and Britain. This was heightened after the disestablishment of the Church in Ireland in the nineteenth century. Again in practice a condition of absurdity might seem to have been reached when neither the Prime Minister nor a majority in parliament could even be claimed as Anglican. Such was the state of things after the 1906 election when a majority of non-Anglicans was elected, and Campbell-Bannerman, Asquith and Lloyd George were in turn Prime Minister. Moreover Anglican or non-Anglican, MPs were getting less and less interested in Church issues. Yet the Church had got to have its business seen to: new dioceses to be formed, new regulations about this and that. There had been 217 Church-related bills presented to parliament between 1880 and 1913. Of these 33 were passed, 1 rejected and 183 dropped. Of the latter, 162 were never discussed at all.[6]

The less ecclesiastically interested or party-minded or theologically informed the average MP was, the less likely he would be to see the point in change of any sort. Let the Church exist, so long as it does not cause trouble; let it open public proceedings with prayers, let it crown and bury sovereigns, let it provide learned eccentric dons in the universities, let it discipline boys at school. The average layman was not anxious for it to go far beyond these things and in particular he was not anxious to allow the new wave of clerical Anglo-Catholics to alter services, doctrines, social attitudes and even suggest that the Established Church of this land was not really Protestant at all, but had been Catholic all the time. Acceptance of the Establishment principle went with Erastianism and Erastianism with an old-fashioned, non-sectarian Protestantism, frequently quite bitterly anti-Roman. Of such a kind, indeed its very champion, was Bishop Knox of

Manchester, and not so very different – though intellectually more idiosyncratic – was Hensley Henson, Bishop of Hereford and then of Durham.

For Henson the adoption of any clerically controlled machinery to make possible an at least partial measure of ecclesiastical self-government was effectively equivalent to disestablishment; the Church would no longer be a body for which 'every Englishman has responsibility'. It would become instead a denomination. The complete Protestant, he saw the Protestantism of the 'National Church' – an essentially inclusive sort of Protestantism – guaranteed by the absence of any final authority other than that of parliament. There should be no dividing line between Church and nation. He knew well enough that the tides within the Church were not flowing his way, but – as he saw it – they were mostly clerical tides, which could still be controlled by the nation as such, that is to say by parliament in which the bishops were represented in the Lords but the laity remained very much supreme.

Both in theory and practice this was just the model of the Church which no Anglo-Catholic could well tolerate: for him the Church – the believing Church, led by its bishops and its priests – must be master in its own house, and once master, then it should put the house in order by reasserting in many another way too the rights of Catholic tradition, so long suppressed by the heirs of the Reformation. In theory we would say that a 'Catholic' view of the Church is likely to be an inclusivist and at least semi-established one: heir to the medieval mutual inherence of Church and society; while a 'Protestant' view should be of a 'gathered' Church of believers differentiated from society around it (and such, of course, was the Protestant view of Free Church Protestants). The curiosity of the Anglican scene in the first decades of this century is that it was the old-fashioned Protestant who really stood for the medieval 'Catholic' view of the inclusive Church, the Anglo-Catholic who argued for the 'Protestant' view of a Church distinguished by the explicit faith and commitment (signified by confirmation) of its members.

In practice the Church in England was now too little privileged for its establishment to be any longer very offensive to outsiders, but still too profoundly established in all sorts of subtle ways for disestablishment to be a road which any but the fanatic would easily choose to enter upon. Some of the ways were not so subtle. The presence of twenty-six bishops in the House of Lords was a very real matter when the House of Lords still had much power, there were no life peers, and the hereditary aristocracy was a good deal smaller than with the 'creations' of Lloyd George and his successors it would soon become. Randall Davidson in particular attended most regularly and delivered many important speeches. He was, Cosmo Lang remarked, very much a 'House of Lords man', 'never more, so to say, at home than when he was there'.[7] The bishops in the Lords were their own men, they certainly did not vote on strictly party lines and they did, of course, divide among themselves. Most might tend to vote with the Liberals on issues of social reform, but with the Tories on education, Ireland and the Constitution.

Undoubtedly the most important and tense vote taken in the House of Lords in modern times was that of 10 August 1911, whereby it passed the Parliament Bill and so allowed its own powers to be curtailed. There can be little doubt that Davidson and a majority of the bishops felt strongly opposed to change. It is also probable that, as it had become a party-political issue of the most electrifying intensity, they would really have preferred to abstain. It is clear that Davidson was canvassed repeatedly by both sides. It is also clear that his natural allies in the House were mostly among the out-and-out Tory opposition, the Salisbury-Selborne group, devout churchmen and generally helpful in matters ecclesiastical. Yet he finally spoke out authoritatively in favour of the bill and it passed by 131 to 114, the two archbishops and eleven bishops voting with the majority and two against. It is highly probable that if he had not spoken the bill would have been rejected, and either some five hundred new Liberal peers would have been created, to end Conservative control of the upper House but also render the Lords ridiculous, or government would have been in danger of breaking down. Davidson was desperately anxious that the Crown should not be found standing with the peers against the will of the people or the House of Lords be effectively emptied of its traditional character by a mass creation, so he voted for what he did not like and

earned by doing so a bitter response from the Conservative right
wing.

The history of the Parliament Act shows well enough that if the
Church was controlled by Establishment, it was also thereby
given power, indeed authority, and could still, somewhat ner-
vously, use it. The control was obvious enough, not only in the
difficulty of getting Church measures through parliament but in
the continual area of patronage – the nomination by the Prime
Minister of the bishops, deans and many other senior officials of
the Church. The care mostly taken over this was very great. It was
a curious situation on any grounds. Few, if any, of the Prime
Ministers since Salisbury could be genuinely described as believing Anglican Christians. The dominant British political class
was largely unbelieving. If one thinks of Asquith, Haldane,
Balfour, Lloyd George, Churchill, H. A. L. Fisher, one cannot
well speak in terms of degrees of Christian orthodoxy, but only of
degrees of scepticism. There was hardly a straightforward Christian believer in the front rank of politics in these years. Yet the
concern of these people for the Church was very real, if somewhat
paternalist. Asquith, the willing listener to many an Abbey sermon despite his Congregationalist origins, the man who could
describe himself as a 'dour and unseduceable Protestant' when
faced with the awkwardness of a Roman Catholic daughter-in-
law but who at heart had the profound scepticism of the completely secular mind, showed the greatest interest and care in the
whole field of ecclesiastical appointments, frequently exchanging
a couple of letters a week with Davidson on the subject.

With Lloyd George, however, it could be more difficult. Like
Asquith his was a Free Church background, but unlike Asquith
he had not been socialized into the Establishment world of
Oxford and the Athenaeum and so understood little about the
intricacies of its ecclesiastical wing, and also cared rather little.
Hensley Henson's nomination to the see of Hereford in 1916 was
Lloyd George's first appointment. It produced an uproar from
both Anglo-Catholic and Evangelical on account of Henson's
supposed tendencies to theological modernism. Henson was
already Dean of Durham, but the beliefs of deans do not matter
so much as those of bishops. Davidson had endeavoured to
dissuade Lloyd George from the appointment but unsuccessfully.

Gore appealed to the archbishop to refuse to consecrate and it seems that Davidson did at one stage actually contemplate offering his own resignation. Eventually a way round was duly found to the satisfaction of most consciences but what the case did show up well enough was the extreme vulnerability of the system to the whims of the Prime Minister.

On the whole however the system worked in practice well enough, bringing many distinguished men of varied schools of thought to the bench: some people, of course, inevitably excluded themselves but few so deliberately as Canon Peter Green, a superb parish priest in Salford and author of *The Town Parson*, who declined the see of Lincoln in 1920 on the grounds that the size of episcopal palaces and incomes was a stumbling block. It was a thought, Archbishop Davidson replied, that had never occurred to him before.[8] The way bishops were appointed, and who were appointed, and where they lived when appointed, were all cogs within a much larger system whereby the Established Church had been fitted most smoothly into the English social order.

It would have meant little for bishops to sit in the House of Lords if they did not participate as well in the wider life of the Lords: Davidson, Lang, Gore and others were frequently to be met not only in the Athenaeum but at the political club dinners such as 'Grillion's and 'The Club'. A note in Asquith's diary for April 1923 is typical: 'I dined at Grillion's and had a good talk with the Archbishop of Canterbury, Haldane and Stanley Baldwin – a curious trio – on the latest development of the Einstein theory'.[9] The bishops were at home in this world because they belonged to it by birth, education and relaxation. Over half the bench in 1920 was connected with the peerage or the landed gentry by birth or marriage, and almost all had been at public schools: forty-one of the ninety-three bishops appointed between 1900 and 1939 had been at the ten leading public schools (Eton alone contributed twenty-five bishops in the century 1860-1960)[10] and with a few insignificant exceptions they had all been to Oxford or Cambridge. Moreover they had had no appreciable training at a theological college or anywhere else to give them even a professional differentiation. When not living in their own 'palaces', or staying at Lambeth Palace while attending an episcopal meeting or the House of Lords, they might well be at one or another of the great aristocratic homes across the country. Of course there was hierarchy in all this – the bishop of a lesser see did not behave quite like Canterbury, York or London but then that too corresponded to the hierarchy in the land.

As important for the Church's total involvement in the national establishment as the bishops were many other dignitaries. The English Establishment was centred at once upon Westminster, upon Windsor, upon Oxford and Cambridge and upon the principal public schools. The crucial point is not just that the bishops came from the same schools and Oxbridge colleges as most other members of the ruling class, but that the Church had a most powerful position within all these institutions. The Provost and Head Master of Eton, the Dean of Christ Church, The Dean of Windsor, were – almost more than the bishops themselves – focal points of the inter-involvement of Church and State. One could write much about the subtle significance of the dual roles of Christ Church in this regard; its head the Cathedral Dean, Tom Quad thick with the homes of canons, professors of theology, yet at the same time the most socially élite of colleges, the *alma mater* of many a Cabinet minister. Again, look at Westminster, with the splendid old deanery and canonries just a couple of minutes walk from the Houses of Parliament and think of all the influential people who have been canons of Westminster, such as Henson and Gore. William Temple, already the young darling of the Church, champion of 'Life and Liberty', had not been installed in 1919 in a Westminster canonry to no purpose: it provided just the right ambience for influencing the great and the powerful. So Davidson's future ecclesiastical eminence was assured by his years as adviser to the aged Victoria while Dean of Windsor.

In 1920 Cyril Alington, Head Master of Eton, represents so unaffectedly the way these things were that it is worth our while to pause a little and consider him. Eton, beyond all other institutions, was school to the powerful, the aristocratic, the wealthy. Alington was a Marlborough boy, a Fellow of All Souls, a priest whose formal theological training had been minimal, whose classical education was excellent. With such as him the divide of culture, sensibility and purpose between clergy and laity was small indeed. He had taught at Eton and been Head Master of Shrewsbury. When interviewed in 1916 by the Fellows of Eton prior to appointment, his brother-in-law, Lord Cobham, asked whether in his opinion it was important that a Head Master should be in Orders. He was the only candidate to be so. He answered 'Yes' and was appointed.[11] When seventeen years later Alington left Eton, it was to become Dean of Durham. A priest like Alington had all that the layman had, but also that little extra note of spiritual and sacramental authority which went with Orders. But as the clergy grew more professional, the theological colleges more important, their lay expertise diminished. The great age of the clerical head was almost over and with it the most effective of all the ways whereby the Established Church moulded the nation's leadership. The price of Erastianism may have been very high, the rewards were very great.

Nor, of course, did the matter end at these august levels. The pattern repeated itself right down to the village where traditionally – that is, more or less, since the eighteenth century – the parson had been the next gentleman after the squire with a house to match his position. It was hard to keep it up, admittedly, in the twentieth century but hard too to let it go. 'The grand atmosphere of many country rectories is one of *paupertas ambitiosa*', wrote an observer just before the war, 'the hat-touchings and curt-seyings, the wagonette driven by the gardeners in livery, the girls to have new frocks for the country ball, the sons to be "educated as gentlemen".'[12] The praxis of a sub-squirearchy might be more and more difficult to realize, but it remained normative, even if there were plenty of poor priests, plenty who had no Oxbridge education, and plenty who spent their lives in the very different atmosphere of a poor town parish. They were not, for the group, the influential ones and they did not lessen the depth to which the spirit of Erastian Establishment in a highly class-structured society had affected the shape of the Church and the norms for clerical achievement. There was no more select gathering in the upper academic, and even political, world than that of the fellowship of All Souls at Oxford. Cosmo Gordon Lang had been Archbishop of York since 1908 but like Alington, like Lord Curzon for that matter, he remained a Fellow and in 1920 at the All Souls' Gaudy he sang, as he had done every year since 1898, its traditional and nonsensical 'Song of the Mallard'. When one recalls as well that Lang prided himself on never having set foot inside a shop in York, perhaps the sheer oddity of his annual singing to the delight of the All Souls fellows expresses as well as anything the intimacy of the Church's continued presence in the corridors of power, privilege and wit in the world of 1920.

It was impossible that a Church so constructed should not have been in a very decisive way a Tory Church. This was not so much a matter of the way the bishops voted in the House of Lords or of their public utterances, but of the consequences of so close a class identification. Indeed there may be something in the view that it was the very consciousness of being an Old Etonian that prompted more than one bishop now and then to express radical or vaguely socialist sympathies. Gore might call himself a Christian Socialist, Temple might announce in 1918 in Canterbury Convocation that he had joined the Labour Party – and all power to their elbows; but at the level of the Church's real life, its interests and policies and the way people saw it, the identification with social class and the traditional aristocratic order of English life allowed of no alternative: the Church of England was as clearly Tory as were the Free Churches Liberal. And this was even more true of the laity and of the lower clergy than of the bishops, though of course devout Anglicans were to be found in the other parties – Charles Masterman, for instance, among the Liberals, George Lansbury in Labour. But the lay politicians who more or less doubled in ecclesiastical politics, men like Lord Selborne and Hugh Cecil, were Tories out and out.

There was in fact a natural concomitance of interests. A map of the country showing those parts where Anglicanism was strongest would coincide almost exactly with one of constituencies Conservatives were sure to win. The Conservatives defended voluntary schools (Anglican or Roman Catholic) and the Welsh Church Establishment, the Liberals attacked both. The Anglicans voted Conservative just as naturally as the Nonconformist voted Liberal. On both the above issues, it is worth noting, hard Protestantism was split politically down the middle as it had always been. No one could be more Protestant than Bishop Knox, the fiercest defender both of Church schools and Establishment; yet no one could be more Protestant than Dr Clifford, the fiery Baptist opponent of both. But when it came to Ireland, the thorniest issue that British politics had to face, then as at so many other times, matters were different. The Liberals in alliance with the Irish Nationalists were battling for Home Rule, the Tories in alliance with the Ulstermen were utterly opposed to it. The Free Churches were now torn down the middle: their profound suspicions of Rome, their natural sympathies with Northern Irish Presbyterians, could not but make them hesitate in the cause to which Gladstone had so emphatically committed the Liberal Party. What is really surprising is how loyal Free Churchmen were to the Home Rule cause. On the Anglican side too some Anglo-Catholics at least found their natural sympathies with Home Rule: let us not forget that the flag of Sinn Fein was solemnly hung beside that of St George in Thaxted parish church! An Anglican episcopal conversation in February 1921 at Bishop-thorpe, mentioned by Temple (now a bishop) writing to his wife, expressed well enough the range of Anglican (perhaps simply English) uncertainties. It was when the Black and Tans were at their worst:

> At dinner they got on to Ireland. Ebor fails to see any difference between our action there and the Germans in Belgium. Sheffield thinks extermination of Sinn Feiners the only hope. Durham very uneasy, but could not go against the Government because he has no alternative policy. I urged that the whole question be sent to the League of Nations and that we undertake to accept the decision; but Henson won't face independence, so he can't agree to that.[13]

Even Catholics were divided on Ireland and they too were continually caught on the Tory/Liberal fence: they needed the Tories for their schools, but, being so many of them Irish in background, wanted the Liberals for Home Rule. Yet not all of them: a true Catholic Tory like the fifteenth Duke of Norfolk, the president of the Catholic Union, backed Ulstermen against the south.

Denominational polarization was never politically absolute and the Church of England itself did span the whole range of options from extreme right to extreme left. This did not however alter the fact that its main and characteristic commitment, institutionally rather than personally controlled, was well to the right of centre.

Lang and Temple and Henson all had their views but until his retirement in 1928 Randall Davidson and no one else really controlled, in so far as anyone could control, the face of the Establishment. Perhaps only in the early part of the war, under the impact of the bishop of London's crusading ardour, had that been for a while somewhat less than true. He was Archbishop of Canterbury from 1903 to 1928 and no archbishop since Laud has probably had so considerable an influence in public life. If Canterbury's natural role has almost steadily declined since his resignation, it is equally true that he had raised it to a level unknown to his predecessors, though in many ways he stood as heir and successor to his father-in-law Archbishop Tait. They were both Scots, Presbyterian by early upbringing, and there were Anglicans who could question whether Davidson had really the Anglican mind at all. It is strange how many Scots there were in positions of power in early twentieth-century Britain, including for many years the archbishops of both Canterbury and York. Certainly the Church of England was in many ways profoundly fortunate in Davidson: a man of remarkable balance of judgment, intellectual humility, sense of responsibility and capacity for work. How in his calm, unexciting way he maintained his voluminous correspondence, supervised the pastoral work of his diocese and spent hours almost daily in the corridors of secular power is something of a mystery. He was at heart an old-fashioned Protestant, yet in practice greatly under the influence of the Anglo-Catholics, clerical and lay, around him. He had no comprehension whatsoever of enthusiasm – ritualistic, suffragette, pacifist, nationalist – no great desire to change anything, no natural flair for providing an imaginative moral lead to a nation in crisis. These were serious lacks, the more so as he was temperamentally an Erastian, who saw it as his task not to make trouble – at least public trouble – for the government if he could possibly help it.

How could such a man, one might ask, be other than pretty disastrous as leader of the Church for twenty-five years in a time of great change? Certainly there were things he failed to do, yet the soundness of his judgment, the care with which he sought the facts, his willingness to be guided by the better informed and his great sense of public moral responsibility gave him an influence and a position which were remarkable. His record in the House of Lords on such matters as the Infant Life Protection Act, the Workmen's Compensation Bill, temperance reform, the West African liquor trade, the treatment of Aborigines in Australia, the introduction of Chinese labour into South Africa, is noteworthy. Or take the long and carefully argued letter of 1 August 1916 to Lord Buckmaster, the Lord Chancellor, urging that Sir Roger Casement's death sentence be commuted.[14] His advice was considered by the Cabinet but not followed. It is a letter well worth pondering for the very down to earth sort of 'political ethics' Davidson attempted to put across – unsuccessfully in this case. He never pitched his case on a higher note than he thought advisable in view of those he was approaching. Doubtless he did not understand Ireland or the power of the Nationalist case, yet his speeches in the Lords condemning the reprisals of the Black and Tans were strong enough to earn him a good deal of opprobrium, as still more did his wartime condemnation of reprisals against Germany. His weakness, not in these cases but in some others, was reluctance to state in public what he felt and even wrote in private. Perhaps most serious was his failure to remonstrate against the anti-German 'hang the Kaiser' mania which swept the country, incited by Lloyd George, at the 1918 General Election. He thought it all 'beyond measure mischievous'. As his highly discreet biographer permitted himself to comment: 'It was a misfortune that the Archbishop, though entertaining these opinions, did not proclaim them to the world.'[15] The same, unfortunately, could be said in regard to his misgivings about the Peace Treaty itself.

Davidson's best work was often done when he had been well briefed by one of his unofficial advisers, such as J. H. Oldham, the Secretary of the Conference of British Missionary Societies, on colonial affairs, or Lord Robert Cecil on foreign affairs. For instance, when in September 1918 President Wilson made a major speech backing the proposals for a League of Nations, Robert Cecil, the Parliamentary Under-Secretary at the Foreign Office and a great protagonist of the league idea, advised the archbishop to write an immediate warm reply to *The Times*: 'I can speak for no Government but ... we want a League of Nations on the very lines which he has drawn.' The letter had its effect in preventing the government from replying rather non-committally to Wilson's proposals. Again, Oldham helped him in 1920 to take up the cudgels against forced labour in Kenya and obtain the revocation of a government circular authorizing it. The Bishop of Zanzibar, the fiery Frank Weston, had appealed to the Archbishop and Davidson assured him (4 October 1920), 'You may rely upon my supporting you to the best of my power in all that seems to me to concern the highest interests of the natives.'[16] Oldham was an extremely skilled operator and together they were fully successful in this matter though, inevitably, further Kenyan problems soon loomed up including the particularly tricky one of Indian immigration.[17] How much trouble Davidson was prepared to take over just one among almost countless issues, British, colonial and international, is drily illustrated by one of his brief memoranda on this matter: 'Kenya, 18 May 1923. I have now interviewed Oldham, Andrews, Sastri, Ross, Bishop Willis, Lord Hardinger, the Bishop of Bombay and of course the Duke of Devonshire. I have read carefully General Stones article in the xixth Century for May.'[18]

The Archbishop had become indeed something of an imperial Ombudsman, surely not an inappropriate role and one unthinkable without Establishment. It is odd that he is nowhere even mentioned in either A. J. P Taylor's *English History 1914-1945*, or W. N. Medlicott's *Contemporary England 1914-1964*. As the most permanent member of the inner circle of the ruling few his influence should not be so disregarded.

One of his typically pragmatic and more ecclesiastical achievements was the Enabling Act of 1919, as a result of which the new Church Assembly met for the first time on 30 June 1920.[19] Legislative authority was delegated to it by parliament to deal with many of the administrative matters, such as the creation of new dioceses, which until then had to go individually to parliament and there – so often – failed to receive attention. Its lay members were to be chosen by those on a new electoral role of baptized (but not necessarily confirmed) members of the Church of England. This was certainly a useful piece of administrative reform but it hardly proved an answer to the ardent appeals of the

'Life and Liberty' movement stirred up by William Temple and Dick Sheppard: 'We demand liberty for the Church of England,' cried Temple at a famous meeting at the Queen's Hall in July 1917. Parliament must give its 'freedom to the Church'. It did no such thing. The archbishops had in fact already appointed a Committee on Church and State, headed by Lord Selborne, which had reported in 1916, recommending the parliamentary establishment of a Church Assembly. Davidson, rightly enough, thought that nothing could be got through parliament in wartime. In the meantime up came Life and Liberty, contributing a head of steam to get the measure through in the first post-war year, a rather propitious moment. It might well not have been passed later for there was considerable dislike of even this moderate degree of ecclesiastical self-government both in the dominant secular establishment and in many Church circles. What saw it through was, on the one hand, Lloyd George's lack of interest in Anglican internal affairs (very different from the quite tense ecclesiastical preoccupations of such establishment agnostics as Haldane and Fisher), on the other, the very pragmatic approach to it of Davidson himself and his parliamentary allies, Selborne in the Lords, Selborne's son Lord Wolmer in the Commons. Davidson put it across effectively, 'not as a constitutional change which was going to shatter the chains of an enslaved Church and emancipate us from a hampering bondage',[20] but as a useful piece of improved administrative machinery. Thus it was passed and thus it proved to be.

Hensley Henson had been against the project all along and sneered at it in all its forms, but his comment on the Selborne Committee was as acute as his observations so often were:

> Lord Selborne, as he views his colleagues from the chair, must have felt a legitimate pride in the fact that the chosen eleven should include not only himself, but also his son, his brother-in-law, and such intimate political associates as his kinsman Mr Balfour and the Duke of Devonshire. The atmosphere of the Committee was not so much national as domestic.[21]

Selborne's wife was a Cecil, Hugh and Robert Cecil his brothers-in-law. When Balfour, whose mother was a Cecil, was Prime Minister, succeeding his uncle Lord Salisbury in that capacity, his government had had so many relatives in it that it had been nick named 'The Hotel Cecil'. The Cecils had somewhat receded from the heart of government since those days, making do instead with the lay leadership of the Church. If an ecclesiastical measure, such as the Sheffield Bishopric Bill, was got through parliament, it was largely due to the good offices of Hugh Cecil and his cousin Lord Wolmer, both in the Commons. It was they who planned the new Church Assembly, they who got the bill through parliament and they who subsequently ran the assembly quite efficiently, on strictly Tory lines, ensuring that it never ventured beyond the legislative and the financial. The State might have rejected the Cecils but the Church remained in safe hands. It was certainly not remotely like the 'Life and Liberty' of Dick Sheppard's warm imagination, but they were distinguished hands. The Cecils and their relations were high Tories and high churchmen – they were also highly intelligent, high-minded and pretty unpredictable. Hugh, the cleverest and oddest of the lot, was fanatically devoted to such High Church causes as the law forbidding marriage to a deceased's wife's sister, and the bitterest opponent of the Parliament Act, but also a defender of conscientious objectors. He became in the Church Assembly, in Lang's words, 'the power behind the throne', at the same time representing in parliament the University of Oxford and being, in later life, Provost of Eton. He and his relatives were no common reactionaries and the Church of England never apparently questioned their corporate resolve to run its affairs for the next twenty years.

4

Anglicans

The proudest claim of the Established Church[1] was to be present in every corner of the country: wherever you went there was a church, a parish and a parson, their services might be scorned but they were there, available. This was true; but it was truer of some places than of others. You could not miss the churches of Norwich. If you lived in working-class Sheffield or in a London block of flats – already numerous by the turn of the century – the old sense of the Church's presence with its strongly local, community, village-like model had almost wholly disappeared. English society by 1920 was overwhelmingly urban, the Church of England's clerical deployment and pastoral vision was still fundamentally rural.[2] A great effort had certainly been made all through the Victorian age to build and staff town churches. It is far easier to add than to subtract: with a total increase in clergy many new town parishes could be opened, without affecting the supply for the far greater number of country parishes. But when ordinations began to fall (already from the 1880s, and even more so with the war) the number of suburban parishes was still inevitably growing. Both the countryside and the large urban parishes of industrial areas now began to feel the pinch in a shortage of curates. There were two curates at Long Melford before the First World War; it has never had one since. But if a curate shortage had begun to affect the southern countryside by 1920, its effect on the north was a great deal sharper.[3]

The numbers of the clergy in any area did indeed reflect well enough the Church's subconscious sense of importance of that area and the latter's interest in Anglican ministrations. The peak areas were undoubtedly Oxford and Cambridge where parishes, colleges and theological colleges were all most generously staffed with the clerical élite. The two university cities were the twin pillars of the Established Church upon which everything else depended. Here the clergy were manifestly at home – more so than anywhere else; but this home ground extended with little conscious sense of discontinuity across the southern countryside and the middle and upper-class sections of town life. Here the vicar's place seemed assured enough. But the further you went north, the further you went into the working class, and the further you went into the large town, the poorer became the ratio of priests to people and the more the Church of England was likely to appear marginal rather than central to society, its clergy to be fighting a desperate battle upon hostile terrain. In Durham, Hensley Henson acutely observed, the established religion was not Anglicanism but Methodism.

In South Kensington 34.5 per cent of the population worshipped regularly in an Anglican church at the beginning of the century – not a bad proportion – but only 1.6 per cent in Somers Town.[4] The figures represent an integral socio-structural relationship in the one case, a wholly marginal one in the other. The members of one society lived in a world where they participated in quasi-ecclesiastical institutions like public schools and society weddings as appropriate pieces of their own life style; for the members of the other the Establishment was immeasurably alien, approaching them even at its kindest across the class gap which separated Professor Higgins from Eliza Doolittle.

The rural church was strongest in the south-west and the east. If church attendance was generally much lower in the urban north than the urban south (apart from London) this had certainly much to do with the fact that rural attendance too was lower in the north. The Church of England had long found difficulty in taking the north quite seriously.[5] Perhaps this was initially related to the post-Reformation survival in the north of a strong rural catholicism. Later on it was accentuated by the northern spread of Methodism, the influx of the Irish, and the growth of a large industrial proletariat. Nevertheless the value of the independent Convocation of York as a source of authority and point of reference outside the south-east was a real one, and there grew up in Lancashire particularly a strong low-Protestant Anglicanism with sounder working-class foundations than might be found elsewhere. The late nineteenth century, after the establishment of the new dioceses of Liverpool (1880), Newcastle (1882), Southwell (1884) and Wakefield (1888), would seem to be the time when in the north, as elsewhere, the Established Church was making its most consistent effort to be a pastorally effective church: the age when five vicars of Leeds were raised to the episcopate. But the decline in the number of men in the ministry in the Edwardian age tended to undercut this, for the shortage was soon being felt particularly in the north. There is a profound, almost constant pull in English life towards the south-east, and this has affected the deployment of the clergy as much as anything else, so that whenever there are shortages they are likely to be felt a great deal more acutely in the north than in the south.

Another point: it was still true in 1920 that the sacramental structure of the Church of England operated a curiously decisive, but little noted, social segregation between quality and populace by means of confirmation. 'The children of well-to-do churchmen are confirmed almost as a matter of course, whereas among the wage-earners confirmation is exceptional.'[6] Confirmation was given in one's teens – and was preceded by a certain amount of instruction and choice-making; it was an almost natural part of public school life, but a decidedly difficult thing for a working-class youth. For the Church of England, however, the rule 'no confirmation, no communion' remained an absolute one, thus barring from communion for life a very large proportion of its ordinary members and establishing something of a two-class citizenship within the Church. Possibly nothing was more influential – particularly in an age of increased sacramentalism – in reinforcing the sense that the Church of England was essentially an upper-class body. This was all the more powerful in its social effect, and the more difficult to change, in being in principle a theological rather than a social matter. The comparable effect that pew rents had had, especially in the nineteenth century, in class-stratifying religion could more easily be recognized in its consequences, because, however useful pew rents might be, they did not have the doctrinal potency of confirmation to defy change and so maintain the conformity of church with class.

All this is not to say that there were not many devout working-class Anglicans. There were. There was George Lansbury. There were some absolutely working-class priests trained at Kelham and elsewhere. Probably the middle-sized towns of the south such as Bristol, Southampton and Exeter were the places where you would find them strongest. Religiously minded working people who saw no reason to go Free Church or Roman Catholic had after all little option and there were zealous, indeed almost desperately earnest priests about, to help them. It is only that the system – despite the good intentions of many a bishop – was geared so powerfully the other way and this in a very class-divided society and an age of increasing class consciousness.

Within the gentleman class the division between clergy and laity was a remarkably slight one, the reason for the absence of at least upper-class anticlericalism of the continental type in England. Hensley Henson was entirely correct when in 1900 he remarked that the English form of establishment had 'declericalised the clergy beyond all precedent or parallel',[7] and the more unprofessional they were, the more they 'think, and speak, and act in ways which are essentially similar to those of their Christian neighbours'. Few priests were any longer JPs, but Henson as Bishop of Durham would still need to rebuke a vicar who became Master of the Beagles in 1931.[8] They were declericalized by both what they had and what they lacked: they had the common Oxbridge education, large houses, the style of a gentleman. What they largely lacked was professional training. The theological colleges were indeed now a reality which, in principle, the bishops expected ordinands to have attended (though compulsorily only from 1917), if often very briefly: one term could still be quite sufficient.[9] Geoffrey Clayton, after his years at Pembroke College, Cambridge, went to Cuddesdon in 1908, hoping to be there 'for the long vacation term at least'.[10] By the end of the year he was back in Cambridge as a fellow at Peterhouse. And so short a period of professional socialization was not uncommon. The years at a university, not – maybe – even reading theology, were regarded as basically sufficient, though Oxford and Cambridge had lost the character of Anglican clerical societies which they had largely had fifty years earlier. There was now indeed an alternative professional training available at Kelham or Mirfield, based rather on the Catholic seminary model, but the men going to them – generally without Oxbridge degrees – were the minority, somewhat under suspicion as not the right type, and seldom destined for high place. Probably the most formative training centre for many an Anglican priest was still the home: a quite extraordinarily high proportion of the clergy were sons of priests. Nothing has been more characteristic of the Church of England with its gentle transition from natural to Christian relationships. The influence of the clerical family both as a wider humanizing and Christianizing agency in society and as the communicator to new priests of the spiritual values and pastoral methods of the older generation has been remarkable. It existed before the Reformation, but illegally. One of the greatest sources of Protestant strength has been the recognition that the marriage of priests is, all in all, a spiritual asset for the Church, not a disgrace. But it does of course, hold a priest rather tightly to his class. Marriage tended to reinforce all the worst aspects of class stratification within the clergy.

In 1920 James Hastings had been Rector of Martley, in Worcestershire, for thirteen years and curate for ten years before that to his father John, who became Rector of Martley in 1875. John had succeeded to the living on the death of his father, Henry James, who himself succeeded his centenarian father, another James, in 1856. This James was the founder of the line – he had bought the advowson of Martley in 1791 with the money of his wife, daughter of a Chipping Norton banker. He became Rector in 1795, so in 1920 James Hastings, his great-grandson, educated at Repton and Oxford, had 125 years of family rule behind him as he ministered to his village flock. He was not, as his father and grandfather had been, a JP and chairman of the local bench, but otherwise life does not seem to have been much altered in that very old and rambling house with its outdoor and indoor servants, its lovely garden, its almost organic relationship with the church and churchyard beside it. On a May Sunday of 1907 he noted an 8 a.m. service in the vestry book with eighteen communicants, a little triumphantly as 'First early celebration for generations' and that now became the norm: an important reform and one in line with the general trend in the country, but hardly an excessive one and not one of many. The church itself was very well restored a couple of years later revealing a wealth of medieval wall painting. Hastings was an assiduous visitor, riding round the parish on his horse, but 'the scraps of writing which he has left are indicative rather of his sporting and agricultural activities than of his theological proclivities'.[11] Gardening, local antiquities, campanology, but above all cricket. Hastings was the keenest of cricketers, and Worcestershire village cricket in his day in which the local clergy played with all their neighbours, Stanley Baldwin and Lord Annaby, farmer, butcher and blacksmith, seemed a splendid thing: the symbol of rural *communitas*.

Clergy of the Hastings type were not promoted. Few, doubtless, were as prosperous as he. Nevertheless the village parson, neither Anglo-Catholic nor Evangelical, neither ambitious nor discontented, remained a common figure throughout the land, more rooted locally than the bishops, more representative than anyone else of a tolerant indigeneity of Christian tradition. Hastings' post-first-war income – £852 – was twice that of the average incumbent, and comparable to that of cathedral dignitaries.[12] In 1939 five thousand stipends were still less than £400. Many a local priest was now pretty miserably stretched. He had the Martley model but without its financial buttressing and with less and less of its social status, its squarson self-confidence. The result could be painful for the individual and in the eyes of society increasingly ludicrous. Many a vicar could only make up for his lack of theological expertise, professional training and loss of social status with a double share of the rather nebulous Christianity of the public school: 'Take God on to the rugger field.' Cricket, rowing, fishing, railway timetables, a little Plato, bell ringing: wonderful sidelines, but rather pathetic if they become too central to a priest's mind. The Oxford and Cambridge boat race could be seen as the sacramental focus of much clerical fellowship – so very much part of being nice and gentlemanly and rather ineffectual in worldly terms, of never quite growing up. Of B. K. Cunningham of Westcott House, most influential of all theological college heads in this period, it was said, 'In many ways B. K. was a public school boy to the end of his life, though he lived to be seventy-three.'[13] The consequence of avoiding the Scylla of clericalization and the Charybdis of the secular rat race could be a life-long fixation with the boat race.

How pastorally successful was the gentleman priest? While it is impossible to generalize it seems that in the majority of cases he was very ineffective: he either visited his parishioners very much *de haut en bas* or hardly at all – many a working-class Anglican felt it hardly proper that, as a gentleman, he should.[14] In *England's Green and Pleasant Land*, J. W. Robertson Smith provided in 1925 a remarkably vivid picture of English country life in the Cotswolds. He had a great deal to say about the Church and the clergy, and was exceedingly critical: 'The blunt fireside judgment of the mass of agricultural labouring families on many a parson is that he is witless and lazy, a self-satisfied drone, who, by the advantage of his social position, has secured a soft job.'[15] If the people still went to church, it was not because of anything the priest did but rather because they had 'nowhere else to go'. It was a reason to put on Sunday clothes, it was a dignified building to enter, it was a free piece of respectable socialization, it was perhaps on occasion even the way to draw some spark of inspiration from the Cranmerian vocabulary of a sung matins, from pillars and vaults and monuments, but seldom from the clergy. It is a hard judgment but probably not a badly mistaken one. Robertson Smith's clergy were 'good sorts', they visited the dying, they were kindly, a few were actually saintly, a few were scholarly, mostly in rather irrelevant matters. They were feeble preachers but – more important – many of them were far too obviously concerned with sport and with maintaining class. Some were quite definitely odd. They were a bunch of very ineffectual men.

Were there many exceptions? Of course there were, particularly in some of the large town parishes and particularly, perhaps, among the celibate clergy. Take one such, Peter Green, who in our opening year of 1920 refused to move from his parish of St Philip's, Salford, to become Bishop of Lincoln. Two years later he described, in reply to criticisms of the 'inexcusable laziness of the clergy', a typical Sunday.

> Sunday began at 6.45 a.m. when I went into the church to get things ready for the 7 o'clock Mass, and ended at 9.45 p.m. when, having closed the vicarage door on a parishioner who insisted on coming in after Evensong to discuss some troubles he was having with his wife I turned to the supper I was too tired to eat. The day had included, in parish church, mission

church and hospital, eight services and five addresses. Monday began with a ward Celebration in the hospital, followed by another in church. It closed when, at 9.15 p.m., I got in from my last sick case to attack the day's correspondence. I actually had forty minutes for breakfast, but against that must be set that dinner was taken in fifteen minutes in a restaurant, between a meeting of the school trustees and hearing confessions in church. And when I got in to tea at 7.10 I found (I declare before heaven I am writing the truth)

   (a) A man with passport papers to be filled up;

   (b) A day school teacher with a grievance;

   (c) Two women with pension papers to be filled up and signed;

   (d) Three boys wanting swimming-bath tickets;

   (e) One man and one lad wanting letters to possible employers, as both were out of work;

   (f) A boy with a Convalescent Home letter to be filled up.[16]

Green was widely esteemed 'the best parish priest in England' and he himself believed that many existing priests should never have been ordained. Yet he was not alone in his understanding of what it meant to be a vicar. With the vast range of his concern – personal, social, spiritual – he was a genuine representative of the Church of England at its very best, but so were the more numerous gentleman oddities described by Robertson Smith.

It was to remedy the gentlemanly amateurism of 'the average clergyman' that Fr Kelly developed at Kelham in the 1890s a quite (for the Church of England at least) new type of theological training – one entered by teenagers without university degrees and taking up to eight years. It was a hard community life, aiming at forming professional priests to cope with any 'old washerwoman' in a back street and it provided its men with theology 'co-ordinating the ideas of natural theology, such as Aquinas handles them, with the Maurician treatment of Church and Sacraments – the Incarnation and the Atonement marking the points of transition'.[17] It was all quite different from a jolly romp reading for an arts degree at an Oxford college followed by a month or two at Cuddesdon or Wells. The bishops did not care for it, especially for accepting men without university degrees, but with some shortage of priests they could hardly stop it, and by 1920 Kelham was the largest of Anglican theological colleges and the most significant, committed by its structure to challenging the class barrier.

It had a short term ally in this in the institution set up after the war for four years in a derelict prison at Knutsford under the direction of F. R. Barry, with the assistance of Tubby Clayton and Mervyn Haigh. The shortage of ordinands at the end of the war was acute, yet there were hundreds of ex-servicemen anxious to be ordained but without the financial wherewithal to get to a university in the traditional way. Archbishop Davidson guaranteed them special free training and this was provided at Knutsford; 675 candidates went there, of whom 435 were ordained. The obvious immediate effect was to rescue the Church of the 1920s from an immediate crisis in clergy, but Knutsford's wider significance lay in its approach to a less class-conscious type of priesthood than had been the norm hitherto. Sadly it was not followed up.[18] The model theological college for the next twenty-five years (1919-44) would be Westcott House, under B. K. Cunningham, described by an admirer as 'the veritable prince of all principals of theological colleges'.[19] Cunningham was a wise and much loved man and, like the staff of Knutsford, anxious to get away from identifying Westcott with any heavy sectional loyalty within the Church. It would, unlike Kelham, be able to find room for the Evangelical as well as the Anglo-Catholic, but Cunningham, unlike Kelly, would quite deliberately maintain the tradition of the 'English gentleman in Holy Orders'. He dreaded professionalism and clericalism of any sort but could never begin to see that his alternative was a class model very civilized but subtly subversive of the Church's social catholicity. Life in Cambridge relieved by a summer of fishing and shooting in Scotland went with deep humanity, sanity and priestly commitment but it reinforced rather than alleviated his church's primary weakness.

The tradition of a laicized clergy went hand in hand with that of a church-minded laity, the 'ecclesiastical layman'. Shaftesbury for Evangelicals and Gladstone for high churchmen were the devout nineteenth-century prototypes. A national Church was, in all sorts of ways, a lay-controlled Church – from parliament to the most local patronage. The upper class was not disposed to forget this and ecclesiastical battles from the latter years of

Victoria on, behind the immediate questions of rubrics and doctrine, were largely issues of lay versus clerical power. The Anglo-Catholic clerical resolve to wrest ecclesiastical freedom from lay and Erastian control could seldom be faulted ecclesiologically and it was frequently successful. The long term danger would be a loss of lay interest. Lay control went with lay concern just as too great a clerical control goes with lay boredom in ecclesiastical matters.

To a large extent, however, it was a common enterprise. Nowhere is this seen better than in the growth of the public schools. What the expanding middle classes needed most in late nineteenth-century England was suitable boarding schooling for its children – on the model of Eton and Rugby, but a good deal cheaper. 1870-1914 was the golden age of the public school. The Empire was now so large that a great many playing fields were needed to train England's sons to police it all. Old grammar schools were revived and changed in character, and dozens of new schools appeared, almost all including a large chapel and a manifest commitment to the Anglican Establishment. The hard core to both Anglican life and the ruling class's life was constituted by the inner ring of public schools, not only Eton, Harrow, Rugby and Winchester but – quite as important from the Church point of view – schools like Westminster, St Paul's, Shrewsbury, Marlborough, Oundle and Repton. Almost all had clerical headmasters as a matter of course, some of them future bishops. Thus, to take a celebrated example in 1914, William Temple was succeeded as headmaster of Repton by Geoffrey Fisher: thirty years later the same succession would take place in the see of Canterbury. It was the steady enlargement of this institutional area by such developments as the Woodard schools which needs to be noted here. Canon Woodard was a single minded and extraordinarily successful Tractarian clergyman resolved to provide boarding education for the professional and trading classes. The vast chapel at Lancing, dedicated in 1913, was symbolic of the whole enterprise but by then that was only the centre of a network of thirteen public schools, including four girls' schools.[20] Perhaps in no other area of life was the Established Church so clearly growing rather than declining in the England of the early twentieth century. It was doing so by demonstrating its utility to the more affluent laity and, quite often, securing its affections, but it was doing so too by a further consolidation of its already dangerously over-weighted class alliance. To strike a contrast: Church day schools had fallen in the number of attenders by a full third, over a million children, between 1903 and 1923.[21] There were sound educational grounds for this. Nevertheless the consequences of the two continuing developments would be massive in the further establishing of the Church of England's upper and middle-class image. Against such processes the almost desperate counter-ploys of slum priests in the Guild of St Matthew or the Christian Socialist League would avail very little. Quintessential public school religion was Anglican with an emphatically Protestant and rather vaguely Evangelical note. The dominant stress upon 'muscular Christianity' was often in truth rather upon muscular stoicism – 'Stoicism making use of Christian phraseology', Kitson Clark has called it.[22] The reigning values were those of athletics, sartorial perfection, the bearing of pain, the future leadership of inferior brands of humankind.[23] 'Play the Game' was the simple message which flowed over the schoolboy in countless headmaster's speeches, school songs, in Newbolt's poetry. It was, maybe, an appropriate ideal for the servants of a gentleman's empire; its adequacy for the Church of England was more arguable.

The common religion of the English laity in the nineteenth century – and of most of the clergy too – remained emphatically Protestant. Tractarianism had made very limited inroads upon the common man; indeed the less religion he had the more sure he seemed to be that he was a Protestant and that the increasingly determined Anglo-Catholicism of the late Victorian age was some sort of treason, if not to God, at least to England. Low church episcopal appointments were always popular. Yet all the evidence suggests that Protestantism as a national religion was moribund, providing no coherent alternative between an agnostic liberalism, which had rejected all Protestantism's most characteristic beliefs about the Bible and salvation, and some form of revived catholicism. If Randall Davidson in fact favoured the Catholic movement across his long archiepiscopate, it was not in the least because he was at heart a Catholic, far from it, but because there was no alternative within sight. The Anglo-

Catholics had pastoral vigour, social ideas and plenty of interesting leaders; the Evangelicals had none of these things. Bishop Ingham, secretary of the Church Missionary Society, was forced to admit to Davidson in 1911: 'There are really so few leaders in what are known as the Evangelical ranks.'[24] Henson, writing of much the same time, and again with no love to lose for the Anglo-Catholics, had the same to say:

> Perhaps . . . the most potent of the favouring circumstances which assisted the advance of the neo-Tractarians was the depressed condition of their rivals. The Evangelicals were exhibiting all the marks of a moribund party. They were out of touch with the prevailing tendencies, social and intellectual, of the time . . . Not the choice of Government, but their own inferiority in personal quality, was the key to their weakness in the hierarchy.[25]

To some extent this was the consequence of the preponderant missionary concern of late nineteenth-century Evangelicals – it had creamed off their best men overseas for several decades. Anglo-Catholics, with their slighter missionary preoccupation, were less affected. Year by year the noblest young men in the Cambridge Inter-Collegiate Christian Union (CICCU) had set off for Africa, Asia or Australia, leaving little that was exciting to head Evangelical ranks at home.

Bishop Knox retired as an old but still vigorous man from the see of Manchester in 1920. He had long been the real leader of Anglican Evangelicals, the last major Protestant champion upon the episcopal bench: the pure Protestant Tory, as unyielding to Nonconformists over Church schools as to Catholics over novel devotions, incense, vestments and the like. He had led thousands of Lancashire men to London to demonstrate their opposition to Liberal attempts to upset the 1902 Education Act and in 1920 he had just engineered a petition to the archbishops signed by 100,000 laity to protest against changes in the communion service. In Bishop Knox the voice of old Protestant England still thundered forth, but his only two sons to take to religion both went intensely 'Catholic' and then, to his father's misery, Ronald his most brilliant child even joined the Roman Catholic Church. 'Between ourselves, Winnie, I cannot understand what it is that the dear boys see in the Blessed Virgin Mary,' the bishop complained helplessly to his more sympathetic daughter.[26]

The Evangelical movement had been most intimately linked with the Victorian empire and a whole range of attitudes and values very markedly on the wane by 1920. Faced with the complexities, the ambiguities, the cynicism of the twentieth-century world, it tended to fall back on to Erastianism and a very simplistic moralism which even bishops whose inner sympathies were far more on the Protestant side of the fence found unworkable. Bishop Knox had no successor – or rather in William Temple he had a remarkable successor of a very different mould – but one of the strange recurring qualities of English religion in the twentieth century right up until at least the Second World War is the wistful sense of an abandoned majority: the ebb of the Protestant ethos, the religious lining of the national myth, Elizabethan and Victorian, a popular religion which was becoming little more than a gut reaction yet still able on occasion to burst forth with a fierce flicker of anti-Romanism.

The heart of the change in terms of religion was a different approach to the celebration of the sacraments. John Henry Newman was ordained a priest in the Church of England on 29 May 1825 but he did not celebrate communion until 7 August; in his own parish he did not institute a weekly Eucharist until 1837. That shows well enough the starting point for the Catholic movement of sacramentalization. Communion was then quite a rare event in Anglican churches: one of the more curious sequels to the Reformation being that, while the Reformers themselves had called for frequent communion of the laity, in fact communion became in most churches very infrequent for all. As a form of religion the Protestant contrast with Roman Catholicism centering upon its daily mass was emphatic – though in truth the Catholic laity remained no more communicating than the Protestant! Anglicans may not have reached the once a year norm of many a Scottish church, but no more than quarterly celebration was regular. In reaction to this Anglo-Catholics in the course of the nineteenth century became more and more committed to the weekly, and then daily, celebration of mass. In 1853 only twelve cathedrals had a weekly celebration. In 1877 St Paul's, at that time a pioneer among cathedrals with a strong neo-Tractarian presence among its chapter, began a daily celebration. Westminster Abbey, the nation's central shrine, started a daily celebration in 1901:[27] that is probably a fair enough date to indicate the effective victory for this central plank in the Anglo-Catholic programme.

Frequent celebration was not necessarily seen as a surrender to an Anglo-Catholic vision of the Church but in its context it was and would anyway make little sense without a 'high' theology of the sacrament itself. Increased ritual and devotions appeared as but the obvious consequences of accepting a more and more Catholic view of the Eucharist and its significance. The more the Eucharist was seen as central in corporate Christian life and devotion, the more inadequate some of the traditional post-Reformation prayers and rituals surrounding it appeared to be, and the more necessary it seemed to supplement or replace them by others chosen from the medieval past or the Roman Catholic present: the eastward position of the celebrant, candles, vestments, incense, reservation, confession . . . there seemed to be a certain spiritual cogency leading from one to another; it was a logic which not only made the Eucharist central to church worship in a way that had not quite been the case previously for the Church of England but which also interpreted the Eucharist in a strongly sacralist manner, stressing – as contemporary Roman Catholicism did – the sacrificial ritual rather than the communion meal. There was plenty of justification for the popular fear that a profound shift was going on in the overall character of the Established Church and this in an unmistakably Rome-orientated direction. The absurd 'spikiness' of the most outré Anglo-Catholics in imitating every current Roman practice (such as not giving communion at high mass, multiplying weekday celebrations at side altars and even giving communion under only one kind) certainly did not help matters and the more 'moderate' or old-fashioned Tractarians were as aghast with some of the more obviously ultramontane of innovations as they were adamant in defence of what seemed to them the basic points. But apart from personal preferences the main line of advance was steady and apparently irresistible. Roughly speaking by the turn of the century, a weekly communion, the eastward position and candles on the altar had triumphed, while vestments had been adopted in over two thousand churches where twelve years before they were not accepted in six hundred,[28] but permanent reservation of the sacred species was still fiercely resisted, as was any stress upon sacramental confession or alteration of the actual rite of communion. Effectively here was a movement with a vigour and a determination which the bishops could hardly have controlled at the best of times, but least of all when they were themselves tied by a parliament overwhelmingly uncomprehending of what it was all about.

Reservation of the sacrament for purposes of devotion appeared for long as the sticking point which neither parliament nor a majority of the bishops were prepared to tolerate, yet upon which the logic of Catholic belief had equally to insist. To reserve the sacrament for communicating the sick was so reasonable (and, since early Christian times, so traditional) that the more pastoral bishop found it hard to refuse: the alternative, a brief but basically complete Eucharist each time a sick person requires communion is simply not practicable in a busy parish where sick communions are a daily occurrence. The crucial underlying factor here was the Anglo-Catholic devotional concern for frequency of communion. But if the consecrated bread is reserved for the sick, it must signify an enduring sacramental presence of Christ, and to reverence it is natural and appropriate. To pray before it, and even to exhibit it in special devotional services such as 'Benediction', seemed as natural to the Anglo-Catholic – influenced as he also was by current Roman Catholic practices – as it seemed abhorrent to the Protestant and even to many a more old-fashioned Tractarian. The intensity of conviction upon each side in this matter over many decades is striking. More than any other issue at this period, it came near to tearing the Church of England apart.

Previous to the war the official Church position was to forbid it absolutely, as Archbishop Frederick Temple had done in 1900, but that had not worked – it had not been obeyed and the reasons for disobedience both of principle and of practice were too deep for the bishops to enforce obedience, even if they had all really wanted to, which they did not. So in 1911 they drew up a 'Draft Rubric' to permit temporary reservation for the communion of the sick 'so that they be not used for any other purpose whatsoever'. Such a compromise was not likely to work but if it broke down as quickly as it did, it was much due to the war and the growth in Anglo-Catholic devotion which the strains of war produced. There can be little doubt that Evangelicalism did not prove a very comforting religion in the trenches; Anglo-Catholicism fared better with its sacramental objectivity and its prayers for the dead. Winnington-Ingram of London, the episcopal Trojan Horse of Anglo-Catholicism across many decades, felt that the solace of prayer before the reserved sacrament could not be refused to 'the tide of human grief and anxiety . . . the longing to get as near as possible to the Sacramental presence of Our Lord'[29] In 1917 a thousand priests signed a memorial to the archbishops opposing the denial of the right of access for purposes of devotion to the sacrament: 'Compliance with such a restriction cannot rightly be demanded and will not be given.' A hundred of the signatures came from the diocese of Oxford where Bishop Gore, torn between his own Anglo-Catholicism and his authoritarian temperament, was still endeavouring to maintain the official line.

Anglo-Catholicism triumphed first in the south-east just as – nearly four centuries earlier – Protestantism had first prevailed there. In 1920, when Bishop Knox retired, Anglo-Catholic enclaves north of Warwickshire remained few and far between. An old-fashioned Protestantism still prevailed in the province of York, though the presence of Archbishop Lang was just beginning to make a difference.

No man apart from Davidson had greater weight on the episcopal bench than Gore, who disliked both benediction and the lawlessness of the younger Anglo-Catholic clergy, but when the bishops solemnly discussed whether they should forbid genuflection before the blessed sacrament he could only declare, 'I have genuflected since I wore black velvet breeches, and I shall genuflect until I die.'[30] For a bishop to genuflect but to deny 'Benediction' to his clergy was not a very tenable position. The truth was that Anglo-Catholicism had now penetrated far too deeply among the clergy and devout laity and if its practices were ever to be moderated effectively, this would have to be done convincingly on Catholic, rather than Protestant, grounds.

Gore was prepared to fight 'for the full liberty of vestments, white or coloured' and indeed that battle had effectively been won by 1920, but Bishop Knox its great opponent was not so mistaken when he wrote, 'Universal adoption of the vestments of the Mass inevitably meant re-establishment of the Mass. It was the Mass that made vestments vital to Anglo-Catholics.'[31] It was indeed the centre of a whole complex of beliefs and practices, an integrated system of religion. A shift on the mass went with a shift on praying for the dead. In 1917, under pressure for prayers for those killed in the war, for the first time Forms of Prayer were issued by Anglican authority containing explicit intercession for the departed. Again, only Knox and Chavasse, the two Lancashire Evangelicals, protested among the bishops. In a sermon at Westminster Abbey on All Saints day 1919 William Temple declared, 'Let us pray for those whom we know and love who have passed on to the other life . . . let us also ask them to pray for us.' Here again the Catholic view had triumphed, yet Temple did not regard himself as an Anglo-Catholic.

The strength of Anglo-Catholicism lay not just in the sincerity and obstinacy of its protagonists; it lay rather in the wide coherence of its view of religion – liturgical, doctrinal, social, institutional – and in the great well of resource it could draw upon, not only that of contemporary continental Roman Catholicism but also the medieval and patristic past. British Protestantism had by and large simply lost touch with too many large areas of Christian tradition and experience, and it was spiritually damaged by its negativeness, if not hostility, towards by far the largest group of contemporary Christians. Anglo-Catholicism took many forms, some more, some less attractive, but it represented an intense desire to recover the deep sense of sacrament, ritual and symbolism, the concern with prayer, mysticism and monastic asceticism, a theology of the Church, the consciousness of communion with the majority of other contemporary Christians rather than of a self-righteous criticism of them, the willingness to listen to the whole past (rather than Scripture and Reformation alone), an openness to art, music and literature. With some it was a severely theological movement, with some predominantly a ritualistic one, with others the primacy was aesthetic or social or ascetic, and its strength lay precisely in this variety. It came in waves, so that a man radical in his youth like ̄ Gore could by his old age seem rather out of sympathy with the younger generation. It was a vast tide, flowing in apparently almost irresistibly, and doing so just because it could enfold such very different people: the most rigid theological conservative as well as the most adventurously modernist, the Tory as well as the Marxist – Hugh Cecil as well as Conrad Noel. They were one in their commitment to an intensely Catholic view of the Church of England.

The relationship of the movement to Rome was necessarily ambivalent. Inevitably it learnt much from Roman Catholicism, and some of its members in every generation – Ronald Knox in 1917 was only one of the most recent – joined the Roman Catholic Church. At the same time the very nature of the enterprise almost forced the Anglo-Catholic to be at least a little anti-Roman, at times rather pettily so, but many could also offer a thoroughly sound critique of Rome's contemporary weaknesses, and some including Gore himself had quite a deep anti-Roman sentiment.

Institutionally in their theological colleges and religious orders Anglo-Catholics had provided a most invigorating new element to the Church's life, while their leadership – Bishops Gore and Talbot, Professor Scott Holland, Fr Kelly of Kelham and Frere of Mirfield among others – was without any possible rival in its combination of learning, pastoral seriousness and sheer range of vision. Nor was it simply an in-turned ecclesiasticism. Almost all the movements of Christian socialism, and the groups of men at work in places like Oxford House in Bethnal Green, were Anglo-Catholic. Gore had preached a theology of liberation, if somewhat academically, for many years. If this had made little effective social difference to England, it had immensely strengthened the movement to be able to put beside its liturgical preoccupations the social gospel of a Stewart Headlam or a Conrad Noel.

More than anyone else Charles Gore both represented and was responsible for the vast transformation of consciousness that was going on in the Church of England in these decades. He had been made Bishop of Worcester in 1902, transferred to Birmingham to head its new see in 1905 and then again to Oxford. He retired –

after many earlier threats to do so – in 1919. A singularly angular and jerky character, impetuous with a tendency to histrionics when gripped by one or another crisis of conscience, he had all the spiritual masochism and odd, almost cruel, quirks as well as the bubbling, rather childish yet also highly sophisticated humour of the over-committed celibate. A natural radical, yet a natural authoritarian too, he was able to continue both throughout life because he had also the detachment of an aristocrat and an intellectual whose personal ascendancy within the Anglican ecclesiastical Establishment was unchallenged for a quarter of a century. Gore was at his worst as a very autocratic bishop coping with particulars of policy about which he did not at heart agree anyway, at his best as a prophet, transcending party leadership. He had distanced himself sufficiently from current Anglo-Catholicism to be the guide to whom Randall Davidson almost instinctively turned, by whom the young Temple was frequently influenced, the one senior ecclesiastic to be recognized by Church and nation as a living representative of that evasive but decisive category, 'religious genius'. The first Principal of Pusey House, the founder of the Community of the Resurrection, President of the Christian Social Union, keen supporter of women's suffrage, of Welsh disestablishment and what have you in radical causes, Gore was at heart a rather old-fashioned Catholic who when still at evangelical Harrow had learnt 'to make his confession, to love the Mass, and to fast on Fridays'. Flanked by his close friends, Edward Talbot, first Warden of Keble, first Bishop of Southwark and then of Winchester, and Professor Henry Scott Holland in Oxford, Gore had transformed Tractarianism from a near fundamentalist and high Tory movement still on the margins of Anglican life into something central to the Church. He is indeed an enigma, and not least in the respect which even his most unsympathetic contemporaries, a Henson or a Headlam, showed for him. Perhaps he can best be seen as successor to Newman, able to do for the Church of England what Newman could not do because of his conversion to Rome. Gore had no conscious sympathy with Rome but that very and manifest absence enabled him to catholicize his Church the more effectively. Like Newman a great admirer of St Philip Neri, he was often compared by Henson with St Charles Borromeo: 'He was, indeed, of the stuff of which the great leaders of the Counter-Reformation were fashioned.'[32]

The Church of England had three Victorian patriarchs over-shadowing it in 1920: its primate, Archbishop Davidson; Charles Gore; and Viscount Halifax. Lord Halifax was by then already over eighty. He had been President of the Church Union almost continuously since 1869. He represented a rather different type of Catholicism to that of Gore: so conservatively orthodox in theology that he had his suspicions of the latter just as Gore had his suspicions of von Hügel. He was far more sympathetic towards Rome than Gore, but far less sympathetic towards socialism. 'The layman par excellence', Maurice Reckitt could call him,[33] and Halifax as a great nobleman had been able to preside over the fortunes of Anglo-Catholicism and negotiate with bishops, archbishops and cardinals over a period of fifty years. But here too the personal heart of the matter lay in his devotion to the Christ of the mass:

> The picture rises up before me of many an early Mass in that rather dark, private chapel at Hickleton which he loved so well. I have always found that, however early I went to the chapel to say my preparation before Mass, there was always kneeling in the front row of seats on the right, and wrapped in the French cloak which he always wore, quite still, and almost invisible, the venerable figure of Lord Halifax . . . There was an intensity about him and the sense of entire recollection when he was praying. . . . During Mass he made the responses quietly but audibly; he received the Holy Communion with deep devotion, and, returning to his prayer desk, knelt again and remained quite still. I have known him not to leave the Chapel for his frugal breakfast for two hours after he had received our Divine Lord.[34]

Halifax, Gore and even Davidson were all aged, even archaic figures, in 1920. They were not such as to speak persuasively to the common England of post-war society. For this all were agreed one should look to someone else – the hope alike of Establishment and of renewal. In November 1920 William Temple was offered the see of Manchester. He was then not quite forty but already for at least a decade he had been a name in the land. Son of an archbishop of Canterbury, golden boy of Rugby and

Oxford, President of the Workers' Educational Association from its start, Headmaster of Repton, member of the Labour Party, Canon of Westminster, leader of the Life and Liberty movement, author of numerous books, major contributor to the notorious liberal theological symposium, *Foundations* – what was William Temple not?

> A man so broad, to some he seem'd to be
> Not one, but all Mankind in Effigy:
> Who, brisk in Term, a Whirlwind in the Long,
> Did everything by turns, and nothing wrong,
> Bill'd at each lecture-hall from Thames to Tyne
> As Thinker, usher, Statesman, or Divine.

That was Ronald Knox's amusing description of Temple in 1912: one Oxford don of another, where there was not too much sympathy between the two, but Knox does convey unerringly the sense that Temple always produced of a staggeringly all-embracing vision and energy. In 1920 almost everyone turned with confidence to Temple as he set off, not only for Manchester, but for obvious leadership of English Christianity across a long generation.

5

Ecumenical Beginnings and Missionary Continuations

In 1899 a Baptist minister in south London, F. B. Meyer, wrote to ask the Anglican Bishop of Southwark, the immensely respected high churchman Edward Talbot, if he could possibly look in at the centenary celebration for their Sunday School Society. It catered for more than four thousand Southwark children. Talbot had been Warden of Keble, was the friend of Gore, the confidant of Davidson. Meyer was an unusually irenic person, particularly friendly to the Established Church.

> Would it be quite impossible for you to look in? [he pleaded]
> We are some of your other sheep . . . it would be a noble act of
> Catholicity . . . Is not the time come when such an act would be
> understood and appreciated by thousands outside the churches
> as an expression of true Christianity?[1]

For Bishop Talbot it was, however, quite impossible; 'a matter of clear principle'. To show any regard for Baptist Sunday schools would be to countenance 'the breach of unity which is so colossal an evil'. As we progress through the twentieth century and witness Anglican bishops slowly giving up the Talbot position and adopting the Meyer view of catholicity and then, still more recently, Roman Catholic bishops beginning to do the same, it is well to remember where we start; with the devout, learned, apparently inflexible Bishop Talbot, the Baptist Sunday schools of Southwark and that 'matter of clear principle'.

If things in 1899 were already just beginning to change, it was very largely due to the Student Christian Movement, an interdenominational organization which only began in the 1890s and was, by 1920, in the middle of its greatest period.[2] If Anglo-

Catholicism was one powerful movement effectively changing the face of English religion in these years, the SCM was the other – overlapping with it, conflicting at times, coalescing at others, wider in impact. Without the SCM the great Edinburgh Missionary Conference of 1910, generally and correctly regarded as the real start of the modern ecumenical transformation of Christendom, could never have taken place – at least with the assurance, the scale, the width of vision and support which it possessed. It was the World Student Christian Federation which had in the preceding twenty years created the new ecumenical consciousness focused in that meeting. Moreover, as regards the English presence at the conference, without the careful salesmanship of the British SCM leaders the hesitations of many people, still far from won over to the ecumenical option – Anglo-Catholics especially but the archbishop of Canterbury too – would not have been overcome. Edinburgh 1910 marks with confident optimism the first great step forward into what was to be in truth an ecumenical century, yet its own rather simple commitment to immediate world evangelization concealed problems about the road ahead which would in due course be painfully exposed.

When the SCM began in the 1890s, it was named initially the Inter-University Christian Union and then, a little later, the British College Christian Union. Under Victorian Protestant inspiration, its principal bases were Cambridge and Edinburgh, its early meetings at Keswick linked with the celebrated annual Evangelical Convention. The concern was with volunteering to go overseas as a missionary and with personal holiness, the basis a non-denominational commitment to 'A belief in Jesus Christ as God the Son and as Saviour of the World'. The watchword was 'the evangelization of the world in this generation'. In its start the SCM formed part, then, of that remarkable, if fairly brief, flowering of evangelical missionary zeal among British university graduates in the closing decades of the nineteenth century – in earlier years missionary candidates had been recruited from less elevated ranks. It was remarkable too in providing so quickly a bridge of communication between younger Protestant Christians of all churches: it may seem odd to regard that as remarkable, but as we have seen at the start of the century the amount of friendly communication between Anglicans and Free churchmen in any other context was minute.

There was no National Union of Students until well after the First World War and no denominational student chaplaincies either. In these circumstances, with a growing number of universities and the sense of a burgeoning and forward looking student world, national and international, the SCM – just because it was there and already denominationally unfrontiered – came to have a quite extraordinary importance. Of the 50,000 students in any form of higher education in pre-1914 Britain, 10,000 were members of SCM. But its concern and emphasis had already significantly shifted from its Keswick linked origins. From the start it included many (particularly among the Scots and English Free churchmen) who were no 'evangelicals' in the rather narrow 'converted' or 'born-again' sense. The larger it grew, the wider became its clientele, drawing now on Anglo-Catholics as well as many young people who, while seriously interested in religion, had not committed themselves intellectually to full Christian belief. It moved its conference away from Keswick. On the negative side a smaller and smaller proportion was seriously intending to volunteer for foreign missions. On the positive side a 'social consciousness' completely absent in the first years was coming to be seen as a crucial part of the movement's mission just at the time – 1907-9 – when its name was changed to the 'Student Christian Movement' from the 'Christian Union', though many of its constituent groups retained the old title.

The growing Anglo-Catholic participation in this predominantly Protestant organization, while being a considerable step forward from one point of view, brought with it an apparent step backward from another. In the early days of the movement intercommunion had been accepted quite easily by evangelical Anglicans and Free churchmen. With an Anglo-Catholic presence this was no longer possible without controversy and, for a long while, it ceased to happen. Much of the inner agenda of the twentieth-century ecumenical movement has been hinged upon sharing, or not sharing, eucharistic communion. It may seem odd that we start our story with a step apart yet it should be noted that at the time Evangelicals were, for the most part, rather unsacramentally minded. Intercommunion, it may be said not unfairly, was easy enough for them just because it signified relatively little. When the issue of intercommunion returns as the most pressing element upon the ecumenical agenda around the middle of the century, it is within a very different theological context which gave the sacrament a far richer meaning than it had possessed in Keswick circles. If Catholics of any sort were to be won to it, it had to appear as a response to that richer theology rather than a denial of it. In which case the SCM's withdrawal from its earlier position may be fairly judged a genuine case of *reculer pour mieux sauter*.

The change of name, the wider clientele, the doctrinal shift in emphasis, combined to produce, as such developments so often do, a reaction of alarm and the formation of rival polarities: one group, the larger, inclusivist; the other, evangelically exclusivist. In the eyes of the latter the SCM seemed no longer to be standing unambiguously for the Evangelical absolutes – the verbal inspiration of Scripture, substitutionary atonement, the profound sinfulness of man, personal conversion, the imminence of the physical return of Christ: the full traditional Protestant package. It was inevitable that the SCM should be affected by the same intellectual and moral issues – the basic pressures to reshape the theological vision integrally if it was to survive at all within twentieth-century culture – which the wider Christian world was having to face. It stood indeed upon the frontier of such issues, and it is not surprising that the development of its thinking proved unacceptable to conservative Evangelicals, first and foremost in their Cambridge heartland. The CICCU founded in 1876 had long been a principal pillar of the Student Christian Movement. No other group had so acute a sense of being the conscience of the whole, the watchdog of Evangelical orthodoxy, the recipient year after year of emotional missions delivered by great American preachers – for already British evangelicalism was to a significant extent a wing of a religious movement centred in the United States. So here after a long discussion, and despite the efforts of many to find some middle way, the CICCU committee decided by 17 votes to 5 in March 1910 – the very year of the Edinburgh Conference – to disaffiliate from the SCM. Its president had to write sadly to the General Secretary of the SCM, 'I am now branded as a narrow evangelical and an anti-Student Movement man, whereas I have wasted a whole year fighting for the other side.'[3] Why bother about all this? The schisms of student bodies have often a short life and singularly little importance, but such was not the case in this instance. The separation between SCM and CICCU not only remained permanent despite numerous attempts to close the breach but out of it came one of the most fundamental divisions within modern British Christianity: the opting out by conservative Evangelicals from the wider interdenominational fellowship long symbolized by SCM.

At the time such a rift was realized only in Anglican Cambridge: a student challenge at the heart of scientific thought and modernist theology. It would have made little sense in the less fraught atmosphere of Presbyterian Edinburgh, and for years CICCU remained a very small body in comparison with SCM, without any corresponding group in most universities. The 1920 state of both movements was symptomatic. The SCM had never been more active: Tatlow, its General Secretary, could boast in 1919 that he received twenty thousand letters a year. In men like J. H. Oldham and William Paton it was providing some of the most influential Christians of the age – thinkers, administrators, ecumenical strategists. Paton was the first secretary of India's Christian Council, Oldham secretary of the International Missionary Council. The burden of such missionary responsibilities should not, however, conceal the fact that among the rank and file of SCM any intense missionary concern was quickly fading; it was now but one interest among many where formerly it had been the point of the whole thing. The old 'watchword', 'the Evangelization of the world in this generation', still crucial at the Edinburgh Conference, seemed to have been killed stone dead by the war. It meant nothing to the mass of post-war students, its sound was exceedingly fundamentalist, and the SCM committee decided to drop it. When this was announced in the 1922 Conference, there was simply no comment.[4] David Cairns, one of the most forceful and perceptive of SCM's leaders, summed up the situation as he saw it in 1920 as follows:

> The conscious aim of the founders of the Student Christian Federation was the evangelisation of the world in this generation. They were not thinking of the threatening danger of the world in this generation at all. But they were in the grasp of a

mightier, deeper and more loving Purpose than they knew, and they are still![5]

Thus was justified the post-war SCM man's concern with the League of Nations, with Irish and Indian nationalism, with wages, housing and unemployment at home rather than with the preaching of the gospel to the unevangelized.

The ecumenical future of Britain was decisively forged within the SCM: a co-operative effort, largely a lay effort, and quite as much Free Church and Scottish as Anglican. What it did was never again undone. The standard bearers of the new ecumenical consensus – William Paton, William Temple, David Cairns, Donald Fraser – had found their gospel within the SCM and little by little carried it to the heart of all the major non-Roman churches of the land.

For some it was a false gospel. CICCU would not be reconciled. Look at Cambridge in 1919 and the revived CICCU led by two undergraduates, Norman Grubb and Godfrey Buxton:[6] for them 'a simple devotion to the Kingdom of God' meant going to China or India to preach the one gospel of salvation, not social work in a London slum nor politicizing about the rights of natives. The negotiation over reunion between CICCU and SCM was described by Grubb and may be regarded as a classic Evangelical statement of the ground of division; quoted again and again:

> After an hour's conversation which got us nowhere one direct and vital question was put; 'Does the SCM consider the atoning blood of Jesus Christ as the central point of their message?' And the answer given was, 'No, not as central, although it is given a place in our teaching.' That answer settled the matter.[7]

The SCM had 'as a Movement apostasized from the truths upon which it had been founded'.[8]

That December 1919 Norman Grubb sailed for the Congo with the wife he had just married, Pauline, to join his father-in-law C. T. Studd on the 'Heart of Africa Mission'.[9] Studd, thirty years before, had been the hero of one of the great heart-throbbing Evangelical stories to be recalled to generation after generation of students. Captain of the Eton cricket team and then of the Cambridge cricket team, he had distinguished himself as no other undergraduate had ever done in the history of the game. Special trains would bring Londoners down to watch Studd play – maybe beside Grace – as when in a game in 1882 against Australia he scored 118 in one innings and took five wickets. After listening to the American evangelist Moody, Studd volunteered for the China mission, together with Stanley Smith, the stroke of the Cambridge boat. Five others joined them, they became the immortal 'Cambridge Seven' and toured the universities of Britain before departing in glory in 1885 to join Hudson Taylor's Faith Mission in inland China.[10] Studd in fact left China after some years, had a later spell in India, but in 1910 had set off on yet another expedition, this time to Africa, without his wife. There he remained until he died, combining intense missionary zeal with a very gloomy opinion of his converts and a marked inability to work with anyone else. For Studd sin was rampant everywhere and of the 500 Africans who came to his church in the Ituri forest on a Sunday, he doubted whether ten would ever get to heaven. From this tormented man, the *crême de la crême* of Evangelical Cambridge, developed the 'Worldwide Evangelization Crusade'. It would be carried on by Grubb and backed by those who refused to allow Christian mission to be translated from the phraseology of sin and salvation into one embracing social consciousness and race relations. Studd's later life was relatively little known. The heroic departure of the 'Cambridge Seven' established him, nevertheless, in the standard mythology as a leading figure of the 'Evangelical Peerage' – a line beginning in Wycliffe and passing through Ridley, Tyndale and Charles Simeon.

Frederick Temple, William's father, when an undergraduate at Oxford in 1841 expressed the hope that England might assume 'the sublimest position ever occupied by any nation hitherto, that of the authoritative propagator of the Gospel over the world', and Archbishop Benson, his immediate predecessor in the see of Canterbury, had told the London Missionary Conference of 1894, 'The Church of England is now charged with the world's Christianity'. All rather confidently imperialist. In fact the Church of England had never been the best of recruiting grounds for missionaries and the supply, such as it had been in the heyday of the late nineteenth century, was growing somewhat thinner by

1920, yet it had by no means died out. That very year young Max Warren, just sixteen years old and at Marlborough, heard the news of his missionary father's death in India and committed himself for life to the same calling – to become in due course the outstanding mid-century leader of the missionary movement. All across the world there was still in 1920 a remarkable range of British missionaries at work from all the churches; bishops, teachers, doctors, Bible translators, nuns. The effect they were having upon the growth of non-western Christianity was quite considerable. Most of them were neither so imperialist in the assessment of their role as the words of Temple or Benson (not themselves, of course, missionaries) might suggest, nor nearly so fanatically evangelistic as Studd. They tended to be firmly paternalist, their minds rather over-protected by their missionary labours from many of the more troubling intellectual pressures of the twentieth century. It could be argued that the missionary movement at its zenith in the later nineteenth century had been for two generations the adventurous vanguard of modern western Christianity. If that is so it had not survived world war. There was a certain unmistakable mental mediocrity settling down upon the world of the missionary societies by 1920; they had pioneered untrodden paths, geographical and ecumenical, they had mastered unwritten languages, they had on occasion even challenged imperialist rapacity, but now, more and more, they were becoming rather too obviously the contented house cats of the colonial system.

To this conformism, at once religious and political, there were however significant exceptions. In Rhodesia Arthur Shearly Cripps[11] was already a thorn in the flesh of the white settler world – poet, holy fool, radical lobbyist, poverello – and for a while in the early 1920s, helped by his rather more moderate friend, the Wesleyan John White, he actually influenced the Rhodesia Missionary Conference in a fight for African rights.

Still more remarkable was the career in India of C. F. Andrews.[12] Cripps and Andrews were Oxbridge high Anglicans in inspiration, and both went overseas at the beginning of the century under the auspices of the Society for the Propagation of the Gospel. In 1914 Andrews startlingly repudiated his priestly orders. 'No longer call me Rev, put plain Mr,' he told his friends,

93

so asserting his institutional disaffiliation from the Church just as Cripps, a decade later, would surrender his bishop's license and remain henceforth simply a 'Christian missionary'. For both, the official missionary Church was just too complacently colonialist. Andrews, who had gone out to India to teach at St Stephen's College in Delhi, now took up residence in Tagore's ashram at Santiniketan. It was to be the nearest thing he had to home for the remaining twenty-five years of his life. An intimate friend of Tagore and Gandhi, Andrews could not be ignored by the British government because of this quite unique relationship with Indians. By 1920 he had already achieved, almost single handed, the abolition of the system of indenture. In the wake of the Amritsar Massacre, while looked upon as a renegade by most churchmen, Andrews was almost the only Englishman Indians did still trust. Like Cripps Andrews was struggling – not only in India but throughout the Empire – with one dreary issue after another of race relations and colonial misgovernment, but far nearer to the heart of them both was the irresistible urge to find a new spiritual and human relationship with the non-western world. They had gone out to teach; they really did remain to learn. And because they did so they were understood and loved by those they came among and are still remembered where a thousand others are forgotten. For Tagore Andrews's friendship was 'a gift of God beyond all price', while Gandhi could think of no better suggestion to Lord Mountbatten when viceroy than that he should act 'as C. F. Andrews had done'.

Andrews and Cripps were obviously in no way typical Anglican missionaries. They were in arms against the preconceptions of most of their Christian contemporaries, missionary or otherwise. Yet, eccentric upper class, even neurotic individualists as they were, they represented too at its greatest and freest a tradition of spiritual vision which Anglicanism seemed good at fostering. They moved out from the centre of an Establishment, powerful, Erastian, conformist, to challenge it most absolutely – and often not ineffectually – by the sheer quality of a religious commitment, love of neighbour, intellectual integrity, a flow of poetry affecting every aspect of life. At the time no other ecclesiastical tradition produced holy men of quite such prophetic power, quite so capable of recognizing in the eyes of the indentured coolie, crouched, scarred, terror-stricken, 'Thy glorious face'.

Most missionaries found it hard to sympathize with the unbridled enthusiasms, whether mystical, political or evangelical, of Andrews, Cripps or Studd. Yet the man who, almost unseen, was in 1920 having the most influence on the evolving direction of the British missionary movement was hardly less remarkable. He worked neither in Africa nor in Asia but mostly in an office just off Sloane Square. J. H. Oldham had been born in India, and had worked there for a few years in the YMCA; he was a member of the United Free Church of Scotland and an Oxford graduate. Somewhat deaf, very much an SCM man and a layman, he had risen through its ranks to be secretary of the Edinburgh Missionary Conference, of its continuation committee, and then of the International Missionary Council, as well as editor of its journal, the *International Review of Missions*. By 1920 he was the spider at the heart of almost every non-Roman missionary web, the mind who could best interpret the future, the tactician who could handle both C. F. Andrews and the Colonial Office, the international ecclesiastical statesman in comparison with whom almost every bishop appeared immeasurably provincial in outlook. It was Oldham who, early in 1919, pointed out to Randall Davidson that there was no reference to freedom of conscience or religion in the League of Nations covenant, enabling the archbishop to write off on the matter 'in the nick of time' to Lord Robert Cecil in Paris, who then got it inserted in Article 22 on the Mandated Territories. It was Oldham who saw to it that German missionary property was exempted at Versailles from confiscation for reparations. It was Oldham who was carrying the weight of the subsequent tricky negotiations involved in enabling the missionaries themselves, expelled from their colonies during the war, to be permitted to return. It was again Oldham who successfully marshalled the archbishop and the forces of Church and Liberal opinion over the Kenyan labour issue, and subsequently over a wide and difficult range of Kenyan problems: thus the Colonial Office Declaration of 'African Paramountcy' in 1923, a key statement for the future if frequently disregarded in practice, had in fact come via Davidson from Oldham.[13]

In Oldham as in John R. Mott, his American counterpart,[14] we see emerging quietly and efficiently the new consensus: an explicit gospel most certainly remained at its heart, indeed in a fairly uncomplicated way, but it was now embedded within the recognition both that 'the message' carried with it, in one way and another, responsibility for a vast range of other matters – educational, political, economic, racial – and that most of these matters simply could not begin to be tackled effectively other than in an inter-denominational way. The protagonists of the new consensus were fortunate in finding so very willing a listener on the throne of St Augustine. Davidson, who in his earlier years as archbishop admitted to a friend that he had never met Dr Clifford, the redoubtable Baptist, and asked what sort of a man he might be, was by 1920 in frequent and intimate consultation with Free Church leaders. Doubtless his own background – Edinburgh, Church of Scotland – helped him here a little to relativize the claims of the Church of England.

It did not diminish the Anglican position. To the contrary. The Archbishop of Canterbury had never previously been so international and ecclesiastically important a figure. Apart from the Pope (who was indeed all too suspect in the eyes of the powerful and progressive) there was in 1920 no other ecclesiastic in the world with in any way comparable a position. The political power of Britain and the extent of its empire, the defeat of Germany and therefore the ecclesiastico-political weakness of the heartland of Protestantism, the denominational fragmentation of America, the dawn of ecumenical co-operation, the experience and personality of Davidson himself, all this contributed to making of him, pro tem, something of a mini pope to whom Christians in distress throughout the world would naturally turn. None more so than eastern Orthodox Christians caught between the collapse of the Turkish Empire and the Russian revolution. If he was unsuccessful in his efforts to achieve an independent Armenia or save its people from massacre by the Turks, he did help to prevent the expulsion of the Oecumenical Patriarchate from Constantinople which the Turks were demanding at the Lausanne peace conference of 1922. It was Davidson's public telegram to the Patriarch at this point, 'The continuity of the Patriarchate in Constantinople is profoundly important to the whole Christian Church', which greatly reinforced Curzon's resistance to this demand in Lausanne and helped persuade the Turks to abandon it.

1920 was the year of the Lambeth Conference's *Appeal to All Christian People*, one of the rare ecclesiastical documents which does not get forgotten with the years: probably the most memorable statement of any Lambeth Conference. Lang's idea in origin, and admittedly far from immediately practical, it gained the support of the whole range of the Anglican spectrum – including that of 'dear old Halifax' (though not of the fastidious Dean Inge who thought it all 'rather pitiful')[15] – because at just the right moment it expressed, and on the whole generously expressed, the new wind blowing across Christendom: 'We do not ask that any one communion should consent to be absorbed in another. We do ask that all should unite in a new and great endeavour to recover and to manifest to the world the unity of the Body of Christ for which He prayed.' In 1920 too, Oxford University at last allowed non-Anglicans to receive its higher theological degrees – a belated allowance as some of its finest theologians, at Mansfield College, had long been non-Anglicans. To inaugurate the new era Dr Selbie, the Principal of Mansfield, and Baron von Hügel were awarded honorary doctorates of divinity. From now on, even Oxford was recognizing, English theology must be the work of Free churchmen and Roman Catholics as well as of Anglicans. That was the 1920 spirit at its best.

The problem, of course, with noble appeals is the difficulty of implementing them. In the following years, despite a warm Free Church response to the tone of the *Appeal*, rather little came of it. Lambeth had still linked its vision of unity to the acceptance by other churches of the 'historic episcopate', in some form not too prelatical or monarchical. In practice this proved then as in many subsequent circumstances a seemingly insuperable bar to any great advance in the institutional relationship between the Church of England and non-episcopal churches. The *Appeal*, a distinguished Free Church scholar would comment a few years later, 'seemed to alter things, but in cold, actual fact it did not. With the magnificent and unconscious sleight of hand that comes from centuries of practice in the *via media* the Anglicans took back what they seemed to give, and, as usual, wanted it both ways'.[16] That may seem a hard judgement. Certainly the Anglican leadership for the next twenty years made little attempt to follow up the *Appeal* in any very effective way, and was perhaps not too interested in doing so. Here, as elsewhere, if there was an immediate post-war dawn, it proved something of a false one. Yet on the longer view, the *Appeal* was pointing a prophetic finger at futures far beyond the lifetime of Davidson or Lang and it would be recalled with gratitude fifty years on.

It was certainly not that there was no responding throb within the Free Churches. Indeed J. H. Shakespeare, secretary of the Baptist Union, was the most deeply and consistently ecumenical of all the Church leaders of the time.[17] In his many years as secretary he had done much to reorganize the Baptist Union. He was in some ways very much a denominationalist, but while serving the Baptist Union with great efficiency he had become more and more convinced that denominationalism had outlived its usefulness and was now increasingly destructive of religious effectiveness: 'A divided church cannot speak effectively to a divided world.' In 1918 he published *The Churches at the Cross-Roads*, echoing the title of George Tyrrell's final posthumous work. It is in principle one of the most important books of twentieth-century English Christianity because it sets out so clearly the logic of the forthcoming ecumenical movement. Shakespeare had long argued for full unity between the Free Churches, but now he was going still further: Anglicans and Free churchmen must unite too. The initial division of 1662 was a mistake which it was high time to overcome. To do that, Shakespeare recognized, the Free Churches must be prepared to accept episcopacy. When two years later the Lambeth *Appeal* said just about that, Shakespeare was able to describe it (to Lang) as 'the finger of God': the recovery of communion was for him the one overriding *desideratum*.

Few Free churchmen really agreed and many strongly disagreed. If intercommunion was to come, it should be without preconditions: 'Fellowship at the Lord's Table must precede, not follow, attempts to unite episcopal and non-episcopal churches,' declared that very moderate Baptist scholar, Wheeler Robinson. But to that Anglicans would not agree. Thus the ecumenical impasse, so often repeated in subsequent years, was quite explicitly present at the start of our era. Shakespeare, almost the only man at the time who really tried to resolve it, thereby effectively lost his following, and no subsequent Church leader has ever committed himself so valiantly to an ecumenical solution at variance with the tradition of his own community.

For the time being, a long time being, very little would be done by Church leaders beyond expressions of polite good will. They knew well enough that the folk in the pews did not desire it. The form of most men's Christian loyalties remained so tightly bound to particularities of belief, ministry and worship, and these particularities drew so much of their sense from the historic sunderings of the religious past that an appeal upon general grounds to a new unity from leaders or theologians, with all the generous concessions inevitably required therein, met with next to no sympathy from the common church and chapel-goer. In the 1920s that still included, for the most part, bishop and moderator too.

The ecumenical wind would continue to blow but it would mostly be felt for the next couple of decades not so much within the churches themselves as in a growing range of new movements and institutions: 'Faith and Order', 'Life and Work', the International Missionary Council. All such were stoked in Britain by, more than anything else, the young men and women of the SCM.

6

The Free Churches

On 16 November 1918 King George V and Queen Mary attended the post-Armistice Thanksgiving Service of the Free Churches in the Albert Hall. It was the first time a reigning British sovereign had ever attended a Free Church service and it was as welcome a signal of social acceptance as the immediately preceding exclusion of the Free Churches from the National Thanksgiving Service in Westminster Abbey had been painful.

The 300 page Report on *Church and State* produced in 1916 made only the most passing reference to the existence of Nonconformists – a fact which revealed far more about a certain blindness of Anglicans in regard to the actual limitations of 'the National Church' than it did about the state of Nonconformity. Free churchmen at this period were apt to claim a full half of the nation; that in English terms was something of an exaggeration, but they certainly included a good half of the Englishmen for whom religion meant anything very much. They also included the Prime Minister as well as his predecessor: there had not been a genuinely Anglican Prime Minister since Lord Salisbury left Downing Street in 1902. Moreover they were an ancient constituent of the national life. Of Congregational churches in existence in 1920, 292 claimed to date back to the seventeenth century; of Baptish churches 122; of Presbyterian 22; of Unitarian 160.[1]

The Free Churches represented within the national life from the seventeenth to the twentieth centuries, and in a very remarkable way, an alternative tradition:[2] an alternative form of religious expression and ecclesiastical organization to the Anglican, but also – across the specifically religious and ecclesiastical – they stood for a whole other England, social and political, an

England for long somewhat suppressed by the Anglican, Tory, aristocratic, landed and academic establishment, but of late an England which had made its voice heard more and more emphatically through the Liberal Party as well as through its own pulpits and newspapers. It was the England of the skilled artisan and of the middle classes, especially – at least until recently – the lower middle classes. In 1900 there was still not a single Free churchman in the House of Lords, though by 1920 there were several. Only from the 1850s had they been admitted to the ancient universities, only from 1871 to university offices in general – and even then they were excluded from very many which remained tied to Anglican orders. Only in 1920 would they be admitted at Oxford to higher degrees in divinity.

The characters and dividing lines between the two ecclesiastical Englands were then clear enough, and a certain arrogance upon the one side was naturally matched by a certain bitterness upon the other. One had been born with the privileges; the other had had to struggle for its rights every inch of the way. And yet this other England was by no means revolutionary; it had its radical wings; it naturally tended to support the political party which stood for change; yet it was profoundly conservative too; the England of the small man, the independent in town and countryside, but still the man who either had or aspired to a little property – and sometimes had a good deal; the England of Birmingham and Manchester and Yorkshire industrialists. Almost certainly the strength and flexibility and essentially nonrevolutionary character of English society, as also the absence of any really deep-seated hostility to the Christian religion as such, all derived in large measure from this profound duality within English Christianity, English Protestantism: the persisting inability of the Erastian and episcopal Church to monopolize the nation or its religious tradition. The constant interplay of the two, unkind as it often was, State Church and Dissent, Erastian and Free Church, Episcopalian and Nonconformist, church and chapel, forged between them and not one nor the other alone, the central lines of English religion and indeed – to a fair extent – of English culture and English politics too.

The long post-Reformation struggle within the national

Church to decide how far the religious revolution should go, was concluded, after the brief radical victory of the Independents under Cromwell, by the Restoration in 1660-2 not only of King and House of Lords but of bishops and Prayer Book. Those unable to conform, including over two thousand ministers, were ejected and harassed. With the coming of William III the harassment ended, but the dissenters remained excluded from the world of privilege. They had themselves hardened into various groups, of which the principal ones were Independents (Congregationalists), Baptists, Presbyterians and Quakers. Of these only the Presbyterians believed in the importance of a connexional authority above that of the local congregation, and they – in the course of the eighteenth century – moved largely into Unitarian doctrine. The real core of 'Old Dissent', both Independent and Baptist, was utterly congregationalist: against the authority of bishop, king or pope it set that of the local church and Christ and his Spirit in and above that local church, the congregation of believers gathered there.[3]

As the eighteenth century wore on the old dissenting communities grew manifestly smaller, until the evangelical revival responding to the great growth of population and the social dislocation of the early Industrial Revolution suddenly produced an intensely emotional outbreak of new religious 'enthusiasm' within the Established Church. There John Wesley had wished to remain, but he failed to do so: his 'Society of people called Methodists', from being a group of revivalists within the State Church – a 'society for the spread of Scriptural Holiness' – became instead the 'New Dissent', reluctantly forced into building its own chapels, ordaining its own ministers, celebrating its own communion services. Methodism itself had soon split into a number of different bodies – mainly, if curiously, because its Wesleyan core, controlled for decades by Jabez Bunting (who stood to Wesley a little as Brother Elias stood to St Francis), was devoted to clerical authoritarianism in Church order and Toryism in politics. More radical and populist elements were simply driven out. Yet it spread like wildfire in the late eighteenth and early nineteenth century, especially in the years of the Napoleonic wars and in northern parts of the country where the Old Dissent had penetrated least. But at the same time the Old

Dissent – at least Congregationalists and Baptists – began expanding again, so that the first half of the nineteenth century was all in all a time of enormous Free Church growth. This was the generation in which it was finally settled that the Church of England would not (apart from a few small fringe groups) be the only Church of the nation, but could be instead no more than a large and privileged denomination, one among a number. For both 'Old' and 'New' dissent growth at this time was as much rural as urban, particularly in the north where Anglican rural ministrations were rather thin, especially in such phenomena of the industrial countryside as mining villages. Presbyterianism revived too in the nineteenth century but on a smaller scale and largely as an extension of Scotland: widely regarded as the Scottish Church, it was strong in Northumberland, present in London and Liverpool, elsewhere very weak. In the exciting rough and tumble of mid-nineteenth century religion, just as in that of the seventeenth, other new groups appeared: the Brethren, the Church of Christ, and then, far more visibly and as a brashly evangelistic as well as humanitarian offshoot from Methodism, the Salvation Army; but numerically, none of these grew large. Roughly, the proportions of the main Free Churches were now: Methodists (all combined) 10; Congregationalists 5; Baptists 4; Presbyterians 1.

Old Dissent had its heartlands in the southern half of England – it was too much a part of the Reformation ever to have penetrated very effectively far north – but it was very weak in the south-east, never a strong dissenting area, and in Cornwall.[4] Its two main centres of rural and small town strength were the east Midlands and the south-west. In the former the Free Church belt (that is to say, Congregationalist and Baptist) stretched from Leicestershire and Northamptonshire across Bedfordshire and Cambridge to Hertfordshire and Suffolk; in the latter it extended from Devon and Somerset to Wiltshire and Gloucestershire. But the most influential urban centres of the new congregationalism were Birmingham and Manchester.

Methodism tended to fill the gaps. In the south its greatest centres of rural strength were Cornwall, the Isle of Wight and Norfolk. It too only feebly touched the countryside round London. Its major strength was in the north, from Lincolnshire,

Derbyshire, Staffordshire and Shropshire to Durham mining villages, though less in Lancashire than in Yorkshire.

Influence and proportionate numerical presence of the Free Churches were not, however, quite the same thing. The latter might be high in some rural areas, such as Lincolnshire or Gloucestershire, where the Established Church's presence was a great deal stronger. If 20 per cent of the population went to chapel in a countryside where almost everyone attended a church of some sort, the wider influence of chapel was not as great as all that, significant as such a pattern of rural dissent undoubtedly was in strictly religious terms. But if 20 per cent of the population went to chapel in an industrial town, where most people hardly went to church at all and the Established Church seemed almost a foreign intruder, then the influence of the Free Churches, their wider penumbra, could there be preponderant. Such was the position of towns like Bradford and Oldham, of Nottingham and Sheffield, of Bolton and Halifax, of Manchester, and of Birmingham, that 'very Mecca of Nonconformity'.[5] Here the most influential place of worship in the whole town was undoubtedly the Congregational church of Carr's Lane, for long the pulpit of Dr Dale, Joseph Chamberlain's spiritual mentor, a pulpit which could still be described in the 1920s (just a little anachronistically) as 'one of the commanding ecclesiastical positions in the British Empire', or 'the Vatican of Independency'.[6]

By the last decades of the nineteenth century the weight of the Free Churches was shifting very noticeably away from the countryside and into the town. That, of course, was the way the population as a whole was moving, and as the industrial towns proliferated and the suburbs spread, the Free Churches grew within them as a duck in water. Congregationalists and Wesleyans appealed especially towards the upper end of the middle-class spectrum, Baptists a little further down, Primitive Methodists down again – they and the Bible Christians (since 1907 part of the United Methodists) were the most consistently working-class of any of the major Free Churches. Conversions still took place, particularly in the industrial north, but these were in practice no longer by any means the main source of recruitment for any of these churches. That was now the Sunday school. The Free Church of the early twentieth century in the age of its greatest ascendancy was built upon the Sunday school: 'Sabbath Schools are England's glory', declared a popular hymn. They were certainly above all a Free Church glory. In 1907 the Wesleyan Methodists had 1,000,819 Sunday school scholars, the Primitive Methodists 470,095, the United Methodists 315,723, the Congregationalists 723,580, the Baptists 583,290, the Presbyterians 87,313.[7] That makes 3,180,820 in all, as against the Church of England's 2,334,000. The Sunday schools had proved in their time a very effective means of social and religious influence, drawing countless children whose parents were never themselves chapelgoers, but they were also a vulnerable, even a volatile one. Up to 1906 their numbers had risen very steadily but they would now start to fall, and quite fast. Free churchmen had perhaps still more reason to fear the Education Act of 1902 than they realized. As weekday school improved in seriousness the less attractive would be the Sunday school.

For the feel of Nonconformist society in early twentieth-century England, Wesleyan Methodism especially, with its severe moral standards, tight frontiers, preoccupation with work and good money, one can hardly do better than turn to Arnold Bennett's Staffordshire novels. Take *Anna of the Five Towns*, the first of the series.

> The yard was all silent and empty under the burning afternoon heat, which had made its asphalt springy like turf, when suddenly the children threw themselves out of the great doors at either end of the Sunday school – boys from the right, girls from the left – in two howling, impetuous streams ... Many of the scholars carried prize-books bound in vivid tints, and proudly exhibited these volumes to their companions and to the teachers ...[8]

Thus the story begins in a Wesleyan Methodist yard surrounded by the various connexional buildings – chapel, school, lecture-hall, chapel-keeper's house – which formed the heart of a circuit in one of the five towns of the Potteries. In the Sunday school lay the key to the whole business, the focal point at which the evangelistic pedagogy of the lower middle class brought to bear its moral persuasion upon the children of the workers – delightful for some in the treats it provided, hateful for others in the pressures it ceaselessly applied.[9] Through its doors one was drawn into the improving, humanizing world of the men's Bible class, the Sunday school sewing meeting, the chapel teas, the annual outings, the bazaar and – from time to time – the Revival and the Revivalist: that classic institutionalized expression, spoken of with bated breath, of the Spirit's primacy over man and his institutions. From Holman Hunt's 'The Light of the World' hanging above the dining room fireplace to *Janey's Sacrifice or the Spool of Cotton*, a Sunday school prize-book, this world was all of a piece. It existed on the interface of skilled artisan and petty industrialist, self-contained and self-assured, intensely local: glorying in honest work, pietistic in speech, unhesitatingly intolerant in its insistence upon conformity to the norms of Nonconformity.

The impression given by the Free Churches in the early years of the twentieth century was one of great confidence, of still growing numbers, of increased wealth, of a proliferation of well-built Gothic churches and large 'Central Halls'. 'Retrogression is not in our vocabulary. Forward is upon the banner of every organisation of the Church', so wrote the young Baptist minister of the Barking Road Tabernacle, West Ham, in 1900.[10] It seemed true enough. Contrasted with the decline in London of Anglican Church attendance the Baptists could appear in the *Daily News* census of 1903 as 'the one really growing religious body in the metropolis . . . wander where you may, there is nowhere a symptom of Baptist decline'.[11] The vitality was still clearly there, yet it was becoming rather too predominantly – at least in the south – a middle-class one, and this would prove dangerous. The Congregationalists, whom Charles Booth called, the same year, 'more than any other the church of the middle classes',[12] provided, as in much else, the central paradigm. Their immediate glory was the greatest; their subsequent fall would be the sharpest. In Free Church history one sees a very steady tendency to move 'upwards' socially across the generations, slowly sundering a body's vital links with the social strata in which it had first been nourished, until identity is smothered by the embraces of the establishment. This upward movement was especially characteristic of the industrial town – a flexibly stratified society ideally suited to it. Nonconformity remained most genuinely working-class within the village community, above all within the nonhierarchical society of a mining or fishing village. Here the virtues of the Protestant ethic were least destructive of Free Church proletarianism. Elsewhere the Edwardian age was the greatest moment for the social and political prestige of the Nonconformist, but by no means the greatest moment for his evangelistic vitality.

With advance up the ladder of the middle-class went the tendency to rural withdrawal. The end of the nineteenth century was an age of steady rural depopulation. As the labourers left for the cities and so many of the old cottages collapsed, the parish church survived but many a village chapel was unable to do so. The Primitive Methodists reported in 1896 that in the preceding twenty-five years there had been a decline of 280 in the number of their rural societies, and every Free Church was experiencing the same thing at one and the same time as their suburban boom.[13] So while the total numbers of the Free Churches were still rising and indeed mostly reached a peak around 1906, the structure of their membership was changing in several ways that might well provide cause for concern.

To understand aright the character and membership of English Nonconformity it is necessary to bear in mind its very special relationship with both Wales and Scotland. Effectively Wales was one country with England, as Scotland was not, and the Free Churches vastly benefited from that oneness. Wales was one part of the kingdom in which they could undoubtedly claim to be the majority; even so it was a bitter fight to secure the disestablishment of Anglicanism in Wales, though secure it they did by law in 1914 – the one and only real gain the Free Churches sustained from the government in which they were most strongly represented. How much they benefited from that gain is questionable. But the point for us here is that Wales provided a rich base both in personnel and in political control. The Free Churches had to be respected everywhere that bit more because of their weight in Wales, and if a Free churchman who constantly appealed to his religious heritage was Prime Minister in 1920, that would be hardly conceivable were it not for his Welsh Nonconformist base. There was a steady flow of Welsh people to other, richer parts of the country, and with it went a steady flow of ministers. One has only to think of Hugh Price Hughes, J. D. Jones or C. H. Dodd, to realize what English Nonconformity of the early twentieth century owed to Wales.

The case of Scotland was different but not less important. Scots were overwhelmingly Presbyterian and while the small Presbyterian Church of England was largely stocked by Scots, there was not otherwise quite the same easy interchange of personnel. But there was a natural alliance in sympathy between Scottish Presbyterians and English Free churchmen against Episcopal pretensions south or north of the border, and the alliance was particularly strong with the large Free Church of Scotland established after the disruption of 1843. English and Welsh Free Churchmen could obtain the degrees in Scotland from which they were long excluded at Oxford and Cambridge or where – even when legally included – they still felt not quite at home. The divinity faculties of Edinburgh, Glasgow and Aberdeen were important for English Free churchmen: they could be relied upon as academic allies, and as at times providers of staff for theological colleges in England. There would be considerable to-ing and fro-ing between Scotland and Mansfield College at Oxford, Westminster College at Cambridge. Fairbairn, Mansfield's first Principal, John Oman of Westminster, and Forsyth, greatest of Free Church theologians in this period, were all Scots. By the late nineteenth century the English Free Churches were near-mortally weak in theology. The Scottish connection could not eliminate this weakness, but it did alleviate it.

When we recall the many links with Scotland and Wales, we realize that in the United Kingdom English Nonconformity was in a far less exposed and wholly underprivileged position than would have been the case if it had faced the Established Church with the national frontiers enclosing England alone. The political and indeed moral weakness of the Church of England was, ever since the unions with Scotland and Ireland, that it claimed a relationship with government which could plausibly be justified in terms of only one of the four parts of the United Kingdom but which had legally covered two others and dominated the Establishment ethos of the whole. The profound linguistic and psychological ambiguity between 'England' and 'Britain' whereby Britons fight but England wins the war, or the King of England rules over Britain, but is crowned only Anglicanwise in Westminster

Abbey, lay at the heart of the relationships and misunderstandings between the Church of England and all the millions of British Christians who were not Anglicans. Symbolically the Church of England could still in 1920 sweep the board when it would, ignoring rivals, as in the 1918 thanksgiving service in the abbey, but in terms of hard politics the government of the nation might be a lot more anxious to conciliate Presbyterians in Scotland, Catholics in Ireland or Free churchmen in Wales than to defer to the sensitivities of Lambeth. At the end of the day the domesticity of Establishment could mean weakness, indeed captivity, rather than power.

What really in religious terms divided the Free Churches from the Church of England? It was not so much a matter of doctrine. Both old Anglicanism and the Old Dissent had been largely Calvinist. With the coming of the New Dissent there was change on both sides. Wesley rejected Calvinism and if many Calvinist evangelicals remained Anglicans, the Church of England as a whole was coming to reject it too. Nineteenth-century Nonconformity then, like the Church of England at the same time, was partly Calvinist, partly not, but both were increasingly not. It was not this that separated them. Yet the Free Churches were undoubtedly in several ways more emphatically Protestant than was the Church of England and prided themselves on being so: 'The real religious principle of Protestantism has been in the care of the Nonconformists', claimed Forsyth.[14] The heart of Anglicanism lies in the Book of Common Prayer and the episcopate: a given order of prayer and a given order of Church government – given and therefore not free. For the Free Churches, for their laity most especially, what was given was the Bible and no more. The authority of Scripture was the one supreme doctrine, preaching and hymn singing the only communal church practices which had not been effectively devalued.

For the Free churchman the Church of England had not freed itself from the basic grip of priestcraft, manifested both by a fixed liturgy and by episcopal rule. For him preaching was crucial, the heart of his worship, rhetoric the one endlessly admired skill; for the Anglican it was of marginal importance. By the late nineteenth century a contrast between sacrament and sermon had in fact come to represent pretty well the heart of the religious difference between Anglican and Nonconformist. It had not always been so. The sixteenth-century reformers themselves, Luther and Calvin particularly, had taught a fairly balanced doctrine of word and sacrament. Subsequently, however, there was a steady tendency to diminish both the significance and frequency of communion. This happened in the Church of England as well as the Free Churches, but the centrality for Anglican practice of the Book of Common Prayer restrained the tendency to some extent and, under Tractarian influence, a return to a richer sacramental doctrine and more frequent practice had decisively affected the Church of England by the beginning of the twentieth century. The Free Churches, on the other hand, had not only long been satisfied with a rather thin Zwinglian doctrine of the sacrament (many did not care even to use the word 'sacrament'); in the nineteenth century they had been irritated, rather than stimulated, by Tractarianism so that they had moved by and large in a still more anti-sacramentalist direction. The hymn had almost taken over as the supreme expression of communal devotion, while communion faded into near insignificance, a mere appendix or after-thought to real worship, its doctrine reduced to a bare memorialism, its symbolism minimized in all sorts of ways as by the multiplication of separate little cups. Forsyth, both Protestant and sacramentalist, could protest that 'mere memorialism' is 'a more fatal error than the Mass, and a far less lovely', but on this – as much else – he was hardly heard.

Eucharistic minimalism only formed part of a far vaster negativity displayed by pure unestablished Protestantism towards the wider practices of religion and the relationship between religion and life. Everything other than a literalist clinging to Scripture and to the central Evangelical triangle of divine wrath, human sinfulness and substitutionary atonement, tended to be cut away except for social concern. Poetry, symbol, the liturgical year, even the celebration of Christmas – all this was profane and to be excised from true religion. Nothing reveals the ruthless negativity of pure nineteenth-century Protestantism better than Edmund Gosse's account of his intensely devout father's hatred of Christmas: 'The very word is Popish,' he used to exclaim, 'Christ's Mass!' pursing up his lips with the gesture of one who tastes asafoetida by accident.' When one year he discovered that the maids had to some slight extent celebrated Christmas within his house by making a plum-pudding, he seized its remains in fury and flung them upon the dust-heap. 'The suddenness, the violence, the velocity of this extraordinary act made an impression on my memory which nothing will ever efface.'[15] Of course, few Free churchmen applied the principle in their private lives with the stark, near-paranoid ruthlessness of Philip Gosse, but it had been applied almost equally systematically, if less consciously, to impoverish the collective practice of their religion. Nonconformity, admitted Bernard Lord Manning, its most sensitive interpreter, had become a 'somewhat crude affair, morally bracing but aesthetically weak and intellectually nondescript'.[16]

Not sacrament, but sermon. Victorian and post-Victorian Nonconformity thrived on listening to the famous preacher. Externally its churches might be neo-Gothic but the characteristic centrepiece for its architecture internally was an enormous and dominating pulpit. If in the twentieth century one could no longer be swept away by the voice of Spurgeon at the Metropolitan Tabernacle, one could listen to Hugh Price Hughes at the West London Mission, Sylvester Horne at Whitefield's Tabernacle, J. H. Jowett at Carr's Lane Meeting House, or J. D. Jones at Richmond Hill, Bournemouth. There was really no end to great preachers and the very texture of Free Church religiosity was derived from the art of preaching, the experience of being preached to, discussion of the sermon at the Sunday dinner table. It had become, declared a perceptive chairman of the Congregational Union in 1919, the 'golden calf' of Nonconformity.[17]

Again, between the Anglican and the Free churchman lay the nature of Church authority: of the way Christ's authority over the Church is mediated. By bishops, king and parliament, said the Anglican – the low churchman stressing king and parliament, the high churchman the bishops. By none of these, said the quintessential Free churchman. For him, authority under Christ was in the congregation, in the local church and nowhere else. That was most true for the Congregationalist, the Baptist and the Primitive Methodist. These best represented the Free Church position in all its purity, while the Presbyterian and the Wesleyan were more

'Anglican', more ministerial and, in their origins at least, more Erastian.

The Anglican, stating the case for a national Church, denied that any Englishman could be excluded from it: it became almost more a matter of geography than of people. It had to be, by definition, the Church of all: the good and not so good; the willing and the unwilling; the converted and the indifferent; the Anglican and the non-Anglican – for the latter could still be a churchwarden.[18] In earlier days you were punished for not attending; in later days you were at least always welcome to attend. The building is there, the vicar is there, the service as by law established is recited. The congregation is welcome, it is also – in a way – almost redundant. The Free churchman began at the opposite end: with a 'gathered' congregation. Maybe no building; no minister unless and until the congregation had 'called' one. The Church of England covered the land, its Church the church of each village, of Toller Porcorum, Ottery St Mary or Sixpenny Handley. The Free Church was there because a group of free-born but fairly humble Englishmen had obstinately insisted on worshipping together in another way, in paying for a building, in supporting a minister, and all this despite the disapproval of the powers that be.

Whichever way you look at it – theological, historical, economic – you get back to the point of freedom. A personal and group freedom to be religious in the way they believed God wished them to be. They stood for a freedom seen theologically and evangelically (though they were, most of them, intolerant enough to those of other persuasions in the seventeenth-century day of their power), but they expressed it at every turn as a sociological and political freedom too. Whatever they had thought previously, early twentieth-century Free churchmen contrasted their freedom with the shackles of Establishment and Erastianism, and they saw it as a necessary evangelical condition for the Church, and not so different, perhaps, all in all, from the freedom the Great Charter had centuries ago claimed for the medieval Church.

> It seems to us as monstrous that the State should domineer over
> the Church as that the Church should domineer over the State
> ... We can no more tolerate the interference of the secular

power than could the Popes of the Middle Ages. On that side of the protest and struggle we wholly agree with the Pope,

declared Hugh Price Hughes, the most outstanding of Methodist leaders at the turn of the century.[19]

At the English Reformation [wrote Forsyth] there were but the two alternatives – a royal Church or a Roman Church, Erastianism or Catholicism. If you resented the royal supremacy you could realize the freedom of the Church only in a Catholic form, and between Henry and More our heart is all with More.[20]

The heart of the freedom of the Free Churches was their sheer refusal to be dictated to in matters of religion, by the State, by bishops appointed by the State, or indeed by the rich and the powerful of any sort.

They had had a few of the latter but, in a very emphatically class-divided society, theirs was not the top class. A sense of religious protest could hardly fail to go very often with a sense of social and political protest. This was not the case with Wesley himself nor with Jabez Bunting. 'Methodism hates democracy as much as it hates sin,' declared Bunting. But the high Toryism of the early leadership, however well it cohered with Wesley's intensely other-worldly spirituality, gave way quite quickly to political attitudes which cohered equally well with Methodism's actual state of being a Free Church inevitably at loggerheads with squire and parson in the village, the large parish church in the town. By the second half of the nineteenth century Free churchmen were providing the heart and soul of the Liberal Party and then, too, of the early Labour movement. This fitted the seventeenth-century origins of Old Dissent. The Free Church stood for the right and duty of the small man to speak up in Church and State alike, for the equality of commoners and against any alliance of squire and parson or of Downing Street and Lambeth Palace.

Alas, freedom is something infinitely easier to claim than to possess. The Free Churches may have been right to denounce Erastianism and the freedom they did build up in so many ways is impressive, particularly because of its own very diversity and multiplicity. Yet it had its hard limits too. Freedom of one sort can so often involve bondage of another. Contrariwise, an unfree relationship to the State may bring with it, as a sort of almost necessary compensation, considerable internal freedom and acceptance of diversity. The Anglo-Catholic movement would have fared less well in a non-Erastian Church. Anglican internal freedom was due, doubtless, not just to Erastianism and to a long-standing commitment to comprehensiveness but also to a certain boredom of the secular rulers now controlling its still Erastian structures, but it was there nevertheless. Politically the Church of England was very unfree, but intellectually at least it was probably the freest Church in Christendom.[21] A fully Free Church status, unprivileged and unsupported in relationship to the State and society, went on the contrary only too easily with profound internal lack of freedom. The absence of much external legal structure has almost to be compensated for by an internal sectarian rigidity in which there is next to no room for the deviant or the dissident and a very large number of negative command-ments. Such was too often the state of the nineteenth-century Free Church, its mind and policy most emphatically controlled by elderly traditionalists, its atmosphere quite other than 'free'.

In fact, then, freedom was far from all on one side. The most unfree of all ecclesial conditions might, of course, be a *tertium quid*, that which combined the structured and politically privileged rigidity of the large hierarchical Church with the sectarian, one-party, intellectual rigidity proper to the sect. It was the tragedy of the Roman Catholic Church in this its most ultramontane period to combine both forms of unfreedom: the concordat (where it existed) upon the one hand, the Index upon the other. Yet here too, despite all the structures, the freedom of the Spirit as we shall be seeing from time to time, kept breaking in.

The pure model of the Free Church was the single Independent or Baptist congregation uncontrolled in any way by higher ecclesiastical authority. And such had been the basic reality for centuries in those two traditions, though never in Presbyterian-ism or Methodism where ecclesiastical authority was settled instead in the 'Connexion', the yearly conference of ministers (or ministers and laity). Nevertheless small independent congrega-tions can become narrow indeed, they can also desperately need financial help from richer brethren elsewhere; moreover they do need trained ministers, and how can that be done without the maintenance of theological colleges by an organized 'denomination'? The history of Free Churches is, to a very considerable extent, the history of a movement from the congregational to the denominational model. In the early nineteenth century Baptists and Congregationalists each began to link themselves by a 'Union', but it was really a century later in the early twentieth-century heyday of Nonconformist confidence and power that this process so progressed as really to alter one sort of religious animal into another. C. H. Dodd, looking back on his childhood at the end of the last century in a long established Congregationalist community in Wrexham, saw it as 'the last days' of the old Independency.[22] In 1916 by 'the Sustentation and Ministerial Settlement Scheme' the Baptists divided the country into ten areas each with a General Superintendent, while a minimum stipend was guaranteed for every minister. This was the work of J. H. Shakespeare, Secretary of the Baptist Union from 1898 to 1924, and very much a new organizational broom. So too among the Congregationalists Moderators were introduced in 1919 for the different provinces of England and Wales. With them also there was now to be a minimum stipend for the ministry. The effect of all such measures, reasonable and necessary as they were, was, in institutional terms, to centralize and so in some very real way de-congregationalize the Church. J. D. Jones was one of the leaders here: a temperamentally conservative Welshman, who had studied at St Andrews and ministered all his life in Bournemouth. In truly Congregationalist terms his work, as that of Shakespeare and a whole generation of Free Church clerical leaders, was no less than revolutionary. Nonconformity was rendered viable in relatively large scale modern terms but at the cost of much that was most characteristic to it. Subjected no longer to the unfriendly political pressures of the past but under increasing economic and social pressures, above all those of far greater social mobility and cash turnover on all sides of life, the Free Churches were becoming denominations both more closely akin to one another and to the national Church itself.

Co-operation was steadily growing not only within the traditions but between them. There is a risk all along in speaking of the Free Churches as in some way a single group but certainly the danger of false simplification was a good deal less in the 1900s than in the 1800s. In doctrine relatively small differences would remain apparently insuperable for a long time to come but in ethos, in political and social action, in a sense of shared community and public point of view, there was now a marked sense of unity. The National Free Church Council, led by Hugh Price Hughes and John Clifford, was founded in the 1890s, and when its image had become rather too political, it was – a little curiously – supplemented in 1919 by a second body, largely due to Shakespeare's advocacy, the Federal Council of Evangelical Free Churches.

In Methodism the Connexion had always exercised authority over the individual congregation and the circuit. The exercise of that authority had, however, produced a whole series of schisms in the course of the nineteenth century away from the still rather Anglican-minded and clerically dominated main body of Wesleyan Methodists. By the end of the century besides the most considerable group of Primitive Methodists – the 'Prims' or 'Ranters' – there were also the Methodist New Connexion, the Bible Christians in Devon and Cornwall, the United Methodist Free Churches, the Wesleyan Reform Union, together with other independent Methodist churches, not to speak of the Countess of Huntingdon's Connexion, which had been separate and Calvinistic from the start. The multiplicity illustrates well enough how the Independent principle of Congregational autonomy had affected the 'Connexional' principle of the New Dissent. But with the twentieth century 'Independency' would become increasingly unfashionable, the 'Connexion' of a nationally organized Church, the model for all – even Unitarians. It is not surprising that Methodists, so fissiparous in the earlier nineteenth century, were now anxious to unite. In 1907 the United Methodist Church was established, merging three of the larger 'liberal' (that is lay and congregationally controlled) groups, the Bible Christians, the New Connexion and the United Methodist Free Churches. A still wider union was talked of, with the 'Prims' or even with the Wesleyan mother Church itself.

This organizational change of emphasis proceeding quietly if apparently irresistibly was not unlinked with a major change in the intellectual activity and academic status of Nonconformists.

The standards of education desired for both ministers and the children of the better off laity had greatly risen in the last generation. The cream of the theological colleges was now being moved to the old universities: Westminster, Cheshunt and Wesley at Cambridge; Mansfield and Regent's Park[23] at Oxford. Mansfield, opened in October 1889, as the principal Congregationalist college in the country and built with great distinction, represented perhaps better than any other institution the arrival of Nonconformity in the world of established learning. Free Churchmen might still be excluded for another thirty years from Oxford's higher degrees in divinity, for such is Oxford's way, but at Mansfield and Westminster by 1920 it is probable that one could find the ablest theological teachers anywhere in England: John Oman at Westminster, C. H. Dodd and Wheeler Robinson at Mansfield. That year Dodd published his first work, *The Meaning of Paul Today*. He would soon be recognized as the greatest British biblical scholar of his age.

Mansfield was the creation of Birmingham and Manchester, the most forceful centres of Nonconformist power, wealth and culture. It was followed up by the establishment at Manchester University – itself an institution whose origins lay in Dissent – of a new Nonconformist-inspired centre of theological studies: first the John Rylands Library, and then in 1904 a Faculty of Theology with A. S. Peake, a Primitive Methodist layman, appointed to the Rylands Chair of Biblical Criticism and Exegesis: the first Nonconformist Professor of Divinity at an English university. Peake's appointment was all the more natural as all three main Methodist churches had theological colleges in the city: Didsbury for the Wesleyans, Hartley for the Primitives and Victoria Park for the United Methodists. The rise of the red brick universities in these years provided the obvious environment for non-Anglican intellectual achievement.

In Birmingham the most striking development was not in the university but just next door, at Selly Oak. It began in 1903 when George Cadbury turned his home at Woodbrooke into an open centre of Quaker studies. A group of independent colleges quickly grew up around it: Kingsmead, founded in 1905 as an interdenominational mission college; Carey Hall, a missionary training hostel for women; Fircroft, a workers' college of adult education, West Hill, a Teachers' Training College with a strong Free Church bent. In 1919 the Selly Oak federation was formed, with as yet no single Anglican constituent. Woodbrooke had proved within a couple of decades the seed of a mini-university of a new type, predominantly though not wholly religious in character, with one focus on overseas mission, another on social service at home. It was probably the most creative instance of Free Church educational enterprise in this its greatest age.

Selly Oak represents pretty fairly the dominant concern of Free Church intelligence: it was practical and it was social. It was indeed the age of 'the social gospel' and a rather rapid fading away of any strong doctrinal under-girding would seem in retrospect the truly disastrous weakness of the period. Of one man at least, however, that could not be said. P. T. Forsyth, Principal of Hackney Congregational College from 1906 until his death in 1921, was probably the greatest British theologian of the Edwardian age, indeed almost the only one (apart from Tyrrell) whose theological work can really be profitably read for its own sake seventy years later. Forsyth was some sort of forerunner of Karl Barth. While by no means uninterested in social issues he was increasingly anxious to warn his contemporaries against reducing the gospel to a vague ethical concern, to a liberal watering down of incarnation and atonement, of Church and sacrament. Although treated with great respect in his latter years, Forsyth was in truth the great 'odd man out' of early twentieth-century Nonconformity – much as Newman had been the odd man out in English Catholicism. In the next generation his message would be appreciated in a way it never was in his lifetime. His struggle to restore to the evangelical tradition a Catholic sense of Church and sacrament was largely unheeded by Nonconformity in its euphoric heyday, but it would constitute a very large part of the agenda for churchmen of several traditions in the generations that followed. If the Free Churches crumbled so fatefully and so rapidly in the wake of their institutional zenith it was, it would seem, in large part because their inner religious life consisted now of little more than institutionalized emotionalism and moralizing.

Yet no one could well question the propriety of serious social concern on the part of the early twentieth-century churchman.

The need in the slums of Edwardian Britain was clear enough. The energies of the Free Churches were not only spent in constructing new chapels by the thousand across the land, they were also greatly channelled into the struggle for a better world. The old and new concerns of evangelicalism mix with strange fire in the most unpredictable of late Victorian religious heroes, William Booth, founder of the Salvation Army. At his funeral in 1912, sixty-five thousand people walked past the coffin resting in Clapton Congress Hall beneath wreaths from the King, the Queen and the Kaiser. A former Methodist minister of the New Connexion William Booth combined the simplest of salvation/ damnation theologies with a burning human concern for the wretchedness of the present material state of the poorest classes. 'While there is a drunkard left, while there is a poor lost girl upon the streets, while there remains one dark soul without the light of God, I'll fight' – that was his last message delivered at the Albert Hall on his eighty-third birthday, a few weeks before his death.[24] The almost accidental discovery of a military model in speech, dress and mode of organization proved extraordinarily appealing. The numbers in the Salvation Army were never large but its public image was immense, and whatever else the Army was it was not middle class. It represented perhaps better than anything else the last vigorous thrust in the long evolution of popular English Protestantism.

A more predictable and very much more middle-class face of the social concern of Nonconformity is to be found in such as George Cadbury, C. P. Scott and John Scott Lidgett. Cadbury was a recognized patriarch by 1920, a man of eighty-one. Heir to an old Quaker family tradition and highly successful manager of its chocolate factory in Birmingham, 'the service of God', he used to say, 'is the service of man'.[25] He was not only behind the development of the Selly Oak colleges, he had made Bournville into a model factory and a model village: pioneer of the weekly half-holiday and of the garden as an adjunct to the urban working man's home. Modern Nonconformity was the denizen of the suburbs and the essence of the middle-class suburb is the provision of a unity of house and garden in an urban context for the relatively unprivileged individual. It was Cadbury who extended that formula to the working class, as it was Cadbury who even into his seventies was still rising early every Sunday morning to teach reading and writing to Birmingham working men in the adult school for which he was responsible – 'Class XIV'. Perhaps still more important Cadbury was almost the only Birmingham Free churchman of significance who refused to succumb to Joseph Chamberlain's gospel of imperialism and who indeed bought the *Daily News* to oppose the Boer War. As he later said, he hoped it would be 'of service in bringing the ethical teaching of Jesus Christ to bear upon National Questions'.[26] In the exhibition it sponsored of sweated industries, the funds it opened for the Bethesda strikers and for the starving in London's East End in the winter of 1904-5, just as in its attitude to war and to empire, the *Daily News* and Cadbury stood emphatically, honourably and by no means ineffectually, for that much criticized, and often fairly criticized animal, 'the Nonconformist conscience'.

Of all 'Nonconformist' newspapers the *Manchester Guardian* was queen. In 1920 C. P. Scott had been its editor for forty-eight years.[27] The Scotts were an old Manchester Unitarian dynasty. Unitarians had founded the *Guardian* in 1821. Scott was the grandson of one Unitarian minister, brother and uncle of two others. The *Manchester Guardian*, like Manchester University and the greater part of Mancunian civic life, had almost grown out of Cross Street Chapel, the original Dissenters' Meeting House, turned over the generations Unitarian. Here was dissent at its most secular, its most assured, its most unparochial. It had generated the quintessentially liberal paper with an international reputation. It had retained its 'conscience'. Whether that was still a 'Nonconformist conscience' was not quite so clear.

With Scott Lidgett, the third of our trio, we move back just a little into ecclesiasticism. Very much a Wesleyan Methodist minister, he was also, like Cadbury and Scott, a man of newspapers – editor for many years of the *Methodist Times*. For half a century he appeared little less than the incarnate personification of British Methodism. 'The greatest Methodist since Wesley', people delighted to call him. After early years as a circuit minister he had chosen Bermondsey as his place of work and there in one of London's dreariest areas founded in 1890 the Bermondsey Settlement as 'a colony, evangelical, but with the broadest possible educational and social aims'.[28] Others – Anglican clerics especially – had established such religio-social settlements before him, such as Toynbee Hall and Oxford House, but they seldom, like Lidgett, then remained there for fifty years.[29] Lidgett was not a creative thinker but through an extraordinarily lengthy and intensely vigorous life of work for his Church, for ecumenical relations, for the School Board of London County Council, for the Senate of London University (in the 1930s when, already in his late seventies, he became its Vice-Chancellor), but above all for the social health of Bermondsey, he represented at the very heart of the largest of Free Church traditions and with great authority what we can call the coming consensus in twentieth-century British Christianity: the consensus in ecumenical and very mildly socialist good works.

The public effect of the Nonconformist conscience extended, however, far beyond the efforts of gifted individuals such as these, and it was – very largely, it would seem – a political effect. It has been claimed that Methodism in particular was a major stimulant to movements of social and political reform in British history; it has been claimed too that, as a lower-class affair stressing personal holiness and other-worldliness, it on the contrary inhibited such movements. How far was Nonconformity the ally of radical Liberalism, and Methodism the womb of the Labour Party? We are not concerned here with the origins of Methodism, any more than with the political and religious Independency of the seventeenth century. For the decades of its greatest expansion after 1900 there can be no doubt that Nonconformity was a highly politicized phenomenon, and the nature of and reasons for that politicization must now be considered, for it is pretty central to the course of English religious history in the first part of the twentieth century.[30]

'The political love-feast' was part of life in Downing Street in 1920. The term referred to the breakfasts to which Lloyd George would invite Free Church leaders: Robertson Nicoll, J. H. Shakespeare, Clifford, Scott Lidgett and the like. Despite the deep distrust many now felt for him, he could still bewitch them again and again with the rhetoric of Welsh Nonconformity in all its emotional passion: 'the greatest Bible-thumping pagan of his generation', his son called him.[31] Lloyd George was not a religious man but he shared fully in the religious culture of dissent. He dearly loved a fine sermon and that fondness stood him again and again in good stead. Before accepting the invitation to one Downing Street breakfast the clerics required and received an assurance that the papers were mistaken in reporting that the Prime Minister played golf on a Sunday. They were presumably ignorant of the fact that he was, as likely as not, coming down from his mistress's bed to join them at table. For Lloyd George the Nonconformist constituency was all important. That year he had sedulously addressed the General Assemblies of Baptists and Congregationalists, Presbyterians and Wesleyans, eloquent in praise of Wesley here, of Spurgeon there. It was this constituency and the crisis of the war which had brought him to the top, and it was Nonconformity he hoped would keep him there. It did not. He had already split the Liberal Party from top to bottom, and it was in fact almost the end of his time in office, of Liberal England, and of Nonconformist political power. They all went down together. But how had they ever arrived at this rather extraordinary situation?

The late nineteenth-century Liberal Party was sufficiently upper class to be largely Anglican or moderately agnostic in its national leadership but in the constituencies the driving force was overwhelmingly Free Church. And the ministers were as committed as the laity. At a political meeting in Leicester in 1889 the young 'Forsyth swept us off our feet in the rage of his passionate defence of Mr Gladstone'.[32] Later in life Forsyth might stand a little more detached from immediate politics, but that speech was characteristic of the political commitment of Nonconformity; Mr Gladstone, the high church Anglican, was forever having to walk a tight rope between his ecclesiology and his political constituency. All the causes of the Liberal Party, except for one, were such as naturally to appeal to the Nonconformist: middle-class democracy, trade and industry, an end to upper-class privilege, the rights of the small man, a certain rationalization of society. All this might seem little linked to the spiritual doctrines of Methodism, but it was only too clearly linked to the human and material interests of Methodists. Little by little the Liberal Party had redressed the specifically religious grievances of Nonconformists – over the vote, universities, marriages, graveyards, and the rest – against steady Tory resistance, but the alliance of the two was a far wider matter than that. The only really tricky issue was Home Rule for Ireland. Nonconformists were not naturally tender to Roman Catholics and it was not easy to remain loyal to Mr Gladstone's alliance with Irish Nationalists, particularly when Irish Protestants – Presbyterian above all – were ranging themselves more and more recklessly upon the other side.

Birmingham, the city of John Bright, the first great parliamentary Nonconformist since the seventeenth century, was by the end of the century the city of Joseph Chamberlain. Chamberlain was a Unitarian. Birmingham was the very pillar of political Nonconformity but when Chamberlain broke with Gladstone on Home Rule and went into alliance with the Conservatives, he carried Birmingham with him. And it was never Liberal again, which must warn one against an over-simplified view of the Nonconformist political role. Elsewhere Free churchmen were mostly loyal to the Liberal Home Rule commitment but it was often a source of misgiving and bitterness – particularly when they saw the Irish in 1902 vote as Catholics for Balfour's Education Act, the very *bête noire* of the Nonconformist conscience.

Gladstone's Home Rule failure and the defection of Chamberlain had left both Liberalism and political Nonconformity in deep disarray. It was in fact the Education Act more than anything else which rallied the ranks. From a national view the Act might be a great step forward in providing a decent system of education for everyone, while co-operating with, rather than battling against, the greatest nineteenth-century provider of primary education, the Church of England. But in Nonconformist eyes the unforgivable was now to be legalized: such schools, Anglican and Roman Catholic as well, were to be assisted from the rates. The Established Church would be strengthened, the faith of Nonconformist children undermined. The Baptist John Clifford of Paddington took the lead in resistance. A better natural fighter or a more moralistic man it would be hard to find. The Act was passed and a Passive Resistance Movement was championed by Clifford: refusal to pay part of the rates. Many Free churchmen, Wesleyans especially, thought this misguided. Baptists were the strongest resisters and in the next years a few were even sent to prison for their refusal to pay: P. T. Thompson of Leicester, it was claimed, on eight separate occasions. Indignation over the Education Act revived Nonconformity and the Liberal Party with it. Numbers went up, by-elections were disastrously lost by the government, Free Church political mobilization proceeded with a deliberation never known before, and in the 1906 General Election the Liberal Party won one of the great victories of modern times. One hundred and eighty-five Nonconformist MPs were returned, almost all of them Liberals. Of that election the Methodist Sunday School General Secretary commented, 'After the wilderness the Promised Land. And we have entered Canaan at last . . .'[33] It must have seemed like that. 'There is no getting away from the fact that ours is a Nonconformist Party, with Nonconformist susceptibilities and Nonconformist prejudices', declared Edwin Montagu (a lapsed Jew) to Asquith (a lapsed Congregationalist), rebuking him for inviting a young lady, a dancer of doubtful reputation, to a garden party at 10 Downing Street.[34] It was a famous victory.

Yet most of the leading men among the '200 Nonconformist MPs' of whom the rather pompous Wesleyan Robert Perks, about to become a baronet, claimed to be the chairman, were indeed lapsed. No one could doubt the Nonconformist background of Asquith, Birrell, Simon, Lloyd George, Haldane: Augustine Birrell and Sir John Simon were sons of ministers, Asquith belonged to an inner network of Congregationalist families, Lloyd George had been brought up in the most intensely religious of Baptist homes: but did any of these men actually believe in or privately practise the Christian religion? It would seem not. What practising Nonconformists there were in the Cabinet were men of the second rank, like Walter Runciman. The great test was of course the schools issue. It had marshalled the Free Church ranks and given the Liberals victory; here above all they expected their reward. The government tried. Birrell and then Runciman sought hard to find a new formula but faced by the resistance of the Church of England, the House of Lords (and of course – not that it mattered much – the Roman Catholics), they gave up. The Cabinet was far more concerned with other things: Home Rule, social reform, the budget, the House of Lords itself. Even Lloyd George, who had more and more taken on the role of the Nonconformist conscience incarnate, ever since his championing of its cause in 1902, did not really care much for the schools issue. No more, on the other hand, did the Nonconformist leader care greatly for the social reforms he was bent on pressing through.

1910 was the crucial year for Liberal government. Lloyd George's Budget, like Birrell's Education Bill, had been thrown out by the Lords. It could simply not proceed with such a stranglehold by the second chamber, now almost entirely Conservative. Hence the need for the Parliament Act to limit the power of the Lords and for two General Elections in one year to demonstrate the Liberal mandate to force through such a constitutionally revolutionary measure, if necessary through a royal creation of several hundred new peers. The nation faltered, the Liberals lost a great many seats, but if they retained as many as they did – sufficient with Irish help to get the bill through – it seems probable that it was still the Nonconformist sense of crusade, of moral outrage with the Lords and their powers that saved them. That sense of crusade was somehow necessary to match the high moral purpose upon the other side, among Hugh Cecil and the 'Diehards'. Back in 1903 Sylvester Horne had declared the House of Lords to be 'an effective instrument against popular privilege and progress'.[35] And so it was being proved again. Lloyd George described Dr Clifford as the 'General appointed to command the Nonconformist forces in this expedition against the House of Lords', and Clifford did not let him down. In the January 1910 election he addressed, on average, two political meetings a day, frequently on the same platform as Lloyd George. Despite considerable Free Church disillusionment with the 'holy alliance' as Lloyd George called it, the alliance was still very much a reality, supported emphatically by most leading Free churchmen, and particularly by Robertson Nicoll the formidable editor of the most powerful Nonconformist paper, the *British Weekly*. Without their help would the Liberals have pulled through?

January 1910 is memorable too for the election to parliament for Ipswich of a Congregationalist minister, Sylvester Horne. Sylvester Horne! At the hour of Liberal and Nonconformist need in came to the House of Commons this 'troubadour', the 'knight pilgrim', 'our Galahad', 'this gay and gallant cavalier of the

Cross'.[36] And that was really the impression he made. Minister of Whitefield's Tabernacle in the Tottenham Court Road, a man full of vitality and fresh ideas and great confidence, one of the new generation of Oxford educated Free churchmen, Sylvester Horne's election was something quite new: 'Since the days of Praise-God Barebones I question whether any minister in charge of a church had been returned as a member of Parliament until my own election in 1910.'[37] If one could not trust the professional politicians, why not elect a minister instead, a man who could speak with as much spiritual fire as the prophet of high Toryism, Hugh Cecil? Horne was actually chairman of the Congregational Union that same year, and his election to parliament may be taken to represent the high point of Nonconformist politicization. The motives were fine, but it did not work. He made little impact in the House, while finding himself questioned in his ministry. He resigned from Whitefield's Tabernacle in 1913 and died suddenly the next year. It is hard to know which way, with all his talents, Horne would have gone had he lived: perhaps neither further into politics nor back into a regular Church ministry.

If 1910 witnessed in some way this last great romantic fling of Nonconformist politicization, it also witnessed a sharp turn to the tide. Probably the most effective instrument for the political mobilization of Nonconformity had been the National Free Church Council, whose secretary was Thomas Law. That year Law fell victim to depression and drowned himself. His successor F. B. Meyer was consciously committed to re-establishing more emphatically religious priorities – social concerns, yes, but not party political concerns. The Free Churches must be rescued from the political trap before it was too late. In this he reflected a far wider sentiment. The crusading temper that had bound together Free Church life and a fairly narrow range of political causes had suddenly waned. The Liberal Party was no longer the only plausible option for a politically active Nonconformist, while the more religiously minded were conscious of the ravages that politicization had made on evangelism.[38]

Disillusionment with the Liberal alliance, then, had set in well before the war. The Marconi scandal had not helped. Yet it was the war which killed it. Conscription was one point. Lloyd

George was the man responsible and he had had his way, but it was something profoundly antipathetic to the Free Church tradition, especially to Congregationalists and Quakers. Distressing too was the ill-treatment of conscientious objectors. Next came his somewhat bizarre scheme to nationalize the liquor trade: a government monopoly of alcohol proved a horrifying thought and Lloyd George had to drop it. The schism with Asquith also did its bit to confuse the ranks. John Clifford, now a very old man but still Nonconformity's most uninhibited clerical leader, had had enough and in the 1918 election he gave his backing to Labour. Lloyd George could not willingly let his most potent political card slip thus from his hand. Hence those 'love feasts' in 10 Downing Street in 1920. Hence his appointment of Geoffrey Shakespeare, son of J. H. Shakespeare the Baptist leader, as his personal assistant. Hence all those eloquent addresses to Free Church General Assemblies. Even as late as the mid-1930s old worthies like Scott Lidgett could still succumb to that siren voice. Neither Lloyd George nor they quite understood that the age in which they could help each other was long past. The 'holy alliance' had proved an increasingly costly religious liability. The immense achievements of the Liberal government between 1906 and the war are clear as day, and gained in the face of the most determined political opposition any modern British government has ever faced. They reflected well enough the most enlightened wing of Free Church opinion. But for the most part the Nonconformist leadership had far more restricted interests: in temperance and a repeal of the Education Act. It flung itself into politics with considerable naivety, but not with ineffectualness. There would hardly have been a Liberal landslide in 1906 without the priming of the pumps by Nonconformist indignation over the Education Act and a lot of Nonconformist hard work too. It is probable also that without the Nonconformist sense that the powers of the House of Lords constituted a moral outrage, the Liberal Party would have faltered in 1910 and the Parliament Act would never have been passed. The whole of Britain (including the Lords) benefited from that, as did Wales (including the Anglican Church) benefit from disestablishment, and Ireland was at least set to benefit from the more unenthusiastic, yet sustained, Nonconformist conviction that the Gladstonian tradition must be maintained, that justice required Home Rule.

These were major contributions and one has no right to jeer at or silently overlook, as is often done, the intervention of the Nonconformist conscience in British Liberal politics. Yet with every year that passed the over-simplification in it all became clearer, till neither side was benefiting, only perhaps Lloyd George. The complexities of modern party politics were simply not matter for an extended moral crusade and all the zeal of a Clifford or a Horne could not make them so. The rank and file felt let down over education, uninterested in most of the rest, bewildered by the recurrent scandal: in place of the shining armour of 'our Galahad' one had the Marconi case, the scheme to nationalize the liquor trade, the Lloyd George peerages, a 'Hang the Kaiser' campaign, the Black and Tans, Jingoism. By 1920 the whole experiment was essentially over. If the war had done anything to religion, it had generated such disillusionment as to end decisively a state of politics in which a religious cause, preached by ministers, could somehow inflame a large part of the nation: but it was not only the war, the inherent contradiction of the alliance ensured that it could not last. Perhaps only the genius of Lloyd George had rendered it effective for as long as it was.

Kingsley Wood, a Wesleyan solicitor, entered parliament in 1918 as Conservative MP for West Woolwich. He was a good churchman and sound on improving things but there was nothing charismatic about him. It was the political road which one half of what survived of Nonconformity would increasingly take, as Birmingham had already taken it. The other half went Labour. And was there any particular meaning in that? Methodist miners and farm labourers and such like had had little cheer in the old Liberal Party. It was not really surprising that, if middle-class Nonconformity turned increasingly Conservative, working-class Nonconformity should hearken to the young voice of the Labour Party. Labour drew water from several sources but certainly a principal one was Free churchmanship, and many of its early leaders were nourished here. Going ILP at the turn of the century was not seen as a betrayal of the old political tradition of chapel, even if some Nonconformists who did so fell away from their religious affiliation as they turned nearer to the politics of class conflict. But many of the most active propagators of the Labour cause were strong Methodists. That is where they started and where they remained too. Take Jack Lawson, the miners' MP. He entered parliament on a by-election in November 1919 as member for Chester-le-Street. He had been a Durham miner for nearly twenty years since the age of twelve. For him, Methodist 'hymns and sermons may have been of another world, but the first fighters and speakers for unions, co-op societies, political freedom and improved conditions, were Methodist preachers. That is beyond argument'. In Methodist mining homes he learnt to talk 'pit-work, ideals, the Bible, literature or union business', and even to carry around in his pocket a copy of Thomas à Kempis's *Imitation of Christ*.[39] Or consider Arthur Henderson, in many ways the architect of the Labour Party: at one and the same time lifelong trade unionist and lifelong Wesleyan lay preacher. It would be hard to disentangle the one from the other. If 'Uncle Arthur' was of all British Foreign Secretaries by far the most personally committed to the cause of peace and disarmament, and the only one to receive the Nobel Peace Prize, that does not sound particularly characteristic of Methodism (as it would, for instance, of Quakerism), and yet in Henderson it was clearly the form his Methodism as much as his socialism took; and behind Henderson in the inter-war years were quite a number of Free Church Labour MPs who were fully committed pacifists – men like Charles Simmons and Wilfred Wellock, both Methodist lay preachers.

The Nonconformist relationship with Labour was not institutionalized in the way it had been with the Liberal Party, and Labour MPs probably took a less active role in higher church affairs than had their Liberal counterparts, but for a generation the actual weight of inspiration in personal terms may well have been greater. The inspiration was not to be found exactly in Methodist origins – they were far too supernaturalist and even overtly Tory; indeed when they looked back at all, early twentieth-century Methodist Socialists cast their eyes, just as Sylvester Horne did, on the seventeenth not the eighteenth century. It was rather that in the industrial north Methodism had generated communities of serious independent-minded, idealist, yet very down-to-earth working men, the best of bases for a pragmatic socialism.

Two figures may serve as well as any to conclude this discussion. One was T. R. Glover, one of the few senior Nonconformist figures in the University of Cambridge. He was a Baptist, loyal but liberal, and a Fellow of St John's. In 1920 he was elected Public Orator of the University, the first Nonconformist to hold the post, and Bernard Manning, another Cambridge Free churchman, wrote enthusiastically, 'I shall vote for you, as the candidate who represents in a comprehensive way all my politics: the "Good old Cause"; "The Glorious Revolution", "What Mr Gladstone said in 1886", and last but not least that glorious thing, the "Dissenting Interest" '.[40] Manning doubtless had tongue in cheek, as he wrote these lines. Had the Dissenting Interest really won through with a world in which a Baptist could at last hold senior office in Cambridge University? Or had it, somehow, faded into insignificance? Glover, as a good Baptist, had followed the Clifford line in not paying his full rates, though as a respected member of the upper class he had not suffered for it. This was now to change. On 19 January 1921 Glover records: 'Paid rates in full after seventeen years of Passive Resistance, which has done nothing; I think the times require rallying to any kind of state.'[41] The Nonconformist lion was now ensconced comfortably enough in the university just as he was (in the shape of Lord Runciman) in the House of Lords, but had not his teeth meanwhile been pulled?

Our second figure is a humbler one. The local secretary of the National Union of Railwaymen at Darlington in 1920 was Simeon Hardwick. He was an LNER storekeeper who had received such formal education as he had at a National School in Yorkshire. He was a Primitive Methodist, a class leader, a Sunday school teacher, a Young Men's Bible Class teacher, a circuit steward. He had also, since 1918, been the first chairman of the Darlington Labour Party, as well as chairman of the district branch of the St John Ambulance Association and secretary of the NUR's Orphan Fund. Doubtless he was not so very unusual in all this: his combination of biblical doctrine, socialist politics and sheer wide humanitarianism was characteristic enough of the working-class Protestantism of the north of England. He was rather more unusual in the 'addresses' he found time to give on 'wasps, beetles, ants, spiders, butterflies and moths'.[42] Of such is the kingdom of heaven.

Roman Catholicism[1]

'His aversion from the Roman Catholic faith was dour and inveterate,' wrote Winston Churchill of the Conservative leader Arthur Balfour.[2] Of Asquith, Balfour's Liberal rival, it is said that he had two lifelong aversions, eating rabbit, and the Roman Catholic Church. Move further down the social scale: in a lower middle-class Methodist Edwardian home, 'the word "Catholic" was almost anathema'.[3] Stones and a shouted, 'That's for your b . . . Communion', could still be the experience of a Catholic child in such a world.[4] One could go on and on accumulating such evidence. Roman Catholics at the beginning of the twentieth century were in fact to be found in every side of the national life from the Premier Duke and the Commissioner of the Metropolitan Police to the tramp seeking shelter beneath Westminster Bridge, yet in religious and even political terms they were felt, and felt themselves, to stand extraordinarily apart, the object of profound latent suspicion able to burst forth from time to time (as at the London Eucharistic Congress of 1908) in an almost paranoid gust of popular hostility, evoking memories of gunpowder, Titus Oates and the Gordon Riots. If the gap between Anglican and Free churchmen was real enough, that between them both and Roman Catholics was intellectually and psychologically far far deeper. Theologically too Henson in the 1920s had no doubt at all that 'the continuing conflict' with Rome remained 'the governing ecclesiastical issue' facing the nation.[5]

The early twentieth-century Englishman, secularized as in many ways he might now be, was then still very conscious that at the Reformation his country had chosen the Protestant side. It was not a particularly theological consciousness, rather one of emotion and a sense of political and ethical righteousness, of being loyal to the national history. Freedom, honesty, parliamentary government, progress in ideas and in industry, all this in some vague but powerful way was bound up with the commitment to Protestantism. That was the message of the great ages of national history, the Elizabethan, the Cromwellian, the Victorian, and it was the message of the Act of Succession. Every sovereign for generations until George V had sworn to maintain the established Protestant religion in a form of words extremely offensive to any Roman Catholic.

Yet from first to last a small minority of Englishmen, from Thomas More onwards, had adhered resolutely to the other side, to papal authority and the Latin mass and to all that went with them, and this despite decades of bitter persecution and centuries of deep discrimination. The absolute Englishness of the core of Catholic dissent, of this alternative tradition of More and Cardinal Allen, Alexander Pope and John Lingard and Archbishop Ullathorne, needs to be stressed. It was in no way a foreign mission. Its major institutions were, certainly, upon the Continent with seminaries in Rome, Douai, Lisbon, and Valladolid, with monasteries and convents to be found in many towns of France, the Low Countries and Germany. But all these institutions had been established from the sixteenth century on by English people and were maintained by English people: a remarkable, perhaps indeed unique, example of the survival in exile across centuries, of the structures of a society persecuted on its home ground. To them English people came across the channel; in them they lived as contemplative nuns and monks, teachers, schoolboys and seminarians. Some of these institutions returned to England at the French Revolution, others survived on the Continent into the twentieth century and indeed even to today.

The Catholic community at home which supported them was weakest in the south and east, strongest in the north. Apart from the homes and villages of a few stalwart landed families Catholicism quickly crumbled in the counties south of a line drawn between the Wash and the Bristol Channel. But where the Church of England and the 'Old Dissent' too had always remained relatively weak, there Catholicism retained its greatest strength – above all in western and northern Lancashire and in parts of the north-east, especially Durham. Preston was and is the most Catholic town of England: in such parts old English Catholicism survived by no means just as a matter of a few aristocratic families and their retainers; it was on the contrary the healthy religion of a normally structured society. Nevertheless it was important for Catholics that, unlike Nonconformists, they were represented at the very top of society and in the House of Lords as well as at the bottom. The Duke of Norfolk, premier duke and earl, had an odd but clearly recognized position as a sort of lay head of the English Catholic community. This was greatly reinforced by the forceful character and personal piety of the 15th Duke, who succeeded in 1860 and died in 1917. He had presided over the community for many decades as President of the Catholic Union and chairman of the Catholic Education Council; he had built the two cathedral-like churches of St Philip's at Arundel and St John's, Norwich. In an age of aristocrats through him and his like the Catholic Church slotted into the ruling English establishment in a way that the Free Churches did not. The fifteenth Duke did, after all, own some fifty thousand English acres. He had been a member of Lord Salisbury's Cabinet and had meticulously supervised two coronations. Besides the duke there were some forty other Catholic peers – some recent converts, others representative of the oldest lines of recusancy. The Catholic landed families were still a powerful reality in 1920: a world of inter-married names having splendid old homes with hiding places and country estates and persecuted ancestors. There were still Scropes at Danby, Tichbornes at Tichborne Park, Bedingfelds at Oxburgh Hall, Stonors at Stonor Park, Petres at Thorndon Hall, Plowdens at Plowden Hall, Throckmortons at Coughton, Blundells at Little Crosby (where the old boast remained that there was not a pub, a pauper or a Protestant in the village), and so many more. The old group of gentry families had been strengthened by nineteenth-century converts in the wake of the Oxford Movement; they were now educated at Stonyhurst, the Oratory, or Downside; they went to Oxford; they voted Tory. They were in fact a characteristic part of English upper class life and their most distinguished contemporary member, Sir Hugh Clifford, was in 1920 Governor-General of Nigeria.

From the 1840s Catholics of English stock had, however, been far outnumbered by Irish immigrants driven by poverty, the potato famine, lack of work in Ireland, industrialization in England, to flood into the big cities of this country. By the second half of the century they constituted some 80 per cent of the Catholic population, were mostly extremely poor and had settled principally in southern Lancashire, a few London ghettos and such other northern towns as Bradford and Leeds. They had also greatly reinforced the old Catholic population on Tyneside and Teeside, and to a lesser extent were to be found in Birmingham. Of course many lapsed completely from the practise of their faith. Nevertheless in the second half of the nineteenth century the English Catholic bishops had faced up gallantly to the enormous task of providing priests, churches and elementary schools for this new flock and – by and large – had succeeded. The Irish of this mid-century migration were poor, rural and ignorant with an ungroomed medieval Catholicism surviving tribally centuries of ill-use. It was something very different from the informed religion of the English Catholic church-goer. The Irishman did not impose his religion on England so much as receive it anew from the hands of the host community in the form of regular church-going, catechism classes and – in due course – primary schooling. Just as the middle-class Nonconformist endeavoured to domesticate the bulk of the native proletariat – none too successfully – into habits of evangelical piety and industrial seriousness, so too did the English Catholic community domesticate – on the whole rather more successfully – the Irish immigrant into the religious practice proper for an urban Catholic proletariat in a Protestant land.

By 1920 there was a Catholic community in England and Wales of over two million, served by almost 4,000 priests (2,500 diocesan; 1,400 regulars of whom Jesuits and Benedictines were the most important), with 400,000 children in Catholic schools.' The achievement in the thirty years before the war had been a staggering one. In 1880 there were 1,946 priests in England and Wales; in 1900 2,856; in 1910 3,835; so the number had been doubled in thirty years – a growth possible only through a large intake of men from Ireland. The total proportion of Catholics in the country had not greatly grown in these years but their institutional framework had been immensely strengthened and this was starting to show, for instance, in a steady rise in the proportion of marriages performed in Catholic churches: 42 per thousand in 1909; 52 in 1919; 60 in 1929. But, to put this into proportion, there were still rather more Methodist than Catholic marriages in 1919 (20,804 to 19,078) and eleven times more Anglican (220,557).

Of the Catholic population a good 900 thousand were in Lancashire, above all Liverpool, where the Irish immigrants had reinforced the indigenous tradition. Only here was the Catholic proportion of the population really significant in national terms. Around London was another half million (the diocese of Westminster's estimated 300 thousand can be compared with Liverpool's 440 thousand). Elsewhere industrial northern towns all had their quota, the rural south very little indeed. The middle class remained thinly represented anywhere; the Catholic community was a society of the poor, headed, a little uneasily, by a few aristocrats. But the poor did go to church, unlike, for the most part, the Protestant poor – doubtless by no means everyone every Sunday, but often and with conviction. A Tyneside social survey in the 1920s concluded that 'It can scarcely be doubted that the Roman Catholics are the strongest denomination on Tyneside'.[6] On Merseyside it was much the same: Anglican and Nonconformist church attendance was quickly falling, the Roman Catholic rising. Its predominantly working-class membership contrasted sharply with other churches. On Merseyside under half the Free Church and Anglican congregations were manual workers; 83.8 per cent of Catholics were. And the contrast would be still more striking if 'manual workers' were to be divided into skilled and unskilled: the latter were to be found in plenty in Catholic churches, only by ones and twos elsewhere.[7] The Catholic class structure was in fact completely different from that to be found in all other major churches, and this gave both strength and weakness. It undoubtedly provides the principal key for the very different demographic history of the churches in the following forty years.

The Catholic clerical system worked extremely well in these circumstances. Celibacy and lengthy seminary training undoubtedly distanced priests socially from their usually working-class origins, but it was rather to take them into a class apart than to merge them with the bourgeoisie. They retained their basic upper working-class social commitment, while their ministry was acceptable across all the classes. If they dominated the laity in things ecclesiastical, the manual labourers who came to their churches wanted no different. They needed leadership and their clergy who were vastly better educated than they were, gave it. In other, and many continental, circumstances the same system produced anti-clericalism, but not here because of the basically underprivileged character of the whole Catholic community. A working class laity wanted its priest sons to have social status and it benefited from the leadership they gave just as it benefited from the Church schools, the sense of community and Irish links in an alien world, the care of the sick, of orphans and of the poorest provided by numerous sisterhoods. If Catholic secondary education for the working class was extremely limited (about 40,000 places in 1920), the best of it was provided by the same sort of priestly staff to be found in the public schools for the small upper class. The young Duke of Norfolk might be educated at the Oratory and young Lord Acton at Downside, while Alfred Hitchcock and John Heenan were educated (and, of course, fortunate to be accepted) by the Jesuits at St Ignatius, Stamford Hill. Classwise they were a chasm apart, but religionwise and even educationwise not so much. The universality of clerical control was also here a great equalizer.

A Church largely consisting of unskilled manual workers had, not unnaturally, a religiosity very different from that of middle-class Protestant congregations. The latter subsisted on the written and spoken word – the King James Bible, the hymn-book, the Book of Common Prayer, the well prepared sermon, even, for the more old-fashioned, *Pilgrim's Progress*. Upper-class Catholics might match this with a layman's missal, Bishop Challoner's *Garden of the Soul*, the *Imitation of Christ* or even the Douai version of the Bible, but these were minority tastes. Working-class Catholicism was upheld by quite a different pattern: the rosary, Friday abstinence, the confessional box, the lighting of a candle before a statue of Our Lady, a brightly coloured picture of the Sacred Heart in the home, the wearing of the miraculous medal, the diocesan pilgrimage to Lourdes. Hymns too had come to have their place, and *Faith of our Fathers* or *God Bless our Pope* could be sung lustily enough when processing down Protestant streets on the parish's annual feastday. There was a combination here of ancient pieties and nineteenth-century continental devotional innovations; together they served effectively to maintain a religious ethos in the home, however poor, at once lay in appeal yet open to clerical influence while insulating one within a world intensely foreign to that of one's Protestant neighbours.

Lay pieties and ecclesiastical worship only mildly overlapped in that the laity were compelled by Church law to attend the latter. No one questioned that the mass should be in Latin, that lay participation in it should be almost entirely silent, that communion should be in one kind, that priests should be celibate and dressed in black cassocks. Doubtless a few people did question these things in their hearts and some quietly disappeared from the Church, but within the Church's normal circles any challenge to the whole hard, objective, apparently unchanging order of hierarchy, creed and sacrament was simply unthinkable. Catholic order was fitly symbolized by the solemnity of high mass: an almost atrophied sacramentality, an intensely clerical worship, an absence of the 'Word'. Catholics had distinguished preachers, like Bernard Vaughan or Bob Steuart, but the sermon had become an afterthought in Catholic worship, an appendix almost unrelated to what lay around it.

While Catholics shared some of the sectarian characteristics of Nonconformity, they differed profoundly over morality. The pious Free churchman had a horror of alcohol, dancing, cards, the theatre, and observed on Sundays a still more disciplined lifestyle. The pious Catholic, on the contrary, might well both drink and dance. He might play cards with the local clergy when they visited his home, and if he did not play tennis on a Sunday it was only so as not to upset Protestant relatives or neighbours. Perhaps as a consequence the Catholic would not find loyalty to his faith so hard to reconcile with life in the modern world as would the Protestant.

It would be foolish to play down the other-than-English quality of much in the Catholic Church at this time, to forget the extent to which early twentieth-century Liverpool had taken on the character of Belfast, riven between the green and the orange, to ignore the long lines of Irish names in a priests' directory –

Connolly, Corcoran, Doherty, Flannagan, Kelly, Murphy and the rest. But then, any list of Nonconformist ministers in an English town had too its striking proportion of the Welsh – Williams, Hughes, Davies, Jones, Jenkins, Morgan.[8] It was, after all, a United Kingdom, and if for the Catholics the Irish contribution was numerically predominant, outside the ghettos of the biggest cities the tendency to go native and English was a steady one. Both of John Heenan's parents were Irish, but his Englishry is clear enough and, where blood mixed, the indigenization could be still more decisive.

The Church was led by Englishmen too and mostly pretty local ones. Cardinal Bourne was a Londoner, born in Clapham; McIntyre and Leighton Williams, two Birmingham archbishops appointed in the 1920s, were both born in Birmingham, Pearson of Lancaster was born in Preston, Henshaw of Salford in Manchester, Thorman of Hexham and Newcastle in Gateshead, Singleton of Shrewsbury in Birkenhead. One could continue the list. Certainly there were a few Irish bishops like Cotter of Portsmouth and Keily of Plymouth but they were never numerous. It would be absurd to call the English Catholic community of the early twentieth century an 'alien' one (though not too well informed observers have been prone to do so) but it was, of course, one with many very significant overseas links. Many of its priests had been trained abroad and they shared with some of the laity an almost over-selfconscious sense of belonging to an international world. Bourne himself had studied in both Paris and Louvain, McIntyre of Birmingham had been a student and later Rector at the English College in Rome, Keating of Liverpool was a schoolboy at Douai in France. The other way round, a great many priests and nuns permanently at work in England came from the Continent, among them such distinguished scholars as Anscar Vonier, the German abbot of Buckfast, and Fernand Cabrol, the French Abbot of Farnborough, where the Empress Eugenie had lived for fifty years and was buried in 1920 in the monastic crypt beside her husband, Napoleon III, and the Prince Imperial.

Cabrol and the Empress Eugenie represented the French connection as did Vonier the German. Then there was the Spanish. The leading Catholic academic at Oxford was Francis de

Zulueta, since 1919 Regius Professor of Civil Law, and Fellow of All Souls. He had served in the Worcestershire Regiment in the war and was brother-in-law of Sir Henry Bedingfeld of Oxburgh. His cousin, another Francis de Zulueta, was a Jesuit. No one could be more at home in both the English Catholic and the academic establishment, yet he was a member too of a great Spanish dynasty, his brother Pedro being Attaché at the Spanish Embassy in London where his cousin, the Marquis Merry del Val, was ambassador. The ambassador's brother was a cardinal, Pius X's Secretary of State, his mother a de Zulueta. All these people had been educated to a large extent in England – the cardinal at Ushaw, the ambassador at Beaumont – and while doubtless this type of aristocratic internationalism was exceptional it gave a certain tone to the community and affected the attitudes and relationships of many others. There was a continuity here which ran from Irish labourers in Bethnal Green to Spanish-named cardinals in Rome and wove together Italian ice-cream vendors, French and Belgian nuns, priests of many an international order, exiled royalty.

In comparison with the situation in many other countries, in England the Catholic Church was led to a remarkable extent in its wider, more secular life by the laity, not the clergy. This may sound surprising, particularly in view both of what has been said about the clerical position especially in the parishes of the Irish Diaspora and of Cardinal Manning's very forceful efforts to impose upon the community what he saw as the proper Roman model. But the English Catholic community had existed long before Manning and outlasted him. The independent attitude of its lay leaders, both gentry and intellectuals, was not easily altered. Manning had feared the Anglican influence of Oxford and Cambridge and endeavoured to prevent Catholics from going there; but his alternative Catholic University in Kensington proved an absurdity and following his death and lay pressures the bishops and Rome gave way quickly enough. It was the lay sense, quite as much as the clerical sense, of what was right which in the long run prevailed. It is striking that the most influential journals – the *Tablet* and the *Dublin Review* – were always lay edited, a state of affairs hardly imaginable upon the Continent, and the principal writers in the community – Lord Acton, Friedrich von

Hügel, Wilfred Ward, Hilaire Belloc – were also lay. It was the presence of an informed, socially influential laity which had really made Newman's very isolated position in clerical terms a tenable one and which, a little later, limited the ravages of the anti-Modernist purge: Cardinal Bourne knew well enough that the laity would not endure too harsh a clerical rein: they shared too deeply the liberal attitudes of their Protestant neighbours.

The position in the universities illustrated all this very well. Catholics were now not only permitted by the bishops to study at Oxford and Cambridge, they had also opened halls of residence for young clerics and established an Oxford and Cambridge Catholic Education Board, effectively led by its more distinguished lay members. In sanctioning this the Church authorities had really turned 180 degrees. In 1918 Anatole von Hügel, the best known Catholic at Cambridge, wrote to 'Sligger' Urquhart of Balliol, Oxford, a letter in which he referred to 'the latent mistrust' of the laity, 'which we all feel in ecclesiastical circles'.[9] Anatole von Hügel and Urquhart were the most cautious and responsible of laymen. They sensed the mistrust, but were not deterred by it. In the case at issue they were in fact intervening over a question of clerical, not lay, education – that clerics should be free to attend a university before ordination – and they, not the Roman Congregation which had issued a contrary instruction, won the day (doubtless because the more educated clergy agreed with them). Even in 1920 the laity could discreetly steer the ship in directions very different from the Ultramontane ideals laid down by Manning fifty years before, ideals which had officially swept all before them in early twentieth-century Rome.

The politics of the community reflected this freedom of the laity. It was united on the need for Catholic schools and an end to anti-Catholic discrimination (as over the alteration in wording of the Coronation in 1910, so as to remove its unpleasantly anti-Roman character), but beyond that it divided by class, ethnic background and a very varying approach to national issues. There were few Catholic Liberals, though they included the only Catholic anywhere near the front rank of English politicians in any party until well after the Second World War: Lord Ripon. A convert in middle life, he became Viceroy of India and a senior member of Asquith's Cabinet.

The Catholic community in England, while far from being politically powerful, could still split three ways; English, upper-class, Tory; Irish Nationalist; working-class Labour. In the pre-1918 parliament, the last in which southern Irishmen took their seats, there were ten Catholic MPs from England, seventy-eight from Ireland. British parliamentary politics for the last half-century, ever since Parnell, had been most powerfully influenced, at times almost dominated, by the Irish Nationalists and their alliance with the Liberal Party. English Catholics had absolutely no comparable political weight, but had in the past benefited at times from the parliamentary presence of their Irish co-religionists, as over education, and of course the majority of Catholics in England were of Irish blood and, mostly, Nationalist supporters. Their spokesman in England was the MP for Liverpool's Scotland Division, T. P. O'Connor, a man of independent ways and a successful journalist who had first entered parliament for Galway in 1880.

But from the 1918 General Election onwards there were no more southern Irishmen sitting in the House and the Catholic presence was drastically reduced. From then on it consisted of a small Conservative group and, at first, an even smaller Labour one. They could not be in much greater contrast. The Conservative parliamentary party of the post-war years was moving fairly steadily away from its old bastions among landowners and into the world of commerce and industry. The former remained a sizeable group, but a smaller one than hitherto (10 per cent of Conservative MPs in 1939 as against 23 per cent in 1914), and one less close to the leadership. It was to this more old-fashioned minority that the Catholic MPs belonged. They were led by Lord Edmund Talbot, Conservative Chief Whip and shortly to become President of the Catholic Union. No Tory was more true blue than the average English Catholic of the old tradition, and this very much included upper class theological 'liberals' like Wilfred Ward and Baron von Hügel. In Catholic circles theological liberalism seldom went with political liberalism, nor was there any real equivalent to the Anglo-Catholic socialist seam: Chesterton's political radicalism faded the nearer he came to Rome. The sixth Earl of Mexborough compelled the officiating priest in his chapel at Arden Hall to pause during the Leonine prayer to St

Michael, 'Thrust down to hell Satan and all wicked spirits who wander through the world for the ruin of souls', while the earl inserted the words 'and Lloyd George'. Such eccentricities were part of the tradition, and the sentiment would have been widely shared.

In the mid-1920s there were sixteen Catholic MPs representing English constituencies. Lancashire was the only area in which Catholicism was politically important (to which, to a more limited extent, Tyneside could be added), and the five Catholic Lancashire MPs are worth recalling as they express pretty well between them the political face of the community. Their doyen was T. P. O'Connor, the Father of the House. Born in Athlone, a Liverpool MP from 1885 to 1929, he was very much the type of the Irish bucaneer who had made good and was, on his home ground, absolutely untouchable politically. There were two Conservatives, heads of the most eminent recusant families of the north-west: Francis Blundell of Crosby Hall represented Ormskirk, and Sir Gerald Strickland of Sizergh Castle stood for Lancaster. Both were men of some distinction. Blundell had been a friend of de Zulueta at Oxford, had married a daughter of Wilfred Ward, was a man of highly sensitive conscience and the very model of a Christian landowner in the care he showed for his tenants. Strickland was more the politique. He had, on his mother's side, inherited property and a title in Malta. Chief Secretary of the island for twelve years, he had negotiated with the Vatican the arrangements whereby the British government exercised a veto on the appointment of the archbishop. Subsequently he had been a Governor in Australia and in the 1920s combined membership of the House of Commons with that of the Maltese Legislative Assembly. In 1927 he became Prime Minister of Malta, his major concern being to keep at bay Italian and Fascist influence, even though that meant clashing pretty gravely with the Archbishop of Malta and even with the Pope. Strickland was a dominating and international figure in comparison with whom most English MPs must have appeared distinctly parochial.

The two Labour members could not have provided a more striking social contrast. Joseph Tinker and James Sexton were both from the poorest of the poor. Sexton, 'The dockers' MP', representing St Helens since 1918, had begun work at the age of eight; Tinker, MP for Leigh, a miner, had begun at ten and was down the mine by twelve. A couple of incidents in Sexton's life illustrate well enough the strains and loyalties in the Catholic working class. He had been a leader in the Liverpool dockers' strike in 1889 and an organizer of both the Dockers' Union and the Independent Labour Party. Of Irish blood though English birth, he naturally supported Home Rule, so when he first stood as an ILP candidate against the Liberal/Irish Nationalist alliance, he was loudly accused of betraying 'the sacred cause of Ireland'.[10] Later, within the ILP he found himself defending the cause of Church schools against the Nonconformist secularist consensus rejecting them. For Sexton local socialism was clearly more important than the orthodoxies of Irish nationalism but not than the Church's educational plans in Lancashire, and in the latter cause he could well co-operate with Mr Blundell of Crosby. Both the conflicts and the sustaining unities of English Catholicism here seem clear enough.

The bishops expected loyalty on the schools question and they got it, otherwise they hardly tampered with politics, quite unlike their counterparts in many another country. The clerical control of the Church in England was firm enough so far as it went, but its unspoken frontiers were clear too. And within them there was plenty to do. Up to 1911 there had been but one archbishopric in England, that of Westminster. In that year the church was rearranged into three provinces, Liverpool and Birmingham becoming archbishoprics. Brentwood was made into a diocese in 1917 and Lancaster in 1924. There was very little further alteration in Roman Catholic structures until well after the Second World War. The shape of the Church had been effectively built up by 1920, a mass of new institutions – parishes, schools and convents – overlying the much older structures of penal and early post-penal times. The rapid growth in the number of convents is particularly noticeable – helped to a considerable extent by anti-clerical laws first in Germany and then France which had brought so many continental nuns to work in England. The Catholic community had as a consequence a range of girls' boarding schools far beyond that of any other section of English society, but of course many of these schools had a considerable number, even a majority, of non-Catholic girls. Very probably the Church in England had, in proportion to the number of Catholics, more convent schools than the Church in any other part of the world and the effect of this on the character of religious practice was not inconsiderable.

Of all its institutions Ushaw College, the very extensive range of seminary buildings and splendid library standing high on a hill a few miles outside Durham, had been the most influential. Here was the training house for the priests of the north, manifestly self-assured, at home, old-fashioned, in the tradition of the Douai from which it came, academic in a rather unexacting way, a little gone to seed.[11] William Browne was its President. Of north country recusant stock he had come to Ushaw as a boy in 1865 and lived there until his death. He had been Prefect of Studies from 1897 and was President from 1910 until 1934. He was, his biographer tells us, 'limited in his views and in his interests',[12] but a man who represented and carefully passed on a sturdy common man's form of northern Christianity. Whatever William Browne was or was not, his was hardly an 'alien' religion, yet more than anyone else he was responsible for the training of the priests of the next generation. William Browne is a reminder that Chesterton was not being too paradoxical when, while still an Anglican, he invented his most popular hero Fr Brown 'a very short Roman Catholic priest' sitting with a large shabby umbrella and several brown-paper parcels in an Essex train, 'so much the essence of those Eastern flats'. Fr Brown was wholly an Englishman.

Nor was Cardinal Bourne, dry old stick as he doubtless seemed, particularly alien. As we have seen he came from Clapham, and his father had worked in the Post Office. He studied at Ushaw and then in Paris and Louvain, so he lacked any close personal experience of Rome which may have helped him keep his intellectual balance during the difficult years of the Modernist crisis, but put him administratively at a disadvantage. He often felt that others were conspiring in Rome behind his back, especially Cardinals Gasquet and Merry del Val. He became archbishop in 1903, the same year as Davidson, and continued at Westminster until his death in 1935. Temperamentally he was not unlike Davidson who could almost have adopted Bourne's motto: 'I never start anything. But I never stop anything'.[13] He was a moderator, lonely, intensely cold in disposition, but anxious in a quiet way that the Catholic Church should participate more actively in national life,[14] and rather worried about the ravages of the anti-modernist witch-hunt. When he insisted that there were no modernists in his diocese, he was only half believed in Rome, but he protected von Hügel and his circle with fair success. Cardinal Vaughan's preference as his successor had not been Bourne but Merry del Val. If the latter had been appointed to Westminster the anti-modernist purge might have been less thorough-going in Rome, but it would have been a great deal fiercer in England.

The name and influence of Merry del Val must remind us that in all truth, if William Browne and Francis Bourne were English enough, it would be idle to deny that there were some pretty sharp 'alien' winds blowing through the Catholic Church in England in these years and we must now turn to consider them. Merry del Val stands for them and their great appeal well enough. He had been born in London where his father the Marquis Merry del Val had been secretary to the Spanish Embassy. There was English blood on his mother's side and he was partly educated in England and technically a priest of the archdiocese of Westminster. In his own opinion he was 'English to all intents and purposes'.[15] In fact he was trained for the Roman curia and never left its service. As Cardinal Secretary of State through the whole of Pius X's pontificate he had been a man of quite exceptional power and the architect of the anti-modernist reaction, though at times slightly restraining its most extreme exponents. A distinguished recent ecclesiastical historian has described him in the following way: 'The priest of pious and austere habit, the refined and urbane aristocrat who was total in his dedication to the Holy See and blandly impervious in his opposition to all modern movements.'[16]

Merry del Val always kept his eye on England. He had been Secretary to the Commission on Anglican Orders in 1896 and in close consultation with Gasquet, and indeed Cardinal Vaughan, had drafted the bull *Apostolicae Curae* declaring them 'absolutely null and utterly void'.[17]

Another member of the same commission, Gasparri, had favoured a more moderate and open view which would not so utterly negate Anglican convictions and the hopes of Lord Halifax and the Abbé Portal who had, perhaps naïvely, raised the matter in the expectation of a positive verdict. For the next thirty years papal politics would be something of a long duel between Gasparri and Merry del Val. For the latter a conciliatory approach towards modern thinking of any sort could only be the most dangerous nonsense: thus Portal was 'practically picking faith and principle to pieces by preaching Liberalism in religion'.[18] In correspondence with Vaughan, Merry del Val was constantly critical of a 'spirit of liberalism and revolt' which he detected in England, and when, in 1907, the English hierarchy sent a joint letter of loyal submission to the anti-modernist encyclical, *Pascendi*, Merry del Val in reply could still criticize 'one sentence which does not come very opportunely now, I mean where it is said that there is little or nothing of modernism amongst Roman Catholics . . . there are not many English Modernists, there is quite a sufficient number of them'.[19]

Merry del Val represents at its most uncompromising the ideology, ultramontane and anti-liberal, which for years had been pressed upon the English Church, and he is personally enormously important both because of the great power he long possessed and because of the fascination he exercised over devout English Catholics. He seemed to represent Catholicism in all its power and purity. He could perhaps wean them from the more open ways of their fathers more effectively even than the convert Manning, and when he died they prayed for and expected his canonization. Yet of course the Romanization of the English Church was a vastly much longer matter than the influence of Merry del Val. It went back to Cardinal Wiseman, the first Archbishop of Westminster, and its greatest protagonist had been Cardinal Manning. One of the master figures of the first Vatican Council and an ultramontane of the firmest conviction, he had no sympathy for the moderate and so-called 'Cisalpine' traditions of the English Catholic community. Like many a convert, but so unlike Newman, he came to despise not only the Church he had left but also the apparent compromises of the Church he had entered. For him, as for his ally in Rome, Mgr Talbot, English Catholicism needed to be Romanized anew. And they largely succeeded in doing so. His opponents, Bishops

Clifford, Errington, Goss, members of the Vatican I minority and genuine representatives of 'the old party', would have no successors. Goss of Liverpool declared emphatically that the testimony of Manning 'is opposed to the teaching of English Catholics. Truth, simple English truth, seems to have parted from the whole faction'.[20] Whether or not Clifford, Goss and their fellows were theologically wrong, Manning right, it was certainly they who represented at the time the historic tradition of English Catholicism. For Manning and Talbot it was a dangerous tradition, too English to be other than quasi-heretical, and Newman was the more suspect in that not only had he failed to repudiate sufficiently his Anglican past, but had also come to sympathize with this English Catholic tradition, a sort of crypto-Anglicanism. 'Every Englishman is naturally anti-Roman,' declared Mgr Talbot. 'To be Roman is to an Englishman an effort. Dr Newman is more English than the English. His Spirit must be crushed.'[21] To which Manning replied: 'I see much danger of an English Catholicism of which Newman is the highest type. It is the old Anglican, patristic, literary, Oxford tone transplanted into the Church . . . it is worldly Catholicism.' What Manning wanted instead was 'Downright, masculine and decided Catholics – *more* Roman than Rome, and more ultramontane than the Pope himself'.[22]

If this programme of radical Romanization was to be achieved, a new type of priest had to be made and the spirit of the seminaries had to be altered. So Mgr Talbot, planning the new chapel at the English College in Rome, had written in the 1850s: 'It is impossible to put the Roman spirit into the students without a church in which they can have their Quarant'ore, their altar of the Blessed Virgin and St Joseph and other Roman devotions.'[23]

Now, fifty years later, the revolution had largely succeeded. Men like Clifford and Goss had died and been replaced by bishops of a very different stamp. Goss had prophesied that with the passing of the Vatican decrees the bishops would degenerate into 'satraps dispatched to their provinces' and the reality of twentieth-century episcopal behaviour did not prove him so wide of the mark. The triumphant ultramontanism of Manning, Vaughan, Gasquet and Merry del Val so affected the clerical mind that the older tradition of the English Catholic clergy almost disappeared in an act of collective amnesia. The ideal was now to be a 'Roman', and the *Venerabile*, the English College at Rome, was the chosen instrument for putting the finishing touches to the new model. In 1917 Mgr Hinsley was made Rector of the *Venerabile*, and in many ways rejuvenated the College. It was about to become, as it had never quite been before, the breeding ground of the English episcopate. Hinsley was a likeable Yorkshireman, but ecclesiastically a Roman of the Romans, the friend of Amigo, the protégé of Gasquet. '*La chiesa Catholica in Ingilterra ha bisogno dello spirito di Romanita*' 'The Catholic Church in England needs the Roman spirit', wrote the latter in a special petition to have Hinsley made a bishop;[24] and so he was, with Merry del Val to consecrate him, assisted by Amigo. When reading John Heenan's memoir of Hinsley, or his own subsequent autobiography, *Not the Whole Truth*, one is struck by the sense of elation with Rome. Much of this was due to Hinsley himself. A man of the people and intensely honest and warm, he harmonized, indeed anglicized, ultramontanism. For Heenan and a whole generation of enthusiastic young men trained in the post-war *Venerabile* to be a 'Roman', to have 'the Roman spirit' was the great thing. The Church in England would owe them much, however true it might be that in them, Manning and Talbot had truly conquered. The Roman spirit of the Venerable English College implied an interest in Roman life and antiquities, in Italian food, wine and (a little patronizingly) politics, but, more important, an uncompromising loyalty to current papal teaching and to the person of the pope, an almost complete lack of interest in theological thinking, a strong group spirit combined with a rather self-conscious Englishry fixed on Christmas productions of Gilbert and Sullivan and summer cricket matches with the British Embassy. The *Venerabile* cultivated above all a very strong commitment to 'the conversion of England'. It was to be, undoubtedly, the most influential clerical institution within English Catholicism for the next forty years, carrying far and wide the single ideal of 'Romanita', so very different from that of the old tradition of a Lingard or a Clifford.

The English College of Hinsley was, of course, but one part of the steady pressure of ultramontanization which was transforming English Catholicism, subordinating ever more absolutely local church to papacy and laity to clergy while at the same time segregating Catholics, so far as possible, from the dangerous influences of other churches and modern ideas.[25] It was a combination of the papal monarchy of Pius IX's reign and the anti-modernism of Pius X's and it was at work at every level of episcopal appointment and clerical formation, spirituality, doctrine, law. It had few more effective instruments than the convent school with its French nuns, absence of theology, but unquestioning commitment to the new Catholicism; an intense devotion to the Pope and to everything connected with Rome, novenas, indulgences, canonizations, eucharistic congresses, pilgrimages to Lourdes, all that was most characteristic of ultramontane spirituality – the absolute stress upon ecclesiastical obedience as the sum of all the virtues, coupled with an often heroic personal self-immolation and other-worldliness, an apparent ruthlessness in the treatment of people.

Antonia White's *Frost in May*, an autobiographical novel describing the Sacred Heart school at Roehampton just before the First World War, provides an extraordinarily vivid picture of the ultramontane convent world – and here one which had only just previously been ruled by the great Mother Erskine Stuart. *Frost in May* really needs to be read side by side with the *Life and Letters* of Mother Stuart, so much light do they throw upon each other. There is no reason to think that *Frost in May* does not provide a fair picture of Roehampton, and indeed of the convent school ethos almost anywhere – it is in fact in many ways a great tribute to it – yet when one reads the *Life and Letters* one cannot but realize that it is a partial, indeed a rather exterior, picture of the nuns and their achievement, as Antonia White herself came later to realize.[26] Such a school presented a model of Catholic life at its purest to the devout lay person and it impressed its ideals and spirituality upon the élite of Catholic womanhood in a way that had seldom been the case in earlier ages. The quintessential heart of this religious world was solemn Benediction of the blessed sacrament on a high feast in the convent chapel: the court of the great king, the girls all kneeling devoutly in their white veils and gloves before the golden monstrance, the many hundreds of candles lit around the altar, the clouds of incense, the Latin hymns. Here was ultramontane Catholicism at its most appealing to many a convert, its most appalling to many a Protestant.

There were certainties here not to be despised, especially at a time of such manifest religious uncertainties elsewhere. And they appealed to many, including some of the most brilliant. Ronald Knox became a Roman Catholic in 1917. He had long tried to be an Anglo-Catholic but came to the conclusion that it was Rome or nothing. The simplicity and clarity of the Roman claim to authority was intellectually important; and it was not diminished for converts but rather enhanced by the growth of internal autocracy. Knox wrote to his father, the Protestant Bishop of Manchester, comparing the Church of Rome to a shop window in which there was no need to examine the goods because there was a sign over the door, THIS IS THE TRUE DEPOT ORDAINED BY CHRIST HIMSELF. 'I should not have used the metaphor,' the bishop sadly commented.[27] Knox's conversion was to a view of Church authority of ultramontane simplicity; no one was less worried by the unmitigated absoluteness of the anti-modernist oath, which he took with positive delight; most intellectual converts for the next forty years – and there would be many and brilliant ones – decided upon substantially the same grounds.

The legal instruments of the new Catholicism were the *Ne Temere* decree of 1908, the anti-modernist oath, and the new code of canon law. Hitherto in Britain Catholics could marry validly in a Protestant church. *Ne Temere* ended this, tightening up the sense of social separation between Catholics and Protestants and producing a deep feeling of injustice among non-Catholics in the whole mixed-marriage field. The anti-modernist oath 'against all liberal interpretations whether of scripture or history', to be taken by all priests before ordination or entering into office, was designed to ensure everywhere an almost fundamentalist orthodoxy. At the same time the new code of canon law, promulgated in 1917, ensured the ironing out of local *differentiae* of all sorts in favour of Roman uniformity. The Rome-trained liturgy professor at Oscott seminary in the 1920s would pick up Bishop Challoner's venerable *Ordo Administrandi Sacramenta*, the handbook of the English Church for two hundred years, in one hand, the *Rituale Romanum* in the other. 'Don't use this,' he would say of the former, 'use that.' It was symbolic of what was happening on every side.

Yet for many, and in very real ways, the ultramontane revolution was liberating and pastorally creative. The new canon law was easy to use in comparison with the previous confusion: most English priests indeed were probably hardly aware until then of what canon law said about almost anything. The old order had been somewhat patrician and cliquish; this was indeed part of Manning's objection to it. The new ultramontanism could seem aristocratic enough in the international connections of Merry del Val but really it was far more working class, even populist – it swept away tradition and privilege in order to get on with the job. Manning not only had the confidence of Rome, he also had that of the London dockers. Furthermore by a series of decrees Pius X had encouraged the laity to come to frequent, even daily, communion and declared that small children from the age of seven or eight should come too. Perhaps when the consequences of most other events of his reign have faded away, this one great decision will stand, out of which so much has grown. The implications of these decrees have hardly yet been fully appreciated. But they did begin the renewal of the sacramental centre of Catholic life, stimulating the liturgical movement, and in a strongly non-élitist direction. Where, as in Britain, the new ultramontanism encountered a naturally vigorous, working-class Church, the pastoral consequences could be remarkable.

Again, if the English bishops insisted that there was little or no modernism in England, they could not unreasonably have claimed too that there was little or none of that sense of a repressed laity associated with ultramontanism. Cardinal Bourne played it all very coolly so that the growth of clerical ultramontanism really did not impinge too heavily upon the laity. Maurice Baring was no fool. He had become a Catholic himself in 1909; when Chesterton was received in 1922, he wrote to him as follows: 'Space and freedom: that was what I experienced on being received; that is what I have been most conscious of ever since. It is the exact opposite of what the ordinary Protestant conceives to be the case.'[28] That witness deserves to be pondered, but it comes from someone unconcerned with clerical discipline or theological thought.

The negative pressures of the new ultramontanism were directed against both the old English tradition and any signs of new liberalism. Against the former it overwhelmingly prevailed, but on the latter front new ideas would keep breaking out, though it was not easy. Following the deaths of Newman and Tyrrell there was almost no clerical theological work going on in the English Church. What there was could be looked for at Downside where the monastery included a fair number of scholars besides its abbot, Cuthbert Butler, or among the Dominicans whose provincial was Bede Jarrett. He refounded Blackfriars at Oxford in 1921 (exactly 700 years after the foundation of the first Blackfriars there in 1221) and the year before began its monthly review (*Blackfriars*), both of which were to have so stimulating an influence in coming years. What these centres provided, however, at that time was some form of historical scholarship and spiritual teaching, less slippery ground than theology proper. Downside's brightest academic light, Dom Hugh Connolly, was eminent in patristics, the least dangerous of fields. On the main intellectual and ecclesiological issues, which had so exercised the modernists and alarmed authority, almost nothing was happening. *Pascendi* and *Lamentabili* had snuffed out for a while a whole movement of thought. One man they had not worried. Hilaire Belloc represented the dominant Catholic mind of 1920 only too well. No one was less of a theologian than he: a brilliant but embittered apologist and partisan historian, a man of many gifts, betrayed, perhaps, by his loyalty to the least healthy traditions of contemporary French Catholicism. His supreme antithesis, Baron von Hügel, international 'bishop' of the modernist movement, as many thought him, had escaped condemnation, perhaps just because he was lay (and a baron!), yet also because of his profound Catholic piety, temperamental caution and naturally conciliatory mind. But his circle was, in Catholic terms, a dying one, his friends and correspondents increasingly non-Catholics. A letter that Abbot Butler wrote to him in 1922 is devastatingly revealing of the reason why:

> In regard to what you say about your regret that I am not giving myself to early Christian things – years ago I recognised that these things – Xtian origins, New Testament, History of Dogma, etc. – have been made impossible for a priest, except on the most narrow apologetic lines. A priest can publish nothing without 'imprimatur'. The only freedom in Biblical things and the rest is that of a tram, to go ahead as fast as you like on rails,

but if you try to arrive at any station not on the line, you are derailed. . . . When the Biblical Commission got under way, and the *Lamentabili* and *Pascendi* were issued, I deliberately turned away from all this work – my being Abbot made it not apparent.[29]

In the words of Edmund Bishop, perhaps the greatest English Catholic scholar of that age, 'deep darkness has settled all around one, and hopes, how bright and vivid . . . are utterly crushed, stamped upon – nay! Anathematised!'[30]

If von Hügel ended up so very much alone, and under such deep Catholic suspicion, he yet remained sufficient in himself as a witness to the onward flow, despite everything, of the living Christian intelligence. There was no other Catholic alive in England in 1920 with whom in influence we can compare him: 'Our greatest theologian and the ablest apologist for Christianity in our time', Dean Inge not inappropriately described him.

If it was ever given to a man to transcend the great religious and national divides of history, then that man was Friedrich von Hügel. Undoubtedly English, yet the son of an Austrian baron, the complete European with intimate friends in Italy, France and Germany; a married man, father of several daughters, yet profoundly sympathetic towards celibacy; the author of magisterial volumes on mysticism, who yet most fully appreciated the social and sacramental character of Christianity; the total Catholic who would be unthinkable without the debt he owed to Protestant friends like Troeltsch and Kemp Smith; the intellectual radical, the social conservative. He stands as an angel at the gate of our period, the great reconciler, seer of a new whole Christianity, overarching the divisions of the medieval and Reformation centuries, but firmly rooted in the transcendent God, the historic incarnation, the Eucharist. Above all, he was a man of prayer. Cuthbert Butler described him in his obituary notice,[31] sitting in church, 'the great deep eyes fixed on the Tabernacle, the whole being wrapt in an absorption of prayer, devotion and contemplation'.

Behind the statesmanlike, irenic figure of the lay aristocrat lurked that of the lonely, provocative convert priest, his friend George Tyrrell. By 1920, dead of Bright's disease at the age of forty-eight, he lay in his grave in an Anglican cemetery because of the unyielding refusal of the Church to allow his burial in Catholic ground. By his own wish nothing was to be written there but his name, the fact of his Catholic priesthood and the emblems of chalice and host. Born an Anglican, converted to Catholicism in 1879, ordained a Jesuit, the friend of Loisy, Brémond, von Hügel, of many worried intellectuals, and Anglican priests, Tyrrell was a rather shy man, quite unambitious, owner of nothing but a few books and a restless mind. He 'feared nothing in this world,' said Brémond at his grave, 'except the faintest shadow of a lie'.

The evolution of Tyrrell's thought across a series of important books spanning hardly more than ten years was towards an ever clearer differentiation between the Catholicism he upheld and both a naturalist 'Liberal Protestantism', and the 'medievalism' of Roman ultramontanes and neo-scholastics. There cannot be much doubt that his was the most theologically innovative and yet essentially orthodox mind at work in the modernist crisis, and, since the death of Newman, the Catholic Church in England has had no other priest comparable in theological stature. Caught between the scholarship of his age and the Rome of Pius X, lacking von Hügel's protection of laymanship or a temperament able to withdraw from the eye of the storm into areas of less embattled study, he was marked down for martyrdom. For several years, after summary expulsion from the Society by the Jesuit General, he was unable to say mass. Finally, on criticizing the encyclical *Pascendi* in *The Times*, – 'this Encyclical [neither] comes from or speaks to the living heart of the Church' – he was, for the last eighteen months of his life, deprived even of communion; this without any explanation as to what he had said to justify Bishop Amigo in taking so cruel a step. Yet he obeyed. Some years earlier Tyrrell had written an article *Beati Excommunicati*, foretelling the fate but also the duty and ultimate consolation of those unable to keep silence in face of ecclesiastical absolutism.

In such circumstances the appeal of a return to the Church of England was an intensely real one, and Tyrrell felt it; 'Church of my baptism; Church of Westcott, Hort, Lightfoot, Church, Liddon, Taylor, Leighton, Coleridge; Church of better-than-saints, why did I ever leave you?'[32] Yet he resisted that call though ground down by the most intellectually obscurantist and institutionally ruthless phase of all modern Roman history, and his final book, *Christianity at the Cross Roads*, published posthumously, is surely his greatest work, the most maturely orthodox, and perhaps all in all the finest apologetic vindication of Catholicism ever written in English. Yet no one has been more neglected: liberal Catholics dared subsequently to stand up for von Hügel, but who would even mention, save with bated breath, the name of Tyrrell?[33] Too obedient to Rome even in his persecution to be comprehensible to non-Romans, too fearlessly critical of Rome to be other than anathema to every ultramontane: the traitorous voice within the walls.

To the little group gathered on 21 July 1909 around his grave in the churchyard at Storrington, to Baron von Hügel and his daughter, to Fr Maturin (the only English Catholic priest to be there), Maud Petre, Wilfred Blunt, a few Anglican priests and other old friends, the Abbé Brémond gave one short address:[34]

> You see the place we have lovingly chosen for him, since another place was refused to us. You see the place. He used to like it, and, many a time, when he was living in the Priory, here he came, reciting his breviary in the very same path beside which they have dug his grave. As you see, it stands half-way between the two Churches, the one in which he died and the other in which he was born. On this side, separated from us by a tiny wall, the Catholic Church; on the other, the Church of Keble, of so many of you who have been so discreetly kind and so courageously true to him . . .

No other English Christian of the twentieth century has been so harshly treated, none other privileged to share so utterly in the condemnation and lonely death of the Saviour. In none else has the harshness of ecclesiastical oppression been so clearly shown – even to the grave. And yet was Philip Waggett, an Anglican priest, mistaken when he wrote at once to von Hügel, in so great apparent contradiction to immediate evidence? 'Such a life and death cannot fail to do something – perhaps very much – to shake the ice of separation and misunderstanding. . . . It makes one unhappy that we who do nothing, live on, and he who attempted so much is gone.'[35]

PART II

The 1920s

8

Politics

Britain in the 1920s was trying hard to be a Conservative land but not quite succeeding. If the clock could only be put back to 1914, bar a few post-war amenities, how pleasant it would be: that was perhaps the dream of twenties society. The unpleasant things had been disposed of or were being disposed of – German militarism, the Irish question, Welsh disestablishment, even the poor. Could one not now enter without much trouble into a social Utopia with the help of all the nice new things science and progress had provided us? The start of the decade was admittedly a time of post-war frustration and at first even intense fear lest the red bogey might not appear here too, but at least by 1924 things were settling down and prospering, both at home and abroad, and there seemed little reason why they should not go on getting better and better. Real wages were rising for most people. There were more cars and radio sets and decent little three-bedroomed houses on new estates and buses in the countryside and State scholarships for the bright but poor, and crosswords, detective stories and talkies to while away the time. 'Things are getting better,' sang Cecily Courtneidge, 'better, better every day.' If the old industries – farming and coal above all – were running down badly enough, there were new ones developing, like car and wireless manufacturing, and a pretty steady drift of population from village to town and from north to south. Away from the slummy early industrialized towns of Lancashire and Yorkshire, the road from Wigan Pier led to a semi-detached haven in the home counties, a suburbanized village, where as likely as not, 'twenty men of us all got work on a bit' of the squire's motor car.[1] The upper class had not lost its nerve but it had modernized its modes of patronage. It was an age of optimism, intellectual,

social, political. There were great social problems still unresolved, undoubtedly, but it was widely, if smugly, felt that at
home they were being faced as fast as the nation could afford,
while abroad the League of Nations was little by little inaugurating a new order of rational harmony. The action of Winston
Churchill, as Chancellor of the Exchequer in 1925, in putting
Britain back on the Gold Standard and restoring the pound's
pre-war parity to the dollar was somehow symbolic of the way
things were meant to be in the 1920s. Not a revolutionary age.

That may seem a little surprising. After all, Britain was a
democracy for the first time and had demonstrated this by
allowing the Liberals, the old but basically élitist party of reform
and new ideas, to crumble rapidly away while establishing
Labour as the new alternative to conservatism. When Labour
came first to power in 1924 over half the members of the Cabinet
were working class. Its MPs had been noisily singing the 'Red
Flag' in the House of Commons only a few months before. A
government led by Ramsay MacDonald, Arthur Henderson and
Philip Snowden must have seemed a pretty revolutionary phenomenon, and Asquith was bombarded with appeals to ally the
Liberals with the Conservatives and so 'save the country from the
horrors of Socialism'. In fact the Labour governments of 1924
and 1929 were very much minority governments, only allowed to
survive on good behaviour for as long as they did, and were firmly
led by the moderate wing of the party. Labour in the 1920s was in
full control of its major bases on Merseyside, Tyneside, Clydeside
and South Wales – decisively wrested from the Liberals – but
these would never give it a majority in parliament. For that to be
achieved, it required a scale of support in the south-east, the
Midlands and among the middle class which it did not yet possess
and could only obtain by demonstrating, to some at least of the
aspiring middle class, its unrevolutionary character.

Doubtless the collapse of the Liberal Party – so central to
contemporary England in 1906, so irrelevant by 1926 – had a
great deal to do with the long feud between Asquith and Lloyd
George, and with the intense ambiguity of role which long
surrounded the latter to the bewilderment of the Liberal world,
but there was far more to it than that. Universal adult franchise
and the organization of the working class through the Trade

Unions made it impossible for the old Liberal Party with its upper middle-class leadership to continue as the principal party of reform. Perhaps Lloyd George could have transformed it into the effective vehicle of working class consciousness if he had wished to do so, but his own political separation from the Labour movement and the large scale organization of the Labour Party after 1906 removed this from the realm of practical possibilities. Once Labour grew, the Liberals could hardly not decline. One might fairly say, their work was done. The only thing which could have delayed this would have been an intransigently reactionary Conservative Party in which erstwhile Liberals could not find a home. It was here that the new conservatism of Baldwin and Neville Chamberlain was so important. Baldwin, the industrialist turned countryman, the master of the fireside chat on the wireless, the man of conciliation, was the ideal Conservative leader to welcome the new recruits. He led the party from 1923 until his retirement in 1937 and was Prime Minister from May 1923 to January 1924 and from November 1924 to June 1929 – over half the decade. More than anyone else he represents the political mood of the 1920s. There was no rejection here of the Liberal reforms of the great post-1906 era. They were simply taken for granted. Post-war Conservatism was far from the last-ditch Toryism which had fought tooth and nail against Lloyd George's budget or the limitation of the powers of the House of Lords, or squirmed at the thought of giving women the vote. The new conservatism in fact took to a full democratic electorate far more easily than did the Liberals and probably benefited particularly from the female vote. By and large it continued, where money was available, the gradual implementation of the welfare state, initiated by Lloyd George, and even the small reforms Labour was able to commence during its months in office in 1924 the Conservatives largely continued – in the fields of housing and education. In principle, from 1924 on, the parties were agreed that the provision of decent houses was a responsibility of government, though any effective slum clearance scheme would still be a long time coming. The Labour leadership, and Ramsay MacDonald above all, was emphatically gradualist in its approach to righting Britain's ills, and it would be hard at that level to find any great divide in approach between MacDonald and Baldwin: 'In all essentials his outlook is very close to ours,' declared the former of the latter. Amazingly different as the social background of the two party leaderships now was – so that the earlier difference between Tory and Liberal could seem slight in comparison – the dominant mind of the two parties was extraordinarily similar, so that the final state of 'National' government, the coalition of MacDonald and Baldwin which ruled the country in the 1930s, with at first overwhelming electoral support, was not really half so strange as in retrospect it seems or as the tougher core of Labour found it at the time. But if it responded to a 1930s rather than a 1920s crisis, it reflected a 1920s rather than a 1930s sense of consensus and the 'liberalization' of both parties for, strange as it may seem, the Liberal Party a-dying had not unsuccessfully bequeathed the cause of liberalism to both its rivals.

And yet, of course, at the heart of the 1920s stands the General Strike, the nearest that modern British society has ever come to class war. A paradox maybe, but not in contradiction with what has been said. In the England of the 1920s, as much as in many a previous age, there were two nations. The prosperous, possessing nation had grown a great deal larger and rather more homogeneous than it had ever been before. It was too large, too hopeful, far too widely based to be dispossessed, especially as it was no longer seriously divided between town and countryside, trade and aristocracy, Established Church and Dissent. But there was another nation too. Millions of people were far too poor, far too remote socially or geographically from the mechanisms of advancement and novel opportunities for entertainment, far too miserable in their living conditions, far too effectively trapped within the mouldering legacy of the most ruthless stages of the Industrial Revolution, for a gradualist, 'safety first' approach to mean anything to them. The miners were the single largest, most obvious case, but the inhabitants of all the major slums of Britain and most farm workers too belonged to this other nation for whom a 'golden age' of the mid-1920s was no other than the bitterest of bad jokes. There were always over a million unemployed, and unemployment had little of the cushioning which had been built up around it by the 1970s. In particular, the mining industry was in an appalling state. It had suffered greatly from overseas competition including the effect of the German payment of 'reparations' in coal, and, if any industry required rational reorganizing – almost impossible without nationalization – it was this one. Nationalization was in fact the recommendation of the chairman and majority of the Sankey Commission, appointed by the government in 1919. It was an enduring tragedy that Lloyd George did not grip the nettle at that moment – the one moment before the Second World War when it could really have been carried through. National control of national interests was coming to be taken for granted in the 1920s in the case of new products, even by the Conservatives who established a national monopoly body for both broadcasting and electricity. Refusal to apply the principle to coal not only prevented the rational reform of an industry absolutely vital to the country, but also left its workers in conditions depressing beyond the acceptable norms of the age. Its problems had been debated for years and the crunch staved off by various government subsidies and commissions, but to no avail. By the mid-1920s, when the crisis could finally be deferred no further, government in Britain was no longer radical enough to contemplate a single measure of reform so considerable as the acceptance of full responsibility for the coal industry. Yet it could not escape responsibility either, because the mine owners were not only demanding a reduction in wages, but also a lengthening of the working day beyond the legal limit, and that required legislation. A final Royal Commission presided over by Herbert Samuel and reporting in March 1926 recommended no nationalization, no further government subsidies, but equally no lengthening of the working day. The rather complicated tinkering with the system it did propose was hardly welcome to either side, now committed to do battle.

'Not a penny off the pay, not a minute on the day': such was the miners' simple position, and hardly a revolutionary one. For sticking to it they were locked out on 1 May 1926. The General Council of the TUC was committed to supporting them and did so, if unenthusiastically, with the result that a general strike began two days later after the breakdown of incompetently conducted final negotiations between the Cabinet and the TUC – a breakdown more or less engineered by the hawks in the Cabinet. The workers called out responded magnificently: they obeyed the strike call, they were cheerful; with very few exceptions they avoided violence. The upper classes responded still more determinedly: they would beat the bolshies as they had beaten the Germans, and, of course, they did. Volunteer workers destroyed the strike's cutting edge while armoured cars drove through the streets of London just to make the basic issue of power quite clear. Churchill and Joynson Hicks, the two chief Cabinet hawks, effectively got their way. There was next to no class war on the strikers' side, just a deal of deference and even a good humoured willingness to play football with the police; on the side of the upper class there were plentiful signs of class war – which, of course, tallies with the view that the finest Marxist is the capitalist rank and file. What is certain is that the General Strike was in no way an attempt to overthrow the constitution or indeed effect any political change at all; it was no more than a matter of poor men standing loyally beside the poorest when driven too hard to the wall. But it seemed to be more; it rallied against it the effective consensus of the governing class and after ten days it was called off. Conservatism not only had won but was seen to have won. The miners themselves stuck it out on strike for six months and were only driven back by starvation. Their cause was a good one, but the means chosen were ill-advised. In the months of negotiation their leaders had shown an inflexibility which would not work, the power of their withdrawn labour being less than they imagined. The union leaders with a future would take a rather different road. Ernest Bevin of the TGWU had, of course, supported the General Strike, but it was not his way. A man of negotiation and compromise, of playing the establishment's own game, he would end at the very top with as good a claim as any to be the representative Englishman of the mid-twentieth century. But then he had in the south-east a wider, more flexible power base than had the miners, a constituency already sharing in the new prosperity. The unions would indeed lead their troops little by little into the valleys of affluence, but the road of 1926, the head-on national confrontation, would not be tried again.

What happened at home was happening, to a very large extent, abroad as well. Revolutionary Ireland was already a quiet, conservative land before the twenties were out. Bolshevist Russia had been neatly cordoned off in the east, while the rest of Europe was – it seemed – at last being pulled together in a more or less realistic and democratic manner. The Treaty of Locarno in 1925 – a non-aggression pact between France, Belgium and Germany, guaranteed by Britain and Italy – had its symbolic value as an acceptance of frontiers and of national equality by the main powers of Europe. Germany entered the League. Its democratic constitution was working, its economy reviving. The political tone of Europe in the later 1920s was conservative but not reactionary; indeed one of the most encouraging things was that in France as in Germany and in Britain some of the pre-war reactionary forces had rallied to the cause of gradualist reform in a democratic context. Catholics in France were more reconciled to the Republic than they had been for generations; Catholics in Germany were a crucially positive force making for the stability of the Weimar Republic. 'The age might yet become a golden, or a platinum, age at any rate,' thought old Soames Forsyte in Galsworthy's *Swan Song*,[2] certainly not one for starry-eyed illusions. Nobody could really envisage another war: there was just nothing to fight about. And if the world's economy was not booming, it did seem to be getting fairly steadily better. Doubtless it was all very brittle really, the League feeble and incompetent, feelings in Germany and France infinitely more sensitive than moderating politicians wanted to recognize, the frontiers of Versailles just made for crises of bullying, all sorts of dangerous ideas in the air. But it did not seem like that. 'Peace in our time' – social peace, international peace, colonial peace – did not seem improbable. On the contrary, with a little give and take, it seemed almost achieved. One must not pass straight from the war to the agonizings of the 1930s; indeed it is the very relaxation of the mid-1920s which gives the latter their plausibility.

Yet the fragility was there all along and it would not take much, after the economic crash of 1929, to sweep far out of sight Soames's golden, or at least platinum, age. The first and one of the most basic causes of that fragility was, of course, the isolationism of the United States. In March 1920 the Senate had refused to ratify the Treaty of Versailles by the necessary two-thirds majority, and America never entered the League. Without the presence of Russia either, the League never could achieve that world status it required if its moral prestige was to compensate for its legal weakness. But the isolationism of America did much more than that. It politically and psychologically unbalanced the world that its greatest economic power was not carrying the responsibilities which its role in the war had shown were now inescapably America's. If Europe ran amok again America would not be able to shrug its shoulders however much it might like to do so. Refusal to participate meanwhile both stalled America's international education and greatly weakened the rest of the world's mechanisms for coping with disaster. American economics – a phoney financiers' boom in the 1920s followed by the Wall Street crash of June 1929 – was indeed a principal cause of Europe's ills. In almost every field of life, intellectual and religious as well as political, the inter-war decades were marked by a strange sense of ambivalence in regard to the condition of America: she had so clearly arrived in an international position of near primacy and yet psychologically could not quite cope with that position, so that what actually emerged as the American contribution proved strangely contradictory, gushing and naïve at one moment, ruthless and even barbarous at another: an emotional anti-colonialism, Frank Buchman's Movement, Prohibition enacted yet not enforced, upon the one hand; the judicial murder of Sacco and Vanzetti in 1927, the staging before great crowds of public executions, an unashamed colonialist grip upon Central Latin America, Ku-Klux-Klan lynchings, on the other.

The underlying political unsoundness of Soames's platinum age was due, almost equally, to the neo-nationalist tendencies of our European neighbours. Parliamentary democracy was the orthodoxy of the post-Versailles world, but it did not exactly go to the heart of every central or southern European. Faced with the spectre of Bolshevik Russia and western Communist parties too, and the consequent threat to the existing interests of the privileged classes, but also with the vast social unsettlement caused by the war, many people were looking for more heady medicine than a Chamber of Deputies. The emergence of a wave of 'Fascist' parties – violent, populist, nationalist, ruthlessly anti-Communist, linked with big business but also anti-Semitic – was the consequence. It was the characteristic expression of right wing sentiment in a post-monarchical era and like many right wing movements it could draw powerfully and emotionally upon religious tradition and fears at one moment, turn and rend the Church a minute later.

The model for all this was, of course, Mussolini's Fascist Party in Italy. It was in October 1922 that Mussolini's Black Shirts marched on Rome and he was asked to form a government from which any democratic element very quickly disappeared. It was government by violence, intimidation and demagoguery. Fascism triumphed because its enemies were so divided among themselves and, mostly, so poor in leadership. In the early days there was no other reason why the movement should not have been resisted and disarmed and, even as late as the murder of Matteotti in June 1924 a determined alliance of anti-Fascists might still have rallied the nation. What prevented this every time was the moral schism dividing Socialists and Catholics. The crucial element here was undoubtedly the *Partito Popolare*. Ever since the ending of the Papal States in 1870 the papacy had first discouraged and then forbidden Catholics to participate in an Italian order which flouted the Church's traditional privileges, thus enhancing the social gulf between the religious and non-religious sides of the nation and more or less forcing the latter, including, of course, Socialists, to maintain a fierce anti-clericalism. This ban had been enforced with particular rigidity by Pius X. The champion of an alternative Catholic attitude was Don Luigi Sturzo, a Sicilian priest and probably all in all one of the most significant figures in the whole of twentieth-century Catholic Church history, as well as one of the most unusual. For many years General Secretary of Catholic Action, he had come to exercise upon the Church in Italy a personal influence almost comparable to that of the pope. A cool and rational person and a most unclericalist priest in politics, Sturzo was striving for a profound renovation of Italian society – the depressed south above all – in regard to which the restoration of ecclesiastical rights and privileges lost since 1870 took a very low priority. Yet he was an obedient priest too, and there lay irreconcilables.

At the end of the war Sturzo went to Pope Benedict, explained that after the co-operation of the war years it was unthinkable for Catholics to continue to boycott Italian politics, and obtained the pope's agreement for the founding of a new party, which quickly

won more than a hundred seats in parliament. Sturzo, its undoubted leader, did not, however, enter parliament himself. The
party was inevitably a coalition between 'Right' and 'Left', but its
main core was remarkably loyal to Sturzo's own line. Hardly had
this happened than the Fascist wave broke upon Italy, while Pope
Benedict died and was succeeded by the more authoritarian Pius
XI.

Hitherto Mussolini had been bitterly, indeed almost ob-
scenely, anti-religious and anti-clerical in his utterings. This
suddenly changed. He began instead to laud the positive value of
religion while bitterly denouncing Sturzo, whom he recognized
as his most dangerous enemy, for his 'materialistic, tyrannical
and anti-Christian politics'.[3] Mussolini soon made it clear to the
Vatican that if he were to control Italy the Roman question could
be settled very well, to papal satisfaction, and on coming to
power he was quick to impose the teaching of the Catholic
catechism in State schools. All this made Pius XI, who had no love
for democracy anyway, quick to lean on Catholics to welcome
Mussolini and on the *Partito Popolare* not to attempt any sort of
an alliance with the Socialists (who were, admittedly, many of
them singularly averse to collaborating with Catholics even at a
moment of such dire national peril).

In August 1923 an outstanding parish priest, Father Giovanni
Minzoni, was murdered by Fascist thugs. The Pope made no
comment. The *Osservatore Romano*, in a brief report, volunteered the information that Mussolini had been saddened by it.[4]
The very next week the Eucharistic Congress at Genoa was
magnificently celebrated with full Fascist support. The message
was clear. On, apparently secret, papal orders Sturzo resigned the
Secretary-Generalship of the party in July 1924 and went into
exile in October, from which he would only return an old man in
1946. What remained remarkable was the strength of grass roots
Catholic support, among both clergy and working class laity, for
Sturzo and the *Partito Popolare*, even when it had become quite
clear that both the Vatican and most of the bishops had withdrawn their sympathy.

So Mussolini got his way. Italian democracy disappeared
under the pressure of murder, the administration of castor oil and
the Vatican's decision to back him. It is clear in retrospect that the

only force strong enough to have held Fascism in check would have been a whole hearted Catholic commitment to democracy, including a willingness to co-operate with Socialists. Pius XI was interested in neither. What he was interested in was some sort of symbolic reversal of the papal defeat of 1870 and this he got by the Lateran Treaty, signed with a flourish in February 1929, establishing the State of the Vatican. It was hailed upon both sides as a masterpiece of diplomacy. Yet its main provisions were obvious enough. Effectively the Vatican State had been an operational reality for years before 1929 with a growing diplomatic corps attached to it, and the treaty did little more than tie up the loose ends. It was for this reason that Pius's real concern had been quite as much with a concordat: he had insisted that the two must go together, and the concordat provided the Church with (for the twentieth century) extraordinarily exceptional privileges throughout Italy, especially in the fields of marriage and education. For many secularly minded Italians the whole thing was nothing less than a sell-out of the *Risorgimento* to the Church, but Mussolini was astute enough to know that a privileged church is a captive church. It could well become effectively a docile auxiliary for the forward march of Fascism instead of the rather independent force Italian Catholicism had often been in the 1920s. When the Vatican became more critical of Fascism in the later thirties, it would find that this had indeed happened and it had in consequence largely lost any constituency to turn to within the nation. The Treaty had provided Fascism in Italy with the certificate of respectability it required in Catholic eyes and this, once acquired, could not easily be taken away again. And not only in Italy. The fate of Italy was to be paradigmatic for the fate of Central Europe a few years later. All across Europe Catholics in the 1920s were wobbling between a commitment to democracy and a commitment to some sort of populist nationalism, usually more or less anti-Semitic and militarist. If democracy could be sold down the river by the Church in Italy, it could hardly with integrity be supported by Catholicism elsewhere. Yet, if the Catholic commitment to democracy was not fostered, the very threat of Communism would almost inevitably result instead in a coalescing of Catholic and Fascist forces which would place the latter, not the former, in power.

For the time being the strongest expression of Catholic democracy was the German Centre Party and much of the temporary success of the Weimar Republic must be put down to its existence, to its willingness to co-operate with Socialists (what in Italy Sturzo had not been permitted to do), and to the work of such men as Fr Brauns, a Catholic priest who was Minister of Labour between 1920 and 1928 in twelve successive governments. The Nazis were kept out of power all through the 1920s. Clearly this was by no means an approach dear to all Catholic hearts outside Italy. On the contrary, in Poland, in France and elsewhere, an anti-Semitic nationalism could prove much more agreeable. The *Action Française* of Charles Maurras was really much more typical of inter-war political Catholicism – though Maurras was an atheist and his movement, to the horror of so many French Catholics including not a few bishops, was very forthrightly condemned by Pius XI in 1926. The Pope was much more perceptive of events outside Italy than within.

The deeper implications of the Lateran Treaty were discussed with moderation but great perception in an editorial of the Anglican *Church Times* (22 February 1929), which is well worth recording here:

> It is, no doubt, a captivating idea that practically every child in Italy will be taught the Catholic Faith; but is it quite in accord with the spirit of our Saviour that the police should drive the children of unbelievers to compulsory Catechism? ... We cannot forget that modern Nationalism is the enemy of Catholicism. His Holiness so proclaimed it when he condemned the *Action Française*. But how does the Nationalism of Signor Mussolini differ philosophically from the Nationalism of M. Maurras? Is M. Maurras's real fault that he has as yet failed to create a Nationalist monarchy or dictatorship? At least, the alliance between Pius XI and the Duce of Fascism suggests anxious thoughts. We cannot help wondering whether the Vatican has not too lightly turned its back on the ideal of the free church in the free state.[5]

Few people in Britain, least of all English Catholics, saw it all quite like that. Neither the true significance of Don Sturzo nor of the treaty was understood. *The Times* and the *Telegraph* had welcomed Mussolini. The fragility of the European order was not recognized, nor the demonic powers about to be unloosed, nor the decisive role that freedom-loving Catholics, confident of the sympathy of Rome, might well have played. All in all the gap here between institutional religion and even a moderate socialism was still far too large. It would leave the road wide open across 'the man of Providence' as Pius XI chose to describe Mussolini, to carry Europe to war, to Hitler's hegemony and to Auschwitz, but in 1929 as Catholic and Fascist alike celebrated the Lateran Treaty, few could have dreamt of that. Indeed the devout reader in England was comforted instead by the rumour that the duce had developed a quite particular devotion to St Teresa of Lisieux, the Little Flower.

In such circumstances the world might seem not so far off the golden age. 'The millennium's nearly here,' remarked Sir Laurence Mount to Soames Forsyte. 'Education's free; women have the vote; even the workman has or soon will have his car; the slums are doomed . . . sport's cheap and plentiful; dogma's got the knock; so has the General Strike; Boy Scouts are increasing rapidly; dress is comfortable; and hair is short – its all millennial.'[6]

Added to which, in Italy the trains now ran on time.

9

Social Thought

Christian concern with the social order was nothing new but in Britain by the 1920s[1] it was attaining upon several sides a self-consciousness, a public airing of a large-scale and semi-official kind, a diversity of fairly clearly specified schools of thought, such as to suggest that it had come to maturity in a way it had not in the pre-war phase when Bishop Westcott presided over the Christian Social Union with great enthusiasm but equal vagueness as to what its several thousand members actually hoped to achieve. There was in that period a somewhat gushing commendation of socialism by bishops and other clerics who could hardly have countenanced any actual hard measure of socialist reform. The charming figure of Scott Holland, canon of St Paul's and then professor at Oxford, Gore's dearest friend, was at the centre of all this: a mood of clerical sympathy for the poor from whom the Anglican clergy – particularly the more privileged yet often more socialistically inclined – was so profoundly separated. The young William Temple declared in 1908: 'The alternative stands before us – Socialism or Heresy; we are involved in one or the other.' If such simplistics were true, who could fail to be a Socialist? Few bishops had the courage to admit, as did Lord William Cecil at the Pan-Anglican Congress that year, that he felt 'almost out of place in speaking as a person with no belief in socialism'. G. K. Chesterton, at the time a willing protagonist of the new Christian social consciousness, parodied a speech of Scott Holland's pretty aptly:

> He said he was a Socialist himself,
> And so was God.

But things were different after the war. The forward-looking consensus of the early years of the century had been pierced on several sides. First, Lloyd George's social reforms in the last pre-war years were hard, concrete things involving a rise in income tax, the start indeed of the welfare state. Did one actually support them? Some winced already at that point. Secondly, the arrival of the Labour Party as a major parliamentary group still further replaced dreams by a limited, perhaps apparently dreary, reality. Did one support the possibly realizable socialism of the Labour Party? Some hundreds of clergy were willing to give it a try[2] but not the thousands of the old Christian Social Union. Thirdly, the socialist revolution had come – in Russia. It was violent, atheistic, Communist and very unpopular in England. All in all to call oneself blithely a Socialist in the 1920s was a very different thing for a warm-hearted cleric, who in fact probably voted Tory when election time actually came round, from what it had been twenty years before.

Those who did so were committed in a way they had not been a generation earlier. When Chesterton wrote his amusing poem about the Christian Social Union's meeting at Nottingham at which Gore, Scott Holland and he himself had spoken, they were all close friends and allies together, with Conrad Noel, Charles Masterman and many another enthusiast. But the ways had parted them. Chesterton had reported of Gore's speech at Nottingham:

> [He] said he would be happier
> If beggars didn't beg,
> And that if they pinched his palace
> It would take him down a peg.

Gore had in fact refused as Bishop of Worcester to reside in Hartlebury Castle but by the time he was moved to the diocese of Oxford he had succumbed to the ways of Establishment sufficiently to settle without protest into Cuddesdon Palace. Things were not so simple. Scott Holland, delightful but not exactly practical, was dead. Charles Masterman had turned Liberal politician, worked closely with Lloyd George and was really the creator of unemployment insurance but had been damned by Chesterton's friends in no uncertain terms for dirtying his hands in practical politics. If Masterman had moved one way – into the political mainstream under the Liberal banner – Conrad Noel moved another: into the clear sighted, if slightly batty wilderness of the far left. No more for him the 'mild and watery' ethos of the Christian Social Union. From 1910 to his death in 1942 Noel was vicar of Thaxted in Essex, hardly the nerve-point, one might think, of social change but from Thaxted's pulpit he preached without flinching the gospel of 'Catholic socialism' – daily communion, plain song, country dancing, a united Ireland and the class war: 'In the age-long warfare between rich and poor, God has always taken sides'.[3] So on St George's day in Thaxted church three flags were displayed, that of St George in the centre, and on either side the Red Flag and that of Sinn Fein.

While much of the Anglo-Catholic movement was spikily unconcerned with anything other than highly ecclesiastical matters, it remains true that most of the consistent Christian concern with social evils and almost all Christian socialism from the late-nineteenth century on, was more or less Anglo-Catholic in inspiration. It is not surprising. Just as the conservative Evangelical tradition – pure Protestantism as it had come to seem – tends to stress individual salvation in religion and the importance of individual initiative in social and economic life, so a Catholic stress upon the corporate aspects of the Christian faith tends to go with a belief in the value of collective responsibility. Incarnation, sacraments, church and a revival of what was seen as the medieval socialist protection of the poor against the capitalist: that, more and more, was the heart of the Anglo-Catholic message in this its most lively and most influential period: the famous words of Frank Weston, Bishop of Zanzibar, at the Anglo-Catholic Congress of 1923, are important because they really do express a conviction of real weight in the life of his time:

> You cannot claim to worship Jesus in the Tabernacle, if you do not pity Jesus in the slum. . . . It is folly – it is madness – to suppose that you can worship Jesus in the Sacraments and Jesus on the throne of glory, when you are sweating him in the souls and bodies of his children.[4]

Essentially it was this Anglo-Catholic inspiration which moved bishops like Gore to veer towards socialism; intellectuals like

Maurice Reckitt to attempt to create a 'Christian sociology' or like Tawney to guide Labour Party policy; radical clerics like Noel to wave the red flag; or slum priests like Basil Jellicoe to get down to the grind of actually improving the conditions of the very poor. Remove the Anglo-Catholic inspiration and very little indeed would be left of Christian social endeavour in this period.

Much of this was ineffectual at the time and unmemorable in the retrospect of history. Excellent as the Industrial Christian Fellowship was in intention, dedicated as its charismatic propagandist of the twenties, 'Woodbine Willie' Studdert-Kennedy, clearly was,[5] the fruits of their work may be hard to discern. Studdert-Kennedy could make an amazing personal impression on those who heard him but his message was completely woolly – against capitalism, against socialism, against violence – but with next to no practical positive content other than a religious appeal. Again, the far more academic 'Christendom' group of thinkers, busy in the 1920s and 1930s endeavouring to outline a Christian or Catholic sociology, achieved next to nothing of significance. Not wholly separate from them was the Distributist League founded in 1926 with Chesterton as president. Basically, 'Christendom' was an expression of Anglican neo-medievalism; Distributism an expression of Catholic neo-medievalism. In both groups there was the same desire to avoid both capitalism and Marxism and to draw on pre-Reformation inspiration. In both groups there was a mass of discussion but an almost complete absence of realization – of the relating of what was said to the realities of the twentieth century. Only odd brave opters-out like Eric Gill actually carried the word across on a small scale to the working life of at least a handful of people. In regard to social issues this was not Chesterton's great period. He had become a Roman Catholic in 1922: his approach to Rome and unfortunate degree of dependence on Belloc seemed to weaken his earlier acute, indeed prophetic, sense of England's social woes. Chesterton had been in his time a great prophet both of what was wrong with society and of how things should be: but a prophet especially in poetry. His poems of the immediate pre-war period, among them the 'Ballad of the White Horse', 'The Secret People', and 'The Song of the Wheels', may well represent the most enduring literary expression of the Anglo-Catholic vision of how

England should be. The last named, written for the rail strike of 1913, was perhaps Chesterton's finest word to society, just as his *Ubi Ecclesia* of nearly twenty years later represents his finest word to religion. As he moved into a narrowly Distributist camp, he became less of a prophet to the nation without becoming any more practical.[6]

Christian Socialism, Christian Distributism, Christian Sociology were the minority interests of a clerical and lay élite largely Anglo-Catholic in inspiration. The great majority of Christians in England saw the relationship of religion and society in much simpler terms: the call to patriotism in war; to man voluntary services in the General Strike; to contribute moderately to the emergency relief of the very poor; to defend the sabbath and vote Liberal; to maintain not only Church schools but the social order, the very class structure which Conrad Noel was crying out against, and vote Conservative; such was the limit of social concern for most Christians in the 1920s. And they had their prophets too, if somewhat odd ones. It is difficult perhaps today to take Dean Inge or Bishop Henson with due seriousness[7] – yet they were serious, highly intelligent and powerful figures in their time and far more listened to, just because the middle-class layman in the pew naturally agreed with what they had to say, than the Liberal or radical churchmen who were endeavouring to find a new approach to the ills of modern industrial society.

Herbert Hensley Henson, Bishop of Durham, was in many things the near reverse to Charles Gore, though equally intelligent: the grammar school boy enjoying the privileges of the Establishment without any of the bad conscience to which the more upper-class cleric now seemed prone; the acute critic of all and sundry – of Davidson and Gore and Temple and the Oxford Group; the fly in every ointment, quick to point out the illogicalities and absurdities of other people's views about the Church and society but with little of a positive policy to offer of his own. As a critic of the nonsense clerics were too often happy with, Henson had a very real value. It is more difficult to say the same of his still more distinguished friend, Dean Inge. Formerly the Lady Margaret Professor of Divinity in Cambridge, and Asquith's choice for the deanery of St Paul's, he was – Asquith felt – 'one of the few ecclesiastics in these days who is really interesting', if full of 'kinks and twists'.[8] The scholar of Neoplatonist mysticism, the derider of institutionalism, the immensely self-satisfied column writer in the *Sunday Express* and *Evening Standard*, Inge was quintessentially the gifted upper-class amateur, exemplific of almost all the defects from which the Church of England was currently suffering. His social attitudes, however, were really a caricature of his Church – exemplifying the Establishment by exaggerating it to absurdity. He was a great believer in eugenics – rather a left wing concern at that time but Inge combined intellectual left-wingery with political right-wingery (much as Henson did, though less acutely). So eugenics meant for Inge discouraging the poor from having children while persuading the middle class to keep up production. 'The servant problem' he saw as 'a matter of national importance', for the lack of servants was distracting the more comfortably off from getting on with child-producing and 'our young middle class couples are not those who ought to be deliberately childless'.[9] An article in the *Evening Standard* of 9 February 1921 on public schools and a small beginning to State scholarships to universities for working-class children revealed Inge's message even more uninhibitedly:

> In the past the public schoolman has been exposed only to the natural competition of his own class, recruited very sparingly from below. But now our sons have to meet the artificial competition deliberately created by the Government, who are educating the children of the working man, *at our expense*, in order that they may take the bread out of our children's mouths.[10]

When the Archbishop of Canterbury mildly expostulated over this, Inge thought it 'most unfair and improper'. Inge was, of course, to put it frankly, rather silly: silliness, as we will see more than once, was at the time rather a characteristic of the clergy and particularly of Anglican clergy. It is particularly prone to emerge where the Christian gospel is preached from a position of considerable personal affluence. The gap between the demanding nature of the gospel and the comfortable state of its proclaimer is made a lot worse by the tendency of the upper-class cleric to pontificate about matters on which he is a complete amateur. There are, of course, other streaks in clerical silliness: the absence of professionalism required by the stress on a priest's status of gentleman has driven many a miserable cleric to cover it up with the pursuit of gimmicks of various degrees of absurdness. Anyway, Inge, despite his great cleverness, was plainly rather silly especially on social matters; but the significance of his particular line was that while it was quite out of step with current Anglican talk, it was only too clearly in line with the reality of the Church of England: a very middle-class body, specializing in the successful public school education of middle class children.

Inge was read, and lauded by the many who agreed with him. But he belonged to no school and was at the end of the day merely one man who gained a temporary notoriety and was then quickly forgotten. Such was the case with everyone outside what we may call the two central groups of reformists, one the Student Christian Movement, the other, people of Anglo-Catholic inspiration and socialistic sympathies.

The problem was how to communicate the central convictions built up by those two groups to the Church at large. For such a task William Temple, now Bishop of Manchester, was a godsend. He had drawn upon both; for years an SCM man, he was not considered an Anglo-Catholic yet some of his closest confidants were, and more and more he came to express the consensus of these two streams of thought in a manner that never seemed partisan but redolent rather of the confidence of a rejuvenated central Anglicanism.

The message had already been outlined clearly enough by the, at that time, famous 'Fifth Report' (there were four others on more ecclesiastical matters) presented to the Anglican archbishops in 1918, entitled *Christianity and Industrial Problems*. It was produced by a commission, which included various bishops, but was probably largely written by Tawney. It represents the clearest ecclesiastical expression of a semi-Socialist approach to the nation's social problems to appear for many years. It discussed unemployment, the control of industry, national education, and much else and was particularly strong on the establishment of a living wage. It suffered from some of the benevolent vagueness characteristic of all such collective and semi-official documents. Henson denounced this 'Socialist tract' (not really so misguided a description) as a 'dangerous pamphlet'. But for the Industrial Christian Fellowship, and then for Temple, anxious to get across the insights of the SCM and his own mildly socialistic convictions about the way the Church's responsibilities in modern society should be conceived, the Fifth Report provided the ideal foundation document.

1924 was the year of the first Labour government. It was also the year of the Conference on Christian Politics, Economics and Citizenship (COPEC), presided over by Temple, which met, all 1,400 delegates, in Birmingham in April. It was massively prepared by twelve commissions producing twelve volume-long reports, quite impossible of adequate discussion within the conference's single week of work. They inevitably varied in attitude and value and most of them were as little significant in themselves as the reports of such conferences usually are. COPEC, like others of Temple's enthusiasms, arose with a wave of excitement but once passed seemed at first to have accomplished little beyond reinforcing the sense of his own unrivalled leadership within the field. The England of the 1920s was not destined to become a Socialist country. The Labour government remained in office but a few months, COPEC's message was even at the time so widely acceptable only because of its extreme vagueness. Temple was always better on the broad sweep than on the hard particularities of contested bastions. Yet COPEC is not simply to be dismissed. Its immediate consequences were small. Its importance lay within a longer process of adult education whereby the leadership, clerical and lay, of the Church was being weaned from high Tory attitudes to an acceptance of the Christian case for massive social reform and the development of a welfare state. In this it and its like were almost over-successful.

What immediate effect did any of the Christian social thinking we have been reviewing have on England in the 1920s? Little enough, it may be answered, when one considers the amount of talk involved. 'Seldom was a satisfactory balance struck between idealism and realism. There was an awful amount of amateurishness and lack of expertise.' Such charges as these of Alec Vidler can hardly be gainsaid,[11] yet when we get away from COPEC, from the Christendom group, from Distributism, there is another side to it. At no time was Oldham more effectively influencing colonial policy from behind the scenes: labour regulations, educational development, refusal to countenance a colour-bar. Of a very different mind another Scottish layman, J. C. W. Reith, the first Director-General of the BBC, was unbendingly shaping that new but soon immensely powerful institution according to what he saw as non-denominational Christian principles, Sabbatarian and moralistic. Each represented a latter-day form of the Protestant conscience within the halls of power.[12] Oldham and Reith shared a profoundly Establishment view of the need for a smooth alliance of religion and politics, though their sense of priorities was worlds apart. But both were highly influential in the development of British society in the 1920s.

We can also look more locally for effectiveness. The most striking example of something very concrete actually done is in the field of housing. The nation as a whole was at last beginning to recognize what an absolute scandal the slums of all our major cities were. Important pioneering work here was being done by the clergy, just as we have seen it being done still earlier by George Cadbury at Bournville. Consider John Wilcockson,[13] a very working-class vicar at Dixon Green in Farnworth between Bolton and Manchester. A member of the local council, leader of its Labour group and chairman of its Housing and Health Committee, Wilcockson was a really forceful local leader on slum clearance through the 1920s and after. Or consider Basil Jellicoe, an Anglo-Catholic curate in Somers Town, complete with cassock and biretta.[14] The St Pancras House Improvement Society was formed by him late in 1924, its aim to buy and renovate housing in Somers Town, one of the worst of London slums. The first major appeal for money in 1926 – for £27,500 – might have seemed unrealistic but the powerful of both worlds were powerfully invoked. On the day of the great appeal there was continuous prayer before the blessed sacrament in the chapel of Pusey House, Oxford. Lower down the power scale Lord Cecil, John Galsworthy and the Prince of Wales were all drawn in, and the money with them. By the end of that year the society had raised over £41,000, by the end of 1930 over £160,000. Where Basil Jellicoe had led the way, similar societies across the country were soon following. It is certainly true, as Bishop Garbett, a genuine authority on the subject, declared in the Canterbury Convocation in 1930, that 'if there were thirty or forty times as many public utility societies at work they would only touch the fringe of the slum problem'.[15] It is also true that every street renewed was a street renewed, one bit of slum the less, and that true reform has always to be the multiplication of hard particulars. Moreover the down to earth concern with such things was giving a new edge to the living parish: the Church would be altered by the housing movement and its successors, perhaps more profoundly – in its sense of priorities of what money should be collected for – than urban society itself. Finally, while such voluntary efforts to challenge a major national problem cannot substitute for State action, they can help considerably to get the State moving – to stimulate a sense of moral outrage with existing conditions and so produce the public opinion which will back major government schemes of slum clearance. And such surely was the case here. Where Basil Jellicoe led, many more have followed in the next fifty years.

The 1920s – the calm after the storm of the First World War, the calm before the quite unexpected storm of the 1930s – may seem in retrospect a sloppy, almost insignificant time when chances were missed and ineffectual attempts made to put the clock back to 1910. Yet decisive choices were made none the less for better or worse and two people may best express what was decisive in the Christian attitude to politics in that decade – Charles Maurras and Henry Tawney.

Maurras, the French conservative ideologist, represents the inhibition of Catholics to accept democracy and the moderately socialist direction which European democracy was veering towards. He stands over against Sturzo and, for a time, effectively he won, with very dire results. Maurras was not only immensely influential through *Action Française* in France, his writings and ideas were carried across Europe and to Latin America, but they represented an approach which was far wider than Maurras's personal influence and seemed naturally to appeal to Catholic societies in a world bereft of its old monarchical structures and threatened by Marxism. The ideology of Maurras was one of Catholic nationalism, populist in its way but hostile to democracy, stressing the values of family and nation, anti-Semitic, anti-socialist, rather military, proclaiming the 'Counter-Revolution' against all the false values it saw attendant upon the French Revolution. There were Catholics in every country struggling to reconcile the Church with democracy and socialism in the 1920s, but almost everywhere they failed quite to carry the day. Democracy could lead to socialism, socialism to Marxist Communism. Maurras set up a coherent alternative ideal which in its main lines bewitched the central core of Catholics and ensured both their continued alienation from western democratic society and that many among them would at least be fellow travellers of Fascism when it arrived. If France collapsed so completely in 1940, it was not just a military or political collapse, it was truly a social one, engendered by the inability of so many French Catholics, at heart supporters of *Action Française*, to man the walls of the Third Republic. Vichy expressed the ideals of Maurras only too clearly – the ideals in fact which were really the most powerful political motivation to be found within Catholic Europe. In due course Vichy killed them as well.

England was, fortunately, not greatly affected by the Maurras syndrome. It had never experienced the profound schism between Christianity and parliamentary democracy upon which it fed on the Continent. Nevertheless the Catholic population was not negligible and was over the coming years to be increasingly drawn in the Fascist direction. The major personal influence here was Hilaire Belloc. A man of great intelligence and force of character, he had committed himself wholly to what he saw as the Catholic view of things and for him that meant the French view. No one could have been much less influenced by Scripture or theology. France meant for Belloc a tradition at once post-revolutionary and very Catholic: Napoleon, his great hero, somehow incarnated the virtues of the Revolution – which the young Belloc had been much in love with – while escaping from the snares of parliamentary democracy. Belloc was at his strongest in criticizing the latter and arguing against the growth of State power, as he did very powerfully and influentially in *The Servile State*. He was at his weakest in offering any sort of sensible alternative to parliamentary democracy. More and more his politics dissolved into a long sneer about the influence of Jews and a sort of unreal longing for some new Napoleonic figure. Certainly, as his biographer admitted, Belloc 'agreed with Maurras more closely than he agreed with any other political theorist of his time',[16] even if to some extent he kept this quiet, especially after the papal condemnation of *Action Française*. When Franco appeared on the scene, he was for Belloc 'the man who has saved us all'.[17]

Belloc was not the only influence making for a certain Fascism in the English Catholic community (at least at its more upper-class levels) in the inter-war years. A warm, if thoughtless, response to the Lateran Treaty and the providential role of Mussolini was inevitable.[18] There had been little if any sympathy for the efforts of Don Sturzo. But Belloc more than most could provide a coherent Catholic outlook, joining the old rather anti-democratic tradition of a Wilfred Ward or a Baron von Hügel with the new wave of continental feeling, adding the anti-Semitic touch and passing it across to the younger generation with great confidence as the true Catholic political vision. Non-Catholic Christians in England would seldom adopt anything like the full Maurras approach, although as the lines hardened in the 1930s anti-Socialists would find it increasingly difficult to avoid this completely.

But if Maurras represented the most characteristic response of continental Catholicism to the political problem in the inter-war years (despite being himself an agnostic), Tawney represented most clearly and decisively the commitment of the on-going centre of English religion at once to democracy, to an increasingly Socialist and egalitarian vision of society, and to a renewed Catholic theology as precisely the required under-girding for the first two. In this Tawney demonstrated how false were the dichotomies of the Continent and indicated the only way forward, other than Fascism, for England and Continent alike. And he did this at the level both of scholarship and the immediate effective guiding of the minds both of politicians and churchmen.

Certainly the 1920s were Tawney's great decade.[19] He straddled it quite amazingly yet also very quietly. In 1918 he was much responsible for the writing of the archbishops' Fifth Report which, as we have seen, set the tone for most Anglican post-war social thinking; the following year he was a member of the Royal Commission, chaired by Sir John Sankey, appointed to report on the running of the coal industry. The report of the chairman and of the majority recommended nationalization – a recommendation largely due to Tawney and Sydney Webb and ignored by government. In 1921 his major work, *The Acquisitive Society*, was published (Crossman's 'Socialist bible'). In 1924 the year of the first Labour government, he wrote the Labour manifesto, *Secondary Education for All*. In 1926 his classic of historical interpretation, *Religion and the Rise of Capitalism*, appeared. In 1929 he wrote Labour's manifesto for the General Election preceding the second Labour government, *Labour and the Nation*. In 1931 his third classic, *Equality*, was published.

Behind that list of major publications was the mind of a man tirelessly guiding government, Labour movement, Church and academic community towards a new society, at once fully democratic, consciously socialistic, and fully in accord with Christian belief. In effective intellectual terms it is doubtful whether anyone else had a remotely comparable influence on the evolution of British society in his generation: if there was someone it was his friend and brother-in-law Beveridge, or his equally close friend William Temple.

How amazingly fortunate that Tawney and Temple arrived as schoolboys at Rugby the same day, went up to Balliol College, Oxford, the same year, worked closely together in the following years in the WEA and were friends for life. Tawney quietly provided Temple with solid meat to undergird his social enthusiasms (though Temple certainly dodged some of it – particularly Tawney's preoccupation with equality); Temple provided Tawney with an immensely valuable link to ecclesiastical leadership. The importance of the friendship of two such men is something the historian must surely emphasize: all the more so since the unobtrusiveness of Tawney's character ensured that it, as so much else in his life, hardly appeared to the public eye.

Tawney was co-operative enough with friends like Reckitt and Eliot in the 'Christendom group' and the Anglo-Catholic Summer School of Sociology, but while they were only too clearly gifted amateurs, he was very much a professional academic, a distinguished economic historian and professor at LSE. They moved, however, increasingly apart: they in a medievalist and apolitical direction; he into full acceptance of modern society and full participation in the modern political process. They remained in a rather religious atmosphere but a pretty ineffectual one; he entered more and more into the workings of secularized politics, in which he effected a great deal, besides being hailed as something of a saint by colleagues and disciples who most often did not share his faith.

What Tawney, Temple, Oldham and their like did ensure was that twentieth-century society's movement away from the individualism and imperialism of the nineteenth century into a more socialist condition did not, in Britain at least, produce any sharp schism with Christianity. On the contrary the churches were prepared for the change which was indeed guided in large part by such as Tawney himself. In line with his friend Bishop Gore and so many fellow Anglo-Catholics, he showed moreover that the change from individualism to collectivism as a model for society could not only be tolerated by Christians but also, if you shifted your Protestant conception of Christianity in a more Catholic direction, seemed actually required by it. A very gentle, rather self-effacing, consistent, intensely morally minded layman, Tawney may come nearest to qualifying as the Thomas More of the twentieth century.

The General Strike

The General Strike of May 1926 had an importance in social history and in national mythology which makes a consideration of Church attitudes and influence at this precise moment valuable and enlightening.

Archbishop Davidson was drawn well within the circle of the storm.[1] He was now in his late seventies, as naturally cautious as ever and as remote from the world of the miner, yet his sense of bearing a national responsibility and his willingness to stick out his neck just a little from time to time, his humility too in listening to the advice of other men whom he trusted, more forward looking than himself, all these things had grown rather than diminished with the years. On 5 May, shortly after the strike began, he expressed his own opinion of the 'unwisdom and mischievousness' of the strike in a speech in the House of Lords, but then on the 7th he met a delegation of Church people including Scott Lidgett, Bishop Garbett and Canon Kirk, director of the Industrial Christian Fellowship. They convinced him that a far more even-handed approach was called for and the result that same day was the publication of a document in the Archbishop's name entitled *The Crisis: Appeal from the Churches*. This called for a return to the status quo before the strike began, involving 'simultaneously and concurrently' the cancellation of the strike, renewal by the government for a limited time of financial assistance to the coal industry and withdrawal by the mine owners of the new wage scales which they had issued and which were the immediate cause of both lockout and miners' strike. Coming when it did it represented a sound intervention, non-partisan, helpful, quite a degree removed from the Establishment position, a genuine attempt to speak for and to the nation. It certainly did not go so far as to imply any endorsement of the strike or its justice. Baldwin did not like the 'simultaneously and concurrently', wanting the ending of the strike to precede anything else, but otherwise he did not disagree: Davidson and Baldwin (both Harrow men) were seldom far apart.

Yet the response to the appeal was little short of extraordinary: in an atmosphere in which the middle and upper classes had lined up so fiercely against the working man, Davidson's words were seen (despite his far stronger anti-strike statements of two days before) as betrayal by the one, as a wonderful gesture of sympathy by the other. Denounced for mixing politics and religion, in letters hastily dispatched by lifelong churchgoers, he was actually cheered in the streets of London by the working class: an uncommon experience for an archbishop of Canterbury.

Strangest of all was the action of the BBC. The Archbishop wished to broadcast his appeal, and surely no one in the country, other than the king, had more natural right to speak to the nation in such a crisis than the primate. Yet Reith, the Director-General, refused to allow him to do so.[2] Davidson at first presumed that this could only have been done on instructions from Baldwin, but such was not exactly the case. Churchill was at this point in his most arrogantly pugnacious mood, leading a cavalry charge against the common man. Editor of the *British Gazette*, the government's special paper, he was as provocative as he could be in his campaign for the unions' 'unconditional surrender'. For him the BBC, despite its unmistakable support of the government's position, was far too willing to quote union leaders and provide a fair measure of unbiased information. Reith claimed to be frightened that if he allowed the Archbishop of Canterbury's message to be broadcast to the nation, this could provide the excuse for Churchill to force Baldwin's hand and commandeer the BBC. The full enormity of thus censoring the Church's leadership at the high point of the nation's greatest internal crisis seems never quite to have been appreciated by Reith, by the government or even by Davidson himself. But it did worry the Labour Party and Lloyd George who raised the matter in the House of Commons on 10 May after which Davidson's message was at last broadcast the following day – when it no longer much mattered.

In public, Davidson was prepared to go no further. In the judgment of many a churchman he had already gone a great deal too far: the strike was a challenge to the constitution, the strikers were the next thing to rebels and revolutionaries; the task of the Church was not to mediate between right and wrong, but to encourage the stout-hearted to resist the revolution. Cardinal Bourne's message was far more to their taste. His statement from the pulpit of Westminster Cathedral at high mass on Sunday, 9 May, was unambiguous. The General Strike was 'a direct challenge to a lawfully constituted authority . . . a sin against the obedience which we owe to God . . . and against the charity and brotherly love which are due to our brethren'.[3] That message was carried to the nation the same evening by the BBC and produced an enormous reaction. How far away was the Cardinal of Westminster from the radical leadership upon social issues which Manning had offered forty years before. If the Church of England was moving to the left, that of Rome was following the opposite direction. Many a Labour Catholic felt bitter enough about Bourne's declaration, and one at least walked out of the cathedral as he delivered it, but the welcome it received upon the other side was almost ecstatic. In the view of the Dean of St Paul's, 'The Bishops have come out of it (the strike) very badly, bleating for a compromise while the nation was fighting for its life. Cardinal Bourne won golden opinions by saying what our Bishops were too cowardly to say: "This strike is a sin against God." '[4]

Inge's friend Bishop Henson of Durham felt quite as strongly. Bourne's message was 'clear, relevant and useful', while Davidson's was 'obscure, unwise and likely to do much harm in the future'.[5] It is to be remembered that a considerable part of the Durham coalfield was actually owned by the bishop and chapter of Durham and administered by the Ecclesiastical Commissioners. The bishop's splendid home of Auckland Castle was in the very middle of it, so that one could indeed dig coal for oneself in the park from outcropping seams, and many needy people did so, to the anger of the bishop. He was not amused to hear of a vicar's wife buying coal cheaply from a miner which had 'almost certainly been stolen from my Park!'[6] Henson at least was not remote from the real life situation behind the strike.

The miserable conditions of the miners – most of whom had

long ago forsaken the Established Church for Methodism[7] – could distress the bishop but they did not affect his judgment. What did worry him was the 'immense and unprecedented sacrifices' the nation had made to prop up the industry – all of twenty-two million pounds (3 May). What did worry him was the power of the unions which he could only compare with what in ecclesiastical terms he hated most – the papacy; 'Will the tyranny of the Trade Union,' he asked himself, 'perish as that of the Popes perished under the disgrace of its own excesses? The servility of the working population is not less than that of the medieval population' (4 May). What did worry him were the local union officials moving around the villages outside his castle gates encouraging their men, until his fury reached new heights:

> These poisonous agitators have the field to themselves, and their criminal talk passes unchallenged. We can trust nobody. The sedulous preaching of 'class consciousness' has not failed of its effect. Even the clergy, who might have been regarded as the obvious champions of individual rights and responsibilities, are as servile as the rest. Indeed, in many places, they are the mere parasites of the Labour Party. (6 May)[8]

Hensley Henson represents one extreme of the ecclesiastical reaction to the strike; a minority view probably, though almost certainly far more of the clergy – at least in the south – would have agreed with him than he was prepared to admit. The other extreme – real support of the strike and the miners' cause – was far more of a minority view. The Catholic Archbishop Keating of Liverpool, president of the Catholic Social Guild and with an outlook very different from Bourne's dry Toryism, declared of the miners' position: 'The poor must live; and if private enterprise cannot provide the worker with a living, it must clear out for another system which can',[9] but there were few bishops in any Church prepared to commit themselves to so clear a view, and among the clergy only a handful. Naturally Conrad Noel of Thaxted and a few of the curates trained there under him came out uninhibitedly on the strikers' side – and one or two were barred from their ministry as a result. One Congregationalist minister at least was quite carried away by it all. D. R. Davies, an ex-miner himself, was at that time minister of a congregation in Southport, someone with strong Socialist leanings. The strike got

189

him, and he announced that the next Sunday evening, 9 May, he would preach on 'Christianity and the Miners' Claim'. The church had a seating capacity of over 400 and a normal congregation of under 100. That night it was absolutely packed as Davies made his way with difficulty to the pulpit and the words poured out from him in a great flood of eloquence: 'The miners are altogether right and the owners are altogether wrong', at which the congregation broke in with a loud 'hear, hear'.[10] For the next two years Davies preached on – his congregation was transformed, new members joined, old ones resigned, as his message became more and more wholly secular, until in 1928 he resigned his ministry in bewilderment, betrayed by the simplicities of his own enthusiasm. Was he more or less foolish than Bishop Henson? He certainly paid more heavily for his convictions.

The General Strike ended in a matter of days, the miners' strike went on for many months and the role of mediation in the latter was a naturally attractive one for socially minded ecclesiastics. An ad hoc committee convened by Kirk of the Industrial Christian Fellowship and including Gore, Temple, eight other bishops and a variety of Nonconformist leaders, came to be called the Standing Conference of the Christian Churches on the Coal Dispute and attempted in July to mediate between owners and miners.[11] The former were uninterested – the tide of victory was running strongly, they felt, in their direction now – but with the latter the Standing Conference achieved some sort of agreement, consisting essentially of falling back upon the recommendations of the Samuel Report. It took its proposals to Baldwin who did not respond favourably. And what were the ecclesiastics to do then? Canon Kirk believed, not unreasonably, that if a powerful Church committee set itself up to interfere in the coal dispute, was cold-shouldered by one side but arrived at some sort of settlement with the other, then it had acquired the duty of backing the miners on this basis. The miners' leaders almost certainly anticipated this, but Temple and his fellow bishops disagreed: such was not their job, they claimed.

It would seem that this was the real moment of Church failure and that Temple, more than anyone, was responsible for it.[12] He saw his role and Church authority's role here as elsewhere in terms of finding consensus, agreement, reconciliation, and he was himself good at doing so, if in rather high and idealistic terms. But what when reconciliation is impossible because one set of fellows is sitting firmly on the backs of the other set? Until they are got off, talk of reconciliation must be empty. In some sense liberation has to come first, but to help with that can mean an at least temporary commitment to one side and to particular policies, not just general principles. If the churchmen were not willing to go so far because it was not their 'own job', then they could better have stayed out of the whole thing. In the circumstances the role simply of mediator was not a practical one (when one side refused to participate) and it could hardly be said to exhaust the role of the Church as outlined by COPEC. But COPEC too had not measured up very well to the hard particularity of the nation's crisis: Charles Raven, secretary to its Continuation Committee, had issued a letter declaring that the General Strike showed that 'we are out of touch with God'. If you are going to propose a Church role in politics, it is no good to fall back on such vagaries of spirituality at the critical moment. Temple's contribution was not much more to the point. There was a profound impracticality, indeed a blindness to the facts, in his preoccupation with conciliation. Faced with hard, practical, highly divisive issues involving the bread and cheese of poor and heavily burdened men, the generalities of COPEC were of little use. Churchmen have either to get beyond the basic principles, or even the 'middle axioms' Temple was so fond of speaking about, to pin themselves publicly with all the dangers involved to certain quite particular courses of action – as old Davidson tried himself to do in an interim way when the strike was still fresh – or they may as well keep out.

Nor should it have been so difficult to settle on certain points. The mine owners could only win if the government agreed to repeal the law as it stood and permit the reintroduction of an eight-hour day. Resisting that repeal was hardly revolutionary and it presented a ground the Church could well have occupied. It did not do so. Beyond that was a deep failure to understand what it was all about – tolerable or intolerable conditions for a large group of very hard-working men. The ecclesiastics were mostly far too remote to realize just how bad those conditions actually were and therefore how justified would be nationalization, seemingly radical and yet the only at all plausible road towards improving them – not that the strike had been a demand for anything as considerable as that. The Sankey Commission had long ago recommended nationalization, and it should not have been very hard to see and to say, as Archbishop Keating did, that nationalization was still the only viable Christian solution. Short of that there could at least have been a public commitment to the compromise proposed by the Standing Conference. As it was, the failure of the churches to do anything significant in the strike, beyond Davidson's interim proposal, coming as it did just two years after all the fanfare of COPEC showed only too revealingly the latter's weakness.

Of course almost everyone's attention was diverted by the claim that the General Strike threatened the constitution of the country. Potentially a General Strike could certainly do so. In fact this one very much did not – in so far as it had any constitutional aim it was to prevent the laws of the land from being changed under pressure of the mine owners. It was easier, however, for ordinary Church people to think about a threat to the constitution, as the *British Gazette* bade them to, and to see the strike's failure as a victory for law and order, than to face up to the working conditions and ownership of a major but ailing industry which lay incredibly far away from the real experience of most churchmen.

When the strike was called off and the news given on the BBC, Blake's 'Jerusalem' was read immediately by an anonymous voice, to be repeated by orchestra and choir. The symbolism was splendid and comforting but the reality of what had happened and was still to happen in the mining villages of Britain was very different.

Ecclesiastical Life

'You see that men go to Chapel. . . . The rule is that men go forty times in a term and the Dean sees the list of attendances every week and goads on the laggards.' Such were the instructions given to the new Dean of Oriel College, Oxford, in 1919 by its Provost.[1] Could the line of religious conformity really be held in such a way? No, it could not. Already next year an obstreperous young undergraduate at Selwyn, Cambridge, Alec Vidler, would be promoting an appeal against compulsory attendance at chapel even in that still most clerical of colleges. In the 1920s compulsory chapel started to crumble at Oxbridge, just as the tradition of the clerical Master crumbled: as old heads of college died, they were replaced by laity and very possibly unbelieving laity, such as H. A. L. Fisher, the new Warden of New College.

The institution of the Established Church was crumbling on many a side, there can be no doubt about that: not only in Oxbridge colleges, but across the country where in the twenties the number of Anglican clergy was declining by some hundred a year. Yet the crumbling in such an extensive, unwieldy edifice could still be overlooked – could best be overlooked, when there seemed so little to do about it. The Church Assembly indeed was now at work, but this work was very different, very much drier and less creative, than the enthusiasts of 'Life and Liberty' had envisaged. Effectively it relieved parliament of some chores and enabled the Church to carry through without difficulty administrative measures such as the creation of five new dioceses in the middle of the decade: Blackburn and Leicester in 1926, Derby, Guildford and Portsmouth in 1927: the last new dioceses the Church of England would create at home. From then on processes of diminution rather than expansion would become the norm.

The creation of those new dioceses is, nevertheless, something to be noted: one expression of the not inconsiderable pastoral revolution that the Church of England had been carrying through in an unrevolutionary way. Take the north central area of England, certainly never an Anglican stronghold, and consider the six new dioceses it was given in under fifty years, from Southwell (1884) and Wakefield (1888) to Sheffield (1914), Bradford (1919), Leicester and Derby. The national Church had certainly not thrown its hand in – quite the contrary. In places like Leicester and Sheffield one has the impression that the public influence of the Church of England, weak in the past, was actually growing in this period.

What was declining most evidently was the central non-party Church of England man. In a way, Henson, like his friend Bishop Headlam, represented the type well enough, a Victorian survivor, much of whose sharp-tongued diatribes against almost all that was going on around him was due to the consciousness that his kind of religiosity – traditionally Protestant, yet suspicious of enthusiastic Evangelicals almost as much as of Anglo-Catholics, highly national in sentiment – was fading away. He claimed a national constituency, but increasingly discovered that it no longer existed – for the successor state to Victorianism was no form of Protestantism, but agnosticism. What vitality there was in the Church, especially among the clergy, was now chiefly to be found in one form or another of the Anglo-Catholic movement, and while much of the Church's leadership from Davidson down still distrusted Anglo-Catholicism to a greater or lesser extent, more and more it found that it had few other serviceable tools at hand.

Certainly the Church led by a very elderly Davidson and at York a prematurely aged Lang was hardly in a creative mood. It had its – often rather over-wrought – heroes, many of them former war chaplains, like Woodbine Willie, Tubby Clayton of Toc H, and Dick Sheppard. One has a picture of them rather desperately battling against a tide with hearts aflame but often pretty little sense of what they themselves even hoped for. There was, maybe, too much despair in their own hearts and too little theology in their heads for the job in hand. A new public school of grandeur if rather muted religiosity could still be founded at

Stowe; a pointer to the future could well be provided in the ecumenical *Cambridgeshire Syllabus of Religious Teaching in Schools*, prepared in 1923-4 and highly influential for the approach to the subject in the post-Second World War period; Lambeth could still speak with wisdom and authority – the encyclical letter of 1930 bears comparison with the teaching of Vatican II! But it was certainly not, ecclesiastically, an exciting age. Even ecumenically, where the 1920 Lambeth *Appeal to all Christian People* might have been expected to make a difference, movement in practice could be back as much as forward. Archbishop Davidson might address the annual conference of the Wesleyan Methodists in 1923 – surely a step forward – but when it came to something nearer the bone, such as intercommunion or at least 'open communion' at Anglican altars, this seemed more difficult than ever: allowed at SCM conferences in the 1890s, it was emphatically forbidden in the 1920s.

Here, as in much else, the explanation lies in the advance of Anglo-Catholicism. In fact, nothing else of comparable importance was taking place in the Church at the time – and admitting Free churchmen to Anglican communion was not something Anglo-Catholics appreciated. So to the progress of Anglo-Catholicism and the reaction to it we must now turn.

The 1920s can indeed be seen as the start of the golden age of Anglo-Catholicism. The hard and painful battles had mostly been won and Anglo-Catholics were truly beginning to enter into their inheritance – to be no longer a barely tolerated party but the central moving force within the Church, reshaping its ethos and symbolism so that the Church of England, as known and taken for granted by the latter part of the twentieth century, would be quite significantly different in a number of important ways from the Church of the Victorian age. The strength of Anglo-Catholicism lay in its width and diversity. Intellectually it had grown well beyond the very rigid Tractarianism of Pusey and Liddon, and it is fitting that the most serious journal of the new Anglo-Catholicism, *Theology*, should have been founded in 1920. Two trends in particular were evident. One was a revival of Thomism. When Kenneth Kirk, one of the ablest of the younger Anglo-Catholic theologians, published his *Principles of Moral Theology* in 1920, he explicitly borrowed its ground plan from the *Summa Theologica* of Aquinas, while at the same time criticizing later Roman Catholic moral theology which had 'lapsed into an almost complete authoritarianism'.[2] Such an approach was very different either from traditional Tractarianism or from the servility to current Roman norms which some high Anglo-Catholics displayed and it was the pointer towards a whole school of Anglican theology with a Thomistic bent which was to flourish over the coming decades. On the other side Catholic modernism had enormously influenced the younger Anglo-Catholic generation. For them Tyrrell had opened all sorts of doors towards a more flexible understanding of the way Catholicism had in fact emerged and how it was to be defended, even if this led for some towards a form of religion in which ritual and social concern remained but dogma had been largely washed away.

In 1918 the festival of Nine Lessons and Carols was devised for King's College Chapel, Cambridge, by its new dean, Eric Milner-White. From 1928 it would be broadcast every Christmas. A new national institution thus came into existence and would soon be accepted as just another timeless piece of English religious tradition, yet it was in fact but one fruit of the wider renaissance in worship and culture stimulated by Anglo-Catholicism. Milner-White, a person learned in many things besides music, such as stained glass, can be linked in creativity with Percy Dearmer, Professor of Ecclesiastical Art at King's College, London, or again with Wilfred Knox, Bishop Knox's youngest son, a brilliant New Testament scholar, as unworldly as he was odd. Like Milner-White, Knox was a member of a society of Anglican celibates, the Oratory of the Good Shepherd, a society with few rules, many eccentrics, but a sustained concern to find a pattern of religious life within the Catholic tradition which should not inhibit the freedom of spirit of its members. Joseph Needham, historian of Chinese science and Master of Caius, spoke of Wilfred Knox as 'a demonstration of how to combine a deep attachment to devotional and liturgical traditions with a totally liberated and fearless search for the truth'.[3] Ronald and Wilfred Knox as young clerics had been the closest of allies, until Ronald's reception into the Roman Catholic Church in 1917. One might compare the two as intellectually characteristic of their two communions in England in the period between the wars when both were thriving. Ronnie, personally more brilliant and famous, was sharper in mind; yet somehow a great deal less 'totally liberated'. He was indeed the utterly faithful convert of ultramontane Catholicism, precise in ecclesiastical dress and theological expression, almost uninterested it often seemed in social problems or the intellectual questions of dogmatic belief discussed around him except to make some sophisticated joke about them. Wilfred's cares ranged wider, his clothes were in disorder, his books were far fewer. His holiness was manifest while Ronnie's was partially concealed beneath acquiescence – not only in clerical decorum but in the country house life of the Catholic aristocracy into which he was adopted. Yet Wilfred Knox, far from being characteristic of Anglicanism, was, rather, a living protest against its dominant ethos and the ways and ideas of such as his Cambridge contemporary, B. K. Cunningham of Westcott House. In Vincent MacNabb you can find a Roman equivalent to Wilfred, just as you can find plenty of Anglican equivalents to his brother.

The Oratory of the Good Shepherd was one of the smallest of the Anglican religious orders flourishing in the 1920s. This was the great age of Mirfield, of Kelham, of Anglo-Catholic congresses and summer schools, even of Anglo-Catholic bishops, including Anglo-Catholic celibate bishops – Gore, Lang, Frere, Garbett. Perhaps the most decisive figure in all this was Cosmo Gordon Lang. Archbishop of York from 1908 to 1928 and Archbishop of Canterbury from then until 1942, he catholicized the Church of England probably more than anyone else, and largely without giving offence. When appointed to York he was already publicly committed to advocating the legalization of the 'Six Points' – eucharistic vestments, the lighting of candles upon the altar, the use of wafers instead of common bread for Holy Communion, the eastward position of the celebrant, the ceremonial mixing of water with wine in the chalice, and the use of incense: the main outward symbols which in the mind of Catholic and Protestant alike distinguished the mass of the one from the communion service of the other. But it was not just that the Archbishop of York, or Winnington-Ingram, Bishop of London, was resigned to the legalization of such things for others. On the contrary, they clearly accepted them at heart as constituting the liturgical norm. Henson might complain of 'Anglo-Catholick lawlessness', when denouncing innovations introduced by the Dean and Chapter of York,[4] but when the 'lawlessness' had reached that far the battle to resist it had been truly lost. During his episcopate Bishop Knox prided himself on keeping such 'lawlessness' under control in Manchester with barely ten churches in which eucharistic vestments were worn,[5] but under his successor, Temple, the Catholic tide flowed in there too – though Lancashire Anglicanism has a natural 'lowness' not easily displaced. At Chesterfield, a rather grimy Derbyshire town, Geoffrey Clayton became vicar in 1924 of its splendid old parish church.[6] A man of formidable character, and very much a churchman, he would quickly be appointed archdeacon and then in the 1930s be called to a bishopric in South Africa. No one was temperamentally less lawless than he, but within months the last full matins had been sung at 11 a.m. and replaced by a solemn Eucharist, complete with vestments and incense. But it was Archbishop Lang who canonized the new norms. At York and again at Canterbury he was the first archbishop to wear a mitre since the Reformation and to make of the cope the normal liturgical dress for bishop or archbishop.[7] Henson might still protest in 1932 that he did not even 'possess a mitre'[8] but he could not hold back the catholicizing tide. The splendour of the celebration in York Minster for the 1300th anniversary of its founding in 1927 produced something of a new norm for Anglican liturgy.

Cyril Garbett, Bishop of Southwark in the 1920s and Archbishop of York by the 1940s, illustrates excellently what was going on. 'I am no Anglo-Catholic,' he declared and many would regard him as quintessentially the sound conservative Anglican. Yet he lived in cassock, wore vestments in his private chapel, cope and mitre in his cathedral. Incense and reservation did not much worry him. The standard both of what constituted deviant 'Anglo-Catholicism' and what had become part of standard Anglican practice went up decade by decade. Even Lang, under whose wing so much became acceptable, had his sticking points: reservation, yes, but exposition or benediction of the sacrament, no. Incense, yes, but he would not bless incense:

'there are some things I don't do.'[9] When we remember that
when he went to York in 1908, seven out of the nine bishops of
the northern province were Evangelicals, it remains surprising
how much he did do. The 'moderate' Anglo-Catholic of the
1920s, like B. K. Cunningham at Westcott or Eric Graham at
Cuddesdon, might laugh at birettas and rosaries, but cassocks
and daily celebration of the Eucharist in college were now taken
pretty well for granted. Cuddesdon, most Establishment of all the
theological colleges (Lang, Garbett and many other of the
bishops had been there), might like to be thought old-fashioned
Tractarian rather than new-fashioned Anglo-Catholic, but under
Graham it was going more Anglo-Catholic none the less. There
was really no alternative and it was turning out the most reliable
sort of Anglican priest available, as even that old Protestant
Henson had to admit: he wanted Cuddesdon men for his diocese,
and was resigned to their being 'Anglo-Catholick' so long as 'not
papistically minded or of lawless habit'.[10] Cuddesdon under
Graham expresses the way a moderate, but quite clearly recognizable, Anglo-Catholicism now became little less than the Anglican clerical norm.

Many an Anglo-Catholic, however, was now only too 'papistically minded'. The Anglo-Catholic Congress in July 1923, of
which Bishop Frank Weston of Zanzibar was the chairman and
shining light, showed this clearly enough. He was a man who
loved the dramatic gesture; medieval in his ascetic devotions,
authoritarian in his ministry, naïvely self-assured in the accusa-
tions of heresy he flung against fellow Anglicans, Frank Weston
was a missionary with a great heart, a maker of images capable of
drawing an immense personal response from others.[11] For a
week the Congress overflowed the Albert Hall into Kensington
Town Hall and the Queen's Hall. It had begun with solemn high
mass of the Holy Ghost in St Paul's Cathedral, its presidential
address was delivered by the Bishop of London, and when Bishop
Weston suddenly and apparently unpremeditatedly produced a
telegram for the pope: '16,000 Anglo-Catholics, in Congress
assembled, offer respectful greetings to the Holy Father, humbly
praying that the day of peace may quickly break', it was received
with loud applause.[12] Two days later Fr Frere, Superior of the
Community of the Resurrection, made a mild protest, 'Messages

of this sort do more harm than good.' Only three months later Frere was appointed Bishop of Truro, at Davidson's urgent request – he needed a spokesman upon the bench for the latest wave of Anglo-Catholicism.[13] Lang already represented an older point of view and Gore, despite his continued acceptance by Anglo-Catholics as their great father figure, was still more remote from much of the current enthusiasm. Henson commented on Frere's appointment otherwise: 'That, on the morrow of such an orgy of lawlessness as the Congress represented, Frere should be raised to the Bench can mean nothing less than the total collapse of Anglican discipline.'[14] It meant far more that Anglo Catholicism was now accepted as properly Anglican.

Was there no effective Evangelical counter-movement in the Church of England at that time? The answer must be, very little. Never was Evangelicalism weaker than in the 1920s – in vigour of leadership, intellectual capacity, or largeness of heart. Its only clerical leader of any real power was the old and now retired but still redoubtable Bishop Knox. His successor as episcopal leader of Evangelicals would in due course be Christopher Chavasse, son of his friend the old Bishop of Liverpool and in the twenties vicar of St Aldate's, Oxford. A good man no doubt, but a limited, rather dull, essentially backward-looking person, of whom, when at length he became Bishop of Rochester, his sympathetic biographer had to admit: 'He sought to maintain Bishopscourt as far as possible like the establishments of the bishops of his boyhood; to continue the habits of dress which he felt belonged to the dignity of that office; to encourage no familiarity from his clergy, from the dean to the newest curate . . .'[15] And before Chavasse's appointment in the late 1930s Evangelicals were even less effectively represented on the bench. There was in general not only an absence of inspiration and a social conservatism but a pettiness in the atmosphere of party, apparent not only in the continued CICCU insistence upon the most narrow criteria for doctrinal orthodoxy, but in such events as the 1922 crisis and schism within the Church Missionary Society. Never had CICCU in fact been weaker – 'in comparison with 30 years before and 30 years later the CICCU was small', even its chronicler has to admit;[16] and its really sectarian character is suggested well enough by the way its missionary sympathies could be transferred away from the main mission societies to bodies so small and uncompromising as Studd's World Evangelization Campaign. If CICCU was weak in Cambridge, outside Cambridge there was, through most of the 1920s, no Christian Union at all, except at some London medical schools, and even there conflict soon prevailed about the inadequately clear orthodoxy of other Evangelicals. Thus the General Committee of the London Inter-Faculty Christian Union was complaining in October 1924 that the Inter-Varsity Conference of Evangelical Unions was weak on 'such important truths as – (a) the universal sinfulness and guilt of the human race, (b) the *necessity* of the atoning sacrifice of Christ to each individual'.[17] In fact the Inter-Varsity Fellowship of Evangelical Unions had the greatest difficulty even in existing until the very end of the decade, let alone falling into heresy.

The typical conservative Evangelical of the 1920s felt himself hemmed in on every side: Anglo-Catholicism, the SCM, the social gospel, liberal Evangelicals of various hues, all presented a threat producing a still more introverted, orthodoxy first and last, state of mind. Yet curiously for a while he almost fell victim to what was truly the greatest threat of all – that from Frank Buchman. CICCU had in every generation looked for inspiration from the American revivalist preacher and when, in the early 1920s, Buchman turned up in the colleges of Oxford and Cambridge he appeared at first – and indeed more than at first – just what the Evangelical movement needed. Bishop Henson, in his usual trenchant way, described Buchman as 'a typical product of Transatlantic Protestantism and English Evangelicalism, uniting the aggressive egotism of the first with the emotional appeal of the other, and adding an element of practical capacity more commercial than religious'.[18] The Evangelical movement in the 1920s was for long, despite its preoccupation with doctrinal purity, almost hypnotically attracted to and curiously confused about Buchman's 'Oxford Group' (or 'First Century Christian Fellowship' as it was earlier known). Many a young Christian Union devotee, like Julian Thornton-Duesbery of Balliol, passed little by little out of orthodox evangelicalism via the excitement of Country House parties 'planned under the guidance of the Holy Spirit' into the undoctrinal moralism of the 'Four Absolutes' to which the message of Moral Rearmament eventually came down.

Certainly Evangelicalism was in general in no state of health to do battle effectively with the Anglo-Catholics for England's Protestant heritage. If Knox seemed too old and Henson too dry for such a role, the cloak of Protestant champion was seized for a while by that very odd, and in orthodox Evangelical terms, unacceptable, bishop, Ernest Barnes of Birmingham. He was the first Labour government's first contribution to episcopal appointments. Barnes, like Ramsay MacDonald, had been a Pacifist during the war and, again like him, had been one of the few to attend the first party the German Ambassador gave in London after the war. He was, then, a generous man and a distinguished mathematician, with, however, a rather limited knowledge of theology, and so liberal an evangelical as to be far better described as a modernist. Where most modernists were rather conservative politically, Barnes was a radical, yet his wide and generous sympathies did not include the Church of Rome nor the Anglo-Catholic movement. He was prepared to put up with a certain amount in this direction as befitted a man so liberal in other directions, but he had an almost paranoid hostility to the doctrine of transubstantiation (about which he knew very little), and whatever he saw as connected with it, reservation of the sacrament especially, benediction or devotions of any sort before the reserved sacrament most of all. It was all for him 'pagan sacramentalism', 'magical superstition', 'a recrudescence of fetish worship', 'the language and ideas of the ancient mystery-religions, with a little Christian colour-wash'.[19] He expressed these views with a crudity and a frequency which offended his opponents, as much as their often unfair personal attacks wounded him. His attacks on Catholic superstition, as he saw it, were so phrased as to include in contemptuous condemnation the beliefs of many who saw themselves as very far from accepting transubstantiation. They also displayed ignorance: 'Catholics pretend', he declared in October 1926, 'that a priest using the right words and acts can change a piece of bread so that within it there is the real presence of Christ. The idea is absurd and can be disproved by experiment.' Inevitably, in the diocese of Birmingham, where he was following two bishops with considerable

Anglo-Catholic sympathies, he came into fierce collision with a portion of his clergy, and a series of unedifying newspaper battles with threats of legal action ensued.[20]

What matters chiefly to us in the battles of Bishop Barnes is their link with the national scene. Barnes was quite right in seeing that what was still a minority among the clergy, and a far smaller minority among the laity, was fast changing the fundamental character of the Church of England's worship and so of the heart of its life. He was right too in seeing that the bishops as a whole were in process of surrendering point by point to this forceful minority because they could find no alternative. He saw too that the key issue in this development, at least in the 1920s, was that of reservation: a matter not even included in the Anglo-Catholic 'Six points', now virtually conceded, of an earlier decade. By the mid-1920s the bishops, who were by now also committed to a revision of the Prayer Book, were aiming at a package deal. They hoped by making some considerable concessions to Anglo-Catholic demands to reach a position which all the clergy could then be expected to obey. There was some sense in this, but also some make-believe. There was, in fact, an old 'Anglican' tradition in the Scottish Episcopal Church, of reservation without any public devotions – reservation solely for the sick. The bishops aimed at such a compromise. If continuous reservation was made legal, then services in connection with the reserved sacrament could be effectively prohibited – so they argued, but implausibly. Anglo-Catholic extremists, influenced not by the restrained Scottish Episcopal tradition but by current Roman practice, if allowed half a loaf legally when they had already taken a whole one illegally, would not be encouraged thereby to surrender the other half. As Bishop Knox remarked, 'These good Bishops were like men trying to turn tigers into tame cats by feeding them on buns.'[21]

In June 1926 the House of Bishops by a large majority did just that: continuous reservation was to be allowed, but no service in connection with it other than the communicating of the sick. The likelihood of such a rule being respected or observed may be gauged when one remembers that even old Gore, who as a diocesan bishop had endeavoured to enforce the old rulings, admitted that he personally felt 'the need of the Blessed Sacra-

ment openly reserved and wholly delight in it. I feel no compunc-
tion in saying my prayers to Our Lord in the Blessed Sacrament.'
If prayers, then why not a service too? Why deprive the laity,
asked the committed Anglo-Catholic, of what Bishop Gore
himself felt the need?

It is curious that among the bishops on the bench at the time of
the great Prayer Book controversy, the most actively opposed in
the name of 'the religious heritage which comes to us from the
Reformation'[22] should have been Barnes. He represented in truth
a curious combination of old-fashioned English Protestant prejudice and a sort of pseudo-scientific modernism which has
quickly dated. Essentially he was a bad champion for the old
Protestant cause just as many of the spiky Anglo-Catholic clergy
he was battling with in his diocese were bad champions of
true Catholic sacramentalism. And, perhaps fortunately for
the Church of England, in the longer run neither of these sides
won.

Nor in the shorter run. The issue here was the revised Prayer
Book with which was included permission for continuous
reservation. The matter of liturgical revision dominated the
thoughts of the Anglican episcopate throughout the 1920s. From
a scholarly point of view, the main point of the revision was to
bring back the prayer of consecration to a form more comparable
with the historic liturgies of both east and west, so that in
particular the prayer would no longer come to an abrupt end with
the words of institution. From an episcopal and administrative
point of view, however, the main point was to make some
concession in a 'Catholic' direction (often without any enthusiasm) in the hope of weaning Anglo-Catholics from greater
excesses: in particular, it was hoped, not unreasonably, that with
a more 'Catholic' Anglican prayer of consecration Anglo-
Catholics would give up the practice of using the Roman canon,
as some hitherto had done. Anglo-Catholics were nevertheless by
no means wholly happy with the proposed revision and some, led
by Darwell Stone, even argued for its rejection because it did not
go far enough. Evangelicals, all the more Protestant-minded
people and in general the conservative argued equally for rejection on the grounds that the old Prayer Book was known and
loved, that it embodied the Protestant religion of England, and

that no concessions should be made to a movement which was subverting that religion to the benefit of Rome.

The change could not be made without the consent of parliament, though it had first to pass the Church Assembly. A principal mistake of the reformers was perhaps to propose the new book as a substitute for, instead of an alternative to, the 1662 version, thus developing a sense of loss – including literary loss – as against one of gain. In consequence the matter became one in which three issues were intricately involved – liturgical reform as against liturgical conservatism, catholicizing tendencies as against the maintenance of unquestionably Protestant standards, ecclesiastical autonomy as against parliamentary control of the Church.

It is remarkable how overwhelmingly the new Prayer Book was passed in the Church Assembly, despite the fierce resistance of a minority: 34 to 4 in the House of Bishops, 253 to 37 in that of the Clergy, 230 to 92 in that of the Laity. Archbishop Davidson, now approaching eighty, remained 'lukewarm about the whole project'.[23] For him the old Prayer Book was entirely satisfactory. Nevertheless he was committed to the revision, because he had been convinced by his advisers – Lang, Temple and others – that it was the right thing. His influence had much to do with its so successfully passing the Church Assembly, his lukewarmness may well have had much to do with its defeat in parliament. The voting figures in the Church Assembly cannot, nevertheless, be principally so explained. If bishops, clergy and laity accepted it there by such large majorities, it was because they were convinced (and they included Temple, Henson,[24] Headlam, and many others who were far from being Anglo-Catholics) that it was the right thing and that, when it went to parliament, the mature judgment of the Church itself would be respected.

That did not, however, prove to be the case. The two principal lay Evangelical hawks opposed to the measure, Joynson-Hicks (the Home Secretary and one of the principal Cabinet hawks against the General Strike two years earlier) and Inskip (the Solicitor-General) were both members of the Church Assembly. Defeated there, they transferred their opposition to parliament. The bill passed the Lords, where the three-day debate (12-14 December 1927) provided a splendid expression of the Established Church, laymen and bishops, discussing the pros and cons of liturgical change with great maturity. The debate itself almost justified Establishment. In the Commons the reverse was the case. The discussion was briefer, poorer, more vituperative, full of irrelevancies. The bill was twice defeated (December 1927 and June 1928). This rejection was a response to a campaign not just within the Church but within the country as a whole: a whipping-up of latent Protestant sentiment against what was being characterized in cruder and cruder terms as a sell-out to Rome. In fact, led by Hugh Cecil, a majority of the Church of England men in the Commons voted in favour, most of them unenthusiastically loyal to their bishops. The majority against consisted of an Anglican Evangelical minority reinforced by Welshmen, Scots and Ulstermen plus an Indian Communist Parsee, Saklatvala, the member for Battersea North. Roman Catholics abstained. Lang remarked of Joynson-Hicks's speech that 'with great skill [it] reached and inflamed all the latent Protestant prejudices in the House',[25] but the most powerful intervention of all was probably that of Rosslyn Mitchell, the Labour MP for Paisley and no Anglican, described by Davidson as an 'ultra-Protestant harangue'. 'In one generation, with that Deposited Book,' Mitchell declared, 'you can swing over all the children of England from the Protestant Reformed Faith to the Roman Catholic Faith.'[26]

In the country, however, the true leader of the opposition was old Bishop Knox, also now eighty. Backed by the *Protestant Parson's Pilgrimage*, he had come out of retirement to address meetings in the Albert Hall and throughout the country and to organize a memorial signed by over 300,000 adult communicants – 'an army of illiterates generalled by octogenarians', as Henson described them. Anglo-Catholicism remained far weaker among the laity than among the clergy, liturgical conservatism far stronger – a factor the experts ignored then and later at their peril. Bishop Knox was the Archbishop Lefebvre of the 1920s: the whole-hearted theological and liturgical conservative emerging from retirement with much lay support to defend the old order of worship which the constituted leaders of the Church had decided – rather half-heartedly – it was advisable to ditch. 'Wake up England! The Reformation is at stake.' To the devout Englishman, he claimed, 'the Prayer Book was almost sacrosanct', it was 'the embodiment of a great national deliverance from Papal dominion'.[27] Two Scottish archbishops could not be expected to appreciate that! After the House of Commons vote, Rosslyn Mitchell wrote to Knox: 'To you more than any man is due the decision of the House of Commons. The generalship of the octogenarian has resulted in a great victory.'[28] For good measure every MP who voted against the bill was presented with a Bible, beautifully bound with gold edges and a golden illustration of the Houses of Parliament on the cover. It was a famous victory but it resolved nothing.

What defeated the Prayer Book measure were the bogey of continuous reservation, the campaigning of Bishop Knox and the nation's remaining fears of Romanism. What was to be done now? Henson, at heart the deepest Erastian of them all, argued bitterly for disestablishment with his usual sharp clarity of mind.[29] How could the Church allow itself to be overruled by parliament on the very shape of its worship? But few were prepared to follow him over that. Effectively the whole issue was relegated to limbo. Davidson issued a statement, agreed to unanimously by the bishops, that it was 'a fundamental principle' that the Church 'retain its inalienable right, in loyalty to our Lord and Saviour Jesus Christ, to formulate its Faith in Him and to arrange the expression of that Holy Faith in its forms of worship'. Beyond that theoretical, but significant, assertion that there were limits to Erastianism, disestablishment was not sought, and the new Prayer Book neither authorized nor withdrawn. After much delay, the bishops rather lamely declared that they thought it might legally be used in dioceses where the ordinary authorized it, using the special authority he had in liturgical matters. Had he? But could they prevent its being used anyway? Could a Prayer Book accepted overwhelmingly by the Church Assembly really now effectively be banned? If the revision had been an attempt to restore discipline to the Church by compromise, its rejection in such a manner could only open the way to greater indiscipline than ever. Davidson retired, an old and weary man. Lang moved from York to Canterbury: the half-hidden protector of the Anglo-Catholic advance, but equally the subtle courtier prelate, he was neither the man to enforce the decision of parliament, nor to challenge it. The Church of England could not but suffer from such a state of affairs. Clearly the Enabling Act had not brought it 'Liberty', but to pursue liberty would – it seemed – cost too high a price. There were, anyway, in the coming years, other, more desperately important, things to think about than liturgical revision, and it may be questioned whether the anomalies created by the fiasco of the Prayer Book were much greater than those already existing in the Church. Each party would continue to go its own way, commissions would report ineffectually from time to time upon the subject of Church-State relations, while the country as a whole would continue its slow slide away from organized religion. Best to avert one's eyes from constitutional and liturgical anomaly than to enter the unchartered fields of an agonizing reappraisal.

One fact which may somewhat have helped to influence the anti-Roman fears of the Prayer Book controversy were the Conversations at Malines.[30] While two Protestant-minded octogenarians – Archbishop Davidson and Bishop Knox – had been battling over the Prayer Book in England and over the defence of England's Protestant heritage, two Catholic-minded old men had been getting together in Belgium to seek a way to do no less than reunite the Church of England with the Roman Catholic communion. The underlying audacity of the Malines Conversations of the 1920s really takes one's breath away. Halifax had for half a century been the accepted lay leader of Anglo-Catholicism. Mercier was among Catholic continental prelates an outstanding intellectual – the chief inspirer of neo-Thomism in Louvain in the late nineteenth century. Back in the 1890s Halifax and his French friend, the Abbé Portal, had endeavoured to obtain Roman recognition of the validity of Anglican priestly orders. The scheme had backfired, and, despite some sympathy in Rome, Cardinal Vaughan and his young allies, Merry del Val and Gasquet, had used the occasion to bring about exactly the opposite result – in the bull *Apostolicae Curae* of 1896 Anglican orders were condemned as invalid more emphatically than ever before. Now in their old age, with Mercier to help them, Halifax and Portal were trying again, encouraged in part by the return of a more favourable atmosphere in Rome. For, just as their 1890s initiative could be explained in part by the slightly liberal tone of Leo XIII's pontificate after that of Pius IX, so now Benedict XV and then Pius XI were moving somewhat away from the extreme intransigence of Pius X. Pius XI's Secretary of State was no other than Cardinal Gasparri, who in earlier days had been one of the more open members of the Commission on Anglican Orders. He had replaced the intensely conservative Merry del Val, who saw in him a real danger to the Church's orthodoxy.

The first conversation between Halifax, Portal and Mercier took place in 1921 and was of an entirely unofficial character. Following it they set about seeking official authorization from both Rome and Canterbury and this they obtained. Davidson had had the 1920 Lambeth *Appeal for Unity* translated into Latin and forwarded to the Pope. He was certainly not an enthusiast for ecumenical initiatives in that direction nor had he, understandably, great trust in Lord Halifax, but he judged it right to go forward with such an initiative cautiously, on the precise condition that the Vatican was prepared to grant equal authorization. And at the time it was. Pius XI responded encouragingly to Mercier's report on the first meeting – 'I see only good in these meetings' – and on 22 November 1922 Gasparri was able to write to Mercier that the Holy Father 'authorizes your Eminence to tell the Anglicans that the Holy See approves and encourages your conversations and prays with all his heart that God bless them'. This was passed on to both Archbishop Davidson and Cardinal Bourne, but never published; so when the Conversations were resumed in 1923 they had upon both sides an official but confidential character.

As a meeting of the two churches, they were unfortunately sadly unbalanced. Halifax, Frere and Dean Armitage Robinson – the original Anglican team, all high church – could not conceivably be regarded as representative of the Church of England at that time, while upon the Catholic side it was a disastrous mistake not to include an Englishman (such as the Dominican Bede Jarrett)[31] and not to keep Cardinal Bourne far more adequately informed than was done. Mercier was, in fact, gravely lacking in understanding either of Anglicans or of English Catholics. He never realized how unrepresentative Halifax really was, and he quite brushed aside the inevitable misgivings of such as Bourne, instead of realizing that without the latter's help little real progress could possibly be achieved. There was also a lack of theological weight upon both sides, though this was somewhat remedied in 1925 with the addition of Gore upon the Anglican side and Mgr Batiffol upon the Catholic.

The failure to cultivate Bourne was all the more foolish as he had some slight sympathy for what was being done. At least he had no love for its principal critics and, unlike them, had made no attempt to prevent the Conversations from taking place. For Cardinal Merry del Val, of course, it was all madness. Mercier was 'in a dream and all at sea', while Gasparri was 'mischievous' and the victim of 'extraordinary delusions'. In these views Merry del Val had surely the agreement of many English Catholics, including the editor of the *Tablet*, Ernest Oldmeadow, but for a time the opposite viewpoint was dominant in Rome.

So the Conversations were permitted to go forward. The high point was undoubtedly the 1925 meeting when the cardinal presented the famous paper written by Dom Lambert Beaudouin, the most far-sighted Catholic ecumenist of the time, on 'The Anglican Church, not absorbed but reunited'. Hitherto the Roman Catholic position had been to deny any true corporate existence as Church to the Church of England. The only way to unity seemed Newman's – that of individual submission. Now suddenly Mercier was sketching a whole different perspective, a perspective which loyal Anglicans could basically accept but which ultramontane Catholics could only regard as little short of treachery. As Frere said, it 'took our breath away'. Of course, it was all a dream, but cannot dreams come true? Certainly such a dream could not come true in the 1920s, far from it. Catholicism was really moving in quite a different direction. The great celebrations of the Holy Year in 1925 with the institution of the feast of Christ the King, and the canonization of Teresa of Lisieux demonstrated an utterly different outlook, to which a concern to conciliate Protestants was very foreign. The 1,200 pilgrims from England led to Rome by Bourne were addressed by Cardinal Merry del Val in St Peter's and by Cardinal Gasquet in St Paul's. The fervent populism of the Holy Year was a world away from, and a far more immediately powerful force than the ecumenical aspirations of the aged Belgian cardinal. Mercier died in January 1926 and there was no one to replace him in such work. In England opposition to the Conversations was mounting on several sides. Bourne could not really stand out against his brother cardinals in Rome, and in York at Easter 1927 made a speech which could only appear aggressively anti-Anglican. Yet in York Minster the episcopal ring of Mercier witnesses today to a different message. When Mercier was dying, Halifax hurried across the Channel to his bedside and the Cardinal dictated a final message for the Archbishop of Canterbury: '*Ut unum sint*: it is the supreme will of Christ, the wish of the Sovereign Pontiff: it is mine, it is yours. May it be realized in its fullness.'[32] Then he took the gold ring from his finger and gave it to Halifax, who wore it on a chain round his neck until he died. Welded into a chalice it was presented by his son to York Minster and is used there on three days each year – St Peter's, and the anniversaries of the deaths of Mercier and Halifax.

Meanwhile the Conversations were terminated and the Supreme Pontiff showed his wish clearly enough by issuing the encyclical *Mortalium Animos* in January 1928, which brusquely rejected the road of conversations of every sort: 'Such efforts can meet with no kind of approval among Catholics.' In 1930 the *Osservatore Romano* went so far as to publish the quite untrue statement that 'these conversations never had on the part of the Holy See the least shadow of official or semi-official character or any sort of mandate or commission'. Davidson, who at the start had struggled so hard to ensure that such a statement could not afterwards be made, had surely not unreasonably written to Lang in April 1922, 'We must take care not to rush effusively into intercourse in which we have to deal with very clever – I do not want to say crafty – people.'

In December 1926 Lord Hugh Cecil wrote to the Archbishop of Canterbury:

> The really striking thing is the concessions the Romans seem ready at least to consider: I expect the Ultramontanes will be extremely angry. But, as I said, what people fear is that Malines is meant to lead to our all 'going over to Rome' as a body. And any reminder of Malines is therefore unfortunate, just while Prayer Book revision is going on.[33]

In the Commons debate on 15 December a letter from Cardinal Mercier was actually read out by an opponent of revision. So, on the one hand, the Conversations may well have contributed to the stirring of the Protestant conscience which produced the rejection of the Prayer Book, upon the other to the publication of that very anti-irenic document, *Mortalium Animos*. The dislike with which they were viewed by many an English Catholic was almost venomous. They were, one may well conclude, both unrealistic and counter-productive. Yet they took place. A programme had been stated, and a few people at least were convinced of its prophetic significance. Fifty years afterwards *Mortalium Animos* was almost forgotten and had entirely ceased to be authoritative, the rejection of the Prayer Book no longer mattered one way or the other, Dom Beaudouin had been hailed by Pope John as the teacher of the true ecumenical road, and the Malines Conversations stood out as a beacon pointing the churches forward, a source of inspiration frequently adverted to in scores of other conversations. Surely the foolishness of two old men was a symbol almost of the foolishness of God.

If the 1920s saw in the Prayer Book controversy a crisis of Erastianism which challenged the basic character of the Church of England with a painful explicitness unparalleled since the seventeenth century, yet finally altered nothing, and in the Malines Conversations an ecumenical initiative as wildly audacious as it too appeared ineffectual, they witnessed as well one extended ecclesiastical process which did succeed to its authors' immediate satisfaction in seriously altering the national religious scene, but which in retrospect seems a little dull. That process was Methodist reunion.[34] These three things had all much to do with the basic religious phenomenon of the passing of old English Protestantism under the multiple pressures, not just of an advancing secularism, but also of a reviving Catholicism. Methodist reunion was indeed urged by many precisely as the creation of a Protestant bastion to withstand the ravages that Anglo-Catholicism was making within the Established Church, but itself contributed in its measure to the loss of the stoutest citadel of English Protestantism: congregational freedom.

The nineteenth century had seen the splitting up of the religious movement begun by Wesley into a main body, the Wesleyans, and a considerable number of smaller but thriving offshoots. The Wesleyan principle had been one of 'pastoral supremacy' of a ruling conference consisting solely of ministers. Closer in mind to high church and traditional Catholic principles, they stood for the authority of minister over laity and of central ecclesiastical authority over the local congregation. Over these principles Methodist unity had broken time and again as the more fully Protestant-minded had hived off to found smaller churches of their own – and, for the most part, churches lower in the social scale than that of the rather middle-class Wesleyans. Nevertheless by the end of the nineteenth century Wesleyans had admitted the laity to a second 'Representative' session of their conference, while the 1907 Union of Bible Christians, Free Methodists and the New Connexion into the United Methodist Church had already done much to curb congregational freedom and local tradition in the interests of a national denomination with an increasingly professional clergy. Upon both sides the sensible thing seemed to be to go further and reunite. In the years from 1906 to 1920 the absolute numbers of all the Free Churches were falling year by year: their peak had passed, quickly passed, and even though there was some temporary recovery in the 1920s, they had all become conscious of the arguments for ecclesiastical 'rationalization'. 'Overlapping' had come to be seen as an undesirable nuisance, instead of a symptom of vitality. Was it really desirable to have three competing Methodist chapels in a single Lincolnshire village? The expenses of running separate theological colleges and central administrative offices, the burden of maintaining independent denominational newspapers – such things were becoming increasingly onerous and, it seemed, increasingly pointless. The more progressively minded thinkers in all the churches found it hard to justify Methodist division in terms of their theological differences. Would not a United Methodist Church make much more impact, both religious and political, upon the nation? The Liberal election victory of 1906 had seemed the high watermark of Nonconformist national influence. In retrospect sadly little of value to Free churchmen had come of it. Could it not be that the cause of the failure lay in Free Church disunity? If Methodists were united in one great Church, they would surely have a national influence which five or three divided churches could never claim. Sir Robert Perks, the Wesleyan who had chaired the '200 Nonconformist MPs' in the heady days of 1906, was the chief lay Wesleyan proponent of Methodist union and lived to become as an octogenarian the first lay vice-president of the United Church. Methodist reunion may then, in some way, be seen as a carry-over from 1906.

It was also to be a great blow for English Protestantism. The Church of England seemed to be succumbing to Anglo-Catholicism. Many Free churchmen were heated opponents of Prayer Book revision, seeing it not as an internal Anglican affair but as a challenge to the nation's Protestantism by crypto-Romanists. The only effective answer to 'the Romeward movement' of the Church of England was a reunited Methodism which might even emerge as the one true Protestant Church of the land. So Perks could argue that, once united, 'The Methodist Church . . . would help to save England from Roman Catholicism and Anglo-Catholicism'.[35] For others reunion was not so much something anti-anyone, but rather a necessary stage in the re-union of Christians all round. The great leaders of Methodist reunion, Scott Lidgett and A. S. Peake above all, were liberal progressives in the full ecumenical tide, men helping to form the emerging Christian consensus of the twentieth century, rather than defenders of the intense but narrow loyalties of nineteenth-century sects. Christian unity could over-arch the small differences which had produced the division of the past, without requiring surrender one way or the other. And upon unity depended evangelism, mission, the forward movement of the Church. Decline was God's judgment upon Christian quarrelling, growth would necessarily follow reunion. It was hoped and believed that 'a Revival will coincide with the coming of Methodist Union . . . with the consummation of Union a great forward movement on quite unprecedented lines is anticipated; is indeed inevitable.'[36]

There were of course the doubters, what came to be termed the 'Other Side', strongest among Wesleyans, but present in all three churches. Support for unity was strongest in the suburbs where Methodism had been growing most effectively in the early twentieth century and where the differences between the three seemed least significant. Opposition was strongest in old rural areas where ancient animosities remained very real, numbers were down and union was likely to result in the recognition of 'redundancy' – the closing of chapels and the amalgamation of congregations where circuits were numerous and overlapped. Local loyalties made some Primitive Methodists and old Free Methodists fear and resist union, if few could say, as did J. H. Standeven, a Primitive Methodist of Skipton who had spent £20,000 on the Ebenezer Chapel, Halifax: 'I am thoroughly opposed to Methodist Union and shall do all that I ever can to prevent Ebenezer Chapel, Halifax, which is my gift, being taken over by any union; it is going to remain *Primitive Methodist* as long as I have any influence.'[37] Nevertheless the two smaller churches – Primitive Methodists and United Methodists – were overwhelmingly in favour of union. It was only among the Wesleyans that there was strong concerted, and almost success-ful, resistance. It was predominantly clerical resistance and reflected the fear of Wesleyan ministers that their role and status would be diminished in consequence of union with the more lay-minded traditions of the other churches. For them it was essential that a separate ministerial session be retained in confer-ence – something quite foreign to the Prims; on the other hand, the latter had always practised lay administration of the sacra-ment in chapels where no minister was available. This was foreign to the Wesleyans and constituted, perhaps, the most crucial dividing line between 'Protestant' and 'Catholic' concep-tions of congregation, ministry and sacrament. The Wesleyans stood with the Anglicans, Catholics, Orthodox, all the historic traditions of Christendom, in reserving the presidency of the Eucharist to the ordained, even though they did so less in terms of the need for 'orders' than for 'order'. Primitive Methodists held to the contrary practice on grounds of the primacy of the congregation and the basic relationship of sacrament to Church rather than to ministry: the needs of small congregations rather than the availability of ministers should be the decisive criterion. In the years of negotiation the Wesleyans secured their separate pastoral session and so a bicameral legislature for the Church, but the Prims retained the right of lay administration of the sacrament which was thus passed on to the United Church.

Formal negotiations between the three Churches were begun in January 1918; various schemes were put forward and agreed over the next years, but it was soon clear that while a majority – at least of the members of Conference of all three – wanted union, the 'Other Side' was too considerable to be disregarded. In 1925 it was agreed that union should depend upon a 75 per cent vote in favour in each conference. Whereas this was at once accorded by the Primitive and United Methodists, the Wesleyan Pastoral Session failed to provide it for the next three years. Only in 1928 after further concessions to Wesleyan tradition was it at last obtained, and that by one vote. Full union was deferred until 1932, but the crucial decision was that of 1928. John Scott Lidgett, elected first President of the new Methodist Conference, may be judged principal architect of unity and inspirer of a new model. A Wesleyan to the core, he had been carried as an infant to receive the blessing of Jabez Bunting, the great Methodist organizer of the first half of the nineteenth century, as he lay on his death-bed. When President of the Wesleyan Conference in 1908, Lidgett could claim to have been personally acquainted with fifty of the ninety-one presidents who had occupied John Wesley's chair, and after that he was amazingly to see another forty-four holders of the office. In 1932, a man of seventy-eight, he was not only President of Conference, and almost lifelong chairman of the London South district of his Church, he was also the effective proponent of every type of local social involvement, a member of London County Council and now Vice-Chancellor of London University, an institution he had served for many years. Lidgett was a man of great abilities, unending energy and rather simple convictions. His liberal ecumenical principles and their implementation inevitably undermined the narrow old patterns of Protestant congregationalism and fundamentalism, but he stopped short of any sort of Catholic sacramentalism or preoccupation with the wider international ecumene or more agonizing moral issues of the age. But Methodists, having moved so far, were not going to be able to stop there with him.

Of course, the internal problems consequent upon union were only too considerable. To unite the churches on the ground at local level was painfully difficult. A place like Ludlow, whose circuit now included fifty-three chapels mostly with pretty small congregations and just four ministers, points the problem at its most acute. In an area of long established Methodism every building was hallowed and had its own little congregation most unwilling to be moved. In the first eighteen years of union over 1,500 Methodist buildings were closed.[38] Undoubtedly – if paradoxically – such closures were all in all a gain, but the battles to achieve them were time consuming and often painful, and more chapels still should have been closed than were, if the 'rationalization' was helpful, the 'great forward movement' never materialized: the years following the union were ones of overall numerical decline, not growth. Furthermore in general the majority tradition triumphed in a rather ungenerous way over the minorities. Wesleyans constituted almost 60 per cent of the united Church but filled far more than 60 per cent of the leadership positions. The smaller churches had wanted union most but lost most through it. It was the small minority of Methodists remaining outside the Union who also remained most Protestant.

Reunion propelled the more free and inherently Protestant tradition within Methodism back into an intrinsically 'Catholic' direction. Certainly the aim was not to catholicize; rather it was to create a massive national bastion of Protestanism able to withstand the growing Catholic movement. Yet, paradoxically, reunion was itself institutionally part of that movement and, far from protecting its members against neo-Catholicism, it tended to draw them still further into its orbit. One need not question the wisdom of reuniting, though many of the arguments put forward at the time were of doubtful validity, but one can hardly doubt too that, in a broad perspective, 1932 was a step not in the recovery but in the continued decline of traditional English Protestantism.

Over the border in Scotland that platinum age of relative optimism, the late 1920s, also had its ecumenical successes when in 1929 the United Free Church and the Church of Scotland were reunited, ending the main schism among Presbyterians which had lasted for nearly a century, since the 'Great Disruption'. The 1920s furthermore saw an immense advance in international ecumenical consciousness – the springing into life of major ecumenical institutions and pressure groups of a permanent

kind: Faith and Order, Life and Work, the International Missionary Council. Their leadership, drawn largely from an SCM
milieu, was a sort of triumvirate: British, American and Scandinavian. One of the greatest weaknesses of the time was the
inability of German Protestantism to take its part. The religious
leader of Europe up to 1914, it had been immeasurably bruised
by the war, as German Catholicism was not, and in the 1920s it
could co-operate confidently neither with the new German
democratic political experiment nor with the international
Christian community. It withdrew rather into a sullen nationalism linked with the maintenance of evangelical purity.

Equally in Britain the spell of German intellectual superiority,
so immensely strong up to 1914, in both the religious and secular
fields, had been irreparably shattered by the war. Germany had
been Britain's Protestant partner, essentially a senior partner.
There was no one really to fill the gap. In future the alliance
would be more with the United States. The American Evangelical
influence on Britain had long existed and to this was added the
sectarian influence and the ecumenical influence. It was often not
quite clear to which of these Frank Buchman, so intimate a
presence in Britain in the 1920s, so vapid in retrospect, quite
belonged. Then one can think of Nancy Astor, Britain's first
woman MP, a fervent proponent of Protestantism in her own
estimation and still more fervent an apostle of Christian Science
and of the wisdom of Mrs Eddy. But the leading American figure
upon the ecclesiastical scene in the 1920s was undoubtedly that
of John R. Mott, a sort of generally accepted lay pope of the
earlier ecumenical movement.[39] He not only kept going for a very
long time and with indefatigable energy an enthusiasm for
conferences, tours and revivals of all sorts, he was trusted as a
personal counsellor by people in every continent. He managed
moreover to combine international ecumenical statesmanship
with a close involvement in domestic American politics. Of
mid-western, middle class, Methodist background, Mott managed the world with a cool, slightly naïve optimism, which well
fitted the mood of the 1920s. He had founded the World Student
Christian Federation back in 1895. He had conducted a three
week evangelistic campaign at Cambridge and Oxford in 1898 –
in the tradition of Moody, but less emotional. He had chaired the

World Missionary Conference at Edinburgh in 1910. He was the close friend of Woodrow Wilson, a strong supporter of Prohibition through the 1920s and the mobilizer of Republican opposition to Al Smith on this issue. A great moralizer, he believed in 'the Kingdom of God', accepted 'the Social Gospel' and saw both as pretty closely linked not only with American democracy at home but American hegemony elsewhere. Mott represented very well the main American religious approach in these years, so far removed from the German, practical, optimistic, intellectually a bit naïve. One can, not unreasonably, compare him with Buchman. Both were globe-trotting preachers, rather over-confident that their message could resolve the world's social problems. Mott was, without doubt, a more significant and responsible person than Buchman, though the latter was probably better known in Britain. Both were very bland. Between them they help to explain why orthodox Evangelicalism, so dependent on its American springs, appeared almost moribund in this period. An admirer remarked that 'Mr Mott has an unrivalled gift of making the obvious sound really impressive.'[40] It is the obviousness rather than the impressiveness of what he said which now remains with us.

American religion of this sort could never achieve the intellectual influence upon Britain of pre-war Germany. Without it the British churches themselves had to take the lead, as they did internationally in the inter-war years with considerable confidence and to an extent probably never realized either before or since – at least since the age of Boniface! Temple, Oldham, Paton, Headlam, Bell, were pre-eminent among the leaders of Christendom in those decades and we may close this discussion of ecclesiastical life in the late 1920s with the meeting of the International Missionary Council at Jerusalem, at Easter 1928, for it reflects well enough the mood of the time, its strengths and its weaknesses. How splendid to be able to have once more a major Christian Conference in Jerusalem, with a secure British military presence around, and a sense, however ephemeral, of the rejections of history having been rolled back. This was the first successor to the great Edinburgh Conference of 1910, and of it, too, John Mott was the chairman. The mood was optimistic, the central theme was the challenge of secularism, the leading intellectual figure William Temple, who wrote its central message with superb lucidity and shone in its assemblies as in such assemblies he always did. Ecclesiastically this was surely the high point of the platinum age. It was a great gathering, an encouraging gathering, a forward-looking gathering, but its rather liberal-sounding consensus would at once be denounced by German theologians. Theology, Churchmen and nations were all again about to fall apart.

The Intellectual Battleground

'The fate of our Christianity is visibly hanging in the balance,' declared A. E. Taylor the Platonist at the Anglo-Catholic Congress of 1920. Among academic philosophers of distinction he was in 1920 extremely unusual in being also an orthodox believing Christian. Engrossing as controversies over the Prayer Book or Methodist reunion might be for many people, it is necessary to recognize that the principal intellectual (as distinct from social) orthodoxy of England in the 1920s was no longer Protestantism, nor was it catholicism or any other form of Christianity. It was a confident agnosticism. It is important to be clear about this. The period of our consideration does not witness a slow crumbling intellectually of religious belief; rather does it start with an emphatic presupposition of disbelief, from which – if you were reasonably intelligent – only the clergy, Roman Catholics and a few eccentric neo-medievalists were expected to be exempt. There is the old story of the undergraduate of the period who rushed to his tutor at Oxford one day to say, 'Sir, I've just discovered that I believe in God. Oughtn't I to be ordained?' The point behind the story is that in such circles only the clergy, who were professionally committed to doing so, still believed in God: an exaggeration, of course, but one symbolic of the time.

It was difficult not to be at least an agnostic. Orthodox Christianity appeared for very solid reasons increasingly implausible to the intelligent man. To believe meant standing out against every single one of the giants of modernity, the prophets who had established the framework of understanding wherein which intellectual discourse, the whole modern civilization of the mind, seemed now established. Ever since the middle of the Victorian age a climate of disbelief had been building up. For some decades Christian thinkers in England had endeavoured vigorously to withstand the tide but most of the ablest were dead before the turn of the century and while on individual points they had salvaged the credibility of faith – at least in clerical eyes – they had by no means won the public battle. Religious thinking was more and more simply abandoned among the wise as essentially primitive and, in the modern world, redundant – it could be eliminated on the principle of Occam's razor, the law of parsimony. It was simply no longer needed. The Edwardian years in particular were ones of a rapid, if still slightly veiled, spread of the new agnosticism – the atheism of the leadership mellowed into the agnosticism of the led – and the agonies of the First World War both showed up organized Christianity at its most bombastic and least plausible, and relaxed some of the conventions which, hitherto, had obscured the spread of disbelief. The 1920s as a consequence, were the first decade in which the intellectual overturning of Christianity effectively achieved by the previous generation could be, and was, openly accepted as a fact of modern life.

Much began with Darwin. Victorian middle-class Christian belief depended overwhelmingly upon a most simplistic acceptance of the absolute reliability of the Bible. In the light of Darwin and, in subsequent decades, in the light also of biblical scholarship, that reliability was irremediably punctured. While learned clerics could argue the toss, win points from time to time and establish new lines of defence to their own satisfaction, none of that greatly diminished the loss of confidence in the intellectual reliability and moral authority of Christianity. To Darwin add Marx, Nietzsche, Freud and Durkheim, four atheists.[1] Together these five, in their different fields, had created by the early twentieth century an apparently irresistible consensus. These were the prophets of enlightenment, whose authority a Modern Man could hardly dare to question in the Edwardian age. The intellectual cream of Edwardian youth – as exemplified by that somewhat precious group of Cambridge 'Apostles' gathered round G. E. Moore – was overwhelmingly agnostic. Whichever form of reductionism was preferred, whether religion was to be interpreted with Marx as the opium of the people, with Durkheim as the symbolic representation of social reality, or with

Freud as 'the universal obsessional neurosis of humanity', mattered little. God was dead and religion an illusion, a hangover from primitive society, pointless if not even harmful for modern man. Late Victorian literary pundits like Bernard Shaw and H. G. Wells, scholars and poets like Gilbert Murray and A. E. Housman, historians like H. A. L. Fisher, politicians like Asquith and Haldane and Churchill, all alike took this for granted. The cultivated upper class of their generation, the mentors of post-Victorian England, were post-Darwinians to a man, and, being so, tended to share the basic imaginative limitations of Darwin's highly intelligent sons as described by a grand-daughter. 'They were quite unable to understand the minds of the poor, the wicked, or the religious.'[2] Maybe that is too hard a judgment – a few at least might sympathize with the minds of the wicked, one or two might have known what it was to be poor, but the religious – no; there at least the post-Darwinian consensus was seldom breached. The young philosophers like Bertrand Russell, the young historians like G. M. Trevelyan, the young anthropologists like Malinowski, the young poets like Rupert Brooke, the young novelists like D. H. Lawrence, E. M. Forster, or Virginia Woolf, all set out to interpret human life with this great and solidly acquired consensus now firmly behind them. There is no God, religion was but the delusion of a primitive past, and while the institutions of Christianity may remain for a time socially useful in the manipulation of the lower classes, they are destined to fade away quickly enough as we advance further into the modern world of almost unlimited freedom, rationality and science, physical and social. Everything of significance in life must be secularized.

Of giants alive in 1920, James Frazer symbolizes it all, perhaps better than anyone else on account of the range of his appeal and his central concern with religion itself. He did not merely dismiss religion or explain it away in the rather abstruse and difficult terms of continental philosophy or sociology. He described this 'long tragedy of human folly' in masses of fascinating detail. The *Golden Bough* was almost the bible of the 1920s: the book of religion par excellence. The anthropology of religion as here revealed seemed irresistible and Christianity appeared to sink into utter incredibility in this vast sea of ritual and myth of which it was now seen to be but a continuation. In *Kyrios Christos*, W. Bousset had already endeavoured to show with great learning that New Testament christology derived from the mythology of pagan religions in the Middle East. In asserting such things the scholars of religion were only putting the coping stone on an intellectual edifice of atheism constructed right across the board of the sciences – an edifice absolutely central to the early twentieth-century mind yet one the recognized proponents of Christianity seemed incapable of challenging, or even of acknowledging. Modernity had simply no place for religion in general or Christianity in particular.

Many an intellectual, many a bright young thing looked back on Christianity and the religion of childhood with genuine nostalgia, but nostalgia is not enough to live on. For Christian belief could be substituted idealist philosophy, art, personal relationships or even spiritualism. Miriam, the soulful churchgoing young lady in Lawrence's *Sons and Lovers*, symbolizes the religion that men still encountered in youth only to reject in maturity, if occasionally with some regret. Paul Morel has to set out on his lonely way without her. For Virginia Woolf even insanity could be a substitute for religion, as she once suggested to Forster.[3] Lawrence's gospel of emotional passion freed from the constraints of reason was again a substitute, and seen as such, for the dreary Nonconformity he had fled from; the brilliant libertinism of Bloomsbury was a substitute for, a 'positively theatrical reversal'[4] of, the Evangelical puritanism of the Clapham Sect from which its leaders derived. The mocking of Victorian religion in Lytton Strachey's *Eminent Victorians* was, yet again, another way of facing up to the ghosts of the nursery.

Classwise and in many of their convictions and enthusiasms, D. H. Lawrence was far indeed from Bloomsbury, and both were far from the Fabians, or from old-fashioned Liberals like Asquith and Gilbert Murray or bright young dons like Jack Haldane or Julian Huxley at New College or King's – the Oxbridge pacesetters of the moment – but in relation to religion they were all as good as one. The religious survivor in such circles was absolutely the exception. The significance of this agnostic near-consensus was precisely that it crossed so many boundaries, embracing groups and people otherwise anything but sympathetic one to another. For the learned, the serious, the chic and the beautiful, religion might on occasion be regretted like other attractions of childhood, it might be pandered to for the sake of social stability, it might still be a fascinating subject for scholarly enquiry, but for the current needs of today's educated man, it was simply out.

Where the new non-religious establishment did meet and respect fellow human beings who did not share their convictions (and it had, of course, to do so even at New College where R. H. Lightfoot was not only chaplain and Dean of Divinity, but junior bursar, sub-warden, tuition secretary, tutor for Admissions and secretary of the Benefices Committee[5] – clearly the clergy still had their uses!) there was really very little to be said beyond pained recognition of an almost undiscussable chasm: 'the dyke that separates us is one that cannot well be crossed by either of us', wrote Sydney Cockerell to Dame Laurentia McLachlan of Stanbrook Abbey in February 1924.[6] Bound together by friendship and a love of medieval manuscripts, they were sundered by the dyke separating the certainty of old religious convictions surviving in a Catholic monastery from the certainty of agnosticism apparently victorious outside cloister walls which found religious belief to be inherently impossible for a 'modern cultivated man' such as the extremely learned and charming curator of the Fitzwilliam Museum. There were, of course, lots of intelligent people who still believed in religion. There were a few temperamentally more conservative colleges – like Corpus at Cambridge, Christ Church at Oxford – which rather prided themselves on being Christian. There were scores of second-rate dons who had never read a word of Marx, Nietzsche, Freud or Durkheim and who still comforted themselves with a mix of the New Testament, Plato, Browning and rowing. There were even a very few outstanding lay Christian believers – Taylor, Lindsay, Ernest Barker, Tawney, Chesterton – but it was pretty clear that it was they who were now the dissenters, intellectual oddities, objects of veiled sarcasm from the enlightened. Agnosticism, if with some a regretful agnosticism, was the common ground of almost all first rank intellectuals. It was the message of all the foundational texts of modern culture. Moreover this was now a public fact and its attraction appeared almost irresistible to the brilliant young.

Moral values were a delusion, and politics and religion a waste of time. I had now given up saying my prayers. Anthony too had a father a clergyman and we both resented the fact that our parents assumed us to be Christian, though neither of us would have dared to stand up in their presence and die for lack of faith . . .

So Louis MacNeice and Anthony Blunt at Marlborough in the mid-1920s.[7]

Or take the following incident in 1923:

. . . a door opened and Bet heard her mother's slippered feet padding softly along the corridor. 'Darling,' said an anxious small voice, 'Father says, *Is he a Roman Catholic*?' 'No,' said Bet sleepily, 'he's an atheist.' 'Oh, thank goodness! I must tell Father, we couldn't sleep for worrying . . .'

This snatch of conversation occurred on the last night that Bet spent in her parents' home before her marriage,[8] the writer and bridegroom being E. R. Dodds, a classical scholar and later Gilbert Murray's successor as Regius Professor of Greek at Oxford. His agnosticism would not prevent him from interpreting Greek religion with great empathy. It may be noted that Bet too was a convinced agnostic yet they were married by her brother, an Anglican priest and later a bishop.

There was nothing odd about the agnosticism of young Dodds and MacNiece. It was simply characteristic of the climate of the 1920s, testified to in autobiography after autobiography, an integral part of the secular optimism of the age. A new heaven was arriving – at least for the middle classes – full of art and a new sincerity and sex and motor cars. The inhibitions and superstitions of the past were happily fading away, politics did not matter much, peace was assured and there was still a sufficiency of servants. The optimism of the 1920s certainly touched the churches, at times in silly ways, but it was clearly enough a mood which owed them nothing, had very little time for them, and indeed flourished in a world to which they did not and could not safely belong.

Yet the descent towards atheism had been made easier in that it was for long a covert descent. It remained very much a Protestant atheism and there was no social divide between the Protestant believer and the atheist as there was between them both and the

Catholic. Old Bishop Knox was far less upset by the atheism of his eldest son Dillwyn than by the Roman Catholicism of his younger son Ronnie. Duff Cooper remarked that for his generation there were only two religions: Roman Catholicism which was wrong, and the rest which did not matter.[9] When Bertrand Russell wanted to stand for parliament before the war and was interviewed by a local Liberal committee, he was asked whether he was a Church member. No, he was an agnostic. Was he prepared, nevertheless, to go to church from time to time? No, nor was his wife.[10] What was decisive against his selection was not his agnosticism but his quite unusual refusal to hide it just a little. Agnosticism seldom prevented others from going on occasion to church. On the contrary. Agnostics could tell a good sermon from a bad one, subscribe to Church funds, read the lesson and take participation in the public rituals for granted. Religious ritual was perfectly acceptable if indulged in for political, social, or aesthetic purposes. It only should not be indulged in for religious purposes. Bertrand Russell and, by the 1920s, a good many other people, caused a social divide by refusing to attend church services at all, but the Roman Catholic had long caused an almost worse divide by insisting upon attending, and really believing in, an alternative ritual. In this he was anathema almost equally to the Protestant believer, like Bishop Knox, and the Protestant agnostic like Asquith, to Bet and to her parents. And in their down-to-earth English way they did not much distinguish between their fairly contradictory reasons for condemnation. Catholicism clearly challenged the intellectual consensus as Protestantism did not do – on the contrary, a devout agnosticism was easily judged to be a sort of logical progression beyond Liberal Protestantism as the latter was beyond Reformation Protestantism. Many an atheist looked back gratefully enough at his Victorian clerical father. Here there was no social divide, surprisingly little intellectual challenge and much willingness to keep the old rituals going in church and college. Where challenge came from Catholicism, Anglican or Roman, it was alike to Protestantism and to agnosticism, and both felt incensed. For modern men other religions did not matter but Catholicism was wrong.

There was something rather schizophrenic about this new

world view. Atheist, intellectually and morally radical as it thought itself, particularly in regard to personal life, the new élite was for the most part politically and socially very much at home in the status quo. If it protested at all on that front, its protest was singularly ineffective: in a Bloomsbury drawing room or an Oxford senior common room, revolutionism was not to be deplored but it was irrelevant, the milieu being immersed in what could be salvaged of Victorian privilege and Edwardian comfort. If revolution were to be encouraged it should be abroad. This schizophrenia was particularly noticeable in regard to Soviet Russia. Here, after all, was the real revolution and Lenin, the greatest atheist of all, at work. For some this was indeed the ultimate enemy, but for many an apolitical 1920s intellectual the Russian Revolution was regarded as a great achievement of enlightened atheism, seen through very rose-tinted spectacles. Utterly ruthless, barbaric, tyrannical as Leninist Russia was and Stalinist Russia continued to be, the 1920s upper-class English atheist, very content to be ruled by Mr Baldwin at home, seldom saw it as such. The bond of progressive atheism could cover a multitude of sins.

Somewhat apart from all this, but arguably little less disastrous for Christian faith, was the underlying influence of Hegel: an almost controlling influence in British philosophy for fifty years.

Hegel is difficult, for most of us probably impossible, to understand. His philosophy of *Geist*, of spirit, affirmed Christianity to be the Absolute Religion, but in fact challenged the specificity of historical Christianity by its contrast of idea and fact. The heart of traditional Christian faith has lain not in the affirmation of the absoluteness of spirit but in that of the particularity of the historic incarnation. Hegel's philosophy stood behind the British idealist school, dominant above all in Oxford, in the late-nineteenth and first years of the twentieth century: T. H. Green, Edward Caird, F. H. Bradley and Bernard Bosanquet are the principal names. Far from claiming to explain religion away, they were in their own way its sympathetic apologists, as against any merely utilitarian or materialist philosophy. The whole idealist endeavour was to assert the primacy of spiritual reality, of what they liked to call the 'Christian Principle', but this could not be done – in their view – in the traditional terms of Christian theology.[11] It seemed impossible and ridiculous to tie the onward development of the human spirit, so manifestly progressive and expansive in the nineteenth century, by claiming finality for a figure who lived and died nineteen hundred years earlier, particularly when historical criticism was blurring the form of that figure more and more. It was the 'Christian Principle', not any particular historical manifestation of it – important as Jesus Christ might be – which really mattered, and this principle was essentially one of divine immanence rather than transcendence: the spirit within man as within all reality rather than a personal Father above him. At a time of growing scepticism British idealism with its deep reverence for 'religion' and Platonism of a sort, was welcomed by many a churchman as ally and friend. Yet in appearing to be so, it was also the philosophical undermining of Christianity as a faith centred around a singular historic person: particularity, awkward as it may be, and the stumbling block to many a seeker of good will, is at the very core of the 'Christian Principle'. Remove it and you are left with something looking less and less like Christianity. Here was a friend as dangerous as many enemies. Idealism has in the end to be seen as a high-minded and plausible way of retaining Christian values without Christianity.[12] It could provide a sufficiently religious note – of a Platonist or even pantheistic kind – to satisfy the needs of a first generation of post-Christians, many of whom still respected religion while finding it impossible actually to believe.

Early twentieth-century man still needed something: atheism was, for many, too hard a road, and so the crumbling of orthodox forms of Christian belief went with the survival of much religious yearning, pantheistic, spiritualist or mystical. Poets like Bridges and Masefield, philosophers like Whitehead, scientists like Sir James Jeans, all wanted something 'spiritual', something with a religious overtone and some sort of verbal continuity with the Christian past, even though they had for one reason or another rejected as unacceptable the transcendence coupled with historic accessibility of the Christian god. Admittedly reverence for Hegel was lessening from the turn of the century and crashed with the First World War[13] – philosophers being no more immune to political sensitivities than lesser men – but the legacy of British idealism very much survived. At its lowest it constituted a diffused vague pantheism substituting intellectually for religion among the temperamentally anti-materialist; at its highest it may be found in the writing of Whitehead and Collingwood. Whitehead may well represent better than anyone else the mental mood of the 1920s in its most religiously sympathizing form. Here was a distinguished mathematician and philosopher, co-writer with Bertrand Russell of the *Principia Mathematica*, who did after all want to find a place for the spiritual, for religion of a sort, in the modern scientific world. There was a somewhat complacent optimism here again, characteristic of the 1920s, when all his best-known works were written, an optimism to which the Christian apologist responded only too optimistically: 'Whitehead's respect for religion was spoken of with respect,' Maurice Cowling has well remarked,[14] but what a poor hand the Christian apologist believed himself to hold that he found such a card worth playing. The religious patronage of Whitehead or Collingwood was almost as deadly to the survival of Christian faith as the attacks of their opposite numbers – Russell or Ayer.[15]

Whitehead moved in the 1920s to America. In Britain the new philosophic wave, rejecting idealism of any sort, would be increasingly logical and linguistic, claiming uninterest in any metaphysical question. While in its mode and the initial concerns of its propagators it was a great deal more remote from 'religion' than idealism, it would in course of time prove less inimical to orthodox Christianity.

Meanwhile the idealist mood of early twentieth-century British philosophy had greatly affected the theologians. The more that historical criticism seemed to undermine the old hard certainties of Bible and tradition, the more 'religion' was being re-located in a mystique drawn especially from Plato, Hegel and a rather partial reading of St John's Gospel. The first quarter of the twentieth century was not a great age for British theology, at least Anglican theology. Almost the only writings of the period to remain memorable and readable are those of non-Anglicans – Forsyth, Tyrrell and von Hügel. Gore, the most powerful intellectual within Anglicanism, had made an adventurous contribution to theological thought in early life in the *Lux Mundi* symposium of 1889. Upset by the reaction to that book, he was, ever afterwards, excessively cautious and dry, as was Headlam – probably the most respected but least creative of the academic theologians in the post-war period. The Oxford and Cambridge schools of divinity contained men like Burkitt, Streeter, Bethune-Baker and Sanday, of immense biblical and patristic learning but of rather little sustained theological skill. These men were 'Modernists', but their 'modernism' was something a good deal more remote from traditional Christian belief than the mystical and sacramentalist Catholic 'modernism' of George Tyrrell (of which they were mostly highly suspicious). Moralism, idealism, and a rather simple theism combined to fill the gap left by the apparent demise of biblical fundamentalism and supernaturalism, in the wake of a very uncritical acceptance of 'Science'. The modernist had, above all, no time for miracles. A conference of the Modern Churchmen's Union at Girton College in 1921 was the high point of this academic wave and it provoked much interest at the time. Take the words of Dr Major, the strategist and most insistent propagator of Anglican modernism:

> We believe that there is only one substance of the Godhead and the Manhood, and that our conception of the difference between Deity and Humanity is one of degree. The distinction between Creator and creature, upon which Dr Gore and the older theologians place so much emphasis, seems to us to be a minor distinction.[16]

For the demystification of theology that certainly takes some beating. The important thing for us in such a statement is that it represents a peak in the demystifying of Christianity: its reduction to theism of a sort, a belief in the after-life and individualistic morality – the final unrevolutionary kernel of Protestantism. Science, it seemed, left no room for more. Biblical scholarship, the study of world religions and scientific materialism appeared to have undermined the foundations of traditional Christianity, and modernist clerical scholars of this sort were sincerely endeavouring to save what they could, to re-establish what Sanday called 'Reduced Christianity' on a basis of post-Hegelian idealism and moralism.

Unlike many of the older theologians, the modern churchmen really had been affected, profoundly affected, by the intellectual culture of their age. But in endeavouring to wrestle with it while interpreting the Christian faith, they seem mostly to have had too inadequate tools and to have given away too much too easily in the process. Their negative criticisms were often to the point, their positive constructions suffered from a vagueness and a dull lack of any great sense of mystery feebly inadequate to bear the weight of Christian spiritual experience. The resultant theology might seem a tolerable middle way for learned but doubting clerical scholars, anxious to retain some ground for their ecclesiastical status and mild piety, but it was not a faith strong enough or coherent enough to appear as an intellectually convincing option, something to which to convert the unbeliever or to rally the unclerical ranks of ordinary Church people drifting towards agnosticism. Modernism was, however, the most characteristic theology of the 1920s.

William Temple's mental training was certainly in the Oxford school of Hegelian idealism under Caird, the Master of Balliol. Together they represent the most religious side of the idealist school. Temple was a man for all subjects; he was also by commitment a modern man – and this is well expressed in a famous response to Ronald Knox. Knox, in *Some Loose Stones*, had criticized *Foundations*, a somewhat modernistic pre-war symposium to which Temple had contributed, pointing out one seeming principle behind the work of Temple and his fellow authors as, 'How much will Jones swallow?' Christian belief is to be so restated as not to go beyond what Jones, a 'modern cultivated man', may find acceptable – but as a matter of fact, the 'modern cultivated man' could increasingly not find any religious belief whatsoever acceptable, so such an approach was bound to leave increasingly little on the table. Anyway, such was Knox's criticism, and to it Temple replied head on: 'I am not asking what Jones will swallow: *I am Jones* asking what there is to eat.' That is to say Temple identified himself, and very genuinely, with modern man in all his questionings, while Knox – like many another of the more obviously orthodox, Catholic or Evangelical – had emphatically rejected the package of modern culture. Certainly Temple-Jones never seems to have asked himself whether he had not in an earlier meal already swallowed rather too much of the modern mind. Knox was self-consciously reactionary, Temple modernist (in its widest sense), but Temple was also a profoundly religious person and temperamentally optimistic. He still looked for some immediate synthesis of Christian faith and modern culture and endeavoured to outline such a synthesis in *Mens Creatrix* (1917) and *Christus Veritas* (1924). There is a wide-ranging scope in these works combined with a sure faith in the singularity of the historic incarnation which remains impressive, even if there are odd traces too of the sort of Hegelian fusion of the divine and the human such as we found in Dr Major. In the twenties Temple was trying to show that the world's 'immanent principle' was signally manifested in Jesus Christ. It was an optimistic age and Temple's an optimistic endeavour. He was, one feels, in tune with the 1920s as he would not be in the increasingly divided and anguished years that followed. But he seems to have greatly underestimated the agnostic character of the contemporary Jones and even the growing lack of interest in philosophic idealism.[17]

Temple once cheerfully described himself and Chesterton – two very fat and jovial men – as Tweedledum and Tweedledee, but Chesterton may well have succeeded, where Temple failed, in effectively addressing 'Modern Man'. If so, it could be not only because Chesterton had gifts of imagination and a mastery of language beyond Temple's but also because he was a great deal more critical of modernity. 'To the young people of my generation, G.K.C. was a kind of Christian liberator . . . a beneficent bomb', Dorothy Sayers later remarked.[18] If there was one man at that time who could speak the whole Christian message and yet be heard by society as a whole, that man was Chesterton, at once journalist and seer. And probably the writings of no one else survive even half so well.

In 1922 G.K. was converted to Roman Catholicism. One could think that the consequence might have been to make his social teaching more effective, but greatly to limit his freedom in regard to any deeper apologetic. In fact the opposite was the case. Under the influence of Belloc his social and political stance hardened into a visionary distributism, but Belloc was not much interested in doctrine, and in the intellectual interpretation of man, religion and modernity Chesterton flowered in his latter years more than ever before. His masterpiece, *The Everlasting*

Man, was published in 1925. It is probably the most impressive piece of Christian literature of the decade, and a very influential one. Chesterton's Christ was grounded in a richer human field than Temple's and challenged far more convincingly the religious, historical and sociological grounds for disbelief. *The Everlasting Man* may well be compared with *Mens Creatrix* but it is vastly more satisfying. Chesterton knew less about philosophy than Temple, but he understood a great deal more about religion.

The following year saw the publication of what may well be regarded as the second major Christian work of the decade: *Essays Catholic and Critical*. The editor was E. G. Selwyn, the influential editor of the monthly *Theology*, the contributors being a group of younger Anglo-Catholics. Essentially they represent a new school almost inconceivable in the pre-First World War period. Few of its authors were as yet well known, but most were to write a very great deal in the next twenty years and to be, indeed, the kernel of a school of theological thought at once more roundly Catholic than anything going before it but also far more critically liberal than any of its orthodox predecessors. Effectively it gave back to the Church of England a viable theology of the supernatural, modifying the crudities of earlier Anglo-Catholic attitudes and producing a corpus of scholarship, at once creative and essentially orthodox, which could be the pride of any church and demonstrate a more than passable recovery from the theological doldrums of the preceding years. Most of this still lay in the future but a 1920s symposium, to which Wilfred Knox and Lionel Thornton, J. K. Mozley, Eric Milner-White and A. E. Rawlinson contributed, could not but be a foretaste of many exciting things to come. Perhaps the two most immediately important essays in the book were those of A. E. Taylor and Sir Edwyn Hoskyns.

Bishop Gore was seen one day on the stairs at Mirfield hugging to his breast a volume of Hastings' *Encyclopedia of Religion and Ethics*, in an ecstasy of delight. It was the twelfth volume, published in 1921. Asked the reason for this behaviour he replied, 'A. E. Taylor's article on God.'[19] It was indeed a splendid article and so was that in the *Essays* entitled 'The Vindication of Religion'. Taylor, an English Platonist, was at that time Professor of Moral Philosophy in Edinburgh. He was perhaps the only orthodox Christian among the leading English academic philosophers in those years (which may explain why he never held a senior post in an English university – Scottish circles were less anti-Christian) and his clear restatement of the rational grounds for Christian theism within a context of modern thought was immensely valuable in its perceptive clarity and the skill with which the author neither claimed too much nor surrendered the truly important positions. Hoskyns was a young and little known Cambridge scholar in 1926; his quite brief article on 'The Christ of the Synoptic Gospels' is, nevertheless, little short of epoch-making in that it signals the turn of the tide in New Testament scholarship, from positions which in one way or another had rendered traditional Christian orthodoxy almost impossible to one from which tradition could, on the contrary, be well vindicated. His conclusion that 'the characteristic features of Catholic piety have their origin in Our Lord's interpretation of His own Person', rather than in a transformation of early Christian attitudes under the decisive impact of one form or another of Middle East paganism, was miles away from the 'fairly widespread agreement' among scholars of the preceding generation, but it would be supported by much British scholarship in the following twenty years.

In 1926 the tide, then, was for the discerning eye, just on the turn.[20] That can be claimed but no more than that. The books referred to here were important certainly, but all the same they were essentially the work of dissidents in the intellectual world of the 1920s. Taylor, Temple, Chesterton, Inge, were voices of weight, but they were very much the exceptions in a society where the Christian Church remained institutionally most important but in which Christian belief was profoundly discredited among the intellectual élite. It may be that the clergy, including Temple and Inge, did not quite realize this but Taylor and Chesterton most certainly did. They knew their isolation, they knew they were defending a cause which was regarded as little more than a joke by the ablest of their contemporaries, so contradictory was it to the whole body of modern science and received wisdom.

Yet the tide was on the turn and we may conclude this discussion by considering two converts to Christianity of the late

1920s, who were to have a very powerful influence on religious life in Britain over the next thirty years. Both came right out of the heart of the contemporary culture, from circles which took for granted atheism as being integral to 'the intellectual climate common to our own age'.[21] The first is T. S. Eliot.

Eliot was a brilliant young American, with an extraordinary flair for literature and a resolve to become very English. He was welcomed into the world of Bloomsbury, and from the autumn of 1922 was editor of a new literary magazine, the *Criterion*, as well as being a poet with a quickly growing reputation. Eliot's work drew upon a mass of symbolism and myth, increasingly religious. Can religious symbolism really make sense in an agnostic world? Eliot found that it could not and that the fashionable contemporary non-religion did not satisfy. He moved as a consequence from a spiritual identification with Bloomsbury towards one with a mythical 'Good King Charles's Golden Days' – the tradition of Anglican religious culture best formalized in the early seventeenth century and the household of Nicholas Ferrar in Little Gidding. In 1927 he was baptized and confirmed in the Church of England to the horrified amazement of his friends who were simply at a loss as to how to react to such strange behaviour. Thus I. A. Richards, with whom he was staying in Cambridge one weekend, wrote 'we were suddenly made aware of our total inability to advise on (or even discuss) the character of the various Services available on Sunday Mornings'.[22] Virginia Woolf's comment was equally revealing:

> I have had a most shameful and distressing interview with dear Tom Eliot, who may be called dead to us all from this day forward. He has become an Anglo-Catholic believer in God and immortality, and goes to church. I was shocked. A corpse would seem to me more credible than he is. I mean, there's something obscene in a living person sitting by the fire and believing in God.[23]

The case of C. S. Lewis is still more paradigmatically symbolic. Brought up on the rump of British Protestantism, in a particularly dreary Belfast form, he abandoned it with relief for atheism at his prep school. Fed on Frazer's *Golden Bough* and such like, he could declare confidently at eighteen that, 'All religions, that is all mythologies, to give them their proper name, are merely man's own invention – Christ as much as Loki.' There was now, he could inform his correspondent, a 'recognised scientific account of the growth of religions', and he accepted it.[24] In later years Lewis was able to look back on his youth and comment mockingly: 'Really, a young Atheist cannot guard his faith too carefully. Dangers lie in wait for him on every side.'[25] But in fact he guarded it well enough for quite a few years, though tending back through a 'watered Hegelianism' to the acceptance of a non-personal 'Absolute'. Then in 1926 Chesterton's *Everlasting Man* gave Lewis, for the first time, a Christian point of view which really made sense and made sense of things generally, and to that was added the same year the devastating admission by a hard-boiled atheist that the evidence for the historicity of the gospels was really rather good (perhaps he had been reading Hoskyns). ' "Rum Thing," he went on. "All that stuff of Frazer's about the Dying God. Rum thing. It almost looks as if it had really happened once." '[26] Christianity had been believed to be something utterly different from other religions by the old orthodox Protestant so that it could be absolutely true, the rest absolutely false. Frazer and his school had shown the two to be inextricably linked – and all, then, equally pointless and equally false. But what if all were in some way true, only Christianity the truest of them all? The very same material, the same links and similarities could be looked at again and seem to point in quite a different direction. Comparative religion far from undermining Christianity might actually render it more credible.

> You must picture me alone in that room in Magdalen, night after night, feeling, whenever my mind lifted even for a second from my work, the steady, unrelenting approach of Him whom I so earnestly desired not to meet. That which I greatly feared had at last come upon me. In the Trinity term of 1929 I gave in, and admitted that God was God, and knelt and prayed.[27]

It would take Lewis two more years to move from theism to Christianity, but it was for him a natural, indeed near inevitable, development. Like Eliot, committed to theistic religion, he soon found himself 'inexorably committed to the dogma of the Incarnation'.[28]

In their conversions to orthodox Christianity, Lewis and Eliot were undoubtedly and even self-consciously adopting something of a critical, even reactionary, anti-modernism *vis-à-vis* the consensus of their clever contemporaries. Now the most clearly reactionary position of any Church was that of the Roman Catholic and it can usefully be asked – as they were indeed asked from time to time – why they did not become Roman Catholics. In Rome there had been no truck with modernism and this was proving its great attraction for reactionaries, for all who refused to submit to the great corpus of modern certainties, including such brilliant converts as Ronald Knox and Evelyn Waugh. Lewis was greatly influenced in the course of his conversion not only by Chesterton's *Everlasting Man* but by close Catholic friends like Tolkien and Griffiths. If Eliot had not comparable Catholic friends he quickly adopted a more self-consciously 'Catholic' and reactionary position than did Lewis. His considerable dependance upon Maurras was certainly not typically Anglican and reminds one instead of Belloc. Yet his penchant for a self-consciously 'royalist' rather than democratic social model to link with his Christian belief, if it owed much to Maurras, mirrored too the royalism of seventeenth-century Anglican divines for whom 'Kings are by God appointed'. The *Action Française* of Maurras had anyway just been condemned by Pius XI and Eliot's urge to be thoroughly English in his religiosity could hardly have been satisfied by Roman Catholicism, at a time when ultramontanism reigned supreme. Again, Lewis's residual Northern Irish Protestantism made him very unresponsive to the ritualism and clericalism of Rome or indeed to the ritualism and clericalism of much of Anglicanism. He was and remained a very lay, and rather Protestant, Anglican, in his religious practice still more than in his belief and apologetic.

There can be little doubt that the influence of Eliot and Lewis was very much greater in the long run on account of their becoming Anglicans and not Roman Catholics. It is true that Christopher Dawson, whose most influential book, *Progress and Religion*, was published in 1929, was a Catholic. Dawson's influence was wide indeed – and still more among non-Roman Catholics than among Catholics – yet he was refused a professorship at Leeds in 1933 effectively on account of his religion. If he had been a less retiring figure, he would have felt the limitations more acutely. It was from within the Established Church, and not from elsewhere, that the main religious battle of the coming decades would still have to be fought in this country. It was important that a deliberate intellectual rejection of the common mind of modern man should not lead as a sort of corollary to the embracing of ecclesiastical ultramontanism. That this continued to be the case was the achievement of Anglo-Catholicism, despite its many distinguished losses to Rome. In the inter-war period Roman Catholics had neither the national position nor the ecclesiastical freedom to be the principal protagonists for English Christianity. If more Anglo-Catholics had 'poped', if men like Lewis and Eliot had felt that the Church of England was now so modernist that an orthodox Christian committed to the Catholic tradition could no longer remain within it with honesty, then Roman Catholicism would only have been marginally strengthened while the cause of Christianity would have been immeasurably weakened. Above all, in the Anglican camp it would prove far easier than in the Catholic to overcome the modernist/reactionary divide, to show that a Christian could be orthodox without being socially reactionary or belittling the immense positive achievements of contemporary scholarship, modern without kicking away the supernatural. At the start of the 1920s the intellectual prospect for Christianity as a living component of contemporary culture had looked grim enough on almost every front: anthropology, philosophy, biblical studies, history, poetry, the novel. In many areas the battle was indeed hardly being fought at all. What major figures survived, such as von Hügel and Gore, were old and rather tired. Ten years later the situation can have seemed at the time little better, though ecclesiastical attention was distracted by internal squabbling and the débâcle over the Prayer Book. Yet in fact the ranks were being reformed and this just at a time when the consensus of the secular majority was about to fall apart under the far more intense pressures and partisan loyalties of the 1930s.

PART III

The 1930s

A

13

Domestic Politics

The New York stock market collapsed on 24 October 1929 to trigger off a major economic depression throughout the world. It seems hard to imagine a more absurd chain of events or one more clearly indicting the capitalist system, but so it was. Unemployment soared, political extremism spread and a hitherto moderately hopeful world situation became very quickly a frighteningly unpredictable one. In Britain the effect was muffled, as so often, by the stability of the structures and the underlying moderation of the central body of public opinion. There were over two million unemployed by the middle of 1930 and nearly three million from the summer of 1931 until early 1933. The minority Labour government, in office since June 1929, could not cope with the consequent dilemma of how to reconcile its principles with the Treasury's insistence that unemployment benefit must be reduced, and it gave way in August 1931 to a National government, still headed by Ramsay MacDonald but effectively Conservative. That was the point – we may mark it pretty precisely – at which, for Britain, 'the Twenties' gave way to 'the Thirties'. Most Labour MPs rejected MacDonald's policy and were in their turn rejected by the nation. From then until his retirement as Prime Minister in May 1937, Baldwin was the decisive figure in British politics as he had been through most of the twenties. The General Election of 1931 gave the Conservatives and their allies over 60 per cent of the votes and over 500 of the seats – a victory unparalleled in any other British General

Election in modern times – and four years later, in November 1935, they did only a little less well, retaining 432 seats. Labour had made some recovery, the independent Liberals had faded further into insignificance. What matters is that a large majority of the nation backed Baldwin and his 'National' government all through the 1930s. The response to crisis was not – as in many countries – incipient revolution, it was not even a call to strike: few decades have had fewer serious strikes than the 1930s. It was a call for the sensible and the better off to close ranks behind a man whose motto was to 'avoid logic, love your fellow men . . .' The old Tory rural England and the old Liberal middle-class England and the new England of suburbia were all behind Baldwin. And with some reason. Despite later myths and nasty jolts from the foreign news bulletin, the 1930s were quite a good time for the middling Englishman who resolutely refused to be unduly perturbed by the ideological battles of the Continent.

If wages had fallen a little, prices were down more and the real income of the employed was steadily rising. A national slum crusade was launched, not ineffectively, in 1933. Never had so many houses been built, decent houses with their little gardens. In the twenties the annual average of new houses was 150 thousand; it reached 200 thousand by 1932, 300 thousand by 1934 and never fell below that figure again until 1939. House prices were cheap, mortgage rates low. Such houses were mostly in the south-east where unemployment was slight and mounting prosperity unquestionable. If in 1934 unemployment among insured workers was 44.2 per cent in Gateshead and 67.8 per cent in Jarrow, in High Wycombe it was only 3.3 per cent, in St Albans 3.9 per cent, in Coventry 5.1 per cent. There was more time for recreation. Little as it may seem to our latter-day eyes, a week's paid holiday was a great advance from no week off. It was in the 1930s that this became not universal but fairly normal and with it the youth hostel, the commercial holiday camp (the first Butlin's opened in 1937), and the weekly visit to the cinema. The latter was certainly the lushest symbol of the nice new world open to the millions of Britain's majority who voted for Baldwin. It was already an established institution in the twenties, when old theatres and concert halls were being turned into cinemas, but it attained its full chromium-plated splendour only in the thirties –

the populist temple of pleasurable modernity. In every High Street such a palace raised its beckoning head: weekly attendance at the parish church might be crumbling ominously, but weekly attendance at the Odeon or the Ritz was almost *de rigueur* for 1930s man. And behind the 'parish church' of the cinema stood the new cathedrals: in the middle of the decade in just eleven months rose the greatest – Denham Studios in south Buckinghamshire, the creation of Alexander Korda and the largest monument of the British film industry. Here, behind the thousand-foot long frontage, *The Scarlet Pimpernel*, *The Thief of Baghdad*, and *The Shape of Things to Come* were produced. Things to come: the majority England of the 1930s still believed in good things to come. With its eye firmly on the main chance, it backed Baldwin, it backed Chamberlain, it backed Alexander Korda.

There were however two other Englands, far less contented. The one was the third of the nation worst hit by the depression; the industrial north shared this privilege with Wales, Clydeside and Northern Ireland. It is curious that a period which showed the greatest parliamentary unity we have ever experienced outside war was the age in which in modern times the division of the country into two separate nations was most marked. It was not perhaps that the condition of people in the north was materially so much worse now than it had been earlier, because it had long been ghastly, in work or out of work, and heavy unemployment in much of the north was not an invention of the 1930s. This time unemployment certainly lasted longer, was more heavily concentrated in certain areas and went, indeed, with a new hopelessness as the industries themselves upon which the people depended for the little they had were so clearly decaying; but it was also the case that the marked improvement in living conditions of the south-east was pointing up more emphatically than ever a difference which had always existed. The one was getting richer, the other still poorer; and the two nations seldom met, except when hunger marchers from the north were viewed uneasily as they tramped, unavailing yet dignified, through the streets of some southern town. There seemed plenty of hope for the people of High Wycombe in the 1930s, but none at all for those of Jarrow or Gateshead or the mining villages round Bishop Auckland: of the thirty-three pits in that area, normally employing 28 thousand men, seventeen were abandoned and the rest only partially at work, with 6,500 men, not all on full time. At West Auckland only a hundred men out of a thousand had had work in seven years.[1] If the bishop of Durham in his palace of Auckland Castle lived surrounded by such a depressed world, the physical proximity did little to bridge the gap of experience and incomprehension. Smoky England on the dole standing numbly in a soup queue, its children unlikely to pass educationally beyond the primary school, was a world unbelievably remote from public schools and Oxbridge colleges and bishops' palaces or even from a nice new semi-detached in High Wycombe. Only Hitler would break down the middle wall that lay between them.

Others however would have liked to try. There was a third England in the 1930s – that of the ideologically committed, of the outraged, of the idealists, stirred up in admiration, loathing or simple fear by the depression at home and the spread of Fascism abroad. We will return to this group, limited in number, but with an importance vastly beyond its numbers: Communists, Fascists, Pacifists, Re-armers, Oxford Group. Here were the intellectuals, the writers, the prophets, rather too many of them. Where the majority was apathetic, they were strident; where the majority was blind, they were only too aware of the approach of either disaster or a great new order. It would be impossible to describe the 1930s while ignoring the new intense politicization of those years. The danger is that with the rise of Nazism and the shadow of the Second World War falling backwards, nothing else is thought worthy of notice. It remains necessary to pay due attention to the more prosaic life of the nation and of the Church, the world which still deferred to Baldwin, Lang and Dawson of *The Times*; later we will turn our minds to these new complexities.

1936 was the year of the Jarrow Hunger March. It was also the year of the Abdication. In January George V died and was succeeded by the Prince of Wales, Edward VIII. Edward wanted to be a modern kind of king. The rather decorous traditionalism of his father had irked him a little. He liked brighter clothes, smaller houses, aeroplanes, sympathized with the unemployed and wanted to marry a twice-divorced American lady named Mrs

Simpson. Baldwin, ageing but still Prime Minister, decided that this last would be a disaster. He was backed by the Cabinet and the Dominion governments and presented the king with a straight choice: not to marry Mrs Simpson or to abdicate. Edward had hoped that at least a morganatic marriage might be possible (Mrs Simpson becoming his wife but not queen). He had his sympathizers, most important of whom was Churchill, who would have liked to put up a fight, but the king was no fighter and faced with his government's conviction he abdicated without a struggle but not without honour. The nation as a whole knew nothing about the matter until in December it was almost over. News of the crisis was followed within a week by the king's abdication on the 11th, in favour of his brother the Duke of York, and departure from the country.

There can be no doubt that this was a political not a religious decision. There can also be no doubt that Archbishop Lang, who was of course consulted by Baldwin, wholly agreed with Baldwin's view – the alternative he described as 'a sort of nightmare'. Some even accused Lang of having imposed the abdication, which he might theoretically have been able to do by refusing to crown a king married (or about to be married) to a divorcee. Yet Lang's role was certainly not of such a kind, though his broadcast to the nation on Sunday, 13th, gave it an appearance of greater weight than it had actually had. Baldwin described this broadcast as 'the voice of Christian England', but it was not. Lang, unfortunately, was a master of words, of an eloquent but oily kind, easily betrayed by his very facility with them.

> What pathos, and what tragedy, surrounds the central figures of these swiftly moving scenes! . . . With characteristic frankness he has told us his motive. It was a craving for private happiness. Strange and sad it must be that for such a motive, however strongly it pressed upon his heart, he should have disappointed hopes so high and abandoned a trust so great. Even more strange and sad it is that he should have sought his happiness in a manner inconsistent with the Christian principles of marriage, and within a social circle whose standards and ways of life are alien to all the best instincts and traditions of his people.[2]

Such emotional moralizing at a moment when everyone felt bruised and in need of silence was far too histrionic to be the voice of England, too judgmental to be authentically Christian. It produced intense bitterness among many, and Henson's unfaltering judgement of 'bad taste . . . arrogant egotism . . . affectation of pontifical moralising . . . lack of generous feeling'.[3]

No archbishop had ever been closer to the royal family than Lang. He had been George V's most intimate confidant and was by his side when he died. He was not wrong to see the marriage of his successor to Mrs Simpson as a nightmare both for himself and the Church. The religious importance of the monarchy in the twentieth century must not be underestimated and that importance has depended at once upon ceremony, upon belief and upon moral example. Edward's proposed marriage threatened the constitutional position and inner being of the Church of England as probably no other single event has done this century. In the often strongly agnostic atmosphere of the political establishment the Established Church has been immensely fortified by the support it has received both from the ritual and from the personalities of the monarchy – George V, George VI and Elizabeth II especially. Their own Christian beliefs and model family life have given authenticity to the recurrent royal rituals when Church and monarchy are seen as united and together still central to the life of the nation. Had Edward been permitted to marry Mrs Simpson and remain king, the public significance of the Church of England could not but have been immeasurably diminished. Effectively a divorce would almost inevitably have resulted between monarchy and Church to the grave weakening of both. Instead the opposite happened. The broadcasting of the coronation of George VI in May 1937 proved a great religious experience. Religious and royal ritual, when well-conducted – and no one in the world does it as well as Anglicans at their sober but traditional best – seems particularly adapted to radio and, still more, television. But the religious strength of the monarchy present beneath the pageantry has derived from the great consistency which three generations have shown in their unassuming commitment to Christian worship, the practice of Christian marriage and a very high sense of public duty.

What mattered most, the abdication or the Jarrow hunger

march? Each in its way represented a life and death struggle within one segment of national life – the monarchy upon the one hand, the northern poor upon the other. The abdication still draws more historical coverage than the hunger march, despite easily appearing an élitist and superficial topic in comparison with the desperate plight of the Jarrow unemployed. Yet such is England. The Pilgrims of Grace in the sixteenth century were no less expendable than the Jarrow marchers. The north has never ruled England, still less the northern poor. The monarchy has, and the abdication conflict represented a genuine challenge to the Establishment's inner logic in a way that the marchers did not, a challenge to the linked traditional forces that in an unwritten alliance still governed the land. The proletariat was not about to win the class war, it did not – poor, dear, depressed thing that it was – even dream of doing so. It just wanted a little work and a little more bread. It is not wrong, though it is sad, that a historian – even, and particularly, a historian of the Church – should almost brush them aside with a condescending smile and turn back to the world of Stanley Baldwin and Cosmo Lang.

14

The Church of England

'What a great man he must be, seeing that we all discuss him so much,' Temple once remarked (maybe with tongue in cheek) of Cosmo Lang, whom he succeeded both at York and at Canterbury.[1] Lang was indeed a fascinating topic for discussion, a man of so many characters, the inner workings of his personality hidden far more mysteriously than in most great ecclesiastics beneath the varied public roles which he played through a long and highly successful career with such masterful virtuosity. No man this century has been longer an archbishop in England than this Glasgow lad. Of no other is it so hard to assess his true significance.

As a young man he shone in the world of intelligence as a Fellow of All Souls; he slaved for years in the slums as a curate in Leeds and as a model parish priest in Portsea. As an archbishop he cultivated the houses of the very rich and the plaudits of the very powerful. Each part he played meticulously to perfection but it was the proud, pompous prelate that, by the thirties, appeared to the world to have long prevailed. The knowledge that he had practised his signature as Archbishop of Canterbury, 'Cosmo Cantuar', for years before it was his, and that after using it for the first time authentically was able to write, 'This has always seemed to me, and to others, a very happy and euphonious signature', is deeply distasteful. A close friend who once said of him: 'He might have been Cardinal Wolsey or St Francis of Assisi, and he chose to be Cardinal Wolsey',[2] provides a fearful indictment but one that seems to come cruelly close to the mark.

Lang excelled as the extremely able religious figure operating within some forum of the secular establishment and able to impart, smoothly and painlessly, the appropriate spiritual note,[3] be it to the Trustees of the British Museum (of whom he was a most successful ex officio chairman), the joint parliamentary commission upon the Indian Constitution, the Lord Mayor's Banquet, the Fellows of All Souls, or simply the House of Lords. A far cleverer man than Davidson, though hardly a more original or learned man, he lacked his predecessor's sureness of touch, combining unctuousness with snobbery in a way that left a bad taste in many people's mouths.

Lang had been twenty years Archbishop of York when he was appointed to Canterbury in 1928 and it was perhaps a pity that Baldwin regarded him – as of course did many other people – as the obvious successor to Davidson. Someone of the younger generation – Temple or Bell or Garbett – might have been a better choice. A sentimental high churchman, Lang always avoided being ecclesiastically controversial, while in fact quietly presiding over the transformation of Anglican ritual from the Protestant to the Catholic. As Archbishop of Canterbury he provided no effective leadership for the Church in either its ecclesiastical or its social dilemmas. That is not surprising. He was a Victorian, flanked on the episcopal bench by too many other distinguished Victorians – Winnington-Ingram in London, Headlam in Gloucester, Henson in Durham. All were men who had made their mark before the death of Queen Victoria but were badly at sea in the very different world of the 1930s, if by no means in agreement in the mode of their conservatism: Lang and Winnington-Ingram had patronized the incoming Anglo-Catholic tide, while Headlam and Henson were disturbed by it. The last two agreed in many things – natural allies, it long seemed, in the defence of a broad Protestantism, as in distrust of William Temple and all he stood for, though they came to disagree sharply over Nazi Germany. Lang, Headlam and Henson all sensed in the 1930s that the Church of England as they had known it – a body truly central to the affairs of the nation, naturally recruiting into its clergy many of the ablest young men at Oxford and Cambridge, highly hierarchical, intellectually tolerant, a genuinely Established Church – was fading away. The House of Commons vote of 1928 seemed to have left the Church without any tenable view of its own spiritual authority but nothing was being done about it. Henson recognized this the clearest and the most gloomily. For him the Church was 'moving like a rudderless vessel over a rock-haunted ocean' and at the end of the decade he published a pessimistic account of it all which he considered but 'a faithful picture of an effete establishment'.[4]

Headlam's response was to try and put the clock back – cling on to parish schools, resist the professionalization of the clergy produced by the theological colleges, block any shift to the left. He was not imaginative. Formerly Professor of Theology in London and Oxford he was a learned but a dull theologian. When Dorothy Sayers forsook detective stories for religious writing, Headlam expostulated, 'Why should she? I can write all the theology that is necessary but I can't write detective stories.'[5] Yet forty years on, who would even think of turning to Headlam's theology? *The Man Born to be King* may still be read. Lang's response to the malaise of the Church was to do as little as possible: *après moi le déluge*. Hold on as long as possible to the way we have known it. Different as these men were in their formal opinions, they shared a common presupposition about the way things were – more a social than a theological presupposition – a view of the Church national, Tory, and somewhat despondent.

The group of laymen who governed the Church in alliance with the bishops right up to the end of the decade saw matters little differently. It was indeed the lay Tory control of the Church Assembly which ensured that no odd outburst of some liberal cleric should unduly disturb the policies of the Establishment. The Church Assembly of the 1930s was not accidentally located at Westminster: the bonds which tied it to parliament and to the Conservative Party within parliament were strong and fully at work. Some dozen Tory MPs, half of them Eton or Winchester boys, were members of it, but still more important remained the effective control of business in the House of Laity by the Cecil family and their relatives. The earl of Selborne, who had chaired the Ecclesiastical Commission of 1916 which had initially proposed the assembly, remained chairman of the House of Laity until the 1940s. His father, the first earl of Selborne, had been a distinguished Lord Chancellor in the 1870s; a high churchman of great piety and an authority on hymns, he had chaired the House of Laity of the Province of Canterbury and wrote in his old age *A Defence of the Church of England against Disestablishment.* His son, the second earl, faithfully continued in that tradition, and he was not alone. Five of his family were members of the House of Laity: his son Lord Wolmer; his son-in-law Earl Grey; his brothers-in-law the Marquess of Salisbury and Lord Hugh Cecil; his sister-in-law Lady Florence Cecil. Another brother-in-law, Robert Cecil, chaired the Church-State Commission of 1936. Selborne, Hugh Cecil and Grey were members of the Standing Committee of the Church Assembly. Grey was chairman of the Central Board of Finance, Hugh Cecil of the Standing Orders Committee. If one adds to the group a few other powerful long-sitting laity such as Sir Philip Wilbraham, Bt, secretary of the assembly from its inception until 1939, Lord Daryngton, vice-chairman of the House of Laity, and Richard Denman, MP for Central Leeds (Westminster and Balliol), who were also the three Church Estates Commissioners, one is faced with the picture of a lay oligarchy of high Tory commitment effectively managing the Church's government for twenty years. To it they devoted much time and a most conscientious sense of responsibility. Their links with parliament both enhanced the status of the Church Assembly and controlled it. Their aristocratic independence, political experience, wealth and public position at once effectively silenced other lay elements in the Church and maintained a rein on episcopal innovation. The Church of England in the 1930s, it is not too exaggerated to say, was controlled less by Lang and Temple in tandem, than by Lang and Hugh Cecil. It would be entirely naïve to point to the moderately radical opinions of Temple or Bell as proof that the Church of England had now a left-wing rather than a right-wing slant. It is rather the case that the establishment of the Church Assembly and its control by the believing aristocracy ensured a more consistently Conservative Church in the period after the First World War than in preceding decades.

As the national character of the national Church quietly diminished, the shrinkage was upwards rather than downwards. In Oxford and Cambridge, in the political establishment, in intellectual circles, in the public schools, there was a noticeable revival of Christianity, Anglican Christianity above all, by the later 1930s. In the nation as a whole, however, the Church's position was slipping steadily enough. There were over 500 thousand Anglican baptisms annually in the twenty-five years before the war. The figure went below 500 thousand for the first time in 1916; after 1922 it never reached it again until after the Second World War. In 1932 it fell below 400 thousand and remained there throughout the decade. Confirmations had been well over 200 thousand almost every year until 1928. Thereafter they never reached that figure and had decreased to 157 thousand by 1939. Forty per cent of elementary school children were in Anglican schools in 1900; 22 per cent by 1938. The process of contraction which Anglicanism was undergoing was undoubtedly in this period reinforcing the existing imbalances. Chaplaincy in public schools was becoming a rather more effective and serious ministry; the Church's presence in Oxford and Cambridge was considerable as ever. It was in regard to the elementary schools, the new universities, the inner cities of the industrial north, the rural working class, that the Church's continued withdrawal was most apparent.

The battle was not, however, going unfought. The 1930s episcopal bench was filled not only with distinguished septuagenarians but also with a number of very able younger men, George Bell (Chichester), Kenneth Kirk (Oxford), Cyril Garbett (formerly Southwark, in the 1930s Winchester), William Temple above all. The odd fact is that in several ways the decade was a time of marked Anglican revival, of renewed life and confidence, of some distinguished leadership. If confirmations were down ordinations were decidedly up. If the shackles of Establishment inertia still clung heavily to the institutional Church and if processes of decline, begun much earlier, were manifesting themselves even more ominously than in the past, there was by the 1930s a more coherent and convincing response to such challenges than previously – a theological, liturgical, pastoral and social response. This could hardly have been the case without the presence of William Temple, now as Archbishop of York arrived almost at the peak of his career. If Baldwin was anything but adventurous in moving Lang from York to Canterbury, he certainly counterbalanced this by transferring Temple from Manchester to York at the age of forty-seven.

We do not want a history of English Christianity in the first half of the twentieth century to look little more than a history of William Temple. That would, of course, be a great misrepresentation and yet it is hard at times to stop it from seeming a little like that, so considerable and far ranging were Temple's activities. This is perhaps the best moment to consider his personality in the years of his greatness, so obviously contrasting in many ways with Cosmo Lang (yet both were Balliol men, both were greatly influenced by the philosopher Edward Caird and both had had to struggle hard with doubt before ordination and the serene convictions of maturity). Lang was born humbly and cocooned himself with the trappings of high society; Temple was born to the purple and glad as archbishop to open his own front door. Lang, like Davidson before him, felt thoroughly at home in the House of Lords; for Temple it seemed a slightly alien environment. He felt far more at home when addressing the crowds on Blackpool beach or over the BBC, or chairing some ecumenical assembly. Such comparisons may seem unfair to Lang who was after all a brilliant and faithful defender of the tradition with which he had identified himself. Maybe as many a convert his fidelity had come close to caricaturing it; but he had done his best and if, in retrospect, one feels that he had overvalued the advantages of being at home with worldliness in a highly civilized and spiritual way, yet that has been after all a very principal characteristic of the upper Anglican clerical tradition. Barchester was no invention of Lang's. Only, by the 1930s, other things were really more important. Lang stood as final sentinel to the *ancien régime*. Temple who knew that régime through and through and was far too mellow to despise it, yet stood all his days for a new and different order, irritating and depressing to some, irresistible to others. He was the ecclesiastical Pied Piper who carried off the curates, while the old men – Henson, Headlam, Inge – shook their heads in repudiation of all he stood for. Yet he was no populist either.

'To a man of my generation an Archbishop of Temple's enlightenment was a realized impossibility,' declared Bernard Shaw. Temple was a modern man, as Gore, Lang, Henson, Headlam were not. He was modern intellectually, but still more socially, in his personal behaviour, able to participate with sympathy, with a sense of real identification and confidence, in the new world of the Labour Party, the BBC, the cinema, a League of Nations world. Nothing is more important to remember about him than that he was president of the Workers' Educational Association before ever he was ordained. There was a quite extraordinary wholeness about Temple, a profoundly serious concern for all things and everyone: the interpretation of the gospel, the immediate needs of the common man, the reunion of Christendom, philosophy, the educational system, the Church's pastoral care. He was, most probably, less of an original thinker than he appeared in any of these fields, but he was a leader in all of them. With superb intelligence, infectious enthusiasm and endless activity, he seized on the new ideas of the SCM, the WEA, friends like Tawney and Oldham, or overseas thinkers like Niebuhr and Maritain and flung them forth in crusade upon crusade of which he was always the leader. Temple provided leadership as no one else in the Christian Church of the twentieth century has quite managed to do. He gave it not only to the Church of England but in an increasingly wide measure to the whole Christian ecumene. This was made possible by a remarkable range of qualities. The first was his sheer intellectual mastery of so many areas of thought. The second was his exceptional skill to knit together the contrasting. He was always the recognizable Liberal, yet always too the equally recognizable Establishment figure and somehow he never lost for long the confidence of left or right. He was the reconciler who, in his own words, had the 'habitual tendency to discover that everybody is quite right',[6] and somehow to succeed in demonstrating such discoveries with acceptable formulas. The third was the calmness of his own life, the cheerfulness, the great laugh, the sense of rock-like unhysterical conviction, the perennial approachableness.

Had he no faults? They were the reverse side of both his qualities and his achievement. So genial, so unpompous, so peaceable, so successful a man could in the last analysis not quite cope with the demonic, or just the obstinately unreasonable. Must there not be some rational formula to resolve each difference? He lacked in his own harmonious life the experience of passion, grave conflict, sheer tragedy. In the conference room he could always find an answer but faced at the time with the Treaty of Versailles, or the General Strike or the advance of Nazism, he tended to temporize, to pour out a mass of sophisticated verbiage which neither really enlightened nor alleviated the conflict. He was then a man for consensus, for a progressive consensus, and where he could carry a consensus – above all within the newly developing ecumenical circles – he marched cheerfully forward. Where he could not do so because issues were too intractable, human divisions too sharp, he shrank instinctively from any sort of sectarian or party leadership, retreating rather within the banal or simply into the pursuit of other causes. He was not a man to be in a minority. He lacked the hard, always potentially partisan quality of leadership to be found in Churchill or Bell.

Encouraged in part by Temple's genial inspiration, much was happening that he could not quite have taken up himself. The revival of Anglican Christian life after the scepticism and disarray of the 1920s first fully surfaced with the Oxford Mission preached by Temple in 1931. For F. R. Barry, at that time vicar of St Mary's and probably one of the sanest clerics of the age, it was 'a decisive moment in the history of that generation . . . it was when the "tide began to come in"'.[7] Certainly for many a churchman, however inconvenient the anomalies of Church-State relations might remain, the ship in the 1930s was far from 'rudderless'. Old men might not see or sympathize with what was happening but in fact a new coherent and defensible pattern of Church life was being established, a new relationship with the nation, a new Anglican synthesis. The character of the renewal may, perhaps, best be indicated by a consideration of five symbolic books.

The first was a threepenny pamphlet, *The Challenge of the Slums*, produced by Bishop Garbett in 1933. Garbett really knew what he was talking about, both urban and rural slums, and frequently spoke with great effectiveness upon the subject. He was by no means the most intellectual of bishops but he may well have been the most pastoral, with a sound intelligence and good judgment about what really mattered to people now. What mattered to ordinary people in the 1930s were housing and unemployment, and bad housing mattered to even more people than did unemployment. Here was a down to earth challenge which a caring Church could face pretty unideologically and might get the nation to face. The 1930s was the first decade in which government did start doing something on a reasonably large scale to cope with the problem and the stimulus provided by the Housing Aid societies, pioneered by Basil Jellicoe, Garbett and other churchmen, was by no means insignificant. The national Church was at least showing an accurate sense of what the nation most needed. To point the moral, in Leeds in November 1933 Labour gained control of the City Council and Charles Jenkinson, vicar of the slum parish of St John and St Barnabas and Labour's spokesman on housing, found himself chairman of the council's Housing Committee, just as John Wilcockson had been ten years earlier at Farnworth.[8] Jenkinson might be called a Catholic modernist. Born in Poplar, at one time the disciple of Conrad Noel, he was a splendidly practical man and in no time he was demolishing back-to-back slum houses at the rate of 3,000 a year. He thus 'wiped out' his own parish and in the end had to pull down his own church too. Rebuilding was equally vigorous so that Leeds soon became 'the Mecca of all housing reformers'.[9] Jenkinson was of course quite atypical of the clergy, yet his achievement does suggest both the vigour of Anglican Catholicism at its best and the local role which a strong vicar could still quite easily play on the local scene in the 1930s.

Our second book is *Men without Work*, a 450 page Report on Unemployment published in 1938 by the Pilgrim Trust. The report had been produced by a team of enquirers established by a Committee on Unemployment brought together by Temple and including Bishop Bell, Lindsay of Balliol, Sir Walter Moberly and J. H. Oldham. The importance for us of this document is not just the subject but the efficiency with which it was tackled. It has generally been recognized as 'the best social study of unemployment made in the thirties'.[10] Its value is not questionable and its existence in an area of such major concern to national life is adequate response to people who still assert that social do-gooding of the Temple type is both ignorant and ineffectual. It did however contain its own message for the Church. Here, perhaps for the first time outside the field of education, it had moved from an amateur to a fully professional model in approaching a social problem. *Men Without Work* limited the frontiers of its subject and made a lasting contribution which the

COPEC reports of ten years earlier had too obviously failed to do.

Our third choice is *Murder in the Cathedral*. Eliot was invited to write it by Bell for the Canterbury Festival of 1935 and it was first acted in the Cathedral Chapter House on 15 June that year. It was acclaimed at once, and consistently since, as a major literary and religious creation. The image of the Martyr standing alone for the freedom of the spiritual kingdom, until struck down by the lacqueys of the latest tyrant, while a chorus of wailing women stand helplessly by, was as relevant to the age of the Duce and the Führer as to that of Henry II – or Henry VIII. *Murder in the Cathedral* was only one of a number of remarkable religious works produced in England in the 1930s within the Catholic tradition, Anglican or Roman. In the field of art it demonstrated that Christianity could still work, just as *Men Without Work* did so. Each in its own area proved the contemporary Church to be both efficient and imaginative.

My fourth and fifth books are selected to reveal more precisely what the contemporary Church at its freshest was trying to become. One is Michael Ramsey's *The Gospel and the Catholic Church* (1936), the other *The Parish Communion* edited by Fr Hebert (1937). Both have been highly influential books and together they represent, after decades of Anglo-Catholic *Angst*, something of an achieved position in which Anglican tradition is reconciled with the renewal of Catholic insight. 1928 had left the Church in an impasse over liturgy as much as over authority, but the liturgical impasse had not been engineered by parliament but through the head-on collision of the Anglo-Catholic revival and the traditional worship of the Church of England. The revised Prayer Book had in fact satisfied next to nobody, it was an institutional compromise of a kind which did real justice to neither side. The unrevised Prayer Book was undoubtedly unsatisfactory in various ways, but the only alternative ideal – the ultimate source of most Anglo-Catholic inspiration – had appeared to be the Roman mass of that age, highly clericalist, intensely sacrificial in its stress, a solemn ritual in which the laity had a very limited part to play. Yet on the Continent in some Catholic circles a new liturgical movement was developing, aimed precisely at overcoming these disadvantages. Dom Lambert Beaudouin[11] and the other pioneers of liturgical reform were reasserting the mass as being as much communion as sacrifice, a collective prayer in which the faithful should actively participate and which should really constitute the sacrament and focal point of Church life. The liturgy, they said, cannot be left to priests or monks. Their message was very much that of the early Protestant reformers and when, years later, at the Second Vatican Council it was at last endorsed by the Catholic Church it would have a profoundly revolutionary effect on Catholic life everywhere. If in the meantime English Catholics were deaf to the words of Beaudouin some Anglicans were beginning to take up the message with avidity.[12] *The Parish Communion* was the result. It transformed the Catholic sacramental emphasis in a direction which the heirs of the Reformation could accept. To the impasse of the 1920s it provided a way through. The enthusiasm of Anglo-Catholicism could now be directed less to the remote sacerdotal glory of the 'Solemn High Mass' which any middle of the road Anglican somehow gibbed at, than to a parish communion which could combine what was best in both Catholic and Protestant traditions. The worst polarization in the twenties had been over the Anglo-Catholic yearning for reservation. Now the underlying Protestant fear of reservation was that it went with a pattern of eucharistic belief and devotion which effectively undermined the primacy of communion: in the solemn high mass there was very probably no congregational communion at all; for the latter, as the high point of eucharistic devotion, the spiky Anglo-Catholic seemed to be substituting the adoration of the host in benediction. This has been characteristic enough of post-Tridentine Catholicism, but now the liturgical revival was drawing Catholic sacramentalists back from that extremity to re-assert the primacy of the people's communion, and by doing so to re-establish a basic unity of understanding with the Protestant tradition. Reservation could then again be seen as genuinely a help to communicating the sick and as a bogey the issue largely faded away.

Of *The Parish Communion* a recent commentator has remarked: 'Few, if any collections of essays have had such a dramatic effect on the life of a Church.'[13] If *The Parish Communion* points towards a new Anglican reconciliation in worship between 'Protestant' and 'Catholic', *The Gospel and the Catholic Church* points towards a comparable reconciliation in theology. Michael Ramsey was a young man, clearly within the Anglo-Catholic tradition but equally clearly breaking out of its characteristic narrownesses in both an 'Evangelical' and a more truly 'Catholic' direction to write what has remained a classic of ecumenical theology. 'The recovery of unity,' he declared, 'is hindered whenever Catholicism is identified with something less than itself', such as papal government or Greek theology, and he appealed to Anglican Catholics with their greater freedom, 'to teach the richest and deepest meaning of the word Catholic and to find the *essence* of Catholicism not in particular systems of government or thought or devotion (Anglican or Latin), but in the organic, corporate idea of the Body in life and worship'.[14]

These two books, for all their individual significance, were in no way isolated phenomena. Rather do they represent a growing consensus in the thinking Church of the 1930s and something of a new normative centre for Anglicanism. In this way they succeeded better than the much laboured-over report, *Doctrine in the Church of England*, which was published in 1938 by a Doctrinal Commission appointed back in 1922 and mostly presided over by Temple. It was a pondered, rather dull document, as was inevitable given the drawn out circumstances and varied views of its producers. Its better parts on the Church and the sacraments reflect the new catholicizing trends to be found in Ramsey; most of the rest is – for the late 1930s – rather anachronistically liberal and modernist.[15] It decided nothing, stimulated little. In contrast *The Gospel and the Catholic Church* stands as something of a living synthesis, not untying all individual knots by any means, but pointing forward to the road that Anglicans, and not only Anglicans, would come increasingly to follow.

The Free Churches

In the early 1930s Isaac Foot was Liberal MP for Bodmin. A Plymouth solicitor, a splendid orator, a passionate lover of books and of learned literacy, a devotee of Cromwell and Milton, a West Country Methodist, Foot represented in all its glory, delightfully but rather ineffectually, a disappearing tradition. He was the quintessential Christian 'radical', with his head in the clouds of Whig history, rooted in the traditions of Devon and Cornwall: non-Anglican Protestant in religion, Liberal in politics, old-fashioned in manners. His aspirations were as noble as those of Sylvester Horne and as remote as his from the realities of twentieth-century politics, remote even from what remained of the living lower-class springs of Nonconformity. In his manor house of Pencrebar he could identify with the upper-class radicalism of his seventeenth-century heroes, but if he held the position he had in the hearts of west countrymen, it was in large part because his Methodism gave him a continued way in to the loyalty of men in a very different class from his own. In Cornwall Methodism remained a force, its village chapels open still to the winds of revival, of a native evangelism,[1] so Foot, a powerful preacher and vice-president of the church in 1937, made some West Country sense, but in terms of national politics he was already a glorious anachronism.

The Nonconformity of the 1930s was still recovering from the political bewitchment of Lloyd George. As he receded further and further from the centre of the political stage, so did it – perhaps with some relief. It had passed through the brief decades of seeming political significance to grow in maturity, even almost to outgrow the pursuit of power.

Methodist reunion, accomplished at the beginning of the

1930s, certainly did not bring with it the national centrality which, it had sometimes been predicted, must follow the unity of Wesleyans and Primitive Methodists. It brought with it a sense of rather elderly achievement – well-earned rest after a long day's work, appropriate enough for its septuagenarian leaders like Scott Lidgett or Sir Robert Perks. There was much the same feeling diffused by the celebration surrounding the centenary of the Congregational Union in 1931. What had gone was the sense of daring, of desire to scale the heights of national life or to convert the world. Nothing is more significant than the deliberately restrictive policy over ordinations which the United Methodist Church at once embarked upon. Out of the 168 candidates selected for 'further testing' in 1933 only fifty-five were accepted for ordination and much the same was true for the next ten years. By the early 1940s a shortage of ministers was actually developing in consequence and the number was eventually allowed to rise to nearly a hundred.[2] The point is that caution, retrenchment, moderation and good sense were now to be the deciding qualities of Free Church polity in regard to their own and national affairs. The appointment of Donald Soper in 1936, when only thirty-three to lead the Methodist 'West London Mission' from Kingsway Hall might well disguise this at the very centre of national life, for nobody's ministry can ever have been much more vigorous, outgoing and uninhibited than Soper's. Yet, despite his very extensive influence, he would always be the exception, even the *enfant terrible*, whose activities do not really reflect the reality of an increasingly staid and elderly Church.

Methodist unification was accompanied by a growing sense of wider Free Church unity. When in 1936 Leslie Weatherhead, a Methodist, was offered and accepted the ministry of the City Temple, the great Congregational church in Holborn, this was unanimously approved by the Methodist Conference, so that he did not lose his Methodist Church membership but even in due course became, while still there, President of Conference (in 1955). At the same time antagonism towards the Established Church and its schools, and even towards Catholicism and its characteristic practices, was fading away. In 1935 the Methodist Sacramental Fellowship was founded and the following year a

Free Church Symposium on *Public Worship*, edited by Nathaniel Micklem, showed that here too the principles of the liturgical revival were beginning to bear fruit. In scholarship C. H. Dodd, Manson and Micklem were merging the Free Church contribution more and more with the Anglican. Dodd's appointment as Norris Hulse Professor at Cambridge in 1935 signals both the full national recognition of Free Church learning and its near-inevitable harmonization within the emerging synthesis, both ecumenical and Catholic. In some ways Free churchmen were still the pace setters in Christian attitudes: Dodd in scriptural studies; Weatherhead in the reconciliation of religion with the new psychiatry; Bernard Manning and Maurice Powicke in the understanding of the relationship between the Middle Ages and the Reformation; Micklem, Oldham and Paton in interpreting and responding to the contemporary world. If the Methodist Arthur Henderson was, as Labour's Foreign Secretary, the most committed peacemaker in politics, the Presbyterians Paton and Oldham were more responsible than anyone else for the development of ecumenical institutions and a Christian sense of international social responsibility. Temple or Bell might stand in the limelight, but it was Paton and Oldham who, behind the scenes, did most to build up the confidence and the network of commitment from which the World Council of Churches was soon to emerge.

The strength, the sanity, the scholarship, the spiritual seriousness of the Free Churches in the England of the 1930s are then very clear. Their contribution to society rested undoubtedly upon a multitude of apparently thriving little chapels, still keeping up much the old sectarian life of Sunday schools and faith-teas and lantern lectures and revivalist preaching. Methodists still hired a special train to bring their members to Bradford or wherever for the annual conference. It was none the less true that this age of maturity was an age of decline, and for the wider understanding of the course of English Christianity, the fact of that decline is highly important. To it we must now turn.

In 1943 D. W. Brogan remarked in *The English People*: 'In the generation that has passed since the great Liberal landslide of 1906, one of the greatest changes in the English religious and social landscape has been the decline of Nonconformity.' It was, then, already unmistakably evident by the early 1940s. What had happened and why?

In the 1920s and 1930s the smaller and new sects undoubtedly prospered – Christian Science, Seventh Day Adventists, Jehovah's Witnesses, Assemblies of God,[3] Elim Foursquare Gospel Alliance.[4] The Association of the Churches of Christ – a small movement of basically Baptist congregations, which began in Britain in the 1830s – reached its maximum membership, 16,596, as late as 1930. 'The inter-war years were the heyday of Churches of Christ', its historian can remark,[5] but for the larger, older, more institutionally established bodies, the story is very different. The membership statistics of the principal Free Churches register a high watermark around 1906, followed by some years of slight ups and downs; by the 1930s the downs are becoming steady and apparently irreversible. Take the Baptists:[6]

1906	434,741
1916	408,029
1926	416,665
1936	396,531
1946	354,900

Relative to the rising total population of the country the fall was of course more serious than these figures suggest. Moreover with the numerical decline went a marked shift in geographical and class structure: away from the impoverished north, into the more prosperous but less deeply committed south-east. It is almost platitudinous to locate a thriving Methodism in Durham mining villages, a thriving Anglicanism in rural south-east England. But compare two areas of roughly ninety thousand people in the mid-1930s for Free Church ministerial provision: one in the north, Chester-le-Street, a Durham mining area, and one in the south, the Isle of Wight. The former had just seven ministers in all (6 Methodist, 1 Congregationalist); the latter thirty-one (17 Methodist, 8 Congregationalist and 6 Baptist).[7] The Isle of Wight was, admittedly, an old Methodist stronghold. But new congregations were multiplying in London suburbs and all across the prosperous south-east, yet they were not sufficient in number, or, still more, in real hard-core Free Church loyalty to compensate for the erosion of interest among the membership and the sheer ministerial withdrawal in the old working-class strongholds of the north.

Perhaps still more important, though related to this socially upward and southward movement, was a decline in the wider constituency, the penumbra, of Nonconformity. At the start of the century the full membership was very far indeed from being the totality of the effectively Nonconformist section of the population. Through the Sunday schools and numerous other activities vast numbers of other people were closely tied up with the Free Church community, and it was from the Sunday schools that full members were mostly recruited. Yet the Commission on Sunday Schools of the Methodist Conference in 1939 had to admit the 'serious decline' in Sunday school attendance, and declared that 'Unless the Sunday School can be revitalised, the future of the Church itself is threatened'.[8] It was indeed, but still more was its social influence.

Despite the painstaking launching of a 'Forward Movement' here, the reorganization of ministerial training there, nothing could in fact now stem the rapid wider shrinkage of the Nonconformist community, and it was that, more than the actual membership decrease, which made it so clear by the Second World War that the public significance of the Free Churches for English life had immeasurably diminished. The life of the community seemed simply to be ebbing away in the majority of churches. D. R. Davies returned to the Congregational ministry in 1939 after twelve years of ideological freelancing and was struck by the intervening decline of every sort – in the size and fervour of congregations, the interest in supporting missionaries, the lower intellectual quality of the ministry, the overall discouraging pressure of a constant shortage of money.[9]

The last serious attempt to treat Nonconformity as a politically significant force in the nation was Lloyd George's *Call to Action* of June 1935. Signed by the editors of the chief Nonconformist papers and such other ageing pundits as Scott Lidgett and J. D. Jones, it was widely seen as the 'Free Churches' Call to the Nation'. In theory it was a non-political move. In fact it was Lloyd George's desperate way of trying to get back to power on the old Nonconformist card which in the past he had played so effectively. But it could work no more. As a political constituency, at least outside Wales, Nonconformity no longer existed, and Scott Lidgett wholly failed to drum up Methodist backing for his old political ally. The structure of politics in England had changed remarkably with the collapse of Liberalism. The latter's Nonconformist base had split three ways. While a rump remained faithful to the Liberal Party as late as the 1950s, much of the middle-class Nonconformity of the south and Midlands, Wesleyan and Congregationalist especially, had moved naturally enough into the post-war Conservative Party. The latter, the party of Bonar Law, Austen Chamberlain and Baldwin, was indeed now their natural home: its rural and squirearchical base was declining, its urban middle-class constituency expanding. If Joseph Chamberlain could carry Birmingham, the ancient Mecca of Nonconformity, into a Conservative Unionist alliance already by the end of the nineteenth century, the rest of middle-class Nonconformity could quite easily follow thirty years later. The Conservative-Anglican alliance had in fact declined. It no longer kept the Free churchman from feeling sufficiently at home as a Tory. Nevertheless it did, as an ethos, still exist. If one could join the Conservative Party, one's old political adversary, could one not join the Church of England too? The realignment of politics was a catalyst encouraging a realignment of religious loyalties as well.

The other, and more working-class, half of the old Nonconformist-Liberal constituency went, of course, into the Labour Party and provided much of its spirit and several of its finest leaders. Nevertheless, this alliance, too, was in trouble. There were a score or more of Labour MPs who were at the same time lay preachers, strong on temperance and respect for the sabbath. But, at the local level, the two causes increasingly pulled apart. Labour meetings found room for a glass of beer. The good Methodist could sadly not approve where the working-class Catholic felt quite at home. Attitudes to temperance and alcohol may well have not a little to do with the growing Catholic presence in trade union leadership, the declining impact of the Nonconformist.[10] The young man of left wing inspiration and Free Church background was now most likely to be an agnostic. This had been a phenomenon within Nonconformist political leadership from the start of the century. It was now one of the rank and file.

This political realignment in inter-war England went with major social and cultural changes, equally to the disadvantage of traditional Nonconformity. There was the erosion of small communities, in which it had flourished; the cultural shift to the cinema, the radio and more serious elementary schooling, hence away from a mass of Church-organized leisure activities, the pleasure of listening to clerical oratory, and the mystique of the Sunday school. The battle over temperance and sabbath observance was increasingly alienating. The Free Churches were no longer strong enough to impose their viewpoint, only to ensure a great deal of ill-will, together with a psychological separation between their approved social world and that of the national consensus.

Again, ecclesiastically, the Free Churches had owed a great deal of their support to a very proper sense of outrage at the privileges of the Established Church and the way in which Anglican clergy shared in class privilege. Nonconformity fed upon the moral indignation of the lower class outsider, but as the privileges faded so did the indignation. By the 1930s both were largely things of the past. An intellectual like Micklem or Manning might still see the constitutional fact of Establishment as adequate ground for dissent, but for many people the issue had ceased to be a significant one. But if the old reasons for attacking the Church of England had largely faded away, then why not actually become an Anglican? The natural claims of the parish church reasserted themselves over those of chapel, especially for young people taught by movements like the SCM no more to cherish separations. Here as elsewhere ecumenism pointed towards the larger body.

In religious and social terms, after all, the Church of England was looking a great deal more attractive than it had done in the past: the Church of William Temple, Bishop Bell and T. S. Eliot, was a Church one could easily want to belong to – a Church with scale, leadership, spiritual vitality, theological diversity and at least something of a social conscience but without the secularization which the 'social gospel' had largely brought with it in Free Church life. The liturgical movement and the beauty of Anglican worship were again a draw. The Free Churches were having their sacramental revival too but somewhat feebly, hardly able to compete with the Church of England when it came to the beauty of buildings, church singing or sacramental ceremonial. They had not in fact much heeded Forsyth's warnings of a generation earlier. By and large they had too little doctrine and too little sacrament left. Micklem's *Public Worship* was quite untypical of 1930s Nonconformity. What was typical was the bromide *Manual for Ministers* produced by Congregationalism in 1936, of which Micklem remarked – almost understating the truth – that it was 'careful to say nothing that might offend the least believing member of any congregation'.[11] Soft forms of modernism, anti-Catholicism and the social gospel had eaten very deeply into the heart of the Free Churches, Congregationalism most of all. If people tended to find their way back to the Church of England, it was due less to the fact that they might there feel free to believe less than before (though that could be true), but rather that they were there encouraged to believe more than before and to worship more profoundly.

In 1943 E. L. Allen published a worried but revealing article:[12]

A few years ago one of my best friends, a Presbyterian minister, resigned his charge and 'went over', as we say in these cases, to the Church of England ... Shortly after, a Baptist Minister who, as pastor of a Union Church, had been uncompromising in his adherence to the principle of believers' immersion, re-appeared as an Anglican curate. Shortly after again, a Methodist minister remarked in the course of conversation that the position in his family was a singular one, since all his sons and daughters were confirmed members of the Church of England: within six months he had followed them. Congregationalists could relate many such incidents ... Ex-Free-Churchmen are everywhere in the Church of England; they live in bishops' palaces, hold canons' stalls, and lecture from professorial chairs ... Is it not time that we faced seriously this disconcerting fact of the drift towards Canterbury?

Two outstanding new bishops of the 1930s had in fact previously been Free churchmen: Rawlinson of Derby (appointed in 1936) was earlier a Congregationalist, Kirk of Oxford (appointed 1937) a Methodist. If leading Free churchmen did not themselves go Anglican, their sons could well do so – as likely as not under the influence of a public school. Such were Michael Ramsey and David Paton, two of the most stimulating young Anglican priests of the 1930s. Many others, of course, became agnostics: the post-Second World War leadership of the Labour Party would consist very largely of men without religious commitment, yet who were sons of devout Free churchmen, like Isaac Foot and Wedgwood Benn. One gets the impression that Nonconformity was simply crumbling away, unable any more to justify itself in the eyes of a questioning intelligence, Christian or non-Christian. If Leyton Richards, minister of Carr's Lane, that most famed of Congregationalist chapels, from 1924 to 1939, chose to end his days as a Quaker, this may not signify a precise rejection of Congregationalism, but it does suggest that anything very compelling was now lacking within it.

Perhaps the odd career of D. R. Davies is as symbolic of the mood of the age as anything. His Congregationalist ministry in the 1920s petered out in disillusionment after his rather heady involvement in support of the General Strike. Years in the wilderness followed. Unemployed, he discovered Karl Marx: 'Marxism came to assume for me the significance and proportion of a holy revelation.'[13] And so to Spain, where he witnessed a Nationalist bombing, but was then disillusioned in his Communist faith by the Stalinist purges in Russia. In 1937 Davies was reconverted to Christianity and was soon received back with enthusiasm into the Congregationalist ministry, only to become once more dissatisfied, but this time he moved 'Right' rather than 'Left' and in 1940 became an Anglican. He was ordained by William Temple the next year. In his rather intense way Davies experienced the whole cycle of traumas of the 1930s, but the point here is that in the end it made a Congregationalist into an Anglican. Others followed other ways. Nothing could be more prosaic and low-keyed than the career of J. K. Nettlefold, the Unitarian minister of the Octagon church in Norwich until he too in the mid-1930s decided he would rather be an Anglican: 'I wanted a larger sphere, to be a member of a bigger Christian society.'[14]

Some of the deep troubles of Congregationalism can be sensed well enough in Nathaniel Micklem's account of his years as

Principal of Mansfield College, in *Historia Calamitatum*.[15] He was appointed Principal in 1931, one of the brightest younger lights of his Church, yet he was clearly ill at ease in his ministry and, for long, pretty unpopular with many of his fellow Congregationalists. It is not hard to see why. Socially Micklem, like many others, had moved too far up the scale. His father was a prosperous Liberal MP, and he had been educated at Rugby and New College. One would have expected him to become an Anglican in such circumstances, but he disagreed with the idea of the Establishment and remained a Free churchman. Nevertheless, socially and intellectually he was only too clearly an Anglican, and had failed to fit in either at Selly Oak or in a Manchester parish ministry. Theologically he had moved in a very Catholic direction; he gave lectures on St Thomas Aquinas, encouraged students to attend courses by the Dominicans at Blackfriars, and threw himself into the liturgical movement. Why do all this and remain a Congregationalist? Either, it seemed, you kept apart and stagnated or you entered into all the movements and struggles of the age, and traditional Congregationalism appeared increasingly irrelevant.

Each such consideration on its own is hardly decisive or adequately explanatory of a truly major shift in English religious consciousness. Together they may suffice. One young man who was converted from Presbyterianism to the Church of England in these years, and later became an archbishop, declared: 'Becoming an Anglican meant for me the one word, *liberation*. I was liberated from a narrow sectarianism; I was liberated from a bigoted anti-intellectualism; and I was liberated too from an unreasoned and unreasonable puritanism.'[16] Protestantism flourished in the 1930s in Scotland and the United States and even in Wales. In England in its Free Church form, it was rapidly disintegrating. This cannot be explained in terms of the general decline of religion. In many ways the 1930s were a strengthening rather than a weakening decade in its wider history. To some extent at least Anglicanism was reviving, as was the intellectual commitment to Christianity as a whole, while English Roman Catholicism had never had it so good. But for the Free Churches it was the end of an age. A brief frenetic epoch of national prominence, almost centrality in national life, had led to an excessive politicization of concern and secularization of internal life. Once Lloyd George was rejected by the nation, the Liberal Party broken and bedraggled, the tides of politics and religion had flowed on in other channels. Decline brought growth in spiritual maturity and a new detachment. Nathaniel Micklem wrote a most generous work on the persecution of Roman Catholics in Nazi Germany. What English Catholic of the 1930s could have written such an objective study of the plight of German Protestants? Who else could have contributed as efficiently and unselfishly as William Paton to the growth of autonomy in the Church in India? Who could have set up the great international Oxford Conference of 1937 on Church and Society from which came the World Council of Churches, as skilfully, yet also as selflessly, as Oldham and Eric Fenn? The English Free Churches were, at one and the same time, shrivelling denominationally and pioneering the mood of the new ecumene. There was loss in the one and gain in the other, but perhaps without the loss there could not have been the gain.

Roman Catholicism

Cardinal Bourne died on 1 January 1935. He had presided over the Catholic Church in this country for more than thirty years, drily and unimaginatively, but seldom foolishly or dictatorially. A lonely man, he had done his best to resist the worst represssions of ultramontanism but was little loved or appreciated either in England or in Rome and his memory was unfortunately perpetuated by a biography written by his closest lay collaborator, which only served to emphasize his dreariest traits: 'A dull and narrow account of a humourless and rigid man. Absurd in adulation mingled with spitefulness against all non-Roman Christians. Parochial Romanism at its worst.' Such was Archbishop Garbett's comment on Oldmeadow's Life of the Cardinal.[1] It was fair enough comment but it is worth remarking that the spitefulness and parochialism were Oldmeadow's a great deal more than Bourne's.

To succeed him a Yorkshireman of seventy, who had not lived in Britain for years, was brought back from Africa and Rome. Arthur Hinsley was certainly an unexpected choice for the see of Westminster, his replacement of Bourne rather like Pope John's replacement of Pius XII. Bourne was as cold and almost as remote, though by no means as intelligent as Pope Pius; Hinsley, like Roncalli, first appeared as the elderly stop-gap, drawn from an apparently conservative and ultramontane stable, but then belied expectations. Hinsley, like Pope John, was a man of the people, coming to the top in old age, of a naturally positive, warm, fatherly disposition, a priest who had outgrown ecclesiastical fears and had somehow come to see that Church windows needed to be opened, that lay people could be trusted and Christians of other traditions welcomed as brothers.

Hinsley's background was profoundly Roman and ultramontane. He was recommended for the episcopate, originally by Gasquet, precisely on account of his 'Romanitas' and his selectors may well have hoped that, whereas Bourne had on occasion proved a little recalcitrant in the matter of following the Roman line, Hinsley would be its authoritative exponent. In this they were mistaken. No archiepiscopate was effectively less ultramontane or clericalist. His giving away of control of the *Tablet* to a group of laity was almost formal repudiation of Vaughan's buying it up sixty years before in order to ensure control of its editorial policy. His appointment of David Mathew, an able young Oxford historian, as auxiliary bishop of Westminster, of Christopher Dawson as editor of the *Dublin Review*, and his desire to appoint Ronald Knox to a bishopric, all showed a great freshness of approach, an absence of fear of men whose minds had been formed within the national universities. Still more important was his increasingly close co-operation with Anglican leadership and his encouragement in due course of the Sword of the Spirit movement, an encouragement that went with deep trust in such lay people as Professor Binchey and Christopher Dawson. The obvious Englishness both of his religion and his loyalties quickly made him nationally popular. Lang was probably the first Archbishop of Canterbury in modern times to have any sort of sympathy with Rome. He helped arrange Hinsley's membership of the Athenaeum and so for the first time something like a 'private wire' came to exist between Lambeth Palace and Archbishop's House, Westminster, though Hinsley's natural sympathies lay far more with the less cautious Bell.[2] In all this Hinsley was nevertheless far from characteristic of the way the tide was flowing in the Catholic Church in the 1930s. In many ways his successor as Rector of the English College at Rome, Mgr Godfrey, was far more typical, and the following entry from the Senior Student's diary at the College in April 1931, after Godfrey had taken over, is only too indicative of the general approach: 'Rector put up notice about Protestant Bibles. No one should buy or retain same in the College. All centres of Protestant propaganda in Rome must be avoided.'[3] Hinsley might feel it possible even to pray with his separated brethren but Godfrey, soon to be appointed Britain's first Apostolic Delegate (as a sort of counterweight to Hinsley's 'liberalism'?), and eventually to succeed to the see of Westminster himself, would insist upon a very different line.

Even in his time Hinsley's influence was then limited. The Catholic Church in England is not a centralized body and the general tide of Romanization and disassociation from all other churches, recently reinforced by the encyclical *Mortalium Animos*, and fully supported by Godfrey, could not be reversed by a single man. The Sword of the Spirit fostered in Westminster would find itself treated very differently elsewhere. The most powerful figure in the English Church lived not in Westminster but in Liverpool, still the most populous Catholic diocese in England. Archbishop Downey incarnated the Liverpool Irish Diaspora. 'Do not forget, Your Eminence,' Downey once remarked to Cardinal Griffin, 'that I rule the north.' That rule was to be demonstrated by the most extraordinarily ostentatious cathedral which could conceivably be built. Lutyens's plan was designed to put not only the Anglican cathedral at Liverpool but even St Paul's, even St Peter's, in the shade. The dedication was to be to Christ the King, the entire plan being based upon a Roman triumphal arch. Here was triumphalism at its most vulgar and uninhibited, a wildly costly scheme, the money for which would have to be screwed out of the numerous but mostly far from affluent Catholics of the archdiocese. Twenty years later only the crypt had been built and a later archbishop had to decide regretfully that the original plan was simply prohibitive. In the end Downey did not rule even Liverpool. Yet at the time it was by no means the only over ambitious and triumphalistic Church project being produced. Prinknash Abbey, newly established, promptly embarked upon a plan which would outscale Gloucester Cathedral, and Douai put up part of an abbey church which, if ever completed, would have been almost equally vast. The great church at Buckfast was completed in 1938. Such plans combined a desire to restore the glories of the medieval past with a not unnatural sense of competitiveness. They were at last outdoing the Anglicans.

It was, however, one side of the very great sense of confidence that was now filling the Catholic Church in England. They were years of quite rapid advance on almost every side. In 1910 there were 3,835 priests in England and Wales and by 1925 this had only risen to 4,031, but by 1940 it would be 5,652 and by 1950 6,643. The rise of 1,600 between 1925 and 1940 really transformed the pastoral effectiveness of the Church in this country. While many new priests were undoubtedly coming in from Ireland, the ordinations within the country (which did include some Irishmen) reached their highest point in 1937 with 170 seculars and 81 regulars.[4]

Where hitherto the English Catholic community had been somewhat bottled up in Lancashire and the main towns, it was now rapidly spreading out into new suburbs and smaller country places. Take for instance the opening of new churches in Southwark diocese in the 1930s:

1930	Morden
1931	Banstead; Biggin Hill; Edenbridge; Purley
1933	Mongeham; Deal
1934	Ash; Aldershot; Carshalton Beeches
1935	Lancing
1936	Bexley Heath; Bostall Park; West Wickham
1937	Blackfen; Cheam; Petts Wood; Sidcup; Stoneleigh
1938	Beckenham
1939	Send; Woking.

Or, again, compare the number of Catholics fulfilling their Easter duties in a number of parishes in the Northampton diocese in 1931 and 1949.[5] This was a part of England where hitherto Catholics had been particularly thin on the ground.

	1931	1949
Aylesbury	131	782
Bedford	640	1,660
Cambridge	752	2,134
Dunstable	40	440
Luton	440	2,243
Slough	689	2,407

Priestwise, the Northampton diocese had 67 seculars and 29 religious in 1926, 145 seculars and 68 religious in 1946.

What were the causes of this remarkable growth? The 1930s were not a time of significant immigration, though the late 1940s would be. Previous to the First World War a quite high proportion of Catholics lapsed from religious practice, often because there was simply no church anywhere near where they lived. Catholics were now moving, like people in general, from the north-west to the south-east. The growth in the number of priests, of churches and of schools meant that the likelihood of lapsing after such a move was considerably diminished from the late 1920s. The impression is that the ultramontane pastoral system, as exemplified by the new canon law, the very unyielding regulations about mixed marriages, and the activities of the Catholic Missionary Society, was working pretty effectively. By the 1930s there were some twelve thousand converts a year, doubtless many of them partners in mixed marriages. Catholic opposition to birth control almost certainly had as its consequence in this period a significantly higher birth rate for Catholics than for the general population: probably at no other time was there so objective a contrast in social mores between Catholics and others. The overall consequence was a quite marked strengthening of the Catholic presence, numerical and institutional, in almost every part of the country, and just at a time when other major churches were, statistically, in unmistakable decline. When large new numbers of immigrants arrived in the post-war years of the late 1940s the Church would be ready to cope with them, and to expand still more emphatically.

Numerical growth brought with it qualitative change. The very considerable expansion in the public schools under eminent headmasters, like Sigebert Trafford and Christopher Butler at Downside, Paul Nevill at Ampleforth and Ignatius Rice at Douai, was having its effect, but so was the development of very much better grammar schools in the major towns. There was a noticeable growth in the number of Catholic dons at Oxford and Cambridge and the number of priests who studied at Campion Hall at the one and at St Edmund's House at the other. If in politics Catholics remained rather insignificant, in some other quarters, such as the Foreign Office and *The Times* newspaper, they were well represented. In a curious way Catholics were now coming to occupy a somewhat privileged position in the life of the country. It was recognized that they were different and that their differences should be almost over-respected. They had to have their schools, their mixed marriage regulations, their lobby for

Catholic political causes abroad. The government had learnt that it was almost never worthwhile tangling with the Vatican, that Catholicism was an extremely powerful and well organized force in many parts of the empire and that, for European politics too, good relations with the Vatican could be extremely useful. This sense had really been communicated to the wider governing class, and hence old Protestant prejudices and new liberal fears about the Catholic Church were offset by what one Anglican historian has described irritably as the 'tacit convention that the Roman Catholic minority in this country, which plays so little part in public life even in proportion to its numbers, should be treated with an obsequious deference, such as is not awarded to any other Dissenting body or even to the National Church'.[6]

Where the Catholic Church of the period could most rightly be criticized was for the narrowness of its institutional concerns. The worst areas of unemployment and acute urban deprivation were also areas of the highest Catholic density. On Tyneside, Merseyside and Clydeside it was above all Catholics who were unemployed. If in such places Communists got votes it was of necessity largely Catholic votes, but there was next to no specifically Catholic voice of protest raised. Doubtless local priests helped organize soup kitchens, but beyond that, what? There were no priests walking south by the side of the hunger marchers. There was no episcopal thunder over the state of the nation: Cardinal Bourne was too Tory for that. There was no incipient liberation theology in the seminaries. Christians of other churches might be wrestling with the positive challenge of Communism; Eric Fenn in the SCM was admitting just how much of an opium religion had been; but not the Catholic clergy. It was a world away, so preoccupied over mixed marriages and birth control and anti-Communism that it had no word to say even when its own strongholds were devastated by mass unemployment. Here again the change from Bourne to Hinsley made some difference. The latter's speech to the dockers in 1936 presented a stark contrast in attitude to Bourne's position ten years before.

Vocal Catholics certainly seemed to care little for such matters. Their clearly constituted sub-culture was both upper class and rather apolitical, their ablest leaders being either literary free-lancers or located within Catholic rather than national institu-

tions. For all Douglas Woodruff's successful early career at
Oxford and as a sub-editor of *The Times*, it is not really surprising that he found his definite home in 1936 as editor of the *Tablet*.
Christopher Dawson edited the *Dublin Review*, Michael de la
Bedoyere the *Catholic Herald*, Victor White *Blackfriars*: a distinguished foursome. The Catholic intellectual world was an
exciting and even brilliant one by the late 1930s, functioning
through its many journals, its several publishing houses, its
schools, its clerical university halls and its network of literary
figures.[7] It was a highly confident growing world of clerics and
converts, but it was a world which impinged only through its
books upon the national life. Apart from these the rest of society
could, quite easily, hardly know of its existence.

The cultured English Catholicism of the 1930s took it almost
for granted that 'modern culture' – the more or less necessary
concluding phase of the post-Reformation evolution of western
civilization – was anti-God and anti-man and that the only
tenable religious and Christian alternative was that of Roman
Catholicism. It was believed that this was becoming more and
more obvious, and the succession of distinguished converts
reinforced the conviction. Little attempt was made to distinguish
positively within the complexities of the Protestant thought
world. Catholics were tremendously conversion-minded and
seldom pondered developments outside their communion except
in terms of conversions which might result. The conversions of
the period were certainly significant: no one can speak lightly of a
group which included Maurice Baring, Ronald Knox, G. K.
Chesterton, Sheila Kaye Smith, W. E. Orchard, Alfred Noyes,
Rosalind Murray, Arnold Lunn, Eric Gill, David Jones, Evelyn
Waugh, Graham Greene, Manya Harari, Frank Pakenham. The
list could be greatly extended. Most of the converts, like most of
the cradle Catholics, steered clear of theology in any very exact
sense and very few upon either side had the slightest worry about
ultramontanism. In a critical sense they were rather ahistorical
and atheological: that is to say they accepted the current Roman
Catholic position in doctrine and practice as almost unquestionably right in all its details, and argued accordingly. Its very
authoritativeness was what appealed. They found in it a sure
framework for spiritual progress, literary creativity and political

stability, but also for an ordered and coherent view of the world to replace the increasing intellectual and ideological confusion evident outside the walls. They tended to argue that Anglo-Saxon democracy was a step-son of Protestantism and somewhat over-rated. The authoritarian character of the Church inclined them to approve of authoritarianism in the State too, and they looked upon Mussolini, Franco and Salazar at least a great deal more benevolently than did most other Englishmen. In all this the influence of Belloc upon a long generation of friends and disciples was unquestionable. He had a confidence, a provision of histori-cal information and a commanding sense of strategy which impressed itself upon others, even those of more subtle intellec-tual discrimination than himself. By the 1930s his creative period was long past, his more tiresome characteristics still very much in evidence.

When Chesterton died in 1936, Fr Vincent McNabb sang the *Salve Regina* and then kissed his pen – a fitting tribute from the most uninhibited priest of his age to the most creative layman of his age. Chesterton was not Belloc. He had much less of a school, but he brought into the Catholic Church a hardly rivalled insight, a rich Anglo-Catholic inheritance and a continuing creativity which did much to enlarge the sights of the younger generation. For an enlargement of sights was, despite everything, going on. Catholics were not only reacting against the Protestant-secularist world around them, they were also beginning to react away from the tight constrictions of their own past, the anti-modernist witch-hunt especially. Maisie Ward ended the second volume of the biography of her father, Wilfred Ward, with a resounding epilogue celebrating the end of 'the siege period'. It would now at last be possible to utilize 'all that was really valuable in the thought of the Modernist period'.[8] Algernon Cecil, yet another distinguished convert, reviewing the book in the *Tablet*, declared that the epilogue 'falls upon the ear like the sound of a reveille warning the faithful that it is now indeed high time to awake out of sleep'.[9] The awakening was going on, being very much helped by the French Catholic renaissance of these same years. Claudel, Mauriac, Bernanos, Maritain, Gilson were all writing in the 1930s and their books were being translated into English and published by Sheed & Ward, and others. Even some quite valuable theological work, by de La Taille and Masure on the mass, was getting across the Channel and into English Catholic heads. New theological ideas were just starting to appear in articles in the *Downside Review* and *Blackfriars*. All in all the English Catholic writer with the greatest influence was probably by the late 1930s Christopher Dawson, despite his rather retiring character. His better scholarship and more subtle vision were gently ending the reign of Belloc and he was influential in non-Catholic as well as Catholic circles.

Young Dominicans, the progeny of Bede Jarrett, like Victor White, Gervase Mathew and Conrad Pepler, were beginning to show that English Catholic priests really could be trained and function effectively on an intellectual wavelength which non-Catholics were able to tune into as well. The renewed Thomism of Maritain and Gilson was, indeed, more widely influential in England outside the Catholic Church than within it, and in most things the hierarchy remained impervious enough to inspiration from Europe north of the Alps. The continental liturgical movement might be influencing the Anglicans and even the Congregationalists, but it would take the war to move a Catholic bishop to countenance the apparently revolutionary 'dialogue mass'. Clearly, in the late 1930s the English Catholic intellectual revival had a long way to go and its future was by no means certain; nevertheless, it existed: it had some institutional and clerical base, especially at Downside, Blackfriars and Campion Hall, and it was in tune, if not with the hierarchy as a whole, at least with the new openness being shown by the archbishop of Westminster. The Sword of the Spirit, the English Catholic response of the early war years, would not have been possible without Cardinal Hinsley, but, equally, it would not have been possible without a new group of educated lay Catholics, anxious to participate almost ecumenically in facing the great social and moral issues which confronted the world. Christopher Dawson and Barbara Ward provided no mean contribution to the general marshalling of the Christian consciousness in the nation in these years, and this did not make them peripheral to Catholic Church life. It was Hinsley's great, if brief, contribution to ensure that. Of course there were clear theological limits to the breakthrough, such as it was, limits which are sensed clearly enough in a little book by

A. C. F. Beales, *The Catholic Church and International Order*, a 1941 Penguin: a heavily ultramontane view of the papacy enabled the author even to praise the *Syllabus of Errors* and the encyclical *Quanta Cura* of 1864, two of Pius IX's more disastrous pronouncements, for their 'astonishing foresight'. Beales was very much a Sword of the Spirit man, he was also perhaps too recent a convert not to take Roman claims rather over-seriously.

A writer in the *Congregational Quarterly* just after the war spoke enthusiastically of the 'growing spiritualising of the Roman Catholic witness in England and France. Jacques Maritain has written for all the Churches. . . .'[10] Nevertheless he saw too the gap between the movement and the continued preoccupation with institutional power characteristic of the Roman Catholic hierarchy: 'Barbara Ward and Maritain are not those who set the pace.' That too, especially after the death of Hinsley, was true and there for the time we must leave the story, though not without considering a few of the more outstanding cultural achievements of Catholicism in the 1930s.

The first figure one cannot avoid speaking about is Ronald Knox.

> Mary of Holyrood may smile indeed,
> Knowing what grim historic shade it mocks
> To see wit, laughter and the Popish creed,
> Cluster and sparkle in the name of Knox.

From 1926 until almost the war, 'Ronnie' was Oxford's Catholic chaplain, sparkling – at least to the observer – as he sat on the fender and lit his pipe in the splendid study at the Old Palace. Sadly it did not only shock Chesterton's 'grim historic shade', but Knox's own utterly Protestant father, the bishop, who in those years was successfully marshalling the troops to throw out Prayer Book reform in the House of Commons. The 1920s were, then, the last decade of the old Protestant Knox and the first decade of the new popish Knox, a writer of detective stories, of odd literary puzzles and devout sermons, but not of theology. In Knox the new intellectual confidence of English Catholicism for long found its showpiece – brightest of all pre-war young men, most orthodox of all priests. There is something rather sad about the absence of surviving significant work from Ronald Knox. One book at least has its own incomparable brilliance, *Let Dons Delight*. It stands upon the border of belief and culture while exhibiting a deft, self-debunking humour. It was too much of an Oxford game to be widely appreciated, yet too subtly Catholic in its message to be wholly agreeable even within the academic circle. It remains his one major unflawed achievement.

Knox began his translation of the Vulgate Bible on St Jerome's day, September 1939; he completed the New Testament by 1942 and the Old Testament in 1948, writing its preface on St Jerome's day of that year. The work had been commissioned by Hinsley and the hierarchy. It was hailed enthusiastically when it first came out, the New Testament at least being much read. It is remarkable as the work of one man, as also for its vigour and intelligibility. Yet it was in principle a flawed work, even an absurd one. To translate from St Jerome's Vulgate, and not directly from Greek and Hebrew, into modern English, was an extraordinarily retrograde exercise. Perhaps only British Catholic bishops at this time could have proposed it, or a scholar, at once so able and yet so loyal to the ecclesiastical system he had embraced as Knox, could have accepted it. Knox thought he would be remembered by his Bible; in fact no translation has fallen more rapidly into oblivion.

For quality of literary craftsmanship, *Let Dons Delight* can be put beside three other works, all of which received the Hawthornden Prize: Evelyn Waugh's *Edmund Campion*, David Jones's *In Parenthesis*, and Graham Greene's *The Power and the Glory*. Here were Catholics powerfully contributing to the enduring literature of the nation. Original and yet intrinsically Catholic, it was a contribution immediately recognized at large as significant and able to be ranked beside that of Eliot or Auden. In literary terms at least it was simply not true that Catholics still played 'so little part in public life even in proportion to their numbers'.[11] The part they played was, in fact, out of proportion to their numbers and would remain so for a while.

If Christopher Dawson embodied a new tide of lay Christian social thought and Graham Greene could translate with the expertise of a great master the intricacies of the Catholic spiritual vision into the existential agonies of modern man, and Ronald Knox represented a clerical scholarship maimed by not being allowed to take theological freedom quite seriously, David Knowles represented something different again. It was the paradox of the truly great clerical scholar who came partially to grief with the Church not on account of any compromising with liberal and Protestant ideas but rather due to a sort of excessive spiritual ultramontanism, impatient of the lax worldly tendencies he detected even in his own Benedictine order.

Downside Abbey in the inter-war years was a community of many remarkable men, several of them of outstanding spirituality and learning. Among them all none was more brilliant, more learned or more devout than the young Dom David. In 1932 he himself described Downside, not absurdly, as 'the Athens of English Catholicism'.[12] Here he wrote his first books, *The American Civil War*, and *The English Mystics*. In an odd way this seems to symbolize his personal problem well enough: the world was a matter of war, extremely interesting but utterly secular, and soon, he would decide, quite foreign to the proper interest of the monk: the Church on the other hand would stand or fall by its most other-worldly activity, mystical prayer. His theology made him, as the years went by, contrast more and more severely the 'natural' and the 'supernatural'. Between the two there could be no 'compromise'. Downside, he believed, did compromise, by its school and by its generally world-consecrating ethos – characteristic, of course, of the Benedictine tradition. Knowles, in his early years apparently happy in Benedictinism, seemed to switch his inner loyalties towards a more Carthusian and world-denying model. He wished to reform Downside, and persuaded some other still younger monks that they should follow him. Downside, however, did not wish to be reformed and Knowles grew strange in his behaviour and increasingly impervious to monastic control. In September 1939 he finally walked out of the daughter community at Ealing, in which he was living, and his own monastic life was never resumed. He had been far from impeccably treated by the various abbots who had ruled Downside in these years, but he had himself behaved in a way so strange and increasingly unreasonable that one is almost forced to conclude that his judgment was at the time gravely disordered. His bitterness against Downside remained intense even thirty years later. Yet at the very time all this was going on he had been writing at

Ealing that mature, wise, humane masterpiece of learning, *The Monastic Order in England*, published by the Cambridge University Press in 1940. It was suggested at the time that Dom David was suffering from schizophrenia and the more one ponders the contrast between his public writing and his private life, the more one is forced to conclude that this was indeed the truth. A recent writer has judged Knowles's historical writing as 'one of the most compelling Christian productions to have been published in England in this century'.[13] It is not too high praise, and it is why one cannot ignore his work here. Certainly no other English Catholic priest in this century has made a comparable contribution to the field of scholarship and to a Catholic reinterpretation of English history. Yet this contribution was made from a position of prolonged personal crisis in which Knowles, like Tyrrell thirty years before, was facing suspension and excommunication by the Church. The difference between the two is not just that Knowles was treated a great deal more gently than Tyrrell; it is also that his conflict with the Church (formally mended twelve years later) basically derived from his being on the 'right' wing, not on the 'left'; from a spiritual mentality, an implicit theology which was too profoundly 'ultramontane' even for an ultramontane Church. The force of Ultramontanism is always to separate Church and world, and the Benedictine ideal, which instead draws them together, has always been spiritually anti-ultramontane. It thrives on history and growth as on the interaction of natural and supernatural. Knowles the historian celebrated all these things, but Knowles the monk and theologian rejected them, calling for greater intransigence just at a time and in a place where the move was at last towards less, not more. There were too many paradoxes here, to be worked out in a mind so very strong and so intensely committed to a narrow ideal. His life was maimed by the tension but his books, superbly chiselled, benefit from the anguish while escaping all but miraculously from most of the contradictions.

In an odd way Eric Gill was Knowles's religious antithesis, searching for near fusion between the spiritual and the material, where Knowles sought separation. Sex, it would appear, was totally taboo in Knowles's world. Gill thrived on it. Since 1928 he and his family and various friends had been living at Pigotts, in

Buckinghamshire, the third and last home for the Christian community, the 'Cell of good living' he had striven so earnestly to create.[14] He certainly had his faults, and as seekers after an 'alternative community' Gill and his friends were not so unusual. Nevertheless he and his greatest 'disciple' David Jones had between them a significance which far transcends that of any other such movement. Gill was the master, socratic in discourse, phenomenally productive in lettering, sculpture and drawing, a man with a total social theory who effectively fused his life and artistic achievement with his ideas. As Jones said of him, Gill 'worked as though one should and could, make a culture exist'.[15] His ideas about work, pacifism, sex, and the ordering of society challenged the Catholic Church, to which he emphatically belonged, with a directness provided by no other Catholic writer of the time; and his sculpture at its best, as in the Westminster Stations of the Cross and the great bas-relief in the League of Nations Hall at Geneva on 'The Re-Creation of Adam', can be counted among the major Christian artistic achievements of this century.

David Jones was very different; thirteen years Gill's junior; at first profoundly influenced by him but then pulling away in a still more intensely personal direction, to an almost romantic flamboyance of word and pictorial detail, where Gill was committed to a classic purity of design. Some of Jones's paintings are fascinating, but it is in his writing – represented in the 1930s by *In Parenthesis* – that he creates with intense difficulty, both for himself and for his reader, what is almost a new art form, combining poetry and prose, imagination and scholarship, religious symbolism and history in a way that is unique and decisive. Both Gill and Jones owed much to the Catholic culture of their time – Maritain, de la Taille, the English Dominicans of the Jarrett tradition. Both were struggling sacramentally to interpret the strange interplay of nature and supernature, not with the mystical antithesis of a Knowles, but through a texture of earthly signs centering upon the richest of them all, the mass, what Jones called a 'complex of mysteries of inexplicable splendour'. In both there is to be found not only an artistic achievement of the highest level, but a freedom to re-work Catholic orthodoxy, an ability not to be intimidated by the standard Catholic position of their time, which makes them still strangely fresh fifty years later.

Much in English Catholicism was parochial, legalistic and utterly third rate. But enough has been said to suggest that at the time of its great expansion, despite both the unimaginative institutionalism which so affected some of its leaders and the absence of much that is to be appreciated in other churches, it yet provided chunks of light and wisdom, almost incomparably valuable, rich contributions to the specifically religious and symbolic life of the nation.

Theology and Culture

Having considered the churches separately let us now turn to review the wider intellectual scene in its religious and theological dimension.

The thirties opened in a mood of considerable silliness and closed in one of great seriousness. 1933 was not only the year Hitler came to power and the British Union of Fascists began to make its mark with its uniformed blackshirts, deliberate violence and anti-Semitism. It was also the year that Frank Buchman's Oxford Group probably made its greatest impact. That autumn it was blessed with much publicity by Archbishop Lang at Lambeth and Bishop Winnington-Ingram at St Paul's. It can hardly have appealed personally to Lang, with its watered-down Evangelicalism, gushing public confessions and rather brash social note, but he doubtless told himself that the times were out of joint and new initiatives, claiming a modern note, must be encouraged. Anglican clergy, with as so often the exception of Bishop Henson, were for a time remarkably willing to believe in the Group. The Holy Spirit was thought to provide the most direct and least painful of guidance in the most expensive of hotels to the best brought up of young men. So B. K. Cunningham at Westcott House could record 'quite the most wonderful term in my experience of thirty years. . . . Six of our best men went through a deep spiritual experience in and through the Oxford Group House Party'.[1] Like many another admirer, Cunningham would come to learn better and to find the Group's 'Familiar childish stories and experiences' 'pitiable',[2] yet the Group would continue for many years to capture loyalties, including those of many scholarly clerics,[3] to confuse Evangelical ranks with its pseudo-evangelical jargon, and to flirt with Fascism.

Buchman was but one of the slightly odd religious and secular 'prophets' who glimmered with a brief deceptive brilliance in the general unsettlement of the early 1930s: one can think of such now mostly forgotten oddities as Orage, Mitrinovic and Major Douglas, Oswald Mosley, and Hewlett Johnson. It is difficult to classify such figures, but in their different ways they all express something of a sense of the bankruptcy of conventional wisdom, secular or religious, and a rather frenetic search for new solutions. Neither the comfortable secular certainties nor the comfortable modernistic religious certainties, both characteristic of the 1920s, stood up very well to the cold winds of the thirties. The central line of descent of received modern wisdom appeared to lead into the Communist Party and then, for those for whom the ghastly reality of Stalinism could not be permanently ignored, into one or another form of agonized reappraisal. If such reappraisal did not occur, one might either become a Russian spy or simply resist the known truth in a way that could undermine the whole credibility of the intellectual life. Take J. D. Bernal, a brilliant scientist with a superbly versatile mind, heir – if ever there was one – to the modern orthodoxy of non-religion, yet victim thereby of a most naïve and gullible Marxism, a man still able to believe in the goodness of Stalin in the 1950s. It was the ability of the protagonists of modern scientific atheism, so confident of itself in the 1920s, to provide such obvious nonsense in the subsequent decades, which helped undermine the old Victorian certainties and ease the way for the intellectual revival of religion – and a religion which prided itself, far less on taking science seriously, as the Inges and the Majors had been trying so conscientiously to do, than on taking the Bible, Revelation, the cross and the supernatural seriously. How on earth, the observer of 1920 might well ask, could we come back to that?

The central tide of English thought and culture in the 1930s was flowing quite perceptibly in one large direction: from irreligion to religion, from liberal or modernist religion to neo-orthodoxy, and from Protestantism towards Catholicism. If the 1920s already suggested some hint of these movements, with the obvious intellectual superiority of Anglo-Catholicism over Evangelicalism within the Established Church, with the steady trickle of distinguished converts to Rome, and with the rediscovery of Christianity by a few young agnostics like Lewis and Eliot, by the 1930s the whole thing is quite unmistakable. 'Oh for an unforgettable vision,' declaimed Malcolm Muggeridge theatrically in 1938.[4] For late 1930s man, agonized by Hitler upon the one hand and Stalin upon the other, increasingly frightened by what was just around the corner, the secular vision had indeed faded and he was more and more inclined to look out for God instead, to hope for the reassurance if not of some unforgettable burst of light, at least of the tempered optimism of the crucifix. Many, and Muggeridge was among them, failed at the time to find quite such a faith; yet others, including some of the most influential figures in contemporary culture, succeeded in doing so and their collective return to Christianity – little considered as it has been – represents one of the more significant characteristics of the 1935-45 years. Even for the Catholic Church, to which the most distinguished converts have usually been Christians of another denomination, and often Anglican clerics, the thirties presents an exception. The characteristic thirties convert story was the odyssey of a lay agnostic, not of an Anglican priest: *The Unknown God* of Alfred Noyes, *The Good Pagan's Failure* of Rosalind Murray, *Now I See* of Arnold Lunn, were all works of former unbelievers. And so was Sherwood Taylor's *The Fourfold Vision*. Taylor was a historian of science, later director of the Science Museum in South Kensington. A resolute agnostic, he had been commissioned by the Rationalist Press Association in 1937 to write a book on Galileo. Four years later he became a Roman Catholic.

John Middleton Murry represents, perhaps as well as any one, the edging back into religious faith of a fair section of the intellectual élite in the course of the 1930s. For him, as for Vera Brittain, it was the influence of the charismatic figure of Dick Sheppard and the ethos of the peace movement which proved the main channel of religious rediscovery. 'The signing of the Peace Pledge', he wrote in 1938 'has meant for me a gradual passing into an entirely new sense of the reality of Christian Communion'.[5] A 1920s agnostic, Murry by the end of the 1930s was even thinking of being ordained. If Dick Sheppard was the guru for some, Charles Williams could be for others. Auden walked into his London office one day in the late 1930s and it seems was reconverted to Christianity on the spot.

> For the first time in my life [I] felt myself in the presence of personal sanctity. I had met many good people before who made me feel ashamed of my own shortcomings, but in the presence of this man – we never discussed anything but literary business – I did not feel ashamed. I felt transformed into a person who was incapable of doing or thinking anything base or unloving.[6]

Admittedly Auden's conversion to Christianity in 1940 did not, to the outward observer, 'transform' his life, nor perhaps did it make a great humanist poet into a great Christian poet. But it was certainly not meaningless nor insignificant. From then on upon his mantelpiece there stood a crucifix. The central figure of the literary left of the 1930s, Auden had found his world in dissolution. With the spiritual collapse of English left-wing secularism in the agony of the time, its heroes turned into refugees. Auden was such a refugee painfully groping for a better, less fragile key to ultimate meaning in the crucifix on his mantelpiece.

Auden's case can be paralleled by those of Jack Clemo the deaf, and soon to be blind, Cornish poet; Joad, the radio philosopher; Frank Pakenham, the Socialist don; Arnold Toynbee – writing his middle, very Catholic volumes of *A Study of History*; Martin Charlesworth, the brilliant historian of the Roman Empire. The list could easily be extended. But Sherwood Taylor, Middleton Murry, Vera Brittain, Auden, Clemo, Joad, Frank Pakenham, and Charlesworth present a curious enough assortment of celebrities – poets, scholars, philosophers, a liberated woman. Their conversion to Christianity in these years had relatively little significance or consequence ecclesiastically. It was seldom very decisively conversion to a Church and it brought none of them into the ranks of the clergy or into that segment of the laity which co-operates quasi-professionally with the clergy. Its religious, cultural and intellectual significance was all the greater for that. It witnesses collectively to the breakdown of the agnostic consensus of the enlightened and to the growing sense that a belief in supernatural religion really was an intellectual option for modern man. If this was the case, it was not only that alternative traditions were taking such an awful bashing, it was also that a high and distinctly powerful Christian culture, centering upon a revived theology, was clearly thriving in the England of the 1930s, just as it was in the France of the 1930s. Politically decrepit as the France of the Third Republic might be, a Catholic renaissance was flourishing within it in a way that was certainly influential for her neighbours: Christian novelists and dramatists like Mauriac, Claudel and Bernanos, philosophers like Maritain, Gilson and Mounier, theologians like Masure and the young Congar, seemed to share in some sort of common conspiracy, at once very French and very Catholic, to redraw the image of religious man. To them may be added the Russian exile in their midst, Berdyaev.

For England all this was the more important as the German religious influence penetrating across the Channel was now more limited and under suspicion. German Christianity, caught in the web of Nazism, was as a whole rather an object to be assisted than any great source of guidance. If the First World War smashed the old Anglo-German religious axis, the thirties came near to creating an Anglo-French one. The reinterpreted Thomism of Gilson and Maritain, the new theology of the mass of de la Taille and Masure, the delving into the working of religion in the soul of man of Mauriac or Bernanos, were all just what the English Christian of the 1930s felt that he needed, as he sought to escape from the legacy of both his ancient Protestantism and his more recent modernism. The English Christian was now only too happy to share the insight of a liberal French Catholic over almost everything except the pope.

This was, of course, by no means the only large source of inspiration. On the contrary, it was paralleled by a wide continental Protestant reassertion of doctrinal orthodoxy led by Barth, as also by the very powerful impact of certain writers from the past – great Victorians unrecognized by the Victorian age. The most important of these were Gerard Manley Hopkins, Kierkegaard, Maurice and Forsyth.

The first edition of the poetry of Hopkins was published forty years after his death, by Robert Bridges in 1918. But the twenties were not really Hopkins territory and it was with the second edition, introduced by Charles Williams and published in 1930, that the Victorian Jesuit became a major influence upon Anglo-

Saxon culture. Reprintings followed almost every year. The power alike of Hopkins and of Kierkegaard was rooted in existential intensity, a personal experience of faith and *Angst*, communicated with great verbal originality. Both were spiritual extremists and Hopkins was a supreme master of poetic diction. Their appeal was by no means merely to the Christian, but the content of their message was intensely religious and strangely contemporary to the hopes and fears of the 1930s. They helped enormously to ground the new Christian culture in a soil more profound than that of its alternatives. Maurice and Forsyth were both undergoing 'rediscoveries' at the same time, as Victorian prophets of a Christianity at once biblical and Catholic. To these names and influences must be added that of Reinhold Niebuhr, the greatest single theological influence upon the decade – far greater than that of Barth. Barth was too Protestant, too emphatically divisive of grace from nature, to be wholly welcome in English circles. Niebuhr appeared to offer a more subtle model, as emphatic as Barth in rejecting the fashionable liberal Protestantism of the previous generation, but without falling back into what could seem a new fundamentalism. Niebuhr provided too a gospel fully sensitive to social reality which yet escaped from entombment within any one single socio-political option, be it Liberal, Socialist or Pacifist. He seemed just what the age of ideological struggle needed, if Christians were to keep their heads above each incoming wave. Niebuhr provided in theology for the more Protestant-minded much of what Maritain provided for the more Catholic-minded, somewhat as in the wider field of culture Kierkegaard offered upon the one side what Hopkins did upon the other. Yet of course all these influences overlapped and coalesced.

The mix in these years is not easy to descramble without grave oversimplification. If the Christian culture of Eliot, Waugh, Greene, Gill, David Jones, Lewis, Charles Williams and suchlike had a good deal in common, it was also full of the sharpest contrasts. For the most part it was the religion of converts. Artistically it was amazingly creative. Doctrinally it was rather intransigent. Politically it had come near to opting out. The political Christians of the age were not the converts and were, on the whole, just a little less doctrinally orthodox. Such were A. D.

Lindsay, the Master of Balliol, Walter Moberly, Vice Chancellor of Manchester University and chairman of the University Grants Commission, and J. H. Oldham. These rather older men owed far more to the greater theological liberalism of the pre-1930s era and could at times have some slight difficulty in adjusting to the more precise orthodoxy of the younger generation.

Theologically, the moment of transition may be dated with reasonable precision to 1933-6. In 1933 Karl Barth's Commentary on Romans – the great trumpet blast of theological counter-revolution – appeared in English, translated by Sir Edwyn Hoskyns. Soon after a number of long-lasting liberal figures retired – Dean Inge from St Paul's, Burkitt and Bethune-Baker at Cambridge being the most notable. Charles Raven had been appointed Regius Professor of Divinity at Cambridge in 1932 and he was surely liberal enough, a guarantee of 'modernist' continuity. His case is, therefore, worth considering. Raven arrived back in Cambridge, an egregiously self-confident young cleric, prepared to sound from this high vantage point a resounding trumpet call in favour of a 'New Reformation' appropriate to the modern scientific age. He was well informed, even brilliant, while deeply, even stridently, committed to Pacifism, the ordination of women and every progressive cause. Yet to this trumpet call almost no one seemed to respond.[7] He found himself instead swimming irritatedly against an incoming reactionary tide. As E. L. Allen, himself no sympathizer with these movements, had to admit a few years later: 'Since 1936 conservative tendencies have gained ground all along the line, and even those who are critical of Barth and Brunner will often swear by Niebuhr.'[8] By the late 1930s Raven, for all his brilliance and pursuit of relevance, found himself regarded as irrelevant, 'almost entirely alone and unwanted'.[9] Ecclesiastically he was singularly out of tune with the spirit of the age: modernistic liberalism appeared as a rather tired and conservative option, while theological conservatism appeared as the exciting radical option for bishop and student alike: 'Worm-eaten with liberalism' was Eliot's damning phrase of condemnation for the old guard. Hitler and Stalin had made the old religious mix of mysticism and social concern, both often of a vague sort, doubts about precise doctrines, a stress on love, rowing, and being a gentleman, seem as a package a rather too inadequate way of asserting Christianity. The German pastors of the Confessing Church were calling for support, but they did not want it from liberals. The voices of Barth, Niebuhr and Maritain were rallying the ranks, and Raven, the 'unrepentant liberal', found himself 'unwanted'. The SCM Press, manned by more old-fashioned liberals, at first actually turned down Niebuhr's *Moral Man and Immoral Society*, and *The Interpretation of Christian Ethics*, until persuaded otherwise by some of SCM's own young Turks.[10] The theological swing of the pendulum had come remarkably quickly.

Its motivation was derived from two rather different sources. The first was hardly theological. The wider cultural swing back towards both religion and orthodoxy in religion precedes the swing back of the theologians. Eliot, Lewis, Waugh, Gill were not theologians and they were not really much influenced by contemporary theology. They had first rejected, in youth, traditional Protestantism whether watered down in a liberal way or not; they then rejected the secularist substitute and returned from it to a full-blooded 'Catholic' orthodoxy. The lay need for this, as the thirties wore on and the secular gospels of the age appeared more and more disastrous, steadily increased. It was not created by the theologians. Nevertheless the theologians, or some of them, had been going this way too, so that it was possible for the two developments to meet and support each other. In a journal like *Christendom*, begun in 1931 as the organ of the rather Anglo-Catholic 'Christian sociology' group, with Maurice Reckitt as editor, Berdyaev and Maritain, Eliot, Charles Williams and Christopher Dawson were joined by young theologians and philosophers like Eric Mascall and Donald Mackinnon. They did not share a common programme by any means, but in their various ways they did reflect something of a common mood and theological direction.

Contrasts certainly remained. Eliot and Lewis might seem to the remote observer to have a great deal in common. They themselves did not find it so and Lewis, in particular, disliked Eliot (perhaps because of course they did have rather too much in common). For some, if you wanted to recover orthodoxy, the only sensible thing to do was to submit to the authority of Rome:

thus Gill and Lunn, Rosalind Murray and Sherwood Taylor, Evelyn Waugh and Frank Pakenham. For others, particularly the more theologically minded, that seemed impossible. There were just too many not unimportant, if still secondary, things about which Rome was wrong. If the thirties was a politicized decade, the new Christian theologians and intellectuals were not. There might be a bit of Fascism here, a bit of Communist sympathy there, but for the most part what is striking is how little they had to offer to political man. And Lewis, at the end of the day the most lastingly influential of all these people, was the least concerned of them all to relate religion to politics. If the Oxford 'Life and Work' Conference of 1937 produced about the most serious approach to the problems of society which the Church anywhere had yet managed, the men responsible – like Temple, Oldham, Moberly and Lindsay – had been only rather marginally touched by the new theological current. It is true that they were supported by younger men, mostly from SCM circles and influenced by Niebuhr. Nevertheless the basic inspiration of the Oxford conference was considerably removed both from the younger clerical theologians and from such as the Oxford Inklings, gathering at the Eastgate to listen to a section of Tolkien's *Lord of the Rings*, a nativity play by Charles Williams, or a chapter from Lewis's *Problem of Pain*.

Probably as good a witness as any to what we may rather loosely call the revival of orthodoxy of a supernaturalist kind may be detected in Alec Vidler, who in 1939 began his long editorship of *Theology*.[11] Vidler has been one of the most reliable of theological barometers in the last sixty years.[12] A young liberal Anglo-Catholic in the twenties, he had moved by the late thirties towards a sort of semi-Barthian supernaturalism from which he was writing books with such titles as *God's Demand and Man's Response* (1938), and *God's Judgment on Europe*. 'To be a Christian, in the authentic biblical sense,' he declared unequivocally, 'is to find oneself by God's free gift and transcendant initiative received into his eternal kingdom.'[13] Or take Arnold Toynbee's almost Barthian conviction expressed in volume VI of *A Study of History*, published in 1939: 'We may and must pray that a reprieve which God has granted to our society once will not be refused if we ask for it again in a contrite spirit and with a broken heart'. In the theologians of the thirties there is no blurring of natural and supernatural in some sort of liberal Christian humanism. The world is sinful and judged as such. The Church, with its sacramental fellowship, is seen as God's saving initiative within and against the world, a new creation through the incarnation, cross and resurrection. There were, of course, many variants on such a view – some more, some less biblically fundamentalistic, some more Catholic, others more Protestant – but a common note is unmistakable. Observe it in D. R. Davies's *On to Orthodoxy*, Temple's Lent Book for 1939, or again, in a fully Free Church setting, with Nathaniel Micklem, who changed from the 'liberal' who wrote *Open Light* in 1919 to the 'Barthian' who wrote *What is the Faith?* in 1936, and collaborated with Bernard Manning and others in addressing to their fellow Congregationalists a letter in which they recalled the centrality of incarnation, resurrection and sacraments as against the 'liberal' social gospel which was all, they believed, that many Congregationalists were being offered.[14] Observe the return to a great confidence in the overall historical reliability in the New Testament. Take first that remarkably challenging little book of 1930, Frank Morison's *Who Moved the Stone?* Take secondly the really seminal scholarly work of Edwyn Hoskyns. Then move on to the Congregationalist C. H. Dodd, Norris-Hulse Professor at Cambridge from 1935, who did most to convince the common Christian, and scholars too, that first-class modern biblical scholarship really could be reconciled with, and indeed support, a traditional belief in Christ. His great continental predecessors and contemporaries, Harnack, Schweitzer, Bultmann, had all in one way or another appeared to undermine that belief. Dodd, with his conception of 'realized eschatology', his insistence upon the overall reliability of the New Testament, his reassertion in due course of historicity even in the fourth gospel, provided a good deal of the biblical arm for the wider return to orthodoxy, while helping to avoid the pitfalls of Barthianism. What he was saying, of course, many other scholars were saying too but his was the most accessible work written with a particularly pastoral and intelligible touch so that it is not quite to be wondered at that the SCM Study Conference of 1937 produced its famous *mot*: 'Thou shalt love the Lord thy Dodd and thy Niebuhr as thyself.' It is true that a new brand of biblical scholarship basically opposed to historicity – form criticism – made its English appearance at this point with R. H. Lightfoot's Bampton Lectures of 1935, *History and Interpretation in the Gospels*. But what is striking is how little impact this made at the time. It was not in line with the spirit of the age, but it would become so in the next 'liberal' phase of English culture, thirty years later, when Lightfoot's best pupil, Dennis Nineham, would be standard bearer for a development clearly opposed to that which we are now considering.

Side by side with the movement in biblical scholarship was that in the theology of the Church, the sacraments and the liturgy. 'In the period on which we now enter', noted E. L. Allen, 'the Church came to occupy in the minds of Protestants a position which had once been thought to be peculiar to Catholics.'[15] This was indeed the beginning of the high summer of Anglo-Catholic theology. It had been maturing for decades. Now it had arrived, both in the universities and in the religious orders. We have seen it in Michael Ramsey's enduring masterpiece, *The Gospel and the Catholic Church*. Behind Ramsey were some rather older scholars like Lionel Thornton of Mirfield, Hebert of Kelham, Dom Gregory Dix of Nashdom Abbey, Kenneth Kirk, Bishop of Oxford, as well as brilliant young priests like Eric Mascall and Austin Farrer. While this school undoubtedly retained an occasionally almost petty, anti-Protestant, anti-Nonconformist note, it was a great deal less narrowly partisan than earlier Anglo-Catholics. One reason for this was its increasingly biblical character; a second what it owed to Maurice and Forsyth; a third, the growing together of the Anglo-Catholic with the SCM thread in Anglican life. The Anglo-Catholics were now beginning to find themselves the natural centre of Anglicanism, providing both bishops and university professors; and greater responsibility produced on the whole greater tolerance. The Thomist thread was also increasingly explicit. Anglo-Catholic theologians were very happy to learn from Maritain or Père Clerissac, just as they were willing to co-operate with Oxford Dominicans. The enterprise of Thomist renewal seemed something in which all could co-operate on equal terms. We may sum up what was happening in the intellectual life of Christians in some rather despondent words of Dr

Major, who had been for so many decades the standard bearer of Protestant liberal modernism:

> Today Liberal Christianity is spoken of with contempt; as something which is discredited as it has proved itself to be futile. The Liberal Gospel, the Liberal Jesus and the Liberal God are derided, and the theologies of Neo-Thomism, Neo-Calvinism, Neo-Lutheranism are claimed as infinitely more deserving of faith and obedience.[16]

Thus had modernism come and gone.

If Anglican Catholics plundered French Catholicism for its Thomism and Belgian Catholicism for its liturgical movement, and could even learn quite happily from an English Catholic like Christopher Dawson, the traffic remained somewhat one way. English Catholics were few indeed who could willingly and openly learn from their separated brethren. Still, undoubtedly, in objective terms the ranks were closing as an explicitly sacramental and eucharistic theology became more and more central to Anglican and even Free Church Christians.

The theologians we have been speaking of were priests and religious. Perhaps still more worthy of notice was, however, the lay theologian. If a priest looking back in the early 1940s on his youth in Oxford forty years earlier could remark, 'Oxford as Oxford had no religious influence on me, and men did not speak of God as they do now',[17] one suspects that the increased godliness of the university was due less to the clergy than to the laity. The SCM had been doing its work for decades and it was now beginning to be possible to speak again, as one certainly could hardly have done for any year of this century before the late 1930s, of 'the impressive number of Christian intellectuals in universities and elsewhere'.[18] Maybe the élite of this group saw themselves at the time as philosophers rather than as theologians – the model of the theologian as cleric dies hard and, to a large extent specifically theological chairs were still reserved to the clergy. Nevertheless when one thinks of Dorothy Emmet, H. A. Hodges, A. D. Lindsay and Donald Mackinnon (following of course in the steps of A. E. Taylor and Ernest Barker), one cannot but sense that something very significant indeed was developing in the intellectual life of Britain: a new professional lay appropriation of Christian belief at a very high level of intellectual expertise, at the same time almost non-partisan, non-denominational and non-backward looking. The modern disciplines of mind were wholly taken for granted but it was not thought, as earlier generations of clerics had tended to do, that this required some vast watering down of the content of Christian belief. These lay theologians mostly owed a lot both to Niebuhr and to French Thomism; they owed something too to the Oldham tradition, to the SCM, to the Oxford Conference of 1937, and they mostly took for granted the 'Catholic' theological side of the Church of England. But they represented the coming together of all these things within non-clerical circles of scholarship, in which the majority orthodoxy remained decidedly secularist. Like Lewis and Charles Williams in their own rather different ways, they were an avant-garde returning cautiously but not unconfidently to territory long effectively abandoned to the other side.

Over all this very remarkable period of Christian intellectual revival, William Temple presided. In no way did he initiate it. A man of the pre-1914 generation, he had struggled for his faith with modernism and learnt his philosophy from the British Hegelians. His social concern was at the start an idealistic but shadowy socialism. He remained, however, all his life a man of tempered enthusiasm, resiliently skilful in grafting into his thinking new patterns of ideas. He was not consciously an Anglo-Catholic and yet from Gore and Tawney, and many other close friends, he absorbed more and more of Anglo-Catholic ecclesiology, just as he had absorbed the ecumenical ideal through his long involvement with the SCM and a lot of social thought through the WEA. Once he had absorbed he led. Now in the thirties he was learning again, this time from Niebuhr and Maritain. His address to the London Aquinas Society on 19 October 1943, on 'Thomism and Modern Needs', was one of the last things he did in this life and it is, perhaps, a little symbolic. Ecclesiastically his relationship with Cardinal Hinsley pointed forward to possibilities hitherto almost unimaginable. Equally, his lecture on Thomism printed in *Blackfriars* was thought by its editor 'in a sense to mark the confluence and reunion of the Anglican and the Catholic philosophical tradition'. Moses who had led his people so far, had now to die, unable himself to enter the Promised Land. For a time his death, and Hinsley's, would bring to a close an almost over-promising moment of religious history. Yet in fact the intellectual work attempted in that period, 'the confluence and reunion of the Anglican and the Catholic' intellectual traditions, together with a comparable reunion of the Christian and the English intellectual traditions – neither in any way complete, but both challenging, insistent and not easily undo-able – left the mental climate of the nation, and especially the climate of religion within the nation, surprisingly different in the early 1940s from what it had been twenty years before.

Ecumenical Advances

If among the religious thinkers of the 1930s there was an increasing transcendance of denominational frontiers towards a catholicism with a small c, so that in retrospect it seems almost irrelevant to which church C. S. Lewis, C. H. Dodd, A. D. Lindsay, Christopher Dawson or even Michael Ramsey belonged, it was still more true that the very considerable institutional achievements of the decade were ecumenical, not denominational. The Church of England subsequent to the rejection of the revised Prayer Book and under the primacy of Lang was sunk in a profoundly 'wait and see' mood. If, in the interchurch field, the crucial test of growth in consciousness of Christian community had now become the urge to share eucharistic communion at least in some circumstances, the very negative regulations on intercommunion produced by the Convocations of Canterbury and York in 1932 were indicative that such growth had not progressed very far within the Established Church. Methodists had reunited but the effort to do so seemed almost to have exhausted them. The churches, as churches, had all a remarkably dull history in the 1930s, yet at the same time one of the most creative and decisively important developments was going on in the new intermediate area of the ecumenical movement.[1] What had hardly existed at the beginning of the century and seemed still in the 1920s something new, marginal and fluctuating came suddenly in the thirties to capture, almost for good, the centre of the stage. The young SCM pioneers of the pre-1914 period – Oldham, William Paton, William Temple – were now the ecclesiastical statesmen of Protestant Europe, dexterously creating the structures for the Church of the future. In other fields of life the thirties were the great dissolvent and it would be hard to point to statesmanship whose fruits have survived the following decades. For the ecumenical movement the reverse is the case. Faced with the fearful challenges of the time, the need to provide a Christian leadership which somehow answered the taunts of Fascism and Nazism and which might in some way assist Christians in Europe to withstand the totalitarian assault, the captains of ecumenism were emboldened to press ahead more than might otherwise have been the case and to put through a plan for a single unified international body which could represent the churches, hopefully all but the Roman Catholic, throughout the world.

The senior statesman in all this was certainly Oldham. Since the Edinburgh Conference of 1910 he had been secretary of its Continuation Committee and then of the International Missionary Council, until in 1934, recognizing the increasingly menacing state of the world, he became instead chairman of the Research Committee of the 'Life and Work' movement and, in practice, holder of 'the most strategic position in the ecumenical movement as a whole'.[2] He was in reality for the best part of three decades the *éminence grise* of international Protestantism. It seems that a Belgian colonial minister once found it hard to understand what importance this rather deaf British Presbyterian layman might have until someone compared him with the Cardinal Secretary of State! Surprising, doubtless, to the Belgian minister but pretty apt. Yet he had been, hitherto, a Secretary of State without a pope and without a curia.

The pope *in petto* was undoubtedly the ubiquitous Temple. Oldham's junior by seven years, he also had been at the Edinburgh Conference, if in the humbler role of an usher. In subsequent years no one participated in more ecumenical conferences than Temple, a truly pontificating figure – pontificating in the precise etymological sense of bridge-building. 'I seem to have written what opens the door for the progressives while perfectly satisfying the conservatives,' he remarked a trifle complacently at Jerusalem in 1928 of its crucial document. From the Faith and Order Conference at Lausanne the previous year his role had become clear. He was chairman of the Lausanne Continuation Committee and presided over all its meetings held at one or another continental health resort, but what was so important about him was the ability to be interested in, and somehow identified with, all the three main strands of international ecumenism: Faith and Order, Life and Work, the International Missionary Council. Other people held to one or another of these, only Temple managed to straddle them all.

William Paton was the third major British founder of the modern ecumenical world. In the twenties he had been the initiating secretary of the National Christian Council of India; from thence he returned to Europe to take over, little by little, Oldham's responsibilities as secretary of the International Missionary Council, while Oldham moved into the field of Life and Work where, with the President, Bishop Bell, he set about preparing the decisive Oxford Conference of 1937. Paton was a less subtle person than Oldham and more interested in ecclesiastical administration. David Cairns once had a dream of him answering two telephone calls at the same time, one from the Archbishop of Canterbury, the other from the Archbishop of York.[3] He could be likened to a pocket battleship, the forceful, almost ruthless creator of a new ecumenical institutionalism – in India, throughout the missionary world, and finally in Britain.[4] Oldham was the Athenaeum Whig, quietly devising the new strategies, spotting and bringing together the 'people who really mattered'; Temple was the public figurehead, the authoritative spokesman who could not be gainsaid; Paton was the selfless, highly efficient bureaucrat, administrator-general of ecumenism. Together, they changed the ecclesiastical map of the world. It was a decisively British contribution and yet by chance in the moment of achievement they so faded away that when the World Council actually materialized after the war, its principal architects were already simply a part of history.

The central ecumenical event of the 1930s was undoubtedly the Oxford Conference of Life and Work held from 12 to 26 July 1937 upon the theme of 'Church, Community and State'. It had been prepared with meticulous care by Oldham and his young assistants, Eric Fenn and Visser 't Hooft. Its thinking represents the most mature ecclesiastical approach to social and political problems of the inter-war years – an approach immensely sobered by the gravity of the international situation around them. There were no delegates from the main churches of Germany. Pastor Niemoller had been arrested just twelve days before the conference began but his absence was more decisive for the delegates than his presence could possibly have been. The conference message (inevitably drafted by Temple) expressed the underlying preoccupation of the German Confessing Church: 'The first duty of the Church, and its greatest service to the world, is that it be in very deed the Church. . . .'

The ecumenical movement had grown with the League of Nations and must have seemed at times in the comfortable twenties but a pale religious reflection of the League's secular aspirations. But now the League was breaking down, its aspirations scorned. Faced with the challenge of Nazism and stiffened by the revival of a more conservative theology the churches of the thirties and still more the ecumenical movement of the thirties saw themselves as Church over against the world, in a near-Barthian way, different from that of the theologically rose-tinted spectacles and natural/supernatural assimilationism of earlier years. Let the Church be the Church. Yet how could the churches, so many and so integrated into national secular structures, be the Church? The ecumenical movement and its earlier international organizations long claimed to be in no way a replacement for existing churches. In a profound way, however, in the thirties the movement felt called to make of itself a unified body precisely so as to fulfil the first duty of the Church and witness in faith and with independence to the world of sin, modern ideology, and secular tyranny when the Churches could, or would, not do it.[5]

The decisive resolution of the Oxford Conference of Life and Work within this context of international ecclesial need was to establish in union with Faith and Order a World Council of Churches. The latter movement met the following month in Edinburgh under Temple's presidency, and passed a comparable resolution. Here there was some opposition, an opposition led by Bishop Headlam. Headlam too had long been an international ecumenical leader, especially within Faith and Order. He saw ecumenism as confirming and recognizing the good within the denominational order as it existed, rather than in rushing into seemingly revolutionary new institutions. Moreover he deeply distrusted Temple's Socialist leanings and in no way shared the general sympathy for the German Confessing Church. Headlam, a firm Erastian, disliked almost everything which a World Council was likely to stand for and he felt, in point of fact fairly correctly, that Faith and Order, in many ways a rather conservative body, was being hijacked by the more pragmatic and politically minded leadership of Life and Work.[6]

The following May at a meeting in Utrecht, again chaired by Temple, the draft constitution and doctrinal basis of the World Council of Churches was already drawn up. Temple became chairman of its provisional committee while Paton and Visser 't Hooft were appointed its joint General Secretaries. Later in 1938, the very year in which the League of Nations Assembly held what was to be its final depressing session, the World Council of Churches ('In Process of Formation') moved into Geneva, where Visser 't Hooft took up residence while Paton, still secretary of the International Missionary Council (holding the same year its major meeting at Tambaram in India), remained based in London.

Visser 't Hooft was a Barthian. Tambaram was dominated by the theology of another Dutch Barthian, Hendrik Kraemer. A neo-Calvinist theological tide was now flowing in ecumenical circles on the Continent, in regard to which the old British hands felt only half at ease.[7] It was they who had had the vision and created the machinery but that machinery might now pass them by. The separation between Visser 't Hooft in Geneva and Paton in London, a fairly minor one in time of peace, became for other reasons as well quite decisive in time of war. They were theoretically co-equal secretaries, but in practice 't Hooft acted more and more as the World Council's sole secretary. Paton's close links with the British government and very straightforward commitment to the war effort inevitably inhibited a fully international role within the new world situation. His sudden death in 1943, just a year before Temple's, did but ratify an arrangement which the war had made inevitable.

In Britain itself the ecumenical bandwagon could now roll securely on. In 1940 the Church Assembly passed a resolution, proposed by Temple, welcoming the establishment of the World Council, and two years later the British Council of Churches – the national counterpart to the World Council – was solemnly inaugurated with a service in St Paul's Cathedral at which Temple preached. The preparatory work for it had largely been done by Paton but Temple was inevitably its first president. In his enthronement address in Canterbury Cathedral a few months earlier, April 1942, he had spoken of 'the great new fact of our era' – the ecumenical community. It had now arrived and the deaths of the primate and of the ecclesiastical pocket battleship, devastating as they certainly seemed at the time to Christians of progressive sentiment, could not conceivably undo the work that had been accomplished. Yet it had not been an inevitable achievement; indeed without Oldham, Paton and Temple it is more than likely that no World Council would have been established for many years, if ever. No one else could easily have taken the lead, and it would have been only too likely that without the very skilful manoeuvring of the three principal actors, the far more cautious line of Bishop Headlam would long have prevailed in ecclesiastical circles.

Nevertheless behind the leaders there was a whole young generation of highly capable Christians committed to the larger ecumenical cause. It is sufficient to list some of the SCM secretaries of the 1930s – Lesslie Newbigin, Eric Fenn, Alan Richardson, Ambrose Reeves, Oliver Tomkins, Ronald Preston, David Paton, Alan Booth. Here were men of great ability, Anglicans and Free Churchmen, who out of their SCM experience would carry forward a sense of ecumenical community far stronger than had ever hitherto existed. They and their like would in many ways be decisive for the development of the churches across the next quarter of a century as they worked to implement a vision which had been essentially delineated during the stress of the 1930s. Certainly not again until the 1960s would there be a comparably creative period.

In the winter of 1939 Max Warren, then vicar of Holy Trinity Church, Cambridge, found himself administering communion to Professor Dodd (a Congregationalist), Mrs Dodd (an Anglican) and Franz Hildebrandt (a Lutheran), who were kneeling side by side. The churches – at least the Church of England and the Lutheran – did not sanction intercommunion, and a few years earlier such a thing could hardly have happened. Now it seemed – at least to the chosen few – right, obvious, unavoidable. Crisis and war produced a new *communitas*. The ecumenical advance of the late 1930s was not just an institutional matter, enormously important as that was, it was also one in the collective consciousness of a small but sufficient Christian élite drawn increasingly from all churches, for whom the denominational barriers, so formidable even at the end of the First World War, were now appearing as a rather ludicrous inheritance from an archaic past.

B

Preface

Our focus hitherto in this part has been upon the domestic history of England and the internal life of the churches in both their separate existences and their common concerns. It is true that our survey of Christian thought and of the advance of the ecumenical movement has required a good deal of reference to the wider international scene and the ideological conflicts of the period, but our interest in these remained their impact upon one side or another of specifically Christian life. We have now to shift our focus to concentrate rather upon the conflicts themselves – in many ways the most crucial for western man in the twentieth century – and the involvement of English Christians within them. This second half of our 1930s survey is then a good deal more political in orientation than the first half and, all in all, more political than any other segment of the book, apart, perhaps, from its immediate sequel, the account of the Second World War.

International Politics

Decades may be delusions but few decadal characterizations appear more convincing than that contrasting the comfortable apolitical culture of the twenties with the sharply divisive political commitments of the 1930s when Fascist blackshirts marched down English streets, idealistic poets went to fight and die in Spain in a civil war magnified into an epic of universal dimensions, and Cambridge apostles were recruited as lifelong spies of Soviet Russia. All this was, doubtless, in Britain essentially élitist activity, the great majority of British people remaining stodgily uninterested in continental ideological warfare. Here as elsewhere, Fascists and Communists truly needed each other, their mutual vilification giving them a *raison d'être* which they otherwise lacked.[1] Nevertheless, the mini-confrontations and marches of Britain imported into this country the major realities of the Continent, from the effects of which neither government, intellectual, religious leader nor common man could eventually escape. The 'heroic' uniformed posturings of Sir Oswald Mosley aped the typical politician of the 1930s: the charismatic 'Leader'. The personality cult, the kissing of babies, the deriding of intellectuals, the vast open air gatherings of passionate supporters – such was the new type of leadership introduced by Duce and Führer, a leadership easily adaptable to the claims of any organization at once populist and totalitarian.

The vast instability to which Europe was now subject had as its immediate cause the slump, a largely artificial disease engendered by American capitalism. But if Europe was now a subject prone to reacting hysterically and uncontrollably to such infections, this was in large degree due to the fact that the religio-political traditions of much of the Continent had been so devastatingly overturned by the First World War, leaving a vacuum both of stable institution and ideological identification. Only if the churches in the major countries had really set themselves to harness a genuine democracy to their essential needs, as Don Sturzo had so clear-mindedly attempted to do, might this have been avoided. But German Lutheranism was far too profoundly tied to German nationalism, to authoritarian and militaristic government, for it to take the democratic plunge with conviction.[2] German Catholicism was a good deal more willing to do so, possessing in its Centre Party an old and respectable tradition, and what stable government did exist in Germany and elsewhere in central Europe in the 1920s owed much to Catholic attempts – half-hearted and over-clericalist as the Anglo-Saxon observer may easily judge them – to establish stable, rather conservative democracies. If they failed and, failing, brought down with them into Fascism and world war their whole society, it was that they had too little time and too much was stacked against them: the harshness of Versailles, the feebleness of the League of Nations, the economic devastation of the Depression, the near-absence of any Catholic-Protestant co-operation, the anti-democratic preferences of the Vatican. Pope Pius XI was a good man, far, far better than most of those with whom he had to deal, and yet if there was one man who might have had it in his power to prevent the agonies from occurring and did not do so, but rather created circumstances which in due course produced the Second World War, that man was Pius XI. His personal tragedy was that in his last year, by then almost impotent to affect the course of history, he seemed himself to see it so, to sense that ten and fifteen years before he had terribly misjudged the times and the movements. It is unlikely that he saw that such misjudgment derived at least in part from his own highly despotic nature combined with the near-inherent political preferences of an institution as authoritarian as the Roman Church. He did see that he had misjudged Mussolini and Hitler, but not that he had done so because in many ways they too faithfully reflected, even pandered to, his own preferred conception of authority.

Behind all these things, apparently unchanging, the object at once of the most unalleviated fear and the most uncritical adulation, lay Communist Russia. The progressive consensus, stretching far beyond the narrow ranks of committed Communists, long retained a starry-eyed conviction that Stalin's Russia was somehow the standard bearer of the future paradise, instead of being what in fact it was – one of the most ruthlessly systematic of all tyrannies, worse than the tsardom it replaced, an inhuman police state crushing its erstwhile believers at least as mercilessly as its long-time enemies. It was the simple inability of the progressive West European intellectual, the typical Left Book Club man, to use his considerable faculties to face up to the truth of where the Russian Revolution had gone so horribly wrong (and so early wrong), that most gravely vitiates the wider integrity of the outpourings of the left in the 1930s.

While the Conservative judged Russia more accurately, his conclusions were often as disastrous. For the religious it was the systematic propagandist atheism of the Soviets which was most decisive. The atheism of Soviet Russia at that time was not a nominal part of Marx's philosophical legacy. It was a crusading cause which no responsible Christian leader could do otherwise than take seriously. Preoccupation with one formidable danger does not justify blindness to other grave threats. This, however, is just what happened, providing a key motif for much of the religio-political history of the period. Time and again Fascism cleverly played the anti-Communist card to capture at some crucial moment the confidence of ecclesiastical authority and disarm the sentinels who stood by the barricades of Christian freedom, before turning to rend the fools that had so trusted it and to assert a pagan totalitarianism as abhorrent to Christianity as Stalinist atheism.

Adolf Hitler came to power as Chancellor of Germany on 30 January 1933. The economic crisis, the threat seen by many in a growing Communist Party and the slow disintegration of Catholic opposition in the Centre Party, made his victory possible and the manipulation of the last two factors ensured the consolidation of his power over the next few months. In July the British Minister to the Vatican could report, after an interview with Cardinal Pacelli, now Secretary of State, 'His Eminence said that the Vatican really viewed with indifference the dissolution of the Centre Party.'[3] That same month the concordat was concluded and the Centre Party dissolved; the latter event took place three days before the signing of the former in which Hitler gave the Church exceptionally favourable terms educationally. When one considers how long and seemingly ungenerous was the Vatican's negotiation of concordats with more respectable governments, of Poland or of Spain, in the early 1930s, the quite indecent haste with which the concordat was signed with Germany six months after Hitler's first arrival in power and when the traditional political leaders of Germany's Catholics were, many of them, actually in prison, strikes one distastefully.[4] Just as, ten years before, Pius XI struck down the *Partito Popolare* in order to make way for a straight deal with Italian Fascism, so now he did not hesitate before delivering the *coup de grâce* to the Centre Party, Europe's most respected expression of Catholic democracy, in the interests of an imaginary Catholic–Nazi entente which would both ensure the Church a maximum of attainable privilege and an unambiguously hard line against Communism.

The Vatican did not, needless to say, like or genuinely trust the Nazis even at this early stage. Its haste to conclude a concordat with them certainly demonstrated its indifference to the Centre Party, and to the political tradition which it represented; but in regard to the Nazis it demonstrated fear rather than trust and Cardinal Pacelli, only the next month, privately expressed his disgust at 'the actions of the German Government at home, their persecution of the Jews, their proceedings against political opponents, the reign of terror to which the whole nation was subjected'.[5] Nor was there anything unique about the Vatican's response to the Nazi mailed fist at a time when the first concentration camps were being opened and the country flooded with anti-Semitic propaganda. It was indeed less gullible than many. George Bell expressed at the time 'profound sympathy' with this 'great awakening in the life of the German People' that was going on,[6] and Bishop Headlam of Gloucester lauded the Nazis still more emphatically while denouncing their Jewish critics in a letter to *The Times* (24 October 1933) as 'clever, malicious and untruthful'.

The tide seemed to be moving across the world in the Fascist direction. Even in Britain the British Union of Fascists was formed late in 1932: 'We shall prepare to meet the anarchy of Communism with the organised force of Fascism', declared its leader, Sir Oswald Mosley, a former Labour Cabinet Minister, an aristocratic populist with considerable flair for obtaining publicity.[7] Attacks on Jews, marches through London of uniformed blackshirts and a general stress on the existence of a state of 'crisis' were the hallmarks of the British Fascist. The response was remarkably slight – even slighter than that to Communist propaganda. Despite the millions of its unemployed Britain was simply not prepared to consider itself victim of the sort of crisis which Fascist or Communist could fruitfully feed upon.

Abroad the situation was far more serious. Each Fascist advance encouraged greater bellicosity elsewhere. In October 1935 Italy invaded Ethiopia (Abyssinia), a piece of colonialist aggression which the nineteenth century would doubtless have thought little of, but which in the twentieth made a complete nonsense of the League of Nations and all it stood for. The League imposed sanctions, producing no effect except Italian fury. Within nine months the country was conquered. The Abyssinian war was important, not only in the major advance it involved towards a Europe divided into two hostile armed camps, but also, for religious history, in the lamentably high degree of support Mussolini's aggression received from the Catholic Church in Italy. Colonial barbarism proved a splendid tool for the conquest of Catholic sentiment by Fascist nationalism. Bishop after bishop went into ecstasies of patriotism. So the bishop of Cremona, consecrating regimental flags, was happy to declare: 'The blessing of God be upon these soldiers who, on African soil, will conquer new and fertile lands for the Italian genius, thereby bringing to them Roman and Christian culture.' For Cardinal Schuster of Milan the Italian army would achieve 'the triumph of the Cross . . . opening the gates of Abyssinia to the Catholic faith and civilisation'. Such fervent nationalism could hardly please the Vatican, and it probably did not please the average parish priest, who was a lot less obsequious to the Fascists than the average bishop;[8] yet it was not rebuked by the pope either, and his only comments on the war were so ambiguous as to be meaningless. Never was there a more obvious issue for the primate of Italy to speak about emphatically, but he did not do so, leaving his suffragans to express themselves in a way nearly as unanimous as it was blasphemous. Once the war was over, the conquest achieved, the pope lost no time in sending as Apostolic Visitor to Ethiopia a notorious Fascist, in replacing with Italians all the non-Italian Catholic missionaries who had long worked there (including the old French bishop, Mgr Jarousseau, who had spent fifty years in the country). Meanwhile the Protestant missionaries were expelled and the head of the Coptic Church beheaded. The pope further went out of his way to address King Victor Emmanuel as 'King of Italy, and Emperor of Ethiopia'. When, a little later, the German Ambassador to Italy, von Neurath, complained in conversation with Mussolini of the growing Vatican hostility to Nazi Germany, Mussolini gave him a word of advice; grant the Vatican, he recommended, small concessions for cardinals. By these means you will win them over completely. 'Why,' he added, 'they even declared the Abyssinian war a Holy War!'[9]

It was not only the Catholic Church which was discredited by the Abyssinian war, it was also the League of Nations and the western powers. No action was more diametrically opposed to the League's principles than the invasion of Ethiopia. The thoughtful exclusion of oil from the League's sanctions and the disgraceful British-French (Hoare-Laval) proposals for a compromise which would hand over two-thirds of Ethiopia to Italy revealed only too clearly the futility of the League and the sham of Anglo-French commitment to 'Collective Security'. This was probably the last moment at which the ideals, which had theoretically governed the world since the end of the First World War, could have been realistically vindicated. The soft centre of British government, which had its advantages on the home front in muddling through, was revealed on the overseas front now, as time and again in the coming years, in all its ineptitude. European Fascism arrived at the point at which it could unleash world war not only through the feeble-minded collaboration of the Church but also through that of the western democracies.

Next year, 1936, was the turn of Spain. It was also the year of the German military reoccupation of the Rhineland and of a vast increase in tension all across Europe. While the invasion of Abyssinia seemed to most outsiders an extremely clear case of immoral politics, the Spanish Civil War presented a far more complex conflict of values. It began in July 1936 when the army under Franco rose in revolt against the Republican government, and it only ended when Franco captured Madrid in March 1939. It was not a war between Communists and Fascists as such. The government was not Communist but a large alliance of the left, and the rebels were far more than the Falange, the Spanish Fascist organization. Vast atrocities upon both sides, and their very selective reporting by the foreign supporters of both sides, justified each in seeing its cause as akin to a crusade. The anarchist-Communist left wing of the Republican alliance sacked churches and murdered the clergy systematically. This was not government policy, but the government was incapable of controlling its own allies, and the mass murder of bishops, priests and nuns[10] was on a scale to make international Catholic support for Franco inevitable. Yet the murder of Republican supporters by Nationalists was probably at least five times as great. If the Republican government held out as long as it did against its own army, it was because of the very great amount of popular support it received in a land nominally almost entirely Catholic and against a cause closely supported by most Catholic clergy. This counted quite as much as international assistance: some forty thousand volunteers, as well as Russian military equipment. If Franco won in the end it was because of the far larger and more systematic overseas support, German and Italian, from which he benefited. This included tens of thousands of Italian regular soldiers.

The Spanish Civil War divided society within France and Britain more profoundly than any other international issue of the time and both governments prudently decided to stick to non-intervention in regard to the conflict, but foolishly refrained from making other than formal efforts to achieve the non-intervention of other powers. The war failed, however, to achieve across Europe what it might have seemed at one point close to achieving – some general alignment of Christians (or at least Catholics) with Fascists against the 'Left'. It was, of course, essentially the common strategy of Communists and Fascists to make of their conflict the one significant divide in society, and the greater the sense of 'crisis' became in any place the more readily could that view of things be adopted. Yet it was a wholly misleading view, Communists and Fascists being then, as many a time subsequently, far closer together in fundamental ideology than either can be to Christians or to liberals. Both Communists and Fascists fed upon distrust between Christians and liberals, but the logic of the situation slowly drove the latter more emphatically together against their common enemies.

The Catholic Church might feel grateful to Franco, but its trust in him was decidedly limited and its distrust in his backer, Hitler, was by 1937 enormous. In March of that year Pius XI wrote an extremely clear encyclical, *Mit Brennender Sorge*, which was printed in Germany, distributed secretly with superb efficiency to every parish priest in Germany and read from every pulpit one Sunday morning, denouncing 'the war of annihilation against the Catholic faith'.[11] In the last months before his death in February 1939, Pius XI battled still more courageously against both Nazism and Fascism, concerning their disregard of the rights of religion, the totalitarian nature of their government, and especially anti-Semitism. But he could now do little. The role of religion in the early thirties was considerable in the public life of Europe, and it could conceivably have swung the pendulum away from Fascism. But once such movements had gained full power, the possible role of an institutional Church in moderating events immensely diminished.

In Britain very few people positively sympathized with Hitler, just as few ever became Communists. Only a tiny minority entertained the slightest desire radically to change either the political or the economic system of their land. No major country of western Europe had been less gravely divided by the crises of the 1930s. The far left and the far right were good on noise, but both wildly wide of the mark in overall political judgment. Eric Blair returned from fighting for Republican Spain converted into George Orwell, the great literary crusader against totalitarianism of every hue and the advocate of a truly democratic socialism. That was not far off the position for which Tawney and Temple had long been preparing Christians of the middle ground. By the end of the decade the increasing confusion over Spain, German anti-Semitism, and the Moscow trials was pressing even British intellectuals back towards a central national consensus. When war inevitably arrived, and even because it arrived after so unrewarding a period of appeasement, it found a singularly

317

united nation, not a jingoist nation, not a well-led nation or one which had worked things out with great clarity of analysis. But it was a nation which had refused to be divided irretrievably either by depression or by ideology and, when it came to world war and to standing for a while frighteningly alone, this would prove the greatest of advantages.

Communism and Fascism
at Home

How far did English Christians seriously identify themselves with the Communist-Fascist confrontation of the 1930s? There had long been a fairly extensive body of clerical sympathizers for 'socialism' of a vague sort, but most of it was very vague and had rather little to do with anything which could be called 'Communist'. Conrad Noel doubtless kept the red flag flying through these years at Thaxted, but nice as he was he could, not unfairly, be dismissed as part of the 'lunatic fringe' of the clerical world. Communism had not been a serious issue for English Christians in the 1920s despite the Russian revolution. Thus it seems hardly to have appeared in the agenda of the Student Christian Movement, avant-garde as the SCM certainly thought itself in those years. With 1933 and the Nazi suppression of the Communist Party this suddenly changed and Christians found the challenge of Marxism to be, for a while, the outstanding issue. The SCM held an international conference in Edinburgh that year and it was largely devoted to the ideologies of Communism and Fascism. F. R. Barry, vicar of the University Church in Oxford, wrote anxiously to Eric Fenn, the conference organizer: 'Some of our most virile Christians are becoming Communists, and the only thing that will save them from Marxism and dropping Christianity altogether is a positive affirmation of Christian Communism.'[1] As Fenn later remarked, 'It is strange that this should have tarried until 1933, when the Russian Revolution took place in 1917.'[2] Few people in the 1930s in fact pursued Barry's proposal of a 'Christian Communism' very seriously, and certainly not Barry himself. If Charles Raven could declare benignly that 'it is in the better mutual understanding of the two movements (Christianity and Communism), and even, perhaps, in their synthesis that the hope of the future lies'[3] he was here, as so often, a lone and unrealistic voice. Christians converted to Communism mostly abandoned their Christianity quickly enough. The one renowned clerical exception was the dean of Canterbury, Hewlett Johnson. The 'Red Dean' accepted a fairly strait-laced form of orthodox Marxism which he combined, as people did at the time, with wholly uncritical adulation of Soviet Russia. He had been to Moscow and twice to Spain, and while for some people participation in the Spanish struggle brought with it an eventual recognition of the complexity of the contemporary political dilemma, for Johnson it simply enhanced his highly simple confidence in the goodness of organized Communism, in which belief he persevered for the rest of a long life. The 'Red Dean' was a thorn in the side of several archbishops of Canterbury, especially as the wider world, unskilled in Anglican ecclesiastical institutions, tended to confuse the sayings of the dean with those of the archbishop. Nevertheless a certain intrinsic silliness in the preaching of social revolution by a gaitered cleric from the comfort of a cathedral close moderated his influence. The clergy as a whole were anything but inclined to Communism, nor among the laity was there greater sympathy to be found for it than existed in the country generally. Stafford Cripps came closest for a time to representing a Christian commitment to effective alliance with Communism in an anti-Fascist crusade, but the Labour Party was in no way prepared to follow him there. The working-class base of the party was too suspicious of ideological radicalism, moreover its principal Christian element was by now upon its right, rather than its left wing. Christian approaches to Communism were upper class and intellectualist, a fringe expression of the wider phenomenon of élitist radicalism, and one of its more ineffectual expressions.

On the Fascist side there was more support and of a kind that mattered more. After the Berlin Olympic Games of 1936 Frank Buchman could declare, 'I thank Heaven for a man like Adolf Hitler, who built a front line of defence against the anti-Christ of Communism', and many Christians would have agreed with him. The fear of Communism produced ground in which sympathy for Fascism could grow as an obvious reaction. Such sympathy, however, developed almost equally naturally from a right-wing

English Christian tradition, both Anglican and Roman Catholic, which had long been a little contemptuous of democracy: Wilfred Ward, Hugh Cecil, Hilaire Belloc, T. S. Eliot, all in their different ways belonged to it. It might despise democracy, pride itself upon being 'reactionary' and yet not be averse to a populist appeal. Belloc and Eliot had both been influenced by Maurras, and it was doubtless from Maurras that Belloc acquired his anti-Semitism. It is striking how Eliot's critique of Fascism in *The Idea of a Christian Society* (1939) really consists in a dislike of its paganism; one has the impression that, apart from this, it would not be at all bad. Again, Evelyn Waugh could praise the Italians in Ethiopia and Roy Campbell join the Nationalists in Spain, but all this too was individualistic and idiosyncratic and, outside the upper-class Roman Catholic community, it carried rather little weight.

There was, nevertheless, sufficient Anglican clerical sympathy for Nazism for it to merit attention, chiefly because it involved two rather distinguished and influential people: Bishop Headlam and Sir Edwyn Hoskyns. Arthur Cayley Headlam was the most academically heavyweight of Anglican bishops.[4] He had long been Professor of Theology and Principal of King's College, from where in 1920 he moved to become Regius Professor of Divinity in Oxford. When in 1923 he was appointed Bishop of Gloucester, he was already sixty years old. He was a major authority on ecumenical relations in Europe with both Protestants and Orthodox. He was chairman of the Church of England Council on Foreign Relations. Unfortunately he was also an obstinate and unimaginative old man, a poor listener, rather deaf, immensely assured of his own wisdom, and he knew no German (in which he was like his great opponent Bishop Bell). Headlam sympathized with the Nazi Protestant wing, 'The German Christians', because of their anti-Communism, because they had forced the many separate Protestant churches into a unified national Church, which he thought a good thing, on the Anglican model, and because they claimed to be merely adapting Christianity in a 'liberal' way to the needs of the times, as against their theologically conservative opponents in the Confessing Church. Headlam almost wholly misread the German situation, interpreting it through mistaken English analogies. This was perhaps excusable in 1933. It was quite inexcusable by 1938, but he never seriously altered his viewpoint. To be told by Ribbentrop that Hitler was 'profoundly religious' impressed him greatly and he could be counted on to write letters to the press belittling the Christian opposition to the Nazis, urging friendliness as a panacea for all problems and declaring it 'a foolish and dangerous thing' to say that National Socialism was incompatible with Christianity.[5] Headlam's important position as chairman of the Council on Foreign Relations – from which he refused to resign – made his statements of real use to the Nazis and a source of confusion for Christians everywhere. 'The pertinacious apologist of the Nazi Government', Henson, his old friend, bitterly described him.[6] Yet he had, after the early days, very little support in the Church of England. When in 1938 in the Upper House of Convocation of Canterbury Headlam took exception to a resolution proposed by Bishop Bell expressing grave concern over the sufferings of Christians in Germany, he could not even find a seconder. Lang disagreed with him as profoundly as did Bell. Headlam was not a Nazi himself. He did not sympathize with Fascism in Britain. He was not anti-Semitic and not anti-democratic; he was just an obstinate old man, as unable to interpret correctly the situation in Germany as was the dean of Canterbury that in Russia – but whereas the dean really believed in Marxist ideology, the bishop did not believe in Nazi ideology.

Hoskyns is a much more subtle case.[7] He was, as we have seen, an outstanding scholar, at once the interpreter of several schools of German theology, and a key figure in the move back from a more 'liberal' to a more traditional interpretation of Christian origins. He greatly, and rightly, admired the learning of Gerhard Kittel, Professor of New Testament at the University of Tubingen, and a personal friend. Kittel was a very distinguished scholar indeed but he had developed a strongly anti-Semitic theology and joined the Nazi Party with enthusiasm.[8] Hoskyns kept in touch with Kittel, endeavoured to publish his writing in English and sent students to work under him at Tubingen. Such a relationship between outstanding academics in the same field was natural. Hoskyns was neither a politician nor an ecclesiastical statesman, but a don of Conservative political sentiments. Kittel lectured in Cambridge in October 1937, where he had been invited upon the persuasion of Hoskyns. It is unpleasant to think of him wearing his Nazi badge as he discussed New Testament scholarship; but one is not responsible for the clothes of a guest lecturer and Hoskyns himself had, anyway, died several months before the lectures were delivered.

Two years later, on another invitation emanating from Hoskyns's college, Corpus, T. S. Eliot would be giving there his lectures on *The Idea of a Christian Society*. An admirer has described the Corpus of those years as 'a Conservative-Anglican plot'.[9] Hoskyns was its dean from 1919 to 1937, Charles Smyth from 1937 to 1946. They, like others in the college, were not only Christian apologists, they were also avowedly anti-liberal, whatever form liberalism might take. In the thirties, like Eliot and Maurice Reckitt and many a Roman Catholic apologist, they tended to see the Nazi movement as a great wave of anti-liberalism which could at least be hailed as some sort of fellow traveller in the 'Counter Revolution'. It does not make them remotely into Nazis, and in the case of Hoskyns, his poor state of health is not to be overlooked. Hoskyns in the thirties was something of a Barthian, and one of the very few Englishmen of his generation to have been profoundly affected by Barth's classic *Commentary on the Epistle to the Romans*, which he had translated with the greatest care. Yet this is odd, for Barth was the prophet of the anti-Nazi Confessing Church in Germany and, if Headlam had a theological dislike for the Confessing Church and a theological attraction to the 'German Christians', it was because the former was Barthian and the latter 'liberal'. So the two leading Anglican clerics who sympathized with Nazi Germany did so from precisely contrary theological angles. Headlam and Hoskyns shared a dislike of political Liberalism, but while the former linked that dislike with a moderate theological liberalism, Hoskyns (like Eliot) linked it with a rediscovered theological conservatism. Hoskyns's opposite spirit in Cambridge, Charles Raven (by the later 1930s both Regius Professor of Divinity and Master of Christ's), was a 'liberal' in both theology and politics, while Karl Barth was a conservative in theology and an anti-Nazi in politics – a combination comparable with that of many an Anglo-Catholic Socialist. In these four men, all four possible political-theological combinations are, then, to be found. What produced Hoskyns's Nazi sympathies – such as they were – was not, one can conclude, his theological but his political Conservatism, much as – in his own mind – he probably linked the two. Neither Hoskyns nor, still less, his pupil and Kittel's interpreter in Britain, Richard Gutteridge, could possibly be described as a Nazi. With misplaced good intentions they misread the Nazis in their own more gentlemanly image.[10] In the vast intellectual and political confusion of the 1930s their contribution to the general muddlement was small indeed and is only really worth pointing out in order to make it clear that it was not bigger. In the Church of England there was simply no party comparable to the clerico-Fascists of Catholic Italy or the 'German Christians' of Protestant Germany, yet Ulrich Simon's comment upon Headlam is all the same worth pondering in conclusion:

> Doubtless the devotion to law and order and a loathing of anarchy make traditionalists victims to the *poseurs* in the political game. They are easily caught. Headlam was not alone in supping with the devil, accepting a very small spoon of poison before the whole infected meal is served up.[11]

The English Roman Catholic contribution to the Fascist cause was rather more considerable. That English Catholics sympathized with Fascism is not surprising.[12] They had, first of all, some encouragement from the pope and, secondly, the example of so many fellow Catholics, bishops and laity, of southern Europe. The Lateran Treaty had been lauded so intensely in Catholic circles that it was hard not to accept the verdict that the person who had made it possible was, indeed, the 'Man of Providence'. Subsequent tension between the Catholic Church and Fascism in Italy should not be exaggerated, at least not before 1938. Salazar and Franco seemed to fit into the same pattern and, in the case of Salazar, it was at least plausible to argue that here was a really original kind of right-minded dictator, intent not only on blocking the advance of Communism, but on creating a new social order, called 'Corporatism' based on the teaching of the Social encyclicals of the popes. At home Belloc had long preached about the phoney quality of western democracy. Why should not the Catholic world now devise something better? In regard to the specific issue of Nazi Jewish policy there was, unfortunately, plenty of latent, and not so latent, anti-Semitism in Catholic circles at home and abroad, stirred up not only by Maurras and Belloc, but by Jesuit theologians regularly at work in their influential Roman review, *Civilta Cattolica*.[13]

When the Spanish Civil War broke out it was more or less inevitable that the great majority of British Catholics should take the Nationalist side, see the war as a highly justifiable crusade against the murderers of priests and the ravagers of churches, and regard Franco in Belloc's words as 'the man who has saved us all'.[14] Probably at no other moment in twentieth-century history has the English Catholic community, as such, taken up so strongly a political position and to such effect. Douglas Jerrold played, it seems, a key role in arranging for a British aeroplane, ostensibly carrying some tourists from the Canary Islands to North Africa, to pick up General Franco and fly him to Morocco to lead the rebellion. There was an official 'Bishops Fund for Aid for the Spanish Nationalists', and there was no doubt where Hinsley stood on the matter – a photograph of Franco was displayed upon his desk. Douglas Woodruff at the *Tablet* threw himself heart and soul into Franco's cause, just as, in France, the editor of *La Croix* did the same.[15] The strength of Catholic opinion certainly had some influence in keeping Britain non-interventionist, though this was what the Conservative government wanted anyway. The political establishment silently agreed far more closely with Hinsley than with Temple over Spain. Yet Protestant, Liberal and left-wing opinion was vociferously and unanimously anti-Franco. Age-old Protestant suspicions of Catholics, as a threat to the political freedom characteristic of the British tradition, were inevitably revived in these circumstances: 'the Catholic in liberal circles was seen as the enemy of our liberties', Christopher Hollis, a liberal-minded Catholic, later remarked.[16] It was the last decade in which English Catholics would widely be so judged.

Here again, the degree of sympathy for Fascism itself was often decidedly limited. Archbishop Hinsley attempted to defend the Pope for not condemning the Italian invasion of Ethiopia. His argument was pretty inept: 'What can the Pope do to prevent this or any other war? He is a helpless old man with a small police force to guard himself, to guard the priceless art and archaeological treasures of the Vatican, and to protect his diminutive state. . . .'[17] But it was clear enough that Hinsley himself hardly looked upon Mussolini with favour, and that his sympathies lay very much more with Africa, 'that ill-used continent'.

There was still less reason for British Catholics to be sympathetic with Nazism, for the religious bonds which linked them emotionally with the Mediterranean world were here not operative. Nevertheless the fear of Communism easily blinded them to the evils of Nazism, and the pro-Fascist lobby, mounted by a powerful section of the English Catholic intelligentsia, easily covered Germany too. There was far too much anti-Semitism among them already for the Nazi attacks on the Jews to matter very much. One fearful example of this viewpoint can be found in J. K. Heydon's *Fascism and Providence*, published by Sheed & Ward as late as October 1937 – six months after *Mit Brennender Sorge*. Heydon, otherwise a businessman of no great significance, linked Fascism with Catholic Action (in a way that could certainly not appeal to the pope) and especially with the Catholic Evidence Guild. He urged that 'the young movement of Fascism', committed to the goal that 'England may attain the happiness of authority in the Corporate State', should work hand in glove with the 'young movement of the Catholic Evidence Guild' whose parallel goal was 'that England may attain the happiness of authority in the Corporate Church'.[18] As regards Nazism he wrote:

> Upwards of a million of the four million Nazis are Catholics, and Catholic Bavaria is their particular stronghold and birthplace. Fascism in fact is of Catholic origin and no English Catholic has a scintilla of right to condemn the Nazis. Catholics who do, and there are some few who are busying themselves considerably, may be found to be fighting against God.

What is most significant about this appalling nonsense is not that some nonentity could write it, but that one of the principal Catholic firms in London could publish it and that major Catholic journals could review it not unfavourably.[19] Even in February 1939 the *Tablet* in an important editorial could still appeal to Catholics 'not to join or encourage this anti-Fascist Crusade'. In this it was essentially at one with most other Catholic periodicals.

Anti-Fascist English Catholic intellectuals did exist – among the Dominicans and their friends especially – and Fascist sympathies were hardly to be found among the great bulk of working-class Catholics. Nevertheless it was at this point of Catholic Fascist intersection that a significant group of English Christians had most closely identified itself with the principal ideological confrontation of the 1930s. It proved fortunate both for the Church and for the nation that Cardinal Hinsley had himself so little liking for such a viewpoint. When war began not the least of his tasks would be to ensure that Catholics fully re-entered into the national commitment to democracy and anti-totalitarianism. He would be helped in this by a new generation such as Barbara Ward and Richard Stokes, people who were at once ecumenically orientated and politically liberal. They would be able in due course to wean their community from the semi-Fascist fantasies by which in the recent past it had been too largely taken in.

Hinsley's view of Fascism was not far removed from that of the two Anglican archbishops, Lang and Temple. None of the three had the slightest liking for anti-Semitism, or for the general drive of Nazism. All three, however, were prepared at times to give the benefit of the doubt to continental dictators and to sympathize with Headlam's opinion that it would be 'better to abstain from the pleasing task of continuously scolding other nations and attempt to understand them' (*The Times*, 14 July 1938).

One senior ecclesiastic who emphatically disagreed with that sentiment was Hensley Henson.[20] Henson combined an old world political outlook with old world moral values. He disliked bullies. At home he thought Trade Unions bullies and castigated them accordingly. Abroad he knew that Mussolini and Hitler were bullies, the invasion of Abyssinia 'an abominable oppression', the persecution of the Jews the undermining of every principle of genuine civilization. He considered such men wholly untrustworthy and thought it right to say so.

A debate in the House of Lords on 18 May 1938 on the Anglo-Italian agreement to recognize the conquest of Abyssinia illustrates the contrasting viewpoints well enough. Lang spoke in support of the agreement though he did it with what he called 'a reluctance almost amounting to pain'. Facts are facts all the same and what was needed, he believed, was 'an increase of appeasement in Europe'. 'The cause of general peace is something greater than expediency.' This was too much for Henson, who felt disgusted to hear the latest piece of pragmatic diplomacy defended by the primate in terms of high morality. Appeasement grounded on rotten foundations means nothing. 'My Lords, really, as practical people looking coldly at the world and weighing facts calmly in the scales of reason, is it reasonable to trust the word of these dictators?'

Their lordships did not agree. The devout and gentlemanly Foreign Secretary, the Earl of Halifax, the quintessence of Tory rectitude, rebuked the Bishop of Durham for rudeness and much else:

> I do not think that the kind of statement that the Right Reverend Prelate made with great conviction this afternoon, that neither the word of Signor Mussolini nor that of Herr Hitler was ever to be believed, is the kind of statement, coming from one in his position, that does assist the cause of peace.

In May 1938 Henson was the odd ecclesiastic out, chided alike by realist and pacifist, by Tory statesman and Christian radical, for unchristian bellicosity. Two years later his would be the received wisdom.

The growing Christian critique of Fascism, Nazism and Communism in the 1930s was basically a rational and theological one, drawing upon a long tradition of Natural Law, of Christian humanism, of a doctrine of man and of the nature of responsible government. Such concerns underlay the outspoken words of Bishop Henson just as they were central to the Oxford Conference of 1937 on Church, Community and State. They helped to ensure something of a common Christian mind, both in Britain and abroad, at a time of great crisis and uncertainty.

Equally important was the multiplying experience of community with fellow Christians who had actually seen these movements at work, not through the double-talk of progressive sounding rhetoric and the plush beguilement of an arranged visit but daily, in one's own street, cruelly at work. It was refugees like Pastor Hildebrandt, imprisoned friends like Pastor Niemoller, trusted informants like Pastor Bonhoeffer, who really persuaded the British churches of what Nazism meant. For Soviet

Russia there were few such witnesses, but they were not wholly absent. Thus in 1934 a young Russian lady, Iulia de Beausobre, arrived a refugee in London to spend there the rest of her life.[21] She had been eight months in the Lubyanka prison, a year in a concentration camp, where a fellow prisoner had introduced her to that lovely Russian saint, Serafim of Sarov, and nuns taught her to pray. Her account of prison, *The Woman who could not Die*, like Waldemar Gurion's *Hitler and the Christians*, both published in 1938, or Franz Hildebrandt's account of Niemoller published the next year, was really rather more important than anything the Dean of Canterbury or the Bishop of Gloucester might do or say. Here was the Church, alive, suffering, witnessing, and Christians in Britain were not unable to recognize authenticity and to judge accordingly.

Pacifism

Far more appealing to the 1930s Christian than either Communism or Fascism was Pacifism. As the international outlook grew ever gloomier the greatest wave of Pacifism Britain has experienced spread across the country. Outside the restricted circles of the Quakers Pacifism could hardly be said to have existed in England before the First World War. The word had not even appeared in the Oxford Dictionary. It was the war bringing with it the threat and then the reality of conscription, the new all-pervasiveness of a militaristic euphoria, whipped up not only by recruiting sergeants and patriotic ladies but by bishops, parsons and Nonconformist editors, that generated in reaction a spelt-out, almost institutionalized Pacifism which has lasted and deepened from that day to this. The Fellowship of Reconciliation was founded in December 1914, predominantly Nonconformist and Quaker. While it included at that stage a few Anglican lay people like Maude Royden and George Lansbury, its clerical membership was predominantly Congregationalist. The great majority of the 16,000 Conscientious Objectors of the First World War were Christians, but like the Quakers and the Fellowship of Reconciliation itself, they mostly saw their decision as a personal vocation requiring a painful opting out of the ways of the world, rather than a possibly effective way of preventing war or coping with international crises. Despite a few distinguished and mostly Socialist exceptions, they were as a whole by no means a politicized group and their often heroic witness had very little immediate consequence other than to force a reluctant government to accept that the phenomenon of conscientious objection could not be hammered out of existence.

In the 1920s almost everyone seemed committed to the cause of peace, which was not difficult as the likelihood of another war had receded almost into the realms of absurdity. This sort of pragmatic commitment to seek peace by all reasonable means has been labelled 'pacificism', in contrast to the absolutist position of 'Pacifism'.[1] Its principal organ was, of course, the League of Nations and, among Christians, the World Alliance, a not very effective international organization set up 'to enlist the churches' for 'the avoidance of war'.[2] It was ecumenical in spirit, a sort of religious counterpart to the League of Nations, and rather vague as to its exact position. In a world at peace there is after all not too much point or urgency in committing oneself on the precise issue as to whether there are absolutely no circumstances in which it would be right to fight. The Pacifist between wars, it has been remarked, is a bit like the vegetarian between meals: if no one is eating, the question of not eating some things becomes a rather pointless issue. The Pacifist was easily submerged in the broader ranks of the pacificists.

On 10 September 1931 Robert Cecil, the League's most distinguished British sponsor, told its assembly, 'There has scarcely been a period in the world's history when war seems less likely than it does at present.' On 18 September Japan invaded Manchuria, and major wars were seen again to be only too likely.[3] The twenties were out, the thirties were in. Faced with that likelihood the pacificist and the pacifist soon parted company though many an ardent peace-lover might find it hard to decide to which he belonged. The pacificist sought desperately for ways, even warlike ways, of preventing war – economic sanctions, an international army, anything to put some teeth into the League. It proved, unfortunately, altogether too late for that, but as pacificism was splintered upon the rocks of militarism and aggression, Pacifism spread for a while like wildfire, fed by the very fearsomeness of the world situation.

Siegfried Sassoon published *The Road to Ruin* in 1933, including that sombre vision, 'At the Cenotaph'.

> I saw the Prince of Darkness, with his Staff,
> Standing bare-headed by the Cenotaph.
> Unostentatious and respectful, there
> He stood, and offered up the following prayer.
> Make them forget, O Lord, what this Memorial
> Means; their discredited ideas revive . . .

Such was the mood of 1933. Militarism and Pacifism were its near twins. But if, for a while, Pacifism became in Britain as popular as it did, this was the achievement very largely of a single man, perhaps all in all the most extraordinary and genuine of the many British 'prophets' of those years. Dick Sheppard was a canon of St Paul's Cathedral. The Church of England is for the most part too sensible, too accommodating, too comfortable, too gentlemanly to cultivate great tragic figures. Yet Dick Sheppard was a tragic figure: a man of the most intense emotional sensibility but almost no capacity for cool sustained analytical thinking or carefully planned action; a First World War chaplain who had been spiritually devastated by a very few months in France; an almost gimmicky vicar of St Martin-in-the-Fields and a national figure as the first radio priest in the twenties; a very unsuccessful dean of Canterbury; a man in agony from bouts of the most acute asthma and an unhappy and finally broken marriage. Dick Sheppard suddenly precipitated himself, in 1934, into the struggle against rearmament. In a famous letter to the press of 16 October he declared himself 'now convinced that war of every kind or for any cause, is not only a denial of christianity, but a crime against humanity', and asked anyone who agreed with this to send him a postcard saying that he or she renounced war. In the meantime he set off on a Mediterranean cruise while waiting for 500 thousand postcards to fill his letterbox. Fifty thousand did so, and the Sheppard Peace Movement was born.

It was nine months later that the 'new pacifism' assumed some sort of coherent form after a mass meeting in the Albert Hall on 14 July 1935, addressed by Sheppard, Edmund Blunden, Siegfried Sassoon and Maude Royden. From this the PPU, the Peace Pledge Union, was born. Old pacifists of First World War vintage, like Sassoon, Leighton Richards and George Lansbury, were joined by a motley array of newer enthusiasts – Charles Raven and Donald Soper, Leslie Weatherhead and Eric Gill, C. H. Dodd and George Macleod, Rose Macaulay and Vera Brittain. For most of the older people among them – Raven, Gill, Brittain – their First World War experience had a good deal to do with it; nevertheless for them all, Sheppard included, the sharp clarity of their present Pacifist commitment was something very new. What might have been an opinion had become a faith. If the clergy was very prominent in the PPU, especially within its leadership, there were plenty of distinguished non-Christians too, like Max Plowman and Bertrand Russell. But it was Sheppard's magnetic personality which held them all together, transforming Pacifism from the faith of an élite into a mass movement. He could be described, not unfairly, if a little unkindly, as the Führer of the Peace Movement, the charismatic leader whose inspiration was a substitute for any regular procedures of decision making. A man of extraordinary eloquence and charm, capable of throwing a spell over the most varied people, he was yet a man of fits and starts, often painfully indecisive, soft in the remedies he proposed, the gentleman populist, enclosing within the populism a very recognizable type of rather woolly and gushing C. of E. padre. 'Last night I had a dream,' he told a great Manchester audience in the spring of 1937, 'in it George Lansbury and I were playing tennis against Hitler and Mussolini. George had a game leg and I was asthmatic but we won six-love.'[4]

It sounded jolly enough, yet another splendid triumph for the gentleman amateur over all those wogs, but what really had Sheppard to offer 'against Hitler and Mussolini'? The trouble with the absolute Pacifism of the PPU was that it was trying to combine two quite different things: the recent pacificist tradition which actually attempted to prevent war by political means and the older Pacifist tradition of Quakers and the Fellowship of Reconciliation, of personal conscientious objection, which refused to take part in war whatever the circumstances and whatever the consequences. The latter had never pretended that such a course would either prevent an oncoming war or present a solution to the immediate problems which produced war. Apolitical and in tendency sectarian, it could be congenial enough for a Nonconformist but was much less so for a member of the Established Church. The trouble with 1930s Pacifism was that it had moved the context of its protest from a Free Church to an Anglican milieu. Sheppard, Raven and the like were not Nonconformists. They really did want 'to stop the next bloody war'. They had to convince themselves and other people that they could offer an effective answer to the threat posed by Nazism, a realistic alternative in political terms to rearmament. They could have done this logically by claiming that surrender to aggression is socially less disastrous, as well as being more Christ-like, than resistance to aggression, that Britain should be willing – if it came to that – to submit tamely to Nazi conquest or whatever. Some took this line. To do so, however, sounded altogether too unattractive to ordinary people whose support was required for a mass movement. The Sheppard message in consequence was rather that Pacifism could actually prevent war and aggression, that if only we stuck unwaveringly enough to country dancing and knitting here, this would be bound to produce a change of heart and the pursuit of peace over there too. Even Fascists could not indefinitely be impervious to the appeal of such a message. Such a line almost inevitably brought with it a minimizing of the evil of Nazism, a stress instead upon the relative reasonableness of Hitler's claims in the light of the injustice produced by Versailles. The Pacifist found it hard not to be an appeaser, or even not to look at times like a Fascist sympathizer. Some of the most unmitigated appeasers, like Lords Lothian and Halifax, or Dawson and Barrington-Ward of *The Times*, were devout Christians of one sort or another. All spoke the language of peace. In the early thirties Halifax, as Viceroy of India, had appeased Gandhi very creditably; appeasing Hitler seemed little different either to him or his Pacifist admirers.

The attack on the Pacifist movement came from several sides. Realists, contemplating Abyssinia and Spain and the Rhineland, ceased to believe that disarmament made sense politically. Lansbury had to resign, because of his Pacifism, from the leadership of the Labour Party which resolved, on the contrary, to support military sanctions, if need be, against Mussolini. Political Pacifism grew weaker just as religious and philanthropic Pacifism reached its peak. But at the same time, despite the intellectual defence of Pacifism by men as able as Raven, Dodd and Donald Mackinnon, most theologians too were refusing to accept that the Pacifist option was necessarily the right one for the Christian. Both Barth and Niebuhr were emphatically anti-Pacifist and Temple even denounced it as a heresy. With the tide turning, in a Church Assembly debate of February 1937, Sheppard passionately denounced any and every kind of war as 'mass murder, a betrayal of God and a blasphemy against the future of man'.

Most ecclesiastics, being as keen supporters of appeasement as the government, did not quite disagree, and yet they could not quite agree either. The absolute pacifism of the Peace Pledge Union was looking less and less like a workable political or ecclesiastical option, rather more like an incipient millenarian cult.

Then, in October of that year, Sheppard died. For Vera Brittain, with his death 'the bottom had dropped out of the world'. 'So here we are,' wrote Max Plowman to Middleton Murry, 'very literally sheep not having a Sheppard.'[5] Canon Morris, his official successor, was by no means his charismatic replacement. Without Sheppard's personality the movement's national impact not only rapidly diminished, it also fell more and more apart between the appeasers and the opters-out. The appeasers (like most of the nation) welcomed Munich and, with George Lansbury (now admittedly getting very old), might even strain themselves to see in Hitler 'one of the great men of our time'. The opters-out moved into the countryside to seek for peace not through mass rallies and the pursuit of politics but in the cultivation of vegetables in an alternative society. His death only slightly precipitated the crumbling of the PPU.

Many who had embraced Pacifism in 1934 and 1935, or even earlier, were abandoning it. William Paton, a founding member of the Fellowship of Reconciliation, was now convinced that absolute pacifism was 'untenable morally'.[6] F. R. Barry could admit the 'disastrous pressure' he and his Pacifist friends had 'brought to bear on public opinion' in earlier years.[7] Leslie Weatherhead confessed in 1939 that his signing of the Peace Pledge had been 'a refusal to think'.[8] For others it was only the early summer of 1940 which brought a change of mind, especially among the rank and file. Resignations poured into the PPU. The curate of still 'uncompromising pacifism' in 1939 had volunteered for the RAF before a year was out.[9] Political Pacifism, with its inheritance of pacificism, now practically ceased to exist. Surviving Pacifists – and some did survive – no longer suggested that Nazi hearts could be converted if only we would pursue reconciliation instead of war. The alternative to war was recognized by all to be a regime of concentration camps, the indoctrination of the young, the rounding up of Jews and gypsies, if not in Britain at least in most of Europe. Shortly before his death in 1940 Lansbury unrepentantly reaffirmed to Sybil Thorndike that 'it would be better to be over-run by the Germans than to fight'. That was the only coherent Pacifist position which remained. It is a hard position, maybe in practical terms an unrealistic one, but it is also invincible. For the most part the Second World War conscientious objector, like his predecessor of the First World War, was apolitical. It was a personal, spiritual, humanitarian decision, absolute in its refusal to compromise with ifs and buts. Among leading churchmen Charles Raven, Donald Soper and George Macleod remained true to this faith. But it was a small minority that did so, very different from the many tens of thousands who had joined the Peace Pledge Union four years earlier.

Helping German Christians

If Pacifism was one Christian response in Britain to the advance
of Nazism, a concern for Hitler's victims and opponents was
another. Upon the Continent the struggle of the churches with
the Nazi State, the *Kirchenkampf*, proved in the long run to be the
most decisively formative fact of ecclesiastical history of these
decades.[1] Yet Nazism appeared, at least at first, to many good
people in and out of Germany as a welcome and necessary
movement of national Risorgimento. While there were Christians
who saw its truly diabolical character from the start, such
clearmindedness was most uncommon. The anti-Semitism and
general brutishness of the movement were very easily played
down by conservative and liberal alike, as but a passing and
secondary phenomenon. Few indeed were the German ecclesiastics, like the highly conservative but strong minded Cardinal
Faulhaber, prepared to speak out in public any criticism of Nazi
policy in 1933, and even he was somewhat in two minds about it.
Upon the Protestant side there was really no one of much weight,
other than the Swiss-born professor, Karl Barth. In response to
the attempt to impose an Aryan clause upon the Church Martin
Niemöller called into existence a Pastors' Emergency League
which met in synod at Barmen in 1934 and produced a Declaration of Protest, largely worded by Barth, against Nazi interference with the Church. As a consequence the Convocation of
Canterbury discussed the state of the German Church on 7 June.
In the debate Bishop Bell, who from this early stage had already
taken the lead in international Christian concern for the German
Church, quoted twice from Cardinal Faulhaber, the only German from whom he did quote. It was hardly accidental there was
no Protestant leader of comparable importance on record. For

various reasons the Catholic Church within Germany, criticizable as its official response to Nazism was on many counts, was both initially less welcoming to the Nazi revolution and, all in all, over the years more resistant to its influence than was Protestantism. It was, however, upon the Protestant battle that British eyes were focused predominantly, and not unnaturally. By tradition the ecclesiastical and theological links were strong, and the news that German Protestant pastors of impeccable theological orthodoxy were being arrested or harassed raised the hackles of every true-born British parson. While the two countries shared a tradition of Erastianism, the theological character of Lutheran Erastianism – with its commitment to the dichotomy of a 'two kingdoms' theology – seemed to leave the Church particularly helpless in face of a Nazi take-over. The minority of pastors who resisted the take-over with great courage in the name of the gospel had not only the Nazi Party against them but had also to contend with their own often militaristic nationalism and Erastian ecclesiology. British churchmen tried hard to appreciate the predicament even if they found Lutheran and neo-Calvinist thought-processes baffling in their theological obscurity; and British newspapers of the thirties, prompted by the churchmen, devoted an almost inordinate amount of their space to the conflict between the Nazis and the 'Confessing Church' – an amount of space in striking contrast with that given to the murder of priests in Spain, the sufferings of the Church in Russia, or even the treatment meted out to German Jews.

It is, all in all, an odd story. The so-called 'German Christians' (Nazi sympathizers) very easily obtained control of most of the various regional Evangelical churches in the Church elections of July 1933, for German Protestantism widely shared the nationalist, anti-democratic, anti-Communist, and even anti-Jewish sentiments of Nazism. So it was not hard at first to welcome Hitler's coming to power as a rejuvenation of the nation. In September, in line with government policy throughout the civil service and the professions, the Prussian synod even passed an Aryan clause, excluding Jews from the Church's ministry, and in the following months an attempt was made to force the hitherto highly fragmented Protestant churches of Germany into a single centralized body more effectively amenable to State control, exercised through a Nazi-minded bishop, Ludwig Müller.

It was over these two issues that the minority Pastors' Emergency League arose in protest. The Aryan clause was anti-evangelical. The State could not be allowed to interfere with the essentials of the Church. The struggle ebbed and flowed. In the early years the Nazis were prepared to compromise temporarily with internal opposition, in such a seemingly minor area, if a hardline was seen to be damaging their image abroad. The protests, in Britain particularly, organized by Oldham, Bell and Dorothy Buxton, may well have helped provide some respite for the Confessing Church in 1934 and 1935. Two years later such protests were less effective. On the contrary, they rather increased the fury of the Nazi leadership. Pastor Niemöller was arrested on 1 July 1937, tried in February of the following year and acquitted of most of the charges brought against him, only to be immediately re-arrested and detained for the next eight years in a concentration camp. It was right, natural and inevitable that Christian leaders elsewhere should speak out for the Confessing Church and Niemöller became a symbol in Britain, quite as much as in Germany, of the spiritual freedom of religion, the refusal of the Church to be dictated to by a godless State. 'The name of Dr Martin Niemöller is famous throughout Christendom,' wrote Bishop Bell to *The Times* (3 July 1937). 'What is his crime? The truth is that he is a preacher of the Gospel of God, and that he preaches the Gospel without flinching. . . .' Bishop Headlam foolishly declared a year later that in Germany all pastors had to do was not to 'use their pulpit for political purposes'. Pastor Niemöller, he maintained, 'was in confinement because he had stubbornly and determinedly defied this law' (*The Times*, 4 July 1938). To this Hensley Henson thundered back that Niemöller was in fact in a concentration camp after having been effectively acquitted of breaking the law, and continued:

> Pastor Niemöller is the embodiment of a protest which no Christian Church could refrain from making without forfeiting its claim to be christian at all . . . what would the Bishop of Gloucester counsel a Christian minister in Germany to do when confronted with the officially patronized anti-semitism of Streicher and the officially encouraged anti-christian doctrines of Rosenberg? (*The Times*, 6 July and 12 August)

Duncan-Jones, the dean of Chichester, seemed to sum up the simple significance of it all when he declared, 'Even for the unbeliever and the agnostic Niemöller has put Christianity on the map of the modern world from which they thought it had faded.'[2]

Unfortunately the issues involved were vastly less simple than such an account – essentially true as it is – might suggest.[3] The complexity derived largely from the intellectual position of the Confessing pastors. Their protest was not explicitly, certainly not primarily, against Nazism at all – a movement with which many of them had, at least at first, great sympathy. Indeed had it not been for such sympathy Hitler might never have attained power.[4]

The German Protestant Church leadership had found it very hard to accept the Weimar Republic, although things had improved somewhat in its eyes when Hindenberg became President in 1925. Nevertheless the republic remained essentially something suspect, the tool of Socialists and Catholics. Strangely enough for Anglo-Saxons, for whom Protestantism and democracy are often thought to go inherently together, in early twentieth-century Germany Protestantism was really more antipathetic to democracy than Catholicism. The German Protestant leadership was anti-liberal in almost every way, except in theology! Theologically they were liberals brought up in a world dominated by Harnack, but theological liberalism proved a very comfortable bedfellow for conservative nationalism. Moreover if the new Barthians emphatically rejected the theological side of this package for an 'anti-liberal' reassertion of traditional Calvinist theology, this had not affected their political attitudes one bit. On the contrary, it confirmed them in their opposition to political Liberalism. The Nazi revolution was greeted with relief by theological liberals and theological neo-conservatives alike, as a reassertion of the true national and authoritarian tradition, and a safeguard against Communism. As Barth later remarked, the Church 'almost unanimously welcomed the Hitler regime with real confidence, indeed with the highest hopes'.[5] Niemöller himself had voted Nazi for years. Pastors of his type, and that included the real core of the Confessing Church, had steadily underweighed the racialist, anti-Semitic, anti-religious and simply brutal aspects of the movement. To all this the young

Dietrich Bonhoeffer was the great exception. Hildebrandt, one of the Confessing Church's ablest exponents and Bonhoeffer's closest ally, could admit unambiguously in 1939 that, before 1933, the Nazi programme had been fundamentally Niemöller's 'with its vehement denial of all that was meant by individualism, parliamentarianism, pacifism, marxism and judaism'.[6]

After 1933 too the Confessing pastors made no consistent stand against anti-Semitism or most of the other major crimes of Nazism, and they later attacked Barth fiercely for declaring that Czech soldiers fighting against Hitler would be fighting for the Christian Church. In this at least they were, with few exceptions, Lutherans to excess. Lutherans have traditionally both divided 'the two orders' of the religious and the secular quite excessively, and exercised an almost obsequious deference to the powers that be.[7] The Confessing pastors' complaint was a specifically ecclesiastical one – that the Aryan clause in its application to the Church was anti-evangelical. Their opposition to anti-Jewish discrimination was at that point absolute but went little further than that. Their paranoid fear of liberalism and democracy and their highly pessimistic theology of society deprived them of claiming any message within the secular and the political. They consistently affirmed that their overseas champions got them wrong, and they consistently disliked being bracketed with the Catholic opposition to Nazism of such as Cardinal Faulhaber. British Christians thought it obvious and splendid that Catholics and Protestants should stand together: 'Cardinal Faulhaber and Pastor Niemöller are seen to be allies in a single cause' – but the Confessing Church, with its deep suspicions of both Catholicism and ecumenism, did not care for such a comment. Truly, they were difficult people.

But not too difficult for George Bell, the Bishop of Chichester. In dealing with them, sympathizing with them, defending them, catering for their refugees, he was at his best – a man of immense compassion and obstinate consistency in clinging to a cause, with a superb heart well in advance of his rather more mediocre head, as Temple's never was. But if with Bell the heart led, it was linked with his head in a psychology of remarkable calm and domestic peacefulness. From this point of view the contrast with Dick Sheppard could not be more striking: here were two outstanding peace-seeking priests, but Bell was as placid as Sheppard was tortured by emotional intensity. The one possessed peace in his own soul almost to excess, the other was almost despairingly without it.

'You are becoming the real *vox ecclesiae*', the Swedish theologian Brilioth, Archbishop Soderblom's nephew, could remark already in February 1934.[8] Bell's right to interfere derived from his being chairman of the Ecumenical Council of Life and Work at that time. The accurate knowledge with which he spoke owed already not a little to a young German friend, pastor of the London Lutherans, whom he was getting to know – Dietrich Bonhoeffer. But the source of his power in interpreting the Confessing Church to the world derived in large part from his almost over-sympathizing with the German nationalist sense of grievance against Versailles and its consequences. In this he, the Confessing pastors and the Nazis were at one. The agony of the pastors in coming into conflict with Hitler was all the greater because they had hoped for great things from him, and shared so deeply in the tradition of German nationalism. Comparably, the agony of denouncing Nazi Germany's doings was much greater for Bell than for, say, Hensley Henson, because he had developed an emotional sympathy for Germany which was willing to overlook a very great deal. 'Uncle George' really did try to see things through the eyes of his Confessing friends – eyes, then, which remained intensely focused upon the theological intricacies of 'the Church struggle' but were (with the always significant exception of Bonhoeffer) too blind to the strident nationalism, the suppression of personal freedom, the growth of concentration camps, the penetration of anti-Semitism into every area of life. Their anti-liberalism made it hard for them to speak of such things and while Bell himself felt these things acutely, as Bonhoeffer did, he feared to say more about them than his German pastor friends as a whole would wish. And this in some way diminished the power of his witness.

Far to one side of Bell in all this stood Bishop Headlam, the Nazis' persistent defender, somewhat to the other stood a remarkable and very active lady, Dorothy Buxton.[9] For Headlam the whole business was being greatly overplayed. If he did not really sympathize with Nazi ideology, he did very easily believe them to be gentlemen. He could not see why reasonable pastors could not live quietly under such rulers but he found the Confessing Church thoroughly unreasonable, moved by a reactionary theology with which he did not sympathize at all.

Dorothy Buxton was a radical lady, a Quaker with a Pacifist husband, the MP Charles Roden Buxton. They both shared Bell's sense of shame over Versailles. More than almost anyone else in Britain, she struggled to get the facts of Nazi Germany known abroad through constant pamphlets and translations. Of course she took the part of the Confessing pastors, but her concern with the Church struggle was simply part and parcel of her concern with the much wider religious and humanitarian issues of Nazi tyranny. She and her husband are good examples of the spiritual dilemma Christians and humanitarians encountered when faced with Nazism. They were both natural Pacifists. What were you now to do? Stick to Pacifism and seem, politically, an appeaser at any price, or decide that Pacifism had its limits and Nazism was so evil that resistance to it could justify another war? Charles Buxton held to the former line, Dorothy Buxton tended to the latter. Bishop Headlam, no Pacifist, would yet agree with the husband: what was there so evil in Nazism to fight about anyway? Bishop Henson, no Pacifist, would agree with his wife: Nazism was a monstrous tyranny, against which we should all stand up and be counted.

And Bishop Bell? His heart was on both sides. His intimate friendship with Bonhoeffer and so many other German dissidents, his deeply felt concern for Jewish refugees, separated him absolutely from Headlam, and yet still left him with some illusions as to the reality of National Socialism fostered by a near obsession with allied guilt in imposing the Versailles settlement. He lacked the clarity of judgment about the wider situation which characterized both Barth and Bonhoeffer. Bell remained an appeaser not only after Munich, but even after the declaration of war. 'Dear Bishop,' Karl Barth wrote to him, 'I think you are too much a British gentleman and thus unable to understand the phenomenon of Hitler.'[10] What indeed is the peace-seeker to do when faced with 'the phenomenon of Hitler'? That question, unanswered then – or answered diversely by equally Christian and conscientious men – remains unanswered still.

What is, perhaps, most striking in all this, is the limitations, rather than the generosities, of British Christian concern over the evil effects of Nazism. Before 1939 very few people were seriously concerned to help its victims, while even the concern of most of those who were worried remained exceedingly churchy. The persecution of the Jews had begun ruthlessly and without ambiguity immediately the Nazis came to power in 1933. It grew far worse after the Nuremburg laws of September 1935 for 'The Protection of German Blood and Honour'. It reached a still more violent stage of horror with the *Kristallnacht* of 9 November 1938, a few weeks after the Munich agreement. It might well be said that in Germany itself both Catholics and Protestants had sold the pass of any effective moral resistance to Nazism by making no public protest against the first disgraceful attacks on the Jews in March 1933. Indeed some, like Otto Dibelius, tended to justify them. As the anti-Jewish campaign mounted in subsequent years there continued to be an overwhelming Church silence. Even when 119 synagogues were set alight on the *Kristallnacht* no word of protest was uttered by Church leaders. So British Christians were in no way stimulated to help the Jews in their plight by their German Christian brothers, and it was only after the *Kristallnacht* that British Christian opinion really began to wake up seriously to the monstrosity of what was going on and to the large scale need for help. Previous to 1939 British Jewry and the Quakers had struggled almost alone to help Jewish refugees from the Nazis, with the support of only very few other individuals, men like Bell, William Paton, Viscount Cecil. Even the worry of ecumenically minded persons like Bell, Temple and Oldham seemed to be very largely concentrated upon the fate of a handful of German Protestant clergy, to the near-disregard of the tens of thousands of Jews whose whole existence was in peril. Behind the rather emotional Pacifism of Sheppard there was at least something of a mass movement, involving thousands of committed Christians. Behind the little committees struggling to rescue Hitler's victims there was no mass support at all. Early in 1936 Bell launched an appeal for £25,000 for the assistance of Christian refugees. By November only £8,250 had been raised.[11] Such apathy was not special to Britain and the 'International Christian Committee for

Refugees' set up in these years has been judged a 'spectacular failure'.[12] The German Church struggle was by no means unimportant, the Confessing pastors deserved all the support they could get, and the preoccupation with them of sensitive British Christians both then and since is understandable enough. Nevertheless it is still more important to remember that far more terrible things were going on in Germany at the same time about which the churches there were unforgivably silent, and that in regard to them most English Christians, clerical and lay, maintained prior to 1939 a most unjudgmental respect for their political neighbour, while they looked decently the other way from their true neighbour in his desperate need.

Munich and All That

From the end of 1937 there was a new tension in Europe. Hitler's energies were clearly moving towards the expansion of the Reich by force through the annexation of neighbouring States. In March 1938 his troops marched into Vienna and Austria was incorporated into Germany. Almost immediately the pressure moved on to Czechoslovakia. Its considerable Sudeten German-speaking minority appeared to justify Hitler's claims to large parts of the country though what proportion of that minority actually favoured annexation by Germany nobody could truthfully say. France was committed by treaty to Czechoslovakia's defence, as Britain was not, but France would not move without Britain. If France did fight however it was hardly possible for Britain to keep out. Here was the sole more or less democratic country of eastern Europe; it had moreover a powerful well-equipped army. If it was struck down the whole balance of power in central Europe would undoubtedly alter. Was it to be surrendered to Hitler's voracity or were Britain and France prepared to enter upon a major war for Czechoslovakia's sake? It is, in fact, rather probable that if they had stood firm from the start, Hitler would have backed down, at least for a while, and if he had not it is also quite likely that he would have been cast overboard by his generals.

Faced with this threat both the British and French governments were desperately anxious to sidestep confrontation if they possibly could. In this the French politicians, who had more reason to be tough-minded, were probably more craven than the British, but Neville Chamberlain had no intention of going to war if he could possibly avoid it. For him Czechoslovakia's fate was of little practical significance, as was Hitler's ideology, regime and even record of untrustworthiness – unattractive as he certainly found them. He was, very genuinely if also rather unimaginatively, a man of peace – a Birmingham tradesman at heart. To make what warlike sounds one decently could to deter continental dictators was one thing, actually to go to war over the fate of one or another little-known region of eastern Europe was quite another. Several times that September Chamberlain flew to Germany to meet the Führer, mistakenly imagining that his personal intervention would be somehow beneficial. All it did was to bemuse the world while increasing his personal responsibility for the very bad terms arrived at in face of Hitler's steadily mounting demands. When he finally returned from Munich on 29 September, where he had agreed to the immediate dismemberment of Czechoslovakia at a conference at which no representative of Czechoslovakia was even present, he could declare with an air of confident complacency that he had brought back 'peace with honour . . . peace in our time'.

It is arguable that Chamberlain had little alternative in September 1938. Neither Britain nor France was psychologically ready for war, nor did Britain believe herself to be ready militarily (she was certainly a good deal more so a year later). Czechoslovakia meant too little to us anyway and the Sudeten Germans provided Hitler with enough of a just cause to deceive the innocent. It is, however, indisputable that the decisive factor in the whole settlement was Hitler's will backed by the threat of force and nothing else, that one of the better ruled countries of Europe was cruelly abandoned by its friends to dismemberment and ruin, and that this in no way provided a basis for 'peace in our time'. The main charge against Munich was not just that it was appeasement but that it was a very amateurishly mishandled bit of appeasement involving a great deal of deceptive double-talk. Even if Chamberlain was not himself deceived, he endeavoured to deceive the nation as to what had really happened.

It is also indisputable that the nation as a whole enthusiastically responded, welcomed Munich with great relief and hailed Chamberlain almost ecstatically: 'No conqueror returning from a victory on the battlefield has come home adorned with nobler laurels than Mr Chamberlain from Munich yesterday', began Geoffrey Dawson's editorial in *The Times* on 1 October. In retrospect it must seem astonishing how nearly universal and unqualified was the expression of gratitude to Chamberlain for so soothingly gilding the sell-out, and this, not only in Britain but throughout the world. He and Lord Halifax, his Foreign Secretary, held the absolute loyalty of the Conservative Party for the policy of appeasement, and the Conservative Party at that point stood very nearly for the whole nation, swept as it was (and is from time to time) by a great wave of honest emotion: peace had been preserved. Duff Cooper, First Lord of the Admiralty, resigned, the one dissident voice in the government, declaring that Germany had been 'allowed, in disregard of treaty obligations, of the law of nations, and the decrees of morality, to dominate by brute force the continent of Europe'. With that Mr Attlee and the Labour Party rather quietly agreed, and so more emphatically did Churchill: 'We have sustained a total and unmitigated defeat.'

There was, then, some significant dissentient voice in the country right from the start. But from the churches there was almost none, even the redoubtable Henson maintaining an uncomfortable silence.

Dean Duncan-Jones of Chichester, certainly one of the only really well-informed priests in England of the state of Germany, had sent telegrams at once to both archbishops asking them 'to voice the conscience of England in protest against most shameful betrayal in English history'.[1] His request was more than ignored. Archbishop Lang, both on the radio and in the House of Lords, was at his most unctuous and almost blasphemous in his oft-repeated expressions of gratitude at once to God and to the Prime Minister. 'More than one member of Parliament said to me today as we all trooped into the lobby: "This is the hand of God."' (*The Times*, 29 September 1938.) For Chamberlain, he declared in the Lords, 'no praise could be too great'. Temple, Bell, Hinsley, all agreed with him. Not one expressed any serious hesitation about the rightness, indeed the near-miraculous wonderfulness, of Chamberlain's achievement. It is worth pondering why the immense amount of thought and verbalization which Temple in particular had put over the years into the issues of social and political morality had not helped him now, at the moment of testing, the *kairos*, to speak a word of critical warning to the nation when it might have been most unpopular, yet most opportune.

A young German Jew, now a refugee and a Christian, Ulrich Simon, was training to become an Anglican priest in those months. Years later he recalled the agony of it:

> A witch-hunt after these many years serves no purpose, but the shame of a false theology remains. Here was an exquisite example of false prophecy. Every ingredient of pious treachery. . . . On the Sunday following the news the Dean of Lincoln preached at a solemn thanksgiving service. He held the congregation spellbound by ascribing the turn of events to God's wonderful providence. I ran out of my stall, feeling sick to the point of convulsion . . .[2]

In the Church it was only a few lesser figures who stood up to make their protest. One such was the Revd St John Groser, vicar of Christ Church, Watney Street in the East End. In a letter to the Anglican *Guardian* of 7 October he expressed his indignation:

> Blackmail has succeeded. The threat of force has triumphed. . . . That Mr Chamberlain should talk of 'peace with honour' when he has surrendered to this blackmail, torn up Article 10 of the League Covenant without reference to Geneva, and sacrificed the Czechoslovaks in order, as he says, to prevent a world war, is bad enough; but that the Archbishop of Canterbury should say that this is the answer to our prayers . . . is beyond endurance.[3]

In 1938, at least within the Church, both the right wing and the left, both the Establishment and the radicals, were appeasers. Only the odd man out questioned the wisdom of Mr Chamberlain. For the clergy as a whole, peace, to be pursued by all means and at almost any cost, was the overriding preoccupation of the thirties, whether or not they subscribed formally to Pacifism. It was of course a fine preoccupation, if stoked, often a little unhealthily, by a guilt complex about both the clerical jingoism of the First World War and the Treaty of Versailles. The sense of guilt over the latter had indeed steadily spread, the further away one got from the historical reality – at the time when it was happening, regrettably few people had felt like that at all. In much the same sort of way people afterwards would feel horribly guilty about Munich. It would haunt British consciousness as disastrously as the reaction to Versailles.

That month of October there was a by-election in the city of Oxford, one of the great by-elections of the century. It was fought, as very few elections ever have been fought, on foreign policy. Quintin Hogg, a brilliant young Tory, Eton, Christ Church and a fellow of All Souls, son of Lord Hailsham, Chamberlain's Lord Chancellor, was the Conservative candidate, standing wholly as Chamberlain's man. He was 'a National candidate in the National interest', pledged to support in the fullest degree Mr Chamberlain's 'brave and devoted efforts in the cause of peace'. Upon the other side the Labour and Liberal candidates had withdrawn in favour of A. D. Lindsay, the Master of Balliol, who stood as an Independent Progressive precisely to challenge Chamberlain's foreign policy as crystallized at Munich and to assert the 'disastrous consequences of the policy of surrender to aggression pursued by the government'. It was no normal party election. Liberals and old Labour men were among those backing Hogg while 'lifelong Conservatives' canvassed for Lindsay, and some young ones as well, including an enthusiastic undergraduate named Edward Heath. The Master of Balliol had only just ceased to be Vice-Chancellor while Lord Halifax, the Foreign Secretary and Chamberlain's closest accomplice in appeasement, was the university's Chancellor and a fellow of All Souls too – as was Dawson of *The Times* and, of course, Archbishop Lang: those were All Souls' most intensely political days. So the university was inevitably deeply embroiled. Letters of support came from heads of colleges to either side: H. A. L. Fisher of New College stood behind Hogg, Sir William Beveridge of University College and Maurice Bowra of Wadham behind Lindsay. A. P. Herbert, the university's own Independent MP wrote to say that to elect Lindsay 'would be to strike a dagger labelled "Oxford" into the heart of the Prime Minister', while Harold Macmillan, a Conservative MP, wrote to say that if he were in Oxford he would 'unhesitatingly' vote for Lindsay. 'A vote for Hogg is a vote for Hitler', some left-wing propagandists chanted to the former's fury, yet it was an argument constantly used by the Chamberlainites that their leader now knew the Führer so intimately that he could manage him where others could not.

Hogg was elected, though not by a very large majority. 'It is not my victory. It is Mr Chamberlain's victory.' Both candidates wanted rearmament. Neither wanted war. Hogg certainly claimed time and again that he alone was truly a peace candidate;[4] Lindsay replied that you would not get peace through the sort of easy surrender of other people's rights that Munich represented. There had been no alternative to this other than world war, answered Hogg.

Hogg, now Lord Hailsham, has all his life been a very typical Tory (as Chamberlain was not). Yet here he was, the standard bearer of appeasement. Lindsay was all his life a rather typical intellectual left-winger. Yet here he was, the standard bearer for a militant line against foreign dictators. In this somewhat bizarre situation it is of some interest to us that both men were unusually emphatic in their commitment to Christian faith. Lindsay, recently author of the Archbishop of Canterbury's 'Lent Book', was not only one of the most influential academics of his generation but a man whose interwoven Christian and democratic ideals were brought to bear upon almost every side of public life in a long and distinguished career. Hogg was to become the outstanding Christian Tory of the next half-century, a most skilled upholder of the wisdom of our ancestors. But such wisdom, as it has prevailed in this country since 1940, above all in specifically Conservative circles, has in fact held Lindsay to have been right, Hogg mightily mistaken. Those who beat their breast with shame in 1938 over Versailles and thanked God for Chamberlain, 'the pilot who weathered the storm', would soon be beating their breasts with shame over Munich and thanking God for Churchill, 'the pilot who weathered the storm'. The mental and spiritual disarray of the time, inevitable as it may have been, is all too painfully obvious.

While the election campaign was building up in Oxford that mid-October, in Austria the Catholic Church and the Jews too were being subjected to a sharp new wave of Nazi violence. The next month, November, saw the worst pogroms yet to take place in Germany when on the night of the 9th, 119 synagogues were set on fire and 20,000 Jews arrested. In March the remainder of Czechoslovakia was gobbled up and Hitler entered Prague. At that point a great many British eyes were opened: not that it was really anything different, just that it proved to be one morsel too much. German pressure was now building up on Poland, and the British government, feeling it must make some positive gesture, offered Poland a fateful guarantee. Chamberlain probably thought of it far more as an opportune warning, a deterrent to Hitler within a diplomatic game, than a commitment which might have to be fully met not many months hence. Halifax, on the other hand, seems to have seen it differently. Shrewder and more experienced in international terms than Chamberlain, for him one Munich was enough. A great appeaser in 1938, it was he rather than Chamberlain who stiffened the government in 1939 and eventually, in 1940, ensured the succession of Churchill.

The British guarantee to Poland was quickly, and wholly unexpectedly, out-trumped in August by a German-Soviet treaty of friendship and on 1 September 1939 German troops crossed the Polish border. For two days Britain hesitated. Chamberlain would still have avoided war if he could: in the small terms of the immediate crisis going to war about anything in eastern Europe seemed so inherently unreasonable. You could only defend Poland with Soviet help but this the Poles had never actually wanted. To 'save' Poland, therefore, was beyond our ability. Why fight for something you cannot achieve? But he was now caught between his bit of paper and the nation's honour; where he might have dodged, parliament would not let him. Faced with the demonic there comes a point when it is a nonsense to rationalize further about practicalities. The free man's only possible response seemed a simple act of faith: it should not pass. On 3 September Britain declared war. Peace, appeasement, Pacifism, the League of Nations, were all swept aside and the Church had, for once, very little to say. It had exhausted its wisdom.

PART IV

—◆◆◆—

1939–1945: The War

The War

In September 1939 the first phase of the war came and went. Germany invaded Poland. Britain and France declared war on Germany. Germany, with Soviet help, crushed Poland. What was one to do then? For what exactly was there to go on fighting? To rescue Poland from the clutches of Germany and Russia seemed quite impossible and months of 'phoney war' with little sense of purpose but a good deal of false optimism followed. Then, in April 1940 Germany overran Denmark and Norway. In May dissatisfaction with Chamberlain's rather anaemic leadership brought about his resignation and Churchill's appointment as Prime Minister at the very moment that Germany invaded Belgium and Holland, broke through the French lines at Sedan and advanced to the sea at Abbeville. Mussolini entered the war on Hitler's side. France quickly crumbled and on 22 June the aged Marshal Pétain concluded a humiliating armistice: the north of the country was handed over to German occupation while the south would be ruled by a puppet government in Vichy.

Western Europe was now ruled by Hitler from Warsaw to Brittany, and Britain stood alone. The first thing, as France collapsed, was to rescue the army from the Continent. Almost miraculously, this was largely achieved: the two-thirds north of Abbeville escaped from Dunkirk at the beginning of June, the one-third to the south from a number of ports between Brittany and Bordeaux later in the month. In July began the Battle of Britain as German planes attacked the airfields of the south and then, from September, London. That summer and autumn the threat of invasion lay over England as it had not done since Napoleon's Grand Army camped on the French coast a hundred and forty years before. But it never came. Fighter Command won the Battle of Britain and the navy did not lose control of the Channel. The blitz would go on night after night through the first half of 1941 but it quickly ceased to be part of an invasion plan. Britain had survived the fall of France and, led by Churchill, was now obstinately committed as a nation to nothing short of victory – in the circumstances a superb but seemingly impossible goal.

There was simply no way in which Britain and the Dominions could now defeat Hitler, yet there was equally no honourable alternative to resolving to do so and none was considered. It was the greatness of Churchill to transform so hopeless a predicament quite convincingly into a moment of supreme national exhilaration and even hopefulness. In temperament he was superbly matched with the hour, a fighter by instinct and by nationalist gospel. An essentially simple man, an agnostic with a touch of pantheism, whose true religion was the secular saga of English political and military history (he knew and cared nothing about the Church), Churchill both chronicled in his writings and personified in his career one, but only one, of the central strands of the nation's experience. An aristocrat imaginatively enthralled with war, who had rejoiced to take part in his youth in the last great cavalry charge of British history, at Omdurman, a man who loathed compromise, be it with striking miners, Indian nationalists or Adolf Hitler, and whose utterly characteristic gospel of hope was a simple, 'we shall fight': Churchill was the exact antithesis of the cautious, peace-loving Chamberlain. As representative of Britain, he was a dangerous anachronism, for his Britain was the Protestant and Imperial England of Elizabethan and Victorian days, ruling the sea, defying continental despots, taming lesser breeds around the world. How very different was Churchill as an expression of 'Englishry' from Temple or Bevin, his greatest contemporaries. Probably they could appreciate him rather better than he could appreciate them. In normal situations of peace Churchill was, frankly, a disaster – Englishry deprived of both its deeper religious roots and its pragmatic adaptability. But 1940 and 1941 were not normal years and in the abnormality of our greatest modern crisis Churchill was incomparable.

He needed to be. If the air battle by day was won in the summer and autumn of 1940, the blitz by night reduced more and more of

Britain's towns to ruins. Thus on 14 November the cathedral and eight other churches in Coventry were devastated together with the whole of its inner city. The worst night of all was that of Saturday, 10 May 1941: the House of Commons was destroyed and Westminster Abbey, Westminster Hall, Lambeth Palace, Charterhouse and the British Museum were all gravely damaged. The most sacred symbols of the State lay under threat. 'Nothing saved', wrote Rose Macaulay of her London flat, also destroyed that terrible night. 'I am bookless, homeless, sans everything but my eyes to weep with . . . What does one do?'[1]

That May and June were the most dire months of the war, the wide horizon offering even less comfort than a year before. Rommel was threatening Egypt, the British army in Greece was routed, then came the fall of Crete. Any remaining hold on the Mediterranean might easily have gone, but if that had happened – if Suez had been conquered – could Britain ever have begun to counter-attack? Following the fall of Crete *The Times* published on 13 June a first leader under the heading *Sursum Corda*, commenting upon a speech of Churchill's to the leaders of the exiled governments in London assembled in St James's Palace. 'The spirit of the gathering', it declared, 'was that of Alfred in Athelney.' To which it added the words of the Blessed Virgin to King Alfred in Chesterton's 'Ballad of the White Horse':

> I tell you naught for your comfort,
> Yea, naught for your desire.
> Save that the sky grows darker yet
> And the sea rises higher.
> Night shall be thrice night over you;
> And heaven an iron cope,
> Do you have joy without a cause,
> Yea, faith without a hope?

If at that point Hitler had pressed on with full strength in the eastern Mediterranean, he could hardly have lost the war. But his lust was not there. The next month Germany invaded Russia, and Britain had once again an ally with whom victory might eventually become possible. Still more was this the case six months later when on 7 December Japan attacked Pearl Harbor and brought the United States into the conflict. Devastating as the immediate catastrophes were – two great battleships, the *Prince of Wales* and the *Repulse* sunk just three days later; Hong kong, Malaya, Singapore, Burma, soon lost – in principle the war could now hardly not be won. Britain, Soviet Russia and the United States together were not to be defeated. The hubris of too many victories had brought Hitler to an absolute miscalculation. Britain, which in 1940 could not win, was now, by no positive achievement of its own, other than the refusal to admit defeat, upon the winning side. This was not, however, at first by any means obvious. Through most of 1942 the tide of battle still flowed the other way. It was only towards the end of the year when the Germans were decisively defeated at El Alamein and then at Stalingrad that it was clear the tide had turned. On 15 November 1942 the church bells were rung throughout England for Montgomery's victory at El Alamein and more symbolically for the removal of the threat to national existence which had hung over the country since June 1940.

Nearly two further years would pass before the opening of the 'Second Front', the landing of the allied army in Normandy in 1944. Five developments in this central period of the war need to be pondered. The first is the steady hardening of the Allied war aim into one of Unconditional Surrender. This was not indeed so far removed from Churchill's simple commitment from the start to 'Victory' and nothing less, and it was in that uncompromising and pugnacious simplicity that his instincts had always differed from those of Chamberlain, Lloyd George or Halifax. Nevertheless, the interpretation of 'victory' continually hardened and in the end it was Russia and America, rather than Britain, which insisted upon there being no negotiated peace of any sort with anyone. 'Unconditional Surrender' became stated Allied policy at the Casablanca Conference between Churchill and Roosevelt in January 1943. It was Roosevelt's phrase.

Less than two months later, many months of the most complex conspiracy reached their maturation when on 13 March Fabian von Schlabrendorff, a German officer on the eastern front, placed in Hitler's plane leaving Smolensk a bomb he had received from Hans von Dohnanyi. Dohnanyi was a senior official within the *Abwehr*, the Military Intelligence Department. He was also the brother-in-law of Dietrich Bonhoeffer, theologian and fellow-conspirator. The bomb failed to explode.

A further unsuccessful attempt was made to kill Hitler just ten days later. A fortnight after that Dohnanyi and Bonhoeffer were arrested. The final attempt at assassination, by Count von Stauffenberg in July 1944, was probably less politically significant, but if Hitler had been killed in March 1943 there would have been an attempt, led by General Beck and Admiral Canaris, to overthrow the Nazi government. It may seem improbable that it could have succeeded, but it is really impossible to speculate about what would have followed upon the sudden death of Hitler. Would the Allies really have stuck to their war aim of 'unconditional surrender' if a non-Nazi military government had come to power in Germany, motivated by the sort of ideas which filled Dohnanyi and Canaris? Again, it is impossible to say. Certainly, the steady Allied refusal to recognize publicly that such an eventuality was a possibility and a desirable one, must gravely have weakened the chances of anti-Nazi Germans gathering sufficient support. If the Allies had publicly encouraged such a possibility, the likelihood of it must considerably have increased. The consequences of such a coup could, of course, in 1943 have been enormous: far smaller casualties upon both sides, the delivery of millions of Jews from the gas-chamber, the saving of eastern Europe from permanent domination by the Soviet army, even a Britain less ruined economically than the war eventually left her.

It may be that all these things were now in the tragic trajectory of history unavoidable. 'Unconditional Surrender' quite certainly made them so. The policy might be intended to ensure that no Nazi would escape retribution though it did not do so; it also ensured that Poland, for whose cause after all Britain went to war in the first place, would be handed over at its end to Stalin, Hitler's ally of 1939. It is strange and horrifying how little Britain cared about the fate of Poland once Soviet Russia had become her ally.[2] The resolution to crush Germany absolutely, whatever the cost, entailed the corollary of swallowing Soviet ambitions whatever the cost. Neither before nor since has there ever been in Britain such a large measure of pragmatic agreement between the Establishment and the hard left.

The second development was the 'Final Solution' – the genocide of the Jews. Their exclusion in Germany from every sort of dignified work and normal life in the course of the 1930s naturally led on, in Nazi logic, to their systematic extermination, especially when it became clear that no other country in the world had any willingness to open its doors to hundreds of thousands, let alone millions, of central European Jews. It had been decided upon in principle as far back as 1938.[3] From 1 September 1941 all had to wear the yellow star sewn upon their coats. Their mass 'evacuation' to the gas camps began almost immediately afterwards, starting with those in Berlin. Most of Poland's three million Jews would be dead by the end of 1942, but it would not be the turn of the Jews of Rome until October 1943, and the fate of many of those in south-eastern Europe, in Hungary above all, was still open in 1944. In all up to six million people were thus exterminated in Auschwitz and elsewhere. Earlier crimes of Nazi tyranny pale almost into insignificance when compared with this colossal commitment to 'anti-life', perhaps unique in history for its methodically controlled and 'scientific' character. It was certainly an awareness of this development which did much to stimulate the German conspirators; while the Allied governments were also made well aware of what was going on, it did not equally affect their attitudes.

The middle period of the war was that in which the British strategic air offensive against Germany was built up, partly to demonstrate that in the years before the 'Second Front' we were not sitting idly waiting. It was, as a matter of fact, Britain, not Germany, which began the indiscriminate bombing of enemy cities and then systematically pursued the policy of area bombing with ever greater intensity. 'There is one thing', wrote Churchill already in July 1940, 'that will bring Hitler down, and that is an absolutely devastating, exterminating attack by very heavy bombers from this country upon the Nazi homeland.'[4] If it was Churchill who originally sponsored this policy, it was Air Chief Marshall Sir Arthur Harris who stuck to it from then until the end, despite the very heavy losses which Bomber Command suffered. The initial aim, to destroy specific war targets, was quickly widened: 'The civilian population around the target areas must be made to feel the weight of the war,' declared the War Cabinet a good two weeks before Coventry went up in flames.[5] As British bombs grew heavier and heavier the inner cities of Germany, the old and beautiful ones very especially, were devastated even more completely than Coventry had been, and thousands of the more useless sort of civilians were killed. However, industry, placed upon the periphery of cities, suffered relatively little, and it is now fully admitted that the effect upon the German war effort of British bombing was extraordinarily slight – hardly, in fact, comparable even with the loss of bombers involved.[6] Here, more than at any other point, Britain at war abandoned the attempt to follow moral or Christian principle; here also the British war strategy proved most mistaken and ineffective in hard pragmatic terms. The country owed its survival to Fighter Command. To Bomber Command it owed very little.

On the home front it is remarkable how civilian in mood, how cool, how creative, how concerned with the future Britain managed to be in those middle war years, when the outcome of the conflict was very far from obvious. The war had greatly altered the state of the nation. Years of heavy unemployment ended almost overnight. Women, even the mothers of young children, flocked to work and into kinds of paid employment they had never entered before. Manners were relaxed. Strangers were spoken to in trains. American soldiers were entertained enthusiastically. Illegitimacy and the sale of contraceptives rose steeply. Society's sexual and marital barriers, just like its class barriers, were breached with the relative impunity of war. It was an age of *communitas*.

As Hitler's bombs ploughed into the worst of slum properties they helped create the will to build a new and less unequal society. Already in 1941 a new approach was being prepared for the nation's system of education. Sir William Beveridge's *Report on Social Insurance* was published in 1942, the basic planning document for a welfare state. In 1944 R. A. Butler's great Education Act was passed through parliament. Churchill was not much interested in such things, but the 'liberals' within his party, like Butler and Macmillan, were. Essentially they represented a national consensus, neither specifically Conservative, Labour, nor Liberal: the consensus to go ahead with the moderated socialism of a welfare state and to ensure that the miseries of the great Depression never returned. This was certainly a consensus to which Temple and Tawney (Beveridge's brother-in-law) had contributed a good deal, and its arrival meant that when the war was over, the lines of social and political advance pursued by Attlee's Labour government would in fact already have been clearly marked out in a non-partisan way.

Finally, the period following the entry of the United States into the war brought a decisive and permanent shift in the public balance of world power. American participation guaranteed British victory at the price of British leadership. And not only leadership in war but in peace too. It was, of course, only the steady isolationism of America throughout the inter-war period which had left to Britain the appearance of a primacy within the western world which, in hard terms of economic power, had already been lost. Pearl Harbor shifted the capital of Anglo-Saxon democratic councils from London to Washington and it began a period of quickly growing and manifest dependence of Britain upon America: military, economic, political, cultural. The post-war world of Britain, even its culture and religion, becomes unintelligible without a constant awareness of the American presence and impact to a degree that was not at all the case for the pre-war world.

So the war changed – in its fortunes, its aims, its likely consequences. In June 1944 came the long-awaited Allied invasion of France. In August Paris was liberated. By September the Rhine was reached. Despite still powerful German resistance throughout the winter and the launching of rocket attacks upon London, the end was now in sight. The fate of the world was settled when Roosevelt, Stalin and Churchill met at Yalta in February 1945. The frontiers of Europe were to be redrawn. Poland was to be handed over to the nominees of Stalin. A United Nations Organization was to be established. Three nights later, in one further devastating spree of British aerial destruction, Dresden – filled with refugees fleeing from the east – went up in flames. 'Dead, dead, dead everywhere. Some completely black like charcoal. Others apparently untouched, lying as if they were asleep. Women in aprons, women and children sitting in the trams as if they had just nodded off.'[7] Next month the Allies crossed the Rhine and in April Nazi power finally collapsed, but not before those Germans who had endeavoured to save their country, and Europe too, from disaster had been duly punished for doing so. On the 9th Admiral Canaris, Hans von Dohnanyi and Dietrich Bonhoeffer were executed; on the 23rd they were followed by Dietrich's brother Klaus, his other brother-in-law, Rüdiger Schleicher, and his close friend F. J. Perels, legal adviser to the Confessing Church. One week later Hitler killed himself. On 7 May his successor, Admiral Doenitz, signed terms of unconditional surrender.

The war with Japan was still not over and was expected to last a year or more. That it did not do so was due ostensibly to the development of the atomic bomb. The Americans dropped one upon Hiroshima on 6 August and a second on Nagasaki on the 9th. Together they killed nearly two hundred thousand people. On the 14th Japan surrendered. The war was thus quickly over, avoiding a lot of hard fighting, but at the price of a cheque which all future humanity would have to honour: the price of living in the shadow of atomic war. The rockets which struck London in the winter of 1944 and the atomic bombs which struck Hiroshima and Nagasaki six months later were infinitely more sophisticated weapons than any available to either side in 1939. In six years mankind had come a very long way in the art of killing. The war had not only brought about the deaths of nearly fifty million people (of whom only 400 thousand were British), it had produced weapons able wholly to transform man's experience of war and to mount a threat to his very continued existence on earth unimaginable in any former age. Henceforward a cataclysmic end of the world would no longer be just a religious theme of divine intervention but a secular theme of human expertise and folly. Truly, as Bonhoeffer suggested, writing from his prison cell, the world had come of age.

The Churches Abroad

Nazism and the war presented the churches of Europe with their greatest challenge in this century. It was a challenge which for the churches in Britain was at once relatively indirect and unambiguous. On the Continent, and especially in Germany and in regard to the papacy, this was not so. The challenge was immediate and yet also, to many eyes, it still managed to be clothed in ambiguity. Yet in point of fact the crisis par excellence of Christian identity and ecclesiastical relevance had at last arrived, and it would at this point be parochial not to pause in our history of English religion and to look first, at least briefly, at how fellow Christians in Europe, Catholic and Protestant, came through the war. Not only is this the proper context for a consideration of English wartime religion and its problems, it is also a basic factor for the understanding of post-war Christianity everywhere.

In Germany in the early 1930s many Christians had welcomed Nazism even with enthusiasm, but by 1939 attitudes had greatly changed. The pagan ideology and sheer cruelty of the movement had become too apparent. Real Nazi sympathizers had distanced themselves from the Church, for which indeed Hitler no longer pretended to see any point, while Church people were nearly all to a greater or lesser extent conscious that they were now part of a body suspect in Nazi eyes. This was more true of most Catholics than of most Protestants. Among Protestants it was intensely true for the small surviving core of the Confessing Church, but between the main body of the Protestant Church and the State there was relatively little conflict. Yet even within the Confessing Church an intercession list of August 1939 included only eleven people arrested and three in concentration camps, though there were 121 'ministerial prohibitions', 150 prohibitions on movement of one sort and another, and 44 prohibitions against preaching.[1]

By the end of the war there were some four hundred German clergy in concentration camps and over 90 per cent were Catholic (despite the fact that Germany itself was over two-thirds Protestant): 360 German Catholic priests in concentration camps was a lot and it demonstrates, together with the quite considerable number who were executed, a sharp and conscious conflict between Church and State. Catholic priests usually share a strong common consciousness and group loyalty and they were not divided into two almost opposed camps in the way that Protestants were between the Confessing minority, who included nearly all those in prison, and the non-Confessing official Church. Between the latter and the State tension probably indeed diminished with the war. Hitler gave explicit instructions that the Church should not be upset unnecessarily. Furthermore the war itself encouraged some closing of ranks. If Bonhoeffer could tell Visser 't Hooft on a visit to Geneva in 1941, 'I pray for the defeat of my country',[2] that statement would still offend most fellow German Christians even in the post-war world. Very few had such clear-sightedness about the situation they were now in. All the Christian sense of the duty of loyalty to country welled up to encourage a deeper support for Hitler's government in time of war 'in defence of the Fatherland'. The political group of soldiers and civil servants to which Bonhoeffer belonged, which planned the assassination of Hitler and the overthrow of his government, included some intensely sincere Christians, but in Church terms it was a tiny and quite untypical minority.

However much Hitler hated Christianity, he could not clash too gravely with the German churches in time of war, the Catholic Church as much as any. He needed their support and the loyalty of the overwhelming majority of their members. Yet their leaders made extremely little use of this relatively privileged position. When euthanasia began to be carried out on a large scale within Germany in 1941 Church protests mounted, including some famous sermons from Bishop von Galen, and the euthanasia decree was withdrawn. But it was, it has to be said, Germans who were the victims of the euthanasia. There was no comparable German Church protest about the still greater crimes being committed against Poles and Jews. Bishops von Preysing of Berlin and von Galen of Munster were outspokenly anti-Nazi enough, but they were held on a rein of caution by old Cardinal Bertram, the chairman of the Conference, and by the pope himself. No German Catholic bishop ever needed to be sent to a concentration camp. Here, as in the Italy of the 1930s and indeed in many a land, the lower clergy did all in all rather better than their bishops. The only national Church leadership which could have spoken out in any way effectively about the major crimes of the war was the German, but it failed to do so. It may be noted too that even in such grave circumstances never did Catholic and Protestant leaders come together to give any common message whatsoever.

The name of one martyr may be recalled: Franz Jägerstätter, an Austrian peasant.[3] A small farmer with a wife and three daughters, he was a man of simple but profound piety and very clear political judgment. He saw the diabolical character of Nazism and found himself as a Christian simply unable to swear the oath of obedience to the Führer required of every German soldier. His parish priest and his bishop both endeavoured to dissuade him, with arguments of thoughtful and solid prudence, from so Christ-like a conviction. They failed and he was beheaded on 9 August 1943 in Brandenburg prison. The profound significance of his death lies in the absolute moral power of a single Christian's witness to cut right through, without anything histrionic, the ambiguities of ecclesiastical compromise in the face of evil. And he did so through the medium of conscientious objection – a medium rejected both by the national and the ecclesiastical tradition to which Jägerstätter belonged. Like Thomas More, a father of daughters, he was like More in much else too. If the process of canonization had real contemporary significance, it might have found in Jägerstätter its candidate of predilection.

The full weight of Nazi tyranny fell only exceptionally upon the German Christian. In Poland it was a very different story. In the inner councils of Hitler the Poles seem to have been marked down for elimination, only second to the Jews, and the Catholic Church in Poland was not less ill-treated than its surrounding society but almost more so – for it has historically provided the very backbone to the survival of Polish nationality and freedom.

Hundreds of priests were shot from the first months of occupation and then thousands were arrested. Poland had 10,000 priests in 1939. Of these 3,647 were placed in concentration camps and 1,996 died there. Such figures, of course, only indicate the clerical tip of a policy of near-genocide: over six million Poles died in the war, but certainly no other European Christian Church has suffered worse persecution in modern times.

While Pope Pius XII wrote at least 124 letters to the German bishops during the war, he sent only eighteen to the Polish bishops: that rather striking difference may open the way for some necessary discussion of the most argued-over ecclesiastical issue of the Second World War: the 'silence' of the Pope.[4]

Eugenio Pacelli had been a papal diplomat in Germany for twelve years – from 1917 to 1929, first in Munich, then in Berlin. Subsequently he replaced Cardinal Gasparri as Secretary of State, and when Pius XI died his Secretary of State was quickly elected to succeed him – on 2 March 1939 (Pacelli's sixty-third birthday). His intelligence was acute, his experience and knowledge of international affairs very great. He combined a rather melancholy but profound spirituality with a mastery of the techniques of diplomacy, and a temperamental timidity which frequently reduced the force of what he said by shrouding it in a mystifyingly obscure phraseology. No modern pope (except Pius X) has been more criticized since his death, so it is well to remember that the adulation he received, especially in his earlier years, was no whit less than that subsequently accorded to Pope John or Pope John Paul. Take the following words, written by a highly intelligent English Catholic, and entirely representative of the way Catholics at least – but probably many other Christians too – thought of the Pope during the war:

> The Pope is astride the world today as never before . . . In one and the same career he reveals the utter piety and devotion of a saint, the insight of the true man of science, who will use his discoveries in the service of an ideal, the penetration that comes of fluency in a dozen languages ancient and modern, and the universal charity that can embrace in one overwhelming sentence, the common people of Britain, France, Poland and Germany together.[5]

Pope Pius's undoubted skills were those of the jurist and the diplomat and they were skills of a very high order, but his very commitment to their use came to exclude other roles which might have been more appropriate in the circumstances of the war. He was moreover a man at once preoccupied with Germany and fearful of Communism. The experience of 1919, when a Communist put a pistol to his head on the steps of the Nunciature in Munich, is likely to have had a profound effect upon someone so sensitive, timid and hitherto sheltered in his life. It was an effect, nevertheless, to reinforce rather than to disturb his scale of values and the intensely rational, rather introspective exercise of conscience which all his life characterized him – an exercise grounded on an absolutely sure doctrinal and juridical sense of the ecclesiastical mission and considerable pessimism about human nature.

It would be utterly false, indeed gravely to misread the evidence, to suggest – as some have done – that he sympathized with Nazism. By temperament, by conviction and through the experience of his work as Secretary of State, he was profoundly opposed to it. He knew the German situation extremely well and all through the 1930s he had carried on an almost ceaseless diplomatic campaign against constant Nazi violations of the terms of the concordat. As pope he wished to try again. 'The German problem is the most important for me,' he declared at once, and indeed his near obsession with the protection of Germany's 'Forty million Catholics' from attack by a malevolent government – an attack which he had already experienced as the consequence of Pius XI's encyclical, *Mit Brennender Sorge* in 1937 – appeared to outweigh in his mind most other considerations.

It was paralleled by one other – the pursuit of peace. Upon his coat of arms was placed a dove holding an olive branch – a highly suitable emblem for a pope beginning his reign in 1939 – but as appeasers had discovered already in Britain and elsewhere (and as Mgr Tardini explicitly warned the pope with great perceptiveness), if international peace is to be your first priority, you are driven to encourage one compromising surrender after another. Having decided that his role must be a diplomatic one of working for peace between the nations, he was committed to a position of 'absolute neutrality': to take sides publicly over any issue would destroy any chance of being a diplomatic go-between. Furthermore, to criticize the German government might bring reprisals upon his forty million German Catholics. These two considerations would seem to have been absolute with him, supplemented by the fear that any outspokenness might well increase the plight of Hitler's victims elsewhere and increase their number. Consequently the pope's lips were sealed. Never did he speak out publicly against German aggression, the appalling ill-treatment of the Poles, or the genocide of six million Jews – even about the rounding up of the Jews in his own diocese of Rome he said not one word. The papal silence was without doubt most conscientiously motivated, almost agonizingly so. It was no less a moral disaster, and one made almost worse – if that is possible – by the subsequent well-meaning attempts of ecclesiastics and even scholars to justify or explain it away.

There are at least three good reasons why this cannot be done. The first relates to the way in which the Pope acted upon a grave misunderstanding of the role open to him. There was no serious likelihood of the papacy being able to play a major diplomatic role in maintaining or regaining peace – it had played no such role in this century and no one of importance outside the Vatican wanted it to do so now. The Pope's own diplomatic career and his patient, and not wholly unsuccessful efforts in the 1930s to make the German government respect the concordat greatly deceived him as to what his wider role could now be. In the early 1930s with a Nazi government, still seeking some measure of international respectability, and on the rather limited terrain of the rights of the German Church as laid down in the concordat, the diplomatic approach could have some slight measure of success. In the entirely different circumstances of the 1940s no such approach was of any use at all, but Pius XII, finding it impossible to switch horses, to turn from diplomacy to prophecy, remained imprisoned by his very skills. He was thereby prevented from fulfilling the very role which he had himself, and rightly, declared to be his primary Petrine task, as set forth in his first encyclical, *Summi Pontificatus*, of October 1939:

We feel we owe no greater debt to our office and our time than to testify to the truth with Apostolic firmness: 'To give testimony to the truth.' This duty necessarily entails the exposition and confutation of errors and human faults; for these must be made known before it is possible to tend and to heal them. 'You shall know the truth and the truth shall make you free' (John 8:32). In the fulfilment of this our duty we shall not let ourselves be influenced by earthly considerations nor be held back by mistrust or opposition, by rebuffs or lack of appreciation of our words, nor yet by fear of misconceptions and misapprehensions.

It is according to his own words that the papacy's subsequent record may be judged.

The second reason relates to practical effectiveness. The Pope had only one major asset in combating Hitler's policies but that asset was not inconsiderable. It was the minds and hearts of German Catholics. Of course they would not simply have followed a papal lead; nevertheless many would have been very seriously disturbed in their loyalty to the German government if the pope had spoken out with absolute clarity and, still more, if Hitler had then reacted violently against the pope himself or against the Church hierarchy in Germany. Catholics in every other country could be ill-treated with impunity, it damaged the German war effort not at all, but Hitler could not afford a major confrontation in war with any considerable part of the German nation; he knew it himself and took great pains to ensure that the pope did not precipitate such a confrontation.[6] In this the Pope played into his hands by quite failing to recognize that the German Church stood in a quite different position from the Church in other lands. Instead of realizing that it was the Church he needed to worry about the least, it was the one he remained most preoccupied to protect. This was probably the gravest single misjudgment of his reign, produced at once by his intense love of Germany, his timidity in face of conflict and – one cannot but add – by an apparent inability to recognize just how grave the moral evils of Nazi rule outside the German nation were. He certainly did not approve of Jewish persecution, but seemed not to recognize that it was entering into an order of moral iniquity infinitely beyond the breaking of the terms of the concordat or the detention of some outspoken priest.

The third reason lies precisely here. The greatest crime in European history – greatest in scale, in systematic deliberation, and in its precise opposition to all human and Christian values – was being perpetrated. This, at least in its broad lines, the Pope knew. But he remained silent. He said not a word in public condemnation, not a word to warn the conscience of the many Catholics involved, not one public appeal to Catholics everywhere to protect the millions of innocents in their midst whose lives were in peril. Whether what he said would or would not be in any way immediately effective, whether it would even make things worse for Catholics here, or other victims of Hitler there, should have been in such a predicament for the supreme teacher of faith and morals, sublimely irrelevant. He had outlined his duty most clearly in his initial encyclical and that duty was now at stake. The Pope is essentially by office a teacher, as he is by no means essentially a diplomat or political arbiter, yet the essential and also practicable duty was laid aside for the sake of a chimera, both unnecessary and unobtainable.

If anyone less than the pope spoke out, at least outside Germany, it could do no good. The Catholic bishops in Holland protested vigorously in a pastoral letter against the deportation of the Jews in July 1942, and the arrest of Dutch Catholics of Jewish blood, hitherto exempt, was the immediate consequence. So the Carmelite nun, Sister Teresa Benedicta a Cruce, better known as the philosopher Edith Stein, was taken from her convent on 2 August and murdered in Auschwitz just one week later. We can, perhaps, rejoice that so noble a victim of Auschwitz was at once fully Jewish and wholly Christian, and that the linking of Christians and Jews together in a common holocaust (so that Auschwitz is almost as much a Polish Christian place of pilgrimage as a Jewish one) did much to end a millenium of Christian (including, very definitely, Polish) anti-Semitism. What had been for generations a common and accepted element in Christian life, in France, Germany, Poland and elsewhere, was now almost cut out of the body, revealed at last in its innate infamy: too late to save European Jewry, admittedly, but at least the post-war churches would no longer be afflicted by this moral running sore from their medieval past.

The war in fact shifted the overall balance of political sympathy of Christians considerably to the left. In France Vichy had expressed pretty well the characteristic preference of most good Catholics in the pre-war period, but Vichy was not liked, and few Catholics after the war would hanker for such an alternative to democracy any more. Everywhere Christians saw what a failure to back democracy with any enthusiasm had brought them to, and the typical post-war European Christian would be a democrat as the typical pre-war Christian had not been. He would, too, be willing to work with Socialists, even if he was not a Socialist himself. Christian and Socialist had fought together in the Resistance. A reconciliation of traditions, which in England had taken place gradually and peacefully, presided over by Temple, upon the Continent took place in the cold heat of reaction to Nazism.

The life of the Church altered in these years far more rapidly than it had ever done in peacetime: international contacts between Protestants multiplied, as did ecumenical contacts between Catholic and Protestant. The French worker-priest was a child of the war. In the concentration camp, in the maquis, in the desperate struggle to hide Jews, in the renewal of ideas which the war thrust upon clergy and laity alike, something of a new Church was being born. Certainly the genesis of change can be traced back at least to the thirties clearly enough in the theological, ecumenical and liturgical fields, but the stress of the war provided its own compulsive force to push those ideas into far less restricted circles than they had hitherto affected. The structures and frontiers of society were overturned by Nazi conquest throughout western and central Europe: the structures and prejudices of Christian society were overturned with the rest. Much of both good and evil was irrevocably lost. If the churches were compromised in part and suffered in part, they were also liberated, far more effectively than by the First World War or by any other major event, to rethink their institutional structures, relationship with society and with one another, the formulation of their gospel.

Church and State at Home

There was at the start of the Second World War a marked restraint on the side of English clerics. The crusading ferverinos so characteristic of the mood of 1914 were almost wholly absent. Bishops and priests had learned their lesson; moreover the Pacifist fervour of many of them was too recent for there to be a total switch-about. For the Church, as for the nation as a whole, war was seen by September 1939 as inevitable and just, but it was entered into soberly and rather sadly. Bishop Bell could still, that December, be arguing for a negotiated peace, and he was not alone. At least until the Battle of Britain the Church as a whole qualified, rather than magnified, the moral dimension of the country's struggle: 'To fight Christianly we must fight in penitence.'[1]

There were, of course, priests and laymen who argued that to live Christianly we should not fight at all. They were led by Charles Raven, Donald Soper, George Macleod, and they were treated on the whole fairly decently though, to Raven's chagrin, they were no longer permitted to broadcast their views. The fact that many conscientious objectors were in deep sympathy with the underlying motivation of the war and ready to be the most courageous non-combatants undoubtedly made a difference. But most people accepted the war simply enough as a moral obligation and the more they learnt about the Nazis, the more certain they were. Participation in the war itself was not a moral issue, even if it generated moral issues of various kinds.

One of the earliest of these was the treatment of enemy aliens. It was natural that in the summer of 1940 with the possibility of invasion the presence of numerous Germans and Italians suddenly seemed a threat to be eliminated. 'Collar the lot,' commanded Churchill, and on Whit Sunday tens of thousands were suddenly rounded up, very many of them political and racial refugees from the regimes they were now suspected of serving as a potential 'fifth column'. Their immediate arrest can fairly be justified but hardly the subsequent treatment, their detention in wretched conditions on the Isle of Man, the refusal of our leaders for many months to set about the sifting of the reliable from the unreliable, the actual hostility with which the very victims of Hitler were treated at times by people now at war with Hitler. Remember the British army officer who declared to an anti-Nazi refugee, 'I can respect no man who has no loyalty to his country, especially the country of his birth.'[2]

The two men who struggled hardest to alleviate the lot of the interned were George Bell and William Paton, both of whom visited them on the Isle of Man – visits which brought real hope to many pretty bewildered people, former inmates of concentration camps in Germany. Bell's subsequent interventions in the House of Lords did produce support and after some months the government began to release manifest anti-Nazis. As an issue it was one of the smallest of the war and most easily solved. It is significant because it well illustrated the absence from the first year of the war of a sense of the conflict as being truly one between two visions of humanity rather than one between governments and war machines. It is also significant because it immediately brought George Bell to the forefront as the obstinate little priest who was quite determined that the Church should not sink in war to being 'the State's spiritual auxiliary'. He, if anyone, had taken to heart the lesson of the First World War. He had been Davidson's secretary, and where Davidson had consistently if cautiously taken an independent line – a refusal to countenance reprisals, a reluctance to allow priests to volunteer for military service – Bell was resolved to follow in his footsteps, only in a very much less cautious way.

The most basic issue was that constituted by the nature of our goal in being at war: what could be the terms of peace? Were we fighting Germany or were we fighting Nazism? Could we imagine a negotiated peace with a non-Nazi Germany? Was such a hope realistic or desirable? Were there in fact enough 'Good Germans' to make a change of government in Germany conceivable? To the last three questions the government's answer, at least from the time Churchill became Prime Minister, was a pretty emphatic 'No'. It was made to appear that to suggest anything else was both to enter the realms of cloud-cuckoo land and to be unpatriotic, to be subtly undermining the single-minded thrust of the war effort by suggesting some possible alternative to the total mobilization of the nation for straight military victory.

Bishop Bell thought differently. His Penguin, *Christianity and World Order*, published in 1940, stressed that Britain must not 'let slip any genuine chance of a negotiated peace which observes the principles of Order and Justice' and that 'Germany and National Socialism are not the same thing'.[3] Next year, on 10 May at the Stoll Theatre, with Cardinal Hinsley in the chair, he challenged the government and nation again:

> I am sure that there are very many in Germany, silenced now by the Gestapo and the machine-gun, who long for deliverance from a godless Nazi rule, and for the coming of a Christian order in which they and we can take part. Is no trumpet call to come from England, to awaken them from despair?[4]

Such words greatly encouraged those Germans who were planning revolution but when they tried to discover if there was in the British government any sympathy for such a line, they were offered no sign of hope.[5] Political circles in Britain were simply not prepared in principle to admit that such good Germans as did exist might also prove to be effective Germans. In May 1942 Bell visited Sweden for three weeks. There, quite unexpectedly, he was joined by two spokesmen of German dissident groups, Hans Schönfield and Dietrich Bonhoeffer.[6] The message which Bell brought back to Britain was that certain highly placed Germans (some of them named) were planning a *putsch*, that whatever they might have to say while actually undertaking it, their aim was a just peace and the elimination of Nazism, and that the Allies could greatly help by indicating that they were ready to treat Germany very differently if such an event took place.

Once back in Britain Bell sought with urgency to get this message across to the government, to Eden and Cripps in particular. The response was not encouraging. In Eden's words: 'Without casting any reflection on the bona fides of your informants, I am satisfied that it would not be in the national interest for any reply whatever to be sent to them.' The bishop continued his campaign both in the press and in the House of Lords.

> I could wish [he declared in the Lords on 15 October] that the British Government would make it very much clearer than they have yet done that this is a war between rival philosophies of life . . . and would assure the anti-Nazis in Germany that they would treat a Germany which effectively repudiated Hitler and Hitlerism in a very different way from the Germany in which Hitler continued to rule.[7]

Bell obtained no significant modification of government policy. On the contrary, an unmitigated insistence upon 'unconditional surrender' as the only option grew ever harder.

It is certain that the German resistance leaders had all the cards stacked against them; it is arguable that their chance of success was next to nil but this is not, and was not, certain. The refusal even to consider or to encourage such a possibility effectively reduced any likelihood it might have had, and showed great blindness to the fearful consequences for the whole world of a fight to the finish.

By the latter half of 1942 the fate of Europe's Jews was becoming only too clear. In that year most of Poland's three million Jews were wiped out, and both Polish and Jewish sources were at last getting the information through to Britain to an extent that it was no longer possible for the informed observer to doubt the main lines of the truth.[8] A *Times* article on 4 December could speak of a 'Deliberate Plan for Extermination', and Temple wrote at once to express 'burning indignation at this atrocity, to which the records of barbarous ages scarcely supply a parallel' (*The Times*, 5 December). On the 17th of the month the Allies made a joint declaration condemning 'this bestial policy of cold-blooded extermination'.

The knowledge, then, was there and with it a verbal response. Of that there can be no doubt. What is equally clear is that the policy of the British government (and indeed of the American government) remained steadily opposed to actually doing anything to help the Jews. This is the more remarkable in that it is clear that Churchill personally would have liked to help, but his mind was on other things and his expressed wishes were disregarded. Large numbers of Jewish refugees could only be a nuisance anywhere. That had been the view before the war; it remained the government's view, even now, when it was certain that the alternative to rescuing them was the gas chamber. Even children from enemy countries, it was seriously maintained, constituted a security risk. It was the Jews in Bulgaria, Hungary and Rumania who were easiest to save but they were not – except in the smallest numbers – to be allowed through. To let them into Palestine must exacerbate the Arabs; to send them anywhere else might certainly upset somebody.

In the House of Lords on 23 March 1943, Temple, now Archbishop of Canterbury, made a long and powerful speech moving a resolution urging 'immediate measures on the largest and most generous scale' to give 'temporary asylum' to all Jews able to escape the Nazis: 'My chief protest is against procrastination of any kind ... We stand at the bar of history, of humanity, and of God.'[9] That was, very probably, the most memorable and important speech Temple ever made in the House of Lords. It had, however, next to no effect. The British government – at one moment Foreign Office staff, at another the Colonial Office, at a third the Cabinet – steadily blocked every proposal to help the Jews, whether it be to bomb the railway lines going to Auschwitz or the gas chambers themselves, to admit children into Palestine (beyond the highly limited quotas drawn up in quite other circumstances), or even the Swedish proposal to take in twenty thousand Jewish children until after the war, about which Temple wrote to Eden in May. 'Jewish Agency "sob-stuff" should not be taken at its face value', commented one civil servant.[10] And so, in this at least, Hitler had his way. Nazi anti-Semitism was as successful as it was, one may conclude, because it rang a bell in many respectable Christian hearts, British as well as German.

If Temple took the lead over the Jews, he refused to take it over another hardly less significant issue – that of obliteration bombing: 'I am not at all disposed', he wrote to Bell in July 1943, 'to be the mouthpiece of the concern which I know exists, because I do not share it.'[11] Bishop Mervyn Haigh of Coventry, distraught by the bombing of his cathedral town, actually pronounced retaliatory action – the bombing of civilian populations in Germany –

morally justified. 'These are primarily technical questions', he concluded in an address which moved the editor of the *Church Times* to declare himself 'dismayed and astonished': Haigh was clearly in need of a long rest.[12] If Haigh's words might seem to point towards the mass bombing of German towns on a scale far more devastating than anything inflicted on Coventry, we must remember that in fact the British government had already decided upon such a policy and had begun to implement it before the bombing of Coventy. 'To bomb cities as cities,' wrote Bell in his *Diocesan Gazette* in September 1943, 'deliberately to attack civilians, quite irrespective of whether or not they are actively contributing to the war effort, is a wrong deed, whether done by the Nazis or by ourselves.' And in the Lords on 9 February 1944, commenting on the fearful devastation caused by a series of recent raids on Germany, he declared:

> If there was one thing absolutely sure it was that the combination of the policy of obliteration with the policy of complete negation as to the future of a Germany which had got free from Hitler was bound to prolong the war and make the period after the war more miserable.[13]

On this more than on any other point Bell incurred deep hostility, perhaps particularly because so many bomber pilots were killed in the raids. Here was a 'political priest', as Vansittart described him, criticizing the conduct of the war and suggesting that it was not only our enemies but we who were morally at fault unsupported by Temple, he was backed by Headlam. Peers like Selborne and Cranborne, devout Tories and leading members of the Church Assembly, replied deriding the bishop's pleas about bombing German cities and saving Jewish lives as contradictory and impractical. Yet Bell was regularly better informed than his opponents and his sights were higher. As Captain Liddell Hart wrote to him after his House of Lords speech,

> Your argument may not have suited the mood of the Lords but, as an RAF friend remarked to me, 'A very large proportion of the silent public agree with the Bishop.' Moreover the historian of civilisation, if that survives, is likely to regard it as better evidence for Christianity and common decency, than has been provided by any other spokesman. It represents the longer view and the higher Wisdom.[14]

Forty years later it is widely agreed that the policy of indiscriminate area bombing, so complacently justified at the time as
the most effective way to bring Germany down, save the lives of
the Jews and whatever, was in fact singularly ineffective. Great
cities were reduced to ruins, tens of thousands of civilians were
killed, but the industrial and military potential of Germany was
damaged to a strangely small degree. Furthermore the loss of
British bombers was very high while German morale was
actually hardened by the very ruthlessness of the attacks.[15]

In most of this Bell, as a public voice, was very much alone:
disliked by Churchill, written off by many a moderately informed
man as a holy simpleton, Bell never achieved the sort of mastery
over men or their gatherings – the Lords, the Church Assembly,
even large ecumenical conferences – which Temple so often
experienced. He was probably altogether too honest, too emphatic in his moral judgment, too little affected by the art of the
possible. Much more of a prophet than Temple but less of a
statesman, he was not the Church's spokesman at war because
the Church was seldom really behind him, but he was Christianity's surest spokesman. His mild and saintly manner, the confidence of his utterances, a quiet obstinacy in outspokenness, even
his sheer grasp of awkward facts, were 'acutely irritating' for
many; but for others Bell was the one man in this country who
truly throughout the war 'manifested that glory which the world
crushes though it cannot live without it . . . *Contra mundum*! Bell
led a rational, moral, realistic fight with the world.'[16] So judged a
Jewish Christian refugee. Or, as Liddell Hart wrote in November
1944, after Temple's death:

> You are the man best fitted to succeed Temple – the man who
> could contribute more to that high office than anyone else I
> have ever met. I hardly imagine . . . that the Prime Minister is a
> big enough man to recognise the value of such an appointment
> and swallow his resentment of your attitude to the war. It is a
> supreme tribute to you that your honesty will have cost you the
> chance of attaining the supreme position in the Church.[17]

If Temple had lived one more year and died after the coming of
Labour to power, it is more than likely that Bell and not Fisher
would have presided over the post-war Church. Whether that
would have been a great gain is more questionable. Bell was not

379

best as a presider, as the former of a consensus, but as an unsilenceable speaker of moral truth *contra mundum* and even *contra Ecclesiam*.

The end justifies the means. Such increasingly was the morality of the Allies at war, and perhaps of almost any nation at war, and the end was seen very simplistically as the defeat of the enemy. Within that struggle the crimes of Stalin, the morality of obliteration bombing, a fair deal for the nations of eastern Europe, the survival of the Jews, all such matters appeared to our war leaders and to much of the nation as little more than inconvenient irrelevancies. The wickedness of our enemies was unquestionably to be finally demonstrated by the trials at Nuremburg; the righteousness of our own behaviour had to be equally unquestionable. The concerns of Bell were indeed vaguely shared by many more liberal minded people, for the free critical mind was not killed by the war, but it was for the most part muted and disorganized. Only, perhaps, on one issue was there a notable public divergence between official policy and the moral judgment of the nation. That issue was the fate of Poland as settled by Yalta, by the Russian refusal to assist the Warsaw uprising, and then by the imposition upon Poland of a Soviet-backed government in place of the government in exile which had been present in London throughout the war. Withdrawal of British recognition of that government seemed to many a base betrayal. Here for the first time the nation began to sense that to some very real extent the right way had been lost across the labyrinth of war and that, dead or alive, Hitler would not have wholly lost.

It was the ending of the war that did most to give ground for such a contention, to shatter the moral consensus and to leave the churches as nonplussed as at its start. How could one not rejoice that it was all over but how could one rejoice when over two hundred thousand human beings had been killed by just two bombs at Hiroshima and Nagasaki? No one was ready for this. As it was all over before people could even start writing letters to *The Times*, the question seemed at first almost academic. There was no on-going policy of atomic war to argue about. Bell and others wrote their letters of condemnation; Maude Royden (a First World War and 1930s Pacifist) and others, theirs of justification. Dean Thicknesse of St Albans banned the use of the abbey for a service of thanksgiving: 'I cannot honestly give thanks to God for an event brought about by a wrong use of force by an act of wholesale indiscriminate massacre which is different in kind over all acts of open warfare hitherto, however brutal and hideous' (*The Times*, 16 August). Bishop Wilson of Chelmsford and Bishop Chavasse of Rochester said much the same.[18] Few clerics and few laity agreed with them. The municipal authorities of St Albans offered their thanks to God in a Methodist church instead.

If the atomic bombs had not been dropped the war might have gone on for many months, with 'the sacrifice of innumerable soldiers, sailors and airmen'. 'How dare civilians ask for this?' asked Maude Royden. Was it really 'different in kind' from our devastation of Würzburg or Dresden? But if it was not, so what? Had we not already in bombing Germany long passed the boundaries of morally acceptable violence? Moreover had not the Japanese in fact already put out feelers for surrender? And had the second bomb, at least, any other point than the provision of the military with extra technical intelligence about its capabilities? We regarded the devastation of Coventry with its five hundred dead as a moral outrage, yet it was but a pinprick in comparison with what we inflicted upon two Japanese towns when the explosion of an atomic bomb in an uninhabited place might equally well have brought Japan to surrender. There was 'room for difference of opinion whether the atomic bomb ought ever to have been used', declared Geoffrey Fisher, the new Archbishop of Canterbury, prosaically. The Church was able to offer nothing more than that uncertain note.[19] Yet with a pervasive sense of horror about what had happened, there was too a millenial feeling in the air. The war was over after all. Hitler and Mussolini were dead. The concentration camps were closed. No one knew, or chose to know, about the Gulag Archipelago. Labour was in power. The United Nations were soon to meet. Socialist Russia could be our friend at last. 'We are facing a new era,' pronounced Clement Attlee at the announcement of the Labour victory only a fortnight before Hiroshima, 'I believe we are on the eve of a great advance of the human race.' Soon, very soon, the cold war would begin.

Religious Life

'Mass in Chelsea seemed curiously fictitious; no peon knelt with his arms out in the attitude of the cross, no woman dragged herself up the aisle on her knees. It would have seemed shocking, like the Agony itself. We do not mortify ourselves. Perhaps we are in need of violence.'[1] Such were some of Graham Greene's thoughts as he returned to England in 1939 from Mexico. Certainly English Christianity appeared respectable, quiet, rather unheroic, even cosy when compared with what Christians had come to experience almost as normal during the 1930s in Mexico, Spain, Russia, Germany, or Ethiopia. Yet at much the same moment another literary English Christian, Lewis, contemplating the approach of war, was only too conscious of the agony: 'I get no further than Gethsemane, and am daily thankful that that scene of all others in Our Lord's life did not go unrecorded.'[2] The intensities of English religion, if they existed at all, had been interiorized. Can anyone truly be 'in need of violence'? In need or not, the violence was now about to come, but the strength of the British response to it derived essentially from its lay and civilian character, a reluctance to glorify violence in any form. The image of 'Dad's Army' is not too far from the truth of the national mood. There developed no sharp divide, as there had been in the First World War, between military and civilian, the front and the nation at home. Everyone was in it together. Heroism was widely spread and played down everywhere. The war was not a war-game, it was a business, yet a matter of honour too, increasingly from 1940 a sort of everyman's crusade. 'In fighting Hitler we are truly fighting the Devil, Anti-Christ,' declared A. A. Milne, a converted Pacifist.[3] Hugh Dormer could confide to his diary that, 'The Nazis today are not just the enemies of my State as the French at Waterloo or the Germans in 1914, but they are the destroyers of everything European and Christian and embody the forces of evil.'[4] Young soldier-hero as Dormer was, he voiced here the common mind of Englishmen as marshalled by Churchill in parliament, Montgomery in the field, Bevin in the factory. Yet most of the nation's leaders – Churchill, Eden, Bevin, Beaverbrook, Attlee – were unreligious enough. They still represented the old agnostic consensus of a former age and were appealing now for some sort of Christian crusade in which they themselves only confusedly believed.[5]

The 1914 war had appeared as fruit of the traditional and Christian order of Europe. Clerics had whipped up enthusiasm for it in the earlier stages and the profound disillusionment that followed had been with religion as much as with anything else. But the Second World War seemed rather the product of the secular ideologies that had called Europe's tune so powerfully in the twenties and thirties. Organized religion appeared now both more spiritually mature and far less to blame for the mess we were in. It seemed meaningful rather than sickly conventional to see the fight as one required by human and Christian values, to recognize Karl Barth's 1940 Call to Britain as truly a prophetic expression of the word of God for man today. Fight on. Fighting Hitler meant in a way recommitment to old values, religious and moral. As more and more countries were invaded by Hitler, as the news of concentration camps and gas chambers burgeoned, so grew more and more intense the nation's sense of an unquestionably just cause, of being chosen standard bearers for all that was best and most Christian in our heritage. The 'hour of midnight' 1940 might be, it was also 'our finest hour' when, for a moment, with the free leaders of half the nations of Europe in exile in London, Britain's international role seemed uncriticizable. Moreover the intense sense of unity engendered by the struggle spilt over into other areas of life enabling people to transcend the long inherited follies of the past. 1940 and 1941, in short, provided a rare moment of *communitas*.

A chronicle of small events may help express the war's impact on religious life in its varied ways.

1939 September:

> One unexpected feature of life at present is that it is quite hard
> to get a seat in church – every local family apparently taking the
> view that whether they go or not, at any rate their evacuees
> *shall*. But I don't like to be surrounded by a writhing mass of
> bored urchins who obviously have no idea of what's going on,
> or why . . .[6]

The writer may not have cared for evacuees in the pews, but their
presence in the village started him upon one of the most imaginative of modern children's stories, *The Lion, the Witch and the
Wardrobe*.

1940 June: John Brown, a Yorkshire quarter-master sergeant,
was at Honfleur in Normandy on the 16th, the penultimate day
for the British force in France.

> Woken 4 a.m. by barrage. Great fear that French will capitu-
> late and that we shall be taken prisoners. Took Holy Commun-
> ion at 8 a.m. service outside farmhouse with small table for
> altar. Received a great deal of consolation from it. The guns
> were silent during the service and a bird sang beautifully.[7]

1940 November: After the great raid on Coventry its victims
were buried at a mass funeral at the London Road cemetery with
the crowds shivering in the rain and the sirens wailing out their
warning of another raid. Bishop Haigh strode to the edge of the
trench: 'I am the Resurrection and the Life. How often shall my
brother sin against me and I forgive him? I say not until seven
times but until seventy times seven.' Yet Haigh soon after proceeded to argue in favour of retaliatory bombing.[8]

1941 May: Joan Veazey was a young curate's wife at St Mary's
by the Elephant and Castle. They had married the previous
September in the midst of an air raid and life had been little else
than one long air raid ever since, but at least until 10 May their
own church had survived. That night, as the House of Commons
burnt down and Westminster Abbey and the British Museum and
Lambeth Palace were damaged and Rose Macaulay's library
obliterated and street upon street spread thick with rubble, St
Mary's too was left just a charred shell. As Joan wrote afterwards, they saw

> the beams blazing furiously and then falling one by one, until
> the Altar caught alight and seemed to fold up and die before our

eyes. The church burnt with white hot flames. It was a dreadful sight, and though we tried hard in the beginning to get the fire under control, we failed hopelessly. The windows had gone, the wind changed its direction and fanned the flames to even greater heights. We could hear the cries of the pigeons in the tower but we found it impossible to reach them. The Great Bells fell . . .[9]

Two days later Evelyn Underhill, herself just a few weeks off death, wrote to Mildred Bosanquet.[10]

12 Hampstead Square, NW3: Yes – I am still a pacifist though I agree with you about the increasing difficulty of it. But I feel more and more sure that Christianity and war are incompatible, and that *nothing* worth having can be achieved by 'casting out Satan by Satan'. All the same, I don't think pacifists at the moment should be controversial . . . one can do little but try to live in charity, and do what one can for the suffering and bewildered. We are caught up in events far too great for us to grasp . . .

1943: William Allchin, a young soldier captured at Singapore, first heard the gospel preached at a camp along the River Kwai. 'Love your enemies and pray for those who persecute you.' He began to learn Japanese.[11]

Bishop Wilson of Singapore was taken for torture in the camp at Changi that October. Recalling the floggings he had suffered years before at his public school – one established specially for the sons of clergy – he said to himself as it began, 'Well, thank heaven I went to St John's, Leatherhead.'[12]

When I muttered 'Forgive them', I wondered how far I was being dramatic and if I really meant it, because I looked at their faces as they stood round and took it in turn to flog, and their faces were hard and cruel and some of them were evidently enjoying their cruelty. But by the Grace of God I saw those men not as they were, but as they had been. Once they were little children playing with their brothers and sisters and happy in their parents' love, in those far-off days before they had been conditioned by their false nationalist ideals, and it is hard to hate little children. But even that was not enough. There came into my mind as I lay on the table the words of that Communion hymn:

> Look, Father, look on His anointed face,
> And only look on us as found in Him.

And so I saw them, not as they had been, but as they were capable of becoming, redeemed by the power of Christ and I knew that it was only common sense to say 'forgive'.[13]

1944: Hugh Dormer was a young officer of heroic temper in the Irish Guards, scion of an old English Catholic family, educated at Ampleforth. In 1943 he had been dropped in Occupied France to carry out sabotage and had twice escaped back to Britain via Spain. He rejoined his regiment in time to take part in 1944 in the final preparations in Yorkshire for the invasion of Normandy and briefly resume his diary:

> Evening Mass was said behind a haystack in an open field. All around against the hedges the tanks were camouflaged, pointing in their silence so perfectly the contrast of peace and war. As night fell fires were lit along the lines, serving as a background to the supreme sacrifice that was being celebrated in the corner of the field. As I gazed at the shadows thrown by the Crucifix on the table I wondered how many of these men here would have paid the price of war before six months had passed. But there are worse things than death, would men only realise it. . . . He who would save his life must lose it (24 February).
>
> We drove over to Malton to the St Patrick's Day Dance. . . . The scene inside was very gay with the band playing and the lights and the couples sliding past on the floor. It all seemed so very right and proper to see such carefree festivity like the great ball at Brussels before Waterloo (20 March).
>
> We talked of pine forests and America, of Europe and the English Character, of broadmindedness and patriotism, of Catholicism and Ampleforth (15 May).
>
> I am sending this book away tomorrow, as I think the hour will strike in the next few days and my final journey will have begun. . . . No man ever went to meet his fate more joyfully than I (25 May).[14]

In June the second front began. On 1 July Dormer's battalion landed in Normandy. On the 31st he was killed.

Six weeks later on 8 September another Hugh, an officer in the Welsh Guards, was killed near the Belgian-Dutch border, an equally buoyant though very different young man. Hugh Lister was an Anglican priest trained at Cuddesdon, he was also chairman of the Hackney Wick branch of the Transport and General Workers Union and had proved in peacetime an indefatigable promoter of strikes and organizer of flying squads. As a curate in a desperately depressed part of the East End it seemed the most sensible way to help his flock. In his own amateurish way Lister was the English forerunner of the worker priest, with his tools of trade the house mass, liberation theology and the 'option for the poor'.[15]

His identification with the have-nots of rundown London in the 1930s was as genuine, as dangerous, and as finally simply right as the commitment of French *prêtres ouvriers* ten years later and Latin American liberationist priests forty years later.

1945: Hiroshima. 'A Japanese town, rather more populous than Southampton, suddenly ceased to exist.'[16] Group-Captain Cheshire, VC, DSO, was perhaps the coolest, most fearless, most consistently successful of bomber pilots. In July 1945 he was sent to the Pacific as RAF representative to observe the explosion of the atomic bomb. On 26 July Japan was given a final dire ultimatum. Would they accept it and thus avoid nuclear attack?

> During those final days before the atomic attack [Cheshire wrote later] a more authoritative rumour began to circulate. It said that the Japanese were on the point of surrender. We learnt later that it had been true. Far from causing us to hope that the attacks would be postponed, it only served to aggravate our obsession to see the bombs explode . . . some means should be found of keeping the war going until the attacks had been launched.

Cheshire was not permitted by our American allies to watch the first bomb and the destruction of Hiroshima, but he was allowed to observe the second. On 9 August he watched the mushroom cloud spread over Nagasaki, and back on Trinian Island that night in 'a state of severe emotional shock' he argued with the majority that what had happened was absolutely right: 'We've got to have the biggest and best bombs. That's the first principal of survival.' 'The definiteness of such views', comments his biographer, 'brought down on his head the disgusted fury of men like a New England colonel, whose remorse was as deeply felt as Cheshire's elation.'[17] Cheshire would be haunted for life by the memory of Nagasaki, would become the devoutest of

Roman Catholics and give his life to the service of the handi-
capped, yet – paradoxically – he would not abandon his belief
that the dropping of the bomb was justified.

Across millions of personal responses to the hard facts of war,
air raids, the battle front, internment camps, one senses not only
the seemingly almost unlimited human ability to adjust to the
unusual and the tortuous, not only a simple, almost crusade-like,
heroism, not only a great deal of moral fumbling, but also a
widespread, rather undenominational, reappropriation of
Christian faith as the key to meaning in life. Undoubtedly this had
been prepared for by the intellectual revival which had been
building up in the preceding years. But now it bubbled forth a
great deal more obviously in all sorts of way. Thus, on the literary
front, the war was the golden age of that Anglican lay literary and
theological foursome – Charles Williams, C. S. Lewis, T. S. Eliot,
Dorothy L. Sayers. Sayers only really transferred from the field of
detective writing to that of religious epic and Christian apologetic with the war, while Williams died before it was over. Let us
look, for instance, at some of the published works of 1942, the
year of the turn of the tide. William Temple's *Christianity and
Social Order*, Christopher Dawson's *The Judgement of the
Nations*, Dorothy Sayers, *The Man Born to Be King*, C. S. Lewis,
The Screwtape Letters, T. S. Eliot's *Little Gidding*. From such
titles it is obvious enough that the most critical phase of the
Second World War was a time of very considerable Christian
literary creativity but of a very unsectarian sort. The BBC was its
natural medium. Lewis's *Mere Christianity* was broadcast on five
Sundays at the start of 1942; and *The Man Born to Be King*,
partly in 1941 and partly in 1942 – perhaps the most successful
piece of religious work ever specifically written for radio. *Little
Gidding* was the last, but by no means the least, of Eliot's poetry.
It can well be read as prescribing the very programme for English
Christianity in the midwinter of war – a programme which must
draw richly upon history and memory but not be bound, as Eliot
and Anglo-Catholicism had in the past often seemed to be bound,
by a nostalgic desire to revive the medieval past:

> We cannot restore old factions
> We cannot restore old policies.

Instead: We shall not cease from exploration

> And the end of all our exploring
> Will be to arrive where we started
> And know the place for the first time.

The repeated message of the poem is Dame Julian's famous word of hope:

> And all shall be well
> All manner of things shall be well.

Little Gidding is the last of the *Four Quartets* and when they were published together for the first time in 1944 they provided something of a poetic religious embodiment of the intensity of recent experience, re-creating the past but with a new Christian confidence in the future.

One detects something of the same sort in C. S. Lewis's prolific wartime writing. Despite the war, life at Oxford did continue, indeed his famous Socratic Club was actually founded in 1941 and much of his best-known theological writing dates from these years: *The Problem of Pain* and *The Screwtape Letters* were both largely written in 1940; by mid-1942 the first was in its eighth impression, the latter its sixth; *Mere Christianity* was broadcast in 1942, while *That Hideous Strength*, *The Great Divorce*, and *Miracles* were on the way. The popular religious apologetic of modern Britain was – to exaggerate somewhat – being composed almost at a stroke!

Of all 1942 literature perhaps the most evocative of the mood of the time was a work entitled *Midnight Hour* by 'Nicodemus'. It was a spiritual journal beginning in May 1941 and ending in September. The writer had gone up to Oxford early in the century expecting to be ordained but had then lost his faith. Now years later the traumatic atmosphere of mid-1941 had brought him back to a conviction that he must re-identify himself with the Church and at long last be ordained, despite his continued belief that the Church of England was 'in the main, a compromising pseudo-Christianity'. He was accepted, but then, four days before ordination in Advent, rejected as unsuitable on account of a piece of the diary which he had just published including the remark: 'I believe that they who ally themselves with the Church of England ally themselves with death and go down in spirit to a grave of the spirit'; yet he himself felt called to that alliance, to joining the ranks of those in this 'dying life' of the priesthood.[18] To speak in such a way was offensive to pious ears and he was not ordained but his book did make a profound impression on many. It epitomizes the note of rather tense conversion in that bleak hour, the wartime experience of arriving back spiritually at where one had started long ago and knowing the place for the first time – knowing it indeed as those who had been there all along might not.

Another similarly strange experience was that of Antonia White, the author of *Frost In May*, a subtle and sensitive writer who had abandoned Catholicism and Christian faith in the 1920s. Having decided to go to 'Midnight Mass' at Christmas 1940, the first time for many years, 'simply for its beauty', she entered a church to find out when it would be celebrated (not at midnight on account of the blitz).

> Several people were waiting their turn for Confession. Suddenly, as if some invisible person were pushing me, I found myself, quite against my will, taking my place in the line. I ordered my body to get up and walk out of the church; it simply refused to obey. When my turn came, I automatically went into the confessional. I have never felt more blankly ridiculous than I did when I heard the little grating noise as the priest drew back the curtain from the grille. . . . I came away in a queer state; happy, apprehensive, bewildered and amused at myself. All the same, I did go to Communion on Christmas morning. It was a very blind, doubting Communion.[19]

Fifteen months later, in April 1942, she could still write: 'I can't feel at home in the Church. I understand Tyrrell so well when he felt the Church like a great octopus sitting on his chest'; and a little later, 'To be once more in St Peter's boat is to be subject to such violent seasickness that every few months I am tempted to throw myself overboard.'[20] But she stayed in. In the movement of 'return', characteristic of those years from the mid-thirties to the late forties, Antonia White – like Nicodemus – is interesting because she represents so well one of the basic problems: a profound need for religious faith but a very considerable difficulty in swallowing the current shape and claims of the institutional

Church. She, like Simone Weil, could not in the end not be a Christian even though she found almost insufferable 'this huge edifice of dogmatism and legalism'[21] which belonging to the Church, the Roman Catholic Church above all, imposed upon her. Yet the pull of Catholicism seemed stronger and wider among the uncommitted than had ever been the case. Its authority, its certainties, its sacramental system, its international fellowship, never appeared more valuable. Perhaps the presence of so many Catholic allies in London – Poles, French, Belgians – contributed to this. But at a far wider level, the Second World War, like the first, saw the upsurge of sacramental renewal. The Anglican parish communion, the Methodist sacramental fellowship, fruits of inter-war liturgical thought, responded to the religious needs of ordinary people at war in circumstances where neither the formalism of a traditional matins nor the verbosity of much preaching would well serve. Waugh was not historically inaccurate in inserting at the end of *Brideshead*, symbolic of that time, 'a beaten copper lamp of deplorable design relit before a tabernacle'. People wanted the sacraments, and sacraments closer to them. Among English Roman Catholics popular participation in the 'Dialogue Mass' was at last in some places being permitted. It was accompanied by the publication of Ronald Knox's *Mass in Slow Motion*. It does not really seem surprising to find even Lewis, deeply Protestant by temperament as he was, starting to make his sacramental confession regularly from 1940.

Publicly and institutionally too, the war years were decidedly innovative for Church life. In the previous twenty years the international ecumenical movement had grown into a big tree, and it had done so very largely thanks to British leadership, yet it had not at home greatly affected the churches. Now suddenly steps which hitherto it had seemed easier to put off to a rainy day seemed instead obvious and inevitable. On 16 September 1940 the Free Church Federal Council was inaugurated in the midst of an air raid, replacing the rather confusing duality of National Free Church Council and Federal Council of Evangelical Free Churches.[22] It was only a first collaborative step forward in the development of something which seemed for a moment almost like becoming a common national ecumenical consciousness.

When in August 1941 Archbishop Lang led a mixed delegation of Anglicans and Free churchmen to see R. A. Butler, President of the Board of Education, on the subject of better Christian education in all schools, it was clear that what had hitherto been the major stone of contention between the two traditions was now so no more. The inauguration of the British Council of Churches in 1942, whose architect was Paton, and first president Temple, signified still more firmly the replacement of confrontation by collaboration. The BCC would quickly become one of the key institutions of British Christianity, so much so that it could be claimed that 1942 divides the pre-war and post-war worlds better ecclesiastically than any other date.

Locally, even more adventurous innovations might take place. In Bristol during the war years a group of local ministers – Anglican, Methodist, Baptist and Congregationalist – built up a local ecumenical community, very far indeed in advance either of any previous practice or the rulings of Church authority. In the parish church of St Matthew, Moorfields, whose vicar was a young liberal Anglo-Catholic named Mervyn Stockwood, and in the neighbouring Free Churches, there were united communion services. At Christmas midnight mass at St Matthew the Free Church ministers joined in administering the sacrament.[23] The hurdle of inter-communion would continue to bedevil the churches for many years, yet here, as at Holy Trinity, Cambridge, and doubtless in many an army camp under the pressure of war, it could locally and temporally be overcome. Forty years later Stockwood would still feel he had never subsequently experienced such a depth of ecumenical sharing.

Still less to be expected was a venture in another quarter. On 21 December 1940 *The Times* carried a letter signed by Archbishops Lang and Temple, Cardinal Hinsley and the Moderator of the Free Church Federal Council, George Armstrong. The letter listed, and supported, the pope's Five Peace Points as the only sure foundation for European peace and future social life. To them it added five further points taken from the Oxford Conference of 1937. What concerns us here is not so much the points themselves as the public indication that in face of the national emergency the ecumenical fraternity had widened yet further to include the cardinal archbishop of Westminster. Such a letter was, in fact, wholly unprecedented. In the course of 1940 a remarkable development had been going on among a group of English Catholics in touch with the cardinal.[24] The previous December, in a radio address after the nine o'clock news, Hinsley had declared that while it was quite right for Britain to be fighting the Nazis, the only weapon which could finally win the battle was the 'Sword of the Spirit'. In the following months a number of lay Catholics led by Manya Harari and Christopher Dawson proposed to the cardinal that there needed to be a practical follow-up to such words. While Christians in other churches were thinking forward to the post-war society, many Catholics still seemed to be half hankering – and were accused of doing so – after Fascism. Pétain's establishment of the Vichy regime in June with its harping upon traditional Catholic social values had had· its reverberations across the Channel. Should not Catholics in all honesty admit to being at heart in the Pétain-Mussolini-Franco camp? Could they really be one hundred per cent behind the war effort? To counter such thinking Hinsley saw the need for a strong Catholic democratic initiative, just as did his lay confidants. On 1 August 1940 the Sword of the Spirit was launched at a meeting at Archbishop's House, Westminster, with Hinsley as president, Dawson as vice-president, Barbara Ward and (a little later) A. C. F. Beales (a lecturer, and later professor, in education at King's College) as secretaries. Beales and his wife proved highly efficient organizers and Barbara Ward the Sword's most dynamic speaker, while the underlying initial sense of direction was largely provided by Dawson. A flood of pamphlets were soon flowing forth, non-Catholics were encouraged to join, and an exciting new initiative had clearly got under way to a very wide welcome from other churches, the government and Catholics among the Allies, Poles and Frenchmen particularly. Bishop Bell was especially enthusiastic. It was overwhelmingly a lay initiative. Only a few younger and more academic priests, like the Dominican Gervase Mathew, the Jesuit Martin d'Arcy, and Fr Herbert Keldany of the Catholic Social Guild, were at all active in support. Among the bishops Hinsley was fully backed by his own auxiliary, Gervase's older brother David, but by hardly any others, while in the north the hierarchy and Archbishop Downey especially was suspicious of the whole ethos of the movement:

lay, ecumenical, intellectually progressive, decidedly English and fairly upper class.

Christopher Dawson was at the time editor of the *Dublin Review*[25] and in the January 1941 issue he formulated the outlook of the Sword. It was to be a 'dynamic and prophetic element' within the Church committed to furthering the implications of the 'general realization that social and political issues have become spiritual issues – that the Church cannot abstain from intervention without betraying its mission'. Catholicism could have no truck with totalitarianism, any apparent similarities being essentially deceptive; on the contrary Catholics could and should, on a basis of recognition of natural law, co-operate with Christians of other churches and democratic society generally. Dawson's subsequent *Judgement of the Nations* (1942), developing these themes, was probably the most significant Catholic book of the war years. It was commended by Bell in the House of Lords but condemned by Fr Andrew Beck in the *Clergy Review*.

The great days of the Sword came in May 1941, the unforgettable weekend of Saturday, 10th. It had arranged two well-advertised public meetings in the Stoll Theatre, Kingsway. On the Saturday at three o'clock with Cardinal Hinsley in the chair, Bishop Bell, Richard O'Sullivan and Hugh Lyon, headmaster of Rugby, were to speak on 'A Christian International Order'. On the Sunday with Archbishop Lang presiding, Sidney Berry, Acting Moderator of the Free Church Federal Council, Fr Martin d'Arcy, SJ, and Dorothy Sayers were to speak on 'A Christian Order in Britain'.

The Stoll meetings were extraordinary in several ways. To have an ecumenical platform of this strength sponsored by an English Catholic organization was something which truly needed to be seen to be believed. Perhaps at that date it needed the blitz to make it possible, though it is clear how carefully thought out it was and how exactly it responded to the aspirations of the Catholic laity involved. It was, of course, also only possible because of the extraordinarily open and generous character of Hinsley. The meetings were rendered still more striking by the appalling bombing to which London was subjected that Saturday night; between the two meetings the House of Commons was destroyed; Lang came on the Sunday from a devastated Lambeth Palace and participants to arrive at all had to struggle over heaps of rubble. Bishop Bell's speech on the Saturday was one of the most powerful of his career.[26] Hinsley closed the meeting with the following words:

> Our unity must not be in sentiment and in word only; it must be carried into practical measures. Let us have a regular system of consultation and collaboration from now onwards, such as His Lordship the Bishop of Chichester has suggested, to agree on a plan of action which shall win the peace when the din of battle is over.

At this point Bell whispered to the cardinal, 'Eminence, may we say the Our Father?' and Hinsley at once led the whole assembly in prayer together: 'Our Father who art in heaven'.

It was all too good to be true, or at least too good to last. The cardinal was apparently reproved by his fellow bishops (though not by Rome) for praying with heretics and, when a new constitution for the Sword was adopted in August, non-Catholics were excluded from membership. The resulting disillusion was inevitable and, despite a hastily devised arrangement whereby in future the Sword would co-operate closely with a newly established non-Catholic 'Religion and Life' movement, much was inevitably lost. The Sword's lay leadership tried hard to maintain its line as far as possible but under the pressure of the bishops and canon lawyers its freedom to manoeuvre was steadily reduced. With Hinsley's death in March 1943 it lost its sole powerful protector.

Hinsley had become a national figure, the first Archbishop of Westminster fully to be so, and his funeral was a remarkable ecumenical occasion with Anglican and Orthodox bishops in the choir of the cathedral. Even Downey's panegyric could not obscure the extent to which Hinsley had altered the conceivable pattern of relationship between Roman Catholics and other Christians in this country. But, for the moment, there it was to stop. He had been too much alone, also doubtless too unaware in his grandfatherly optimism and openness to goodness in others (he was particularly affected by Bishop Bell) of the wider implications of what he was doing. His successor, Archbishop Griffin, would be a great deal more circumspect and the Sword would shrink till it became little more than a penknife.

Hinsley had undoubtedly wanted to allow some common prayer with other Christians – at the very least silent prayer or a hymn, like 'Lead Kindly Light', as was in fact authorized practice in Holland – but most of the hierarchy was quite set against this. Hemmed in by Godfrey, Amigo and Downey, he could do very little. They had moreover the full backing of Establishment theologians, especially those of the *Clergy Review*, edited by Canon George Smith, the leading figure at the Westminster seminary at St Edmund's Ware. There can be no common prayer because there is no common faith between Catholics and non-Catholics, nor even a common charity: 'Their charity is not our charity; the words are the same but the content is different.'[27] The Catholic bishops could authorize common action on social issues just as long as this was wholly divorced from anything explicitly religious. Such a divorce seemed to non-Catholics wrong in principle and effectively impossible in practice: the social action of Christians cannot be divorced from the springs of prayer and belief.

If prayer was one sticking point, the issue of religious freedom (with Spain, for instance, in mind) was another. The Free Church members of Religion and Life were anxious, perhaps over-anxious, for a commitment on this point from their somewhat embarrassed Catholic collaborators, and the Sword leadership was anxious to give it. An acceptable draft was actually drawn up by Douglas Woodruff and John Murray SJ, upon the one side, William Paton and T. S. Eliot upon the other, by June 1943; it included the statement that 'there is a natural and civil right to religious freedom'. The draft was warmly welcomed by the British Council of Churches but on the Catholic side there was a long and awkward silence. Griffin consulted Canons Smith and Mahoney and they were not favourable; after a year's delay the statement was politely rejected in July 1944.[28]

By then the national emergency and the state of *communitas* had receded, and the lines of ecclesiastical normality were firmly re-established. On 6 June 1944 Normandy was invaded and on the 8th the Catholic bishop of Nottingham attended a meeting of the Christian Front at which Archbishop Garbett of York was also present. It was on condition that there should be no prayers, even silent ones. The Archbishop commented afterwards: 'It is monstrous that we should have to buy Roman Catholic co-operation at the price of no prayers.'[29] The aberration of Hinsley's one little 'Our Father' was not only not to be repeated, it was not to be mentioned. His Life by Heenan, published that year, does not refer to it.

One enduring fruit of the Sword's brief golden age was the Harvill Press founded in 1942 by Manya Harari and Marjorie Villiers with the encouragement of David and Gervase Mathew. It would become in the next thirty years a principal channel within the publishing world through which the more liberated writing of European Catholicism came to Britain, together with much other exciting continental, especially Russian, literature, including in due course Dr Zhivago.

The Sword of the Spirit, cut short in its stride as it was, remains the most interesting because the least predictable Christian development of the war years. In its concern for a future social order it was, of course, fully matched by Anglican and Free Church activity, by Oldham's Christian Frontier Council, and much else. The Malvern Conference in January 1941, which brought together some four hundred Anglican priests and laity, was the most publicized event of this kind. Unlike the Sword's work at its best, it was, however, a little poorly organized. John Middleton Murry, T. S. Eliot, Dorothy Sayers and Donald Mackinnon were among its speakers; Temple presided but Sir Richard Acland was its moving figure. Acland persuaded the conference, despite some unease, to state its belief that private ownership of 'the principal industrial resources of the community may be [Temple preferred "is"] contrary to divine justice'. During 1942 Temple, now at Canterbury, began a much wider campaign to prepare for post-war society, his chosen allies being Richard Acland, Donald Soper but, most of all, Stafford Cripps. It started with an Albert Hall meeting in September at which he, Garbett and Cripps were the speakers. The selection of Cripps at that point was surely significant and intended to be so. Chips Channon confided to his diary: 'The old Archbishop, heaven knows, was foolish and wicked enough but the obese one is positively dangerous. He now openly preaches Socialism from a platform which he shares with Cripps – Is England mad, and doomed?'[30]

Temple had, alas, developed a new bee in his bonnet – on the reform of the banking system – about which he spoke at length. At a subsequent meeting Garbett amused the gathering when he remarked that he was no financier, but as 'the Bank of England was in the Province of Canterbury, he could leave high finance to his senior brother'.[31] Temple's weakness was always an inability not to be drawn on too many hares at the same time, yet his Penguin Special published that year, *Christianity and Social Order*, remains one of his most important books. Clearly addressed to the nation rather than to the Church, it was a sane, long lasting work (able to be republished with a preface by Edward Heath thirty years later). Together with the Malvern Conference it provided the Church's *nihil obstat* for the moderated socialism which Labour leaders like Cripps, Attlee and Bevin were getting ready to give the nation, and to which Conservative leaders like Butler were hardly opposed, and it ensured that the Church would be ready for this when it came. It proved a valuable legacy, and it is significant that in offering it Temple based himself, as did the Sword of the Spirit, on 'the old conception of Natural Law'.

If 1942 was the year of *Christianity and Social Order*, and of *Little Gidding*, it was also the year of the *Report on Social Insurance and Allied Services*, produced by a committee chaired by Sir William Beveridge. Its purpose was to abolish all known causes of grave want and more than any other document it pointed the way to the welfare state and the characteristic social order of the post-war world. It is worth remembering that one of Beveridge's brilliant young aids was Frank Pakenham, formerly a don at Christchurch. He was also one of Fr d'Arcy's recent converts into the Catholic Church, a man unable to forget d'Arcy's special piece of advice: 'Keep close to the poor'. For many Christians the socialistic option was not the right one; it would weaken, they feared, both personal initiative and family responsibilities. That was both a Catholic and a Protestant fear. It is all the more important, therefore, to recognize how influential was the Christian contribution to the moderate left-turn which the nation was now preparing to take.

On 26 October 1944, with the war so nearly over, Temple died. He was sixty-three and had been Archbishop of Canterbury for just two and a half years. 'The People's Archbishop' had seemed so clearly chosen and so well prepared to lead the churches in Britain and throughout the world in the era of reconstruction. For twenty-five years, more than any other man, he had called the tune in ecclesiastical life, presided over innumerable meetings, formulated acceptable yet challenging statements, written books about theology and religious philosophy and social reform. The sense of loss was acute.[32] His old opponent and critic Hensley Henson, however, saw matters differently: 'I think he is *felix opportunitate mortis*, for he has passed away while the streams of opinion in church and state, of which he had become the outstanding symbol and exponent, were at flood, and escaped the experience of their inevitable ebb.'[33] Subsequent historians have agreed with this rather jaundiced judgment.[34] In fact Henson misjudged the situation considerably. Whatever else happened in the next five years, 'the streams of opinion in church and state' of which Temple was the exponent did not ebb so fast as all that. Labour Britain was just about to begin, the World Council of Churches to meet. The post-war ecumenical scene would have provided Temple with a stage beyond anything which had hitherto been his. Archbishop of Canterbury in peacetime, president of the World Council and chairman of its Central Committee, he would indeed have been *alterius orbis papa*.[35]

Instead, he was dead, as were William Paton and Arthur Hinsley. Each proved effectually irreplaceable and the absence of all three has much to do with a certain ecclesiastical vacuum noticeable in the following years. Of the major ecumenical personalities of the war only Bell survived. He had thrown himself indefatigably into the support of the German Confessing Church in the thirties and then into all the moral problems of the war. He came out of it immensely revered abroad, but at home perhaps just slightly diminished by a whisper of rejection. Yet he seems most certainly, and still more in retrospect than at the time, the outstanding English Christian of the Second World War, as Dietrich Bonhoeffer was the German. It is touching that they were such close friends and that the last recorded words of

Bonhoeffer before he went to execution was a message via a fellow prisoner for the Bishop of Chichester. 'Tell him that for me this is the end but also the beginning.'

PART V

———◆◆◆———

1945–1960

Politics

To exchange the splendours of oratory and the decades of experience of the greatest of war leaders for a very sincere but decidedly uncharismatic little man, seemed to the rest of the world an odd thing for the British electorate to do in the summer of 1945. It never made a wiser choice. Britain was straining forward to peace and a new social order, anxious that the disillusionment and lost opportunity which followed the First World War should not be repeated this time. For that, Attlee was the man. Churchill had no more desire to establish a social democratic Britain than he had to give India its overdue self-government. Attlee was committed to both.[1] The Labour government of 1945 to 1951 was all in all the most competent, effective and honourable reforming administration in modern British history.

For the first time Labour had an absolute majority in the House of Commons; for the first time it had gained such a degree of middle-class support that it could truly be seen to represent the nation as a whole, and the success of its work can be measured by its genuinely national character. No Prime Minister of the twentieth century has been less partisan than Attlee or has had sounder judgment. He gauged his mandate with accuracy and carried it out with a cool modesty which deprived his opponents of any chance of convincing the nation that its affairs were now in the hands of dangerous revolutionaries. No hands were safer than those of this old boy of Haileybury, which, if lacking the panache of Churchill's Harrow, is one of the most respectable of public schools. If Attlee seemed so very reliable it was perhaps due in some measure to the fact that he had no pretensions to being either an aristocratic radical or a rebellious working man.

He came from the most sober of the middle middle-class – just a little above that which in twenty years time the country would come to prefer for its Prime Ministers. With lieutenants as outstanding as Bevin, Cripps and Aneurin Bevan, and with a leader of the opposition as distinguished as Churchill, it is not surprising that Attlee himself appeared so ordinary as to be mediocre, even to his lieutenants themselves. The strength of Labour's achievement lay in being tied to no one man's genius. It was a collective and almost unideological response to the inherent inequality of British society and the unemployment of the thirties, seen in the light of the indigenous socialism of Tawney and of the experience of national community engendered by the war. After the election victory the Labour MPs might gather in the House of Commons to sing the 'Red Flag', but it represented no more than a nostalgic re-evocation of tribal mythology. In the hard light of day the party's more doctrinaire socialists, led at the time by Professor Laski, chairman of the National Executive, were kept very much at arm's length by the Prime Minister and his closest colleagues.

Labour's agenda could be seen as the missed agenda of the 1920s and 1930s: the coal mines were nationalized at last, so too were the railways and the Bank of England, but little else (Iron and Steel, as a last and only half-believed-in fling, in 1951). Attlee, Morrison and Cripps had ceased to believe that massive nationalization would help the cause of social equality. The economy could be controlled more effectively and less dramatically on Keynesian principles through the working of the Treasury. Control rather than ownership was the point; control to bring to an end the massive social misery of the recent past. In this they were largely successful. Unemployment, unknown during the war, hardly reappeared for years; it remained lower than even Beveridge had thought possible. The really large-scale poverty of pre-war Britain was gone for good: where in 1936 Rowntree had found 31.1 per cent of York's workers living below the poverty line, by 1951 it was only 2.8 per cent. The main weak spot here remained the slum areas in the great industrial conurbations, and Labour was not very successful with its housing, but food and health were enormously improved. Infant mortality rates had been 138 per thousand live births at the beginning of the century, they were down to 21 by the 1950s. On the basis of the Beveridge Report the welfare state was solidly erected with its principal glory, the National Health Service, inaugurated in 1948. For this Aneurin Bevan, the most radical of Labour's current leadership, was directly responsible. The health of the nation, which had improved so dramatically during the Second World War, with a fair distribution of basic food, was to be maintained at that level. If education needed to keep pace with health, the achievement here was less complete. The Education Act of 1944 provided a charter for secondary education for all with the raising of the school-leaving age to fifteen and the establishment of a break at the age of eleven. However, while there was certainly a very considerable expansion of good secondary education outside the privileged and fee-paying classes, the hard division which grew up between 'grammar' and 'secondary modern' based on the 'eleven-plus' examination was not a fully satisfactory answer to the nation's needs, and the proportion of really working-class children getting anywhere near a university remained decidedly low.

In evaluating the limitations of Labour's success, it is important to remember that Britain's economic situation after the war was grave in the extreme: assets down, debts up, responsibilities as great as ever. Of the three great allied powers, Russia had suffered by far the most through the war; she also gained enormously by the peace. Britain had suffered much and lost in every way. America had suffered very little and gained everything. The war over and with the cool Truman as Roosevelt's successor, she did not see herself on top so as to help needy old friends, but to make the world safe for the speedy realization of all her hitherto, unspelt out ambitions. The new order was to be centred irremediably upon the US. The United Nations were to be located in New York. The World Bank was not to leave American soil. Lend-Lease, on the other hand, was to be immediately terminated. The British Empire should be decently dismantled, to be replaced so far as convenient by a string of American bases spread across the globe. Neither politically nor economically could Britain say a very firm Nay to much of this. It could only procrastinate while waiting for America to wake up to the fact that Soviet power required that their allies be strengthened not weakened, and this of course soon began to happen. The inauguration of Marshall Aid in 1948 was the result. For Britain the immediate struggle was simply to stay in business; perhaps it was fortunate that her people hardly saw it this way, remaining somewhat mesmerized by the consciousness that they had 'won' the war. For the time being the country was still shorter on food than during the conflict: bread rationing was a post-war phenomenon. The Labour government battled through the economic crisis quite effectively during the chancellorship of Stafford Cripps, but it came nowhere near to achieving any sort of economic miracle. In such circumstances the weight of its social achievement is the more remarkable.

Three books published in 1945 well express the mainstream intellectual mood of the following years: George Orwell's *Animal Farm*, Arthur Koestler's *The Yogi and the Commissar*, and Karl Popper's *The Open Society and Its Enemies*. All three were extremely influential. *Animal Farm* was undoubtedly one of the most prophetic literary works of the twentieth century, whose relevance never seems to fade. As all good prophecy it was rejected by the fashionable pundits of established reputation, like Victor Gollancz and T. S. Eliot. Orwell and Koestler were former intellectuals of the left, emphatically repudiating both what the Soviet Union had turned into and the tradition of left-wing intellectualism which had so persistently mis-read that monstrosity. Karl Popper provided the textbook analysis of totalitarianism and its descent from Hegel, a 'charlatan' whose works were an 'intellectual farce' written in 'gibberish', the father alike of Nazism and Marxism.

For all its singing of the 'Red Flag' the socialism of Attlee wanted nothing in common with Soviet Communism. The prosecution of the cold war was safe in his hands. So was the development of Britain's independent nuclear deterrent: whatever has been thought of it subsequently, it seemed obviously necessary to Attlee at the time. Doubtless it was too late to save the countries of eastern Europe from a narrow party tyranny imposed by Stalin, but Labour probably did as much as the Conservatives would have done to protest and resist. Indeed Ernest Bevin may well be claimed as Britain's finest conservative Foreign Secretary since Castlereagh. No Tory Foreign Secretary of this century has so well personified the British bull dog – as Churchill himself recognized. His task was to harness the United States to the defence of Europe and the non-Communist world, while surrendering as little as possible to America's anti-imperial syndrome. British responsibility in Palestine was hurriedly abandoned in 1948, largely under American pressure and fairly disastrously for the future of the Middle East; but on other matters the growing fear of Russia on both sides of the Atlantic was the necessary lever to bring the two into line. The working of the Marshall Plan for Europe's economic recovery owed much to Bevin, while the establishment of NATO in 1949 may well be seen as his supreme achievement and, for better or worse, the principal foundation of British foreign policy for the next half-century.

The welfare state emerged then into the full light of day, on a basis established well before by Lloyd George and even Neville Chamberlain, linked with a far more widespread and deeply pondered anti-Communism than characterized any earlier phase of British history. This undoubtedly helped both the churches and the middle classes overcome their surviving hostility to the degree of socialism to which the government was committed (though, when vested interests were at stake, that hostility was still fierce enough – as within the ranks of the BMA). Nevertheless, all in all, the inheritance of Temple, Tawney, Beveridge; the Christian Socialist idealism of Cripps; the tough anti-Soviet line of Bevin; the sheer sanity and respectability of Attlee; the fact that at heart Conservatives like Butler and Macmillan could go along with quite a large part of Labour's programme: all this ensured that, despite a not too successful economic strategy, Labour's revolution was the most widely supported and the least seriously challenged of all the great legislative reforms of modern British history. It established a modern, benevolent, and rather bureaucratic shape taken for granted by all British governments until the late 1970s.

Perhaps the most decisive and unquestionably right of all Labour's achievements was the granting of independence to India in 1947. If there was no reasonable alternative, it is also true that the speed and lack of tergiversation with which it was done owed a great deal to Attlee himself and to his choice of Lord

Mountbatten as the last Viceroy. Rapid withdrawal from so vast and ancient a responsibility combined with a last minute agreement to divide the sub-continent into two separate States – India and Pakistan – was an operation too immense and, really, too unplannable not to bring with it some fearful disorder, yet it is probably true that if Attlee and Mountbatten had not committed themselves to a minimum of delay, the overall breakdown of order throughout the country could have been a great deal worse. Since the late eighteenth century Britain had owed much of her world position to the possession of India. Now it had gone and people at home seemed strangely little affected by the ending of this extraordinary relationship, so that the standard histories of Britain mostly understate the significance of what had happened. The development of British Africa may have appeared to offer sufficient imperial compensation for the loss of India, Pakistan, Ceylon and Burma. At the time it did not occur to people how quickly the rest of the Empire would go too. In the earlier 1950s young colonial officials were still being offered a lifetime of work ahead of them administering some African territory. But in regard to India, Attlee had taken a decision which would constitute a decisive precedent for the Empire as a whole: each land could go when it would, provided a majority so desired and some sort of democratic structure, frail though it might be, had first been established. The Commonwealth Conference of 1949 was almost as pregnant as the founding of NATO for the future shape of Britain's relationship with the rest of the world: India and Pakistan could remain within it as republics and therefore, in due course, many another country too. The creation of a multi-racial Commonwealth rendered the dismantling of the Empire a much easier and more positive exercise than it would otherwise have been.

Attlee's Britain was the third of 'The Big Three'. It was also the first State of a battered western Europe. Germany, Italy and France had all been damaged by the war a great deal more than Britain, and Germany was now truncated of its eastern provinces, filled with millions of refugees from the east, and divided into four zones of occupation. The relationship between Britain and her main European neighbours would be increasingly important yet never satisfactorily apprehended. On the Continent out of great disaster grew a greater renewal which, while it in some ways paralleled what was happening in Britain under Labour, was also distinctively different. The principal political phenomenon of post-war Europe was Christian Democracy, an animal of which British people tended to be somewhat suspicious. It was, above all, a Catholic phenomenon though in Germany especially it also attracted considerable support among more conservative Protestants. In pre-war Europe the Catholic community had already demonstrated a strong and deeply rooted tendency towards democracy. But still more powerful, especially in Rome, had been the fear that democracy was Protestant in origin and Socialist, if not Communist, in destiny; that it was closely linked with anti-clericalism and the confiscation of Church schools; that Catholicism, being an authoritarian religion, could only really be at home with an authoritarian government. The concordat signed in 1940 between the Vatican and Portugal represents the last important expression of a Catholic political approach which had hitherto in practice steadily crushed Catholic aspirations towards democracy. The collapse of Fascism, Nazism and Vichy, together with the strong participation of Catholic radicals in the resistance movements, redrew the politico-religious map of western Europe. Effectively the world was now divided between Communist States on the one hand and countries trying to model themselves on the principles of Anglo-Saxon democracy upon the other. The bulk of European Catholics (and Protestants too) were left with little alternative: except for the lunatic fringe, Christians ceased to flirt with Fascism and plunged instead into 'Christian Democracy', with the blessing of Pope Pius XII and under the leadership of Catholic democrats surviving from a former era: in Italy Alcide de Gasperi, Don Sturzo's right hand man from the 1920s; in Germany Konrad Adenauer; in France, Resistance leaders like Georges Bidault.[2]

The most apposite indicator of the immediate post-war mood was the appointment of the philosopher Jacques Maritain as France's ambassador to the Holy See. A devout Thomist democrat who had opposed both Maurras and Franco, Maritain represented at its noblest the leftward-looking tradition within Catholicism that had hitherto been decidedly off-centre both for

Church and nation – especially in France – and suspect at the Vatican. In 1946 he stands instead for an apparent new consensus: the reconciliation of Catholic orthodoxy with political freedom and social pluralism, if not as yet with intellectual freedom and theological pluralism.

In its early post-war fervour European Christian Democracy could then appear as a left of centre phenomenon – at least in its leadership and aspirations, though not so clearly in its grass roots voting power. This was less true in Germany, more in France. Here it was not only democratic but also saw itself as an essentially reforming force, a not unnatural ally of Socialist parties. It was committed to much the same sort of programme as Labour in Britain, though having a less coherent experience to draw upon; its policies were vaguer, the gap between immediate circumstance and underlying attitude greater. In France, moreover, the Mouvement Républicain Populaire (MRP) – just because of its more left-wing character – quickly lost half its electorate to more conservative parties, especially the Gaullists; moreover, the issue of Church schools fatally divided it from the Socialists; while it further failed for long to grasp that democracy at home was not compatible with the continued imposition of French rule abroad. No party suffered more in its integrity from the early 1950s war in Viet Nam. By the mid-1950s its surviving rump had clearly ceased to be a party of the left. In Germany and Italy, where there was no de Gaulle (that is to say, no right wing politician of distinction with an impeccable war record), Christian Democracy was not challenged effectively from the right and remained a far larger party, but over the years – and perhaps for that very reason – it moved no less decisively to the right. If in the 1940s it could look not too unlike a continental version of Labour, by the 1960s it had undoubtedly become the principal continental parallel to Conservatism. This was a natural enough development and did not undermine the basic significance of the phenomenon of Christian Democracy. Sooner or later even Spain and Portugal would have to follow suit and participate in Catholicism's new political mode. The new community of western Europe, growing out of the devastation of the war and achieving in due course the economic miracle which always just eluded Britain, would be united by an extremely solid Catholic political presence in every single country south of Scandinavia, for finally even Gaullism was but a rather right-wing form of 'Christian Democracy', more adapted to traditional France than the MRP. It was not wholly an accident that, when the European Economic Community was brought into being, the beginning of a politically united Europe, it was done by a 'Treaty of Rome'. For many British people 'Rome' still retained an ominous and threatening note; moreover they have seldom cared for the overt relating of politics to religion and did not greatly warm to, or even understand, 'Christian Democracy'. Yet just as it is probable that the Vatican's failure to back Christian Democracy in the 1920s was its greatest missed opportunity of the inter-war years, so Britain's failure to read the new Europe aright and take the lead in a European Defence Community in the early 1950s was her greatest missed opportunity of the post-war years.

As Stalin's iron hand imposed Communist regimes all across eastern Europe, the sense of the need for a united front greatly grew. Any lingering hopes of appeasement disappeared in 1948, after the Communist coup in Czechoslovakia in February and the Berlin blockade imposed in June; the following year saw both the Communist conquest of China and the foundation of NATO; 1950 the Korean war. In Malaya Britain now had a hundred thousand troops resisting Communist guerrilla infiltration. The United States, which had so easily concurred in the abandonment of eastern Europe to Stalin five years before, now plunged into an anti-Communist witch-hunt led by the Catholic senator Joe McCarthy. Nothing quite so hysterical happened in Britain but the antipathy for Communism is shown well enough by the fact that 97 out of 100 Communist candidates in the 1950 election lost their deposits and for the first time for many years no Communist candidate was elected.

By 1950 Labour's appointed work was done. The senior members of its government were old and tired; there was little heart to go further or sense of common purpose between the radical left led by Aneurin Bevan and the old leadership. Its two most outstanding members, Cripps and Bevin, both had to retire in ill health. In April 1951 Bevan and his lieutenant, Harold Wilson, actually resigned from the government in protest against details of Hugh Gaitskell's rearmament budget. Yet the country was strangely reluctant to let Labour go or the Tories return to power. The government had not lost one by-election. They retained control by a tiny majority (of eight) in the 1950 General Election and though they lost that of October 1951 by a small number of seats they still possessed more votes than the Conservatives. It was certainly time for Labour to go, but it was equally clear that the Conservatives had no mandate to undo the work of their predecessors and in fact little desire to undo it either. Their programme was to 'free' the nation from the mass of rather dreary controls which the war had brought and State socialism fostered, and to build houses. The economy was anyway beginning to prosper and the nation to relax: there were 126,000 television licences in 1949, 763,000 in 1951. The Korean war set things back a little but food rationing was at long last phased out in 1953-4. Road transport and the iron and steel industry were denationalized, income tax reduced, controls of all sorts lifted, but the core of Labour's achievement was in no way touched. The Conservative leadership recognized that this was what the nation wanted and had no desire to restart the class war.

Churchill, returning to 10 Downing Street in his late seventies, was less a Prime Minister, more a historic monument, asleep or reminiscing on the past. He was no longer interested in either confrontation or adventure. 'Invest in success', declared Butler, his Chancellor of the Exchequer and general handyman, uncontroversially. The man who had hammered the unions in the twenties was now all for industrial appeasement: settle it, Churchill told his minister, 'on their terms'. As to the new European community, which he had himself encouraged to come into existence with a prophetic speech at Strasbourg, he was now not at all interested in Britain's entry – the Empire must come first. George VI died in February 1952 a few months after the Conservatives had returned to power. The coronation of Queen Elizabeth the next year was not only an occasion of unparalleled splendour, it was also the symbolic rite of passage in which the traditional values of society were reasserted at the very moment when the war and its subsequent austerities could at last be put aside and the age of affluence begin to dawn.[3] For such a ceremony Churchill was the ideal Prime Minister.

The government's principal positive contribution to the new

affluence lay in the field of housing, one of Labour's weaker spots. The Conservative manifesto promised 300,000 new houses a year, which Labour decried as just empty words, but Harold Macmillan was appointed Minister of Housing and soon more than fulfilled the target. The three million houses and more built while the Conservatives were in office vastly enlarged middle England, the houseproud middle class. It is arguable that the concentration on private building was damaging for Britain's real economic expansion and was indeed one of the reasons why this country never achieved growth comparable to that of Germany or France. These things are relative. The British economy in the 1950s did grow by 2 to 3 per cent a year, more than it has ever done before or since in this century, and domestic prosperity grew still more rapidly. Where there were two and a quarter million cars and one million television sets when the Conservatives came to power in 1951, there were eight million cars and 13 million television sets by the time they left office in 1964. Average earnings had risen by 110 per cent, a rise of over 30 per cent on average living standards, allowing for inflation.

It remains true that while Britain's economy appeared to flourish in the 1950s, the growth in affluence was not matched by a comparable growth in production. Elsewhere in Europe, as in Japan, it was different. Europe, especially hitherto industrially backward southern Europe, was hastily breaking through into a modern, urbanized, industrialized society: France, Italy, Spain. A world of peasants was fading almost overnight into a world of high rise flats, pollution, advanced technology. The interface between peasant and technocrat is far more intimate in southern than in northern Europe. Germany, Britain's traditional industrial rival, was modernizing on a different tack. Vastly more damaged by the war than Britain, the will to recover proved more emphatic. By the end of the 1950s Britain was in fact slipping badly back in Europe's economic race. Its industrialization and urbanization had taken place too long ago, its war scars were too relatively mild. On both counts it lacked a sense of novelty or urgency in the thrust of economic advance such as its rivals enjoyed. It also failed to grasp what was happening, how decisively the base of its long international pre-eminence was being eroded.

'Invest in success': the mood of the 1950s remained comfortable, complacent, somewhat neo-traditionalist, its humour that of the Ealing Studios comedies, *Passport to Pimlico*; *Kind Hearts and Coronets*. The Conservatives who had achieved power somewhat insecurely in 1951 were returned with resounding success in 1955 and again in 1959. The world relaxed. Stalin died and East–West relations grew easier. Our African empire, it was quietly recognized as the decade wore on, would soon have to go the way of India, and no one minded too much. The thing to do was to make the process as gracious as possible. Even the foolish fiasco of the Anglo-French invasion of Suez in 1956, undertaken during Eden's brief premiership, disastrously divisive as it was, proved to matter far less than seemed possible at the time. It certainly hastened the pragmatic recognition that Britain's imperial power was shrinking fast – faster than people had imagined even in the gloomy early post-war days. But what would it matter? Macmillan was now Prime Minister and, under the genial mantle of SuperMac, as the Empire shrank, the Commonwealth expanded. Happy little independent States, each endowed with a parliament on the Westminster model, would succeed to the old colonies. Trade would grow. Everyone would be free and content. 'A wind of change' was blowing across Africa and indeed across the world, Macmillan warned the South African parliament in Cape Town in February 1960, a non-racial and democratic wind, but so long as you go along with it, there should be nothing to fear.

There were, of course, some signs in the later 1950s that there might still be things to fear – the Notting Hill race riots in the summer of 1958 being one of the more obvious, and the explosion of Britain's very own hydrogen bomb another. Ever since Attlee, the government had been adept at spending ever greater sums on nuclear weaponry without discussion in parliament or – by and large – anywhere else. Only at the end of the 1950s did the horrifying reality of nuclear war hanging over the world since 1945 start to penetrate the imagination of the multitude. Nevertheless it is impossible not to recognize the sense of controlled content the nation felt at the time. Unemployment never reached half a million. At the end of the decade industrial production was still rising, the balance of payments was fairly favourable, inflation reasonably low, income tax down (and twopence off the price of beer). National service was phased out after the White Paper on Defence of 1957 while, internationally, cold war confrontation was being transmuted in the age of Khrushchev into rivalry over space exploration and a race for the moon. Even divorces, which had been high just after the war, were now well down in a society where a popular song could run:

> Love and marriage, love and marriage
> Just go together like a horse and carriage.
> This I tell you, brother,
> You can't have one without the other.

The avuncular and unflappable character of Harold Macmillan, Prime Minister from 1957 to 1963, provided the ideal coping-stone for this Indian summer of content, a benign and comfortable age. In earlier days he had been more drawn to enthusiasm. As a very young man he was close to becoming a Roman Catholic under the influence of his tutor and friend Ronald Knox (he was the 'M' of Knox's *A Spiritual Aeneid*), almost but not quite. In the inter-war years he had been the Conservative protester, both over unemployment and over Munich, so much so that he was close to joining the Labour Party, almost but not quite. By the early fifties, as Minister of Housing, he had become the most sure-footed of all the Conservative team, and in the post-Suez disarray he righted the boat with remarkable aplomb. A liberal Conservative if ever there was one, he yet now seemed rather less reformist than Rab Butler and more acceptable to the Tory right wing. All things to all men, he was the crofter's grandson who believed in one nation; the Duke of Devonshire's uncle who saw fit to bring the Duke into his government – and got away with it. 'You have never had it so good', he told the nation and though that rather simple message has subsequently produced many sneers, it was yet substantially the truth and people of later, more harassed, generations would look back to the age of Macmillan – so much more comfortable and relaxed than that of Churchill and Attlee before it, more confident and hopeful than the age of Wilson after it – with increasing nostalgia. If the affluence was genuine and widely spread, it was, of course, part of a global movement of prosperity and political relaxation. In its local expression it was firmly grounded upon the maintenance of Attlee's welfare state with which it combined a renewed stress on personal freedom and the celebration of England's past. Macmillan was Britain's last truly imperial premier. He epitomized the central social, political and religious judgment of the age: in everything a little bland, a little too reluctant to delve uncomfortably into the murky deep. Nevertheless beneath the blandness, humanity steadily prevailed.

In July 1955 Ruth Ellis, the mother of two young children, was hanged in Oxford Gaol for shooting her lover. He had been both unfaithful and cruel. She had just had a miscarriage, brought on very probably by his punching her in the stomach. She wanted to die. Eden was Prime Minister at the time and Major Lloyd George, an elderly nonentity, Home Secretary. That such a thing could happen, despite protests, for a crime which in other western countries would certainly no longer have been punished in this way says a good deal about the underlying unimaginative moral conservatism still normative in the mid-1950s. But in fact she was the last woman to be hanged in Britain. The Commons lobby for the abolition of capital punishment had been growing steadily stronger, and the very next year on a free vote there would be a majority for abolition, though this would only become law ten years later. The hanging of Ruth Ellis appears strangely barbaric to the Englishman of the 1980s; to most Englishmen of the 1950s such a thing still seemed in theory justifiable enough, as running a world-wide empire seemed justifiable; both had seemed so for centuries. In practice, however, neither appeared any more quite the right thing to do. Macmillan's genius lay in the skill with which he epitomized a somewhat jaunty Conservatism while in fact keeping the ship of State moving rather rapidly forward. British society was in reality changing fast in the 1950s and woe to them who failed to see beneath the drapery of tradition the emergence of a new and unimperial age.

Church and State

The Education Act of 1944 was one of the most decisive pieces of legislation passed in this century, decisive not only for the country's educational system but also for its religious life. The one great remaining rock of offence dividing the churches, especially Free churchmen from Anglicans, had been schools, as the fierce and prolonged battles over the Balfour Education Act of 1902 and many subsequent aborted negotiations had demonstrated. The issue was a simple one: England had developed a dual system of schools (quite apart from the top layer of fee-paying 'public schools') – roughly half being Church schools (four-fifths Church of England, the other fifth mostly Catholic), the other increasingly preponderant half, those of the local education authority. The nineteenth-century Church had preceded the State in the field of elementary education, but by the end of the century was finding it increasingly hard to maintain and improve its twelve thousand schools. Once the State recognized its responsibility to ensure some decent minimum of education for all its citizens, and its own directly controlled segment of the educational system grew in size and improved in standard, the problem of the Church schools became obvious. As they constituted at that time a full half of the total system, the State was inevitably concerned that standards should improve as much there as anywhere else, but this necessitated either taking them over or subsidizing them. The Church of England was not willing to go along with the one, the Free Churches were bitterly opposed to the other. In that contest of wills the Church of England, allied to the Conservative Party and the House of Lords, largely won the immediate battle through Balfour's unamended Act. It proved in fact to be to the special benefit of the Roman Catholic Church, whose will to maintain its schools through thick and thin was a great deal tougher than the Anglican. For the latter the subsidies were not really sufficient as educational requirements mounted. Church schools increasingly lagged behind in amenities, many hundreds were on the black list and between the wars Anglican schools had been closing at the rate of seventy-six a year. Nevertheless in 1940 there were still over nine thousand of them and there were still many country parts known as 'single-school' areas because the only available school was a Church of England one, to which everyone, willy-nilly, had to send his children.

When R. A. Butler became President of the Board of Education in 1941 there was a general consensus that a new deal in schooling was long overdue. He was just the man – diplomatic, humane, immensely competent – to arrange for that. Chuter Ede, a Labour MP, was his Parliamentary Private Secretary. The one a good Anglican, the other a good Free Churchman, they were a sound combination to crack the religious-educational nut. Churchill advised to reform nothing until the war was over. Butler disregarded the advice and put on to the statute book with full Labour support a comprehensive piece of new legislation one whole year before Japan surrendered. The days of 'elementary' schooling only were to be over for good. The school-leaving age would be raised to fifteen as soon as possible after the war and a secondary course separated from the primary was to be guaranteed for the first time to every child in the land. That was the great aim and the great accomplishment; the question was how to stop its inevitably costly realization from being frustrated by religious divisions.

Already in 1941 an inter-Church delegation led by Archbishop Lang had come to see Butler. It included the Methodist stalwart Scott Lidgett. This in itself indicated clearly enough that there was now a joint resolve (though it did not, of course, extend as far as Roman Catholics) to find a way round the old impasse. The meeting was also significant because at its close the President of the Board asked the archbishop to lead them in prayer. It seemed, even to the churchmen, a surprising thing for the successor of Birrell and H. A. L. Fisher and C. P. Trevelyan to ask but it showed as well as anything how times and moods had changed. It was an 'Agreed Syllabus' of Religious Instruction, such as that drawn up in Cambridgeshire in 1924 and since adopted by more than a hundred local education authorities, which was to provide the ground of agreement between most Anglicans and Free churchmen. Christian teaching on these lines seemed just positive enough for Anglican managers to accept, if a little sadly, that their schools could be handed over to a body which would guarantee such a syllabus, while for Nonconformists the specific of non-denominational teaching was maintained. The all round gain seemed to be more religious instruction, and worship too, than had ever been the case before in State schools. It was the atmosphere of the war, with its heightened sense of the need for a national religious revival and ecclesiastical reconciliation, which made it seem natural for both the churches and the State to take so positive but also undenominational a line towards the teaching of religion throughout the nation's schools.

The Catholics remained apart, requiring continual separate treatment even in the processes of negotiation. They were as determined as ever to keep their own schools and their own Church teaching within them, and they were too important to be simply antagonized. So some way had to be found of accommodating them, without leaving their schools hopelessly inferior to all the others. At the same time the way must not be made too attractive or else Anglicans would be tempted to take it too, in which case the dual system would remain essentially intact with all its inconveniences. Butler had to find a way of voluntarily edging most of the Church of England schools into full national control while offering the Catholics terms which they might grumble about but would still accept. And this is just what he did. He offered all Church schools a choice between two alternatives: to be 'controlled' or 'aided'. The 'controlled' school would effectively be taken over by government and receive full financial support; in 'aided' schools, on the other hand, the Church would retain a majority on the governing body, the control of religious instruction and the right to appoint and dismiss teachers. The local education authority would be responsible for salaries and all the running costs of the school, but 50 per cent of any alteration or improvement must come from the Church. The churches were free to choose which they preferred. There were Anglicans, of whom the aged Arthur Headlam, Bishop of

Gloucester, and Kenneth Kirk, Bishop of Oxford, were the most prominent, who believed that non-denominational teaching would prove useless and that the Church should retain its schools at whatever cost. Headlam worked hard to raise money to do so. For him 'this megalomaniacal Education Bill is a very evil thing'.[1] Temple, who was all for going along with Butler, seemed to Headlam on this, as on much else, to have sold the pass. But the amount of money the Church of England would have needed in order to retain and modernize the mass of its schools was prohibitive. Headlam might admire the line of the Roman Catholic bishops and wish that Anglicans could be as firm, but what was just practicable for Catholics with their far smaller constituency, tighter discipline and intense traditional commitment to schools of their own, was really not a viable option for the national Church, with its poor record of raising money and deep internal doubts as to whether it could properly continue to segregate itself from the nation's own system of schools. The internal logic of a State Church was against it. Was it not far wiser, Temple asked, for the national Church to do its best to ensure a Christian atmosphere and improved standard of education throughout the national network than to restrict its influence to what had long been a diminishing segment of that network and was in places little better than an educational slum?[2]

Temple won, Headlam lost, as was generally the case. Some dioceses, such as Bradford and the Lancashire ones, clung to their schools a good deal more than others, but of the nine thousand Church of England schools remaining in 1944 only some two thousand were to survive as such (and at one time they had looked like falling to around five hundred). The remaining section of public education controlled by the Church of England would hardly be bigger than that controlled by the Catholic Church.[3] Essentially, so far as the Established Church was concerned, the dual system was killed by kindness. The new order was carried through parliament by devout Anglicans like Butler in the Commons and Selborne in the Lords, and was implemented by other devout churchmen, like Temple's great admirer John Maud, the Ministry of Education's first Permanent Secretary.

What were the consequences of the Act? Educationally they

were a vast improvement without the slightest doubt; from a religious point of view, however, the results were less clearly favourable. Archbishop Garbett became increasingly convinced in later years that Temple, over-optimistic and over-trusting as ever, really had sold the pass in 1944.[4] The Church's influence in the educational field rapidly diminished; the Agreed Syllabus might not be too bad in itself (though it consisted of little more than Bible knowledge, and an undenominational Protestantism) but there were few teachers at once interested and competent to teach it. Without Church affiliation or trained catechists Religious Instruction was the least favoured subject on the syllabus. A religious ethos from the old Church schools did not spread across to penetrate the whole system; on the contrary, in Butler's own words, twenty years later, 'the perfunctory and uninspired nature of the religious instruction provided in all too many local authority and controlled schools had begun . . . to imperil the Christian basis of our society'.[5] The quickly advancing secular consensus of middle England in the sixties owed a great deal to the educational choices made in the 1940s.

The one great religious beneficiary of the 1944 Act was the Catholic Church, as indeed it had already been of the 1902 Act. Though the financial burden placed upon it to find half the cost of a massive programme of reconstruction would be formidable, the burden had basically been there already and it would in fact prove to be not quite intolerable (with the aid in due course of Bingo and a change of 50 to 75 per cent in government grants for maintenance and improvement by the Education Act of 1959). The effort to pay for the schools may well have damaged a healthy balance within Church life and clerical concern more gravely than was evident, and it certainly left most dioceses with increasingly heavy debts, but the result was both an actual increase in the proportion of the nation's children attending Catholic schools and – still more significantly – a marked improvement in the quality of Catholic education. The spread of Catholic urban grammar schools across the country is largely a post-1944 phenomenon. It greatly enlarged the size of the Catholic middle class and the proportion of Catholics going to the university, and it is a direct cause of the far wider contribution Catholics were making to the national life from the 1950s, while retaining their own social identity. Butler's Act raised them educationally without submerging them religiously.

Neither at the time nor subsequently would Catholics admit to seeing it in that light. They had been the Act's most consistent critics. In the middle of Butler's principal speech in the Second Reading debate in the House of Commons, Archbishop Griffin, newly appointed to Westminster, was ushered into the Strangers Gallery where Butler caught sight of him. He had just reached the point where he was to reply to the Bill's critics, urging them to dismiss their fears and suspicions. No listener could have been more welcome. 'The best way I can reassure them', he declared, 'is by quoting a verse from the hymn':

> Ye fearful saints, fresh courage take,
> The clouds ye so much dread
> Are big with mercy, and shall break
> In blessings on your head.

Griffin nicely dispatched to Butler next morning a large parcel containing Butler's *Lives of the Saints*, an old Catholic classic.[6] Whether Griffin or Butler himself realized it, the quotation was prophetic: disastrous as the Act might prove for the Church of England, 'the clouds ye so much dread' would indeed shortly and conveniently 'break in blessing' on the head of English Catholicism.

'I thank God for the welfare state,' declared Donald Soper emphatically in his presidential address to the Methodist Conference in July 1953.[7] Many a cleric in all the churches would have agreed wholeheartedly. The welfare state was what progressive Christians had had their eyes on for years. Now it had arrived as the answer to COPEC, to the Oxford conference of 1937, to the Malvern conference of 1941, to Temple's *Christianity and Social Order*. The politico-intellectual pre-eminence in the post-war years of Sir Stafford Cripps, Temple's nearest equivalent on the lay scene, makes the point clearly enough. If there was a clerical radicalism in previous decades, its programme – other than that of a handful of unrepresentative eccentrics – seemed now essentially achieved. Achieved, it naturally lost some of its glamour, though not its worth. Its great surviving representative was undoubtedly Soper, not far off becoming the Labour Party's national chaplain. (He shared the role with Mervyn Stockwood.) A member of the party, a preacher at annual conferences and president of the Christian Socialist movement, he was a national figure, to be heard almost weekly on the BBC. Yet politically and ecclesiastically he was an increasingly idiosyncratic one, for the wider clerical radical note now fades and – for the Church of England particularly – the 1945-60 years can be seen as one of ecclesiastical social conservatism after the radicalism of the Temple era and before that of the 1960s.[8] If that is the case (and it is certainly easy enough to exaggerate the radicalism of the preceding period), it is not to be explained simply in terms of ecclesiastics growing a little wiser after the progressive hot air of Temple's well publicized campaigns. First of all the leadership had altered: Fisher had rather little interest in social or political issues and was clearly no radical; though he was quite capable on occasion of administering a headmasterly rebuke to government – as he did over Suez. Garbett at York was a shrewd and compassionate high Tory who had been a very effective campaigner on certain social issues, housing especially, and could still speak extremely impressively about international issues,[9] but he was now a very old and profoundly conservative person. When he did retire he was replaced by Michael Ramsey, whose brilliant mind was at home in the theological and spiritual rather than political. Social radicals there still were in these years in the ranks of the clergy, particularly in regard to overseas issues, but certainly no one played the major role that Gore, Temple or Bell had played in the past. But, secondly, it was not just a matter of individual personalities – Bell, after all, was still bishop of Chichester and extremely influential abroad in ecumenical affairs – but one of circumstance and mood. Clerical radicals had campaigned over the years for a massive attack on unemployment and bad housing; they had called for the nationalization of certain key industries and for better social security. These things were now being taken in hand. Even Northern Ireland was quite exceptionally quiet. Certainly new issues were emerging – the post-war state of Europe, the colonies, nuclear warfare – and radical clerics would prove in their regard not only noisy but also quite effective, but it would take some years for these issues (other than that of Europe's immediate hunger) to be clarified or to impinge upon the moral consciousness of any large segment of the English churches. Thirdly, the challenge of Communism abroad contributed to a conservative hardening of the ecclesiastical line at home. The characteristic political approach of Christians in these years may be found best in the ex-Communist Douglas Hyde's *I Believed* (1948), or Garbett's *In an Age of Revolution* (1952). English Christianity was certainly not widely McCarthyite, theologians could still insist that Christians and Communists had some things – important things – in common[10] and Garbett, for instance, could still warn of the danger of accepting a too 'rigid, black-and-white concept of a necessary war of ideologies' between East and West.[11] Nevertheless with very few exceptions Christians were agreed as to where the danger lay. The consequence was something of a closing of ranks in a conservative direction. There was in this a fair measure of consensus between Catholic and Protestant such as had not existed in pre-war days.

The social role of the Church in the age of Fisher was then confirmatory, a very great deal more than it was confrontatory. This was by no means merely a response to the Soviet threat, any more than it was merely an indication that to the ecclesiastical mind welfare state legislation had now gone as far as was needed. It represented a far deeper sentiment of the 1950s Church as of the society it belonged to. As imperial power slipped away with every passing year, one senses a deep collective refusal to face up fully to what was happening, a resolve instead to restore and celebrate the past before it was finally too late.

Restoration was, quite inevitably, an important activity of the post-war Church. It was fortunate that of cathedrals only Coventry and the Catholic cathedral of Southwark had been destroyed, but hundreds of churches and chapels, not only in London but in all the main cities, had been bombed out and as a consequence the work of architectural restoration, with financial assistance from government, took up a very great deal of time and mental energy in the next fifteen years. Coupled with this material restoration was the symbolic restoration involved in the coronation of Queen Elizabeth II in June 1953, 'perhaps the most universally impressive ceremonial event in history'.[12] The Church of England, the monarchy, the nation, were bound together in an act of sacralisation whose imaginative impact was profound – it was the first great event to be seen in full by the whole nation on television – but whose meaning and relevance for a highly pluralistic society was, perhaps oddly, left unquestioned. At such a moment England still liked to think of herself as possessing a moral and religious coherence at the level of the nation's public *persona*: Christian and Anglican. It was indeed a very Anglican decade. For three generations the monarchy had presented that image with great sincerity and considerable impressiveness, but the political establishment had done so very much less. What is striking about the 1950s is that Britain now had such a very conspicuously Anglican government: Macmillan, Butler, Hailsham, Home, Salisbury, Heath, Monckton, Powell, were all Anglicans for whom their religion in different ways meant personally quite a lot. Even Iain Macleod, a far from churchy person, regularly attended services in Westminster Abbey. The difference between this Cabinet and one of the first half of the century was considerable. Then the personally committed and orthodox believer was something of an exception, now he was very nearly the norm.

This was, of course, a Conservative phenomenon. At the very same time the Labour leadership was going increasingly secular as its old generation with quite strong religious connections died off – Lansbury, Henderson, Cripps, Attlee, Chuter Ede. Jim Simmons was MP for Brierley Hill, Birmingham, until 1959. A lifelong lay preacher, brought up to worship at the Primitive Methodist 'Tin Tabernacle' in Moseley, Simmons had sung the 'Red Flag' with gusto long before the First World War. His life, he could affirm after retirement, had been 'devoted to three main principles: Christianity, Socialism and Temperance'.[13] There were still MPs like Simmons in the 1950s who had not wavered in that old-fashioned combination but they were no longer very characteristic of the party leadership. The party of Gaitskell, Bevan, Wilson, Crosland, Crossman and Jenkins was a party to which matters of religious belief seemed oddly remote and in which 'theology' came to be used to describe the meaningless, or the unnecessarily complicated. The Conservative leadership of the 1950s was Anglican with an agnostic fringe, the Labour leadership agnostic with a Nonconformist and Catholic fringe, but the 1950s was after all a Conservative decade. To find the dead centre of fifties politics one can hardly do better than read Lord Hailsham chiding Dr Soper for poor theology in the pages of the *Spectator*. Hailsham indeed provides the very quintessence of the fifties as Stafford Cripps did of the forties.

As for the Liberal Party it had still not quite lost its Nonconformist image or ability to muster antique loyalties. At the 1945 General Election the *Congregational Quarterly* had even predicted a Liberal victory. In fact the party was almost annihilated but of the six Liberals still in the Commons in 1950 three were Congregationalists. If the party survived through these decades of its greatest weakness, it was still due in large part to the continued loyalty of many Free churchmen, especially in England.[14] In Wales, however, Nonconformity's principal bastion, there had been an almost communal transfer of loyalty to Labour. Moreover the Free Church Conservative was now no rarity. In 1950 Sir Cyril Black was the first Baptist ever to enter parliament as a pure Conservative, but in practice there had been quite a few Conservative Free churchmen there for years (Tory Methodists had never been unusual). They included Geoffrey Shakespeare and, indeed, Neville Chamberlain himself. While a Nonconformist rump – Baptist, Congregationalist, Wesleyan – remained faithful to the Liberal Party in its post-war wilderness, as a whole the Free Churches were never more apolitical than now when the Liberal Party, their ally of the past, seemed destined for early extinction.

The ethos of society as conceived and cherished by the Established Church's leadership remained firmly old-fashioned, illusory as that ethos often in fact was. It was suffused by a vague romantic rural Toryism still dominant in the imagination of the patronal figures of the decade's religious culture, Sayers, Lewis, Eliot, Rose Macaulay. Cabinet ministers still hobnobbed with bishops in the Athenaeum. *The Times* still devoted plenty of space to episcopal speeches in the House of Lords. Gaiters were still the normal episcopal dress. It is perhaps symbolic that Dorothy Sayers, that formidable church warden and exponent of orthodoxy without compromise, never admitted to the existence of her now fully grown-up illegitimate son. The Church of England was not in the fifties a socially innovative or morally compromising Church. Certainly it was not a hide-bound Church either. It could firmly and convincingly accept the morality of contraception in marriage, it could pay some attention to progressive moral theologians like Gordon Dunstan and Ian Ramsey, but equally Garbett was not far out of line in adamantly refusing to allow people remarrying in a registry office even a subsequent 'service of blessing'. No archbishop ever found turbulent priests more out of place and inappropriate than did Geoffrey Fisher. Perhaps without too great absurdity one might suggest that the most suitable clerically produced literature of this undramatic age was that of the Revd Wilbert Vere Awdry, author of the *Railway Series*, a long and immensely popular set of children's books about talking engines, such as *Tank Engine Thomas* (1949), or *Gordon the Big Engine* (1953). They continued to be written for several decades but their true spiritual home is surely the age when they began. English clergymen had often indulged a passion for railways. Here such harmless pleasantry was being shared with the young, and who can say that it was less worthy of remembrance or even less socially beneficial than the protest of the more turbulent?

That formidable exercise in fantasy, *The Lord of the Rings* was published in 1956 after very many years of gestation. Tolkien's three-volume saga, so rich in detail, so deeply dependent upon the author's Early English and Scandinavian scholarship, so apparently unrelated to either the religion or the politics of contemporary man, might seem to fit hardly at all into the sort of history we are engaged upon. Yet, whether the author intended it or not, *The Lord of the Rings* sublimates almost to perfection a very typical world view of 1950s western man. The theme is the essentially simple world-encompassing conflict between good and evil, in which good finally triumphs but only at great cost. 'The West' is good and 'the East' evil, though many in the West may be corrupted and many in the East, enslaved by Mordor, are not evil in their hearts. While the leaders of the West are great soldiers and statesmen like Aragorn, Elrond and Gandalf, it is the tough, shrewd goodness of the civilian commoner, the hobbits Frodo and Samwise, which is finally decisive. As an allegory of the rather simple way many an English Christian saw the world in the early 1950s it could hardly be bettered, and no year was more fitting for its publication than 1956, the date of the Hungarian uprising.

In July 1956 Edward, Earl of Halifax, aged seventy-five, set up a tall crucifix on Garrowby Hill near his home in Yorkshire. It bore the inscription, 'To The Glory of God, and in Memory of George, King, Servant of his People, 1895–1952'. It was dedicated by the Archbishop of York.[15] Halifax had all his life been an intensely devout Anglo-Catholic, the biographer of Keble, the faithful son of his father the second Viscount Halifax, who had led the Church Union for fifty years and brought about the Malines Conversations. Edward, the first earl, had been Baldwin's Viceroy in India in the 1920s, Chamberlain's Foreign Secretary at Munich, Churchill's wartime ambassador to Washington. No one of his generation, other than Churchill, had had so distinguished a political career, almost the last great aristocrat to move naturally and without the appearance of effort or ambition, at the very centre of the nation's power. And here he was in old age erecting a wayside crucifix to the memory of his king. It was an action that could have been that of any great and pious landlord of Catholic faith for a thousand years previously. It may express as well as anything, and not too self-consciously, that last wistful stand in the 1950s of the traditional order against the irresistible currents of modernity.

On 5 December 1945 the Oxford Town Hall was packed for a meeting organized by the Revd John Collins, the Dean of Oriel. An overflow meeting filled St Mary's. Bishop Bell was in the chair. The speakers were Victor Gollancz, Richard Acland and Barbara Ward. The theme was the involvement of Christians in post-war politics. The most immediately practical resolution was one to formulate a new approach to occupied Germany and to back Gollancz's Save Europe Now campaign.[16] The consequence was the foundation of Christian Action, an organization which would represent the radical wing of Christianity in politics for the next twenty years. Behind all this lay the inspiration of Stafford Cripps, Collins's political and spiritual mentor.

John Collins seemed a fairly typical Oxbridge cleric: Conservative background, minor public school, radical leanings, a bit bored with scholarship, more than a bit unsettled by a wartime spent as an RAF chaplain. He was however somewhat untypical in the vigorous and clear-minded practicality, the straight-to-the-point and obstinate forcefulness which he was to show time and again as the most effective campaigner on the Church's left wing of his generation. His effectiveness derived not only from a combination of clarity of mind, obstinacy and efficiency, but also from his not being too far to the left. Opponents liked to portray him as another Red Dean, but he was no such thing. His radicalism was that of heir to the later Cripps, no more; he had no Communist tinges and considerable respect for democratic niceties. In 1948 Cripps arranged Collins's appointment as a Canon of St Paul's. From then on that would be the base from which he irritated the Establishment and carried on his own particular form of spiritual warfare, right up until the 1980s.

Christian Action's immediate priority was an obvious one: the physical and moral plight of Germany. The Oxford Famine Relief Committee, another new small and as yet amateur group, was already at work on the material side. Christian Action fostered friendly contact at various levels, petitioned for the release of prisoners of war and organized in October 1948 – despite the beginning of the Berlin blockade – a visit to Britain of the Berlin Philharmonic Orchestra, the first such cultural contact in the post-war world: an emotional achievement.

Christian Action saw itself in 1946 as a way of marshalling the marked Christian post-war revival – noticeable especially in university circles – in a politically radical direction. The problem with this was twofold. First, the Christian revival proved theologically conservative and, on the whole, rather little interested in politics one way or the other. Secondly, it is clear that Christian Action itself was a pressure group looking for a cause, but – once Germany was round the corner from famine – having some difficulty in finding one. Then in 1949 Victor Gollancz introduced Collins to Michael Scott, and Christian Action quickly discovered what was to be its most characteristic role: supporting the opponents and victims of apartheid in South Africa. From this point on Africa in particular and the third world in general became increasingly the principal interest of Christian political activism. A new era of Christian concern had begun with Collins and Scott as its chief protagonists.

Michael Scott, like Trevor Huddleston, was an English priest of Anglo-Catholic inspiration who had arrived in South Africa in 1943. Together they soon became the life and soul of the religious opposition to racialism. Scott, a profoundly unsettled but very saintly man, to outward appearances a clerical tramp, had become filled with the simple and uncomfortable passion to identify with, and defend the cause of, the very poor. He had stood by Asian passive resisters in Durban and been arrested; he had lived with a poor African minister, the Revd Theophilus, in an appalling Transvaal shanty-town, and been arrested.[17] In 1950 he was declared a prohibited immigrant in South Africa, but by then he had also been appointed by Chief Hosea of the Herero of South-West Africa (Namibia), the representative of his people at the United Nations, and had succeeded, practically single-handed, in forcing the Herero issue in South-West Africa before the International Court of Justice at the Hague.[18]

The effect of Scott, as also of reading Alan Paton's *Cry the Beloved Country*, upon Collins was decisive. Hitherto he had had little interest in Africa. For the next ten years it would be the centre of his concern. Collins provided an immediate pulpit for Scott in St Paul's Cathedral, and in Christian Action he provided an effective support group, even though the temper of the two priests was so different that they proved unable to work easily together for any length of time. Scott in fact developed his own rather different London-based organization, the Africa Bureau, which became one of the most effective pressure groups in regard to British government policy all through the 1950s. He was helped in this by Liberal patrons like David Astor.

In 1952 in South Africa the African National Congress and Indian National Congress joined in an extensive campaign of civil disobedience against legal discrimination and large numbers found themselves in prison as a consequence. Christian Action was appealed to for financial help for the families of those taking part in the defiance campaign. Collins responded and the money was sent to Huddleston, now a parish priest in the Johannesburg slum of Sophiatown. When in December 1956 156 leading South African opponents of apartheid, including Chief Albert Luthuli and Professor Z. K. Matthews, outstanding black churchmen as well as the political leaders of their people, were arrested and charged with high treason, it was Christian Action that opened a massive appeal for the defence of the accused and the support of their families. It also helped arrange for Gerald Gardiner, a distinguished QC and later Lord Chancellor, to attend the first court hearings and report on them. Five years later, in March 1961, the last of the 156 were acquitted: not a single one of the government's charges had been proved. By then the Treason Trial Fund had raised more than £170,000 sent by Collins to Bishop Ambrose Reeves in Johannesburg for distribution as needed. But there were always more arrests, more people in need of such assistance, especially after the massacre at Sharpeville in 1960, and so Christian Action's Defence and Aid Fund became a permanent institution – one immensely appreciated by South African blacks, and intensely hated by many South African whites.

The nature of these operations is worth considering. First of all, they were within their inevitable limits remarkably effective. The combination of Collins, Scott, Huddleston and Reeves was a remarkable one.[19] Reeves was as efficient in Johannesburg (until his deportation in 1960) as was Collins in London. Huddleston was a publicist of great spiritual power, whose best-seller, *Naught For Your Comfort* appeared in 1956, just when he too had been banned from South Africa. Scott's work in bringing South-West Africa to international attention had been extremely successful, while almost certainly Defence and Aid not only alleviated the sufferings of the Treason Trial's victims but also contributed considerably to the verdicts eventually reached. Their effectiveness lay in a combination of on-the-spot reliability in South Africa and a very capable back-up in London; it lay not only in the power of their general moral critique of apartheid, but in their ability to focus on very particular issues and actually to do something about them. After 1960, with no real spokesman left in South Africa and a different political situation there following Sharpeville, their role inevitably diminished.

In Britain Christian Action had developed a rather special mode of existence. It was clearly a Christian organization and yet was one in no way controlled by any Church authority. Its Christian claims strengthened its hand but infuriated its enemies. It had escaped the temporizing prudence characteristic of nearly all Church organizations faced with awkward political issues. Lord Halifax felt compelled to withdraw his sponsorship when Christian Action assisted passive resisters against the law; the Archbishops of Canterbury and Westminster ceased to nominate representatives to its council; yet they could not silence the organization or nullify its Christian character. After all, not only was it led by a canon of St Paul's, but Lord Pakenham (later Earl of Longford) retained his sponsorship through thick and thin, an eccentric but never entirely off-the-point representative of the Christian Socialist idealism of Stafford Cripps.

Thirdly, all these operations were predominantly Anglican. In the fifties the protest as much as the Establishment was manned by the Church of England. All our four heroes were of Anglo-Catholic spiritual inspiration but – with the uneasy exception of Collins himself – they were not very Oxbridge or natural members of the Church Establishment. Scott was the son of a poor Anglo-Catholic priest and had himself no university education. Reeves had been a Liverpoool vicar before going to Johannesburg; he was rather clearly cold-shouldered on his return to Britain. Huddleston was a member of the Community of the Resurrection and easily dismissed by clerical egg-heads as too gushing a monk. The Anglican Establishment took its cue from Geoffrey Clayton, Archbishop of Cape Town, who while he did not believe in racialism himself, most certainly did not believe in any odd priest shaking the boat. He saw eye to eye in this with the Archbishop of Canterbury. Yet it is the strength of the Church of England, at its best, that it is so unable to control its prophetic mavericks.

The success of Christian Action must be seen within a steady wider growth in social and political concern, especially over Africa, going on among British Christians through this decade, and replacing the predominantly domestic concern of the inter-war years. OXFAM and Christian Aid were becoming large and professional aid agencies. Max Warren, the highly influential

General Secretary of the Church Missionary Society, was quietly educating the missionary world with the discussion, in his thoughtful *News Letter*, of the relationship of Christianity to almost everything else that was going on in human life.[20] John Taylor, one of Warren's bright young men and eventually his successor, wrote in 1957 a popular Penguin on *Christianity and Politics in Africa*. The Church of Scotland took up a strong stand in regard to the politics of Central Africa where it had important missions in Nyasaland (Malawi), and believed that black opinion and black interests were being unjustly overridden in favour of the white settlers of Southern Rhodesia.

Behind the various progressively-minded and Africa-orientated pressure groups of clergy and laity stood the immensely imposing figure of Margery Perham.[21] The 1950s was, very especially, her decade. She had, indeed, an unusually long innings upon the British African scene, from the twenties to the seventies, but the 1950s represent the apogee of her influence – at once Oxford academic, consultant to a dozen colonial governments, the high priest of liberal Christian enlightenment in things imperial. She was a sort of successor to J. H. Oldham in this regard. If British Africa proceeded so peacefully towards political independence, it had a lot to do with the influence of Margery Perham. Month after month her special articles and letters in *The Times* plotted the road the colonial empire had to follow. Now it is not irrelevant that while as a young don before the war her outlook was essentially secular, by the fifties it had turned deeply religious. She had become part of the inner Anglican Establishment, not only Nuffield College's Fellow in Imperial Government, author of magisterial volumes on Lugard, member of the Inter-University Council on Higher Education Overseas, and so forth, but also a keen supporter and soon to be president of the Universities Mission to Central Africa, the high church missionary society founded a century earlier in response to the appeals of David Livingstone.

Perham's persistently reformist fist was certainly well covered by the velvet of her Establishment glove, and that well suited the age of Macmillan and Butler. Perham and Collins did not really differ greatly in the way they wanted Africa to go. They could both rely to a considerable extent on Church opinion which was

433

now being mobilized with increasing effectiveness against racialism and in favour of a fairly rapid peaceful transfer of power from white colonial rule to black democracy. But while Perham, Warren or Taylor were helping to guide public opinion across the board but chiefly in regard to policy within Her Majesty's Dominions, Collins, Scott, Huddleston and Reeves were spearheading the attack at the most critical spot – and one now outside those dominions. If they did, of course, fail to deflect the advance of Verwoerdt's apartheid, they partially achieved what, from the religious point of view, could in the long run be still more important – a public statement, convincing in black eyes, that white Christianity could and should be utterly opposed to racialism. They existentially pricked the myth, as Archbishop Clayton or even the general run of the missionary movement did not, that Christianity was really a piece of the machinery of white domination, and as that myth was itself an important piece of the machinery, their unpopularity with the white dominators was deservedly unbounded.

In 1955 during a tour in Africa Archbishop Fisher had propounded what he thought was the sage observation that 'all men are not equal in the sight of God though they are equal in the love of God'. Somewhat earlier, in a sermon at St Paul's, Canon Collins had declared:

> Let us sympathize with Dr Malan. Let us be charitable to him – this poor, wretched man, hag-ridden with fear. We know that only love can cast out fear; but as well expect a man with *delirium tremens* to discover in his heart the love to destroy his illusion of pink elephants, as to hope that the Nationalists whose hearts are full of fear, can rid themselves of the illusion of white superiority.[22]

The Archbishop's statement enraged all liberals and was severely criticized by Canon Collins. The Canon's statement enraged all conservatives and was severely criticized by Archbishop Fisher. Each received great publicity. The Archbishop's statement, in so far as it was true, was rather banal, but it was poor theology (Fisher indeed was no theologian) and it could easily be taken as a defence of racial discrimination on the old grounds of God having set each man in his estate – castle or cottage, affluent white suburb or rickety black shanty-town. The Canon's statement infuriated because it was judged divisive as well as disrespectful to the powerful. The divisiveness of his approach could be contrasted – to take another extreme – with the much publicized reconciling rituals staged at the time by Moral Rearmament, in Africa as elsewhere. MRA – Frank Buchman's Oxford Group re-named – flourished particularly in this decade, continually claiming to have brought together this and that conflicting group around the world. His birthday praises were sung each year with a full page advertisement in *The Times*. MRA's political approach appealed widely to 1950s Christians, just because, without ignoring the existence of contemporary issues, it made so few precise demands – other than that of anti-Communism. Its demands were really those of the old Protestant personal conversion restated in purely moral and theistic terms. Out of this, social harmony will somehow prevail. Collins, on the contrary, was seen as an interferer in politics and as an instigator of discord.[23]

Archbishop Fisher felt that Dr Malan should be accorded a reasonable deference. Motives should not be impugned. It is a first principle of Establishment to respect establishments, and nothing was more firmly established socially than the churchly world of Dr Fisher. Collins was not respectful, he was always linking things together which should be kept apart. To mix pink elephants with Prime Ministers of a Commonwealth nation was not the sort of thing you expect from a Canon of St Paul's. In this Fisher certainly represented the consensus view of 1950s English Christianity, the Council of Churches as much as archbishops, Anglican or Roman. It was one reason why they paid more attention to Miss Perham than they did to Canon Collins. Yet it could be claimed that Collins did understand the realities of the South African situation and the basic needs for effective Christian witness there, while Fisher, and for that matter MRA, were quite out of their depth. It is also true that if at the time Collins seemed an out-and-out radical, in retrospect across the sixties and seventies he appears mild enough. A canonry of St Paul's is not exactly the wilderness, Sir Stafford Cripps had seen to that, but to the eyes of the ecclesiastical world of the 1950s it seemed a little like it.

Anglicans and Free Churchmen

'The historians of the Church of England may yet recognize that the worst misfortune to befall its leadership in the end of the war was less the premature death of William Temple than his succession by Fisher of London, and not by Bell of Chichester.'[1] This is a severe judgment on the man who governed the Church for the next sixteen years, by possibly its most distinguished lay academic. Certainly if you wanted a successor in Temple's mould, a man of ideas, of political initiative, spiritual sensitivity or ecumenical experience, then Bell was the obvious candidate. Geoffrey Fisher was quite a different sort of person.[2] Let us note first that he was the most Anglican archbishop of this century. Davidson and Lang were Scots of Presbyterian background; Lang, Garbett and Ramsey were all touched by Anglo-Catholicism; Temple had been deeply influenced by the WEA, the SCM, and all sorts of other alien things. In contrast to all of these Fisher was an Anglican first and last, born in a vicarage, not an Anglo-Catholic nor an Evangelical though he certainly, like Evangelicals, saw the Church of England as emphatically Protestant. All his experience had been within. Even Oxford mattered little to him. It was his own public school, Marlborough, and Repton, the public school of which he was headmaster for eighteen years (1914-32) – both particularly Anglican institutions – which shaped him. He had just one non-Anglican loyalty (if you can call it that, for he shared it with many a low churchman): he was a Mason. He lacked charisma, theology or ideology. 'Commonsense' was his favourite expression and the source of his wisdom. He made few pronouncements. Clear-minded, efficient and methodical, humorous in a gentlemanly and clerical way, self assured, autocratic with an affable toughness, he was a man without doubts, without causes, without the slightest *crise de conscience*. He had been, and remained, a most successful headmaster. Davidson, Lang, Temple and Garbett were childless. Fisher had six strapping sons, two of whom became in due course headmasters themselves. He slammed his study and bedroom doors with vigour and regularity but was otherwise unexcitable. His considerable intellectual powers he exercised chiefly upon *The Times* crossword.

During the war Garbett and Temple had promised a great reform of the Church once the war was over. The war ended, the Labour government arrived, something of a religious revival arrived too, but Church reform did not. The Church of England hobbled on with a few partial measures, as it had done at least since the rejection of the revised Prayer Book in 1928, but with next to nothing in the way of overall policy. It is true that a report entitled *Towards the Conversion of England* was produced in 1945 by a commission chaired by Christopher Chavasse, the Bishop of Rochester, and received at the time considerable acclaim. An ineffectual mix of old-fashioned evangelicalism and modern gimmicks, its most striking proposal was for a massive advertising campaign of evangelism to cost £200,000 a year. Naturally next to nothing came of this and in retrospect it could be dismissed as 'a very damp squib'.[3] Faced with the rather dreary reality of post-war England, the Church of England as an institution sat tight, tied on every side by its venerable customs, pastoral amateurishness, and immensely complex separation of powers. It could do little about the state of the nation, and not much more about itself, being short of both money and men.

It was particularly short of curates. It had still 4,554 of these invaluable objects in 1938, but only 2,189 in 1948. Manchester's curates had fallen from 161 to 45, Birmingham's from 178 to 38.[4] Yet without curates large town parishes could be almost paralysed. In general the shortage of clergy was felt far more in the north than in the south; as the Church's effective assets shrank, it clung to its southern citadels while spreading itself thinner and thinner in areas in which its dominion had always been much in question. The plight of the vicar could be worse than that of the curate, trapped with diminished income in some vast historic vicarage with the servants gone, the curate gone, the

Church school gone, only the damp rising.[5] Even his horse was gone and he could seldom afford a car but was left with a cheap bicycle, 'peddling laboriously up a country lane, with his shabby mackintosh flapping in the wind'.[6] The Pastoral Reorganization Measure of 1949 was a partial response to the crisis: clerical stipends were to be raised, livings merged, ten-bedroomed vicarages in due course sold. But it would inevitably be a slow, piecemeal process, incapable of coping with underlying causes. And even if the causes were recognized it was hard to know what to do about them. The national Church could naturally hardly accept the fact that it was at once almost irretrievably alienated from half the nation and institutionally incapable of doing much about it. On 1958 figures 41.7 per cent of the clergy were located to serve 11.2 per cent of the population, while 14.6 per cent of the clergy had to deal with 34.7 per cent. In Birmingham 34 per thousand of the population made their Easter communion in 1956; in London 37; but in the diocese of Bath and Wells 139, and in that of Hereford 172.[7] Most of the parsons were in the countryside shivering in their unheated rectories, most of the people were in the towns. But at least in the villages they were, more or less, wanted and knew what to do. If more were moved to the drearier urban areas they could find themselves simply at a loss, unless their style of ministry was altered most drastically.

The unecclesiastical half of the nation was now being educated as never before. The Church's greatest avoidable failure in these years was probably in the field of catechetics, in not pioneering a new style of religious teaching in State schools to make up for the great diminishment in Church schools and to keep pace with new educational approaches in other subjects. There were plenty of able theologians in the Church in the 1950s but they were mostly far too academic to get down to such tasks as this.

However it is not true that nothing was being done. Probably Bishop Wand's essentially old-style Mission to London of 1949, with 155 missioners let loose on the city and Wand himself free to write the leaders in the *Evening News* for a whole week,[8] was too much of a surface operation to have any great effect, though it would be a mistake to dismiss the impact of all large-scale missions. Some do change the course of life of many people. But they change the course of the Church's life much less and it was this that was felt to require reform if the secularization of society was to be stopped. The only overall reform attempted in these years was the revision of canon law – an enterprise upon which a very great deal of careful thought and effort was expended over many years.[9] It was a characteristic expression of Fisher's primacy: 'the most absorbing and all-embracing topic of my archiepiscopate'. But there were in many places more limited approaches to pastoral reform, four of which we may now consider. Leslie Hunter was appointed Bishop of Sheffield in 1939. An SCM man who had been much involved in Temple's 'COPEC' in the twenties, had established a Bureau of Social Research in Newcastle in 1925, and was caught up in coping with Tyneside unemployment in the thirties, Hunter was perhaps as close to being Temple's heir as anyone within the Established Church's hierarchy. He was not an important bishop – Sheffield was definitely not an Anglican stronghold – and his establishment there in 1944 of an 'Industrial Mission', with E. R. Wickham as its leader, was certainly not at the time a major piece of Anglican policymaking. In retrospect it would nevertheless be recognized as the start of something important in the creation of a 'missionary structure' for the Church's presence in a modern urban-industrial community.[10] It was to provide the model for many subsequent ventures both in England and abroad.

In 1949 in Lincolnshire a considerable amalgamation of small parishes into a single pastoral unit took place around South Ormsby. They started with six churches and went on to twelve – fifteen ecclesiastical parishes – though the actual population involved was still little more than a thousand.[11] The Anglican rural tradition of the single village, parson and church was here being replaced by an approach which had rather more in common with the Methodist way of coping with small communities in an English countryside. To devise a team ministry which could handle quite a large number of small churches and congregations without losing the particular Anglican ethos of pastoral care was a challenge. South Ormsby felt very original in the 1950s; it was little imitated before the 1960s. It would seem fairly commonplace by the 1970s.[12]

A third new approach was the large scale development of university chaplaincies, for much of which Kathleen Bliss, earlier the right hand of J. H. Oldham, was responsible from the late fifties, from her office in Church House. Until the war the Church of England had paid little attention to chaplaincing in universities outside the colleges of Oxford and Cambridge. That area of life was largely left to the SCM. Now scores of priests were being drawn into this field. Somewhat comparable was a more professional approach to chaplaincy work in the public schools. In the old days headmasters and housemasters were often priests, and chaplains would have had little place. As the laity took over positions of authority, the need for a more professional religious ministry became evident. The combination of devout lay headmaster and full-time chaplain (or, often, several chaplains) could make for a far less amateur approach to Christian life in what was probably the most important surviving bastion of the Church of England. A crucial influence here had been that of Spencer Leeson, headmaster of Winchester 1935-46. Appointed as a layman and a recognized specialist in educational problems, he decided to take orders in 1939 and his mind became increasingly concentrated upon how to revivify public school religion as a serious reality. As chairman of the Headmaster's Conference 1939-45, an exceptionally long tenure for the post, he was able to spread his ideas far and wide. Robert Birley's Eton in the 1950s demonstrates the new model.[13] Birley had had plenty of experience before the war successfully modernizing Charterhouse. Christianity was still intended to be, if anything, more not less, 'the essence of the place'. Classical studies and all good tradition could be retained, but there would be far more freedom, less formality, a new technological sophistication. It seems likely that this was an area in which all in all the Church of England actually gained effective strength in these years.

New growth of a very different sort was the founding of the Samaritans by Chad Varah in 1953.[14] Varah, a London curate at St Stephen, Walbrook, was struck by a news item about the number of London's suicides and their helplessness at the moment of crisis. The function of the Samaritans was to be a voluntary group of people manning a telephone round the clock, to which potential suicides could appeal for help. It was not a specifically Church group, but, especially in its earlier years, its Church links were extremely strong. It can be seen as one of the more imaginative developments in the apostolate of Christian care in the post-war years and would include, in twenty years time, more than ten thousand members. But it is to be noted that it was only in 1959 that a second Samaritan group was founded and only in 1960 that it spread outside London. As a major new growth, in terms of numbers and national acknowledgement, it was a movement characteristic of the 1960s rather than the 1950s.

The same was true to a greater or lesser extent of most of the changes we have been considering (with the exception of the public schools). They were all in their different ways aimed at providing more professional and specialized forms of pastoral ministry related to one or another particular aspect of modern society. Together they add up to a fairly considerable and growing shift in the shape of Anglican clerical deployment and pastoral concern. But it was not a shift planned from the top or even particularly encouraged from the top, and in the fifties it was still not too clearly noticeable a shift. In Chad Varah's Samaritans, Leslie Hunter's Industrial Mission or John Collins's Defence and Aid, the shape of a new face of the Church might be emerging, but it was not until the sixties that this face would cease to be that of a few somewhat marginal groups and come near, instead, to constituting the new persona of the Church as a whole.

More central to our present period was the Parish and People movement founded at a meeting at Queen's College, Birmingham in January 1949,[15] with Henry de Candole, one of the protagonists of the parish communion in the inter-war years, as its chairman. It represents the establishment of the liturgical movement as an organized force within the Church of England and its function as a pressure group was complemented in 1955 by the formation of an official 'Liturgical Commission' by the two archbishops. The central aim was to make a 9 a.m. (or thereabouts) Eucharist the principal Sunday service and to relate the rest of parish life integrally to that central sacramental moment. Unlike the development of professional ministries the liturgical movement aimed principally at the ordinary parish and its revitalization, by an escape from clerical and social hierarchy and the dignified rigidities of matins and evensong to a pattern of worship at once more free, more participatory, more sacramental and more Catholic.

Parish and People undoubtedly exercised very widespread influence in thousands of parishes including Evangelical ones, but it had its weaknesses which were rather characteristic of the 1950s Church as a whole. There was a certain absence of punch. It raised no opposition. It was almost over-respectable. This was partly because it was a little weak on theology. It was a reform of practices more than of ideas. While the liturgical movement on the Continent was sustained by a galaxy of theologians and scholars and could produce periodicals like *Maison Dieu*, of really top quality, the Anglican liturgical movement could hardly manage this. Its best scholars, like Dix and Hebert, were already dead or old. Here as elsewhere while the English Church of the 1950s did not lack learning, it did lack a lively interplay between learning and religious practice.[16]

There were exceptions. In 1955 Mervyn Stockwood, a liberal Anglo-Catholic of some brilliance, became vicar of Great St Mary's Cambridge and quickly transformed its liturgy, as much else. Up till then, 'anything but matins was popery'.

> I am glad to think that it was during my incumbency that for the first time since the Reformation the Eucharist became the principal service on Sundays and vestments were worn, while on weekdays there was a daily Mass. In the side-chapel, the Sacrament was reserved, the sick were anointed and confessions were heard.[17]

It is important to realize that there was now nothing *outré* about this sort of liturgy within the Church of England, nothing strikingly partisan, as there would very much have been forty years earlier.

Rather more radical were developments at the parish of Halton, Leeds, described by its vicar, E. W. Southcott, in a work published in 1956 *The Parish Comes Alive*. It was an appeal, more than anything else, for 'the house church' – the celebration of the Eucharist on weekday evenings in private houses up and down the parish. *The Parish Comes Alive* represented the most revolutionary edge of Parish and People, of the movement for a genuinely popular liturgy, and the inspiration for it came quite explicitly from the French priest-worker movement and the Abbé Michonneau's *Revolution in a City Parish*. House celebration in Halton began in October 1952 and by August 1953 John Robinson, a Cambridge divinity don, was writing enthusiastically in *Theology*:

> I shall not attempt to describe what I saw at Halton, except to say that one found the church living at a level at which she can seldom have lived since the days of the Acts. The breaking of bread from house to house and the rediscovery of the *Ecclesia* of God in all its fullness at basement level – these can be described only by sharing in them.

Excited words. It should at once be added – as with Chad Varah's Samaritans – that this remained in the fifties a pretty isolated phenomenon. And even at Halton it had its limits. While Southcott was a progressive not only in liturgy but also in ecumenical relations, nevertheless the two together did not carry him so far as to allow intercommunion. It is certainly worth noting how emphatically he asserted that when, in the 1953 Week of Unity, Methodists and Congregationalists 'attended our Parish Communion' there was never 'any question of communicating'.[18] Just a few years later the house church would become one of the points at which it seemed most morally impossible not to practise intercommunion.

Stockwood at Great St Mary's and Southcott at Halton represent very definitely the way the wind was blowing, but it does need stressing that there were a very large number of parishes, common or garden rural parishes as well as more explicitly evangelical ones in towns, which at the end of the 1950s were still quite uninfluenced by the ideas of Parish and People. In them matins or evensong was still the principal Sunday service. Some of them flourished. Their flourishing was symbolic of the mild resurgence of tradition more than of religious renewal.

The movements of renewal we have considered will have had their effect on religious practice but it would probably be to overevaluate their impact to see them as the principal cause of the undoubted revival of Church life which took place in the fifties. They were rather themselves expressions of a wider revival. The war itself and a concurrent spiritual and intellectual readjustment of society seem to have set the ball rolling. C. S. Lewis could remark of undergraduates returning from the forces that there was a much higher percentage of Christians among them than had been the case in his own generation after the First World War.[19] The general feeling of religious revival or, perhaps better, of restoration, continued for about a dozen years. It fitted well with the dominant mood of the fifties, its politicians, its literary figures, its art. 'The church', declares a character in Pamela Hansford Johnson's novel, *The Humbler Creation*, 'is respectable again. People have to say they believe in God.' It was not just a matter of respectability. When, after thirty years of Anglo-agnosticism, Rose Macaulay returned to Christian faith through sacramental confession and communion late in 1950, it was certainly not a question of respectability but quite a shock to respectable agnostic friends.[20] Growth is noticeable in many of the Anglican, Roman Catholic, and even a few Free Church, statistics of the time. There were 251 Anglican confirmations per thousand people aged fifteen in 1940; 279 in 1950; 315 in 1960. Communion and ordination figures also rose in the fifties, while the Church of England was probably receiving towards fifteen thousand new adult members a year.[21] 'Congregations really do seem to be growing both in numbers and in apostolic toughness.'[22]

It is also true that the wider linkage of the Established Church with the population as a whole was contracting rather fast. Infant baptisms were 672 per thousand births in 1950 (up a little on 1940). They had fallen to 554 by 1960: a very big decline for one decade. If the hope behind Industrial Mission was that it would revivify the Church's presence within the urban lower class, then, despite its excellent intentions, its immediate achievement was slight (Hunter and Wickham had never expected it to be anything else). Furthermore what was at least being seriously attempted in Sheffield was hardly to be found in many other equally important towns. The structure of the new educational system, on the other hand, was universal and it did a lot not only to enhance the long-established secular ethos of the common man, but to give a new confidence to the secularized. It spread afar the rather dated secret that modern educated men did not need even to pretend to be religious.

The milieu where Anglican measures of pastoral reform and rechristianization were most likely to be bearing fruit were the suburban parish, undergraduates at Oxford and Cambridge, the public school, Solihull. There looks to be an almost inexorable law that every effective measure of Anglican pastoral reform also contributes to a narrowing in the Church's sphere of influence, as well as undermining just those institutions and observances which have hitherto provided some sort of bridge to the poorer classes. The public schools are renewed in their youth, the day schools abandoned in their old age. Even the parish communion, so rightly hailed as a pastoral breakthrough, probably contributed to the decline both of church-going among non-communicants and of the Sunday school, one of the Church's best links with the less ecclesiasticized classes.[23] Wickham could begin his important study of church life in Sheffield in 1957 with the stinging words, 'the weakness and collapse of the Churches in the urbanised and industrialized areas of the country should be transparently clear to any, who are not wilfully blind,'[24] yet a southern suburban parish could equally report: 'Our main problem is sheer numbers: 380 funerals, 120 weddings, 200 baptisms, 80+ confirmations per annum . . . the parish magazine goes to over 4,000 houses with the help of 130 distributors . . .'[25] And there were many such parishes. The gap between the material standards of the two Englands was diminishing but not, it seems, that between their religious ethos.

Look at Worcester College, Oxford.[26] Worcester tends to be one of the more conservative colleges but by no means stick-in-the-mud. Its 1950s mood reflected especially well the governing ethos of the age as its Provost, Sir John Masterman, certainly desired it to do. A distinguished figure, urbane but formidably intelligent, an effective Vice-Chancellor, the friend of Macmillan, Provost Masterman remained very much a Church and State man of the old school. For him the chaplain was 'my chaplain', the chapel and its services a personal responsibility. He attended regularly as did the Vice-Provost and many of the dons. The right note was paternalist, believing, but not argumentative or emotional. Here, unlike most colleges, undergraduates were still obliged to attend chapel at least once a term. They mostly went to matins. They had come overwhelmingly from public schools and did not find it so strange. In Masterman's Worcester the ancient order – the assumption that an Oxford college was a religious and an Anglican community and that in this it was true to the country generally – still positively flourished, a little oddly but not too archaically. Moreover, the chaplain of Worcester, be it noted, was only one of some 160 Anglican priests somehow involved in the Oxford ministry, town and gown, of the late 1950s.

The intellectual life of the Church of England can seldom if ever have seemed healthier. Take the contributors to the 1947 *Catholicity* report, and to that of the sixth Anglo-Catholic Congress the next year. In these collections a remarkably brilliant group of men is represented, including Michael Ramsey, then Professor of Divinity at Durham, Dom Gregory Dix, T. S. Eliot, Austin Farrer, Eric Mascall, L. S. Thornton, Donald Mackinnon. They had begun to make their mark before the war but were now nearing the height of their achievement, nearly all producing important books in these years. Gregory Dix's formidable and extremely influential piece of imaginative scholarship, *The Shape of the Liturgy*, appeared in 1945; Thornton's three great volumes of theological synthesis, *The Form of a Servant*, between 1950 and 1956; Austin Farrer's *Glass of Vision* in 1948 and *A Study in St Mark* in 1941; Mascall's *Corpus Christi* in 1955. As a group they created something unusual for Anglicanism – a working school of historical theology, drawing not only on Scripture and the Fathers but very especially upon St Thomas. To one side of them stood some immensely learned biblical and patristic scholars, like Canon Greenslade, Professor H. W. Turner, and Professor Ratcliff, the liturgist; on another side more distinctly philosophical apologists like the engaging young Nolloth Professor of the Christian Religion at Oxford, Ian Ramsey; or Donald Mackinnon.

In less specialist fields of religious literature the position looked even brighter. C. S. Lewis, T. S. Eliot and Dorothy L. Sayers (now translating Dante) produced a continued glow of literary distinction around the Church of England. At a more popular level John Betjeman wrote nice churchy poetry like 'Christmas' or 'Dream of a Church Mouse', while Elizabeth Goudge, one of the most widely read of contemporary novelists, published in 1951 a devout, unerringly orthodox life of Jesus, entitled *God So Loved the World*. J. B. Phillips, a south London vicar, was responsible for a modern translation of the New Testament (starting with *Letters to Young Churches* in 1947) which soon sold four and a half million copies. The range and versatility of Anglican religious writing in these years, from Goudge to the most subtle pieces of Farrer or Mackinnon, was remarkable. It was confident and creative. It was at home in the times, yet for the most part very well rooted in tradition. It was scholarly. Some of it had an exceptional literary quality. When to it is joined the religious literature of the previous twenty years – for there is a literary unity about Christian writing in England from the early thirties to the fifties – it adds up to a pretty impressive achievement.

By the middle of the 1950s it may well have seemed that the Church was right after all to dodge any more radical measure of post-war reform. It had not been needed. The leadership had re-established confidence quite effectively without it. The Captain of England's cricket team in 1954 was ordained in the Church of England in 1955 – David Sheppard, a bright young product of the old Cambridge Evangelical stable. It was a most satisfying moment, symbol of what the fifties seemed all about.

It would be a mistake to underestimate the unquestioned mastery which Fisher exercised in these years; but one can also consider York. Until 1956 the Archbishop of York was Cyril Garbett, now an old man for whom many people felt an almost unparalleled respect. He was a pastor with the most exacting personal spiritual standards, a man with a lifetime's hard slog over social problems behind him, and with just that sensible, mildly reformist, but essentially conservative judgment which appealed to the age. We have noted before a certain silliness in many an Anglican cleric – the silliness of a kind of religious self-confidence too closely linked with the comfortableness of the upper class, rather over-confident intellectually, over-sheltered socially, a middle-aged hangover of the clever silliness of the Oxbridge undergraduate. You may find it on occasion in Temple and Lang and Fisher, even in Bell, not to mention many a dean. You won't find a trace of it in Garbett. Perhaps this has something to do with his not having been to a public school, with his background of a fairly poor home, with his Oxford second. He had been neither don nor headmaster, only a parish priest. A little less clever than many other bishops, he came closer to embodying for his own generation the nation's religious judgment. In him the national Church was still a functioning fact and very impressively so.

All the bishops were not, of course, of the calibre of Garbett though colleagues like F. R. Barry of Southwell and Noel Hudson of Newcastle were men with very similar traits. But take a rather more episcopally conventional figure like Edward Woods of Lichfield. The son of a vicarage, educated at Marlborough and Trinity, Cambridge, an Evangelical (but not too rigid a one), Woods lived in a world which took shooting parties for granted and felt no shortage of money (his wife was a Barclay). He was exactly the class to be a bishop and it really does not surprise one that his brother was bishop of Winchester and his son, in due course, bishop of Middleton. With the Woods we are still very close to the old-fashioned heart of Anglicanism where upper-class and clerical *mores* had quietly gelled into a single whole. Edward Woods was a priest and a gentleman. He was, everyone stressed, very 'lovable'. Yet he was a forward-looking bishop who had become increasingly ecumenical and had taken a very active part in Faith and Order. He fitted the fifties very well.[27]

There was not too much wrong here nor with the younger new arrivals – pretty high-powered professors like Mortimer of Exeter, experienced ecumenists like Tomkins of Bristol. Of these, Garbett's successor at York was the most distinguished. Michael Ramsey had been Regius Professor of Theology at Cambridge. He was certainly far more of a don than most of his colleagues, and also more obviously an Anglo-Catholic than Garbett, but he was a man able to put theology across with authority to a wide audience, someone of outstanding presence and spiritual charisma, a bishop whose pastoral authority was really enhanced by his scholarship. The obvious quality of these men illustrates rather impressively the mature, confident distinction of the upper echelon of the Church of England in the 1950s. A national Church led by such men had not – it could seem – too much to be worried about. It was holding together old and new, intellectual creativity and pastoral reform, even Evangelical and Anglo-Catholic, with far less strain than in the past.

The high point of this ecclesiastical period was the Lambeth Conference of 1958.

> We, Archbishops and Bishops of the Holy Catholic and Apos-
> tolic Church in communion with the See of Canterbury, three
> hundred and ten in number, assembled from forty-six coun-
> tries, under the presidency of Geoffrey, Archbishop of Canter-
> bury, in the year of our Lord one thousand nine hundred and
> fifty-eight, send you greeting in the name of our Lord and
> Saviour Jesus Christ.[28]

Lambeth conferences have an unlucky habit of being over-
shadowed by some other more immediately exciting piece of
ecclesiastical life. Thus those of 1948 and 1968 suffered a little
from proximity to more important conferences of the World
Council, while those of 1968 and 1978 were even more, and
unexpectedly, shadowed by papal events – the publication of
Humanae Vitae, and the death of Pope Paul. In the summer of
1958 nothing happened to belittle the significance of Lambeth,
but still more to the point was its intrinsically noteworthy
character. On the one hand its theological preparations had been
well done and its resultant teaching, especially the statement of
its committee on *The Family in Contemporary Society*, was
among the ablest to come from any authoritative Church body in
the twentieth century. Its position on the uses of contraception
would be rejected, but not invalidated, by Pope Paul in *Humanae
Vitae*, ten years later: perhaps one of the more unfortunate
modern failures to listen to the voice of a 'Sister Church'. The
bishops of the Anglican communion were speaking at this point
from both a maturely developed formal moral theology and with
the benefit of personal experience. They were, unlike so many
bodies of bishops, a gathering mostly of the married.

The Anglican provinces of West and Central Africa had been
established in 1951 and 1955, and Archbishop Fisher had since
been to Africa to consecrate a number of black bishops: he was
the first globe-trotting Archbishop of Canterbury, and quite
effectively so. Lambeth 1958, it could be said, saw the Anglican
communion discover and affirm itself as an international and
inter-racial Christian fellowship, rather than an almost
accidental imperial and missionary prolongation of the Established Church of the English nation. This was confirmed by the

appointment of its own executive officer the following year: an American. The conference showed that Anglicanism, despite the intensely English character that it had often retained overseas, would find no insuperable difficulty in adjusting to the end of empire. The approach here had been pragmatic and piecemeal, it had worked, and Fisher could take a good deal of credit for the achievement.

At home the dominant note remained less innovative. The chairman of the House of Laity during the second half of the decade may illustrate this almost too obviously. He was the third Earl of Selborne and his election to that office suggests an almost self-conscious determination to maintain the aristocratic and Tory surveillance which the House of Laity had enjoyed from the start, especially from the Cecil family. Lord Selborne's mother was a Cecil. As Lord Wolmer, a very young member of parliament, he had indeed had much to do with the original establishment of the Church Assembly forty years earlier. His father had been chairman of the House for most of its existence prior to his death in 1942, and his grandfather, the first earl, had chaired the old House of Laity of the Convocation of Canterbury. Before entering the Lords, Wolmer had been a long-standing feature of the Commons representing for over twenty years that part of his native Hampshire which stretches from Aldershot to Selborne. He was a member of Churchill's wartime government, Minister of Economic Warfare, and together with his first cousin Lord Cranborne performed in the Lords the task of rebutting Bishop Bell's frequent criticisms of government policy. Since 1949 he had been president of the Church Army. An eminently respected and experienced peer, who had given so much of his life serving Church causes, Selborne must have seemed an almost inevitable choice for the chairmanship of the House of Laity. It was so utterly consistent with the way that House had always been.

The function that the Earl of Selborne fulfilled nationally continued to be played locally across most parts of the country by his peers. Take south Yorkshire and the diocese of Sheffield: the south Yorkshire coalfield and Sheffield itself were, as we have seen, anything but Anglican strongholds; for that reason the diocese was, perhaps, all the more firmly supported by the local aristocracy. We have observed one great and very pious south Yorkshire landlord, the Earl of Halifax, erecting his tall crucifix at Garrowby in 1956. His neighbour, the eleventh Earl of Scarbrough, was little less distinguished. He was low in churchmanship where Halifax was exceedingly high. His uncle, the tenth earl, had been a pillar of the diocese from its foundation in 1914 until his death in great old age at the end of the Second World War: *ein fester Burg*, Bishop Hunter described him. His heir, Lawrence Lumley, was everything that one could desire of an intelligent and public-minded English nobleman. Member of parliament in his youth and then Governor of Bombay for six important years, he was now a major-general (his only book was a *History of the Eleventh Hussars*), Lord Lieutenant of the West Riding, President of the South Yorkshire Scouts Council, chairman of the Governing Board of the School of Oriental and African Studies and patron very especially of orientalist activities. The year that Lord Halifax set up his crucifix, Lord Scarbrough was the Queen's Special Ambassador to the coronation of the King of Nepal. A Knight of the Garter and Lord Chamberlain of the Household, Scarbrough was also Grand Master of the United Grand Lodge of English Freemasonry. He practised that brand of decidedly Protestant and unritualist churchmanship which never sensed conflict with the rituals of the Masonic Order. Like his uncle, the eleventh Earl gave a great deal of his time to the work of the diocese of Sheffield, being chairman of its Board of Finance all through the fifties. He would later add to that the High Stewardship of York Minster. Figures of the Selborne and Scarbrough type still quietly steered Anglican Church life in the appropriate direction in most dioceses, while providing very freely of their time and their money.[29]

The tone of this rather Anglican decade,[30] and Anglican of a benignly conservative hue, may also be glimpsed through a look at some of its novels. Here the picture is less encouraging. Rose Macaulay's *Towers of Trebizond* (1956); Barbara Pym's *A Glass of Blessings* (1958); Iris Murdoch's *The Bell* (1958); Pamela Hansford Johnson's *The Humbler Creation* (1958), have a good deal in common.[31] They are all distinguished pieces of writing concerned with contemporary Anglican life. In each the Church appears on the surface as a relatively prospering institution with a decidedly traditionalist orientation. If there are any new initiatives, their character is mostly one of medieval revivalism – a lay monastery with very old-fashioned rules or an absurd missionary journey to Turkey. Of course there is an element of caricature here, especially in *The Towers of Trebizond*, the amused and sophisticated in-talk of the half-agnostic. Beneath the surface of Anglo-Catholicism, it suggests, there lies some rather wild fervour but also a considerable layer of Anglo-agnosticism. A Church apparently very much in business turns out in each case to be really rather worm-eaten. Anglo-Catholicism in particular appears still more rundown than querky, its ideals fading, its claim to represent historic Catholicism in England none too convincing in face of the mounting attraction of 'Going over to Rome'.[32] Between Rome and agnosticism the impression given is one of a nice, rather ineffectual, socially respectable but bewildered rump not far off its last legs. The over-earnest lay community at Imber collapses in moral disarray. The vision of Trebizond retains its mystic power, 'the pull and power of the Christian Church on the divided mind',[33] but has a 'hard core' just too difficult for most modern people to make their own. The London parish so gently depicted by Pamela Hansford Johnson, a sort of upper middle-class village deep in a seedier portion of the West End, is only just keeping its head above water. 'The number of people in this district even dimly interested in the Church', Maurice, the vicar, regretfully recognized, 'let alone showing an active interest, is minute. So, do let us stop pretending that the eyes of half London are concentrated upon us and poor old Kate'. . . . 'But isn't that', said Libby, 'an ostrich-like approach? People are concerned. They must be. We are still the leaders.' 'Oh, no,' said Maurice impatiently, 'we're not.'

Look at Archbishops Fisher and Garbett, at Lords Selborne and Scarbrough, at Sir John Masterman, at Margery Perham and Robert Birley, at Dorothy Sayers and C. S. Lewis, and the Church seemed still to be the leader, seldom reactionary but rather reassuringly conservative. You knew better where it stood than in the slightly disturbing days of William Temple. The Church of the 1950s was not a disturbing phenomenon. It seemed too sure of itself to be that. Archbishop Fisher could confidently declare as he retired, 'I leave the Church of England in good heart', and only some hard-pressed vicar might reply, and half to himself, 'Oh, no, we're not'.

One part of the Church of England certainly was in good heart and that was its Evangelical wing. It had not always been so. Go back to the 1920s and no side of English religious life seemed more depressed – inturned, lacking in leaders, unable to appeal widely even to its normally favourite undergraduate clientele. That was true not only of England. Evangelicalism in America was similarly in a bedraggled state between the wars. The SCM in both countries had been its great creation at the start of the century, but the SCM with its increasingly liberal theology, social concern and ecumenical openness, even to such unconverted sinners as Anglo-Catholics, had strayed badly from the true path. In Cambridge an independent, purified Christian Union had early resolved to get back to the narrow way, but until the end of the twenties it had very little success in convincing people elsewhere that the SCM no longer represented the true ideals of the movement as they had been prior to Moody's death in 1899.

It was not until 1928 that the Inter-Varsity Fellowship of Christian Unions was effectively brought into being and only after that did it become established in Birmingham, Leeds, Durham, Hull, Southampton. In each place SCM members protested at the splitting of student Christian ranks. In this struggle between the inclusivist and the exclusivist approach, the latter often failed to take root in the tolerant twenties, but as the thirties advanced, it grew steadily stronger.[34] By 1934 a young man named Donald Coggan could already edit a book on the advance of the Inter-Varsity Fellowship, *Christ and the Colleges*. Here the vast achievement of the SCM could be effectively disregarded. By 1939 the Christian Union was active in almost every British university, had its own publishing house, the Inter-Varsity Press, and large headquarters in Bedford Square. That June its international conference was held in Cambridge with more than a thousand students attending. The Evangelical revival was well under way.[35]

The importance of all this nevertheless lies less in what was achieved before the war than in the foundation it laid for the far greater expansion of the post-war years, particularly under American influence. The revival was clearly not an American importation, yet it owed a great deal to repeated American contributions. For CICCU's first great mission after the war it brought Donald Backhouse across the Atlantic to pack Great St Mary's, but it was the impact of Billy Graham that was really formative for the Evangelicalism of the subsequent decades. The modern American Evangelical revival, 'The Fourth Great Awakening' as it is termed, began with Graham's crusade in Los Angeles in September 1949. Such at least is the standard mythology. From then on the world of Billy Graham grew ever larger as he developed into the model of a twentieth-century evangelist.

For Britain the great moment was undoubtedly the spring of 1954, when for three full months Graham conducted the 'Greater London Crusade' at Harringay. It had taken more than eighteen months of meticulous preparation, backed by all the resources of Evangelicalism both in Britain and in America. Graham arrived on 23 February. Three days later he was entertained at a House of Commons dinner presided over by Lancelot Joynson-Hicks, son of the Joynson-Hicks who had been Home Secretary in the 1920s and most formidable lay opponent of Prayer Book revision. Joynson-Hicks had followed his father at once in Evangelical churchmanship, assiduous membership of the Church Assembly, a seat in parliament, the family firm of solicitors – Joynson-Hicks and Co. – and the chairmanship of the Automobile Association. A House of Commons dinner presided over by him provided for this young and still rather little-known American preacher precisely the correct initiatory note of Evangelical continuity and Establishment benediction.

On 1 March, the opening night at Harringay, Graham declared that he saw the beginning of what could be 'a sweep for God through Britain'. Within five years, he added, 'I am convinced there is going to be a spiritual awakening such as you have not seen since the days of Wesley.'[36] All the way down the Piccadilly Line, we are told, were train loads of happy people singing: 'This is my story, this is my song. . . . Praising my Saviour all the day long'; the theme song of the revival. Was it really like that? There can be no doubt that Harringay was a quite remarkable success. Graham's audiences in those three months totalled over 1,300,000. On the final Saturday in May both the Wembley Stadium (with 120 thousand) and the White City (with 65 thousand) were filled to capacity as Graham preached his final message, with the Lord Mayor of London upon one side of him and the Archbishop of Canterbury upon the other. That was an achievement which, the *Sunday Times* declared in an editorial, would 'before it happened have seemed incredible'. It is hard to assess the long-term effects of such an event. Amazing as it seemed to participants at the time, it was far too neatly packaged to constitute or even lead to a major 'spiritual awakening' in the nation's life and yet it is true that very many a fervent Evangelical in later years would look back on 'Harringay' as the moment of truth.

One mission – even conducted by Billy Graham – does not make a revival and, important as American preachers have always been for fully fledged Evangelicalism, the revival really depended even more on its local representatives, and more than anyone else on John Stott. If we take the triennial missions to Oxford and Cambridge of the Christian Union in the fifties – a very crucial part of the whole strategy – while Graham preached the 1955 Cambridge mission, Stott preached those of 1952 and 1958 and the Oxford missions of 1954 and 1957. He had become Rector of All Souls, Langham Place in 1950, the church in which the BBC records its daily service. From then on Stott must be accounted one of the most influential figures in the Christian world, standing as he did at the point of intersection of the Evangelical movement and the Church of England.

Anglican Evangelicals provide the core of the Evangelical movement in England and they are, most decidedly, Anglicans and more Erastian than many of their brethren. Their favourite breeding grounds have long been the public schools and Oxbridge. Socially, politically and even in the tone of their worship, Evangelicals can seem almost quintessentially Anglican of a rather Victorian kind. None the less, British Evangelicalism claims to be pure Protestantism and no one can restrict Protestantism to the Church of England. It is only too clear that there are plenty of sound British Protestants outside the Established Church and plenty of non-Protestants within it. The Anglican Evangelical has a strong double loyalty – the 'Evangelical Movement' upon the one hand, his Church upon the other. And this ambiguity is greatly enhanced by the American connection. American Evangelicalism is not Anglican at all. It belongs to a very different kind of religious tradition, far more sectarian, more temperamentally fundamentalistic, in discourse more gushing. The modern Anglican Evangelical belongs internationally on the one hand to the Anglican communion, but on the other he belongs to a movement dominated by the immensely rich Billy Graham Evangelization Association. The ethos of the two really does not tally. It may appear odd that the Billy Graham movement should not have been more closely linked with the private sector in British Protestantism, more distanced from the Established Church. Yet this is not a new phenomenon: the upper-class Cambridge attraction for the non-denominational American evangelist was already there in the nineteenth century, and it seems to have suited both partners.

In the post-war revival of the movement John Stott became the very hinge of this double belonging. Educated at Rugby and Trinity College, Cambridge, the son of a physician of the Royal Household and himself a chaplain to the Queen, Stott represents the quintessence of Evangelical upper-class Establishmentarianism. Yet he is equally one of the controlling figures in the councils of international Evangelicalism, the man who could be trusted to prepare the key paper on 'God's strategy for this age' at the crucial meeting at Montreux in 1960 held to plan the future of the Graham crusades. Again, it may appear anomalous that the officially non-denominational daily service of the BBC is recorded at the very heart of England's Evangelical empire, but this again suggests the duality of Evangelicalism: on the one side it sees itself as straight undenominational Protestantism, on the other as the *pars sanior* of the Established Church of England, while being in fact a network of a tight and exclusivist character. If Stott had not been something of an ecclesiastical statesman, with a considerable sense for the wholeness of things as well as a very fine preacher, he could hardly have played this double, or triple, role across several decades. One thing he has not become is a bishop, and doubtless wisely. A modern Anglican bishop has to relate sympathetically to all wings of the Church of England, and in strict Evangelical eyes an Evangelical who accepts a bishopric, like Edward Woods or even Donald Coggan, is almost bound to be judged sooner or later as something of a sell-out. British Evangelical history in fact is replete with lost leaders – men who, as they grew older, have found it impossible or at least undesirable to stick quite closely enough to the movement's doctrines and norms.

Clearly it has always had a narrower and wider tendency. Its two ablest modern English leaders, Max Warren and John Stott, have both in a cautious way represented the latter. Warren's position was always unusual.[37] As a young man at Cambridge he had insisted upon belonging both to the Christian Union and the SCM – and got away with it. From 1936 as vicar of Holy Trinity, Cambridge, and then from 1942 as General Secretary of the CMS for twenty-one years, he had done all he could to widen and 'liberalize' Evangelical attitudes. He objected strongly to classifying Evangelicals as either 'conservative' or 'liberal', yet in the end if he had to be classified it would be as the latter. It is surprising, perhaps, that he kept the personal influence he did, but in some ways his influence and attitudes were overtaken by the far more strident and uncompromising wave of Evangelicalism unloosed by Billy Graham and already, of course, working its way anew through the British movement.

Warren had a warm lay ally in Sir Kenneth Grubb. Both were at Marlborough. Grubb was President of the CMS from 1944 to 1965, and from 1959 chairman of the House of Laity in the Church Assembly. He was also chairman of the Churches Commission on International Affairs within the WCC, vice-president of the Institute of Race Relations, and a great deal besides. Like Warren, he carried on the more open tradition of Evangelicalism which had nourished the SCM and done so much in its earlier stage for the ecumenical movement, at once liberal and highly Establishmentarian. His brother Norman we have already met as a very uncompromising young undergraduate at Cambridge in 1919 (see page 91). Both were missionaries. While Kenneth remained very much a Church of England man, Norman took over from his father-in-law, C. T. Studd, the leadership of the World Evangelization Crusade, to which he later added the Christian Literature Crusade. Their sister Violet had also gone abroad in the 1920s, to teach botany in China. She returned to become headmistress of Westonbirt for many years and president of the Association of Headmistresses of Boarding Schools. The Grubbs were clearly masterly people, but they illustrate the range of Evangelicalism: Kenneth and Violet at the Anglican and institutional end, Norman as representative of that face of the movement which jibs at Establishment and is preoccupied rather with 'crusades', theoretically undenominational but effectively highly sectarian, while being suspicious of both Catholic and ecumenical tendencies. The strength of Stott was that he reconciled, better than almost anyone else, Establishmentarianism with crusading.

The revival of the 1950s with its 'bash camps' for public schoolboys in the summer holidays, its packed congregations in the Round Church at Cambridge and St Aldate's, Oxford, its increasing takeover through the Christian Union of the principal role in student Christian life from a decaying SCM, had restored to evangelicalism a major and initiating role in English religion. Its predominantly Anglican base was, perhaps, evidence of how far the decline of the Free Churches had now gone, yet the revival could not be wholly Anglican – it did in fact include Baptists particularly, and not unnaturally, as the very heart of American Evangelicalism are the Southern Baptists. But it was Protestant and it represented a major counter force to the erosion of traditional Protestantism and to the advance of one form or another of Catholicism which had been, hitherto, the predominant characteristic of twentieth-century English religious history.

It also fitted closely enough within the American ascendancy of the post-war years. When Graham arrived at Southampton in February 1954 it was, symbolically enough, on board the liner *United States* with its state rooms at his disposal. In his opening press conference he quoted from President Eisenhower and on the first night at Harringay he was accompanied by two American senators. The 1950s were white America's most confident age, Oklahoma's 'Beautiful Day', in which almost the whole world seemed at last to be going its way, in religion as in power and in wealth. The war had been won, the world freed, the United Nations established in New York. If the Soviet Union was hostile and threatening, it could be isolated. If China had gone Communist, rejecting American tutelage, it could at least be excluded from the UN. The World Council of Churches' one plenary conference in the decade was held in America, at Evanston, a suburb of Chicago, and in that environment it very nearly succumbed to a rather partisan note of cold-war anti-Communism. American influence of one sort or another was pervasive almost everywhere. At the most sophisticated and liberal end of the religious spectrum we have the Union Theological Seminary, New York at the height of its influence, with Paul Tillich and Reinhold Niebuhr its most distinguished professors, a centre of world-wide theological influence. The production and export with great gusto of rather simplistic versions of the Christian message was, however, far more characteristic of that moment of American supremacy and its wider political, cultural and economic imperialism.

It was for the United States a rather Victorian age, unquestioning in its moral righteousness, a highly religious and church-going age (the two there being more or less identical as in England they have seldom been). It was a missionary age. America was now the self-chosen standard bearer of civilization, capitalism and Christianity, as Britain had been in the nineteenth century. American missionaries were multiplying throughout the world, from Southern Baptists to Catholics, and if Billy Graham was easily American religion's favourite son, he was by no means the only American Protestant to make a marked impact on British religion in the 1950s. In July 1955 the Jehovah's Witnesses held a five day convention in the Rugby grounds at Twickenham, drawing 42 thousand people: 1,183 new Witnesses were baptized in the nearby Municipal Baths. On the final day the Witnesses' president, N. H. Knorr, delivered his message on 'World Conquest Soon'. The Witnesses had become a fast growing constituent of British religion, just as had the Mormons. The 182 congregations they possessed in Britain in 1914, and 386 in 1928, had now increased to 727.[38]

To turn to a seemingly rather different sort of movement, Frank Buchman's world reputation as a guru of reconciliation was more widely spread than ever. The organizational and propagandist skills of Moral Rearmament had never been more active or enjoyed greater resources than now when it operated from its two world centres of what it called 'The Assembly of

Nations': Machinac Island in the US and Caux in Switzerland. 'The one unfailing light in this dark world is the light of Moral Re-Armament.'[39] Buchman, Graham and Knorr would not have worked well together, yet they represented three streams of much the same phenomenon. Buchman in the twenties had been frequently mistaken by British Evangelicals for a straight revivalist preacher in the Moody tradition. By the fifties the doctrinal content of his message of conversion had almost disappeared in favour of the 'four moral absolutes'. Graham, on the other hand, reasserted a straight biblical fundamentalism, if without the millennialist note which had so bewitched the Witnesses. Nevertheless traditional Evangelicalism had a strong millennialist tendency too and Graham's revival of the old Evangelical watchword, 'The Evangelization of the world in this generation' (which had been dropped by SCM around 1920), was not entirely dissimilar to Knorr's 'World Conquest Soon'. While Knorr undoubtedly represented a sectarian deviation, Buchman and Graham stood rather for different facets of a sort of single state religion of the American empire at the peak of its power and sense of world mission under Eisenhower. Both accepted its political presuppositions and were captivated by its techniques of media packaging – for much of which on the Catholic side Bishop Fulton Sheen could provide a near-equivalent. For all of them the media were coming a little close to being the message.

If Protestantism seemed to flourish on several of these new frontiers, at its most native level it continued to decay. In Manchester in 1950 Union Chapel, a vast Victorian Baptist auditorium, was demolished.[40] It had been built to hold the listeners to Alexander McLaren's preaching – seating for 1,400 and room for another 400. 'The Nonconformist Cathedral of Lancashire' it was called, being always open to more than Baptists. It had stood in its pride for the common culture of northern Nonconformity and its demolition was as symbolic as anything of the collapse of the tradition even in its heartland.

Turn further south. The 'Peculiar People' were founded by James Banyard, a Wesleyan cobbler, in the 1830s. A tiny sect among the rural poor, they rejected all medicine, sang and danced in church, and hardly spread beyond Essex. Elsewhere, there had been other similar little sects. In 1937 there were still thirty chapels of the Peculiar People in Essex and two outside the county but on 31 March 1956 they were dissolved and the small surviving remnant incorporated into the Union of Evangelical Churches.[41] The dissolution of the Peculiar People was, however, just one example of an almost universal disintegration of the small congregations of rural Nonconformity.[42] This did not, of course, mean that all small sects were necessarily at risk: Quaker membership, on the contrary, was higher in the late 1950s than it had been for many decades, but then Quakers are urban middle-class and often rather active participators in society's modernizing process. It was the working-class sect caught within a culturally conservative but also numerically declining corner of society which was in danger.

In Sheffield, another old heartland of Nonconformity, the membership of the principal Free Churches at the beginning of the 1930s was over 21,000: Methodist 15,960; Congregational 3,841; Baptist 1,709. By 1955 it was under 16,000: Methodist 12,528; Congregational 2,037; Baptist 1,070.[43] A decline of a quarter in twenty-five years was decidedly serious. Congregationalism, here as elsewhere, suffered the worst, Methodism the least. In England as a whole Congregationalism had hitherto been more numerous than the Baptist Union and politically far more influential. In the early 1950s its membership fell below that of the latter and from 1955 remained below.[44] Methodism however, like the Presbyterians and the Quakers, actually shared, if mildly, in the 1950s religious boom and its leaders were probably not over-worried about the general state of things. Over the whole period 1945-60 its membership slightly declined but for the middle years there was actually some small increase. Sunday scholars numbered 706,237 in 1945; 816,718 in 1954.

Decline in the industrial north – characteristic after all of society as a whole – seemed partly compensated for in Methodism by growth in southern suburbs but numbers were holding up well enough in many places from Liverpool to Norfolk.[45] Methodism was moving towards being a predominantly middle-class phenomenon. Readjustment was assisted by a considerable exercise in resiting and rebuilding of churches, accomplished with the help both of the government War Damage Commission and the J. Arthur Rank Benevolent Trust. There were far more

461

Methodist university students after than before the war.

Methodism was involved too in a rationalizing reorganization, in some measure the long overdue consequence of the reunion of 1932. From the beginning of the century the traditional Wesleyan Districts were each accorded a 'Chairman' who remained however a minister with a normal pastoral charge. Inevitably the responsibilities of chairmen grew, and little by little they found it necessary to give up a local ministry. This process was completed in 1957 when the Districts were reduced in number and all their chairmen were from then on to be separated from any particular charge.[46] It was a process of moderate episcopalization bringing Methodists one step nearer to the Anglican way of structuring the ministry. (Baptists and Congregationalists had already done much the same with the establishment of Superintendents or Moderators). It was also a measure of stabilization which accepted a certain shrinkage in the Church over the last thirty years but trusted that the decline could now be held.

In the immediate post-war years preaching as both art and edifying entertainment was still alive and cherished. In London Leslie Weatherhead at the City Temple, W. E. Sangster at Central Hall, Westminster, and Donald Soper at Kingsway Hall, maintained the flair and the fame of earlier generations of Methodist orators. At the same time a process of Catholic sacramentalization was now at last developing quite effectively throughout the Free Churches.[47] The belatedly recognized teaching of Forsyth, the initiatives of Micklem and others in the thirties, the general trend throughout ecumenical Christendom were all having their effect. The Free Church theological report, *The Catholicity of Protestantism* (1950); *The Presbyterian Service Book* (1948); the Baptist Neville Clark's stimulating *An Approach to the Theology of the Sacraments* (1956), were some of the significant factors and witnesses in this development of getting the liturgical movement off the ground in the Free Churches. In East London at Highams Park, the Baptist Stephen Winward provided a lively new model for worship with weekly communion and a balance of word with sacrament which was far indeed from customary Baptist practice. A few years later Winward and Ernest Payne would produce *Orders and Prayers for Church*

Worship (1960), whose introduction declared emphatically: 'It is a departure from apostolic worship to celebrate the Lord's Supper infrequently, or to regard it as a brief appendage following another complete service. Christian worship is essentially eucharistic.' What Winward was doing for Baptists, Donald Soper was doing rather more flamboyantly for Methodists.[48] A preacher by tradition, he was rediscovering himself as a priest. From 1950 president of the Methodist Sacramental Fellowship, he could well be described as a Methodist 'Anglo-Catholic'. He habitually wore a cassock. When president of Conference he insisted that the main feature of his 'President's Visit' to any church be the celebration of communion. His two great preoccupations across the years, declared the Methodist *Yearbook* in retrospect, were 'to recall Methodism both to the Eucharist and to the world beyond the Church's walls'.[49]

Soper represented almost all that was alive in contemporary Methodism. For forty-two years superintendent of the West London Mission in Kingsway, he was, like so many of the most outstanding Free Church leaders of the twentieth century, every inch a Londoner. An indefatigable public preacher on Tower Hill, a keen Labour Party man, a long-standing Pacifist, the author of innumerable remarks irritating to the Conservative sensibility, Soper was one of the most out-going of pastors, always as concerned with the world as with the Church. His influence can be seen at its best in 'The Order of Christian Witness' he founded just after the war and in the large range of service institutions which developed around Kingsway Hall. In 1946 he led two hundred and fifty 'London Christian Campaigners' on a mission in Plymouth. A few months later the campaigners were formed into an 'Order' whose first major Evangelical offensive was to Huddersfield the following August. Here, as in all Soper's work, there was a fusion of unfundamentalistic personal evangelism, a vigorous message of social salvation and a strong sacramental, eucharistic, emphasis. Around Kingsway there developed at least thirteen distinct institutions of social service – houses for the rehabilitation of alcoholics, homes for unmarried expectant mothers, for unmarried mothers and their children, for girls on probation, the West London Clothing Store. Soper and Kingsway were rather too vigorously worldly, too professedly radical, to be other than a little untypical of 1950s ecclesiasticism, but they would constitute the very model for a modern religious progressive, a decade hence when Soper himself would be ennobled at the start of Harold Wilson's government as 'The Reverend. the Baron Soper of Kingsway'. The House of Lords was not all in all an unsuitable place for him to be. Remove a few minor idiosyncracies and Soper's Methodism, in its wide social and sacramental character, fits very much within the mainstream of modern English religion, just as the evangelicalism of Billy Graham does not.

Soper was more in the public eye than most of his colleagues, but the ministry of the Free Churches as a whole can seldom if ever have been more distinguished. Scholars like C. H. Dodd, Gordon Rupp and Newton Flew had a rightfully recognized position in national life well beyond that of Free churchmen of any previous generation, and Wesley House in Cambridge in particular, where Flew was Principal (and Rupp would succeed him), was an institution of recognized distinction. The Free Church presence in Cambridge included Dodd as Norris Hulse Professor of Theology, and Herbert Butterfield as Professor (and then Regius Professor) of Modern History.

In Oxford, in a different field, Charles Coulson, both an outstanding physicist and a Methodist lay preacher for over twenty years, was appointed in 1952 Rouse Ball Professor of Applied Mathematics. He was only one, if the most eminent, of a number of Free churchmen distinguished in the field of natural sciences. At these levels the Free Church presence was growing, not declining, and it was no more, as it had been forty years earlier, even in the slightest degree the presence of the outsider. When the World Methodist Conference met in Oxford in 1951 it was somehow symbolic that the patriarch of British Methodism, Scott Lidgett, now ninety-seven years old, should preach from the pulpit of the university church. He spoke for forty minutes and then collapsed into unconsciousness. Methodism had arrived. Was it also about to pass away?

The Methodism of these men was as enlightened, mature, out-going and faithful a form of Christianity as one might find anywhere, yet its problems of continued existence as a separate Church were very considerable, even if a little masked by the modest religious revival, common to the whole nation, of those years. The problems were nevertheless mounting relentlessly. On the one side lay the issue of 'redundancy': hundreds, if not thousands, of small chapels which should have been closed after Methodist reunion twenty-five years earlier, were still clinging to life, 'steadily strangling' effectiveness, to quote Eric Baker, Conference secretary over many years.[50] 'Redundancy' covers the wide field of the old-fashioned, often over-elderly Methodism of small communities, entrenched in places of declining population: for every Methodist member there were five chapel seats.[51] But on the other side, where Methodism did flourish on the new frontier of suburbs, universities, modern thought, it faced a threat almost equally insuperable though less easily admissible. The continual process of assimilation towards 'ecumenical' and 'catholic' religious attitudes subtly undermined, especially for the young, the justification for independent existence. As the sacrament grew in importance, so did the sermon diminish. The mid-1950s can be dated pretty precisely as the end of the age of preaching: people suddenly ceased to think it worthwhile listening to a special preacher. Whether this was caused by the religious shift produced by the liturgical movement or by the spread of television or by some other alteration in human sensibility is not clear. But the change is clear, and if the sermon as a decisive event was gone, had not at least half the *raison d'être* of the Free Church gone too? Leslie Weatherhead could compete on his own terms well enough with Westminster Abbey, the liturgy of Kingsway Hall could not. The more the best Free churchmanship approximated to a form of enlightened Anglicanism – at home in Oxford and Cambridge, unlinked with any particular political party, open to the winds of ecumenism and liturgical renewal, thoroughly middle class – the more it imperilled its institutional and emotional base and claim to a separate loyalty.[52] It had become too tolerant even to be much opposed to what survived of the Church of England's constitutional Establishment.[53] Again, it is very noticeable how even at the level of the Sunday school (always an institution which mattered more to the Free Churches than to the Established Church) there was a very marked shift in balance at this period. In 1921 Church of England Sunday schools claimed 1,780,000 members; Methodist 1,533,000: in

1957 the former figure had become 1,308,000, the latter 699,000.[54]

> An elderly Methodist minister of strong ecumenical convictions lamented to me last year that it was the young people his denomination could least afford to lose who were being confirmed in the Church of England, and he ran through a striking list of ex-presidents of the Methodist Conference whose sons and daughters were Methodists no longer.[55]

Christopher Driver's searing analysis of the state of things in *A Future for the Free Churches?* (1962) can be used to set the scene for the developments of the 1960s; it also remains a judgment upon the 1950s. When the *Congregational Quarterly* ceased publication in 1958, it was saying something about the near extinction of the old sort of reading public in that tradition.[56] Methodism was not yet so reduced. The long term future – even the middle term future – of the Free Churches had, nevertheless, become a question that could very reasonably be asked.

On 23 November 1946 Archbishop Fisher delivered a university sermon in Great St Mary's, Cambridge. It might be regarded as the most memorable statement he ever made. It was an attempt to overcome the impasse in regard to Christian unity (or, at least, Protestant unity) in Britain. Very little had happened on the local scene between the wars, but the experience of the Second World War, the establishment of the British Council of Churches, the termination of most of the old dissension in regard to schools, and the international arrival at long last of the World Council of Churches (its opening conference actually took place at Amsterdam in August 1948), all combined to promote an atmosphere in which some great step forward was widely desired. Yet the old difficulties remained as irreducible as ever: Anglicans could not recognize non-episcopally transmitted orders, Nonconformists and the Church of Scotland could not admit that their non-episcopally transmitted ministries were inadequate. In the wider Christian spectrum Fisher's sympathies lay strongly on the Protestant side, nevertheless as a dyed-in-the-wool Anglican he would in no way compromise over the necessity of episcopal ordination. To overcome the problem he now appealed to the Free Churches, in a memorable phrase, to 'take episcopacy into their own system'. That might not seem too difficult a thing to arrange, seeing that Methodists, Congregationalists and Baptists were effectively in the process of doing it anyway (and in many parts of the world Methodist superintendents were actually called bishops). Fisher, be it noted, did not propose this as a step towards 'organic unity' for he did not in fact want organic unity with other churches, which would inevitably mean changing the Church of England, of which he was not in favour. What he wanted was what he called 'full communion'.[57]

> While the folds remain distinct, there would be a movement towards a free and unfettered exchange of life in worship and sacrament. . . . It is, I think, not possible yet nor desirable that any Church should merge its identity in a newly-constituted union. What I desire is that I should freely be able to enter their churches, and they mine, in the sacraments of the Lord and in the full fellowship of worship.[58]

This may seem, in some ways, a curious proposal. He did not ask for unity: 'My longing is not yet that we should be united.' He did not, furthermore, propose that his own Church should do anything at all. Here was an ecumenical strategy in which the Church of England would do nothing but wait until other Protestant Churches had accepted her conditions by modifying their ministry, and not so as to obtain any complete unity but simply that individuals could share in the worship of other bodies without inhibition. Nevertheless many Anglicans seemed to regard this sermon as containing the very epitome of ecumenical wisdom. Still more curious, negotiations were set on foot as a consequence between Methodists and Anglicans which led, if very slowly, to a recommendation quite the opposite of what Fisher had wanted: 'union in one church'. By the time that report came out (1963) Fisher had retired from Canterbury but he opposed the plan from retirement, to his successor's considerable chagrin. In fact it failed in the end to gain sufficient support within the Church of England, though it was Anglo-Catholics and Evangelicals more than old-time Protestants of the Fisher sort, who rejected it. Fisher's 1946 suggestion had undoubtedly been an eminently cautious one, yet in the light of the failure of every more ambitious attempt to find a way towards 'organic unity' in the subsequent forty years, it could be argued that such caution was not unwise.

The immediate reunion problem with which Anglicans were faced was that over the Church of South India, born after long negotiations in September 1947 through a coming together of Anglicans, Methodists, Presbyterians and Congregationalists. The non-Anglican clergy involved had not been reordained but all the Church's bishops shared in the Anglican succession, and all future ministers were to be episcopally ordained. Should the Church of England at present enter into any sort of communion with such a Church? By 1955, when the question finally reached the Convocations of Canterbury and York, a considerable majority of all CSI clergy had been ordained by a bishop. The issues were subtle: could a Church which for the time being accepted non-episcopally ordained ministers for the same work as those who were episcopally ordained really mean anything much by episcopal ordination? Had it not accepted only the name but not the substance? Yet had not that always been the case for vast numbers of more Protestant-minded Anglicans at home anyway? South India was nevertheless far away, and the predicament of a Christian minority needing unity in face of the large Hindu majority around it was one which provoked sympathy.[59] Anglicans had sincerely entered the union. Were they to be permanently excluded from Anglican communion or, if ordained, from ministering, if they came to England on a visit? Many a high churchman who might not have tolerated such an arrangement in Woking could allow it for South India, so despite earlier protests from the highest of Anglo-Catholics, including the heads of the religious orders, in July 1955 a relationship of 'growing intercommunion' was agreed upon by the Convocations. The agreement did not include permission for the non-episcopally ordained to celebrate at Anglican altars. That remained, as ever, the sticking point. Archbishop Fisher had opened the Convocation of Canterbury with a speech in which he saw fit to divert attention by denouncing the Roman Catholic Church as 'perhaps the greatest hindrance to the advance of the Kingdom of God among men' on account of its practice of 'ecclesiastical apartheid'. Rome forbade intercommunion; Protestants should rightly practise it: such seemed to be the moral. It is memorable as being the last great denunciation of Rome to come from Canterbury. It was followed by the submission to Rome of a small number (about twenty-five) of protesting Anglo-Catholic clergy belonging to the 'Annunciation Group', led by Hugh Ross Williamson and Walton Hannah.

The moral of the story was probably a simple one, though it was hardly recognized at the time by either side. If a fairly limited recognition of a small Church away in South India could cause such a storm in the Church of England, then it was because Anglo-Catholics were now far too central a force in the Church to be overridden in their susceptibilities to any great degree. The Church of England weathered the storm by sticking pretty closely to its tradition of episcopal ordination, rather than by being ecumenically innovative. Yet if Anglo-Catholics were thus obtaining an ecumenical veto in one direction, Anglican Protestants would have it no less in another and the weight of both would be conservative. The significance of this for ecumenical prospects was not exactly encouraging.

In 1957 an agreement was actually arrived at between representatives of the Church of England, the Church of Scotland, the Episcopal Church in Scotland and the Presbyterian Church in England, much on Fisher's proposed lines. It was denounced as 'The Bishops' Report'. Bishops, consecrated by Anglicans, were to be appointed as permanent moderators of presbyteries in England and Scotland. This proposal was violently attacked by the secular press in Scotland and later described as a piece of 'coarse Anglican imperialism of the ecumenical era'[60] by an irate opponent. It was emphatically rejected by the Church of Scotland's General Assembly and nothing came of it. In short, ecumenism might be 'the great new fact of our era', as Temple had called it, but its course was clearly not destined to run smooth.

British churchmen continued to take their part in the international ecumenical movement. Archbishop Fisher was in the chair at Amsterdam in August 1948 at the moment when the World Council was formally inaugurated. Bishop Bell was immediately elected to the council's most important office other than that of General Secretary: chairman of its Central Committee. In consequence the World Council's first Central Committee meeting was held in Chichester. Bell remained chairman until the WCC's second conference at Evanston in 1954. His influence was without doubt of immense importance for its development in these formative years, but it was not a work greatly regarded in England. Bell was followed in the international field by younger men like Ernest Payne,[61] Oliver Tomkins and Norman Goodall.[62] As secretary of the International Missionary Council Goodall, a Congregationalist, carried on the almost apostolic succession of Oldham and Paton through a period of enormous importance in the evolution of the direction and structures of world mission. In due course he saw the IMC merged with the World Council (at the New Delhi Conference of 1961) and became himself Assistant General Secretary of the council. Payne and Tomkins, on the other hand, were both extremely influential in the Faith and Order side of the World Council, particularly at the Lund Conference in August 1952. Here Payne chaired the section which really wrestled – perhaps for the first time – with what had now become a true 'thorn in the flesh' for the ecumenical movement – intercommunion.[63] From now on the question – to intercommunicate or not to intercommunicate – would hang incessantly over every aspect of ecumenical contact, often quite agonizingly. Lund was probably the only really significant Faith and Order Conference since Edinburgh in 1937 and the contribution of British churchmen – Tomkins, Payne, Newton Flew and Thomas Torrance – was immense.

Such roles were certainly crucial in the church history of the period, but they were international roles which seemed at the time to affect England rather little. The leading ecumenical figure in England after 1954 was Payne. Chosen as General Secretary of the Baptist Union in 1951, he became vice-chairman of the World Council's Central Committee at Evanston. He retained both offices until the late 1960s and presided over the World Council's General Assembly at Uppsala. A historian of sound judgment and quiet manner, he fulfilled these duties with admirable discretion despite some disquiet on the part of his Baptist constituency – perhaps more abroad than at home – at so ecumenical a commitment. Payne was a true successor to J. H. Shakespeare, Baptist General Secretary forty years earlier and the most committed ecumenist of his time, but he was no obvious successor to

Bell or Temple and the fact that he was called to play such a role suggests something about the absence in these years of any great interest in the ecumenical cause at the higher levels of Anglican leadership.

After the defeat of 'The Bishops' Report' and the emphatic affirmation of the value and institutional future of the Anglican communion by the Lambeth Conference of 1958, it might seem on the surface as if the ecumenical cause in Britain was not much further advanced in 1958 than in 1938. It remained, one clear-eyed observer complained, an only 'semi-ecumenical age',[64] and fairly content to be such. Perhaps this would be a not too unfair judgment at the level of Church leadership. The British Council of Churches could be praised precisely for its 'reticence' and 'sobriety',[65] not words which suggest a very dynamic or novel function, yet its very existence and that of the World Council too had done much to develop the framework of a permanent ecumenical community which was increasingly claiming the primary loyalty of a determined minority. Intercommunion was becoming something more and more hard to resist either in theory or in practice. The fact that former Anglicans and former Methodists were now in full communion within the Church of South India and also in 'growing intercommunion' with the Church of England as well as with the Methodist Church in Britain inevitably affected the relationship between the latter. On 5 July 1956 a hundred and fifty Methodist ministers and laity shared in communion at St George's Anglican church in Leeds, celebrated according to the rite of South India: by no means a usual event for the fifties, but very much a portent for the future. The number of local Councils of Churches was steadily, if slowly, multiplying. The sense of a single Christian community was advancing perceptibly. It is very much present in the joint Report, *Church Relations in England*, of 1950. It could perhaps be felt most warmly and least self-consciously in the scholarly world when gathered for a patristic or biblical conference. Here it was increasingly drawing in even Roman Catholics. This was notice-able, especially, at the Oxford Conference on the Four Gospels in 1957 at which Archbishops Ramsey and Heenan, both newly appointed (to York and Liverpool), appeared very cheerfully together. In Church relationships, as in other areas of life, a continuing – or even reinforced – rigidity in the public form of the institution only partially hid from view a great transformation of consciousness which was proceeding almost irreversibly beneath the surface.

Roman Catholicism[1]

The Roman Catholic Church in England remained a law unto itself. While throughout the first half of the century all other major churches had declined and were feeling only too painfully the effects of decline, the Catholic Church had grown almost continuously, especially since the late 1920s, and now, in the post-war period, it had never had it so good. It had not lost the ascendancy in its old strongholds of the industrial north but it was spreading continually in the smaller towns and suburbs of the south. It could still claim, as did Hinsley in 1942, to come 'mostly from the workers and from the poorer sections of the community',[2] but it was rapidly developing a sizeable middle class, far more smoothly integrated within the mainstream of English social consciousness than had been the upper-class converts and Irish ghettoes of previous generations. In 1911 58.4 per cent of the Catholic population of England and Wales lived in the ecclesiastical province of Liverpool and only 26.2 per cent within the dioceses of Westminster and Southwark. By 1951 Liverpool's proportion was down to 37.8 per cent, that of Westminster and Southwark up to 52 per cent.[3] The steady growth in the number of priests, churches, Catholic schools, convents, the flow of distinguished converts, the nation's increasingly tolerant acceptance of a large Catholic presence and of Catholic educational claims, combined to give Catholicism a very great confidence, a sense of having the ball at its feet, of being irresistibly set upon the upward path.

The immediate post-war years provided considerable further accessions of strength. The first was the very large number of eastern European Catholics, Poles and Ukrainians especially, who remained in Britain as a result of the post-war settlement of their countries. In 1950 there were ninety-two Polish priests caring for some hundred thousand Polish Catholics in Britain. While the older refugees mostly remained in purely Polish congregations, the younger ones and still more their children were integrated to a very large extent with the Catholic community of Britain. To this was added a large new wave of Irish immigration, but one spread across the country far more than its nineteenth-century predecessors. With the people came more priests: many an English parish of the 1950s was staffed with Irish clergy, secular or regular, just as local Irish papers were sold at the doors of its church, and Irish nuns taught in its schools.

To these in-flows should be added that of many religious orders. The British Empire might be crumbling but it had not gone yet and international missionary societies, themselves at a high peak of resolve and recruitment, recognized the need for missionaries to have a mastery of the English language and of British educational methods in a way that they had previously largely spurned. Thus the White Fathers had had houses in Britain before the war but they had made a rather limited impact. By 1946 they had four: a parish and a provincialate at Heston, west London; two minor seminaries, one at St Boswells on the Scottish border, the other at Bishop's Waltham in Hampshire (their first British house, opened in the 1920s), and a small centre for propaganda and recruitment at Sutton Coldfield in Birmingham. By 1949 this had doubled. They had taken over three large country houses – Monteviot in Scotland, Claughton Hall in Lancashire, and Broome Hall in Surrey – and had opened a students' hostel at the University of St Andrews. These houses were staffed by forty priests as against nineteen three years earlier. To all this they were about to add a ninth residence, a new provincialate at Palace Court in central London. While the primary task of these men was that of missionary recruitment and training, they were also very much available for local pastoral work at weekends. A varied international body including highly experienced French and Dutch missionaries from central Africa, the White Fathers were by the 1950s making a considerable impression on English life both locally and nationally. And this is just one of a number of possible examples. The Catholic missionary world of Britain became indeed quite bewilderingly complex. While hitherto most male British missionaries had been Jesuits or Millhillers, and they were not all in all so numerous, now White Fathers, Holy Ghost Fathers, the Divine Word, Verona, Consolata, and several other congregations were all vigorously competing for vocations. The orders of nuns were still more numerous. The archdiocese of Westminster alone had more than a hundred (at least twenty of whom were primarily concerned with recruiting vocations for missions overseas).

'Rome is building new churches all over Britain and as fast as those churches are built, they are filled . . . even if they celebrate a dozen masses a day.' Doubtless that was an exaggeration, but it remains the impression one intelligent outside observer obtained in the 1950s.[4] Priests were up, conversions were up, marriages were up. By 1961 12.7 per cent of all marriages in England and Wales were in a Catholic Church (in fact the highest figures ever reached) and 9.7 per cent of all people marrying were Roman Catholics marrying in Catholic churches. This meant that 10 per cent of the nation could now be seen as practising Catholic.[5] In 1962 of every thousand marriages in England and Wales 474 were Anglican, 123 Roman Catholic and 102 Nonconformist. Comparison with the 1920s is striking. Then there were ten Anglican weddings and two Nonconformist for one Catholic. Forty years later there were only four Anglican for one Catholic, while Nonconformist weddings were actually less numerous than Catholic ones. This was no sudden change; it had been a steady process continuing all through the 1930s, 1940s and 1950s.

The social impact of Catholicism remained very different between south and north. Some evidence in the Paul Report provides a general impression for the end of the 1950s: in a Kent housing estate Catholic households were only 4.3 per cent as against 8 per cent of Methodists; at Sedgley, Dudley, in Worcestershire 6.3 per cent against 14.9 per cent Methodists, and doubtless there were many more rural places where the Catholic proportion was still smaller. In south Norfolk 2,500 people would attend a Methodist chapel at a major festival, 600 a Catholic church.[6] In such places Catholics remained a relatively insignificant section of the population. But at the other extreme, in the industrial north – Teesside, Merseyside, Tyneside, Leeds –

they constituted about 20 per cent of all households and they were the only ones where religious practice really held up at all. This survived the removal of slum conditions. In Kirkby, a new town fed by Liverpool slum dwellers of the 1930s, half the entire population was Catholic.[7] A survey of church attendance in four Liverpool wards in the early 1960s (South Scotland, Abercromby, Childwall and Speke) gave Catholics 81.6 per cent; Anglicans 10.8 per cent; Nonconformists 4.2 per cent.[8] Doubtless Liverpool was to some extent a special case, even for the industrial north; but not entirely so. The Tyneside pattern was not strikingly different. The strength of Catholicism by the 1950s was that it had achieved a genuinely national spread, had established a strong institutional presence in London, Oxford, Cambridge and the principal cities of the south, but had done this without losing its grip on its old provincial strongholds of the north. It was just this that, a generation or two earlier, Nonconformity had – with the exception of Wales – failed to do.

Politically, Catholics maintained almost as low a profile as in previous decades. At this level there was nothing even slightly aggressive about their new strength. Catholic MPs remained collectively insignificant – fifteen for England in 1949, twenty-four by the early 1960s. They were fairly evenly divided between Labour and Conservative. D. G. Logan, a founder member of the Knights of St Columba, represented the Scotland division of Liverpool from 1929 to 1964, as T. P. O'Connor had represented it from 1885 to 1929. Men like Dick Stokes and Bob Mellish on the Labour side, Christopher Hollis and Hugh Fraser on the Conservative, were intelligent, respected people but there was no one at all near the front rank of politics. As a whole Catholics welcomed the welfare state in practice while maintaining, many of them, reservations in theory because of its failure to apply their cherished social principle of subsidiarity.[9] They appreciated 'Christian Democracy' abroad[10] but had no desire to try anything similar at home; they were active in the trade unions, especially if they detected a Communist hand at work; they busied themselves building schools and paying for them by Bingo, or what have you; they still had rather large families and they were still more or less united in rejecting contraception and cultivating the Safe Period. Their social mobility was steadily upwards, the number of Catholic students at the university was increasing by leaps and bounds,[11] but there was little sign of this upsetting either their ecclesiastical loyalty or their basic relationship to society of a certain privileged ineligibility for most of its top roles.[12]

If Catholicism made any memorable impact upon English society in these years, it was only in the literary field. Not that the main body of the Church or its clergy could possibly be influential in such an area, but Graham Greene and Evelyn Waugh were now accepted as probably the nation's leading novelists and, for both of them, what Greene called 'the big Catholic verities'[13] entered, if in rather different ways, into the central themes of their work. Their books were for a while flanked and paralleled by some remarkable French religious films starring Pierre Frenay. *Monsieur Vincent, Le Défroqué, Dieu a besoin des hommes*, were artistic and spiritual achievements which could somehow be linked affinitively with *The Power and the Glory*, or *The Heart of the Matter*, as convincingly portraying religious and moral issues seen within an essentially Catholic context to a world far beyond that of the Church. Catholics themselves tended to look askance at much of this, preferring the less ambiguous, more indubitably orthodox ground of Bruce Marshall's *All Glorious Within*, the buffoonery of Don Camillo, or – in the film world – productions of those Catholic Hollywood stars, Bing Crosby and Grace Kelly. *The Bells of St Mary's*, with Crosby a curate and Bergman a nun and nothing amiss between them, satisfied the Catholic mood a good deal better than Greene or Frenay but it could hardly challenge the verdict of 'intellectual emptiness' passed by the hostile on contemporary Catholicism.[14] Nor perhaps could that verdict be called in question by what, strangely enough, proved the most popular of all Catholic works of the period, *Brideshead Revisited*. Published in 1945, it was Waugh's most flamboyant trumpet-blast against the times, written in a 'rhetorical and ornamental language' which its author was later to find somewhat distasteful. It is the most deliberately and overtly religious of all his novels, an account of the ways of divine grace in the contemporary world. Of most set intent, those ways are depicted as not our ways. The Flytes are not attractive people. However Catholic they may be, that does not make them less 'flawed' as a family. Whether bigoted, drunkard, or just a rather silly girl like Julia, they are neither effective nor lovable, and their religion on the face of things has made them actually worse. Yet grace saves them all, not out of their drunkenness, bigotry or boredom, but within it. The religion extolled here is intensely supernaturalist, concerned far more with how people die than with how they live. It is as far as possible from the Christianity of Temple or Bell. An unbridled nostalgia, both for the aristocratic past and the supposedly golden 1920s, confuses the message but gives the book much of its appeal. Waugh's Catholic world is one of decaying aristocracy. *Brideshead* has probably owed its popularity far more to the theme of noble decay than to that of supernatural victory, but together they combined to give a hopelessly false impression of English Catholicism, an absurd caricature, encouraged a little by Farm Street may be, but ringing no bells at all for the vast majority of English Catholics.

Ten years later Waugh produced in his *Sword of Honour* trilogy what may well be the finest fictional portrayal of the Second World War.[15] Flamboyance has given way to a more restrained and humorous sense of the working of grace in nature. Where *Brideshead* portrayed a bewitching but incomprehensible otherness, the *Sword of Honour* suggests rather that the Catholic is just the best sort of unassuming Englishman and with that, on the whole, the 1950s were not too disposed to disagree.

The English Catholicism of the 1950s was not then politically or intellectually very influential, and its significance could well be missed by any historian of the period. Nothing, after all, could be much duller than its cardinal leaders – Griffin up to 1956 and then Godfrey. Griffin was the least important archbishop of Westminster of the century, a nice, hard-working nonentity. He was also for much of the time a very sick man. Godfrey was the dominant Catholic ecclesiastic all through these years and no one was more sure of his own mind or had less to offer that was unexpected. He had been Rector of the English College in Rome until becoming first Apostolic Delegate in 1938. From then on his was the deciding influence upon ecclesiastical policy until his death in 1963. A Lancashire man, trained in Rome and one hundred per cent reliable in Roman eyes, as Hinsley had proved not to be, Godfrey had transformed the English hierarchy into a Roman clique by the steady appointment of a single sort of bishop – secular priests trained at the *Venerabile* under Hinsley and himself. Up to the 1930s only a handful of English bishops had been old boys of the *Venerabile*, and those not the most important. The English hierarchy became more homogeneous than it had ever been: Griffin, Masterson, Heenan, Grimshaw and Dwyer – five archbishops appointed in the forties and fifties in Godfrey's wake were all from this one stable, as were Rudderham of Clifton, Resteaux of Plymouth, Ellis of Nottingham, Holland of Salford. The *Venerabile* spirit was that of a clerical élite, isolated by seven long years in Rome with little personal contact permitted outside the circle of fifty fellow students. It was a regime of strict rules punctuated by Christmas theatricals and long summers playing cricket. It cultivated a polite disdain alike for Anglicans and for continental theology. Rome was adored but Italian was seldom learnt. Insularity was as important as ultramontanism.

From the Second World War until the Second Vatican Council the Church in England was entirely controlled by priests of this particular formation while those of other traditions, both secular and religious, felt themselves excluded from the centre of power and indeed just slightly under suspicion as being not quite the real thing. Almost the only non-*Venerabile* bishop of any weight in these years was George Andrew Beck, an Assumptionist and former headmaster of a school in Hitchin, who was brought into the hierarchy to cope with its educational headaches but in due course became a mildly broadening influence in other areas as well.

Godfrey's years at Westminster were christened by its clergy somewhat irreverently 'the safe period'. When he died it was remarked in *The Times* obituary that it could undoubtedly be said of the cardinal that he had never made an imprudent remark. His leadership was hardly such as to grasp imaginatively the undoubted opportunities with which the Catholic Church in England was now confronted. If, nevertheless, to some extent she did so all the same, it was due to a much younger and more

479

vigorously apostolic member of the *Venerabile* group, John Carmel Heenan. 'There is a priest in whom I have perfect trust, and whom I recommend to you – Rev. John Heenan', Cardinal Hinsley had written to Christopher Dawson. A zealous young pastor in London's East End who had just published a not terribly good book about Hinsley his hero, Heenan was chosen in 1947 as Superior of a revived Catholic Missionary Society (CMS), a special team of secular priests entrusted with the task of gingering up Catholicism in England. The team he picked included friends from student days in Rome like George Dwyer and Thomas Holland.[16] From this time on Heenan became a national figure, leader of the Church's pastoral renewal. At one with Godfrey in ecclesiology and loyalties, he brought to the job a vigour, an imaginative practical judgment, and a personal warmth, all of which Godfrey quite lacked. There can be no question that Heenan was the outstanding Catholic ecclesiastic of his generation. A working-class Londoner of Irish background, loyally English in general but lacking any attachment to English particularities, an ultramontane to the core, extremely intelligent but almost contemptuous of priest intellectuals, a man who once told Malcolm Muggeridge that he had 'never had a serious doubt in his life', Heenan seemed to epitomize the self-confident new Catholicism of the post-war period, a Catholicism which yielded intellectually not an inch but which appeared quite at home and seldom out-marshalled in the debating halls and on the television screens of the 1950s.

'Bring back the Mass to every village in this isle' – such was the programme of Heenan's CMS. The Church of England was not so much attacked as ignored as a well-meaning old dodderer. The immediate strategy was less one of conversions than of reactivating the great pool of 'lapsed Catholics' through missions in every parish. The National Mission, organized by the CMS throughout the country in 1949 and 1950, began a year after the great cross-carrying pilgrimage to Walsingham in the summer of 1948. Fourteen different parties of twenty to thirty men had carried crosses for fourteen days from every part of the country, as through almost all its towns, to converge on Walsingham. 1950 was dominated by the celebrations of the Holy Year – and no Holy Year has ever taken so many British Catholics to Rome.

1950 was as well the centenary of the restoration of the hierarchy in England, marked by a great gathering at Wembley Stadium – the largest rally English Catholics had ever produced. 1951 was the year of the First International Congress of the Lay Apostolate in Rome. It was also the year Heenan was appointed Bishop of Leeds and consecrated with great publicity. These events were the high points publicly expressing the pastoral and spiritual self-confidence, even controlled excitement, of a Church come of age and not unwilling to flex its muscles.

It shared in the fighting confidence of international Catholicism in these middle years of Pius XII. Much later a rather sad Frank Sheed could look back nostalgically upon 'the high euphoria of Pius XII's reign'.[17] To people of a later generation that may sound strange, but it was how it seemed at the time and Sheed himself was no starry-eyed romantic but a very keen and well-informed observer of the contemporary scene. Pius XII combined a quality of spiritual remoteness, unyielding ecclesiastical claims and increasingly centralized administration, with a great deal of effective reform and moderately new theology. In biblical scholarship he permitted a freedom unthinkable to Pius X whom at the same time he canonized. In liturgical reform the permission for evening mass, the reduction of the eucharistic fast and the transformation of the ceremonies of Holy Week were of enormous practical value for ordinary Church life. The encyclicals *Divino Afflante Spiritu* (1943) on the interpretation of Scripture, and *Mediator Dei* (1947) upon the liturgy, were destined to be foundation documents for the Second Vatican Council of twenty years later. The appointment of the first black bishops in Africa and the establishment of a non-Italian majority in the College of Cardinals contributed to a new sense of realized catholicity.

In England Godfrey might steer the ship drearily enough from the bridge but the real pace was made by the likes of Heenan and Sheed participating in a far wider movement of Catholic enthusiasm. In generating that enthusiasm no book was more important than Thomas Merton's autobiography, *The Seven Storey Mountain*, published in the United States in 1948 and in Britain the following year under the title of *Elected Silence*.[18] It proved by far the most exciting and influential religious autobiography of its generation, perhaps of this century. It was the story of a mixed-up young Anglo-American intellectual trendy who passed from being a rake in Cambridge (England) to conversion to Catholicism in New York in 1938 and, in due course, to a Trappist monastery. Merton's pilgrimage and his way of telling it harmonized strikingly with the religious mood of the immediate post-war years and helped to fuel a quite extensive movement both in America and in Europe back to the contemplative life. Its message was both fundamentalistic and romantic. The rejection of a self-indulgent, self-deceiving world was the backdrop for a straight re-presentation of the medieval monastic call and the holiness almost inevitably to be acquired thereby.[19] It expressed, for many almost irresistibly, the dominant Catholic spiritual mood of the moment: supernaturalist, uncompromising and neo-traditionalist.

Catholic religious enthusiasm could, of course, take other less world-renouncing forms. The cross-carrying pilgrimages to Walsingham were part of an intense and often extravagant Marian devotion which owed much to a whole wave of little books about Our Lady's appearance at Fatima in Portugal in 1917, but also to the spread of the Dublin-based Legion of Mary and to the American Fr Peyton's world-wide Rosary Crusade. The definition of the Assumption in 1950 was the great moment here. The Marian movement might be devotionally other-worldly but both in the work of the Legion and in much of the Fatima literature it was very closely linked with social work and even political action of an anti-Communist type.

This takes us to a third dimension of enthusiasm – the great post-war expansion of Catholic Action, particularly of Mgr Cardijn's Young Christian Workers and Young Christian Students. The new Christian Democratic Europe was its ideal operating ground but the movements flourished in Britain too, as in Australia and almost every part of the Catholic world. Pat Keegan, a tough young man from Wigan, who led the British delegation to the Lay Apostolate Congress of 1951, was soon to become the YCW's World President.

Monks, Marian devotions and the YCW overlapped quite naturally; they shared, far more than might be imagined, a common theology and view of life, but above all the deepest loyalty to the contemporary papacy. The supremacy of the pope, both in theory and in practice, was never less questioned. The almost mystical aura surrounding the figure of Pius XII in post-war years had much to do with this; it was buoyed up by a sense of martial unity: we were all now in the front line in the struggle with Communism. In eastern Europe even cardinals were in prison. It was part of the message of Mary to the three small children at Fatima that if Catholics prayed hard enough, and especially said the family rosary, Russia would be converted. 1950 was a high point in the cold war. It was also the Holy Year and probably the highest point, at least in the twentieth century, in ultramontane fervour. The definition of the Assumption might alarm non-Catholics but it seemed obviously right to the great majority of Catholics: a flag of triumphant defiance flung forth against the worlds of Stalinist tyranny, liberal Protestantism and agnostic materialism. Catholics knew where they stood and were not disposed to be ashamed.

Two books, very influential at the time, represent the mildly progressive centre of post-war English Catholicism: Frank Sheed's *Theology and Sanity* (1947), and Clifford Howell's *The Work of Our Redemption* (1953). Frank Sheed and his wife, Maisie Ward, had a long innings – from the 1920s to the 1970s – but it was now that they seemed most at home, at the peak of their influence and their rapport with the Church. In pre-war days they had, following in Belloc's steps, leant politically rather to the right. Now, deeply reinvigorated by contact with French worker priests they leant, Maisie in particular, just a little to the left. Sheed, however, was essentially apolitical in his preoccupation with the clear and compelling presentation of theological orthodoxy. In this, as in much else, he was not unlike C. S. Lewis. It was an age in which the orthodox prided themselves on reason not enthusiasm, an age of Thomism when scholastic disputations could be heard even on the radio. Sheed's *Theology and Sanity* represents Catholic doctrine at its clearest, most rational, most convincing, with clerical preoccupations reduced to a minimum – a layman writing for laymen. Yet it remains the most straight contemporary orthodoxy, with hardly a hint of history in it, not a suggestion that anything might be wrong, missed out or one-sided in the current theology, canon law or institutional structures of the Church. The personal morals of popes or bishops might fail a thousand times but such failings only illustrate the overriding divine control of the Church. Sheed, like Keegan, was proof of the thesis that the clergy could trust the laity, that the lay apostolate could work to perfection in unsubservient but utterly loyal terms.

The Work of Our Redemption was important for rather different reasons. Clifford Howell was a Jesuit intensely committed to the liturgical movement and here was a book which really got through to people, appearing at just the moment when it was at last ceasing to be quite true that 'the liturgical revival is still mainly something of which we receive news from others'.[20] If Anglicans, Methodists and Baptists were all being strongly affected in the 1950s by the liturgical movement, Roman Catholics too (from whom on the Continent it all began) were no longer being quite passed by. At least the 'Dialogue Mass', in which the congregation could join in saying prayers like the Creed and Gloria hitherto confined (apart from singing) to priest or server, was becoming a regular occurrence in more lively parishes. Rome itself was revising the liturgy. Evening mass was now allowed. The changes in the Holy Week services approved in the early 1950s signalled a major breakthrough at official level of the case for reform in order to make the liturgy more intelligible and more popular. What had been happening in the Church of England for twenty years, partly under continental Catholic influence, was working its way into English Catholicism too and the mass in particular was now being taught to be – to the shocked surprise of many – not just a sacrifice but also very much a meal. Such was Clifford Howell's message.

Renewal was then at work despite, and indeed within, the cautious, often almost ostentatiously backward-looking note of Restoration and neo-medievalism which so often dominated these years. The Carmelite 'return' to the pre-Reformation priory of Aylesford in Kent, like the Benedictine return to the ruins of Pluscarden Abbey in Scotland and the serious suggestion that even the ruins of Fountains should be re-colonized, expresses this mood exactly. Religious habits were to be seen on the streets, particularly on occasions such as the Walsingham pilgrimage, something which had been studiously avoided prior to the war.

There was a widespread revival not only of Thomism but of recusant studies, and books like the autobiography of John Gerard, the Elizabethan Jesuit, could be best sellers. The note of pervasive traditionalism can be detected well enough even in *Blackfriars*, surely one of the most consciously progressive of reviews, which yet appeared with a staid black and white cover embodying a coat of arms and a motto, quite incredibly different in tone from the flashy *New Blackfriars* of ten years later.

Yet there was often newness peeping up under the oldness. In December 1948 Group Captain Cheshire was received into the Catholic Church after reading Vernon Johnson's *One Lord, One Faith*. His decision to establish a Home for the chronic sick and give his life to their care was virtually a simultaneous one. It was to be at Le Court, a Victorian mansion in Hampshire, and his Anglican neighbour, Lord Selborne, arranged a gift of beds and equipment from the Church Army. By the mid-1950s there were half a dozen further Cheshire Homes, following on St Teresa's in Cornwall, and yet another new development in charity had taken institutional form. If it flowed out of Cheshire's intensely Catholic convictions – a devotion to St Teresa of Lisieux, the Benedictines of Solesmes and the Holy Shroud of Turin were now the staples of his personal piety – it was nevertheless in no way confined to a Catholic milieu. It was not only lay but ecumenical in scope and support: a good instance of the way old pieties and new – but admittedly unradical – practices could coalesce unaffectedly in these years.[21]

The exciting and really formative conference centre of Spode House in Staffordshire was opened in 1953 where its inspirer, the Dominican Conrad Pepler, managed to combine deep spirituality, intellectual freedom and a wonderfully informal domesticity.[22] Here as in Catholic People's Weeks and Downside Symposium conferences and even the pages of Michael de la Bedoyere's *Catholic Herald*, a new world was a little guardedly emerging, conscious of high-powered continental theological allies but conscious too of much official disapproval. Archbishop Roberts returned in 1950 from Bombay, where he had been its last white archbishop, to become an asker of awkward questions and a thorn in the side of the English hierarchy. He was one they could hardly get rid of – a Jesuit archbishop of good character cannot easily be silenced. His *Black Popes* was published in 1954. The *Downside Review*, edited by Sebastian Moore with Christopher Butler behind him as abbot, was in its most distinguished and innovative period, the principal theological channel for the diffusion in Britain of 'the new theology'. However worried Rome might be, Congar, de Lubac, Danielou, Rahner, Bouyer, von Balthasar, were in their greatest, most scholarly and creative period. Congar might be 'exiled' by Roman authority to the safe atmosphere of England. De Lubac's *Surnaturel* or Congar's *Vraie et fausse réforme dans l'Eglise* might be on order withdrawn from circulation. Their ideas could not thus be crushed. Scripture and Patristics were challenging the central place of neo-scholasticism in Catholic theology. At Hawksyard a young Dominican, Cornelius Ernst, was beginning the translation of Rahner's *Theological Investigations* into English. Here as at Blackfriars, Downside and Heythrop, the theological revolution was already under way, but the circle of influence was decidedly limited, the fear of provoking the full scale repression of a new wave of official anti-modernism (already begun by the encyclical *Humani Generis* in 1950) very real. In general the 'New Theology' was suspect and unread. Waugh had heard enough in 1956 to write to Penelope Betjeman about the 'dreadful influence of French Dominicans'.[23]

English Catholic intellectual life was, then, by no means non-existent in the 1950s but its more distinguished components remained, as had long been the case, emphatically non-theological. Fr Copleston's magisterial *History of Philosophy* was, without doubt, one of the great scholarly achievements of the age; with it may be compared the volumes of David Knowles, *The Monastic Order in England*, and *The Religious Orders in England*. Victor White's relating of Jungian psychology with Thomist theology gave inspiration to many, and the list of particular contributions to religious scholarship could be extended. Nevertheless, it is hard to disagree with Abbot Butler's general judgment on the state of Catholic studies at the close of this period:

> What contribution is English Catholicism making, what contribution has it made in our century to the general progress of [biblical] studies? The answer must be: practically none. . . . It

> would be pleasant if we could contrast with our poverty in the
> field of Scripture a large and challenging output in that of
> dogmatic theology. But it is not so. ... Why are we so
> poverty-stricken?'[24]

Outside the very limited circles of a few houses of the older
orders, the English clergy in the age of Godfrey remained complacently and determinedly uninterested in responding to that
question. Why, after all, should they worry? The converts,
including some of great distinction, continued to come in; the
statistics steadily improved. More learned Churches were, on the
contrary, in some disarray. Professor Trevor-Roper might deride
'the intellectual emptiness of modern English Catholicism' but
did a Church whose members could produce *The Anathemata*;
The Lord of the Rings; *God and the Unconscious*; *Helena*;
Enthusiasm, as well as Copleston's *History*, need to worry
about such jibes? It could hold philosophers as distinguished as
Elizabeth Anscombe, gain convert clergy as learned as Canon
Edward Rich,[25] scholars as outstanding as Professor Evans-
Pritchard, poets like Siegfried Sassoon and Edith Sitwell. A
handful of avant-garde clerics might chafe at the seemingly
unyielding intellectual structure of Roman Catholicism which
continued to make theological scholarship so difficult, but it was
just this that many of the converts were looking for – 'Inflexible
authority' (the words are Sassoon's), to which to submit; 'Influence, relief, resultancy from Rome'.[26] Yet it is true that many
of these figures were elderly and near the close of active work if
not of life. If brilliance there was, it was largely the mellow
autumnal maturity of a generation formed well before the Second
World War.

The English Catholic paradox of robust clerical sterility combined with a just slightly precious lay creativity was, after all, no
new one. Was it such a bad thing? Harman Grisewood, director
of the Spoken Word at the BBC, like many another thoughtful
layman, did not find the apparent duality uncongenial. Rather
did the 'exclusivism' of the 'official order' with its 'authoritarianism', 'inflexibility' and 'infallibility' provide the framework for
an experience characterized, he felt, by 'inclusiveness. The
Catholic temper is not prone to exclusivity in the fact-world of
truth and goodness and beauty. She disposes men to an enlarge-

ment of the understanding, not to a narrowing.'[27] Of course, for strong protagonists of the official order, a wider Catholic inclusiveness was not so much virtue as insidious vice. The year Grisewood's piece was published, 1954, Catholics were forbidden to sit on the Council of Christians and Jews, a body set up in the more generous mood of 1942. 'I am afraid catholicism is the enemy of Catholicism,' Evelyn Waugh had written to Lord David Cecil in 1949.[28] Catholicism with a small c and Catholicism with a large C, inclusivism and exclusivism, were demonstrated excellently well in a lengthy correspondence published in *The Times* that November and later republished as a pamphlet.[29]

It began with a lengthy special article[30] on 31 October, which reviewed the state of Roman Catholicism, admired its spiritual power, the 'liberal Thomism of M. Maritain', and the sturdiness of its resistance to Communism, but regretted its administrative and intellectual rigidity and the lack of willingness to co-operate with other Christians, especially manifest, it claimed, in Anglo-Saxon countries. It pleaded that Rome should be prepared 'to discuss ways and means with heretics and schismatics' in order 'to bring into being a revivified Christendom'. What was perhaps most noticeable in the inevitably varied response that followed this appeal was the warmth of many of the Catholic comments – coming admittedly from the sort of liberal and clerical élite which had backed the Sword ten years earlier.[31] Two Anglican writers remarked how 'many Roman Catholics, as your columns have shown, are free of the ultramontane temper, even though they are tied to the Ultramontane doctrines'. Not many Catholics would have gone along with that formulation of their predicament, but the contrast between two tempers is quite clear. Dom Columba Cary-Elwes of Ampleforth was the clearest spokesman of the one in urging 'that the time had indeed come for a *rapprochement*' with 'meetings between representative Roman Catholics and Anglo Catholics' to plan 'the great return, not by way of bargaining but by that of understanding'. Just a day before Dom Columba's letter Bishop Beck had joined in the correspondence, the only Roman Catholic bishop to do so. He wished to explain why it was that Roman Catholics could not rightly even say the Lord's Prayer with other Christians:

United prayer, if it is to mean anything at all, must be an expression of united minds. But a Catholic and a non-Catholic saying the Lord's Prayer could not have united minds or mean the same thing. The Catholic saying for example, 'Thy Kingdom come', would be praying for the conversion of all men to Catholicism; the non-Catholic evidently would not subscribe to this petition. . . . To look for 'reunion' in religion except on the conditions explained by Pope Pius XI in the encyclical *Mortalium Animos*, is to look for a will-o'-the wisp.

In the letters of the Benedictine monk and the bishop of Brentwood were disclosed rather unambiguously the two minds of Catholicism – the inclusivist and the exclusivist. For the time being, while there were in fact a number of unpublicized meetings between Catholic and Anglican theologians of the sort Dom Columba was asking for,[32] and the inclusivist approach was increasing its support, the exclusivist remained in very firm control.

Ten years later the position was not very different, though permission had now actually been accorded for the Lord's Prayer to be said on occasion with other Christians. But the official mood of the Church in England was little changed even if there were now odd rumblings from the Continent where John was Pope and an ecumenical council in preparation. In October 1960 the Beda College in Rome moved to spacious new buildings next to the Basilica of St Paul. Ever more numerous vocations were expected, new seminary buildings were rising everywhere. The Catholic Church was certainly in good heart, solidly expanding in its sound old ways. Mgr Charles Duchemin, who had long planned the move, had been Rector of the Beda since 1928. Educated at Downside and Trinity, Cambridge, Duchemin represented socially something very different from Godfrey or Heenan, but he was no less committed to *Romanitas*. A gentle, selfless, humorous priest of high intelligence but absolutely no interest in theology, he had presided for more than thirty years over the ecclesiastical formation of some of the ablest priests (as also many of the dullest) that the English Church was provided with. He saw to it that they said the rosary, memorized the standard textbooks and cultivated a devotion to Italian cultural trivia. It did not occur to him that much more might be required.

Around him the Catholic Church functioned and flourished as it had done, apparently almost unchanged, for many centuries. The Latin mass he celebrated daily had been altered only marginally since the Middle Ages. Day by day it was said alone with a single server by each of the Beda staff and student priests at side altars up and down the college. *Ratam, rationabilem, acceptabilem sacrificium*, measured, changeless words. The priest stood with his back to any congregation, maniple on left arm, and spoke in lowered voice. All seemed still as it had been when Henry VIII ascended the throne or when, in a seventeenth-century manor house, Catholics gathered behind barred doors to hear the mass of Gerard, Garnet or Henry Morse. Nuns still wore their antique habits, their strange distinctive head-veils. Minor seminaries were still filled with hundreds of small boys from working-class homes trained in their teens in Latin and celibacy. Benediction and rosary, the nine First Fridays, plenary indulgences and the special *toties quoties* indulgence for All Souls: the pattern of popular and even clerical piety remained utterly remote from that of most other Christians in Britain.[33] At the end of every Latin mass, kneeling at the foot of the altar, priests switched to English to pray for the conversion of Russia: three Hail Marys and an appeal addressed to St Michael. 'Do thou, Prince of the heavenly host, thrust down to Hell Satan and all wicked spirits who wander through the world for the ruin of souls'. The Catholic Church remained indeed a law unto itself.

32

Theology and Culture

'The teaching of traditional Christians,' wrote old Bishop Barnes in 1949, 'of course makes no appeal to men and women of modern education.'[1] The good bishop was thirty years out of date for it was noticeable in the post-war years what a considerable appeal very traditional forms of Christianity had for some of the best educated of modern people. The Christian intellectual revival, which had been proceeding steadily from the 1920s, had now reached its peak. Its range of competence had widened as had the professionalism with which it mastered the techniques of modern intellectual achievement. In the post-war years moreover it was batting on a favourable wicket. The non-religious orthodoxies of the inter-war years had been badly bruised by the experience of the war and disillusionment with Communist Russia. There was never a time since the middle of the nineteenth century when Christian faith was either taken so seriously by the generality of the more intelligent or could make such a good case for itself. If the 1920s saw a high tide in the advance of religionlessness among the intelligentsia, the 1950s may represent the furthest point in the swing of the pendulum in the contrary direction. The increasingly evident obsolescence of the mental structures of late Victorian agnosticism was now beginning to affect its credibility even within its most assured strongholds and the young were finding it both possible and creative to combine Christian faith of a fairly traditional kind with every aspect of modern scientific expertise.

'Science without religion is lame: religion without science is blind', declared Einstein. For several of the major contemporary intellectual figures, whose shadow fell across young minds in these years – Einstein, Jung, Toynbee, Wittgenstein – religion remained at the very least a serious contemporary reality. It was no more – as it had seemed for the comparable stars of an earlier generation – something to be dismissed as an anachronistic and temporary survival from primitive times, without any possible place in a modern synthesis.

In retrospect one may feel that the specifically theological side of this renaissance was its least important part. The Anglo-Catholic theological school, which had looked so promising earlier on and contained so many potentially brilliant figures, never quite fulfilled that promise. It produced some work of considerable learning, beauty and maturity.[2] It fortified and comforted the Church at the time but its impact on anyone outside clerical circles was decidedly limited. Its most brilliant figure, Austin Farrer, both philosopher and biblical scholar, was of absolutely outstanding quality; he was nevertheless a little too idiosyncratically enigmatic, too closely confined to Oxford's ways and idiom, to have a really national influence. There was no one quite comparable in weight with continental Catholics like Congar, de Lubac and Rahner, or continental Protestants like Cullmann. There was little genuinely theological wrestling with great contemporary issues – the bomb, the reunion of the churches, the philosophy of Wittgenstein. Theological 'conservatism' in the 1930s had had a radical if simplistic quality; twenty years later it had turned more mature but also somewhat complacent and unchallenging. 'The theological scene was calm to the point of being colourless', says Ulrich Simon of these years.[3] Oscar Cullmann, Barth's younger colleague in Basle, may provide better than anyone the 1950s theological note. He never quite achieved the status of Barth or Bultmann, lacking their systemic originality, but he was a good deal more sensible than either. A sensitive scholar, traditional without being reactionary, quietly irenic, Cullmann corresponded very well with the wider mood of the post-war decade. His books were much translated into English and helped engender a learned tranquillity, but even Barth himself appeared by the later 1950s 'spiritually in these latter days more obviously a kinsman of Canon Raven than of many traditionally minded evangelical Christians'.[4]

A young American studying at Oxford in the early 1950s later recounted his conversion and that of his wife to Christianity and the influences which produced it:

> We read G. K. Chesterton, who with wit presented in *The Everlasting Man* and other works a brilliant, reasoned case for the faith. And Charles Williams, theologian and novelist, who opened up realms of the spirit we didn't know existed, was tremendously important to us both. Graham Greene showed – terribly – what sin was, and what faith was – also terrible. Dorothy Sayers made Christianity dramatic and exciting. . . . We had read T. S. Eliot for years, but now we began to see what he was really saying in *Ash Wednesday* and the *Four Quartets*. . . . And we read the New Testament, of course, in numerous translations along with commentaries. But there is no doubt that C. S. Lewis was, first to last, overwhelmingly the most important reading for us both.[5]

For a great many people this was undoubtedly the case: it was Lewis whose influence was decisive for their return to Christianity, and the sort of Christianity they returned to.[6] No formal theologian or clerical writer was half as important, if we are concerned, not with a history of original theology, but one of religion, of widely shared conviction, of the movement of belief and religious behaviour. In the field of religion no other writer of the mid-century is comparable to Lewis. In the cycle of his writing the post-war years were not the age of the most striking apologetic; that had come earlier. It was the age rather of his fullest spiritual and literary maturity, of the Narnia stories, of the massive volume of historical scholarship, *English Literature in the Sixteenth Century* (1954), and particularly of that lovely, enigmatic meditation upon love and the forms of religion, *Till We Have Faces* (1956). But it was not these less obtrusive works which account for the quite immense influence which Lewis exercised upon the generation of the 1950s. The corpus of his works was now very considerable. It combined a rationally acute but uncompromising faith with scholarship, imaginative creativity and a natural social conservatism in a way very satisfying to many a young searcher after wisdom.

Lewis appealed both to the Catholic and the Evangelical while being identified properly as neither. It could seem unkind to lay stress on the Ulster Protestant background, which he so much disliked, and very wide of the mark to link him with the resurgence of conservative Evangelicalism. Yet Ulster has been one of the perennial breeding grounds of the latter and the more one scrutinizes Lewis, the more it appears that he never quite threw off the constraints of his origins. If the springs of his adult Christian reconversion were at once rather Catholic and rather English, they flowed along channels more firmly dug than Lewis himself may have realized. If one considers the main characteristics of his theological position – an unyielding, rather fundamentalist orthodoxy on the doctrines of God, Christ, angels and devils, redemption and sin; the literal accuracy of Scripture; a near-complete lack of interest in the doctrine of the Church and the ministry; an almost instinctive shying away from the sacraments and from Mary; sheer lack of interest in the social and political dimensions of the faith other than the simple duty to be honest, truthful and generous; a dislike of ritual: these constitute almost exactly the traditional theological package of the conservative Evangelical. It should not, then, be surprising that the latter has subsequently taken Lewis very much to heart with the organization of 'C. S. Lewis Weeks' and so forth.

It would, nevertheless, be absurd to categorize Lewis as essentially a conservative Evangelical in disguise. His case is far more complex than that. What made him such an immensely creative and influential figure was not the hard core of doctrinal orthodoxy which conservative Evangelicals and conservative Catholics largely share anyway but an imaginative genius which flowered out of a predominantly Catholic literary tradition and within a circle of Catholic friends (Roman and Anglican). There can be no doubt that across the years he was quietly moving spiritually in this direction, coming to appreciate more deeply the sacraments and mystical life – even if he found it difficult to write about them – and it is to the point that Austin Farrer, Warden of Keble and perhaps the nearest thing to a genius that Anglo-Catholicism produced in this generation, conducted his funeral. Yet it remains something of a paradox that, while a chief characteristic of the Christian revival of the mid-century was precisely the liturgical and sacramental movement, Lewis – the most powerful single voice in that revival – was almost void of interest in the liturgy and silent about the sacraments. It may well be that his most lasting literary achievement will prove to be the Narnia stories and the almost mystical *Till We Have Faces*: the work of his autumnal maturity. In the latter's Greek context and the mythical Narnia, Lewis seems best to escape the inhibiting consequences of doctrinal precision.

In popular terms the very limitations of Lewis may well have been sources of strength. His remoteness of sensibility from the frills of Anglo-Catholic clericalism and his deep dislike of the Ulster Protestant tradition alike contributed to his ability to be the ideal spokesman for 'Mere Christianity' to Protestant, Catholic and sceptic. No school or Church could be proprietorial about Lewis. In retrospect and for the age of more radical sentiment soon to come, Lewis's deepest limitation was probably his psychological anti-modernism. He was not only out of sympathy with liberal theological scholarship, socialistic tendencies and institutional ecumenicalism, he was consciously out of sympathy with the whole deeper trend of modern civilization. He refused to see himself as a modern man, and described himself as a 'Dinosaur'.[7] Yet that note of neo-traditionalism in so distinguished a scholar and lively an author added to, rather than detracted from, Lewis's appeal through the period we are considering.

The intellectual revival of Christianity did not, needless to say, eradicate the convinced secularism of a great part of the intelligentsia. On the contrary, the alternative tradition continued to flourish in the fifties. The heritage of Hume, Mill, Darwin and Hardy has after all long been an integral element of English conservatism almost as much as of English radicalism. It was certainly no less confident of itself in the post-war years than it had been earlier and it was, perhaps, less muffled: in the past the muffling had often been due to a strange anxiety not to unsettle the servants. Now the servants had departed, so the master's atheism need no longer be disguised. It could also appear freely on the BBC. Formerly there had been a policy of religious preference, established by Reith and enhanced during the war when the number of weekly religious broadcasts trebled. It was abandoned in 1947. From now on 'responsible' attacks on the Christian religion would be permitted and a few years later Mrs Knight's broadcasts on 'Morals without Religion' would produce something of a furore.[8] The novels of Anthony Powell's *Music and Time* series, or C. P. Snow's *Strangers and Brothers*, characterize the 1950s quite as much as those of Waugh or Greene. Both present the picture of a profoundly secular society in which, when religion appears at all, it is as something of a psychological kink. Snow's *The Masters* is based upon the Christ's College of Charles Raven, but whatever the religiosity of Raven it is excluded from the focus of Snow. The intellectual secularism of the 1950s as found in the fiction of Powell and Snow, the history of Hugh Trevor-Roper, A. J. P. Taylor and A. L. Rowse, the philosophy of A. J. Ayer and Gilbert Ryle, continued to take for granted the disappearance of religion as a serious element of life. At no time was Bertrand Russell more widely accepted and respected, though at no time was he himself less radical. Here was a rather different sort of agnostic secularism from the far more ideologically charged and crusading convictions of the inter-war years. The typical secularism of the 1950s (at least in more sophisticated circles) was a somewhat conservative phenomenon, anti-romantic, anti-ideological, a dry man-of-the-world cynicism, as bored with left-wing enthusiasms as with religious credulities (Mrs Knight, in fact, was not at all its proper leader. She reflected rather the crusading ardour of an earlier age). The agnosticism of the 1920s still believed itself radical; that of the 1950s knew itself to be the safest core for a conservative Establishment, more safely immune from radical sympathies than ecclesiastics could ever be. It hardly bothered any more to confound its rivals, it simply laughed at them, sure that there are no ultimate questions worth asking and that the age of affluence must spread across the world as faiths fade and comfortable common sense prevails.

The odd thing about the 1950s is the cohabiting of these two intellectual in-worlds, the religious and the agnostic, each self-assured, each apparently thriving, each rather sneeringly dismissive of the other. What we need to note here are a number of frontier areas, previously accepted territory of the one world, but whose allegiance was now again open to question. The first, and doubtless the least significant, is that of history. The study of British history, even medieval history, had to a very considerable extent until the 1930s an implicitly anti-Christian, and more explicitly anti-Catholic slant. It was essentially what has come to be known as the 'Whig Interpretation of History', the orthodoxy against which Hilaire Belloc, for instance, hit his head so fiercely. It accepted the principle of almost inevitable progress, at least within the British sphere, contrasted the superstitious backwardness of the Middle Ages with the great step forward of Renaissance and Reformation, leading on by inescapable progression to the Enlightenment and the modern scientific world of which Protestantism (particularly Anglo-Saxon Protestantism) had been the (now redundant) foster-mother. The most influential historians, with the exception of the superb but somewhat schizophrenic Acton, had been profoundly non-religious. By the thirties this picture was changing and a new school starting to emerge which in the post-war years had become, at least as regards medieval history, master of the field. Sir Maurice Powicke, Regius Professor at Oxford, brother-in-law of Lindsay of Balliol and a Free churchman, was its father figure. Next to him came E. F. Jacob, his successor as Professor of Medieval History at Manchester and then Chichele Professor of Modern History at Oxford from 1950: a strong Anglican, member of the House of Laity and a Church Commissioner. Among other devout Anglican medieval historians at Oxford were May McKisack and Richard Southern, the interpreter of St Anselm. At Cambridge the most distinguished figure was Dom David Knowles, flanked by Herbert Butterfield, who succeeded him as Regius Professor and produced in 1949 his *Christianity and History*. These and others constituted in the post-war years a formidably learned school of history in close touch with continental scholars like Etienne Gilson and concerned above all with the mental and moral rehabilitation of medieval civilization. The dichotomies between Middle Ages and Renaissance or between Medieval and Modern began to fall away; the papal role in medieval history – especially English medieval history – no longer appeared as a matter of outrageous aggression against an independent national Church; the spiritual and intellectual culture of the medieval centuries was interpreted afresh in a way that seemed exciting and positively significant for the development of western society. On 15 April 1947 the greatest of modern British historians, Lewis Namier, was 'baptised into Christ' in St Faith's chapel at Westminster Abbey.[9] It may not greatly have affected the secularity of his writing, but it is certainly symptomatic of the post-war world that this Russian-Polish Jew and erstwhile leading Zionist should have decided at this time to commit himself to Christian faith.

More unexpectedly the same sort of thing was happening in the school of social anthropology. No discipline had developed more inimically to religious belief. One of its most deeply held presuppositions was a basic contrast between 'primitive society' and 'modern society', in which the former was inherently characterized by religion, the latter by rational secularity. 'Religion' and 'Primitive Religion' became close to being convertible terms, and signified the hard core of mystifying non-rational thought-process which separated 'primitives' from our enlightened selves. It had then to be explained, and explained away, in sociological or psychological terms. Then came Evans-Pritchard. Formed in this school, the most brilliant field researcher of his generation and its most powerfully critical mind, he did with Nuer religion or Zande magic something not unlike what Powicke or Southern were doing with medieval religion: getting inside it and finding it far from wholly alien to modern man. Dichotomy is replaced by a continuity which finds room for rationality among 'primitives' and religion among 'moderns'. In 1944 he became a Roman Catholic and in 1946 Professor of Social Anthropology at Oxford. In 1956 his *Nuer Religion* was finally published. Around him grew up a group of mostly Catholic anthropologists with a strong religious interest – Godfrey Lienhardt, Mary Douglas, Victor Turner.[10] His Aquinas Lecture delivered at Hawkesyard Priory to the Dominicans in March 1959, on 'Religion and the Anthropologists', in which he hammered his distinguished predecessors for their irrational and a-priori models for the explanation of religion, expresses the new situation: social anthropology has simply ceased to be a bulwark of agnostic orthodoxy.[11] Religious belief, even of a quite traditional kind, has become fully tenable in conjunction with a masterly grip upon this field of science. Of course many other social anthropologists remained unimpressed by the religious dimension of Sir Edward's thought, some indeed maintaining that his *Nuer Religion* suffered as a consequence.[12] That is a matter of opinion. What is a social fact is the loss of the agnostic near-monopoly in this discipline and the success of the believing mind in advancing into a field of social understanding long effectively abandoned to the other side.

A third area of realignment was that of philosophy. There had, of course, always been Christians in the philosophy school, including many dons in Oxford and Cambridge colleges. Nevertheless as a contemporary discipline represented by the most powerful exponents of English philosophy it had become predominantly agnostic. With the fading away of British Hegelianism, the ruling school was that of 'Linguistic Analysis', whose most influential exposition was to be found in A. J. Ayer's *Language, Truth and Logic* (1936). At that point 'Linguistic Analysis' had been synonymous with 'Logical Positivism', according to which all metaphysics, all theology, and all statements of religious belief were but meaningless nonsense. By the 1950s some linguistic analysts were becoming rather less sure about that, as one can see in the interesting 1955 symposium, edited by Antony Flew and Alasdair MacIntyre, *New Essays in Philosophical Theology*. Nevertheless a perusal of that work shows a pretty weak theistic defence against a prevailing agnostic confidence that linguistic philosophy had finally demonstrated the meaninglessness of religion. The prime mover of that symposium was Antony Flew and he represents excellently well one way the movement of thought had gone. His father the Revd Newton Flew, was a distinguished Methodist scholar about to retire as Principal of Wesley House. The son was Professor of Philosophy at Keele and an atheist. One of the major pieces in this symposium had appeared in *Mind* in 1948: Professor Findlay's 'Can God's Existence be Disproved?' Professor Findlay thought that it could. His piece is a rather simplistic illustration of the mentality that took it for granted, on quite slight argumentation, that for the 'modern mind' it was 'self-evidently absurd' to attribute existence to God. 'Modern approaches', he maintained, do not 'allow us to remain agnostically poised in regard to God: They force us to come down on the atheistic side.'[13]

Despite undoubted dissentients this was still near to being English philosophical orthodoxy when it was written in the 1940s. Yet curiously the greatest name in modern philosophical history had already punctured that orthodoxy, to the eventual confusion even of the professional philosopher. You and I, dear reader, are unlikely ever to understand very adequately the philosophy of Ludwig Wittgenstein. We may console ourselves with the suspicion that we share that predicament with many a philosopher. He died in 1951. While his early *Tractatus Logico – Philosophicus* might seem to be behind the Logical Positivist orthodoxy of the inter-war years, his enormously influential posthumous *Philosophical Investigations*, on which he had been working during his latter years at Cambridge, left the field far more open.

Findlay, who was certainly none too happy with Wittgenstein's influence, later described him as a 'Pied Piper of Hamelin' who 'has rid one of a plague of rats only to deprive one of one's own dearest children'.[14] How does such a description fit Wittgenstein? 'I am not a religious man,' he once remarked to Con Drury, 'but I cannot help seeing every problem from a religious point of view.'[15] Wittgenstein's supreme function was that of a dissolvent of orthodoxies, particularly of the current orthodoxies of 'the modern mind', the 'dearest children' of Professor Findlay's confident atheism. Wittgenstein had somehow undermined the intellectual consensus of 'the modern mind' with its positivistic domination by a certain type of science. He showed it to be as open to challenge as the religious consensus of any earlier age. One often naïve intellectual arrogance had been replaced by another. Wittgenstein was the small boy looking at the modern emperor's clothes. He succeeded in intruding upon the Anglo-Saxon philosophical consciousness a sense of limitation relevant for the secularist as much as for the theologian, so that while the preceding agnosticism took it for granted that the methodological limitations of linguistic analysis effectively annihilated the meaningfulness of transcendental talk, Wittgenstein's agnosticism related to linguistic philosophy itself. It left the door open for religious faith, and whatever his own position in this regard (the evidence is scanty and ambiguous), it has certainly been central to the lives of some subsequent Wittgensteinians, including his chief literary executor, Professor Elizabeth Anscombe.

Here, as in the fields of history and anthropology, the effect of the developments was not, of course, to convince the majority of philosophers that religious faith was right after all, but it was to alter very considerably the balance of debate. In the age of Donald MacKinnon, Elizabeth Anscombe, Peter Geach and Michael Dummett, modern philosophy could no longer be seen as the natural preserve of the non-religious. The frontiers had been broken open and the to-and-fro battle was taking place again on the very middle of the ground. The, at the time almost successful, attempt of inter-war philosophy to dismiss religion as nonsense had proved to be a very temporary phenomenon.[16]

Little of this formidable intellectual engagement was very noticeable to the churches or their leadership. They were pleased to see some rather distinguished professors coming dutifully to church, they barely grasped its underlying significance. In the field of art as in that of literature, however, the Christian renewal was more widely recognized and more officially patronized. It stretches back to the pre-war years, though they were not, on the whole, a time when creative religious art or architecture was greatly appreciated: ecclesiastical propriety still held rather too close to neo-gothic models. Jacob Epstein and Stanley Spencer were both old men in the 1950s whose greatest work lay long before but they now received a social and ecclesiastical recognition which hitherto had been largely withheld. Spencer, a scruffy uneducated village pigmy, was perhaps the greatest British religious artist of this century. While he did his finest work around 1920, he was not greatly appreciated at the time and it is not unreasonable to include him in our post-war scene after his return to his native Cookham in 1945. With his almost fussy preoccupation with often bizarre detail, Spencer's approach to the expression of religious meaning is another extreme from the modernist simplicity of Epstein. There is a delightful homeliness here, a last undogmatic, unprofessional but absolutely sure-of-itself expression of the church-going village England, so familiar with the Bible that there is simply no separation possible between the two – a type of familiarity perhaps more medieval than Protestant, though Spencer acquired it from years of childhood attention in the little Methodist chapel at Cookham to the sermons of 'Mr Francis the baker'.

> Nothing has for me any meaning of form or shape except it is perceived in this religious joy [he wrote to Elizabeth Rothenstein in October 1953]. Had I not known and been completely

assured that this painting was to form part of a scheme in which there would be a resurrection in which Christ would be receiving the resurrected soldiers, I would not have been able to compose that picture of the man scrubbing the floor.[17]

His was a vision of incarnation not transcendence – a genuinely biblical incarnation culminating in an awfully earthly resurrection in the Berkshire village of Cookham. At times it goes so far as to seem almost ridiculous: the consecration of triviality, the canonization of the village gossip. But it would be a wretched mistake to reject such joyous celebration of human particularity or to insist that creative religious art must necessarily express the transcendent or the symbolic. Spencer was the inheritor, under a compulsive force he simply could not evade, of an ancient tradition of English incarnational vision, the tradition carried down the generations by miracle play and carol singing, the vision of Francis Thompson's 'Lo, Christ walking on the water, not of Gennesareth, but Thames'. He died in 1959, just after being knighted, to his amused astonishment; at work during his final illness on *Christ preaching at Cookham Regatta*.

If Spencer represents the genial spirit of populist traditionalism, Epstein was the arch-modernist, continually affronting sensibilities in the twenties and thirties. His powerful seven foot statue of Lazarus, carved in 1948, was acquired by the chapel of New College, Oxford in 1952.[18] This really begins Epstein's short years of ecclesiastical recognition. In 1953 came his *Madonna and Child* for the Holy Child Convent of Cavendish Square, and then a great *Christ in Majesty* for Llandaff Cathedral, and *Saint Michael and the Devil* for Coventry.

Already in 1944 Graham Sutherland was asked by Canon Hussey of St Matthew's, Northampton to produce an *Agony in the Garden*. He painted instead a *Crucifixion*. It was while preparing for this that he developed his thorn symbolism:

> For the first time I started to notice thorn bushes and the structure of thorns as they pierced the air. I made some drawings, and as I made them, a curious change developed. As the thorns rearranged themselves they became, whilst still retaining their own pricking, space-encompassing life, something else – a kind of 'stand-in' for a Crucifixion and a crucified head.[19]

This was followed by a *Deposition* in 1946, and a *Christ Carrying the Cross* in 1953, by which time he had just been commissioned to prepare a work with a very different kind of symbolism, the vast tapestry, *Christ in Glory*, for Coventry, which – as an exercise in the expression of transcendence – would provide the opposite pole to the kitchen-sink Christ of Cookham. Each has had its critics.

There are ways in which the musical achievement of England's greatest modern composer, Benjamin Britten, can be compared with the work of both Spencer and Sutherland. As he returned to Britain from America in 1942 he was composing the setting for the *Hymn to St Cecilia*, which Auden had written for him. He had just completed his *Ceremony of Carols*. The next twenty years were to see an amazingly rich series of religious compositions. The Aldeburgh Festival opened in 1948 with a performance of his new cantata *St Nicholas*. Ten years later came *Noye's Fludde*, an opera reviving the ancient Chester miracle play and first performed in Orford Church in June 1958. The animals enter the ark singing their *Kyrie Eleison* and leave with a joyous *Alleluia*, but there is a frequent touch of homeliness not at all unlike that of Spencer. Britten's work grew organically out of the soil of Suffolk life and traditional Christian culture, carol and plainsong, Bible story and miracle play, all rendered contemporary. From his earliest *Hymn to the Virgin*, to the *Burning Fiery Furnace*, and *The Prodigal Son*, there is a constant recreation of old religious themes in the context of the moral and spiritual issues of the present day, but often maintaining too a touch of homely frivolity characteristic of the Catholic incarnational tradition: all this with the freshness, the sheer unquestionable originality of a musician of genius.

The pre-eminent visual expression of this cultural renaissance (fuelled by the very considerable amount of money the churches received in compensation for war damage) was Coventry Cathedral. Designed by Basil Spence, dominated by Sutherland's tapestry of *Christ in Glory*, filled with numerous other masterpieces including the splendid baptistery glass of John Piper and Patrick Reyntiens, Coventry was the principal collective artistic achievement of the 1950s: planned – a little characteristically of the fifties – with art more than liturgy in mind. Here (as in the

Catholic cathedral of Liverpool completed just a few years later, a more decidedly sixties sister church) is the scale appropriate to a cathedral, coupled with quality and modernity. 1962 was the year of its accomplishment and that date will do as well as any to conclude a period of confident revival, at times a little too comfortably traditionalist but at moments, too, capable of the very highest achievement. On 30 May 1962 the cathedral was consecrated, the tapestry displayed and Britten's *War Requiem* first performed.[20] Britten's music has its own intrinsic gospel but never more so than in this, the most committed of all his pieces, with its note of tremendous warning. Coventry Cathedral had gone down with the bombs in 1940, now it had risen again with new beauty but as no mere restoration of the past and with no forgetfulness of why it had all happened. At this select moment the glories of the fifties merged with a new spirit of urgency which would dominate, at times creatively, at times disastrously, the climate of the sixties.

PART VI

The 1960s

Politics

In October 1959 the Conservative Party, led by the Prime Minister, Harold Macmillan, won a General Election for the third time in succession, defeating that very earnest Labour leader, Hugh Gaitskell. The relaxed masterliness of Eton, it might be said, had triumphed over the more evident intellectualism of Winchester. The difference between the two was, nevertheless, not a big one. There would have been no great change in policy if Labour had won, yet the victory of the Conservatives did ensure a continuity of symbol. As a consequence it is easier to recognize that the first years of the 1960s form a single unit of political history with the preceding decade. In many other ways too there is no clear divide between fifties and sixties.

In Britain an age of rather unworried affluence had begun in the early fifties, after the austerity of the post-war years, and it continued under Conservative patronage for ten good years. This harmonized pretty well with the experience of the world at large. Tension between East and West had relaxed despite the occasional crisis; in general an atmosphere of liberal benevolence was noticeable upon the wider scene. Khrushchev ruled in Moscow, John Kennedy in Washington, Pope John in the Vatican. They were all, in their different ways, figures of hope, of a new, seemingly more humane regime within their own dominions.

The most striking single alteration in world affairs was probably that produced by the granting of independence by Britain, France and Belgium to most of their remaining colonies, especially in black Africa and the Caribbean. Within the British Commonwealth Nigeria became independent in 1960; Sierra Leone and Tanzania (at that time Tanganyika) in 1961; Jamaica, Trinidad and Uganda in 1962; Kenya in 1963; Malawi and

Zambia (Nyasaland and Northern Rhodesia) in 1964. Parliaments on a Westminster model proliferated, and in most cases a general atmosphere of good will immediately prevailed. If the result was, effectively, to bring the British Empire to an end – apart from Hong Kong, a few odd islands and minor territories and the unresolved problem of Rhodesia – it was done with few regrets within a general mood of self-congratulation that colonialism had finally behaved so decently and that the transition to political independence could be achieved so harmoniously. As, again and again, the Union Jack was lowered and another new flag raised before the erect figure of some member of the royal family representing the Queen, State after State entered the Commonwealth and the United Nations. It helped confirm a sense of international progress while making its own contribution to British euphoria. It was fortunate that the Conservative Party at this, its most liberal moment, was thus able to preside over the demise of the empire. If Labour had been in office at the time much the same process would undoubtedly have occurred, but it would have been far more contentious.

At home standards of living had never risen so fast or so continuously. While a considerable minority of people continued to suffer wretchedly miserable conditions, and this was very easily overlooked, the large majority of the nation for the first time in its history was enjoying a state of some genuine affluence. This was as true of Tyneside, Merseyside, Halifax and Bradford, as of the home counties. Holidays were prolonged. Motor cars, television sets, refrigerators, washing machines multiplied. For the young the conditions that so many of their parents had suffered before the Second World War were fading into unreality. The government of the late fifties had presided over all this with satisfaction but it had done rather little to ensure that the growth of affluence was spread evenly or properly buttressed by suitable new institutions. The approach to education, health, social reform, had been decidedly *laissez-faire*. In the early sixties, however, this noticeably changed. The new Britain required new institutions, and Macmillan's last ministry was suddenly in quite a hurry to provide them. The Robbins Report of 1963 called for the doubling of the number of university students and half a dozen new universities. At once they arose – Sussex,

York, East Anglia, Lancaster, Essex and then Kent and Warwick. A year earlier Enoch Powell, the Minister of Health, had promised that ninety new hospitals would be built in the next ten years. Prisons too were to be drastically modernized – a very long overdue measure. Beeching was reorganizing the railways, Robens the coal mines, Newsom secondary education. Much of this should have come a good deal earlier but there can be little doubt that the Conservative government in Macmillan's final years was the last major reforming administration England was to have for a long time. The structure of the new England which Attlee had shaped in the immediate post-war years upon foundations laid by Lloyd George and Neville Chamberlain was now seemingly completed by the aged SuperMac and a group of bright young ministers – Macleod, Heath, Powell, Maudling. The empire was gone. In its place was to be a prosperous, unsocialist but equitable Britain, its citizens driving around the countryside on the new motorways or holidaying in a united Europe when not listening to the Beatles or otherwise enjoying the pleasures of 'Swinging' London. The early 1960s image of Swinging London, the world's youth capital, may seem a curious one. It was, of course, somewhat unreal, a media creation. Nevertheless it did represent a widespread genuine feeling: that Britain had dismantled the empire but was the better for it, had in fact never had it so good; that you could lose power but still retain supremacy in the arts of peace; that you could even combine the advantages of an Old Etonian Cabinet with populist culture.

The coping-stone of the new order was to be entry into the European community, and this was intended to be the last and most important of all the Macmillan reforms. It would provide the context for the new Britain. De Gaulle thought differently and in January 1963 vetoed British entry. That decision, Macmillan declared, was 'bad for us, bad for Europe, bad for the whole free world'. It represented the first major sign that the new harmony would have its limits, the *Pax Macmilliana* its failures.

It was, of course, inevitable that this genial Conservative paradise would not go on for ever, nor be taken by everyone at its own evaluation. Voices of protest had, indeed, been heard for some time. Through the later fifties the 'Angry Young Men' – certainly well enough publicized and rewarded for their anger –

had been expressing in novel and play the frustration of the new generation with, precisely, the emptiness of affluence. John Osborne's *Look Back in Anger* of 1956 can well be regarded as the best beginning of the new mood – the protest of the newly articulate, rather classless class against its creator, and especially against the élitist trappings of the Establishment that still ruled Britain. Protest they might, and *Look Back in Anger* was written, be it noted, before the beginning of Macmillan's premiership, but for many years protest remained very much a minority occupation.

Its most powerful expressions were those of race riots and the Campaign for Nuclear Disarmament. It was Britain's prosperity which brought to her shores from the middle fifties a great wave of black immigrants which turned her rapidly and unexpectedly into a multi-racial society. 260 thousand Caribbean immigrants entered the country between 1955 and 1962 (nearly 75 thousand in 1961 alone). Their labour was welcome, their presence in large numbers in 'one's own' residential area was often not. The Notting Hill riots of 1958 were the warning sign that a major new area of tension had entered English life.

CND presented unrest of a different sort.[1] For several years at the end of the 1950s and early 1960s the Aldermaston March was the focal point of all political and intellectual dissent. It was Britain's acquisition of her own hydrogen bomb from 1957 which fuelled the movement, but it is noticeable that this was not a period when the immediate use of nuclear weapons seemed particularly likely. The leaders of CND – Bertrand Russell, Canon Collins, Michael Scott – were not politicians. They represented a rather amateur alliance of Christian and humanist radicals. Their following was overwhelmingly middle class, perhaps a little too nice to be very effectual though it included a more ruthless wing which eventually helped bring about its collapse by appealing to fairly symbolic forms of violence. Its greatest victory politically was the passing of the 1960 resolution of the Labour Party Conference at Scarborough, moved by Frank Cousins and resisted by Gaitskell, calling for British unilateral nuclear disarmament. For the most part the CND of that period was strong on rhetoric but very weak on anything which could possibly be pragmatically effective. It was, say the analysts, a matter of expressive rather than of instrumental politics: a blowing off of steam by very intelligent people outside the Establishment rather than a campaign structured actually to achieve its goal, though there was always a polarity here, Russell representing the symbolic role, Collins the pragmatic.

The Aldermaston March of 1961 was the last great anti-bomb demonstration in Britain for nearly twenty years. It is ironic – and not too easy to comprehend – that the seemingly radical sixties from then on mounted so relatively little organized opposition to nuclear weapons.

1963 was the year in which at one and the same time the government's reformism reached its peak and the rather placid prosperity of former years gave way fairly sharply to a more frenetic mood: it was 'the year of the Beatles'. Hugh Gaitskell died in January, the same month that de Gaulle vetoed British entry into the Common Market. He was replaced as Labour's leader by Harold Wilson who had hitherto acted as leader of Labour's left wing, the successor to Aneurin Bevan.

Harold I and Harold II, the ailing king and the only credible heir apparent in sight, were then contenders for power through 1963; the Etonian uncle of the duke of Devonshire and the grammar school Economics don from Oxford – standard bearers, it would seem, of Conservatism and radicalism. Not for nine hundred years had two Harolds wrestled for the governance of England. Would it have made much difference if Harold Hardrada had defeated Harold Godwinson? It seems unlikely, but certainly it made very little difference when Harold Wilson stepped into the shoes of Harold Macmillan.

Those last months of the thirteen years of Tory rule were also the high point of the new media preoccupation with youth, with radicalism, with sex, with a gushing populist turn-about which would somehow sweep away the grouse-moor image of British government and replace it with a glorious combination of Beatle and egg-head Hungarian economist, the inaugurating moment alike of *Private Eye* and James Bond.[2] 'We are living in the jet-age,' Wilson declared, 'but we are governed by an Edwardian establishment mentality' which was now to be replaced by 'a break-through to an exciting and wonderful period.'[3] 'Dynamic', 'exciting' and 'purposive' were, at this point, his favoured adjectives. Macmillan retired due to illness that October and was replaced by the respectable and sensible, but hardly 'breakthrough' figure of Sir Alec Douglas-Home, hitherto fourteenth Earl of Home. Pope John had died four months before. Six weeks later President Kennedy was assassinated. The death of John Kennedy was not only a psychologically traumatic event for people all across the world for reasons few could well explain; it could seem to symbolize the close of an alliance between establishment hopefulness and populist hopefulness. Yet at the time that was not really so: the alliance continued in America in the early days of Lyndon Johnson and his 'War on Poverty', as it continued in Britain in the early days of Harold Wilson and at the Vatican in the early days of Paul VI. Only two years or more later would the liberal establishment wilt and populism turn messianic and anarchic.

Wilson came to power a year later, October 1964, and the rhetoric at least was maintained with some credibility a while longer. Electoral victory, he promised, would be followed by 'a hundred days of dynamic action' to 'get a tired country moving'.

> The accursed power that stands on privilege,
> And goes with women and champagne and Bridge,
> Fell, and Democracy resumed her reign,
> Which goes with Bridge and women and champagne.

Belloc's tart comment on an earlier election goes well enough for 1964. It would be quite untrue to say that the Wilson administration carried through no reforms. It did indeed carry on all the reforms begun by Macmillan. And it added to them, particularly in the area of comprehensive education at secondary level and more technology at tertiary level. Seven new universities were founded in 1966 – Loughborough, Aston, Brunel, Bath, Bradford, Surrey and the City University – and one (Salford) in 1967: an impressive list. No more hereditary peerages were to be created (and no more were – for nearly twenty years). The last hanging in Britain took place in August 1964. The first year of Wilson's government saw the passing of the Murder (Abolition of Death Penalty) Act, as also the Race Relations Act (but not the repeal of the Commonwealth Immigration Act of 1962, so fiercely resisted by Labour at the time as racialist). In 1968 abortions became legal, as did homosexual behaviour in private between consenting adults. Divorce was made far easier. There is, overall, a curiously private character about these reforms but really there was rather little else that Wilson could reform, 'dynamic' as he might wish to be, without touching an order of things which he had in truth no heart to meddle with. The overall note of these years was still one of modernizing transformation – a hasty, self-confident transformation evidenced not only by the relaxation of moral taboos and the creation of comprehensives and polytechnics but by the often ill-considered demolition of the Victorian heart of many a town and its replacement by a burgeoning landscape of motorways, high-rise flats and sheet-glassed office blocks. It remained an era of construction.

Wilson was the dominating figure of British politics for the next twelve years, to be succeeded for another three by his close colleague and understudy, James Callaghan. 'At last we have got a leader who can lie', remarked Richard Crossman with satisfaction after Gaitskell's death. Hitherto the Labour Party had been harnessed to a sense of moral purpose, a simple old purpose deriving from the simplicities of the late nineteenth-century chapel in Nonconformity and Trade Union. It had never been a very Marxist purpose. It had served, and the party had always retained something of the atmosphere of a crusade. It would do so no longer. Wilson was the heir to a revolution seemingly accomplished. The welfare state had been established at home, the empire disposed of abroad. A heavier measure of State socialism was desired only by the few: it was not within the logic of the situation – either Britain's or the Labour Party's – to be an effective option. A little rhetoric might still be forthcoming but no more. There was, in fact, less room for manoeuvre, even for gimmicks, because the economy was beginning noticeably to deteriorate. While the standard of living, the spending power of the common man, was rising fast, production was not. The consequence was a chronic balance of payments problem. For the next twenty years the efforts of government would be predominantly concerned with economic problems themselves, with cushioning society from the effects of a worsening economy or, again and finally, with making society face up to those effects. Anything else would have to take second place.

Of course much of this was very far from evident when Labour returned to power in the middle of the sixties. It was disguised, not only because the current wave of radical enthusiasm was still near its crest, but also because of the engagingly reassuring character of the new Prime Minister. Wilson was extraordinarily good at speaking to the common man; confidently calming and sensible words. He was in this rather like Stanley Baldwin with whom he had much else in common. Behind the words there was often exceedingly little. 'Theology' expressed for Wilson all the theory that he regarded as useless and almost despicable. With Wilson and Callaghan ideology, belief, commitment to a theoretical policy had all more or less ceased to matter. Equally, there was no cruelty, no ruthlessness – at least beyond the achievement of trivia. They were both, very profoundly, men of peace. Their commitment was to decent middle Britain, enjoying the benefits of the welfare state at home, quietly withdrawing from any foolish power role abroad, able to sit back and enjoy contentedly *The Pirates of Penzance*. It was not a bad Utopia. Of course Wilson had to be able to pretend at times to be a more stalwart figure, the upholder of Britain's bulldog past. He could well get himself – as in the confrontation with Smith – 'eyeball to eyeball', to say boo to a goose. He could, furthermore, proudly confide to the nation, pipe in hand, that he had done so. Hopefully, nothing tougher than that would ever be needed again in what must be an increasingly sensible world of post-imperial, post-Marxist politics. In so far as it was so, the country was fortunate to have so humane, so utterly unbellicose a leader. Sadly, however, the world was not quite like that. By the end of the decade the Viet Nam war, conducted by Britain's principal ally, was growing steadily more horrible. Nigeria, Britain's most admired former colony in Africa, had split in civil war. Northern Ireland was fast falling apart. Where Africa had produced easy credit for Macmillan, it provided for Wilson only Ian Smith's intractable Rhodesia. Nuclear weaponry was spreading ominously enough. And what in reality could Wilson do about any of this? He was in truth Britain's first non-imperial Prime Minister. It was obvious that British power mattered less and less.

1968 was the year, not just for Britain but much more for the world as a whole, in which the leftward-looking intelligentsia, the optimistic populist reformism which had provided the consensus characteristic of the sixties as a decade, came finally and decisively to the moment of truth. There were student riots in the spring in Paris and then in many another city; the assassination of Martin Luther King in April and Robert Kennedy in June; the extinction by Russian invasion of Dubcek's immensely exciting experiment in Czechoslovakia – 'socialism with a human face'; the hard slog of the Nigerian civil war; the stormy emergence of the Civil Rights Movement in Northern Ireland. Two weeks after King's assassination Enoch Powell had made a speech in Birmingham on race relations which electrified Britain. 'As I look ahead I am filled with foreboding. Like the Roman I seem to see the River Tiber foaming with much blood.' Already Britons were becoming 'strangers in their own country'. He was dismissed at once by Heath from the Conservative Shadow Cabinet but received 100 thousand letters, mostly of support.

On the religious side such events were matched by the intensely committed and radical meetings of the Latin American bishops at Medellin and of the World Council at Uppsala (where Luther King was to have been a principal speaker), as by Pope Paul's highly controversial encyclical on birth control, *Humanae vitae*. Despite the expression of radical sentiment by student and bishop alike, the hard realities of irresistible power were once more only too apparent – the power of the assassin's gun, the power of American bombs in Viet Nam, Soviet power in Czechoslovakia, papal power over the Church. It was a great disillusionment.

We can discern a fairly clear collective evolution of mood from the late fifties to the early seventies: a specifically English evolution, though much dependent upon the American prototype, and of course in large part shared very much more widely. The prosperity, optimism, and sense of release of the fifties was mostly of a pretty conservative and controlled type. It recognized boundaries. It was the placid contentment of an era of restoration, glad to be distanced little by little from the worst horrors of the past, increasingly confident in its outlook on the future. The secular hopefulness of the early sixties grew out of the earlier phenomenon but altered with remarkable rapidity. From being something rather conservative, it was transmogrified into an ever more shapelessly radical one – anti-élitist, easy going, even ecstatic, self-satisfied, libertarian. 'Permissive' was the word – in regard to sex, art, the whole round of social and intellectual life. The inspiration derived partly from a rejuvenated Marxism – a Marxism liberated from the Soviet model and fed upon the discovery of the writings of the Young Marx – partly from poets and novelists like Virginia Woolf, Brecht and Herman Hesse, but mostly from a sharp, but shallow, highly contemporary sense of being free to deride the past, an explosion of the cynical and the satirical. The mood, especially at first, was not at all unlike that of the twenties, except that it was more vulgar and more credulous. All the traditional values of society were almost systematically derided by a new literary élite posing as anti-élitist. Sir William Haley, at the time Editor of *The Times*, one of the wiser mandarins of the old establishment, berated one of the high points of the new culture, *Not so Much a Programme, More a Way of Life*, as illustrative of the BBC's 'panic flight from all decent values', its 'sick sniggering attitude to life',[4] but there were few people at the time who were not to some extent bewitched by the bright excitement, the confident claim to represent triumphant modernity enshrined in such programmes. Order and optimism remained linked in the fifties, in the sixties they fell far apart. The world of youth, of pop, of irreverence, of unprepared happenings, was all, in sociological terms, a classic case of *communitas*: a brief but intense experience of ecstasy, of unstructured almost incoherent fellowship, a world in which norms are temporarily derided and seem unnecessary. The Beatles, heroes of 1963 and 1964, were in their cheerful, generous way completely dismissive of the structured world of class, Church, institutions of any kind. All the complex pattern of hierarchies seemed for a brief blissful moment boringly unnecessary. For that moment the voice of working-class Merseyside, liberated by affluence but still quite recognizable, seemed more authentically English, yet more cosmopolitan too, than anything else in hearing.

The point of *communitas* is that it is generated at some lively moment of intersection, some temporary breakdown of structure, but that it cannot last.[5] The attempt to prolong it, to treat it as the real world, must inevitably produce pessimism, indeed neurotic breakdown. Its seekers find themselves no longer part of normal society and retreat instead into some mini-community, some make-believe world of their own invention. This is what was happening more and more by the close of the 1960s: psychedelic churches, wife-swap clubs, the world of LSD, Playboy clubs, Zen. For a much wider circle of people who had been deeply affected by the unusual optimism of the early years of the decade, its later years were ones of deepening depression. Almost all the hopeful signs of yesterday had now turned painfully sour. Black Africa was sinking under coups and political mismanagement into a continent of famine, chaos, an amorphous mass of apparently almost helpless misery. The Catholic Church, so buoyant under Pope John, was being torn apart between progressive and conservative. In the United States the technical achievement was as great as ever. In 1969 the first man was landed on the Moon, but socially things were falling badly apart. America under Nixon was heading for the disillusionment of Watergate.

As so often in our history, Britain was spared the extremes: its student riots were mild; its odder religious communities American imports; its governmental linen, drawn as you will from a kitchen cabinet of no distinction, was yet no more than very faintly soiled. Yet Britain was now, more than ever, being carried in the wake of American culture, subject to the ripple effect of all the moods of California, to every new discovery whether of the glory of the 'secular city' at one moment, the horrors of 'Future shock' at another. There was, undoubtedly, a specifically English cultural trajectory of the sixties but it was being continually affected by the greater intensities of American experience – Civil Rights, assassinations, Viet Nam, Watergate. No longer very powerful, certainly less badly led than the States, Britain came out of the decade very much less bruised. The shift from Wilson to Heath in 1970 and then back again to Wilson in 1974 really signified little – only very minor alterations in course. Undoubtedly the hopefulness had faded. The state of the economy was getting steadily worse. Unemployment was beginning to rise. Nevertheless when the sixties turned to the seventies, Britain was not as yet over-conscious of being in a bad way. It was settling down to its new status as a middle-sized power. It still looked forward to the day when it would 'enter Europe' and find thereby a solution to its problems.

Looking back upon the sixties, for Britain at least, they remain for all their faults of over-enthusiasm one of the most humane of decades. Maybe in no other did so few British soldiers have to die abroad in battle. Here the British experience was decisively different from the American: almost four million Americans served in Viet Nam. The sixties demilitarized Britain but militarized America. Hanging ceased in Britain. There was a vast and almost universal growth in concern for the relief of misery at home and abroad. While some reaction might follow against the loud permissiveness, poor taste and general hubris of the liberal Establishment at that time, the underlying revolution in social, especially sexual, attitudes would almost certainly never be reversed. Sexual equality, like racial equality, became in the sixties a practicable ideal. The very first mixed university student hostels were opened in Britain in 1960. Within twenty years even the colleges of Oxford and Cambridge would almost all have ceased to be bastions of a single sex. A strongly sexually segregated pattern of life had been the norm, particularly for the English upper class from school to club. Now even the House of Lords was to admit women. The Church had fitted well into the old sexually divided world and, of all institutions, would find it now most difficult to adapt to the new mode. Intellectually there was a massive public shift away from religion towards the establishment of secularism as the ruling orthodoxy, noticeable particularly in the BBC. For these, and many other reasons, after a rather too comfortable ride through the fifties the churches found the sixties at once challenging and, as time went on, extremely disturbing. To that experience we have now to turn.

The Second Vatican Council

The factor of personality is not something to be ignored if one wishes to make sense of human history, religious history most of all. In the case of Pope John XXIII this is outstandingly true, even though one could not possibly have predicted his extraordinary role in ecclesiastical history before he passed the age of seventy-six. That was his age when, in October 1958, as Cardinal Roncalli, the Patriarch of Venice, he was elected to succeed Pope Pius XII.[1] He was the candidate of the caucus of conservative Italian cardinals, of that there can be little doubt. Pius's long reign had ended gloomily with the old pope in a position of extreme isolation. There was no obvious successor. There was mounting unrest in the Church, a movement of intellectual and spiritual change, particularly in France, Belgium, Holland and Germany. To the outsider it may appear restrained enough in its manifestations but it was causing great concern in Rome, and the Curia, hitherto, had been unable to control it effectively. Roncalli was selected as a safe elderly conservative who could be counted upon not to disturb the status quo unduly while the search went on for a suitable younger man. His wide international experience – he had been papal nuncio in Bulgaria, Turkey and France – made him acceptable to non-Italians, the French especially, but it did not make him – on any available evidence – in the least dangerous or unpredictable.

They misjudged their man. Pope John was not someone of a speculative turn of mind. His literary interests were concentrated upon the pastoral endeavours of Italian Counter Reformation bishops, Charles Borromeo in particular, as upon the history of his own native diocese of Bergamo. He was of peasant stock and had served as a sergeant in the First World War when already a priest. He had a confident unworried, humorous cast of mind, an unusual confidence both in the Spirit and in his fellow men, a shrewd peasant's judgment and a gift for memorably earthy phrases. Perhaps by chance, in the early years of the century, his sympathies, but certainly not his beliefs, had been very slightly enlisted upon the side of the so-called modernists. He was entirely unlike his sensitive, intellectual, aristocratic, ever worrying predecessor.

In some essentially intuitive way Pope John had decided that the Church needed a change. Only three months after his election, on 25 January 1959 (the final day of the octave of Christian Unity), he announced the summoning of a general council. He talked of *aggiornamento* (a bringing up to date), of taking note of the 'signs of the times'. Most of all he talked of the reunion of Christians. And people were quite amazed. Pope John was not elected to say such things, and no pope was expected to say them at all. Probably almost no Catholic expected that another council would ever be called – the defining of papal infallibility had seemed to render it unnecessary. There was no inevitability about the Second Vatican Council. The Catholic Church might well have sat out the storms of the 1960s with hardly a change anywhere, as it had sat out many another storm.

In John's mind, it is safe to say, what was uppermost was certainly not a foreseeing of the next decade but a homely recognition that things had not really been going too well in the 1950s or indeed for many years before that. When the writings of the most outstanding Catholic scholars of the age, of de Lubac, Congar, Rahner and their colleagues, were condemned – if rather ineffectually – by the Holy Office, when these men themselves were forbidden to teach and sent into exile here and there, something seemed clearly wrong. Such scholars were manifestly loyal and orthodox, their fault being simply that they were not narrowly subservient to ultramontane theology. Their links with all that seemed best and most fruitful in the modern Church – the liturgical movement, the lay apostolate, a more irenic relationship with other Christians – were unquestionable. Roman policy in the latter years of Pius XII seemed to have been dictated increasingly by fear, fear linked with a very narrow model of catholicity – scholastic, clericalist, more and more centralized.

Of course, that model was not a new one: it was the ultramontane model of many generations, but it had not for a very long time been possible to contrast it so plausibly within the Catholic Church with another model, no less Catholic, better based in scholarship and far more beautiful. Even within the ecclesiastical universities of Rome ultramontanism had been losing the battle for the minds and hearts of the young.

Teilhard de Chardin was a case a little apart. He had died on Easter Sunday 1955. A very loyal Jesuit, but a thinker of great originality and self-confidence, he had long been under the ban of Rome and no book of his had been published for many years. After his death the ban ceased to be effective and suddenly the later works of Teilhard saw the light including, in 1959, *The Phenomenon of Man*. In an almost exuberantly confident attempt to reconcile the scientific outlook, as he saw it, with Christian belief, his expressions were often vague, his terminology original, and it is hardly surprising that the mind of traditional Catholic orthodoxy found it all very dangerous. Yet how much more dangerous were the consequences of his shabby treatment: his ideas hit the public consciousness in one almighty rush just at the time when they seemed most acceptable, with their large optimistic vision of the future of mankind, charted with a new symbolic language – hominization, the neosphere, the Omega Point. Teilhard's long martyrdom by ecclesiastical autocracy now gave his writings an added glow. He became in no time at all the Pied Piper, able both to lead the children of the Church away from scholasticism and the children of the modern world back to acceptance of religious romance – a romance which clothed a Christian eschatology in a language seemingly drawn from modern science. 'Disease and hunger will be conquered by science and we will no longer need to fear them in any acute form. And, conquered by the sense of the earth and human sense, hatred and internecine struggle will have disappeared in the ever-warmer radiance of Omega.'[2] How true and right that sounded in the early sixties.

Pope John was no theological innovator. His personal thoughts, as committed to his diary, were clothed in the most traditional vocabulary of Catholic piety. But he sensed that Church authority had got to stop fighting its ablest sons and work with them instead. The council was the result. Not that he knew quite how to go about it. Conciliar preparations were largely left in the hands of the curial old guard who diligently prepared draft texts which proved largely unusable and indeed in many cases quite obviously at odds with the Pope's stated aims. Yet in various ways he set about, almost instinctively, shaping the ground for a very different approach. Most important of all, in 1960 he established a new curial office, a Secretariat of Unity, headed by a distinguished German Jesuit Scripture scholar, Cardinal Bea, with Mgr Willebrands, an ecumenically experienced and practical Dutchman, as its secretary. The Secretariat would prove in the next ten years, for all its caution, to be a truly revolutionary unit within the Curia.

That year Archbishop Fisher visited Rome. We have seen Fisher as a firm Protestant, almost intuitively suspicious of Rome:

> I grew up with an inbred opposition to anything that came from Rome. I objected to their doctrine; I objected to their methods of reasoning; I objected to their methods of operation in this country. So I grew up, and I saw no reason for differing from that opinion as the years went by.[3]

When a few months earlier Mervyn Stockwood, the new bishop of Southwark, had visited Rome, called on Pope John and carried a friendly message back to Lambeth, Fisher was not pleased.[4] When Archbishop Garbett had visited Rome in 1945, though something of an Anglo-Catholic, which Fisher was most certainly not, he had thought it quite out of the question to call on the pope.[5] Yet now, after travelling to Jerusalem and Constantinople on an 'Ecumenical Pilgrimage', almost the final episode in his long archiepiscopate, Geoffrey Fisher went to Rome to see the Pope. What had made the difference? 'Without any doubt the personality of Pope John. It was quite obvious to the world that Pope John was a different kind of Pope', someone who could actually be met and talked to 'friend to friend'.[6]

In ultramontane eyes it was all very dangerous. For the pope to meet the archbishop of Canterbury (the first time it had happened since the fourteenth century) might well appear as some sort of recognition of the Anglican communion, even of Anglican orders. When Fisher got to Rome he was therefore informed through the British Minister to the Holy See that there was to be no official photograph, no press release, no meeting with Cardinal Bea or anyone else at all except the pope. It was to be as private as could be. Such were the instructions of the Secretariat of State. It sounded very preposterous.

When John and Geoffrey, two elderly ecclesiastics, had sat down in the pope's study, and had exchanged more formal greetings, the Pope read to the archbishop a passage in English which referred to 'the time when our separated brethren should return to the Mother Church' – a pretty ultramontane view of things. At that point Fisher interrupted: 'Your Holiness, not *return*.' The Pope looked puzzled and asked, 'Not return? Why not?' to which Fisher replied: 'None of us can go backwards. We are each now running on parallel courses; we are looking forward, until, in God's good time, our two courses approximate and meet.' The Pope paused to think about this and then said, 'You are right.' Perhaps this little story indicates as well as any the mind and heart of Pope John, his ability in the context of a personal relationship to move quickly, but rather untheoretically, well beyond traditional positions. In fact Fisher did see Bea and there was a modest press release. Undoubtedly Vatican officialdom had greatly wanted to play down the visit's significance and, perhaps, at the time they more or less succeeded. Nevertheless it was in fact a visit of quite enormous significance for English Christianity. It marks, more than any other single event, the turn of a very long tide. Fisher himself recognized that it constituted 'the final achievement of my archiepiscopate'.[7] His successor recognized that it 'opened a door which will never close'.[8]

The Second Vatican Council was opened by Pope John on 11 October 1962 in the basilica of St Peter's amid immense expectation. A best-seller by a young Swiss theologian, Hans Küng, *The Council and Reunion*, had just outlined vistas of reform almost too exciting to be believable. If there was a bishops' council in Rome, there was a popular council going on far across the Church fuelled not by the rather dull and highly cautious Latin documents which had been placed before the bishops but by the debates of reforming theologians, many of whom were also on the sidelines in Rome. Besides nearly 2,500 bishops and heads of major religious orders, there were also present within St Peter's a considerable number of theological experts (*periti*) including both the major curial theologians and many of those, like Congar and Rahner, who had been near to public condemnation only a few years earlier. Furthermore there were also just over forty (by the final session more than a hundred) non-Catholic Observers, representatives of nearly all the major traditions of Christendom other than the Baptists. From England the Anglican delegation was led by John Moorman, the Bishop of Ripon.[9] The importance of the Observers' presence was very great. While they could not vote or speak in the debates, they received all the papers and were able to make their views heard time and again in all sorts of ways – not least in the St Peter's coffee bar where continual informal discussion could be carried on. This was first of all a demonstration of great confidence; secondly it was an expression of friendship – if not already in existence, then of friendships being quickly created; thirdly it was an invitation to effective dialogue with the inevitable consequence that, time and again, things were said differently in the council's documents because the Observers had preferred it so. When one recalls the Roman bar to discussions on religious matters with non-Catholics for so many years, the refusal to allow any Catholic Observers to attend the World Council's first two conferences at Amsterdam and Evanston (though not the third, at New Delhi in 1961), then the significance of the presence of the Observers at the Vatican Council becomes overwhelming. It provided a quite new model for relationships between Rome and the rest of Christendom which was bound in the following years to become normative at every level and in every part of the world.

The council met for four annual sessions, terminating its work on 8 December 1965. By then Pope John was dead. He had been succeeded by Cardinal Montini, Paul VI. Montini had worked for years in the Secretariat of State under Pope Pius. He had long been regarded as the hope of ecclesiastical liberalism. Finally Pius made him Archbishop of Milan. He removed him from Rome; he did not make him a cardinal; but he had appointed him to Italy's second most important see. Once John had placed a cardinal's hat upon his head, he was universally expected to succeed. His father had been a journalist and a politician, a member of Don Sturzo's *Partito Popolare*, so Montini's background was distinctly modern: urban, middle class, democratic. He had got to know Bishop Bell and at Milan once invited a group of Anglican clerics to stay with him for some days so that he could learn better about the Church of England.[10] He was an admirer of Jacques Maritain and of Jean Daniélou. In the first session of the council he had taken his stand, if a little cautiously, with the progressives, quite unlike most of the senior Italian bishops. He was clearly John's heir apparent but so very unlike him – intellectual, unable to relax, a worrier, frequently unable to make up his mind, never quite confident how to reconcile the liberal reformer he was very anxious to be and the ultramontane of curial training that he was. 'Amletico', Hamlet-like, Pope John had called him. In fact he left the council very largely, though not entirely, to go the way its increasingly progressive leadership wanted it to go, so that in some ways his pontificate hardly began until the council – the centre of all attention – was completed.

There can be no question but that the Vatican Council was the most important ecclesiastical event of this century, not just for Roman Catholics but for all Christians. It so greatly changed the character of by far the largest communion of Christendom (and, by and large, in a direction which we may describe not too unfairly as one of 'Protestantization'), that no one has been left unaffected. The most anti-Roman of Protestants has been forced, if he or she thinks at all, at least to reconsider things. But for Catholics it both provided in its principal constitutions and decrees[11] a body of doctrine which is proving to have greater effective authority than any encyclical or any other document except scriptures and creeds, and it decisively altered the ordinary practice of Church life in a great many ways. Furthermore, it set in motion a process of discussion and change which quickly moved far beyond the official decisions of the conciliar fathers.

The council's first major achievement was the Constitution on the Liturgy, ratified in the second session. It was possible to reach agreement here rather easily because the principles of the liturgical movement had largely been accepted in Rome during the middle years of Pope Pius. All that was needed was to apply them more extensively. Here more than anywhere else was there continuity between Pius, the council, and Paul after the council. Popular participation was the key principle: the liturgy must be such that the laity can both understand and join in. Hence the vernacular was to be brought into use wherever it is of 'great advantage to the people'. Communion under both kinds was to be restored for certain circumstances as also 'Concelebration' (whereby priests celebrate mass together, instead of doing so 'privately', each on his own). The Constitution remained a cautious document, characteristic of the council's earlier thinking. No permission was given for the celebration of the whole mass in the vernacular. This was, however, within the logic of the document, and four years later, in 1967, Pope Paul authorized the saying even of the canon in the vernacular. Within a very few years a Latin mass had become a rarity in most Catholic churches throughout the world. At the same time texts were not only translated, they were also changed and, in particular, many late medieval prayers (like the long offertory prayers of the Tridentine mass) were simply eliminated.

When one considers that the Latin mass had remained almost unchanged for more than five hundred years, that its revision and translation constituted one of the most burning issues of the Reformation and one which Rome had been adamant in refusing, then the speed and decisiveness of liturgical reform in the 1960s becomes really amazing. No Catholic in the fifties could have imagined what was about to happen. No young Catholic in the seventies could easily imagine what church worship had been like twenty years earlier. Almost overnight Catholic worship changed from something in outward form extraordinarily unlike normal Anglican or Lutheran worship to something not far off being apparently identical. In symbolic terms nothing was more powerfully significant than the permission granted to the laity to receive – albeit at first rather rarely – the cup in communion. On no point had Rome been more intransigent in the past in its reaction to Protestant insistence. Even nuns had come and gone, generation after generation, receiving daily communion but never once receiving of the chalice. Now, within a few years, in a typical convent chapel communion of the cup would become again a daily practice.

Doctrinally, the most central and decisive of the council's documents were the Dogmatic Constitutions on the Church and on Revelation. They were fought over fiercely enough, as the conservative rearguard was driven to abandon item after item of scholastic terminology and ultramontane prescription. Preconciliar Roman theology had described the Church as a 'Monarchy'; it had been preoccupied with authority – conceived in very legal terms; it had defended a model of two 'sources' for Revelation – Scripture and Tradition; it had maintained that Christians not within the Roman communion were at best within the Church only 'by desire'. Such teachings and much else were abandoned either implicitly or explicitly in the council's documents. The Church is seen instead primarily as the 'People of God' united by faith and the Holy Spirit, by baptism and Eucharist, rather than by government. The ministry within it is a 'collegial' one of the bishops as a group, carrying on the collective ministry of the original apostles. 'Monarchy' is never once mentioned, though the Pope is, of course, clearly recognized as the necessary head of the college. The Church is a communion and other Christians, whose baptism is recognized, are at least partially members of that communion. The two-source theory of Revelation, in which Scripture and tradition were somehow regarded as equal partners, was wholly avoided. Instead it was stressed both that the Church's teaching office 'is not above the word of God' and that 'easy access to sacred Scripture should be provided for all the Christian faithful'.

It is impossible in a history of this sort to outline adequately the numerous and often subtle shifts in doctrinal emphasis which the council made, or the public and ecumenical consequence of such shifts. Cumulatively their effect was immense in asserting for Roman Catholicism an official theology, including an attitude to the scriptures, which other Christians could both understand and very largely sympathize with. It is certainly true that doctrines formulated in the past and rejected by other communions, such as papal infallibility and the Assumption of the Virgin Mary, were in no way repudiated. Nevertheless even here the context within which they could now be understood might render them rather different in meaning and acceptability. For Catholics unprepared for all this, and that was the case for most in Britain, the changes could be extremely disturbing. It appeared at times as if the bulwarks they had manned for generations, and not unsuccessfully, were suddenly being dismantled by continental theologians and a council of bishops carried away by a sort of ecumenical euphoria only too similar to the enthusiasms which were gripping the wider society in 1963 and 1964. The Roman communion, despite occasional liberal glimmerings, had moved for centuries with great consistency in a single direction. Now for the first time, and in all sorts of ways, that direction had been suddenly, and almost solemnly, reversed.

Whether it was on the subject of religious freedom, or the action of the Church in the modern world, or the appropriate independence of a local church, or the duty of planned parenthood, or many another matter, the council took up positions which were not always worked out in their full implications but which, all the same, were pregnant with significance for the future. Frequently they appeared to be more in line with preconciliar Protestant than Catholic insights. Of course the theologians of Louvain, French Dominicans like Fathers Congar and Chenu, Jesuits like Henri de Lubac, Jean Daniélou and Karl Rahner, had long been preparing the way for the council's doctrinal shift, but they had been under the greatest suspicion for writing as they did. Moreover their writings, in Britain at least, had not percolated down to the man in the pew. Now, almost with the sudden haste of the newly converted, Catholic orthodoxy appeared to be shedding one rather threadbare robe and clothing itself in another – in fact an older and a richer one, less scholastic and medieval, more scriptural and patristic.

At the end of 1965 the council was over. Sixteen documents of very varying merit had been approved. The bishops had gone home. The pope was left with a massive work of implementation. His sincerity in that task is unquestionable and for the next two years the spirit of the council remained decisively operative as many of its chief figures continued at work pouring out upon the Church a mass of post-conciliar directives, above all in the fields of liturgy and ecumenical relations. Yet it soon became clear not only that the attitudes of the Roman Curia had not changed much (so that an antagonism, always noticeable during the council between the curialists and conciliarists, was still very much in existence) but that – with the council over – the curialists were now quickly recovering much of their old predominance. This was the more serious because of two things: the first was that a number of very important, indeed explosive, issues implicitly within the council's agenda had never been explicitly thrashed out, either by design or by accident. The second was that on almost all matters the council had spoken in very general and theoretical terms. It had seldom (outside the Constitution on the Liturgy) come near to the practical and the specific. In particular it had made no attempt whatsoever to establish in practice a 'collegial' rather than a 'monarchical' Church. For centuries the Catholic Church had been structured in an ever more emphatically monarchical way, as the power of the bishops had been whittled down in relation to that of the Pope (though not in relation to those below them in the hierarchical structure). The council's assertion of 'Collegiality' in Chapter 3 of the Constitution on the Church was about the most carefully argued and doctrinally important element in its work. Yet the council dissolved, leaving the Church to function in practice as monarchically as it had ever done. In fact over the next twenty years, despite the calling from time to time of a brief consultative 'Synod of Bishops', there has been no effective diminution of papal power. Collegiality has remained a word. Monarchy has remained a reality.

The ecclesiastical atmosphere, nevertheless, was changed irrevocably. The intense deference, the almost morbid fear of disagreeing publicly with any papal word whatever, simply melted like the snow in spring. If autocracy remained, its subjects had decamped. The atmosphere of freedom which the council had engendered could not now be eliminated. In practice the council wrote the Church's agenda for the next twenty years as much by what it did not say as by what it did. It was to prove in consequence a very stormy agenda. For many the council had already gone too far and the agenda would consist in reinterpreting it so far as possible in consistency with the pre-conciliar Church. For others, including the pope himself, the Council had gone just far enough. It would be unthinkable not to implement it loyally, but equally it would be very unwise to go much further. For a third group, which included most of those who at the time had welcomed the council most warmly, it had on the contrary not gone far enough. It had allowed married deacons but not married priests. It had favoured responsible parenthood but had been silent about accepting methods of contraception. It had time and again proclaimed the rights and particular character of the local church, but it had not said how the latter could be protected from the shackles of Roman bureaucracy. It had declared the bishops to be colleagues with the Pope in the apostolic college, but had left them to be appointed by the Pope or his curia. It had remained extremely vague about how far relations with other churches could really go. It had stressed the active role required of the laity but remained remarkably quiet about women. Could nuns attending mass in their convent chapel even be allowed to read the lessons?

It has to be recognized that in the circumstances it was nearly impossible for the council to resolve all such issues. Its very creativity engendered questions which, in Catholic circles, could hardly have been raised before its work was done. This did mean, however, that the council, authoritative as it undoubtedly was, did not conclude a period of doubt and disagreement but, to a very great extent, inaugurated one. Its years of excitement had engendered a public debate about every aspect of Church life which could not now be stilled.

All this was not, at first, very obvious. The mood of the Church in 1965 and 1966 remained fairly euphoric. So many new doors were opening, it was not yet clear which doors were to remain closed. Let us conclude this discussion with Michael Ramsey's visit to Rome in March 1966. The contrast with Archbishop Fisher's visit of five years before is immense. Where that was furtive, this was immensely public. After an initial meeting and exchange of greetings in the Sistine Chapel, Pope and Archbishop led together an ecumenical service in St Paul's basilica in which, after the singing of the *Veni Creator Spiritus* and the reading of a lesson (Phil. 2:5-11), each said a prayer and the Our Father was recited. They then signed a 'Common Declaration' announcing their intention 'to inaugurate between the Roman Catholic Church and the Anglican Communion a serious dialogue which, founded on the Gospels and on the ancient common traditions, may lead to that unity in truth, for which Christ prayed'.[12] Here was both a deliberate example of prayer in common and a degree of mutual recognition which would have seemed unimaginable a decade earlier. From now on the relationship in England, as everywhere, between the Catholic Church and the Anglican Communion would have somehow to reflect that service in St Paul's. Whatever the future had in store, it must be something very different from the regular mutual disregard which, at the official level and very largely at the local too, had hitherto characterized that relationship.

35

Anglicans and Free Churchmen

Michael Ramsey was enthroned in the chair of St Augustine as the hundredth Archbishop of Canterbury on 27 June 1961. Like Lang and Temple he had come to Canterbury from York. He had been Bishop of Durham before that and earlier still, Professor of Divinity at both Durham and Cambridge. Like quite a number of outstanding Anglican priests of the inter-war period Ramsey came from a Nonconformist family, but his own Church commitment was clearly high, and with the publication of his first book, *The Gospel and the Catholic Church*, in 1936, he was marked out as probably the most distinguished of Anglo-Catholic theologians – an old Tractarian at heart, but a Tractarian clothed in the new robes of biblical theology. His ecclesiastical advancement represented the mellowed arrival of the liberal Catholicism, which had grown from the Oxford Movement, from Gore and then from the theological developments of the inter-war years, pretty close to the heart of Anglicanism. This was possible only by breaking out from the rather stuffy limits of conventional Anglo-Catholicism. The breaking out process had been going on a long time in one way and another. In the case of Ramsey, while he could never possibly identify with the Protestant tradition as such, it was his arrival at Canterbury and an absolutely national role which seems to have helped his submerged Nonconformist conscience to resurface, releasing him from the legacy of a somewhat complacent Tractarianism and allowing him to become a truly national primate. National, too, because he had broken free from the conventional image of prelacy beloved of central Anglican tradition. Where Fisher was seldom seen except in frock coat and gaiters, Ramsey was almost always dressed in a purple cassock – more Catholic and ecumenical, a lot less traditional to Anglicanism, it seemed more congenial to the spirit of the sixties.

More than any senior Anglican bishop before him, Ramsey had learnt greatly from contemporary Roman Catholicism and admired it, especially the Belgian and German liturgical movement, the writings of theologians like Yves Congar and Hans Urs von Balthasar. While at York he had developed an excellent relationship with Archbishop Heenan, and he later co-authored a book with Cardinal Suenens. Perhaps the most cherished moment of his life would remain the signing with Pope Paul at St Paul's-Outside-the-Walls of 'The Common Declaration' in 1966. Yet he retained, just because he felt himself so much a Catholic, an enduring bitterness over the Roman condemnation of Anglican orders and considerable touchiness over the activities of the Roman Catholic Church in England, conversions above all.

Ramsey was less of an arch-administrator than Fisher, far less omnicompetent than Temple, less of a professional politician than Lang. Destined to lead the Church through an exceptionally stormy and uncertain period, he may have seemed at times less immediately effective in the leadership he offered. He had to be, far more than his predecessors, a pilgrim, exploring the way forward for himself also, rather than presiding from some central and assured position. If he was able to do this in a way reassuring for many – and he was surely the first of modern archbishops of Canterbury whose leadership many a Roman Catholic could in practice often accept – it was not only that he was unpompous and unprelatical but also because of his exceptionally deep resources of intellect and spirituality. That deep furrowed forehead and rather firm mouth added too to the sense that here was an authority to be relied upon, whether or not one was an Anglican. It was such an authority as the Church would now sorely need.

That need was not so evident in 1961. It is true that Ramsey said before his enthronement: 'It may be the will of God that our Church should have its heart broken';[1] the words may be judged prophetic, but not seemingly over relevant to the world of 1961. Fisher had just remarked, with his eyes observing sharply enough the present surface of things, that he left the Church in good heart. The *Church of England Newspaper* too had recently declared editorially: 'A new Church of England is being born, a Church efficient, sophisticated and progressive, a Church with money enough and to spare'.[2] The General Assembly, re-elected in 1959, might seem good evidence of that. Sir Kenneth Grubb, very much a man of the world, a man who had served his time as a missionary before becoming both businessman and ecclesiastical statesman, replaced the earl of Selborne as chairman of the House of Laity. The aristocratic note, which had long dominated the leadership of that House, was almost gone. It is worth listing the members of its Standing Committee for 1940 and 1960 to demonstrate how immense the change here was, especially since the 1959 election.

1940: The Earl of Selborne; Lord Daryngton; Col. Sir Robert Williams, Bt; Major Sir John Birchall, MP; Caroline Viscountess Bridgeman; Mr Buckmaster; Viscount Caldecote; Lord Hugh Cecil; the Hon. Mildred Gibbs; Earl Grey; Mr Kelway; Lord Mamhead of Exeter; Mr Albert Mitchell; Lt.-Col. Oldham; Sir Philip Baker Wilbraham, Bt.

1960: Sir Kenneth Grubb; Sir Eric Gore Browne; Mr O. Clarke; Mr W. Coles; Mr George Goyder; Mr T. Levett; Mr M. McQueen; Mrs Ridley; Mr Peter Winkworth.

Not only did the new Standing Committee include no Old Etonian, Harrovian or Wykehamist (as against four; one; one, respectively, in 1940), it included only two Oxford men and none from Cambridge. The Church of England, on this evidence, might seem almost truculently set in 1960 upon projecting a new image: 'efficient, sophisticated and progressive'.

The best-seller of 1961 was the *New English Bible*, an ecumenical work of scholarship written under the chairmanship of C. H. Dodd. It had taken years to produce, a piece of scholarly literature at once orthodox and modern. In May, a month before Ramsey's enthronement, Guildford Cathedral had been consecrated in the presence of the Queen: the first Anglican cathedral to be built on a new site in the south of England since the Middle Ages. It was very large, not untraditional, yet modern. A year later it was the turn of Coventry. At Guildford, and still more at Coventry, we find symbolically expressed this new Church of England: efficient, sophisticated, progressive.

At the same time confirmations and ordinations were at a high

point, though confidently expected to rise still higher. Twenty-six
Anglican theological colleges were at work, training the clergy of
the future. Change, of course, was still needed. This was part of
the logic of the Macmillan age. But change meant growth rather
than decline – like the important new Department of Theology
opened in Bristol University in 1964: a particularly ecumenical
venture whose first professor was a Methodist. Moreover change
could now be undertaken from a position of strength after a
sophisticated analysis of the situation had been obtained. With
this in mind Leslie Paul, a widely versed lay writer and theologian, was asked to produce a comprehensive Report on *The
Deployment and Payment of the Clergy*. He did it most carefully
and sociologically. When published early in 1964 it was hailed as
an authoritative and professional piece of analysis. Unfortunately it was just wrong, based on gravely false assumptions.
Writing in 1962 and 1963, Paul had behind him a decade in
which the number of ordinations and the general state of things –
church attendance, finance, and the rest – had been pretty
steadily improving. Perhaps a little unimaginatively he presumed
that this would continue almost indefinitely. In point of fact he
wrote at the very peak of the movement when decline was just
about to set in, and set in fast. There is something rather pathetic,
indeed a little ludicrous, about the Church turning for the first
time, in this new age of efficiency, to lay sociology to obtain a
thoroughly professional view of what it should be doing with its
priests and how many of them it would have, and being quite so
grotesquely misled.

The figures are as follows: Paul's predicted number of ordinations for the next nine years were what he regarded as a
'conservative' estimate (i.e. on the low side). Set below them are
the number of those who, as a matter of fact, were in due course
ordained.[3]

	1963	1964	1965	1966	1967	1968	1969	1970	1971
Paul Report	642	662	686	713	737	761	785	809	831
Fact	636	605	592	576	496	478	436	437	393

This is perhaps as good an illustration as any of what suddenly began to happen in the Church from 1963, producing within a very few years a situation immensely different from that of the early sixties and going far to justify Ramsey's prophecy, uttered to a still smug age, 'it may be the will of God that our Church should have its heart broken'.

What had happened? What seems certain is that there is no simple answer to that question. It would surely be mistaken to see the statistical decline as a straight consequence of the disturbance produced by the new ideas and sudden religious excitement of those years, and yet it would be equally mistaken to separate the two phenomena too completely. We need at least to look at them both in themselves before attempting to explain their relationship.

First, the excitement. We have seen already something of the secular character of 1963, as also the enthusiasm and sense of expectation generated by the Vatican Council. The religious world of Britain, particularly the south-east of Britain, was undoubtedly caught up in this mood of rather heady and optimistic novelty. The great sign of it all was John Robinson's *Honest to God*. It was one Sunday in early March 1963 that readers of the *Observer* were confronted with a special article extracted from a forthcoming book by a distinguished bishop, entitled 'Our Image of God Must Go'. It is possible that without the almost fortuitous publicity produced by nearly a million copies of the *Observer*, the book might never have made the national, and indeed international impression that it did. It went through four impressions that March and nearly a million copies were sold within three years. Only the Bible could rival it. English religion of the 1960s will always remain more associated with *Honest to God* than with any other book.[4]

Robinson was by no means a natural revolutionary. Born in the precincts of Canterbury, with more clergy ancestors than could be counted, he was quintessentially an Anglican priest and had never seriously considered being anything else. He was also a distinguished biblical scholar, not quite at home anywhere but in Cambridge, though he was now for a few years suffragan bishop of Woolwich – suffragan to his old friend, Mervyn Stockwood, whose curate he had once been years earlier in Bristol. Robinson was a man of exceptional intellectual versatility, an easy writer with a quite special facility for articulating what a great many more people were thinking. He was at heart not unconservative yet with a penchant for appearing a little naughtily radical. In *Honest To God*, which he wrote in hospital in rather a hurry, he picked out some of the more startling themes of the leading radical theologians of the preceding decades – Tillich, Bonhoeffer and Bultmann – and melted them together in a brief 140-page book which almost anyone could read. At other times it might have been disregarded. In 1963 it became a best seller.

Robinson had sensed quite correctly that the 1950s religious revival, such as it was, had really not got through to the ordinary modern pagan at all. On the contrary, the gap between the new secular mentality and the churches seemed greater than ever. His intention was a missionary one. Christianity, if it is to mean anything in the future to more than 'a tiny religious remnant', has got to change its style radically, and learn a new language in which 'the most fundamental categories of our theology – of God, of the supernatural, and of religion itself – must go into the melting'. Perhaps we are even called to a 'Copernican Revolution' in which 'the God of traditional theology' must be given up 'in any form'.[5] He meant to be constructive but for many of his more churchy readers he seemed instead quite unnecessarily destructive. Yet in this, as in several of his other books, John Robinson was with little doubt the most effective writer of popular religious literature since C. S. Lewis, if in many ways Lewis's opposite. Both were highly persuasive. Lewis was a man for the fifties, suspicious of modernity, unwilling to allow the smallest particle of traditional doctrine to be thrown overboard unexamined. Robinson was a man for the sixties, apparently willing to de-mythologize almost anything of which modernity might conceivably be suspicious. He was both denounced as heretical by many an insider and hailed as a guiding light by many an outsider. *Honest To God* was quickly followed by *The New Reformation* (1965) which, comparing the present time with that of the first Reformation, dealt a good deal more positively than *Honest To God* with what Christians should now do – in liturgy, lay theology and the like. At heart Robinson was always quite an old-fashioned believer – as well as being a pastorally minded bishop – though trying on occasion not to look like one. English theological thought by the end of the fifties was moving quickly away from the neo-traditionalism of the last twenty years. In biblical interpretation particularly, under the influence of Bultmann and the 'Form Critical' school, led in England by Dennis Nineham, Regius Professor of Divinity in Cambridge during the sixties and an enormously influential figure in academic circles, a radical questioning of historicity was again in fashion. To liberal theologians at the time their conclusions seemed extraordinarily convincing; to the observer they often seem more a matter of mood than of scholarly decisiveness. The mood of Robinson's books can be found, then, in much other writing of the time – in, for instance, the much discussed symposium entitled *Soundings*, written by a group of Cambridge theologians and edited by Alec Vidler, in 1962 – but nobody else in Britain could express these things so aptly, so attractively for the mass media, so infuriatingly for the conservative.

'We need urgently, all of us whether Anglicans or non-Anglicans, new beginnings. I say deliberately *beginnings*'; so wrote Donald MacKinnon, also in 1962.[6] People were calling for this 'New Reformation' upon every side. One had anyway to keep up with Rome. A new beginning could be made in many ways. There was first the theological, and *Honest to God* would soon be followed from across the Atlantic by the still more radical 'Death of God' theologians; secondly, the pastoral, ministerial and liturgical – the attempt to look afresh at the Church's own daily life and organization; thirdly, the ecumenical – a suddenly surfacing impatience with the stale, often seemingly trivial separation between denominations; fourthly, the turning to the secular: the conviction that religious life should be far less concerned with the Church itself, far more with 'the World' and particularly with the struggle to overcome misery and injustice.

Let us start with the most ecclesiastically acceptable item – pastoral reform. Liturgical change was the first breakthrough point in the Vatican Council, and the Vatican Council was to a very real extent now making the running for everyone else. We have seen also how the Parish and People movement, founded in 1949, had been the chief pressure group for liturgical reform in the Church of England but had taken so distinctly gradualist an approach that by 1960 it seemed to progressives to have become too 'frightfully respectable'.[7] In that year a small new reforming movement calling itself the Keble Conference Group came into being. Its purpose was a far wider and more radical reappraisal of the Church's pattern of ministry. It drew its inspiration from the group of clergy gathering in the diocese of Southwark around Mervyn Stockwood and John Robinson, which was coming to be labelled 'South Bank'. Southwark had long been a pretty religion-less area and by 1960 in its deanery of Battersea, for instance, less than one per cent of the population visited an Anglican church on an average Sunday.[8] That was the background which triggered off *Honest to God* – Robinson's pretty hasty reaction on moving from Cambridge to Woolwich. In Woolwich itself Nicholas Stacey, the dynamic young vicar of its eighteenth-century parish church, St Mary's, was battling to revive the weary life of a tiny congregation, turning the crypt into a discotheque, housing the local Council of Social Services, enclosing the galleries for trans-formation into a coffee bar.[9] In 1963 the Southwark Ordination Scheme was launched, a programme for the training of worker priests. Finally late in 1963, after a good deal of negotiating, the Keble Conference Group was merged with Parish and People at a special joint meeting held that October. The proposal was seconded by the bishop of Woolwich and a new full-time secre-tary was appointed: Eric James, another member of the South-wark team. The aim was to galvanize Parish and People and make it the effective spearhead for a new theology, a new liturgy, a new pattern of ministry, a new laity, new and dynamic social action. The ideas and inspiration were clearly Robinsonian, even if he played little part in what followed. Nevertheless for many people his influence was now both ubiquitous and sinister, the principal source of 'South Bank religion' (a media term for anything original which could be linked with Southwark).

While the new Parish and People's inauguration had been timed to coincide with the publication of the Paul Report, which had been eagerly awaited as offering some sort of a blue print for reform, when it appeared it disappointed reformers with its rather modest proposals. As a matter of fact such major recom-mendations as it did make – for the abolition of the Parson's Freehold and the patronage system, for instance – would not have been implemented even twenty years later, but at the time such recommendations seemed to fall far short of the radical restructuring of the ministry, including its de-professionalization, which reformers believed necessary if the progressive decay of the Church, throttled by its traditional clerical structures, was to be averted. 'The Paul Report does not provide us with a platform', was the conclusion.[10] For the next two years Eric James would stamp the country urging a far more decisive 'new beginning'.

On the ecumenical front still more was happening. It seemed that here, if anywhere, the 'New Reformation' might really be about to take place. Already late in 1961 a group of Anglican theologians, led by Professor Geoffrey Lampe, had stepped so far out of the traditional Anglican line as to appeal for inter-communion in an open letter to the Archbishops of Canterbury and York. They were, of course, strongly criticized for doing so. What is striking is how more and more people of very different backgrounds came in practice in the following years to a conviction that not to communicate sacramentally between Christians (especially Christians who were otherwise doing so much in common) was simply wrong. More than anywhere else the tidal wave of ecumenism during the next twenty years, while it would frequently fail to make much impact on the walls of institutional division, would advance seemingly irresistibly at the level both of personal relationships and of the sharing of the Eucharist. In the sixties the necessity of this would, by and large, prove convincing for Anglican and Free churchmen: in the seventies the same conviction would spread to Roman Catholics too.[11]

In the early 1960s, more than at any other time before or since, the churches in England were very much aware of being part of a wider international ecclesiastical world – of the Vatican Council, of an extremely active World Council of Churches, and of the emergence into the full light of day of many third world churches which had hitherto been somewhat confined by colonial wrappings. This international scene was in all sorts of ways an intensely ecumenical one, in which almost endless conferences were being held and observers from other churches always expected to take part. Moreover in many parts of the world projects of corporate reunion were rapidly advancing: North

India, Zambia, Canada, Nigeria ... When Oliver Tomkins, Bishop of Bristol and the Church of England's senior ecumenical expert, attended the Faith and Order Conference of the World Council at Montreal in July 1963, he reported a feeling of urgent intensity gripping everyone, of not being quite able to keep up with the speed of Church progress: 'the sense of panting along in the rear of events'.[12]

It was at Britain's own Faith and Order Conference, held the next year at Nottingham, September 1964, that this sense of urgency really boiled over. It was the most important specifically British ecumenical conference ever to be held. Five hundred delegates met together in Nottingham University, not – it was noted – in an old-fashioned place like Oxford or Cambridge but in a truly 'modern secular university' properly adjusted to 'the academic and technological needs of modern secular man'.[13] Presided over by Bishop Tomkins, with the veteran Eric Fenn as its chaplain and the veteran Dominican Henry St John among the Roman Catholic Observers, it included all the most experienced ecumenists of Great Britain from Quakers to Catholics. What at this high point of hope could the conference actually suggest? While the Anglican-Methodist Unity talks had for years been slowly advancing, and nobody could underestimate the importance of their coming to fruition, something more precise and more all-embracing seemed required to match the enthusiasm of the hour. That something was met by what Norman Goodall called 'the splendidly irrational symbol of the date "1980"'.[14] Nottingham would always be remembered for that date. On the final day of the conference the following resolution was passed:

> United in our urgent desire for One Church Renewed for Mission, this Conference invites the member churches of the British Council of Churches, in appropriate groupings such as nations, to covenant together to work and pray for the inauguration of union by a date agreed amongst them.
> We dare to hope that this date should not be later than Easter Day, 1980. We believe that we should offer obedience to God in a commitment as decisive as this.

Conference after conference had talked of 'the urgency' of unity, so much so that, it was felt, the verbal currency seemed to be becoming devalued. Nottingham's '1980' for a time revalued it. It offered a covenantal hope for half a generation and if that was in fact not fulfilled, it was not less significant at the time. Nottingham did, furthermore, stimulate a lot of more immediate 'all in one place' ecumenical enthusiasm – the establishment of areas of local experimental ecumenical unity – which spread steadily enough in the following years.

It was within this sort of ecumenical atmosphere that the new spirit was manifested most successfully: at the Nottingham Conference; in *New Christian*, a lively weekly begun in 1965 (it held a conference entitled The World is the Agenda at Birmingham the next year); in the expansion of Christian Aid. But what about the old stalwart of ecumenical life, the SCM?

Ambrose Reeves was appointed its General Secretary in 1962. He had previously been an outstanding bishop of Johannesburg, a very active and efficient opponent of apartheid policies. He had been deported after the Sharpeville massacre in 1960 and had, of course, been much in the public eye. It must have seemed an excellent choice at the time, but in fact Reeves was a tired man unable to reorientate himself adequately both to Britain and to a younger generation. Yet it would surely be a mistake to lay on Reeves the principal responsibility for the rapid decay of SCM in the following years. Decay had undoubtedly set in already in the 1950s. Until then it had been a force of genuinely national significance not only for student life but in its wider Church influence. David Edwards could still write in 1959: 'The SCM today is a powerful force in the universities and colleges where tomorrow is shaped, and it has been like that for over sixty momentous years.'[15] Its combination of liberal orthodoxy, biblical studies, a concern for both Christian unity and social problems, had been just what the inter-war years needed, but times had in fact changed. Perhaps it was just because its message had been so widely received that the organization itself was losing apparent significance. Equally its role of providing a unifying force in Christian student life had been undermined by the advance both of Evangelicals, who had moved into the increasingly powerful and ubiquitous Christian Union, and of Roman Catholics. Even within its own old constituency the SCM had lost ground owing to the multiplication of denominational chaplaincies and student societies, a more or less inevitable

development as redbrick universities grew in size and importance. Perhaps it was because the post-war SCM was losing its old
over-arching role that it had struck out, rather perilously, to win
new support. Already in 1951 it removed any condition of
Christian commitment for membership. While the intention had
been to draw the uncommitted of good will into its ranks, in
practice the consequence was to make it less attractive because it
stood for less. The uncommitted would prefer Student Union
politics anyway. The SCM's theoretical uncommittedness
seemed simply to justify the Christian Union's separation and the
tendency of the committed to go there instead.

In this state of both uncertainty and openness the SCM was
well set to be carried far by the enthusiasms of the sixties,
particularly the enthusiasm for secular action: the world is the
agenda. The appointment of Bishop Reeves must already have
been made with that somehow in mind. Here as elsewhere a
moment of intense excitement was nevertheless followed quite
quickly both by a withdrawal of the less radical and a realization
that there was almost no specific point left to the SCM. Other,
more precise organizations could work far more effectively for
this cause or that. The SCM by the latter years of the decade
would seem to be left almost without message, constituency or
even material resources.

It is not that, in other quarters, the secular concern of the 1960s
Christian was just a matter of ephemeral hot air. On the contrary.
While it took a vast variety of forms, many of them were both
practical and successful. At the centre was the great growth in
Christian Aid, the relief arm of the BCC (so named only from
1964). From 1957 the annual Christian Aid Week had been
growing into an event of national importance. In the fifties it had
an income of some £200,000, by the end of the sixties this had
grown to two and a half million.[16] Other new arrivals of the
post-war years, like the Samaritans and the Cheshire Homes,
spread far wider in the sixties than in the fifties, and they were
joined by more and more such movements: Shelter; the Cyrenians; Cicely Saunders's Hospices for the Dying;[17] numerous
Housing Associations; Amnesty; 'The People Next Door'; the
Notting Hill Group Ministry. To these may be joined the Baptist
agitation in 1961 over Portuguese misrule in Angola. Some of

these were more 'secular' than others. None of them was a specifically Church organization (except for the Notting Hill Group Ministry, a Methodist response, encouraged by Donald Soper, to the Notting Hill race riots) but all owed a great deal to Christian inspiration and participation. The range of concern in such organizations extended from the international and the political in Amnesty and over Angola, to the most local and personal in 'The People Next Door', the Cyrenians, St Christopher's Hospice for the Dying. The Angolan Campaign fits well enough into an older pattern but it would be hard to deny that collectively these and similar works added up to a vigorous and lasting shift in the pattern of Christian life, lay life especially.

English religion of the mid-sixties was being pushed rather fast in quite a number of directions – ecumenical, liturgical, world-orientated, charismatic. Proposals and pilot schemes were jostling each other on every side. In part this sprang from, and yet it was not really made easier by, the increasingly obvious absence of an agreed basic position as to belief or goal. In fact the impression of a sort of snowball effect of growing radicalization at the theological level probably did a good deal to undermine the chances of practical achievement by frightening off the hesitant and the old-fashioned believer. In 1961 Don Cupitt, a young Anglican priest at Cambridge, was arguing for dispensing with the Devil: 'The age-long battle of monotheism against the enslavement of men by superstitious fear' would, he claimed, be 'finally' won by denying the devil's existence.[18] That seemed fair enough and Cupitt stressed that 'God and the devil are different' but a little later God too was being found dispensable. Admittedly the 'Death of God' school of theology was mostly an American fashion and a pretty brief one; nevertheless it was much noised abroad. Coupled with the intense stress of the moment upon the duty of relevance to 'the secular city', it helped at one and the same time to distract religious reformers from the ecclesiastical tasks to which they had earlier been committed and to convince doubters that the 'New Reformation' was set to lead to the total dissolution of religion.[19] As a matter of fact the optimistic vision of a secular city advancing upon the Omega Point faded very fast after 1965. The sort of 'radical' theology which, accepting that mythical vision, had come near to abandoning God had very little to say to a world in greater and greater distress. The Anglo-Saxon theology of the sixties was, in reality (unlike the doubtless less sophisticated Latin-American theology), almost never a truly radical theology.

In retrospect the dominant theological mood of that time in its hasty, slack, rather collective sweep reminds one a little painfully of a flight of lemmings, something not wholly undeserving the charge of *trahison des clercs*. A good deal of the more publicized theological writing in the sixties gives the impression of a sheer surge of feeling that in the modern world God, religion, the transcendent, any reliability in the gospels, anything which had formed part of the old 'supernaturalist' system, had suddenly become absurd. There were plenty of fresh insights but too little stringent analysis of the new positions. Everything was to be enthusiastically 'demythologized' in a euphoria of secularization which was often pretty soft in scholarly rigour. Theologically the early years of the century had returned with a vengeance while the middle years of 'neo-Orthodoxy' seemed simply wiped away. At times it looked as if the authority of the Bible, the Church, scholastic theology and Christian spiritual experience were all alike being rejected as 'irrelevant' and outdated, to leave as the new sources of enlightenment little more than sociology, linguistic analysis, modern Marxism, or the study of other religions. The greatest new religious source of enlightenment was undoubtedly Teilhard de Chardin, scientist-mystic and theological optimist. It is striking that the one major survivor from the theological liberalism of forty years earlier, Charles Raven, was now in old age an enthusiastic Teilhardian.

At times of optimism there often appears to be a link between dogmatic 'radicalism' (dropping the incarnation, etc) and socio-religious radicalism (proclaiming the necessity of justice, cost what it may, etc), but the link seldom seems to survive hard times for very long. By the later sixties the cleavage between the two types of 'radicalism', absent in the early sixties, seemed to be reappearing. There was no very evident social implication in the most demythologized of theologies. Social radicalism, whether Marxist or not, if it sought theological support at all, tended to find it in dogmatically more conservative quarters. Donald MacKinnon, in a penetrating lecture in 1968 in Westminster

Abbey, denounced 'theologians who combine a *soi-disant* theological radicalism with an ecclesiological conservatism'.[20] The social conservative might well stick to Bultmann, the social radical needed something more akin to Barth.

Already by the middle of 1965 there were signs that the New Reformation was not going to come so quickly after all. One senses it in the angry special article in the *Observer*, 23 May 1965, on 'How the Church could survive', by Nicholas Stacey, Rector of Woolwich. He had himself just announced that he would shortly no longer be a paid Church minister. He would soon be paid by OXFAM instead. One senses it in the admission of Eric James in January 1966, after two years of hard work for Parish and People, that 'little broad support existed within the Church of England for a radical movement'. 'Humanly speaking I have little or no hope' for renewal, he confessed.[21] One senses it in the sudden shattering withdrawal by Charles Davis in December 1966 from both his priestly work and the Catholic Church, in which he had served all his adult life. Of course there was still a great deal of Church of England reform of very considerable importance on the way: the introduction of Series II in 1967 (the first new Anglican eucharistic liturgy since the Prayer Book débâcle of 1928); the *Pastoral Measure* of 1968; the establishment of synodical government in 1969; the Chadwick *Report on Church-State Relations* of 1970. The *Pastoral Measure*, an extremely complex piece of legislation, arranged for the union of parishes, the setting up of team ministries and the declaring of churches redundant. The new General Synod, opened by Queen Elizabeth in November 1970, replaced the Church Assembly established by the Enabling Act of 1919. It became the supreme legislative authority of the Church of England and consists of three houses: bishops, clergy, laity. The Commission on Church-State Relations, chaired by Owen Chadwick, grasped the nettle of the basic faults of Establishment as preceding commissions had failed to do. It made two recommendations of considerable importance. The first was that the General Synod, and not parliament, should henceforth be the final authority in all matters of worship and doctrine. The second was that bishops should no longer be selected by the Prime Minister but by a committee or college representing both the diocese and the wider Church. It held that these recommendations did not require disestablishment. They were subsequently accepted in substance (the Prime Minister's role in bishop-making has not been wholly removed but whittled down to choosing between two names selected by the Church). It may be argued that the last serious objections to the existence of the Establishment were thereby removed.

The significance of all this was certainly great. Even so, coming after the heady, often hardly formulated hopes of a few years earlier, it could still seem somewhat like an anti-climax – as the down-to-earth reality of institutional reform must almost always do. Moreover it was clouded by the very sharp statistical decline. It was becoming painfully clear that, rather than being rejuvenated, the churches were in some danger of rapidly fading away.

On the international scene the last great verbal expression of the religious radicalism of the western world in the 1960s was the World Council's Conference at Uppsala in 1968. Martin Luther King had been invited to be the conference's special preacher but was assassinated in April. His murder made him more central to the conference than his preaching could have done and the mood became one of intense, almost anguished commitment to the struggle for justice in the world. The old concerns for mission and church unity might appear somewhat secondary, even slightly *passé*, in comparison. Carson Blake, the new General Secretary of the World Council, was far less of a theologian than his Dutch predecessor, Visser 't Hooft. He reflected the dominance of North American Protestantism in international Christian circles in the sixties.[22] A Presbyterian with an impeccable record on civil rights and ecumenical mergers, he was strong on 'programmes' and social involvement. For Blake there was a 'radical newness' in the World Council's Fourth Assembly: 'A new era' began at Uppsala. 'Whether consciously or not, each member of the Assembly knew in his depths that radical change, creative and destructive, was the mark of the times'.[23] There was an almost apocalyptic mood in the world generally that year. If the optimism of six years earlier had quite perished, the radicalism was still very much alive in many parts – among the Catholic bishops meeting at Medellin in Columbia as much as among the World Council delegates at Uppsala. Even, perhaps, in a milder way among the four hundred Anglican bishops meeting for the Lambeth Conference in July and August: at least, critics could accuse them afterwards of 'a head-first plunge towards ecumenism and unity' which could only lead to 'destruction rather than renewal'.[24] It was, anyway in the case of England, now chiefly a matter of verbal radicalism, for it was becoming increasingly clear that the churches had set their faces against real 'radical change' of almost any sort. The dream of it, however, still remained. Thus that summer there was a splendid production of Baron Corvo's *Hadrian VII* in London and very fittingly all the bishops of Lambeth went to see it in special buses, somehow enacting a spiritual pilgrimage to the sort of papacy they could accept. For one short moment, or maybe only in the imagination, Pope John had made it somehow conceivable. But that, like many another change, was now but a dream. The reality of the papacy in 1968 was very different: the encyclical *Humanae Vitae*.

It is hard to plot fairly the progressive course of depression in the next years: the collapse of institutions of renewal, the fading away of its leaders. Kenneth Slack, General Secretary of the BCC, wrote a little book on *The British Churches Today*, in 1960. He revised it in 1969 and found that 'Passage after passage of the book written in 1960 has seemed strangely optimistic and has had to be excised'.[25] One very major project of renewal however had remained on the drawing board through all these years: the reunion of Anglicans and Methodists.[26] Plans had been going steadily if slowly forward. They began soon after Archbishop Fisher's Cambridge Appeal to the Free Churches in 1946. There had been *An Interim Statement* in 1958, a *Report* in 1963, an approval in principle in both Anglican Convocations and the Methodist Conference in 1965, followed by another three years of rather detailed discussion. The final scheme for a two stage reunification preceded by a Service of Reconciliation appeared in 1968. It included what could be taken as a conditional reordination of the Methodist clergy. Certainly Methodism had come a long way in its commitment to unity. Almost all the real and painful concessions had come from its side. It was agreed that a 75 per cent majority would be required upon both sides. On 8 July 1969 they voted. The Methodist vote was 78 per cent in favour, the Anglican (the two Convocations meeting together in London) only 69 per cent. A minority combination of some

Anglo-Catholics (led by Bishop Leonard of Willesden), some Evangelicals and some old die-hards of no particular school had been sufficient to prevent unity and in the words of one commentator to 'reduce the Church of England from comprehension to incoherence'.[27]

For good or ill the acceptance of the scheme would have greatly altered the face of English religion, basically ending the Anglican-Wesleyan schism after two hundred years. It would have stood out as the principal English ecclesiastical achievement of the sixties and, institutionally at least, it would indeed have constituted 'radical change'. Yet it was no Utopian scheme, had been very carefully worked out, and came close to acceptance. Methodism in the 1960s, while awaiting union, had little history, except for an unprecedented rate of numerical decline. At the end it was left with only a smack in the face.[28]

All across the board rather similar things were happening. Parish and People had lost its nerve, despite Oliver Tomkins taking over its chairmanship in 1967. Both Eric James and Trevor Beeson, editor of its journal, moved to other work. The last published issue of *Parish and People* appeared in December 1968. In 1970 the rump of the movement merged with other small renewal groups – Methodist, Baptist, Catholic, Presbyterian and Congregational – in One for Christian Renewal. Denominations were bravely declared 'to be not only meaningless but a hindrance'. It was wholly ecumenical. It was also almost wholly insignificant. The fate of SCM was not much different. It did not actually cease to exist but its activities were more and more curtailed until, after a semi-Marxist period, it moved into a rather opting-out phase, establishing its headquarters in Wick Court, a remote, antique and – at first – horribly cold manor house in the Somerset countryside. What had once been a movement of national importance, the cradle of illustrious names, became little more than another small, almost odd, expression of the search for the alternative society.

Institutions and Church publications of all sorts, old and new, folded in these years. Among journals, add to *Parish and People*, *New Christian* (the principal voice of the religious left from 1965 until its closure in 1970); *Slant*; *Herder Correspondence* (the two chief Catholic contributions to renewal, the one more Marxist, the other more liberal); together with the venerable *Church Quarterly Review* (high church), the *Hibbert Journal* (old-fashioned liberal modernist), and the *London Quarterly* (Methodist).

In 1970 it was announced that the Methodist Kingsway Hall, the place where Soper had preached for thirty years, was to be sold. Methodist theological college closures were particularly traumatic. At the start of our period there were no less than three such colleges in Manchester alone – Didsbury (Wesleyan), Victoria Park (United Methodist), Hartley (Primitive). The two chief Wesleyan colleges in the nineteenth century had been Didsbury for the north and Richmond in London for the south. After 1932 the United Church wisely merged the three Manchester colleges to create Hartley Victoria. Elsewhere it maintained Richmond in London, Handsworth in Birmingham, Wesley College in Headingley, Leeds, together with Wesley House, Cambridge, opened in the 1920s as a principally postgraduate centre of excellence. To these was later added a new Didsbury in Bristol. That was certainly a fair range of colleges across the country but by the 1960s it had become quite unrealistic. In 1970 Handsworth was closed to unite with the Anglican Queen's College, also in Birmingham, and create the only officially ecumenical theological college in England. Next year was Richmond's turn. Finally, after much fierce debate, even Hartley Victoria had to go, merging with Manchester's Baptist College but retaining its own name. This left no independent Methodist theological institution of any sort in the north of the country. Only Bristol and Cambridge – two relatively new foundations – remained unscathed. The move from north to south is particularly striking.

The Church of England closed Ely Theological College in 1964. This was followed in 1969 by St Aidan's, Birkenhead; Bishop's College, Cheshunt, and Worcester Ordination College. In 1970 Rochester joined the list, and in 1972 two still better known institutions, Kelham and Lichfield. A total list of closures of all sorts by all churches in these years would be very lengthy. What is indisputable is that, while some of these closures and mergers can be honestly defended as positive gain, as a whole they are only explicable in terms of a very sharp shift away from organized religion of the old sort – a shift quite unprecedented in speed and spread. It seems clear that in some ways the shift was linked with both the intensity of attempts to reform the churches in the preceding years and with the widespread failure of those attempts to achieve very much. It was obviously linked too with the tendency of radical reform to be taken over by extremist tendencies which quickly turned into either some new form of liberal agnosticism, Marxism, or even an opting out neo-millenarianism, in each case washing its hands of the existing churches. But it is also true that the shift was linked with, perhaps essentially dependent upon, a movement of basic secularization – a decline in any sort of Church commitment by ordinary people – which had preceded all these more ephemeral tendencies and to which they may indeed be seen as in part simply reaction.

The decline can best be observed through a consideration of statistics. It should, first of all, be repeated that – all in all – there had been no very sharp statistical alteration in the religious practice of England between 1890 and 1960: Free Church figures fell fairly considerably, Roman Catholic figures rose, the Anglican decline was pretty steady but seldom appeared calamitous. Thus in 1895 there were 641 Anglican baptisms per thousand live births; in 1960, 554. They had first risen and then fallen in the meantime, but not dramatically so. Over 60 per cent of all marriages were in an Anglican church in the 1890s; they were still almost 50 per cent in 1960. The Newcastle diocese in 1960 had 39,977 Easter communicants – the highest it had ever had; this represented 6.4 per cent of the population over fifteen, just about exactly the same proportion as that of the 21,216 Easter communicants of 1891.[29] Moreover the very real fall of the inter-war years had been somewhat reassuringly, if really only rather slightly, reversed in the 1950s, so that there was no expectation of the sort of sudden statistical collapse which was now to take place.

In October 1969 Bishop Robinson, always quick to recognize a new trend, published an article in *New Christian*, entitled 'The Dramatic Dip': the national ratio of Anglican confirmations had fallen by 32.2 per cent in six years (the six years since *Honest to God* was published), ordinations had dropped by 24.8 per cent in five years, and so forth. There were 191,000 Anglican confirmations in 1960, a rate of 34.2 per thousand of the population aged twelve to twenty years. In 1970 there were 113,000 confirmations, a rate of 19.7. Anglican baptisms had been 55.4 per cent of live births in 1960; they were 46.6 per cent in 1970.[30] If baptisms fell for the first time well below 50 per cent, marriages solemnized by the Church of England went correspondingly well below 40 per cent. Ordination figures, as we have already seen (page 535) decreased from 636 in 1963 to 437 in 1970. Nor, of course, did the decline cease with the end of the decade. It continued relentlessly for several years more. The 636 ordinations of 1963 would be no more than 273 by 1976.

The Free Churches suffered quite as badly. Congregationalist membership fell by 20 per cent in the decade and Presbyterian by nearly as much. Methodist membership, 733 thousand in 1960, was 690 thousand in 1966; 651 thousand in 1969; 601 thousand in 1972; 557 thousand in 1975: a decline of 24 per cent in fifteen years. The Baptists were less involved than others in the excitements of the 1960s; whether for that reason or not they also declined rather less – by some 13 per cent in ten years.

Within the Church of England the Evangelicals had been least affected by either the Vatican Council or Robinsonianism and, while it is impossible to offer precise figures, it seems clear enough that as a group they came through the sixties in far the best shape. Not John Robinson but C. S. Lewis remained their favourite literature. Certainly, their appeal had more obvious public limits than in earlier years. The Billy Graham Crusade in London in 1966 (centred upon the Earls Court Stadium) lasted a month and cost £3,500,000 but it was in no way a repeat of Harringay and remarkably few people attended. In America, where both the popular base and the overseas missionary commitment of Evangelicalism were still expanding, the old symbols retained their potency. Billy Graham was invited to stay with Lyndon Johnson in the White House for his last night in power and then with President Nixon for his first night there. Parties might change but God – and the public role of evangelicalism – remained the same. In Britain by the end of the 1960s such information would hardly act as a commendation.

But in fact English Evangelicalism was now very much going its own way. While the post-war revival had renewed its enthusiasm it had left its character very little altered: Evangelicals in the

1950s seemed to be saying and doing just about the same things as Evangelicals in the 1920s. Liturgically they still clung to the 1662 Prayer Book, frightened that the slightest change meant capitulation to popery: 'Before 1962 the trends in liturgy for evangelicals were nil – everything was static,' writes their leading authority on the subject, Colin Buchanan.[31] Their wider image, remarks another Evangelical scholar, James Packer, was one of 'archaic theology, spiritual conceit, ecclesiastical isolationism, social unconcern, pessimism about the world and the Church, an old fashioned life-style, and a cultural philistinism'.[32] Those are strong words and that they could be written soon after the end of the 1960s by a mainstream Evangelical leader shows just how considerable a change the decade brought for them too: the radicalism of the time helped to set them on new paths without too gravely disrupting their basic sense of identity.[33]

Already in 1960 a Church of England Evangelical Council was founded, and in the same year Latimer House, a sort of Evangelical think-tank at Oxford. It is noticeable that these were Anglican initiatives. One of the clearest characteristics of subsequent developments was the reassertion of English Evangelicalism as being Anglican, in contrast with the far more nondenominational character of Evangelical institutions generally if they formed part of the great American outreach. In 1963 a new experimental 'Evangelical Eucharist' was published: it was a remarkable sign of change both to admit the experimental and to use the word 'Eucharist'. But the great moment of renewal was undoubtedly April 1967 – the National Evangelical Congress at Keele. It had been prepared meticulously by a committee presided over by John Stott and meeting in his vestry at All Souls, Langham Place. Over a thousand people attended the Congress, acclaimed a 'milestone' because it broke so emphatically with the rather negative note of the twentieth-century Evangelical past. 'Evangelicals have a very poor image in the Church as a whole,' Stott declared in a preparatory address, 'We have acquired a reputation for narrow partisanship and obstructionism. We have to acknowledge this, and for the most part we have no one but ourselves to blame.'[34]

The Keele statement with its stress on the need for social responsibility, for ecumenical attitudes, for a willingness to

experiment, for two-way intercommunion, for a greater sacramentalism, was one of the more important ecclesiastical documents, not only of the sixties but of this century. It so greatly
altered the Evangelical sense of direction. It was the first deliberate and public step towards closing the mental schism with most
other Christians which Evangelicals had been somewhat smugly
cultivating ever since 1910. In particular its statement about the
Eucharist was – always in an Evangelical context – little short of
revolutionary: 'we determine to work towards the practice of a
weekly celebration of the Sacrament as the central corporate
Service of the Church'.[35] Evangelicals were here at last re-
entering, instead of battling against, the central worshipping
development of the century – embracing the principal positive
contribution of Anglo-Catholicism, the liturgical movement,
Parish and People. Just as Vatican II was making it possible for
non-Roman Catholics to be on the same wavelength as Catholics, so Keele made it possible for non-Evangelicals to be on the
same wavelength as Evangelicals. Let us not exaggerate. Keele
lasted two and a half days. Well prepared as it was, formative as it
managed to be, it still pointed the way rather than accomplished a
transformation. How far that transformation would go within a
group for so long set so rigidly in its ways, it would not quickly be
possible to say. What Keele did was to offer Evangelicals a viable
road forward in line with Christendom as a whole, an immediate
not too revolutionary programme which enabled them as a group
to weather the storms of the 1960s rather well. They would still
be faced with basic problems of theology and biblical interpretation which their increased openness on other fronts would
make it all the more difficult to evade, but they would for a while
combine a sense of clear purpose with pastoral vigour and a
willingness to learn in a way that almost no one else could rival. It
is hardly surprising if by 1972, 35 per cent of all Anglican
ordinands were in the six Evangelical colleges.

The Anglo-Catholic party, on the other hand, lay devastated.
This may appear strange because it was in a way the moment of
its greatest victory. They were not only as solidly ensconsed
within the Establishment as ever – Michael Ramsey was the most
emphatically Anglo-Catholic Archbishop of Canterbury yet –
but the whole history of their struggles seemed somehow vindi-

cated in the light of the rapprochement between Canterbury and Rome. They had always looked hopefully towards Rome, however bleakly Rome had looked at them. Now the Malines Conversations were lauded upon all sides while Pope Paul himself could speak of the Church of England as 'a sister Church' and present Archbishop Ramsey after their meeting with his own fisherman's ring. Their goals of reunion seemed at times almost unbelievably close to realization. Yet Anglo-Catholicism was as much a victim of the sixties as the SCM – if half of its goals were now generally accepted (even by Evangelicals), the other half seemed more absurd than ever (all that preoccupation with birettas and incense). Both the changes of the Vatican Council and the new theology cut the ground from beneath so many of the more petty things they had clung to too tenaciously. The narrow anti-Protestant, anti-ecumenist hard line which had characterized so many of their battles – as, for instance, in the long struggle against recognition of the Church of South India – seemed now actually un-Catholic and rather foolishly archaic. Much of the apparent 'Protestantizing' going on within Roman Catholicism proved very hard to take. As a matter of fact traditional Anglo-Catholic culture had been already clearly crumbling in the fifties – it was very noticeable, for instance, in the matter of celibacy, which was fading fast as an Anglo-Catholic ideal. In reaction to the sudden loss of so much of their customary approach, young Anglo-Catholics, like young Roman Catholics, tended to rush into all the enthusiasms of the new theology, which in part grew out of the tradition of liberal Catholicism anyway. *Honest to God* might get a cold reception among the students at the London College of Divinity; it was warmly welcomed by most at Mirfield.[36] While in the stress of the times Evangelicals tended to go more evangelical, young Anglo-Catholics went less Anglo-Catholic and more 'radical'. Anglo-Catholicism as a consequence lost much of its old cohesiveness as a party, split between an obstinate conservative, rather elderly rump clinging to old ways, and a radical but somewhat leaderless younger group, profoundly influenced by Vatican II as by Bishop Robinson and much else, but not seeing at all clearly where now to go.

Donald Coggan became Archbishop of York in succession to Michael Ramsey and he would, in due course, also succeed him at

Canterbury. It was in some ways appropriate. He had been a leading figure in the Evangelical revival from the thirties and Principal of the London College of Divinity before becoming Bishop of Bradford. Yet Evangelicals could still declare that they had not a single episcopal spokesman in the country. Coggan was an able and honourable man, impeccably clerical, with a narrower range of experience than any of his twentieth-century predecessors but successful within that range. He disappointed the clergy but reassured the laity. It was his misfortune that, as a bishop and a scholar, he was a little too liberal to retain the full confidence of Evangelicals but too Evangelical to be quite on the wavelength of either liberals or Anglo-Catholics. Yet he did in point of fact represent quite well the outlook of the common churchman within the Established Church.

But the bishop who seemed most adroitly in tune with the mood of the sixties was not Coggan, nor even Michael Ramsey, but Ian Ramsey, Bishop of Durham from 1966 to 1972, and before that Nolloth Professor of the Philosophy of Religion at Oxford.[37] More than any other ecclesiastical leader of the second half of the twentieth century he resembled William Temple in the breadth of his concerns, the immensity of his commitments, the impression of confident modernity he conveyed, the engaging geniality and optimism of his temperament. Ramsey was a man most suited to the sixties, a quintessential liberal upon every intellectual and social issue, yet no whit less deeply religious for that. Perhaps he spent himself too widely in an age far more specialist than that of Temple to be fully effective in any field, and – just as people were anticipating that he would be moved to Canterbury on Michael Ramsey's retirement – he died of overwork, aged fifty-seven, in 1972. He had been a principal speaker at the Church Leaders Conference at Birmingham a few weeks before,[38] and both his death and that conference – a last exciting but ineffectual display of sixties fireworks – marked as well as anything the end of an ecclesiastical mini-age.

There was still plenty of vigour in many places, not all of them Evangelical. Let us consider two more. The first is the Charismatic or neo-Pentecostal movement.[39] Here again we find ourselves back in 1963 and at All Souls, Langham Place, where

Michael Harper was a curate. The modern charismatic movement (characterized specifically by 'speaking with tongues') began in California in 1959. Unlike the Pentecostal movement of the start of the century, neo-Pentecostalism did not break away from the traditional churches and by 1963 it included several hundred Episcopalians, Presbyterians and Lutherans. That year a Lutheran pastor from California visiting London set Harper on the road to speaking in tongues and to becoming the acknowledged leader of a new movement in English Christianity.

Pentecostalism, it might seem, was almost the exact antithesis of typical 1960s religion. The latter, as we have seen it, was emphatically anti-supernaturalist. It found little or no 'relevance' in miracles, angels, heaven and hell, even petitionary prayer. The Bible, to be usable at all, had to be sternly de-mythologized. It was this-worldly religion, endeavouring to be as 'relevant', as 'secular', even as political as possible. The charismatic movement, on the contrary, was intensely supernaturalist. It was pretty fundamentalist in regard to the Bible and was preoccupied with intercessory prayer – even for such material ends as the lengthening of short legs. It believed emphatically in miracles. It is important then to note that, like so much else, it dates its English beginnings from around 1963, but also that its expansion was far more a phenomenon of the late 1960s and early 1970s.

Michael Harper had been a typical young member of the Evangelical élite. 'Converted' at Cambridge in 1950, member of CICCU, trained at Ridley and ordained in 1955, he was chosen to be one of Stott's curates. When Harper's flat developed into the new centre of British Pentecostalism, however, Stott was not happy. Traditional Evangelicalism is very far from Pentecostalist and the relationship between Stott and Harper reflects a basic tension within Evangelicalism as to whether the charismatic movement is really acceptable. While the two have so much in common, the ultimate issue of authority can hardly not divide them: for the Evangelical it lies in the Bible, for the Pentecostal in the Holy Spirit speaking today. In June 1964 Harper resigned his curacy and four months later the Fountain Trust was established as an ecumenical charismatic institution with Harper as its secretary. It would stand as the principal British embodiment of neo-Pentecostalism beside such American embodiments as the Full Gospel Business Men's Fellowship International (FGBMFI) (Los Angeles) and Melodyland (just opposite Disneyland), also in California.

If neo-Pentecostalism sprang to life in California, it represented the latest form of a very long American tradition of Protestant revivalism. What came to make it seem so different in the course of the sixties and seventies was something else, a typical 1960s phenomenon, the general breaking down of barriers. This enabled Pentecostalism to thrive and spread in churches where, previously, it would not have been tolerated, particularly (from the later sixties) the Roman Catholic. By the end of the decade the charismatic movement had become a mix of typical Protestant revivalism and the more Catholic type of renewal which had burst forth in the Catholic and Anglican churches in the wake of the Vatican Council. It provided a new leaven for the latter, a vast new forum for the former.

In November 1965 the FGBMFI of Los Angeles flew an 'airlift' of several hundred of its members to hold a neo-Pentecostal Convention in London at the Hilton Hotel with a final session in the Albert Hall. If John R. Mott represented the correct model for the exportation of American religion in the 1920s, Frank Buchman in the thirties, Niebuhr in the forties and Graham in the fifties, the FGBMFI might share the honour with, perhaps, Harvey Cox and Carson Blake in the sixties. The airlift was not in vain. By the end of 1965 there were reckoned to be more than a hundred ministers of historic churches in Britain who had experienced the 'Baptism of the Holy Spirit' (speaking in tongues). It is true, nevertheless, that this would remain for the time a relatively small movement until, with the practical collapse of institutional reformism at the end of the decade and the almost simultaneous entry of Roman Catholics into Pentecostalism, it would emerge in the early 1970s as one of the principal forces within Church life as a whole.

Our second example is that of the new churches springing up among coloured immigrants. In one of Barbara Pym's last novels, *Quartet in Autumn*, a rather weary white spinster in London is upset to find the house she lives in has been bought by a Nigerian who turns out to be a priest of the Aladura Church. Dismayed by the very warmth, friendliness and religious enthusiasm of the house congregation meeting noisily beneath her, Letty quickly moves away to lodge instead in the silence of a house belonging to a tiresome but churchy lady in her eighties. This was written, one feels, as a parable of the way things were going.

By the end of the sixties there were forty or more different churches, mostly West Indian, which had sprung up in England in the wake of the immigration. Some were very small but a few had many thousands of practising members.[40] While all were not Pentecostal, the largest were. Take the New Testament Church of God and the Church of God of Prophecy. Both were in origin white North American Pentecostal churches but both were fully inter-racial and had become thoroughly indigenized in the West Indies before arriving in Britain. This was the key to their success here and very rapid spread. The New Testament Church of God had twenty-three congregations in Britain in 1964, sixty-one two years later.[41] In practice in Britain they were all entirely, or almost entirely, black. Immigrants found the existing churches mostly staid, elderly and very little interested in them. They had been Anglicans, Baptists or Roman Catholics in Jamaica, but the great majority quickly ceased to be so in Britain. The new churches offered a far more attractive 'place to feel at home', as well as strong pretty fundamentalistic biblical doctrine, baptism by immersion, a stress on moral holiness, and a close, sharing human community. They also continued to provide – and this, on account of their one-race membership, might easily be overlooked – an essentially universalistic religious faith which combined with their stress on good neighbourliness was bound to make a valuable contribution to good race relations.[42]

The scale of these churches in immigrant areas may be illustrated by a consideration of Handsworth, Birmingham.[43] The first West Indian Church to open in Handsworth was the United Church of Jesus Christ Apostolic which acquired the former Unitarian building in Gibson Road in 1957. The New Testament Church of God moved into the former Methodist Aston Villa church in 1961. By the early 1970s there were eighteen different West Indian churches worshipping in Handsworth. While most met in schoolrooms, five had by then acquired buildings formerly used by white churches: the two already named, the Church of

God of Prophecy, the Light and Life Fellowship and the Church of God (Seventh Day). Moreover the old Seventh Day Adventist church, formerly white in congregation, was now 80 per cent black with a black pastor. The Church of Prophecy with thirty-two different local congregations in the Birmingham area had established its headquarters in Handsworth.

For such churches, while buildings were useful and a source of pride, they were secondary. Here we are back at a true primacy of the congregation – a primacy both over building and over denominational network. We are back, then, very much at what a 'Free Church' really meant in origin. When we record the decline of the old Free Churches, which had indeed so largely lost their function in a middle-class world burdened with buildings and denominational superstructure, it is well to remember that beneath their feet new Free Churches, not at all unlike in spirit the Primitive Methodist or Baptist Congregation of a hundred and fifty years earlier, were springing up on many a side in the less affluent areas of our great cities. Some Churches might be withdrawing from Handsworth but Christianity was not.

Roman Catholicism

It was good to be an English Catholic bishop in 1960. Old prejudices had disappeared. All the doors were open. Numbers had never been so high. Between 1959 and 1964 Catholic infant baptisms were more than 15 per cent of the nation's total live births.[1] In 1961 there were over forty-four thousand marriages in Catholic churches in England and Wales – 12.76 per cent of the total, the highest ever reached. The peak figure for converts to Catholicism in 1959 was 13,735 but the annual figure remained over twelve thousand until 1962. By 1967 9.3 per cent of children in ordinary government supported schools were in Catholic ones, now hardly less than the 11.8 per cent in Church of England schools (recall the 5.4 and 40.2 per cent respectively in 1900) and that was probably not more than 60 per cent of the Catholics of school age in the country. Of course, there were millions of 'lapsed' Catholics around, plenty of Irishmen who had never practised since settling in England; nevertheless, the English Catholic Church did appear to be a considerable pastoral success. It had retained its discipline but lost its harshness and its under-education. It had, and this was important, ceased to make the rest of the community afraid of it. Catholicism was respected as never before and even Free churchmen had almost ceased to object to the provision of very large sums of tax money for Catholic schools.[2] While the Education Act of 1959 made some further concessions to Catholics, it was the Act of 1967 which really gave their schools a new deal: 80 per cent grant not only for repairs and improvements to existing schools but also – and this had never previously been admitted – for completely new schools. Hardly a dissentient voice was raised against thus granting so much of what the Catholic Church had been campaigning for over several decades.[3] Since May 1963 an inter-church group of nine had been meeting twice a year to discuss educational affairs, comprising three Anglicans, three Free churchmen and three Catholics. The educational consensus established between the Free Churches and Anglicans prior to the Education Act of 1944 had now been extended to include Catholics, principally to the advantage of the latter.

Catholics had, it may be claimed, earned this new dispensation by their convincing commitment to the very centre of the English political tradition. They were, of course, quite properly not unanimous in their political loyalties. There was a group of them on the far right of the Conservative Party and there were always some to be found on the far left of Labour, but these were by no means typical of modern Catholicism. By and large Catholics had become liberals with a small l. Their two leading figures in politics, Shirley Williams and Norman St John Stevas (at one time Minister of Education and Shadow Minister of Education – that indicates well enough where Catholic hearts still lay) were effectively as close to one another as two MPs, one Labour, one Conservative, could well be, while being also within the leadership group of their respective parties. George Woodcock, a Preston Catholic, was General Secretary of the TUC from 1960 to 1969 and the architect of what seemed a final piece in the new socio-political order – the reshaping of the TUC, no more as an organ of protest but as one of the principal pillars of the establishment. Add to Woodcock, Charles Curran, Director-General of the BBC from the end of the decade, and William Rees-Mogg, editor of *The Times* (all three people to whom their faith meant a great deal) and it is clear how far catholicism had moved into the moderate centre of national power by the 1960s. A few decades earlier the presence of Roman Catholics in such influential positions would have been regarded by many as constituting a mysterious threat to the safety of the nation. Now it evoked little comment.

Catholicism had in fact come to fit excellently well into England's *ancien régime*. It remained indeed a special case, but then England was full of special cases, from Jews and Cornishmen to south Yorkshire coalminers and dukes. It had worked hard to be accepted, demonstrating itself to be as democratic, as loyal to the monarchy, as supportive of the Empire, as keen on cricket, as unideological as any group – and probably no other church was as at home in all social classes. Rees-Mogg's landed background, Shirley Williams's literary and academic one, Woodcock's proletarian one (he began work as a cotton weaver at the age of twelve on eight shillings a week), could all mesh equally well with one quite recognizable brand of religious faith and liberal social pragmatism. The Catholic Church had managed almost across the board to combine a moderately tough insistence upon its marriage and school disciplines with avoidance of a ghetto mentality. It had finally thrown off the last hint of being an alien or disloyal minority. This was, however, a balancing act. Success upon the one side – social and intellectual integration – was bound to imperil success upon the other – maintenance of adequate group cohesion. The proportion of Catholics entering a mixed marriage was steadily growing: the first year in which the number of such marriages, solemnized in a Catholic church, exceeded that of purely Catholic marriages was 1963. By 1966 the mixed were already 25,000 to 19,000. The decline of a segregated community at this decisive level was proceeding very fast. But that is already to look just a little too far ahead.

At the moment when the Vatican Council first met in 1962 the position seemed almost wholly rosy, whatever statistic one considered. The Church in France might have its grave pastoral problems, just as the Church of England had, but the leadership of the English Catholic Church felt, not unreasonably, that really it had none. Why call a council? The very notion appeared as an oddity, an unnecessary extravagance, even a source of danger: an occasion for firebrands like that young Swiss priest, Hans Küng, to appeal for all sorts of extravagant neo-Protestant 'reforms' which the Church of Cardinal Godfrey seemed quite confident it did not need nor want. Yet things were not really so simple as that.

There was, after all, John Heenan, since 1957 archbishop of Liverpool. Heenan was in this period undergoing something of an ecumenical conversion. 'I remember the earnestness with which soon after Dr Ramsey's enthronement Cardinal Godfrey attempted to dissuade me from accepting an invitation to dine at

Lambeth Palace.'⁴ Already in August 1962, just before the start of the council, Heenan organized a conference on ecumenism at Heythrop with Cardinal Bea as the principal speaker together with local English ecumenists like Henry St John.⁵ Heenan, always a forceful, practical, thoroughly go-ahead pastor, had just scrapped the old plans for Liverpool Cathedral and commissioned instead Frederick Gibberd's 'spaceship', with John Piper and Patrick Reyntiens to prepare the glass for the great lantern. It would soon be completed. Heenan in the early sixties seemed the leader to ride whatever storm might be coming, to harness the new ideas of the council – on ecumenical relations especially – so as to enhance the pastoral strength the Church in England already possessed. Unlike the timid Godfrey, Heenan was, in his own mind, a progressive. He was also a natural leader, every inch a cleric, and yet very much the common man's archbishop, a masterly person with a wry sense of humour, unintimidated by anyone, and an established television personality. When in September 1963 he left Liverpool for Westminster, struggling through the immense crowd gathered at Lime Street Station to see him off, it must have seemed to many that here for once God had matched the man with the hour.

The English contribution to the council was not an outstanding one, not comparable with that of Manning, Ullathorne, Clifford and Acton at Vatican I. Yet it was not insignificant. There is a story, *ben trovato*, no doubt, that two groups of journalists each selected a football team from among the Council Fathers – one was to represent the Conservatives, the other the Progressives. When they compared notes they found that each had selected Heenan to play centre forward. The story has a point. Heenan was a natural centre forward. But on which side? Theologically he was a pure conservative ultramontane, never questioning the theology he had learnt in Rome as a young man and quite uninterested in theological speculation which he felt to be almost unworthy of a priest. His reformism could be vigorous but it derived from pastoral pragmatism and a warm, generous streak in his heart, not from any personal questioning of the absolute rightness of the Roman Catholic system he had been brought up in. In all this he was immensely different from that other leading English figure at the council, Christopher Butler,

Abbot of Downside. He was one of only a handful of genuine theologians to be a full voting member, not just a *peritus*. He saw the problems as Heenan did not. An Oxford Anglican convert, a biblical scholar and, hitherto, a somewhat conservative controversialist, the council was for Butler something of a second conversion. He would now increasingly come forward as the one senior English voice, at once unimpeachably loyal to Rome, yet cognizant of the full weight of contemporary theological scholarship and able to shake himself free of the simplicities of ultramontanism. It seemed a very real cause of hope when, just after the council, Heenan appointed him his auxiliary bishop at Westminster.

Three other Englishmen at the council deserve a mention. John Moorman, the Anglican bishop of Ripon, was one of the few observers to attend all its sessions. As a leader of Anglo-Catholicism, a medieval historian and a scholar of Franciscanism, his experience of the council and the inner workings of the Vatican would enable him to be one of the principal bridge builders between Rome and Canterbury in the next twenty years. Patrick Keegan, President of the World Movement of Christian Workers, was one of the few laymen to address the council – in its third session, on the role of the laity. Another Lancastrian, however, even though he was an archbishop, was not allowed to do so. Archbishop Roberts had been branded as dangerous. In even the best administered of autocracies mistakes occur occasionally and Archbishop Roberts was one of them. No one so honest, so independent, so persevering in his intellectual commitments, so ingenuously frank, should ever have been selected by pre-conciliar Rome as an archbishop – even of Bombay. The institution had long to rue it. In England, where he had returned to live in semi-retirement, he could not be effectively silenced about his favourite subjects, birth control and the atomic bomb, but at the council, through various subterfuges, he was never once permitted to speak.[6] That should not be forgotten when we applaud the breakthrough in freedom which the council did undoubtedly constitute.

For a small minority of English lay people, just as for a small minority of priests, the council was a source of immense excitement and optimism – one sees it well enough in the pages of

Michael de la Bedoyere's newsletter, *Search*.[7] For the stalwarts of the older generation, however, this was seldom so. Frank Sheed had been in the business of the lay apostolate a great deal longer than Keegan and he went to Rome for every session of the council: 'Not often did I come away cheerful. From end to end of the Council I met no optimism, just . . . a trust in the Lord which had more than an edge of bleakness.'[8] That may seem a strange judgment when one thinks of the immensely positive, almost over-optimistic note in many of the council's documents, but they did include such a change of note from the past as a veteran apologist like Sheed, well read and deeply thoughtful as he was, found hard to take.

For many more people the council at the time meant little either way. Their bishops, certainly, did not try to set them thinking. Non-Catholic observers like Bishop Moorman were far more on the council's wavelength than were most of the English Catholic bishops. But if the bishops were at sea, how much more their priests and the great bulk of the laity. The council hardly affected the life of ordinary Catholics in England until the second half of the sixties and then little more than liturgically. Its more serious implementation would hardly begin before the mid-seventies. John Braine's *The Jealous God* is a novel about Yorkshire Catholics published in 1964. It is interesting from our present point of view because it shows so few signs of new winds blowing through the Church. There is no mention of the council nor anything connected therewith. Its world remains that of Catholicism in the fifties – unquestioning dependence on the Safe Period, kindly but highly authoritative monsignors, a persistent consciousness in the background of confession and the fear of hell: all good evidence that in the northern provinces at least, the new ideas were as yet not coming through.[9] Yet the theme of the book is symptomatic of what was lying just below the surface all the same: the crumbling old-fashioned convictions of the intelligent young history master at the local Catholic grammar school faced with a sexual crisis. He is just the generation we shall meet fifteen years later in David Lodge's *How Far Can You Go?* His early sixties plight really represents the strains of a fifties hangover. The strains in ordinary Catholic society depicted by Braine are only one episode in a much longer story but the point here is that at the common level the council had not yet started to make a difference in that story.

English for those parts of the mass either directly addressed to the laity or intended to be said by them (Epistle, Gospel, Gloria, Credo) was introduced at the end of 1964. A fully vernacular mass (including the canon) was permitted in 1967 and became normal the following year. That was really the moment of crucial change, though in not a few places many a mass remained in Latin long after this. Temporary altars were being erected at much the same time so that the priest could celebrate facing the people and he was now to say the canon out loud. In 1970 came the new *Missa Normativa*: the text of the Tridentine mass was not only translated but changed, the long medieval offertory prayers were suppressed, the opening prayers altered, now alternative prayers of consecration were placed beside the Roman canon. At the same time concelebration was spreading fast and the multiplication of side altar masses was starting to look anachronistic, if not a little weird, by the end of the decade. The giving of communion of the cup to the laity was allowed far more slowly and reluctantly and remained all through the seventies very much the exception. Only in a handful of the most progressive parishes did it soon become the norm. Yet all in all this was an immense revolution, carried through rapidly, smoothly, with typical Catholic discipline, but awfully little explanation or enthusiasm. By 1970 the liturgical demands of the Reformation had been, very largely, met. Moreover with the formal liturgical reforms came related changes like the encouragement of house masses and the setting up of parish councils.[10] The obvious and overwhelming contrast between the eucharistic practice of Catholics and of the other Christians had gone for good. From now on the outsider might easily fail to distinguish one from the other.

'I hate the changes in the liturgy,' wrote Christopher Dawson to E. I. Watkin.[11] It was 'a regression into nationalism and a widely unpopular one', declared Douglas Woodruffe, still editor of the *Tablet* after thirty years.[12] 'Easter used to mean so much to me before Pope John and his Council – they destroyed the beauty of the liturgy,' lamented Evelyn Waugh in March 1966. 'I have not yet soaked myself in petrol and gone up in flames, but I now cling to the Faith doggedly without joy. Church going is a pure duty parade. I shall not live to see it restored.'[13] In fact he died on Easter Sunday, eleven days later. 'At the moment it is an iron age', wrote David Knowles to a friend in 1967, 'in which one looks in vain for a prophet or a master in Israel and cant and humbug are very much in evidence. I can now, as a historian, understand how England lost the faith *tempore Henrici octavi*.'[14] They were right at least in deploring the loss of much beauty and dignity in the Latin liturgy where previously it had been well celebrated, in monasteries above all. Plainsong was largely abandoned and replaced with nice, trite contemporary hymns with tunes easy to learn and correspondingly lacking in depth. 'Popular participation' in the liturgy, the prevailing aim of the reformers, would be realized at some considerable loss. But in the typical parish the old Latin liturgy had provided neither beauty nor understanding, only a remote, poorly performed rigmarole during which the parishioners had been encouraged, as often as not, to say the rosary. Even if the replacement was at first feebly done, with ill-phrased translations, it constituted in the majority of places a pastoral and ecumenical change of immense significance for the future ethos of the Church. With the passing of Latin, both the special mystery and the unquestioned clericalism of Catholicism faded fast. The mass and the priesthood seemed no longer so absolutely other from the Holy Communion and the ordained ministry of Protestantism.

With liturgy went ecumenism as the two – the only two – undoubted areas of near-immediate and widespread post-conciliar achievement. A new relationship with other churches seemed what lay closest to Pope John's heart. Cardinal Bea and the Secretariat of Unity represented the very quintessence of the new look and Heenan was a member of the Secretariat from the start. It was here, perhaps only here, that he himself felt personally committed to the new rather than to the old. Other things he would do out of a sense of duty but this from warm personal conviction. 1964 was the year the Decree on Ecumenism was passed in Rome. It was Heenan's first year at Westminster. It was the year in which English Catholics were active observers at the Nottingham Faith and Order Conference of the British Council of Churches – a very great step forward in English terms. It was the year too in which Heenan accepted the invitation of the

Archbishop of Canterbury and the Chief Rabbi to join them in the joint chairmanship of the Council of Christians and Jews, despite the manifested disapproval of Cardinal Ottaviani of the Holy Office. The council had been founded during the past war with Hinsley as one of its chairmen. Later, Griffin had been ordered by the Holy Office to resign from it. Now Heenan was, quite consciously, walking in the steps of his master, Hinsley, in resurrecting the mood of the Sword of the Spirit days of twenty years earlier.

The consequent thaw can be detected at many levels of society. It can be seen in Bishop Butler's invitation to deliver the 1966 Sarum lectures at Oxford on the theology of the Second Vatican Council, in the increase of theological dialogue, in the sudden beginning in all sorts of places to inter-parish co-operation, Catholic, Anglican, Methodist, at such times as harvest festivals and between clergy hitherto not noticeably ecumenical. It can be found too in the multiplication – under ever easier conditions – of mixed marriages and in the crumbling of denominational hostilities at popular level in such corners of the realm as they had hitherto survived, such as Liverpool. A survey of Catholic Liverpool in the later sixties found that 'Intolerance and prejudice have disappeared to an unbelievable extent and the whole attitude between Catholics and Protestants has now changed'.[15] This had been brought about, the researcher claimed, both by the social and educational changes of the last twenty years and by the explicit ecumenical tide itself.

The high and public point of this sudden and effectively irreversible alteration, especially in Roman Catholic/Anglican relations, is undoubtedly to be found in the highly publicized visit of Archbishop Ramsey to Pope Paul in the spring of 1966,[16] with the subsequent rather rapid establishment and operation of the Anglican-Roman Catholic Joint Preparatory Commission, which met already in January 1967 and concluded its Report at Malta exactly one year later.[17] Important theologically as the much more drawn out work of the subsequent ARCIC[18] would be, the truly decisive note was set for the new and 'special'[19] relationship between the communions of Rome and Canterbury by the Common Declaration of Pope Paul and Archbishop Ramsey of 24 March 1966 and then by the Malta Report of 1968.

The work of the Joint Preparatory Commission was important for various reasons. The first was the particular and very deliberate weightiness of the commission which, besides the theologians, included five bishops on each side. Among the Catholics was Mgr Willebrands, himself secretary of the Roman Secretariat for Promoting Christian Unity. Leader of the Anglicans was Bishop Moorman. Whereas most subsequent commissions have tended to be staffed by theologians with simply a bishop chairman, here the two churches appeared to be engaged at the most authoritative level that was practical. Secondly, while the commission was fully and emphatically international, nevertheless upon both sides it had extremely strong English representation (five English Catholics: Bishops Fox and Butler, Canon Purdy, Frs Richards and Hastings; seven English Anglicans: Bishops Moorman and Knapp-Fisher (of Pretoria); Canons James Atkinson, Eric Kemp, John Findlow and John Satterthwaite; Professor Howard Root). In fact, the English members very largely made the running so that here at last was a top level episcopal and theological confrontation (amicable yet also often quite sharp) not only between world or continental Catholicism and Anglicanism but also very positively between the Anglicanism of England and the Catholicism of England, recognized as the most appropriate representatives of their two world communions. There was no longer a sense of fear or of patronizing upon either side. Thirdly, the commission went to work very speedily, held three meetings within a single year, received a good deal of publicity and hence helped generate a powerful sense of momentum at a time when within the Church as a whole a positive tide was still flowing strongly. Fourthly, the final report written at Malta – like nearly all that led up to it – was clearly aiming at the realization of no less than full unity between the two churches and even quite soon. It is, within the genre of such documents, very noticeably orientated in a practical rather than a purely theological direction; yet, while most practically orientated ecumenical documents are aimed at good working relations between churches, this one was aimed at 'full organic unity'. It was because of that aim coupled with the realization that adequate agreement at a strictly theological level must still appear almost impossible to reach within present circumstances, that the report considered the possibility of partial intercommunion as a road to unity. Possibly no other document approved by representatives of Rome has ever explicitly contemplated this approach and this is almost certainly the explanation why subsequently – even though Rome's key ecumenist, Mgr Willebrands, went along with it at the time – muffled objections were raised to the publication of the Report in any official way.

The Malta Report may fairly be seen as the last, and perhaps most generous, expression of the mood of optimism prevailing in the Catholic Church in the years immediately following the council. The mood was, of course, already changing and by the end of 1968 it had indeed been transformed into one of dominant confrontation and pessimism. Bishops and theologians had shared briefly in a state of mutual trust during the *communitas* period created by Pope John (it had, in fact, only really begun in 1963, during his final months after the council's first session); they were now to fall back into a pattern of almost structured confrontation, only too reminiscent of the 1950s. Yet, even if the Malta Report suffered on account of both its own cautiously radical proposals and the Church's decisive shift of mood, it still did in fact light the way, not only for the slow grind of theological discussion carried on by ARCIC, but also for the vast popular Anglican/Catholic realignment which was now going on at ground level all across the world.[20]

In December 1958 a group of radical young Catholics met at Spode House in Staffordshire. As the meeting became an annual event, the gathering in question became known as the 'December Group'. From it, in 1964, developed *Slant*, a bi-monthly journal of the new Catholic left, committed to 'socialist revolution, not just as one aspect of christian engagement, to be ranked in a hierarchy of values and priorities which also includes ecumenism and liturgical reform, but as the central perspective within which the revolutionary message of the gospel can find articulation in our time'.[21]

Slant was in essence a group of Cambridge Catholic undergraduates (and, then, graduates) with a largely Lancashire working-class or lower middle-class background. They combined the cleverness of Oxbridge with hostility to its normal public school stance. They may well be seen as intellectual Beatles, perkily opposed to structure, proclaiming Marxist *communitas* of a highly idealized kind with relish. Their links with the Dominicans and the publishing house of Sheed & Ward made their voice carry relatively far. Minute in their following they obtained for a brief while, in the heyday of verbal radicalism, a reputation out of line with their real importance. They were much more systemic in their thinking than liberals of the Search or Parish and People sort and, of course, like most good Marxists, they despised the liberal approach, yet in practice, in so far as *Slant* proposed any programme for the Church, it was more or less identical with that of such other reformers: decentralization, a popular liturgy, the acceptance of contraception, and so forth. One may fairly, if oddly, compare *Slant* with the Distributists of forty years earlier. Both were almost entirely theoretical in approach, both made no attempt at all to inter-act with any real centre of power, both developed considerable theoretical consistency, both had their Dominican allies.

After six years of often exciting talk *Slant* faded away. Its final issue was dated March 1970. Several of its leaders remained academic Marxists but ceased to be Catholics. In that final issue Eagleton denounced the Church as 'the neo Bloomsbury of the 1960s – small intimate groups of liberal minded men moving within a quiet blend of liturgical aesthetics, moral pragmatism and marginal social radicalism'. It was a clever description but at least as true of *Slant* as of anyone else. There was, he claimed, no longer any ground on which Church and State could effectively interact in Britain to give meaning to Christian radicalism. What was true was that *Slant* had never found (nor, perhaps, even seriously sought for) such ground, yet it did in fact still exist, as another less-trumpeted group, developing at much the same time, demonstrated fairly cogently.

The Sword of the Spirit[22] had struggled on none too effectively through the forties and fifties. It had done a little useful work on the publishing front but had made very little impact nationally or ecclesiastically for a long time. Then suddenly, as the fifties turned into the sixties, it too came back to life. The first sign was a special 'Africa Office' set up by the Sword in 1958 and chaired in that golden age of liberal Toryism by none other than the Conservative MP, Major Patrick Wall. This led in 1962 to the establishment of the Africa Centre at Hinsley House in Covent Garden. The previous year a decision to join in the Freedom from Hunger campaign led quickly to the founding of CAFOD (Catholic Fund for Overseas Development). In 1965 the Sword changed its name to the CIIR (Catholic Institute for International Relations) and the same year set up its own overseas volunteer programme. All this represents something much less intellectually brilliant than *Slant* but much closer to the centre of Catholic life, much more effective and, also, increasingly coherent. The CIIR would soon become one of the most competent agencies of social reform at work in the country and it would enjoy steadily growing Catholic support just because its programme could be seen to concur with that of the post-conciliar Church. The most important Church document of these years was Pope Paul's 1967 encyclical on development, *Populorum Progressio*. Here could be the CIIR's text. Moreover in Barbara Ward and Fritz Schumacher it could hearken to two major prophets, voices of weight far beyond Church circles. Both were distinguished economists. Schumacher had, years before, done much of the drafting of the Beveridge Report. He was converted to Catholicism and to the 'Small is Beautiful' economic approach alike in 1965, the year of Barbara Ward's *It Can be Done* (an approach to the problem of world poverty). Ward had been one of the original founders of the Sword and remained a close ally. By the end of the decade *Slant* was effectively dead but the CIIR was just beginning to flex its muscles as standard bearer of a characteristically Catholic modern approach to international issues – an approach which, in secular terms, one might call radically liberal, unafraid of a socialist alliance but not itself socialist. Its development, with that of CAFOD beside it, demonstrated that it was still possible to find ground for effective action 'twixt Church and State.

The post-conciliar developments we have been considering hitherto have mostly been positive ones. We have now to turn instead to the confrontation and the decline. On 20 December 1966 Fr Charles Davis declared that he was leaving the Roman Catholic Church forthwith.[23] He was the author of several books of theology, the editor of the *Clergy Review*, a lecturer at

Heythrop College, and a very well-known speaker in Catholic societies in Britain and abroad. The shock was immense. Davis had always seemed a rather carefully orthodox theologian, hardly more than moderately progressive. Yet now, precipitated by his conviction that Pope Paul was actually lying over the issue of contraception, he suddenly flung off the whole system, declaring that he had not really believed in it for quite a time. The biblical and historical claims of the Catholic Church were unjustified, while 'the Official Church' was continually saddening him by its lack of concern for truth and for persons: 'The Church in its existing form seems to me to be a pseudo-political structure from the past. It is now breaking up and some other form of Christian presence in the world is under formation.'[24]

Plenty of replies were soon published, some more, some less to the point. Most accepted that the criticisms Davis made of the Church were largely justified, even that the Church was indeed gravely 'corrupt'.[25] Yet was not Davis showing himself somewhat unhistorically minded in not recognizing that this had always been true and really has to be true? Davis gave the impression of being too narrowly a seminary theologian, with little sense of history, literature, or even humour. The very narrowness of his formation linked with a fine mind had produced in him an unbearable sense of strain. He had, after all, been living in a seminary since the age of fifteen and had never had the chance of attending any British university. In him all the faults of British ultramontanism backfired quite disastrously. His explosion represented the sense of claustrophobia that the Catholic clerical system could produce in one exceptionally intelligent and rather narrowly consistent person. It caused special shock because of when it came, only one year after the end of the Vatican Council. Ordinary people were just beginning to become aware of the new openings, the greater sense of freedom, the new respect for other Christians and much else. Yet here was Davis, a better informed man than almost anyone else in the country, declaring the Church simply an archaic 'obstacle' in the lives of Christians.

An element of confrontation was already present in Catholic life before the departure of Davis but from that moment it grew rapidly stronger. The sense of a grand and trusting alliance of bishops, theologians and laity united for the reform of Catholicism, fell tragically away. The Catholic Church and very especially the Catholic Church in England, was now – journalists were noting more and more frequently, adding fuel to the flames with their probing reports – in a state of 'crisis'.[26] It was eighteen months later, in the summer of 1968, that the crisis fully exploded, participating in the general crisis atmosphere of that turbulent time. The powder keg finally responsible for the explosion was Pope Paul's encyclical on contraception, *Humanae Vitae* (29 July).

The pope had prevented the council from debating two particular issues, birth control and the celibacy of the priesthood. He had regarded both as too delicate and threatening to the Church's inner life. They were, in fact, to prove – and perhaps in large part just because they had not been discussed collegially – the most disastrous of Church-renders in the future. Be it noted that in neither case was a simple maintenance of the 'traditional' Catholic position likely to seem plausible. As regards celibacy, western tradition had long excluded married deacons as much as married priests and for the same reasons; the council, by allowing the former, had necessarily undermined the old rationale for the latter. As regards birth control, the council had strongly approved of responsible family planning. It had recognized the moral grounds for limiting the number of children (*Gaudium et Spes*, 50, 51, 52, 87). It had thus moved away from the old position of leaving it all to God to decide. Only a matter of means, not of intention, was now in question. The pope had himself felt the dilemma and to resolve it set up a special commission, largely consisting of lay experts (including the English Catholic Dr John Marshall) to advise him. By early 1967 it was known that a majority of the commission had advised in favour of change: the choice of means should be left to the individual. The International Congress for the Lay Apostolate, meeting the same year, said the same. Pope Paul was now in a condition of agonized hesitancy. He knew that Popes Pius XI and XII had emphatically condemned as immoral the use of artificial methods of contraception and his closest advisers urged him not to appear to diminish the weight of papal authority in any way. He knew also what his own commission had advised him and how widespread that opinion now was throughout the clergy and laity in the

Church. For long he delayed. Finally he came down upon the side of his predecessors and *Humanae Vitae* was the result. He must have expected opposition. He almost certainly did not expect the degree of public opposition, much of it expressed with the greatest vehemence, which the encyclical in fact received. He lived for ten more years but he never wrote another encyclical.

In the past the Catholic Church in England had often seemed distinctly docile in comparison with continental churches like those of France and Holland. Now it was different. A chorus of priests and lay people of every sort spoke out in opposition. Even the *Tablet* (now edited by Tom Burns) was opposed. There were five columns of letters in *The Times* on the subject in the first days of August, overwhelmingly negative. Besides the protests of individual priests – some of whom were suspended for refusing to read the pastoral letters of the more hawkish of bishops (that of the archbishop of Southwark especially) – a letter of nonconformity signed by fifty-five priests was published in *The Times* on 2 October.[27] Now, as sixty years earlier over modernism, the bishops were soon somewhat divided between hawks and doves. Heenan, like his predecessor Bourne, took as gentle a line as he could; Cowderoy of Southwark, like his predecessor Amigo, took the hardest of lines.

The consequence was not only immediate confusion, including scuffles on the steps of Westminster Cathedral between rival groups, but an immense and lasting decline in ecclesiastical morale. A majority of at least middle-class Catholic married people were probably already using the pill (the long delay had encouraged people to make up their own minds) and few now pulled back. Priests found themselves caught between laity and bishops: publicly they were in trouble if they dissented from the encyclical, privately and in confession they could say what they really thought. The whole situation was demoralizing. Few even of its supporters argued for the infallible character of what the pope had said, but what was clear was a resultant sharp decline in respect for papal authority and the emergence of a strange feeling among even many loyal Catholics that they were now, and would hereafter remain, somehow 'against' the pope.

Bishop Butler was the one senior ecclesiastic in England with whom such people might still feel fully able to identify and this on account of a remarkably outspoken interview given by him to the *Sunday Times*[28] immediately after the publication of the letter of the 'fifty-five'. It was entitled, no less, 'The Dictates of Rome'. So clear, weighty and (for a Roman Catholic bishop) unexpected were his words that we will quote them here at some length:

> There is a good deal of evidence that since 1965 the old habits of autocratic action in Rome have survived the Council. A great many Catholics and some non-Catholics, whatever they think of the actual teaching of the latest encyclical (I am not criticising its teaching), are profoundly disturbed by the history of its genesis and the mode of its promulgation. The subject was withdrawn from the Council and given to a Commission of very learned people. The Commission's conclusions were rejected, it seems, in toto. The Synod of Bishops, meeting in Rome last autumn, was not allowed to discuss it as part of the agenda. And then one day the bishops get a document which is published in the entire press the following morning . . .
>
> It is simply and solely to man's conscience that the Christian gospel, the Catholic faith, makes its appeal. And it seems to me that at the very point where authority fails to communicate its message to the conscience, it fails to *be* effective authority . . . The birth control encyclical may turn out to have been the occasion of a great ecumenical advance and not a regression. Because, it is already compelling the Catholic Church to face internal criticism of the encyclical thus making Vatican II a living reality. The Council itself is the only genuine answer to such internal criticism.

The length of that quotation is, one hopes, justified by its significance. It may well be true that Roman Catholic opposition to *Humanae Vitae* was the crucial factor in convincing Christians of other Churches, as nothing else could, that Catholics were no longer – if they ever had been – ecclesiastical robots but fellow men and fellow Christians. If the encyclical very dangerously disrupted the relationship between many Catholics and their leadership, it also established strangely enough new bonds of fellowship and shared experience, a sense in which still committed Catholics could now participate in the 'protesting' note of the Reformation, out of which a new 'ecumenical advance' – to use Bishop Butler's phrase – might come.

If Butler is the best theological commentator on what was

happening to Catholicism in the sixties, Anthony Burgess may have been its acutest fictional commentator. Burgess is an enigmatic novelist but a wrestling with both the good and the bad in Catholicism comes back in his work again and again, especially in the novels of this period (*The Worm and the Ring*, 1961; *Tremor of Intent*, 1966). Upon the one hand Catholicism is crushingly tyrannical, a legalistic, flesh-denying system of human repression, yet it is also basic religion at its richest, flesh-affirming and liberating. The lapsed hero in the one book, Christopher Howarth, the spy hero of the other, Denis Hillier, both finally come back to the Church. They come back straight across the sort of intellectual and emotional religious turmoil with which the sixties were full. In statistical terms such a rosy commentary could hardly be maintained, but in terms of the reappropriation of religion by some – perhaps just enough – people who started off from the confines of a too rigid ecclesiastical system and ended with the same basic beliefs but held within a new condition of freedom, a Burgess view may not be too far from the mark: 'Howarth lost none of his optimism, his trust in his own future based upon the past. There would be wine and love and the self-renewing cycle. And, above all, God and the various sword-sharp manifestations of God.'[29]

For one man there was no rosy view. Cardinal Heenan was not 'spared the agony' of seeing the Catholic Church in decline, disintegrating under the blows of 'neo-modernists and Catholic anarchists'.[30] On the contrary, his last years would be for him 'a crown of thorns'.

Heenan, as he saw himself, was a reformer, a man of the council, never willing to blame either Pope John or Vatican II. He was indeed, for England, *the* man of the council, who had tried to lead conciliar reform at home a good deal further than he can really have liked. He had backed the new university college of Heythrop and appointed Charles Davis to its staff; he had established the pastoral centre of Corpus Christi and appointed Hubert Richards to its staff; he had made Abbot Butler his auxiliary bishop; he had backed the CIIR; he had commissioned the avant-garde new cathedral at Liverpool; he was a personal friend of the Archbishop of Canterbury and of the Chief Rabbi. Why had it all gone so wrong?

> The cult of softness was sedulously preached by theological journalists. . . . Dismayed by the cynicism and apathy of their elders, young people developed a disillusioned view of the Church . . . the barque of Peter was ill-equipped to face a tornado . . . it became fashionable to preach a gospel according to Marx not Mark . . . anti-papal theologians abounded . . . the religious orders were the first to give up prayer . . . theological revolutionaries claimed that the Council was a failure because it had not really changed the Catholic religion . . .

Heenan's pathetic lament went on and on.[31]

Heenan was a humane if over-narrowly clerical man, with a rather rigidly pastoral, almost anti-intellectual model for the priesthood. He was not unlike Garbett, though while Garbett softened with age, Heenan hardened. He could be pragmatic in regard to *pastoralia* but he had no sense at all of the reality of an intellectual problem. He simply could not understand how transubstantiation, the Virgin Birth or papal infallibility might worry a good priest. Ecumenism was a matter of friendly gestures; it could never have occurred to him that it might involve the recognition that in some things, traditionally controverted, Rome could have been wrong, Protestantism right. The Church of the sixties was caught up in a vast theological and moral storm, both the Reformation and modernism replayed and other things too: this was all quite beyond him. His ultramontane training, never questioned, left him helpless. He was ill with meningitis and profoundly bitter.

Davis, Butler and Heenan represent three different English Catholic responses to the post-conciliar dilemma and all three had plenty of sympathizers among the rank and file. The tragedy in England of the post-conciliar Church was a tragedy of devout young people, desperate for the pill, but unable to reconcile it with the confidence in Roman authority they had learnt at their mother's knee. It was a tragedy of a whole generation of able priests – perhaps the ablest the Catholic Church in England ever had – who went down leaderless between Rome and their people; but it was the personal tragedy too of John Carmel Heenan.

The Legacy of the 1960s

The average annual number of converts, aged fourteen and over, to Roman Catholicism in England and Wales in the years 1959 to 1962 was 12,490; for the years 1969 to 1972 it was 4,436. Of these years the first (1959) had the highest figure (13,735) while the last (1972) had the lowest (3,897).[1] What had happened to explain that alarming drop? The Vatican Council, one might answer, or the spread of ecumenism or *Humanae Vitae*; but before we try to formulate an answer in specifically Catholic terms let us recall that statistics for almost all other churches plummeted comparably in the second half of the 1960s. It is true that the Catholic decline became striking a little later than elsewhere (1965, perhaps, rather than 1962); furthermore the Anglican and Free Church decline of the sixties could be seen as essentially the reinforcement of a tendency that had been present since 1910, while the Catholic decline was in contrast to a steady rise over the previous half-century. Nevertheless, the general picture is a common one: a rather stable, if not actually improving state of affairs characteristic of the 1950s seemed almost overnight to be replaced by a near-nightmarish quantitative slide.

What happened in England was quite closely comparable to the pattern discernible in France, Germany, Australia, almost anywhere within the 'western' world. The social, intellectual, religious crisis of the 1960s was specific to no one particular religious tradition, nor to any one part of the world. More widely still, it was not even a specifically religious crisis, it was rather one of the total culture, affecting many secular institutions in a way comparable to its effect on the churches. It was a crisis of the relevance (or capability for sheer survival) of long-standing patterns of thought and institution of all sorts in a time of intense, and rather self-conscious, modernization. If the first long phase of post-Second World War society was a conservative one, an attempt to recreate a fairly traditional world, that phase had gone with a steady escalation of secondary and tertiary education – most of it unquestioningly secular – major shifts in academic preoccupation and a massive rise in the standard of living. Suddenly the mood changed, neo-traditionalism crumbled in ridicule and the pendulum swung rather wildly to the other extreme, the glorification of the modern.

Classics and philosophy – the traditional academic room-mates of theology – ceased to provide a normative core for education and started to seem instead slightly eccentric pursuits. Economics, sociology and politics – all rather unconcerned with religion or concerned only in a dismissive way – were coming to constitute the regulative subjects upon the arts side of a university (on the side of the physical sciences any link with theology was even more remote). The architecture of the new world of knowledge as much as the sheer physical architecture of Aston or Salford simply did not provide the space, as the old had always done, for the pursuit of religion. Compare the role of chaplain in an Oxbridge college and in a new polytechnic. The system made him, however deficient or competent he might personally be, somewhat central to life in the one, ineffably peripheral in the other.

Do not simplify the forces of change or the multiple ways in which they interacted. Ideas and their phraseology flowed hastily forth to express or cloak the onward flow of social *mores*, manners adapted to reflect the latest views: shallow fashions, many of them, coming and going in a matter of months, but drawing the immediate attention from other changes which were proceeding almost as fast but would not pass again for many long decades. A shift in the deepest structures of society was made easier to take, but was hardly caused, by immediate circumstance – the relaxing of international tension, the growth in affluence, the demise of empire. The new structural balance of the sciences, the new campuses, comprehensives, secular optimism (the Kennedy factor), society's new sexual permissiveness, the pill, the return of Hegel as a serious philosophical influence, the discovery of the young Marx, Teilhard de Chardin, Buddhism and Zen, the discoveries at Qumran, Pope John, the passing of corporal punishment . . . these are all inter-acting factors, among many others, in the development of a new cultural consciousness.

Let us, all the same, for one moment simplify things a little wildly to make a point: Pope John represented Catholicism without Roman rigidity; the young Marx and even Khruschev represented Marxism without Stalinism; Kennedy represented American capitalism without disregard for the needs of the third world; Teilhard and Zen alike represented religion without sin and even without dogma; the pill represented sex without unwanted children. Remove Roman rigidity, Stalinism, sin and the rest, and what a nice world it would be and could not Catholicism, Marxism, American capitalism and sex all then go happily together? The early sixties half thought they might.

They were only too obviously years of quickly shifting, volatile, often flabby, thought; yet the shallowness of much that appeared on the surface must not be allowed to conceal the major, deeper changes going on beneath, nor the capacity of the time to give rise and credence to new movements of originality and vigour, if often in contradiction with one another. In the religious field we have detected some five different movements, all of which we can date reasonably well to 1962-4. The first is the most purely theological, liberal or radical in orientation, growing chiefly from Anglican and Protestant ground of a scholarly sort, a return in many ways to the anti-supernaturalism of the twenties and earlier. It was a reaction against the Barthian years. *Honest to God* is the standard text here at the popular level but Dennis Nineham's Penguin, *Mark*, which also appeared in 1963 is in a different and more masterly way at least as important in diffusing widely and authoritatively a highly scholarly, post-Bultmann approach which simply left no room for the old kind of miraculous supernaturalism. Secondly there is the pastoral reform, most obviously at this moment Roman Catholic, but also Anglican and Free Church, with its concentration on Christian living, liturgical, catechetical, ecumenical. It was in no way intended by its principal leaders to have the sort of radical theological dimensions of the first movement, but the two became inevitably and inextricably involved. (For Heenan in his latter gloom, sound reform of the second type had been hijacked by wild men from the first category – and continental Catholic theologians like Louis Bouyer and Jean Daniélou would have agreed with him.) Thirdly, there is a more socially radical movement, particularly the Christian Marxist *Slant*. This took over a good deal of the luggage of No. 2, but mostly despised and opposed No. 1, finding theological conservatism a better basis for social radicalism. Then we have No. 4, the revival of Evangelicalism, less sectarian, less American-influenced, less simplistically fundamentalist than formerly, but still basically itself. It opposed No. 1, learnt a lot from No. 2, ignored No. 3 as absurd. Finally comes No. 5, the charismatic movement. It almost grew out of No. 4 and – at least later on – took over a good deal from No. 2 but was far more dependent on American experience. Nothing could seem more different than Catholic Marxism and neo-Pentecostalism (though they, in fact, shared a common dislike of liberal naturalism), but both sprang to life in 1963-4. Perhaps the deepest divide did lie between naturalists and supernaturalists. 'The mechanisation of the world picture and the rise of a technological culture have proved incompatible with the supernatural elements in Christianity,' remarks Peter Burke.[2] Our divide lies between the 'modernists' who accepted the truth of that judgment and endeavoured to rewrite theology as best they could accordingly, and the 'anti-modernists' who have rejected it. In the earlier phase of the sixties the 'modernists' were dominant and they continued to provide the main note for English theology for the next fifteen years – Nineham, Wiles, Cupitt, were all essentially early 1960s people. Theological naturalism goes temperamentally with a confidently optimistic mood about this world. Evangelicalism and, still more, Pentecostalism were asserting a contrary gospel – a sinful world, a supernaturalist religion. Pentecostalism, in particular, sees special divine interventions everywhere and it also tends to find personal devils at work. Pentecostalism was out on a limb in the early sixties, but as the general mood of society altered to the far greater pessimism of the end of the decade, and as the more journalistic and extreme wing of liberal theology almost faded away with the 'death of God' school, only too obviously the end of a road, the charismatic movement came close for a while to the centre of the religious stage, spreading rapidly even within the Catholic Church. Liberal theology captured the theologians but never really reached the pews; Pentecostalism was largely ignored by the theologians, but captured plenty of pastors. In the seventies, as a consequence, the gap between theologians and pews was greater than ever.

Different and even antipathetic as these various movements were in many ways, they all had one thing in common in their heyday: enthusiasm, a pattern of small rather informal groups, a contempt for structure. They all thought little of denominationalism (even if, in practice, several quickly developed a new sectarian character). They mostly tended towards intercommunion, they were all in their different ways strong on immediate experience, the exciting sense of at last having got it right. The fifties were moderately strong on structure, secular and religious; the sixties despised structure, secular or religious, at first out of optimism towards society, later out of pessimism. The Bonhoeffer of the war years was the father figure of this liminal age, Sydney Carter's songs its preferred music. The return to a general awareness of the necessity and advantage of structure of some sort came slowly, sadly and none too successfully in the course of the seventies. The hopefully structureless sixties – a liminal age of *communitas* – was characterized both by an exceptional fluidity in ideas and commitments and by a parallel and consequent decline in quantitative attachment to any structured church. Structure requires clear divisions – between churches, between religions, between sacred and secular. In a state of *communitas* the divisions and rules are seen to be artificial and hampering, there is instead an intense sense of the unity of everything. 'Well, either religious faith penetrates everything in life or it doesn't. There are some experiences that seem to make nonsense of all separations of sacred from profane – they seem childish. Either the whole of life is unified under God or everything falls apart', so Barbara Vaughan in that splendid sixties novel, Muriel Spark's *The Mandelbaum Gate*. That was indeed a central conviction of those years: the separations of sacred and profane, upon which the hard institutional and moral systems alike of Catholic and of Protestant so much depended, seemed childish. That is the liminal experience and while it lasts it is inevitably confusing, both for those professionally responsible for the maintenance of an ordered, discrete, ecclesiastical system of any sort, and for the sociologists of religion. Without convenient formulas of separation they can hardly do their work. The excitement of the *communitas* experience over, the ecclesiasts would inevitably find numbers down, dykes untended, the whole business of structure requiring to be undertaken anew with depleted resources. The sixties will not come again for a long while but their effect will last a long while and the shape of things emerging in their wake must needs be based upon the underlying shifts in society, the new realizations of religious and moral purpose, achieved at that time.

However heavy the casualties which all the churches suffered in those years, made worse by the striking contrast between the disillusionment so widespread around 1970 and the confident reformist optimism of six or seven years earlier, the lasting acquisitions of those years were, all the same, impressive. In ten years the religious map of England had changed more profoundly, positively, as well as negatively, than in the preceding sixty. The main churches, including both Roman Catholics and conservative Evangelicals, were now linked by what was almost a common liturgy and eucharistic understanding, as well as by a wider sense of fellowship including a shared theological tradition and a willingness to work together which would have seemed almost impossible to imagine twenty years earlier. Concerns of the Christian Aid type had moved from the periphery to near the centre of Church life. The advance towards a single recognizable Christian community, a reconstituted *Ecclesia Anglicana*, had been enormous, even if the pace now greatly slackened due to loss of nerve in a number of quarters.

The most lasting and worthwhile voices of the 1960s were probably those of lay people like Barbara Ward and Fritz Schumacher who had little to say about the Church as such, simply taking it for granted, but who spoke in a confidently unified sixties way about economics and the Spirit, the needs of man, the proper scale for humanity. Schumacher's 'Small is Beautiful' message seems in its own way a recall of the central intuition of Chesterton's Distributism, once again a reminder of how like the sixties were to the twenties.

The crisis of 1960s religion was a crisis of 'secularization', that much used and much abused word. It should not need to be disputed that in many very real ways something fairly called 'secularization' was proceeding extremely rapidly – all the statistics point to it. If 'secularization' does simply and necessarily signify a process of religious decline, full stop, then the mortal seriousness of what was happening for the churches hardly needs demonstrating. If the significance and viability of religion in a given age really does depend on the maintenance of one particular social pattern of ecclesiastical structure and the attendance at church sufficiently frequently of Tom, Dick and Harry, then the sort of negative prognosis one tends to find in observers as acute as Bryan Wilson may be the only reasonable judgment. If, however, the establishing of a stable geography of belief, social and physical, while certainly often inevitable, may yet somehow be inimical to the deeper functions at least of biblical religion, then the inner dynamic of the latter may actually require from time to time for its own deliverance the savage thrust of secularization, the creating yet again – as in Henry VIII's time – of 'bare, ruined choirs'. The old structures, useful as they were, were put up not only to fortify religion but to domesticate it, give it so much and no more, sacralise society this much, secularize religion that much, effectively encapsulate the spirit within a given social and political order. The secularization of society, a cutting down of the old wood of religious structure, may in fact provide for the liberation of religion, allowing it in principle, and in so far as its proponents dare, to relate anew to the totality of the secular. Was the existence of a Barbara Ward, a Mother Teresa, a Fritz Schumacher ('the nearest thing Britain possessed to a secular saint'),[3] more religiously important than the statistics of declining church attendance? In very serious and analysable, if possibly pedestrian, ways the churches had undoubtedly fallen back in these years in their relationship to the wider society. The question that remains unanswered was whether that falling back is not, in terms of a very deep law of the relationship of sacred to secular, a Bonhoeffian intuition, to be seen as a necessary case in a liminal age of *reculer pour mieux sauter*, and whether – as just one small provisional instance – the role of a Schumacher is not evidential of the power of religion still to function quite dangerously enough.

PART VII

---•••---

1970–1985

38

Politics

In the General Election of June 1970 Labour under Harold
Wilson was defeated and the Conservatives returned to power,
led by Edward Heath. He was Prime Minister for only three and a
half years. In February 1974, faced by the miners' strike, Heath
called a General Election and lost. Labour returned to office and
remained there, led first by Wilson and then by Callaghan, until
1979. The General Election of May of that year brought the
Conservatives back again under Margaret Thatcher, and in that
of 1983 she retained power with an increased majority. Meanwhile Labour in opposition under Michael Foot had lurched to
the left, producing a schism of 'moderates' led by Roy Jenkins
and David Owen, who founded a new party, the Social Democrats, soon to join in alliance with the Liberals. This split greatly
weakened Labour but at the 1983 election the Social Democrats,
while polling many votes, won only three seats in England.

Politically the crucial date in these years is 1979. In retrospect
the administration of Heath looks insignificant, a minor island
within a long period of Labour rule dominated by Wilson and
stretching for fifteen years from 1964. Heath, Wilson and Callaghan were all alike latter-day representatives of Butskellism,
the liberal consensus of post-Second World War politics. They
would in fact be its last major representatives. Personally, it is
true, Heath was a very different man from Wilson. He held to the
principles, and manifested the rigidities, which Wilson lacked.
He believed in 'theology'. An honourable man – working class by
background, Balliol by education, a musician by preference, a
churchman by conviction – he was weak at sensing the reactions
of others, a second-rate tactician, rather sadly isolated after the
fall of his ministry. Heath saw himself as the standard bearer of a

'one nation' Toryism, liberal and Christian. The friend and successor of Harold Macmillan and Alec Douglas-Home, he lacked the benign confidence of their more patrician touch. His one major achievement – Britain's entry into the European Economic Community (1973) – was in fact concluded on extremely bad terms and would in future years both fail to provide the expected economic benefits and be a bone of almost continual contention: Wilson was wise to say he would re-negotiate the terms if he returned to power. The Heath years were in general a time when things began to fall rather obviously apart. In Ulster the first soldier was shot early in 1970, in 1972 Derry experienced Bloody Sunday and a long era of violence had begun. World oil prices quadrupled in 1973, while both large-scale unemployment and industrial confrontation seemed set to become almost normal aspects of British life. Disillusionment with the powers that be was greatly enhanced everywhere by the scandal of Watergate and the consequent resignation of President Nixon. It had become a gloomy age.

The subsequent years under Wilson and Callaghan were not memorable. Throughout the seventies things for Britain were getting worse. Northern Ireland with its continual violence and absence of any discoverable solution to the conflict between IRA nationalism and Protestant Unionism was a source of continual moral depression. Industry was in steady decline. Up to the mid-1960s British Industry almost equalled that of West Germany; by the mid-1970s it had fallen to half of West Germany's; even France had overtaken us in terms of world trade. In the first half of the seventies sterling depreciated by over 40 per cent against other major currencies. The rise of unemployment was the principal social consequence of economic decline. Before the 1970s the highest figure it had ever reached since the Second World War was 555 thousand in 1968. By 1972 it was 870 thousand, by 1977 1,455,000, in 1980 it passed two million, in 1981 three million. By 1985 the true figure was probably over four million and still going up. Neither liberal Conservatives nor moderate Labour appeared to have an answer to this in the days of their power.

Jim Callaghan presided over the last years of Butskellism, the benevolent, essentially conservative uncle, unflappable but with really nothing actually to say or do. He kept the country calm, as Stanley Baldwin had done in not dissimilar circumstances forty years before, until the winter crisis of 1978-9 finally swept the calm away with strikes of lorry drivers, oil tanker drivers, train drivers, the staff of *The Times*, and much else. A few months later Mrs Thatcher was in power, the start of a new political age. Callaghan, like Heath, had fallen victim to the unions, forgetful of the old truth that the devil they did not know would be a great deal worse than the devil they did.

The Labour Party, and particularly its right wing, had been in decline for many years – in terms of inspiration, paid-up membership, the number of full-time workers, the percentage of the vote it received in General Elections. Its left wing – Marxist in inspiration and, often enough, seemingly contemptuous of parliamentary democracy – was its only growth point. Similarly the left wing of Conservatism was also disintegrating, a new hard right gathering strength. Mrs Thatcher and the group around her were repudiating in their new look fifty years of Tory leadership: the long Conservative acceptance of a mild form of State socialism. Limiting the competitive incentives of individualism was now judged most un-Tory in spirit and a disaster for the British economy. The consensus which had effectively ruled Britain from the days of Stanley Baldwin, Ramsay MacDonald and Neville Chamberlain, which had found its major prophets in Tawney, Beveridge and Temple, its achievers in Attlee, Cripps, Macmillan and Butler, was no more.

In dwelling upon the contrast in purpose and rhetoric between the new age and the old, let us note first of all the things that did not change. The rise in unemployment had been appalling already under Labour. It simply got worse under the Conservatives. The decline of British industry had been bad in the seventies; in the first three years of the Thatcher government 20 per cent of the remainder collapsed. An ever higher spending upon arms was characteristic of Thatcher but already by 1979 Britain's annual arms bill had reached eight and a half billion pounds, 4.7 per cent of the Gross Domestic Product. It is striking, when recalling the preoccupation with Japanese militarism of forty years earlier and the current obsession with Japanese industrial success, against which British industrial failure was being constantly measured, to observe that by the end of the seventies Britain was at the top of the league for military expenditure as against GNP while Japan was at the bottom. All the major decisions about deeper involvement in nuclear weaponry had already been made by Labour. Equally, government spending on housing had already fallen by 1979 lower than for any peacetime year since the 1930s. The economic theory of Thatcher was quite different from that of Wilson, but the obvious dominance of economics over politics (almost always, in point of fact, mistaken economics) was not new: it was a characteristic of all government from the 1960s. If we consider these things we realize that the last Wilson-Callaghan administration represented but a happy-go-lucky rump of Butskellism: the life had long gone out of the animal. The scene had been set for a new arrival, though Thatcherite rhetoric too would often prove more radical than Thatcherite reality.

Mrs Thatcher entered 10 Downing Street on the afternoon of Friday, 4 May 1979 with the modified words of the 'Prayer of Francis of Assisi': 'Where there is discord may we bring harmony; where there is error may we bring truth; where there is doubt may we bring faith; where there is despair may we bring hope.' The Prime Minister was clearly confident that she could improve on the supposed words of the saint of Assisi.[1] A few months later she voted for the restoration of hanging, though the core of her party – more traditionally Conservative (in the Macmillan mould) than she – would not agree, but the gap between a rather sugary, at times traditionalist, rhetoric and a decidedly unsentimental reality was already clear enough.

It conformed to a new pattern of leadership in the western world. Pope John Paul II was elected later in 1978, President Reagan in 1980. 'The time for counter-attack is long overdue,' declared Mrs Thatcher. 'We are reaping what was sown in the sixties. The fashionable theories and permissive claptrap sets the scene for a society in which the old virtues of discipline and self-restraint were denigrated.'[2] This could as well have been said by Reagan or even the pope. 'Americans are turning back to God', the former declared, to the 'fundamental American values of hard work, family, freedom and faith'. Reagan's mission, commented a journalist in 1980, 'is seen as the reversal of almost fifty years of misguided American liberalism, social and economic'.[3] Jimmy Carter, Democratic President of the late seventies, had been last of the line in America as Callaghan was the last in Britain. Though Carter was in fact a convinced Christian, while there seems little evidence from his personal life that Reagan ever was, the latter was yet able in the new mood of things to appeal powerfully to the 'moral majority' of middle America and the conservative evangelical revival in particular. The western conservative reaction of the end of the seventies was by no means religiously motivated but it did make what use it could of religion in its determination to break open the 'liberal' mould which the Established churches of the Anglo-Saxon world had come so largely to back.

The link between Thatcher and Reagan was not just one of attitude or even friendship but also of the articulation of foreign policy in an increasingly ghastly world. In large areas of the Middle East – Afghanistan, Iraq and Iran, Lebanon – there prevailed a state of almost continuous war. Throughout Asia, Latin America and Africa government was becoming more and more regularly bloody and dictatorial. Torture proliferated, and in Africa famine proliferated still more. The Anglo-American alliance was never tighter, but this tightness when combined with the decline of British power in relation to America's could only produce a dreary subordination. Apart from the little flurry of the Falklands War, Britain's role internationally was being reduced to insignificance precisely by the abdication of freedom to man-oeuvre. In hard reality, as the American military presence in Britain grew ever more considerable, the principal function of this island was to be the main forward base in nuclear war for the air force of the United States. Hardly an enviable role, and one extremely distressing to a great many English people, it satisfied our government.

The welfare state had been constructed over the years on Tawneyish principles of the duty of equality, a moral obligation to help the under-privileged at home, and then too, so far as possible, throughout the world. Thatcherite theory, on the contrary, as learnt from its principal prophet, Milton Friedman,[4] rejected the whole approach as both unrealistic and a mistranslation of the ethical from the realm of the personal to that of the collective. The pursuit of social morality, whether socialist, liberal or Christian, had been, it seemed, one vast self-deception. The hard world of economic life must be directed on quite different lines. This was far more a matter of philosophical belief than of economic demonstration but, faced by the crumbling economy of 1970s Britain, Mrs Thatcher was convinced.

Upon every side the structure of the welfare and semi-socialist State was to be chipped away in favour of the extension of individual or capitalist initiative – in education, health, the social services, the wider concern for the environment, the infrastructure of local government, the ownership of the means of production. While public schools were subsidized by an assisted places scheme and the income tax of the very rich was quite significantly reduced, the charges for meals at State schools, for medicines and dental treatment, were raised, full fees were required from overseas students, university budgets quite gravely diminished. The list of such 'reforms' could be extended indefinitely. At every point it should be set against the size of the military budget – the devastation caused in the universities by the cutting of a few million contrasted, for instance, with the very much greater expense of the Falklands War. Nevertheless it is also true that the cost of the welfare state had grown in the sixties and seventies vastly beyond the dreams of Beveridge and that in some ways at least it had certainly contributed to the ineffectual character of the British economy. Moreover there were still too many people in the Conservative Party who were by no means convinced Friedmanites to allow the Thatcherite axe anything like its full sweep. The welfare state survived a good deal better than the rhetoric, either of right or left, in Thatcher's early days made probable.

A small incident in 1980 may be used as a symbolic model. The government decided to introduce charges on school transport but the proposal was rejected in the House of Lords by 216 votes to 112, a major defeat. Resistance had been led by the Duke of Norfolk, Earl Marshal of England, beside whom stood Lord Butler, now very old and very near to death, the Bishop of London and Lord Soper. Here was an alliance of all that had guided England for forty years, Conservative, Labour, the churches. Butler, architect of the 1944 Education Act, the basic charter of the modern educational system whose principles he believed were now being breached, turned at this last end of his career to speak and vote against a Conservative government. Like Luther, he said, 'I can do no other.'[5] Here, clearly enough, was a frontier dividing middle England from the new brooms and the latter would find that they could not easily ignore it with impunity.

Thatcherite policy might, then, be partially resisted for a while, but – especially after her second electoral victory of 1983 – it was clear that the political and cultural history of Britain had entered a new era to a degree unknown since the 1940s. This was no revamping of Butskellism but a counter-revolution which sneered at socialism and all its works. The welfare state had grown top-heavy and too little loved; the nation's productive base, particularly the old large-scale, labour-intensive, industries, had vastly declined; the middle class had continued to expand in numbers and affluence. The theoretical assumptions behind the reforms of the Attlee, Macmillan and Wilson years were now under question. Christian thinkers found themselves no better prepared than liberal and left-wing ones for this new face of things. It was a suddenly revealed weakness of the alternatives, both in political leadership and theoretical models, which ensured Mrs Thatcher's long period of power – that and her own strengths. Here was a leader who knew her mind, who could unhesitatingly call upon the more militant spirits of the nation's past, Victorian and Churchillian, to justify whatever she did, and who too could act with vigour and efficiency. The south, for the most part, responded with some enthusiasm; the north (including Scotland and Wales) with a bitter awareness of redundancy and rejection. The success of the Falklands War in 1982 and the defeat of the miners' strike in 1984–5 were the principal achievements she could point to. General Galtieri and Arthur Scargill had alike met their match. In each case the immediate economic cost was immense but she has won where her predecessors faced with similar challenges abroad or at home had fumbled and lost. In an age in which so many loyalties and landmarks were going down, in which there was so little room left for natural optimism, Mrs Thatcher – like Ronald Reagan and Pope John Paul – provided for the short term a rallying point, exasperating to the wise, but sufficient in a world left with few alternatives to hold for a while the confidence of many. And here we must leave the story.

The 1970s, or rather their earlier years, witnessed considerable educational progress at tertiary level in the development of polytechnics, the principal colleges of education and the new universities founded a few years before. All in all this may well have been the greatest age, at least in terms of spread, for higher education in Britain. The recommendations of the Robbins Report had been implemented, the age of cuts had not yet begun. Many polys and colleges of education were now teaching for degrees on a large scale. There seemed room for everything and if the stress was increasingly on the new technology there was also, for instance, considerable growth in departments of religious studies. It was their brief golden age too. Only after the return of the Conservative Party to power in 1979 did this start to change, especially from 1981 when university budgets were, for the first time, drastically cut and some small departments began to close. The shift was to education for the computer, making its presence felt everywhere from the primary school to 'New Blood' university lectureships. A profound move away from the arts and towards the most technical side of the sciences was in progress – probably the nation's biggest mental shift at least since the universalization of secondary education half a century earlier. Its consequences would only be fully experienced far beyond the end of this history.

In many other ways too the reforms and new approaches of the sixties came to maturity only in the course of the seventies: development in the scale and professionalism of social work, in the implementation of sexual and racial equality, in a positive approach to the special educational needs of minority and under-advantaged groups, in a serious ecological concern for the preservation of the environment. It was only as the decade wore on that the rise of unemployment, the falling pound and economic recession began to threaten some of this, so that the most imaginative and humane of new initiatives might come to be regarded by officialdom as mere fringe elements of the welfare state which could no longer be afforded.

The huge growth in unemployment from the middle of the decade must be seen as the central fact around which a wider social disintegration was developing. Yet all the blame could not reasonably be laid upon unemployment (as the left would wish) but much too had to be seen as the eventual consequence of the new personal and social *mores* of the sixties (as the right tended to claim). While there was undoubted gain in the new insistence upon personal freedom and sexual equality there was also a heavy bill to pay in social and moral dislocation. In 1963 there were 23 thousand divorces in England and Wales; by 1980 there were 150 thousand. Over a million couples were divorced in the 1970s, the devastating sequel to the Divorce Law Reform Act of 1971. A third of the marriages now enacted were heading for dissolution. By 1976 there were 750 thousand one-parent families. Abortion became legal in Britain, under certain definite conditions, in April 1968. By 1980 there were 140 thousand registered abortions a year and more than a million lives had been legally extinguished before birth over the previous decade. Where there were 200 thousand alcoholics in England and Wales in 1959, there were 600 thousand in 1979. The number of young people in prison almost doubled during the decade. Add to all this the spread of drug taking and the pursuit of pornography. When the nude review *Oh! Calcutta!* was first produced in London in July 1970, with a sort of pseudo-intellectual content, it seemed fearfully cute and adventurous in the attempt to be uninhibited. As the years went on, it appeared more empty and tired but kept going all the same, for want of any decisive reason to stop. Behind it, in less tasteful ways, English society was being bombarded with a quantity of porn unthinkable in earlier decades.

If unemployment was one side of social disintegration, and considerable disruption within the area of personal, sexual and marital morality was another, closures were a third. They were of many sorts. There was a very large number of bankruptcies, often of old and well-established firms, coupled with the take-over of other companies by far larger groupings, frequently foreign controlled. Of course closures, bankruptcies and take-overs were none of them new, but they were happening now in greater number, more hurry and with a consequent greater cumulative dislocation of society. It was not reassuring when leading London newspapers were sold back and forth among international tycoons. Meccano may stand as representative of the large number of high quality British products which disappeared in these years, the Consett steel works for the single large closure leading to mass unemployment in a particular place. Most of Liverpool docks went, together with Grimsby fishing fleets, and an assortment of rural railway stations (Beeching, of course, had already closed many in the mid-sixties), village schools, village shops and sub-post offices, uneconomic coal mines, high street Woolworths, eighteenth-century historic homes, nineteenth-century mental asylums, early twentieth-century cinemas, and later twentieth-century tower blocks. In September 1979 Birkenhead began the odd business of dynamiting tower blocks of flats constructed only twelve years before. Even the number of public houses fell by more than a fifth (6,511) between 1977 and 1981 – in the north it was almost a third. The closure of churches was just part of a much vaster pattern of structural dismemberment.

What was emerging, beneath a pattern of almost totalitarian uniformity at the macro-level – the biggest commercial groups, chain stores, football and snooker championships, a television-watching and computerized world, highly complex but closely controlled by the very few – was a much more splintered, privatized, almost apolitical society at micro-level, a development reinforced by the multiplicity of ethnic and other minority groups with an immigrant background. A certain boredom with almost all the old and central institutions of society – parliament, the major political parties, the unions, the major churches, Oxford and Cambridge – was combined with wide-scale enthusiastic participation in small, sectarian-type groups: single issue politics, small charitable trusts, minute far left political parties, new religious movements and churches together with charismatic house groups in the existing churches. Krishna Consciousness, Scientology, Transcendental Meditation, the Divine Light Mission, the Children of God, the Unification Church: waves of highly privatized, yet often spiritually and socially highly totalitarian religious credulity were flowing into Britain from both America and Asia. They would take their place beside the now considerable communities of Moslems, Sikhs and Hindus, the smaller groups of Buddhists. In almost every city disused Free

Church buildings – Methodist, Congregationalist, Presbyterian – were being reopened as Sikh or Hindu temples. A splendid mosque was rising by Regents Park. William Carey, a Baptist shoemaker, was more than anyone originator of the nineteenth-century missionary movement. In 1792 he left for India and a lifetime of outstanding achievement, to become the inspirer of numerous generations of British missionaries. By the 1970s the Carey Memorial Hall in Leicester was in use as a Sikh temple.

England had never before experienced religious and cultural diversity comparable to that which by the end of our period was almost the urban norm. Only in the village and some wealthier suburbs did the old pattern of a one-culture society remain in any way functional – and yet the village was one of the social institutions which had most declined as a working unit with the mechanization of agriculture, the loss of school, policeman, village shop. Even the elm trees which had for generations shaded the nearby lanes were being felled by the million, victims of Dutch elm disease. The old England, it might be claimed with small exaggeration, had struggled shakily through crisis after crisis from the First World War to the 1960s but it could struggle no more. A shell might remain, some tarted-up buildings, but the reality was now so different that it would be more than ridiculous to imagine that the churches alone might survive the deluge unscathed.

Yet to a remarkable extent the upper class, the nation's ruling élite, had so survived. Its economic basis had changed far more than its internal ethos or effective power. In January 1980 there were 528 thousand pupils in independent schools, 6 per cent of the total for England and Wales. They had a pupil:teacher ratio of 12.7 as against the 18.4 in maintained schools. Mrs Thatcher's first Cabinet, out of twenty-two members, contained only two people (herself and John Biffen) who had not attended public schools. It included six Old Etonians, three Wykehamists, one Harrovian and one Rugbeian. Seventeen were graduates of Oxford and Cambridge. At that point, at least, the Conservative pattern had not changed since the start of the century. Oxford and Cambridge were relatively little affected by the financial cuts which had so devastated some of the poorer universities. For the rich, Thatcher had eased the burden of tax and all her policies were calculated to encourage, not only their economic survival, but also an increase in the power they could effectively yield. This was greatly assisted by the 'privatization' of national assets. Not since the Dissolution of the Monasteries had there happened in this country so vast and reckless a public sale of property to the benefit of the very rich. Around them was a far larger core of south-east England whose standard of living was continuing to rise quite fast: delectable foreign holidays, private swimming pools, all sorts of exciting electronic gadgets, were now within their grasp.

On the other hand the class of the very poor, which had been so considerably eroded from the forties to the sixties, had hardened anew.[6] Those who stood clearly below what contemporary public opinion regarded as an acceptable 'poverty line' were some seven and a half million people, 15 per cent of the population. They included the hard core of the unemployed, were largely to be found in the north (on Merseyside and Tyneside 25 per cent of the population was unemployed, and far more of the very young), and were disproportionately black. Everywhere, however, they included many of the old, the chronically sick, the disabled, young single-parent families. The policy of the welfare state from Attlee to Callaghan had been, somewhat pragmatically, to lessen the gap between rich and poor in pursuit of a Tawneyish ideal of equality. It had never fully succeeded but it had greatly reduced the scale of the problem as it existed until the thirties. Now the gap was widening again.

It is remarkable how little the political revolution was for long effectively challenged, how considerably the new establishment could manipulate – through its grip on the mass media, the short-term fluctuations of the economy, the handling of patronage, the preoccupations of the police – the mood and voting of the common majority. The resistance of Yorkshire miners or the union of teachers could seem as fruitless as that of Yorkshire Pilgrims of Grace, or Carthusian monks four centuries earlier. There was, throughout the community, the loss of an underlying ideology to which people could together turn in confidence, though – without much doubt – the majority of the nation, voting either Labour or Alliance, remained basically committed, just as the churches did, to the philosophy of the welfare state. But the soul had gone out of it. Many Christians might emphatically reject the rather materialist individualism of the new orthodoxy, yet neither they nor anyone else seemed able to present a viable alternative. The moral community, as much as the Christian community, had fallen very low. Protest there was. The campaign against the greatest, most expensive and most dangerous development of all, the advance of nuclear weaponry, went bravely on. CND was as powerful as it had been at the close of the 1950s, led now by Mgr Bruce Kent, upon whom had fallen the mantle of Dick Sheppard and John Collins. Women protested night and day at the American nuclear base at Greenham Common, unsuccessful but unbowed. Numerous studies, in book or on television, analysed dangerous developments in this area or that of society. But the opposition parties remained divided, Labour in particular torn by recurring bouts of internal dissension. To criticize Mrs Thatcher was easy enough, to formulate a truly alternative policy acceptable to a majority of the nation seemed beyond the abilities of her critics. Meanwhile the country remained set upon a course different indeed from what had been pursued, not inconsistently, for many a decade. In such an age is it surprising if the churches, too, should stumble in their course, close their doors, or send forth in some confusion of mind a pained, uncertain note?

Anglicans and Free Churchmen[1]

The closure of doors is unquestionable. Between 1969 and 1984 the Church of England declared 1,086 churches redundant. Some of the more historic were preserved but very many had to be pulled down. In 1976 one church was demolished every nine days. Church buildings are static but populations shift. In one Anglican Manchester deanery 17 churches had been left with just 30,000 people and 14 of them were in due course closed. Inevitably it was the many churches of inner city areas, developed in a hurry in the nineteenth century, which suffered most. Methodists closed 493 churches in the three years 1971-4 and they continued to close others at the rate of more than a hundred annually over the next ten years. Of course many of these chapels should probably have been closed years before, soon after Methodist reunion in the 1930s, and there were still 7,600 Methodist churches in use at the end of our period. Relative to their numbers Catholics had far fewer churches and larger congregations; as a consequence they were not affected by this particular problem. Indeed, while the Church of England erected few new buildings in this period, Catholics were still building not inconsiderably. Nevertheless it was only in 1978 that the greatest of all modern Anglican cathedrals, that of Liverpool, was finally dedicated, after seventy-five years of building. Amazing in vastness, strength and height[2] – something for the religious to be rather grateful for in a somewhat brazenly secular age – Liverpool Cathedral in its finality yet represented an era and a grandiosity of ecclesiastical aspiration already long passed, a product not of the seventies but of late Victorianism.

To turn from buildings to people, Church of England baptisms had been 55.4 per cent of live births in 1960. By 1970 they had fallen, for the first time, below one half of the nation, and by the early 1980s were well under 40 per cent. Confirmations, 191 thousand in 1960 and 113 thousand in 1970 were 96 thousand in 1977 and 84,500 in 1982. In 1961 the Church of England had 26 theological colleges able to accommodate 1,663 people, by 1977 it had only 15 with 769 places.[3] In 1963 636 deacons were ordained, in 1976 273. As a result of the increase of ordinations in the later 1950s and the amalgamation of parishes, the number of curates had noticeably risen in the sixties and reached 3,317 in 1968, but in subsequent years the decline in the number of full-time clergy went faster than that of separate parishes and by 1978, as a consequence, curates were down to 1,823. It is not exaggerated to conclude that between 1960 and 1985 the Church of England as a going concern was effectively reduced to not much more than half its previous size.

Methodist membership[4] fell in the sixties from 733 thousand in 1960 to 651 thousand in 1969, an 11 per cent decrease in nine years; by 1977 it had fallen to 516,798, a decrease of 20 per cent in eight years; and by 1984 to 458,206, a decrease of 11 percent in seven years. Membership was keeping up best in London suburbs and some more rural areas like Cornwall, the Isle of Wight and East Anglia. In Manchester, however, it slipped from 33,725 in 1964 to 18,972 in 1984, a decline of 44 per cent in twenty years. On the other hand, if there were many quickly crumbling Methodist congregations in Manchester, as in other major northern cities and those parts of the countryside where Methodism had never been especially strong, there were also in Manchester, and elsewhere, a far smaller number of lively growing ones, still capable of drawing in new members.

The numerical decline within the United Reformed Church was no whit less serious: its membership at the start of the union was reckoned at 192 thousand in 1973; eleven years later in 1984, at 132 thousand: a decrease of slightly more than 30 per cent.[5]

The Catholic Church in England and Wales had 137 thousand infant baptisms in 1964, but only 70 thousand by 1976. In place of over twelve thousand converts a year received into the Church in the early 1960s, there were less than four thousand by 1972.[6] Marriages had fallen equally seriously. Marriages in Catholic churches were 12.76 per cent of all marriages in 1961 – the highest ever reached – but from that year the percentage fell continuously across the next fifteen years until by 1977 it was only 8.24 per cent.[7] In the diocese of Westminster, for instance, while 7,689 marriages were solemnized in 1967 and 7,598 in 1968, by 1980 the figure was down to 3,499 and in 1981 had reached 3,283.[8] The mass attendance of the estimated Catholic population had fallen from 49 per cent in 1968 to 32 per cent in 1978. The number of priests, nuns and seminarians was also diminishing, if more slightly.[9]

One consequence of the large and steady decline over many years of the number of Anglican priests was that there was now a far less striking difference between the number of Anglican and the number of Catholic priests at work full-time in the country. The Church of England had about 29 thousand priests at work at the start of the century[10] while the Catholic Church had something over three thousand, and the gap only really began to diminish in the 1930s. By the end of the seventies, however, the Church of England (excluding Wales) had 11,337 full-time diocesan clergy, while the Catholic Church (including Wales) had 6,797. The Catholic figure includes a number of religious in no way involved in pastoral work while the Anglican figure excludes the small number of Anglican religious and the much larger number of auxiliary priests. It also excludes the retired, while the Catholic figure is a total one, including such retired as there were. So the two figures are certainly not exactly comparable. Nevertheless it is probably true that there were now only about twice the number of Anglican priests at work full-time over Catholic ones, and that was an enormous alteration of balance.[11]

In general the rate of decline was reduced by the close of the 1970s, and a new more stable situation was developing, though it was seldom halted entirely. It could be argued that the real weight of influence of the main churches upon English society was gravely undermined by this vast quantitative decline in their relationship with people, dating from the mid-1960s and extending through to the later 1970s. In the case of the Methodists (as earlier in that of the Congregationalists) the scale of decline was such as to remove them from being the major national influence they had been hitherto. Considerable as the losses of the Church of England and the Catholic Church have been, they were not as yet comparably crippled. Yet the claim of the Church of England to be the national Church has, of course, been made far weaker – it became in these years what is almost a minority community. Only in counties like Dorset, Kent, Sussex, Hereford and Gloucestershire did its position remain clearly preponderant, while in almost all the major areas of population such as Greater London, Greater Manchester, Merseyside, Tyne and Wear, and the west Midlands, active Roman Catholic Church membership now far outstripped Anglican.[12] The Catholic Church might seem outwardly less affected by quantitative decline, helped both by the fat it had accumulated by steady increase up to the mid-sixties and by the more obvious weakening of other bodies which pushed it steadily forward. Its churches remained reasonably full, though its morale had grievously suffered, but the size, organization and surviving *esprit de corps* of English Catholicism was such that a considerable quantitative revival remained on the cards in a way that, to be honest, with Methodism or the United Reformed Church it no longer did. There was now no way in which the former influence of Congregationalists or Wesleyans in the life of this country was recoverable. Only on Humberside and in the Isle of Wight were Free churchmen now more numerous than either Anglicans or Catholics. Yet it is worth remembering that there were still, at the end of our period, almost twice as many Methodist places of worship as there were Roman Catholic – but they had, of course, far smaller congregations. It is also true that the Free Churches, like the Church of England, retained relatively a far wider penumbra of sympathizers and adherents – based on ancestral connection – than Roman Catholicism enjoyed. This remained noticeable, for example, in opinion polls.

If other churches were declining, one major Church at least had grown very considerably in the seventies: the Orthodox. It was a growth due to conversions as much as to migration. Archbishop Athenagoras II of Thyateira and Great Britain died in 1979, the first important Greek ecclesiastic in England since Theodore of Tarsus in the seventh century. In his episcopate there had been a fourfold increase in the number of Greek churches in

Britain and four auxiliary bishops had been appointed to assist him. At the same time Archbishop Anthony Bloom of the Russian Orthodox Church had become one of the principal religious voices in this country. Here, as in regard to the black churches, it is dangerously easy to overlook the growth while cataloguing the decline.

In November 1970 Queen Elizabeth II opened the first session of the new General Synod of the Church of England in Westminster Abbey in the presence of the Prime Minister, the Leader of the Opposition and the whole political establishment. The character and working of the General Synod quickly came to dominate the Church from this moment and to provide an ethos noticeably different from that of former decades. It also served to distance it from the State. The very authority of the synod, with its own quasi-parliamentary procedures and mounting sense of ecclesiastical power, reduced the sense of dependence upon Crown and parliament. In a way, then, that day in 1970 provided not only the State's blessing upon the new institution, but also a note of farewell: not disestablishment, certainly – neither side was ready for that – but a slightly regretful admission of diminished interest. The Church would now be permitted, very largely, to rule itself, both because that is what it wanted to do and because the political establishment no longer bothered very seriously about this section of its former empire.

When, a few years later, at a moment of crisis, Dr Coggan asked to see the Prime Minister and Mr Callaghan replied that he had no time available for the archbishop of Canterbury, the reply was unprecedented but should not have been unexpected. When 25 March 1980 was chosen months ahead for the enthronement of Archbishop Runcie in Canterbury Cathedral and it was then selected for Budget day, the clash of dates seemed again indicative of the new political insignificance of the Church of England in Conservative as well as Labour eyes. This however was to go too far: after protest Budget day was changed and Mrs Thatcher herself attended the enthronement.

Coupled with the existence of General Synod has been the effective transfer of the selection of bishops from the Prime

Minister to the Church. This had, of course, been urged by some churchmen for a long time.[13] It had also long been resisted both by the State and by the large majority of the episcopate. Now the mood was different. The 1970 Report of the Chadwick Commission on *Church and State*[14] was one of the first things which synod had to consider. The Report had rejected disestablishment (though three members of its commission submitted a minority report in favour). The majority view was that bishops should still be appointed by the Crown while the selection process should essentially become the work of a permanent Church electoral board; half the members of the commission wished to exclude the Prime Minister from the process altogether, the other half wished to retain his or her role of ultimate choice within a short list, believing that without this the Church's Establishment could not continue. In July 1974 the General Synod voted overwhelmingly (270 : 70) that the Church should have the final say in the appointment of bishops. Two years later a compromise was reached between Coggan and Callaghan (with the agreement of the leaders of the other political parties) whereby the Report's least revolutionary alternative was effectively accepted: henceforth a Church committee, attended by the Prime Minister's appointments secretary in an advisory capacity, would send the Prime Minister two names in order of preference, one of which he or she would forward to the queen. If the principle of lay political control was thus maintained, in practice this arrangement came near to terminating the age of the Church's subjection to political patronage (at the level of bishops, though not that of deans!). It did not, however, affect the theoretical supremacy of parliament.

In July 1984 a fairly minor measure passed by synod and sent on to parliament for approval was rejected in the Commons: the first such rejection for many years. The Appointment of Bishops Measure was designed to do no more than abolish the need for the formal election of a diocesan bishop by dean and chapter. The voting in the Commons was 32 : 17. The figures were indeed derisory. The rejection represented in personal terms no more than the displeasure of a quite small number of MPs with the way the Established Church was now going. Enoch Powell made use of the occasion to deliver a small sermon:

> It is possible to have an internally self-governed church in this country, but it will not be the national church, it will not be the Church of England. The Church is the Church of England because of royal supremacy, because there is royal – and that is to say, lay – supremacy. It is for that reason that it is the church of the people and the Church of the nation, and can never be converted into a mere sect or a private, self-managing corporation.[15]

In point of fact the Church had already been largely converted into 'an internally self-governed Church' and it was certainly no longer, except as a figment of the imagination, 'the church of the people'. Yet few people now much desired its disestablishment[16] or to weaken what little remained of its public character whereby in some slight but still real degree the State of England retained a religious and Christian quality. It was therefore prudent to hearken to the sermon, eat humble pie, and not press forward with the measure in question which anyway lacked the whole-hearted support of the synod.

The revised arrangements for the appointment of bishops was part of a coherent new system: the triumph of synodical government was a triumph of self-government, of centralized self-government. The Church Commissioners had been centralizing the control of Church property for a long time. The General Synod's principal arm was the not inconsiderable central bureaucracy of Church House, Westminster. It is all of a piece that the dioceses were not given freedom to choose their bishop (as was the custom of the Catholic past and as is the custom of most provinces of the Anglican Communion). Instead a central electoral college was allotted that task, though it included for each separate nomination a significant diocesan representation. In the past the traditional Anglican near-autonomy of the individual diocese and bishop had only been subject to a political master. The nineteenth and twentieth centuries had seen this slowly change with the revival of the Convocations and then the establishment of the Church Assembly. The arrival of General Synod considerably accentuated this trend, as did the new system of episcopal selection. While conservatives preferred the new arrangement over one of diocesan elections because it preserved the centralized and confidential character of appointments, it –

like the establishment of General Synod itself, with the virtual demise of the separate convocations of York and Canterbury – weakened the sense of the Church as a federal body, of diocesan particularities. The age of the old autocratic, and often idiosyncratic, bishop was ending. Conservative, rather autocratic bishops like Williams of Leicester,[17] idiosyncratic bishops like Stockwood of Southwark, did not much care for it. The latter wrote of the General Synod of 1972 in his diocesan letter: 'I regard it as a disaster, a playground for bureaucrats or bores. Worse still is the time wasted on endless chatter and the money wasted on cascades of memoranda and minutes, stamps, envelopes and secretarial expenses.' Was the authority of a 'Father in God' in danger of being replaced by that of an ecclesiastical computer?

A case can certainly be made against the General Synod on grounds of bureaucracy, a rather mediocre cautious conservatism, the fallaciousness of rule by democratic centralism. On certain key issues it has had a paralysing effect, several times restraining a more adventurous and open-minded episcopate. As a whole its lay membership (as, indeed, its clerical membership) has been elderly and from the educated class. It has contained few aristocrats (Christian Howard and the Earl of March, formerly vice-chairman of the Church and State commission, being the principal exceptions) and few working-class people. Women have been better represented – though only in the House of Laity. The latter had as its first chairman the distinguished lawyer and Evangelical writer, Sir Norman Anderson, director of the Institute of Advanced Legal Studies of the University of London. Whatever defects may be found in its membership, it has represented a credible legislative authority for the Church, and one which has, in a serious way, combined Catholic with Protestant tradition. It may be favourably compared with the almost complete failure of the Roman Catholic Church, in the period subsequent to the Second Vatican Council, to give any proper embodiment to the much discussed doctrine of collegiality. The Church of England has done so. If Anglican bishops seem as a consequence less authoritative and singular than some of them did in the past (and there are other reasons for this too: some decline in their class background, academic distinction and recreational pursuits, also a more modest income), the synod has in its way provided an appropriate locus precisely for the leadership of an imaginative primate (though, admittedly, it has explicitly rejected that leadership in some instances).

There were, then, both gains and losses in the development of the General Synod. What cannot be doubted is that it was a decisive development. The synod's rejection of a number of major proposals was crucial for the whole development of English religious history in this period. It rejected the Anglican-Methodist reunion scheme in May 1972 (it required a 75 per cent majority: the clergy gave it 65 per cent, the laity less than 63 per cent; only the bishops supported it adequately – by 34 to 6); it rejected the ordination of women in November 1978 (despite a preparatory vote in favour in 1975); it rejected the proposal to allow Anglican women priests from other provinces to celebrate in England in 1979; it rejected the proposals for ecumenical covenanting (which again required a two-thirds majority) in 1982; finally it rejected proposals to allow the divorced to be remarried in church, in 1973, 1978 and again (despite a favourable vote in 1981) in 1985. Ramsey had appealed eloquently for acceptance of reunion with Methodists in 1972 and Coggan for the ordination of women in 1978. In each case it was really the clergy, especially a central core of broadly Anglo-Catholic clergy, with some Evangelical backing, which blocked the proposals. In each case the proposals might be seen as facilely attractive conclusions to sixties theology which were losing their glitter in the less progressively-minded seventies and which would, moreover, further distance the Church of England from Roman Catholicism, as also from eastern Orthodoxy. This the ordinary Anglo-Catholic priest was unwilling to agree to, even if many parts of the Anglican communion overseas – far more easily influenced by current ecumenical attitudes and Protestant theology – had accepted them.

Nothing in the seventies was more deeply divisive for the Church of England than the issue of the ordination of women. It was something which society's new-found commitment to the equality of women put at the very centre of the agenda for all the churches. It was hard to construct a very sound theological argument against;[18] it was easy to suggest social and pastoral reasons in favour (perhaps not always such conclusive ones, when the actual experience of Protestant churches which had ordained women was considered). Yet it also seemed clear that – even if liberal Roman Catholic theologians seemed almost too encouraging – the ordination of women was quite likely to damage any prospect of union, or even intercommunion, with Rome quite considerably. By the 1980s it was nevertheless becoming clear that, as Rome became again more uncompromisingly conservative under Pope John Paul, reunion was not anyway a likely eventuality in the medium-future. It is perhaps hardly surprising that at the very close of our period, November 1984, the issue of the ordination of women was once more considered in General Synod and obtained in principle a very substantial positive vote in all three houses. Here as elsewhere the temporizing conservatism of the 1970s might not, after all, prove a very enduring phenomenon.

What emerges in the seventies in the Church of England is, then, a collective government, novel in structure but conservative and cautious in direction. There is little very weighty personal leadership left. Donald Coggan, in his very short archiepiscopate (1974-80) made less impact, ecclesiastical or political, than any of his twentieth-century predecessors. The day both of the great scholar-bishop and of the great politician-bishop (or, indeed, the eccentric prima donna) seemed almost over. Almost the only priest of indubitably national weight, a natural choice for the most senior episcopal appointment, preferred a different role. Owen Chadwick was a historian and theological scholar of exceptional eminence, Master of Selwyn College, Regius Professor of Modern History, Vice-Chancellor of Cambridge University, President of the British Academy, chairman of the last and most influential commission on Church and State. He represented to perfection the rather unclerical and unpartisan tradition of priesthood which, at its pious cultured best, constituted one of the great strengths of the Church of England: that easy yet still high-principled interchange between the political, the ecclesiastical and the academic. When Chadwick retired as Master in 1983 Selwyn College elected, for the first time, a layman (just as Keble had done at Oxford a year or two earlier). The kind of clerical leadership which he represented, powerful in learning and personality, if perhaps just a shade too comfortable, was passing away. It would be quite a loss.

It would be the task of Donald Coggan and Robert Runcie to guide the shaping of this new order while providing some reassurance for doubters. Coggan was good at the second, rather less at the first, being little of a listener or co-operator. What many would regard as his great fiasco, *The Call to the Nation* of 1975, was entirely a personal effort, lacking both preparation and any serious follow-up, yet – like much else that he did – it reassured worriers among the Church's traditional clientele.[19] A sound biblical scholar of deeply orthodox doctrinal conviction and much personal charm, Coggan seemed too simple in judgment to cope with either the theological conundrums or the social confusion of the age. Yet, and this is remarkable for a man who was essentially an evangelical, he somehow grasped and did his best to further what, since the mid-1960s, had become in fact the principal business upon the Church of England's agenda: reunion with Rome. Dialogue was properly carried on with many other churches but there can be little question that ARCIC now stood in a class by itself. Its statements of 'substantial agreement' on Eucharistic Doctrine in 1971, on Ministry and Ordination in 1973, and then the agreed statement on Authority in the Church in 1976, seemed immensely encouraging. The Romeward relationship had been established by Archbishop Ramsey, the Vatican Council and the hard facts of current ecclesiastical allegiance in England, as the absolutely crucial one. Coggan may have missed the nuances in the Roman mind and have exasperated more sophisticated ecumenical colleagues in consequence, but with what *The Times* called his 'headlong approach' in his visit to Rome in April 1977 and his consistent appeals for intercommunion he played his part to maintain the impetus.[20]

Robert Runcie, Archbishop of Canterbury from the beginning of 1980, was however a man more naturally suited to the task. He had been an officer in the Scots Guards during the war and was an MC; a family man, a don at Cambridge in the fifties, Principal of Cuddesdon in the sixties, Bishop of St Albans in the seventies. So he had a particularly wide range of experience when he came to the chair of Augustine and showed this in the confidence with which he handled the media. His most important task would be, perhaps, to reassert the Church's truly public status demonstrating a national concern and availability.

Runcie was a man of the Anglo-Catholic centre, a theologian and a diplomat, who had been especially interested in discussion with eastern Churches, and was the more suited to carry forward the business with Rome in that he had hitherto shown no taint of special Roman-mindedness. His enthronement in the chair of Augustine in Canterbury Cathedral on the feast of the Annunciation, appeared as an expression of western Catholic Christianity almost fully re-established, with several cardinals in the choir near him, the full use of Catholic vestments, the appropriate Marian hymn. Cardinal Hume read the epistle. The central message of Runcie's enthronement sermon was of the Christian duty of love, 'deep unsentimental love – part toughness, part sensitivity'. Only this can give true authority and the example he cited was of Mother Teresa and her authority.

Two months later Runcie and Hume led Anglican and Catholic pilgrims respectively to the shrine of Our Lady at Walsingham – the first time an Archbishop of Canterbury had been there on public pilgrimage. As Runcie processed through the town, behind a crowned statue of the Blessed Virgin, flanked by the Bishops of Chichester and Truro, and surrounded by hundreds of clergy and thousands of jubilant laity, he could afford to disregard the accusing placards of the Protestant Truth Society.[21]

Full reunion between Rome and what Pope Paul VI described as its 'Sister Church' might have seemed only just round the corner; above all, at the almost unbelievable moment in 1982 when Pope John Paul stood in Canterbury Cathedral surrounded by both Catholic and Church of England episcopates, offering to all a warm 'kiss of peace'. Here was the near culmination of a process rooted in Tractarianism, nourished by Gore and countless Anglo-Catholics of many varieties, led further in their time by Lang and Ramsey but, each in his own way, contributed to by every single archbishop of this century. It would be pleasant to see that day as the happy ending of a story, but history seldom provides happy endings and – as we shall soon discover – the enterprise of reunion between Rome and Canterbury, on which the Church of England had come (perhaps almost unconsciously) to stake so much, and which in the England of Runcie and Hume seemed so obviously appropriate, was in fact being faced with counter-movements of no little vigour.

'If some of my own clergy who go around to their endless committees and yak and yak and yak away would only get on with the job of trying to convert their own parishioners, I think that we should not be in quite the state of decline that we are.'[22] Archbishop Heenan would have agreed with this remark of Mervyn Stockwood – one of many examples of erstwhile radicals turned rather sour in the 1970s. His comment does however indicate some of the pastoral characteristics of our final era: on the one hand, increasing use by the Church at every level of modern systems of decision-making (or, at times, decision-avoiding) and appraisal; on the other, a steady distancing of clergy from people. Both were inevitable. Even in parts of English society where, until the fifties, Anglican priests were fairly thick on the ground – rural areas especially – the gap had grown between the Church and the daily life of the community. In most villages there was no longer a priest. The amalgamation of livings, the fading away of curates, the considerable difficulty at times – especially in the north – of filling a living at all, the rapidity with which priests now changed their parish, the disappearance of old-fashioned pastoral methods (Sunday school, clubs), even the erosion of the vicar's social standing, all contributed to making the ministry of the Church of England vastly more marginal to society than it had ever been.[23] Despite early enthusiasm for the 'South Ormsby Experiment' the amalgamation of rural livings had seldom been done very creatively. Not only the townsman but the countryman might now not even know the vicar by sight. The old vicar had been, typically, a graduate, a gentleman living in a large if uncomfortable house, a sort of sub-squire excelling at cricket, where he could mix as an equal with his parishioners while still receiving a fair measure of deference. He was known. The new vicar was more than likely to have no degree at all: in the forty years prior to 1960 38 per cent of Anglican ordinands were Oxford and Cambridge graduates; by 1971 this had fallen to 16 per cent while 57 per cent had no degree. The large vicarages had been sold. Cricket playing was no longer much of a clerical characteristic. The new vicar was living in a comfortable but insignificant house – not necessarily near the church – with an assured but limited income. The image of the gentleman was gone. The vicar had almost ceased to be a figure of fun, but he had also almost ceased to be a public figure at all.

The old social basis of the church might still survive to some extent in certain more conservative strongholds, mostly upper middle-class citadels, comfortable small towns and larger sub-urbanized villages like Solihull or Painswick; but by and large it was very nearly gone, a loss on both sides, and the general decline of the more nominal type of churchmanship as a result was quite inevitable. The majority of the clergy in all the churches seemed to have next to no idea as to how to cope with the frankly missionary situation which now faced them. New approaches to the apostolate – the house mass, the prayer group, retreats, small conferences, clerical commitment to special social needs, and much else – were tried at times and by some, but the toughness and versatility required both in the minister and in his congregation by a genuinely missionary situation were too seldom in evidence. That was the majority picture. There was a minority one, exceedingly different. All churches in the seventies had a number of extremely lively, growing congregations. In the Church of England, take St Michael-le-Belfry in York, or Holy Trinity, Brompton Road, or St Aldate's, Oxford, and a good many more. Here one found congregations so considerable that the clergy could hardly cope. They were mostly Evangelical and Pentecostal, but in both regards only moderately so. They were inclusivist. They excelled particularly in management techniques. They tended to make great use of smaller prayer groups or house masses. They drew in members of other denominations and of none quite easily, and yet they maintained a decided Anglicanism.

Evangelicalism, renewed in the sixties, continued to flourish in the seventies to such an extent that maybe half (and the tougher half) of newly ordained Anglican priests now belonged to it. Behind it the guiding hand of John Stott could still be discerned as it had been for twenty years, nationally as well as internationally – a sort of touchstone of Evangelical respectability. He had become the recognized senior theologian and thinker of world evangelicalism, invited time and again to give the major address, the daily exposition of Scripture, at some thousands-strong, American-sponsored missionary convention.[24] The apogee of this central current of 1970s Evangelicalism was undoubtedly the Lausanne Conference on World Evangelism of July 1974. It was attended by 2,700 picked people and cost over three million dollars ($2,272,000 came directly from the Billy Graham Evangelistic Association). 'This must be a gathering', declared Graham, 'of those totally committed to the evangelical position as we understand it. This should not be a gathering of those committed to liberal or to controversial positions.' 'The planning of Lausanne', wrote one of its principal American commentators, Arthur Johnston,[25] 'isolated the heretical views of the ecumenical movement, exposed their non-biblical foundations, and strongly reaffirmed the primacy of proclamation evangelism'. Clearly on this view the evangelicalism of the 1970s remained what it always had been: self-consciously fundamentalist, anti-ecumenical, suspicious of anything other than 'proclamation'. Yet John Stott was Lausanne's principal theoretician, author of its introductory study, *The Biblical Basis of Evangelism*, and chairman of the follow-up committee, the Lausanne Theological and Education Group. In fact it would appear that Stott had been quietly steering Lausanne in the very directions which Johnston was denouncing: it was due to him that the Lausanne Covenant avoided a commitment to the verbal inspiration of Scripture, made social action a partner of evangelism, and stressed – instead of individual and undenominational evangelism – the collective responsibility of the visible Church. None of this was very acceptable to main-line American Evangelicals. For Johnston, Stott was in point of fact leading the movement back on to the slippery slope which was believed to have been so fatal half a century before in the days of the SCM, so disastrous to the WCC, the very road which had led to the undermining of all the simple certainties of the early missionary movement.[26]

In December 1976 Stott was again the leading theological figure at the PACLA[27] Conference of African Evangelicals in Nairobi and admitted that he had been present as an adviser at the WCC conference in Nairobi the year before: 'It seems to me that evangelicals ought to be in the World Council.' In the 1960s,

Stott admitted at Lausanne, he had still understood Christian mission as only one of 'preaching, converting and teaching', but now, 'I would express myself differently . . . not only the consequences of the Commission but the actual Commission itself must be understood to include social as well as evangelistic responsibility, unless we are to be guilty of distorting the words of Jesus.'[28]

In April 1977 Stott chaired the second Anglican Evangelical Congress at Nottingham as he had chaired that at Keele exactly ten years earlier,[29] two thousand people where last time there were one thousand. His position was now very clear. 'Evangelicals ought to be conservative on the Bible and radical on everything else' – yet not too conservative even on the Bible. The accepted patriarch of English Evangelicalism, he had moved steadily forward in his own thinking and, while doing so, had struggled with skill and determination to liberate evangelicalism from its worst narrownesses and overcome the schism within Protestant Christianity between ecumenicals and Evangelicals, which had dogged it since almost the start of the century. Indeed on almost all the issues where Evangelicals had been accustomed to point the finger at the former, Stott had come down in defence of the wider ecumenical position, always carefully phrased but increasingly unequivocal. Within the world Evangelical movement of the second half of the century he played to Billy Graham a role not altogether unlike that which J. H. Oldham had played fifty years before to John R. Mott. In each case the less flamboyant but more intellectual Englishman was endeavouring to guide the movement into new, less simplistic vistas. What is remarkable is how far Stott was able to go without losing the confidence of Graham. All the same, on the international level it may well be that he did not quite succeed in converting a dominantly American movement to the extent he would have liked. He was bowling on too foreign a wicket.

In England it was different. The ecclesiology which was so unacceptable an element in the synthesis for many an 'undenominational' American missionary, was fully acceptable within an English Evangelicalism which was becoming more and more consciously Anglican. Yet here too there were problems. The more Evangelicals felt freed after Keele to explore new vistas, the more their own party unity and rather monolithic sense of doctrinal certainty began to be eroded. By the end of the seventies it could begin to look as if the Evangelical movement might be going the way of the Anglo-Catholic. Nevertheless, all in all, the line laid down by Keele in 1967 was being pursued: very moderately sacramentalist, socially committed, biblically conservative but not obscurantically fundamentalist, cautiously ecumenical. It did not reject Rome with the horror characteristic of much older Protestantism, but it remained decidedly cautious all the same. The Evangelical movement was still self-consciously Protestant and had none of the often emotional desire for reunion characteristic of Anglo-Catholics. If there was to be unity, Rome would have to change a great deal first.[30] It may, however, well be the case that in England there remains no real alternative for Evangelicalism between an intellectually archaic and fundamentalist sectarianism on the one hand and absorption as a Conservative and biblically conscious wing within an ecumenical Catholicism upon the other. Such may seem to have been the message of our story almost throughout. For America it would be hard to say the same with any confidence but then the basic American pattern of religion has been different from the English ever since the late seventeenth century when the two went contrasting ways.

The Evangelicalism of the 1970s was also increasingly open to Pentecostalism but here too it continued to exercise a certain reserve, though a number of prominent Evangelicals like Michael Harper and David Watson[31] turned into leading figures in charismatic renewal. The more they did so, the more ecumenical they usually became. The Fountain Trust, founded by Michael Harper in 1964 as a sort of ecumenical guiding agency for the charismatic movement in Britain, was dissolved in 1978. Harper moved instead to SOMA, an international but specifically Anglican organisation for charismatics. The Fountain Trust had been a valuable steadying influence, undenominational but not anti-denominational. Its function had been, indeed, precisely to locate the charisma of 'Baptism in the Spirit' within a wider theology and to prevent Pentecostals from hiving off into little ghettos of their own. To a large extent it succeeded. It is true that the charismatic movement looked at times like a refuge for frightened Christians from the intellectual and institutional problems with which the churches were failing to cope: it could provide a sort of euphoria of freedom for people in fact deeply enmeshed in legal and theological bonds which they could not, or would not, break. The mechanisms of ecstatic dancing, the making of strange noises and stirring but not intellectually articulated sounds, the lying about in unusual postures, could all be little more than a reassuring psychological get-away for priests and nuns who were the rest of the time very faithful servants of a system which the reformers of a few years before had wanted to change but had not succeeded in doing. It could all lead too to a one-sided preoccupation with faith healing or, even, just the throwing out of devils. Yet that was only one side of it. The charismatic experience led in many people's lives to a remarkable recovery of joy and faith. It led to a noticeable loosening of denominational prejudice. It enabled conservative Evangelicals to discover the value of a frequent Eucharist, and conservative Catholics the value of sharing the cup. It could bring Catholics and Protestants to share in worship in Northern Ireland more openly than anything else could. It led many people to feel free to intercommunicate.[32]

The charismatic movement was, for the most part, fairly successfully domesticated by both the Roman Catholic and the Anglican churches. It influenced many but by no means a majority of congregations[33] and it did not too gravely divide the charismatic from the non-charismatic. By the end of the decade the likelihood of a major charismatic schism seemed to have disappeared. The Fountain Trust was no longer required. If that is true of the majority, it is also the case that, as the years passed, a strong Pentecostal minority moved in a very different direction. It became harder, more self-consciously institutional, especially among converts within the old Free Churches where the basic sense of a wider Church authority had always been smaller. Here the temptation to go it alone, to become an independent charismatic Church set apart from the old mixed body, proved stronger and all over the country a considerable number of independent 'House Churches' were appearing.[34] The background of some was predominantly Anglican, but more often Free Church. If, in its earlier forms, the charismatic movement had been strikingly open in all sorts of ways – lay, non-authoritarian, susceptible to the personal leadership of women, moderately libertarian in life-style and liberal in theology – by the later 1970s a quite different face was coming to dominate, clerical, autocratic, intolerant of disagreement, theologically highly conservative. The active role of women disappeared. What is most characteristic of the typical house church is the unquestioned authority of its minister. Links with the wider Church (except, possibly, for other house churches) have been severed. Socially it becomes a very strong support group – far stronger than most modern parishes – almost a commune, in this not unlike many other new religious movements of the period, such as the Unification Church. Indeed, the 'Children of God' led by David Berg, while constituting a highly organized international movement of their own, have had a considerable overlap both in membership and in inspiration with Pentecostalism. Through the development of house churches the charismatic movement has become a major source for a new sectarianism, a born-again congregationalism which was long part of English religion but had – prior to this new arrival – seemed, outside the black community, to be not far off its last legs.

There had, after all, been an ancient tradition of English congregationalism. Throughout the country there have always been strict Congregationalists who refused to join the Congregationalist Union with its increasingly centralized character but continued on their own, a church here, a church there. All in all, there were far more of them than one easily realizes, because next to nothing has ever been written about them. Some, of course, did have their wider links. Considering those surviving into the eighties one may think, for instance, of the Independent Methodists, whose secretary lived at Croxton, Stafford: a network of 119 churches and 150 unpaid ministers. Or the Wesleyan Reform Union, whose centre was Sheffield, with just twenty-four ministers. Or the General Assembly of Unitarian and Free Christian Churches with ninety-five ministers and 250 chapels. One may even think of the Congregational Federation, those member churches of the old Congregational Union who in 1972 refused to join the United Reformed Church. Its secretary was in Nottingham. Stafford, Sheffield, Nottingham: that already suggests something about the heartlands of the surviving old independency, but in truth it could still be found in many unexpected places: at the Wyche, on the Malvern Hills. In many a Sussex village. In many an older suburb of an industrial town. Many such chapels have closed over the years, but others have revived recently, strengthened by a new wave of separatedness, the arrival of new members from the house church wing of the charismatic movement.

The surviving old independent chapels and evangelists, tiny denominations like the Wesleyan Reform Union or the Brethren or Elim; the new black churches (not 'black' in principle, but overwhelmingly as regards membership) like the New Testament Church of God or the United Church of Jesus Christ Apostolic, and the new house churches, all represent in somewhat varying forms the basic characteristics of the English Protestant tradition in its unestablished form – Congregationalist, born-again, Baptist, biblically fundamentalist, set apart: the institutional fragmentation of Christianity, forceful, divisive, thriving upon the word of the preacher and the singing of the congregation. It was all in strong contrast with the publicly prevailing ecclesiastical wind of the 1970s. It was particularly important because the dominant ecumenical consensus, despite the most sincere lip service to the contrary, made so easily for uniformity and bureaucratic centralization, and could appear to conform so neatly with the take-over economy of post-industrial capitalism. Undiluted Protestantism stood, on the contrary, for an almost pre-capitalist form of human community, the viability of the separate localized unit – the local church at its starkest. It fitted not at all with the Establishment culture of modern society but rather well with a mass of other ill-financed structures engendered by the increasing multitude of people repelled by the syndromes of centralized control. Among the larger churches really only the Baptists still officially shared in this type of Christianity, and even here it had been considerably modified, organizationally, liturgically and intellectually. The divide between the ethos of independency and a preoccupation with direct evangelism on the one hand, that of ecumenism, the liturgical movement and liberal biblical criticism on the other still came down somewhere round the middle of the Baptist churches.

Elsewhere it was between the middle and the periphery. And in the middle the ecumenical consensus grew and grew.

Attitudes in the pew might still remain a good deal different from that of the leadership. Let us consider an odd course of events in the North Yorkshire fishing village of Staithes.[35] There were always three chapels in Staithes – Wesleyan, Primitive Methodist and Bethel (Congregationalist), and each had a Sunday school. After the national Union of 1932 the Wesleyan and Primitive chapels remained firmly distinct apart from the occasional interchange of pulpits. By 1961 the circuit was in debt and anxious to cut down on avoidable expenses. A Replanning Commission proposed the closure of several chapels, of which one was to be in Staithes, and the Wesleyan was selected. The Wesleyans objected. Deadlock was averted by an agreement to have a trial period in which both chapels remained open but would be used on alternate Sundays. The Sunday schools would be merged. The trial period began in the spring of 1970 and continued uneasily until 1975, when a vote was taken to reopen both chapels each Sunday, which was done. Congregations rose as a result, for some 'Prims' had refused to attend 'Wesley' and vice-versa. The Sunday schools had never in fact been amalgamated. The gap between the priorities of one kind of grassroot and those of the leadership was here revealed with pathetic poignancy. Cost-effective efficiency and the ecumenical ideal of the unity of 'all in one place' were clear enough on one side. They were the principles which had prevailed overwhelmingly at national level. Here, indeed, the Methodist conference had agreed in this very period by an overwhelming majority to unite even with Anglicans. But that meant nothing in Staithes. Here the priority was the surviving consciousness of a very small community, attachment to a particular building, the very attractiveness of sectarian separation. Here Methodists could still not agree to unite with Methodists.

Of course the Staithes Methodists were unusual in their obstinacy. They represented in traditional and rural guise the very sort of Protestant congregationalist religiosity which we have already considered in more novel forms. The real heartland of the new Methodism was clearly not Staithes.[36] It was suburbia – the Church of England's new heartland too and, for that matter, increasingly the Church of Rome's. The London area in the mid-1970s still had 975 Methodist churches. The most thriving were the 213 in the south-west (including parts of Surrey and Sussex) with an average membership of 112 per church, two churches per minister, and an attendance of about 90 per cent. Almost all had their Sunday schools. Here Methodism was holding up well enough, in fairly strong contrast with the 464 churches of East Anglia with a mere thirty-two members per church and seven churches per minister. Almost certainly a study of the two groups would reveal a contrast as much in forms of religiosity as in numbers. The East Anglian churches were old, rooted, almost none received any new members. Their loyalties were predominantly local, to the traditional values and forms of Protestant religion. The congregations of south-west London, on the other hand, were looking less and less different in worship[37] and sense of commitment from their Anglican neighbours. They were very much part of the ecumenical, liturgical and social consensus to which the Church's leadership was itself committed.[38] The Methodist Conference, both in 1969 and 1972, had voted by over 75 per cent for unity with the Church of England, but many an old-time Methodist could not have liked it – and not only in Staithes. Jim Simmons, lay preacher and MP over many years for Brierley Hill, Birmingham, had this to say in his old age (he was almost eighty) of the unity scheme: 'As an old Primitive Methodist I see nothing but disaster in the proposal to accept as christian union the position where the established Church is the whale and Methodism Jonah.'[39] He undoubtedly spoke for one kind of Methodism, an apparently dying world of tin tabernacles where 'Hallelujah! Praise the Lord!' could be shouted with gusto and no embarrassment.

The Methodist Conference was more than ever committed to all progressive causes. In 1971 it voted almost unanimously for the ordination of women. It had first decided to do so long before, in 1938, but nothing was done at the time on account of the war and later of the more conservative mood of the fifties. Under the persuasion of Pauline Webb, conference recorded its intention in 1971 to ordain women but also, with excellent ecumenical manners, to do nothing about it until the conversations with the Church of England were resolved. In 1974 the first women were ordained. From this point of view Methodism was coming into line with a far wider Protestant consensus, for the Congregational Union and the Baptist Union had ordained women for many years.

The wave of institutional ecumenism which had been building up for ten years, having been provided by the Nottingham Conference of 1964 with a target date of unity in Britain by 1980, reached its high point at the start of the 1970s. At that point Anglican-Methodist reunion, so long prepared for, still seemed attainable. In 1970 Queen's College in Birmingham became England's first and only fully ecumenical theological college. In 1972 the Church Leaders Conference at Selly Oak in September was undoubtedly the most ecumenical gathering of churchmen, including lots of Roman Catholics, yet to meet in Britain. Two weeks later the United Reformed Church, the one major institutional achievement of British ecumenism in this period, was inaugurated at Westminster.

Back in 1933 Bernard Manning, one of the wisest and most learned of twentieth-century Congregationalists, declared, 'I have no doubt that union with Presbyterians is the next step . . . I personally would pay almost any price to achieve that union . . . I would bring it about tomorrow.'[40] An attempt to bring it about came to grief in 1951. In the sixties negotiations began again and on 5 October 1972 the Congregational Church in England and Wales (as the Congregational Union had renamed itself in 1966) and the Presbyterian Church of England were at last joined into one under the name of the United Reformed Church: the first interdenominational scheme of full unity to succeed in Britain – forty years after Manning's 'tomorrow'. The Presbyterian Church was small, hardly present at all outside Northumberland, London and Merseyside. The Congregational Church had once been large and powerful. It had now declined in numbers more than any, though it could still count several Labour leaders including Harold Wilson among its more nominal members, and had also become more ecumenical than any. There had been no significant doctrinal difference between the two churches. Both saw themselves as heirs to the tradition of seventeenth-century dissent. Their disagreements had been largely governmental and had been whittled away by twentieth-century developments in both churches. Their union in fact had long been obvious; it had also long been delayed. When at last it was achieved it was within a process of decline which went on unaffected by the merger. Nor was its acceptance unanimous upon the Congregational side. Here some hundreds of congregations opted out and continued as a separate Congregational Federation, comparable in mood with the Methodists of Staithes.

The new Church was uncompromisingly ecumenical. All the leading officials of the Church Leaders Conference would be among its most prominent ministers – John Huxtable, the conference's chairman, Kenneth Slack, the chairman of its steering committee, Michael Hubbard, minister of Carr's Lane church, the conference secretary.[41] Congregationalists could still provide a hopeful avant-garde for the British ecumenical movement though in reality the Church Leaders Conference marked far more the end than the beginning of an era. Slack, formerly secretary of the British Council of Churches, became the URC's first Moderator. Its greatest scholar was the octogenarian C. H. Dodd, the first Free churchman to be a Professor of Theology at Cambridge, a universally respected figure but also, to tell the truth, very near to being an Anglican at heart. Its most international figure was Lesslie Newbigin, Moderator in 1978-9, for long a missionary in Asia, a bishop of the Church of South India, and later a leading figure in the World Council of Churches. He was the one Free churchman in England to be recognized as a bishop by the Church of England. Apart from him, the Free Churches had not taken episcopacy into their system as, back in 1946, Archbishop Fisher had appealed to them to do, while, ironically, the Church of England had taken government by assembly into its system! Men like Slack, Dodd and Newbigin were committed to the full ideal of Christian ecumenism really far beyond their commitment to Congregationalism, Presbyterianism or the URC. The surviving fragment of the Congregational Federation might be but a crumbling and antiquated remnant, yet it could appeal to the ancient logic of Congregationalism. But how, except as one step forward, the construction of a rather temporary tent, could the existence of the URC be justified apart from Anglicanism or even, maybe, Roman Catholicism? The ecumenical ideal, once embraced, could not stop there. That, in fact, the architects of the URC most explicitly recognized when, the very day of unity, a service of thanksgiving was held in Westminster Abbey in which Archbishop Ramsey and Cardinal Heenan promised to join the continuing search for a wider unity.[42]

As a matter of fact, after the union of 1972 no further advance was made at the institutional level – except that in 1980 the very tiny body of the Association of Churches of Christ in Great Britain and Ireland dissolved itself, allowing the majority of its congregations to join the URC. In 1930 the association had had 200 churches and 16 thousand members. Now it had fallen to 75 churches and 3,586 members.[43] Yet as a group it failed to obtain the two-thirds majority of the churches to join the URC organically. Considerable as the tide was in favour of unity in most churches there was nearly always a sufficient minority opposed to block progress, and the institutional leadership was less and less inclined to get bogged down in the seemingly endless intricacies of unifying disparate ecclesiastical bodies. It is true that, as a sort of half-way house, after the failure of Anglican-Methodist unity, an alternative approach, 'Covenanting for Unity', was explored over many years. It was an attempt to avoid the hazards of devising some road to full institutional unity by substituting for it a basic act of corporate recognition: commitment to visible unity, out of which corporate unity could then flow by stages. This approach was formulated in the 'Ten Propositions' of 1976. Yet here again official ecumenism came in due course to be bogged down in issues of episcopal ordination and the ordination of women, over which agreement could not be obtained. In 1982 General Synod failed to accept the covenanting scheme and with that, just ten years after the demise of Anglican-Methodist unity, the last hope of a national way forward within a Protestant framework was abandoned.[44] In the judgment of many an ecumenical old hand, 'with the failure of the Covenant the whole movement which had begun with the Lambeth appeal of 1920 seemed to have come to a dead end', due to 'the lamentable fading of the ecumenical vision in the minds of English church people'.[45] Again, when one recalls how major a role British people had in the formation of the World Council of Churches, it is strange to see how little the World Council and the concerns of Geneva seemed to matter in England by the eighties. It all seemed to have become an irrelevance, and rather a boring one too.

If the institutional record alone be considered it could, then, well appear that the enterprise of Christian unity in England in its traditional and essentially Protestant form had been shown well before the end of our period to be a case of clear failure. The Faith and Order Conference at Nottingham in 1964 had called for unity by Easter 1980. 1980 had arrived. Unity had not. Institutionally the churches were nearly as divided as ever, and each scheme for ending their division had been abandoned. Yet the ecumenical movement in England in the 1970s was in reality by no means a failure. This was because it had in fact discovered a longer goal. All conventional ecumenical planning hitherto had more or less left Catholics out. In the pre-Vatican II world there was no alternative, but it was now becoming clear that no really significant Christian unity in England could be achieved without them. The principal achievement of the period was precisely this recognition: Christian unity without Catholics would simply not be, nor appear to the world to be, Christian unity. Older ecumenical hands often recognised this but could do little about it. In the new context what seemed the immediate way ahead was not so much the reconciling of institutions as their bypassing. Ecumenism had never in fact been more widely influential or less rigidly structured. It was not, indeed, that it took no institutional form; rather that it took so many. Areas of ecumenical experiment ('local ecumenical projects' they were later called) were springing up all over the country: Swindon, hardly a typical ecclesiastical centre, was probably the most advanced. New towns and housing estates were the ideal place for them. Local councils of churches, local covenanting between congregations, Christian Aid, joint theological commissions at almost every level, joint churches, inter-church schools, joint theological colleges, ecumenical institutes of higher education (as in Liverpool and Roehampton), the complete inter-denominationalizing of all university faculties of theology (except Oxford), joint Lenten programmes, the Ecumenical Society of the Blessed Virgin Mary, the Association of Inter-church Families, the study programme 'Not Strangers but Pilgrims'; in such things lies the real ecumenical transformation of the seventies and eighties, and it was one in which Roman Catholics were taking a full part in a way that would have been almost inconceivable even in the sixties. Several secretaries of local Councils of Churches were now Catholics.

Think of Norman Goodall, that distinguished Congregationalist who was William Paton's successor as secretary of the International Missionary Council from 1944 to 1963, spending ten memorable weeks in Rome in 1975 lecturing at the Gregorian University and living at the Venerable English College.[46] Think of the Anglican Bishop Cocks and the Catholic Bishop Brewer on 13 July 1980 confirming candidates of their two churches simultaneously in a joint service held in the shared church of All Saints in Telford New Town. Think of the Anglican and Roman Catholic laity of Much Hadham, Hertfordshire, voting to share the twelfth-century parish church of St Andrew (the Anglicans voted 3 to 1 in favour, the Catholics 4 to 3).[47] Think of the joint celebration of baptism of children of inter-church families which was, by the early 1980s, becoming a quite common feature of the religious scene. Think of Archbishop Worlock solemnly presenting a Jerusalem Bible to the Dean of Liverpool Cathedral at its dedication before the Queen: it was all now so natural, even in Liverpool, previously a centre of particular bitterness. Upon almost all sides the sense of a common Christian community advanced immeasurably in this decade and by the end of it the ban on intercommunion itself between Roman Catholics and others was rapidly crumbling. The Christian obligation to share the body and blood of Christ with fellow believers and co-workers in so many ministries was being increasingly recognized by quite ordinary people as transcending any ecclesiastical veto upon it. At the point of communion Christ was seen as standing above the Church. In this Archbishop Coggan had been, perhaps, the best interpreter of the mind of the common Christian (and even of Christ too!) of the decade. Evangelicals might object to his appeal for intercommunion,[48] just as the Pope and Cardinal Hume rejected it,[49] but increasingly the common believing man, Anglican, Free Church, Roman Catholic, did not. Loyalty to Christ and the unity of Christians was seen as coming, at least on occasion, before and above the denominational divide. Father Michael Hollings, that sturdy spokesman for the free centre of English catholicism, declared as his 'Hope for the New Year' in

1984: 'There should be intercommunion before the end of 1984.'[50] Institutionally there was no hope of any such thing, yet in many a small gathering it was already not hope but reality.

In the judgment of many the ecumenical movement by the end of the 1970s had 'run out of steam'. There was, as we have seen, some ground for that conclusion, yet it seems also true that the opposite was in fact the case. When Michael Ramsey declared in August 1978 that progress within the ecumenical movement had been 'miraculous' and 'only a few more divine miracles – and they do happen – will bring us all to that day of unity in truth and holiness, total unity in the Mass given to us by Jesus',[51] he seemed at least half right. 'A great change has passed over men's minds in relation to Christian unity,' declared J. H. Shakespeare in 1918.[52] In 1942 Temple had declared the ecumenical movement 'the great new fact of our time'. Neither had Roman Catholics in mind. By the 1980s this 'great change' had not only affected Anglicans and Free churchmen vastly more than it had in 1920 or 1940, but it now also included Catholics. A sense of one Christian community with a common mission and a common faith had become central to the experience of all the main churches in England in a way that it had never been previously. And that was a very great achievement.

Roman Catholicism

If in general the first half of the 1970s appears as an age of indecision when the exuberance of the sixties had quite run out of steam, but nothing much had as yet been found to put in its place, this was quite particularly true of Roman Catholicism, both internationally and in Britain. Pope Paul was temperamentally indecisive at the best of times but since the storm over *Humanae Vitae* in 1968, which had in fact never really subsided, and faced with growing disaffection both from conservatives and from progressives, he had entered into a prolonged state of nervous inactivity. The least illiberal and most sensitive of popes, he had no desire to go backwards but equally, surrounded by a conservative curia quietly reasserting its power after a temporary eclipse, no capacity to go forwards. He would never quite condemn rebels; he would write no more encyclicals; he would allow no authority to the episcopal synods he dutifully called from time to time; he would continue – despite suggestions that he might resign – to preside gloomily but not unbenignly over an increasingly distracted Church in which progressives protested that the promise of Vatican II had not been fulfilled, and from which conservatives moaned that the glory of the past, the confidence in authority, the splendour of the liturgy, had sadly departed.

England was no different. Cardinal Heenan's final years were ones of bitter depression. And there was no alternative leadership of weight: Archbishops Cowderoy of Southwark and Dwyer of Birmingham were equally weary leftovers from a previous age, fighting a rearguard action to accept as little as possible of the package of reform. What did come came piecemeal, with little explanation as to the point of it, introduced by priests whose heart was too often not in change at all. The vernacular mass and the reversal of the position of the altar had been accepted. Over other things there was far more contention: the giving of a 'kiss of peace', communion in the hand, the celebration of house masses, lay communion of the cup, each of these became a matter for a long, often dreary battle until, one by one, they were adopted in most parishes (communion of the cup still not being generally offered to the laity but seemed about to come at the end of our period). In this way the changes produced a maximum of disaffection. The Church's leadership received credit from neither progressive nor conservative, while those in the middle were simply bewildered.[1] No serious collective attempt was made by the hierarchy to incorporate the thinking of Vatican II into the life of the English Church until the late seventies, by which time a rather different set of ideas was anyway coming out of Rome. 'Why', asked Frank Sheed in 1974, 'did the bright promise of the twenties, thirties and even forties, fade away into the sadness of the seventies?'[2] It was a question Heenan, Dwyer and many another stalwart of the pre-conciliar age must often have asked themselves.

The background to their alarm was the massive statistical decline which we have already considered. Anglicans and Free churchmen had long been habituated to this sort of thing and it did not have for them quite the traumatic effect it had on Catholics who had hitherto taken for granted that, whatever might be the case in France, Germany or Italy, Catholic statistics in Britain would go up and up. The collapse of mass attendance and a shortage of vocations might have started far earlier on the Continent and be far more advanced, but now that the same phenomena were appearing in England and in the years immediately subsequent to the council, the tendency was to blame it on the council, and this even by people who would never really have wanted to return to the pre-conciliar state of affairs. There was, then, a considerable sense of gloom in many quarters and very few grounds for immediate hopefulness.[3]

It is all the more important, in this context of undoubted depression, to recognize how relatively slightly in these years the principal core institutions of English catholicism were outwardly affected: the parishes, seminaries, schools, monasteries, newspapers. There were few individually significant closures. Above all, the commanding institutions which, since the nineteenth century at least, had shaped the physiognomy of the English Catholic Church remained mostly untouched: Ushaw, Oscott, the English College at Rome; the abbeys of Ampleforth, Downside, Douai, Stanbrook, Buckfast; Stonyhurst, Ratcliffe and other well-established schools; the *Tablet*, the *Universe*. Westminster Cathedral, indeed, became far more of an accepted national landmark with the clearing in front of it of an attractive piazza, and the cardinal who lived in Archbishop's House next door, be it Heenan or Hume, was more of a national figure than any of his predecessors. The seventeenth Duke of Norfolk was still, at the end of our period, just as the fifteenth Duke had been at the start of the century, the devoutly traditional, but also theologically slightly liberal, lay leader, assiduous both in attendance at daily mass and in the fulfilment of a thousand responsibilities, religious and secular.

If some institutions had fallen by the wayside, other major ones had developed in recent years. Heythrop College within London University was now one of Britain's principal centres of academic theology. The main Catholic colleges of higher education, like Strawberry Hill in London, and Trinity and All Saints at Leeds, were now teaching for a wide range of degrees and had become little less than mini-universities while retaining a basic Catholic character. They still lacked distinction but not potential. Add to all this a new network of conference centres throughout the country run by religious orders or dioceses, special institutes like Plater College at Oxford or Blackfriars, also at Oxford – still English catholicism's best centre of living theology – and a remarkably rich collection of journals: *Clergy Review*; *New Blackfriars*; *Month*; *Heythrop Journal*; *One in Christ*; *The Way*; *Downside Review*. The institutional scale of the Catholic Church remained immense and it was under no immediate threat.[4]

Nevertheless there had been some not inconsiderable cuts and, still more widely, a pervasive laicization as the quality of the clergy declined relative to that of the laity. There were many departures from the priesthood between the early sixties and the late seventies including a tragically high proportion of the intellectually ablest members of the younger generation.[5] This included the academic cream of the secular clergy – Anthony Kenny, Charles Davis, Hubert Richards, Peter de Rosa, Peter Harris, and Nicholas Lash, among others – but the numerical decline of the religious orders was far more severe.[6] The years after the Second World War had been ones of a rather hasty growth in the number of religious in this country, often foreigners brought here to staff new seminaries or recruit for vocations, especially for the missionary societies. After 1960 this fell quickly away. Consider the example of the Portsmouth diocese (Hampshire, Berkshire, the Isle of Wight and the Channel Islands). It was served by 164 religious priests in 1926; 252 in 1949; 210 in 1964; 150 in 1978. If we compare the changes between the last two dates, in Hampshire the White Fathers abandoned their junior seminary at Bishop's Waltham with a loss to the diocese of seven priests; the de Montfort Fathers closed their 'Apostolic School' at Romsey, with a loss of nine; and the Benedictines closed Douai Junior School at Ditcham Park, with the withdrawal of five; in Berkshire the Salvatorians left Sindlesham and the Servites Newbury, each with the loss of six, while the Jesuits closed Beaumont with a loss of nineteen. This meant the closure of six institutions with a combined staff of fifty-two priests: men teaching in school or seminary but available, many of them, for pastoral work at the weekends. The only considerable institutions of male religious left in the diocese were the Benedictine abbeys at Douai, Quarr and Farnborough and the Salesian school at Farnborough. The total effect on the Catholic life of Berkshire and Hampshire cannot but have been considerable even though, fortunately for the diocese, the number of diocesan clergy had risen by forty in these years.

Let us take one other example: the history of the Franciscans (Friars Minor) in the diocese of Northampton. Back in 1936 they had a single house in the diocese, a friary at Buckingham with seven members. In 1938 they acquired a small House of Studies in Cambridge, and after the war took over the buildings of the abbey of Benedictine nuns at East Bergholt and made them into a further House of Studies. Following this, in the 1950s the friary at Buckingham developed a boys' grammar school, St Bernardine's College, and for full measure a preparatory school was set up at Stony Stratford. By the mid-sixties they had, then, four houses staffed by no less than thirty-three men: there were twelve in Buckingham for the parish and grammar school, seven at Stony Stratford, four in Cambridge and ten at East Bergholt. By 1978 almost all of this had gone, including both schools and both Houses of Study. Only seven Friars Minor remained – three in the Buckingham parish and four in an Ipswich parish. It is true that their main House of Studies was now part of the new inter-order Franciscan Study Centre in Canterbury, but they only had some five men there. In under fifty years, so far as the diocese of Northampton was concerned, a great wave of Franciscan activity had come and gone.[7]

The 'Minor Seminary' or 'Apostolic School' was the chief institutional casualty of these years. England was still littered with them at the end of the 1950s; twenty years later they had almost entirely disappeared, either closed or transformed into ordinary boarding schools.

On the continent of Europe thousands of Catholic parishes were pastorless by this time. In Britain this was not the case. Indeed the number of staffed parishes was actually still increasing. To cope with the situation the secular clergy were being withdrawn more and more from teaching responsibilities, while the number of one-man parishes was multiplying. There were fewer curates. There were instead, however, an increasing number of 'parish sisters'. The number of nuns had declined quite heavily in the last thirty years, but their deployment had changed still more. Many convent schools were closed. Nuns were moving into smaller houses, far smaller communities, and more direct pastoral work. As a result the total number of small convents was actually growing in these years, at least in the south. In the far north, the diocese of Hexham and Newcastle especially, where the number of religious had always been extremely small, these problems hardly arose and the pastoral changes in this period were far less noticeable.[8]

Nevertheless the principal consequence, or concomitant development, of the decline of the clergy was a rise of the laity. At the beginning of the 1960s all Catholic grammar schools still had priests or religious at their head, and some had many priests on their staff. By the end of the 1970s almost all the day schools had lay heads and the boarding schools were beginning to follow suit.

In March 1980, faced with a shortage of personnel, the Christian Brothers announced their intention to close Prior Park, Bath, one of the better known Catholic public schools. The Old Boys vigorously protested and an agreement was reached instead whereby the Christian Brothers withdrew but the school continued with a lay board of governors and a lay head master. In 1984 a lay head master was appointed at Stonyhurst, most distinguished of Jesuit public schools. By now, apart from the main monastic schools, there was only a handful of priest headmasters left. What had happened in the Church of England a generation earlier had now taken place within catholicism.

Laicization can thus be documented pretty precisely in the educational field. The same thing was happening somewhat less definably across a far wider pastoral and cultural area. The laity were simply taking over larger and larger chunks of Church activity, in a way that would have been commonplace in most Protestant churches for decades but was in pretty strong contrast with the pre-conciliar Catholic pattern. The decision-making of parish councils, the teaching of religion throughout Catholic schools and in Catholic colleges of higher education, pastoral counselling through such organizations as the Catholic Marriage Advisory Council, direct liturgical work through the institution of 'parish ministers', were all examples of this. At the same time there was a sudden surge forward in the Catholic presence in university departments of theology including the appointment of professors like Hamish Swanston at Kent and Nicholas Lash at Cambridge. There was a growing, perhaps alarming, contrast between a highly educated and theologically aware minority among the laity and a clergy which increasingly lacked even a handful of brilliant figures, such as it had had in the past, and seemed in places to be only semi-literate. As in other churches there was also a growing contrast between a relatively small number of extremely lively parishes run by very capable priests, and a rather large number of others in which the standard of liturgy, preaching and pastoral expertise was dismally low. The problem of the Catholic Church in England was hardly yet a problem of the shortage of clergy but it was most certainly one of its competence and increasing age.

Meanwhile laicization went on irreversibly and, with it,

ecumenization. The Catholic laity co-operated with its counterparts in other churches (to which it was, indeed, in quite a few cases, even married!) in a natural way which the clergy less often managed. In fact the Catholic laity was increasingly taking the lead within the total Christian community. In this way the seventies were very far from being a dormant period. It was rather one in which the very weakness of Church leadership actually contributed to a decisive change of balance which did in truth respond well enough to one emphasis of the Vatican Council: the universal priesthood and apostolic activity of the laity. Whether, as a matter of fact, laicization would lead to secularization and the rapid disintegration of the Church's community and structures, it was, at the end of our period, still too early to say.[9]

In February 1968 a society known as the Catholic Priests Association was set up with the purpose, according to its original circular, of helping to 'combat and refute the neo-modernism which is eating at the very vitals of the Church'.[10] Its real leaders were two Sussex parish priests, Fr John Flanagan and Fr Leonard Whatmore. Its first chairman was Fr Alan Clark, also a parish priest and formerly Vice-Rector of the English College in Rome.

That same year Archbishop Marcel Lefebvre, formerly Archbishop of Dakar and Apostolic Delegate to French West Africa, and subsequently Superior General of the Holy Ghost Fathers, a masterful person who had also for many years been, in his own way, a very dutiful servant of the papacy, began his institutional rebellion against the Church's more progressive policies by founding the Fraternity of St Pius X and opening the seminary of Ecône in Switzerland. In his later *Profession of Faith*, Lefebvre rejected the reforms of Vatican II, declaring: 'This reform, arising as it does out of liberalism and modernism, is entirely poisoned. It comes from heresy and will finish in heresy.'[11] All Catholic ecclesiastical life in the seventies, all the painful hesitations of Rome, must be seen beneath the shadow of the unhesitant figure of Archbishop Lefebvre.

In 1970, back in England, a lay movement of not dissimilar outlook, called *Pro Fide*, was founded by the Conservative MP

Patrick Wall. It was a movement clearly linked with that of Fr Flanagan who appeared on the platform at its first national meeting, held in Brighton in June 1971. There were other small movements of a similar tendency,[12] nearly all of which combined religious conservatism with political Conservatism. They were opposed to the socialistic tendencies, the 'welfare state' mentality, which had spread in the Catholic as in other churches. Well to the right of all of these, if that is an appropriate description for something so odd, stood Plaza de Troya in Spain where the Virgin Mary was claimed to make regular apparitions, where a bevy of bishops and priests were ordained through the complicity of an unfortunate Vietnamese bishop, and where open resistance to Rome was justified on the grounds that the true pope had been kidnapped and the figure claiming to be Pope Paul was in fact an impostor. Plenty of English people went to Plaza de Troya on pilgrimage.

The emergence of this wave of conservative dissidence is hardly surprising in view of the quite hasty, and ill-explained, abandonment of practices like the Latin mass which had been until recently so primary in Catholic consciousness and apologetics. If *Pro Fide*'s membership was fairly small, it undoubtedly represented a great many less articulate Catholics, clergy and laity. The dilemma they had to face was how traditionalist Catholics, whose underlying *raison d'être* was bound to be one of loyalty to Rome, could resist reforms approved not only by a general council but by the reigning pope. Within a few months Alan Clark had seceded from the Catholic Priests Association because while, like the CPA, he strongly supported *Humanae Vitae*, unlike them he refused to criticize the rather moderate stand of the English bishops. Within a few months he was a bishop himself and in the process of moving across into ecumenical activities (he became the Catholic chairman of ARCIC) more or less anathema to his former colleagues: he had quickly seen the dangers of an even mildly schismatic stance, especially for those appealing principally for a religion of authority. Lefebvre and, in England, priests like Fr Baker of Downham Market,[13] might refuse to use the new mass rites as dubiously orthodox, appealing from Paul VI to Pius X. Most *Pro Fide* and CPA members deeply sympathized. Nevertheless it seemed clear that there was no possibility of the Church going back on what the council had done, hence Catholic conservatives had either to become practically schismatic, mentally and liturgically isolated within a net-work of independent mass centres, which Lefebvrist priests were endeavouring to set up across Britain during the 1970s, or they had to come to terms with the new order, adopt some sort of Tamworth Manifesto, and go on from there. It was not forbidden to say mass in Latin, and the aim of the Latin Mass Society became to maximize opportunities for celebration in Latin without casting aspersions upon the vernacular. By 1977 in the wake, maybe, of Archbishop Hume's appointment to Westminster, this approach was coming to prevail more widely among conservatives.[14] At an important *Pro Fide* meeting in the Caxton Hall on 29 November 1977, for instance, the principal speakers, Patrick Wall and Paul Crane, took a far more positive approach to the post-conciliar Church than would have been the case a few years earlier; they admitted that all had not been well in the past and outlined a positive programme for conservative involvement in parish councils and main-line Church activities generally. They were, then, ready enough to greet Pope John Paul II when, the following year, he arrived upon the scene: traditionalist but still loyal.[15]

There is some similarity between all this and the Church of England quandary in the twenties: just as then conservative Evangelical laymen like Sir William Joynson-Hicks were pressing their bishops to take a firm stand against catholicizing tendencies, especially in the liturgy, so now conservative Catholic laymen like Patrick Wall and John Biggs-Davison were pressing their bishops to take a firm stand against Protestantizing tendencies, especially in the liturgy.

At the other end of the spectrum there was also activity. 1968 again saw the start of the Catholic Renewal Movement, whose initial purpose had been to help priests threatened with disciplinary action for dissenting from *Humanae Vitae*. Inspiration came from the example of Archbishop Roberts, from the books of Hans Küng and from talk about what was going on in the Dutch Church. Among CRM's leaders was Clifford Longley, religious affairs editor of *The Times*. Its level of activity fell to a rather dispirited low around 1972 but revived a few years later and was

joined by other groups of similar viewpoint such as the Movement for the Ordination of Married Men. While the membership
of these bodies was small they stood – just as did the conservative
groups – for a much wider public. Several well known priests
shared in and expounded their approach which hailed Vatican II
as the great sign of God for our times but believed that its
potential had never been realized nor the nettle of pastoral and
ministerial reform seriously grasped.[16] Perhaps the most potent
single voice from the wing of English catholicism was that of Dr
Jack Dominian, a ceaseless writer on Christian marriage and the
justifiability of contraception. Dominian was in himself so
powerful a challenge to the more conservative that he could be
denounced personally as the 'enemy within the fold, against
which we should all be on our guard'.[17] As a matter of fact the
evolution of religious consciousness among English Catholics
was such that, by the end of the decade, as the Liverpool Pastoral
Congress clearly showed, the principal aims of the Catholic
Renewal Movement had become those of the dominant group of
English laity: more lay participation, more ecumenism, some
intercommunion, some married clergy, the acceptance of contraception. The underlying secret fear of such developments,
both on the part of Rome and of traditionalists generally, sprang
to a large extent from what they thought all this was bound to
lead to: 'Protestantization', becoming 'just like Anglicans', that is
to say open to all the winds of de-mythologization, of *Honest to
God*, and so forth. Could you have a married clergy and intercommunion and not go on to question the divinity of Christ, the
reality of transubstantiation, the existence of angels?

Between these battling camps arose the Catholic Charismatic
Movement. It really began at Duquesne University, Pittsburgh,
early in 1967 and quickly spread to the theology faculty of the
University of Notre Dame.[18] By 1973 the annual Catholic
Charismatic Renewal Conference at Notre Dame had 22
thousand attenders, including Cardinal Suenens. It crossed the
Atlantic quickly enough. Like so many other religious movements of the time it can be seen as one of withdrawal from
political, and even ecclesiastical, activism (characteristics of sixties religiosity), a return to prayer, the creation of community,
personal healing – the 'holy huddle', its critics might label it. In

639

the Catholic Church, as elsewhere, part of its early strength lay in the lack of structure, the room for impromptu female leadership, the openness to ecumenical encounter. At the same time it diverted people from seemingly hopeless battles over structural change in Church or State into a world of healing and spiritual victories. It renewed confidence, hope, and a sense of inner freedom. Theologically it tended to the conservative, indeed often very uncritically so. While in terms of the tradition of Catholic spirituality it appeared at first extremely radical, it was in fact quite easily domesticated within old-fashioned walls and seldom offered any serious challenge to Catholic Church authority. In the context of the conservative/progressive confrontation which provided, in some way, the dominant characteristic of the post-Vatican II period, it was not easy to locate charismatic renewal: more progressive at first, more conservative later on, but never quite one or the other and open – as forms of serious prayer always are – to very different influences.

All three movements persisted in uneasy tension through the latter years of Pope Paul and Cardinal Heenan: not condemned by the Church, not trusted either. There was an impasse and a sense of drift in which some parishes were only too clearly *Pro Fide* in sympathy, others Catholic Renewal, others again Charismatic Renewal. They were awaiting a new lead.

Cardinal Heenan died in November 1975, and in February 1976 it was announced that the new archbishop of Westminster would be the abbot of Ampleforth, Dom Basil Hume. It was, of course, a surprising choice. The last four archbishops had all been *Venerabile* men, and now their successor was not even a secular priest and had never lived in Rome. He was, in a social and educational sense, all that they were not: upper class, the child of a mixed marriage, a public-school boy, a graduate of Oxford, all that Anglican bishops mostly were, a natural member of the English Establishment. Indeed his brother-in-law was at the time secretary to the Cabinet. It was, then, in a way, a rather worldly choice. Yet it was of a very unworldly man.

It is reasonable to suggest that the Benedictines come nearest of all Catholic institutions to being a natural bridge between Rome and Canterbury. It was a Benedictine monk who went from Rome to found the see of Canterbury in the first place. The monks cradled *Ecclesia Anglicana* in the Middle Ages, and what other see anywhere could compare with Canterbury for great monk archbishops – Augustine, Dunstan, Anselm, Theobald? Nowhere else in the world had there been permanently Benedictine cathedrals like Canterbury, Durham and Worcester. Again, the role of Westminster Abbey in the life of England has been unique. The subtle cultural impact of Benedictinism on the Church of England does not seem to have been wholly lost at the Reformation. The monks were never the best of scholastics, their learning was more naturally patristic, but they did very much embody the Thomist principle of the commonsense harmony of grace with nature. In all this central Anglicanism has stood very much with them and against the harder doctrines of both Calvinism and counter-Reformation catholicism. Again, no other country in modern catholicism has been influenced by the Benedictine order comparably with England: nowhere else have monasteries been comparatively so numerous and so central to the life of the community. And perhaps only a Benedictine monastery within the Catholic Church can really compete with, indeed surpass, an Anglican cathedral for the dignity and beauty of worship.

All this is not irrelevant to a consideration of the significance of the appointment of Hume. He was such a very good Benedictine. If anyone in his personal life could somehow overcome the divorce of centuries, here seemed such a one: a quintessentially ecumenical figure, yet unambiguously orthodox in his Roman Catholicism too; a man of the spirit, in whom a profound concern for prayer and a restrained but unquestionable asceticism were the paramount impression; a man of religious commonsense, some self-depreciation, little forcefulness but deep humanity. In all of which he contrasted rather markedly with the accustomed manner of Catholic authority.[19] He was accorded as a result of all this, almost too easily, a quite exceptional position in Church and society, not only in this country but also on the Continent and throughout the world, becoming quite soon President of the Council of European Bishops' Conferences.

The evening of Hume's consecration day in Westminster

Cathedral, everyone trooped over to the abbey and vespers was sung, unforgettably, by a vast assembly of Benedictine monks gathered there for the first time since 1559: it seemed, in the unaffected naturalness with which the monks occupied the choir stalls, an almost theatrically symbolic start to a new and irenic era.

It was also in February 1976 that Derek Worlock was appointed archbishop of Liverpool. He had been an obvious choice for Westminster: the private secretary of three previous archbishops (Griffin, Godfrey and Heenan), and an efficient Bishop of Portsmouth since 1965. Absolutely at home in Rome, Worlock knew the Church's administration both there and in Britain like the back of his hand, and he knew the council's documents too. He was in fact, indeed self-consciously so, the very model of a post-conciliar ecclesiastic. While he lacked any touch of charisma, he had soon established in Liverpool a remarkable working relationship with David Sheppard, the Anglican bishop. For all his good works – and they have been many – Worlock was little loved by either conservative or progressive, while Hume was almost unfairly loved by both. In fact they needed and complemented each other well enough, their first major joint achievement being the National Pastoral Congress which met in Liverpool in May 1980.

But by that time there was a new and highly decisive pope. John Paul II was elected, after the strangely sudden death of John Paul I in October 1978. A Pole of immense physical and spiritual strength, an exhilarating sense of certainty and mission, a varied early experience of theatre and philosophy and considerable success as an archbishop in a Communist-ruled country, John Paul was something of an enigma because of the highly contrasting chunks of modernity and medievalism in his make-up. The first non-Italian pope since the Dutch Adrian VI in the sixteenth century, he came to the papacy filled with the preoccupations of the Polish Church's struggle with Communism. He had been through all the sessions of the council as a fairly young man, but would not appear to have imbibed much of its deeper re-orientations and the sort of experience from which they derived in western Europe, Latin America and the southern hemisphere generally. He had remained profoundly opposed to a diminishment of the traditional gap between the sacred and the secular, clergy and laity, man and woman, church and world. He was also an ecclesiastical centralist. 'Collegiality', so exciting a word twenty years earlier and the chief assertion of the council's main dogmatic constitution, had almost disappeared from Catholic consciousness by the 1980s as papal monarchy and the personality cult of the pope were back with a force, an attractiveness, an omni-presence never known before. Priests were to stay out of politics (except, perhaps, in Poland), liberation theologians and liberal theologians of various sorts were to be investigated and disciplined, clerical dress was to be enforced, clerical marriage abhorred, the liturgical functions of the laity cut back, the active role of women in the Church circumscribed discouragingly. The condemnation of contraception was to be renewed with vigour. The Dutch Church was to be humiliated rather painfully. The canonization of holy priests and nuns to be stepped up. The selection of bishops, to ensure their undeviating ultramontane orthodoxy, was to be subjected to especial attention. The most conservative religious body in the Church, *Opus Dei*, was to be greatly encouraged and privileged, while those which had responded most to the progressive influences of the last decade, such as the Jesuits and the Young Christian Workers, were to be subject to an almost unprecedented degree of interference in their internal affairs. Pluralism was out, the imposition of Roman uniformity was back with all the new efficiency of post-conciliar bureaucracy. And religious conservatism would be linked increasingly with support for political reaction. Vocations to the priesthood increased somewhat, and the more traditionally minded of Catholics everywhere breathed a deep sigh of relief.

All this did not become immediately evident. After the slightly querulous indecision of Pope Paul, John Paul's advent was immensely exciting to progressive and conservative alike. It was not entirely clear at first on which side he would come down. His spirituality and pastoral concern, the sense of a sure hand on the tiller, were indisputable. His pastoral concern included a very real desire for reunion with other Christians,[20] about whom however he knew rather little. Only slowly did it become painfully clear that the direction in which he was taking the Church was such as to make reunion with anyone quite out of the question, an absolutism just a little reminiscent of the Stalinism he had fought so hard against. Even eastern Orthodox Christians whom he was said to be more concerned with than with Protestants could only be alienated by the way Rome was now going. For Christians in general who had put such large hopes in the unfolding of *aggiornamento*, there could now be only the expectation of a long winter.

In England there was, however, a little St Martin's summer before the implications of all this became quite clear. When the National Pastoral Congress met in Liverpool in May 1980 it had been well prepared, chiefly by its chairman Archbishop Worlock. Now, at last, the teaching and spirit of Vatican II were to be deliberately adopted by, and adapted to, the Church in this country. It was a long awaited moment, a sort of culmination of a period which had in some ways, despite the failure of clerical leadership at almost every level, been a great one: an age in which Barbara Ward, Fritz Schumacher and Jack Dominian were prophets and teachers not only for the Church but the nation, in which Rees-Mogg had been editing *The Times*, Charles Curran directing the BBC, Shirley Williams Minister of Education and – at the end – Norman St John-Stevas Leader of the House. It was an age in which the Catholic Institute of International Relations had become a body of truly international reputation and CAFOD a major aid agency. The English Catholic laity had never before been so outgoing, so central to the life of the nation, so rich with distinguished people in its ranks.

The Pastoral Congress reflected this acquired lay confidence. Its two thousand members included many young people, were fairly equally divided between men and women, but were overwhelmingly middle class.[21] They included just one MP, David Alton, a Liverpool Catholic and the president of the Young Liberals. There was an infectious enthusiasm which the bishops who joined in the Congress quite shared. For Hume the Holy Spirit was manifestly at work. Yet its conclusions were next to indistinguishable from the programme which the Catholic Renewal Movement had been backing for years: Catholic entry into the British Council of Churches, the acceptance of the morality of contraception where there were good grounds for its use, some intercommunion (at least eucharistic hospitality within mixed marriages), more lay ministry, communion of both kinds as the norm, a new look at the ordination of married men and of women.[22] Despite the unfeigned spirit of loyalty to the Church manifest in the congress, objectively these conclusions undoubtedly represented what a correspondent in the *Universe* (23 May) described as 'a snub to the Holy Father'. Subsequently, gathered on their own, the bishops welcomed the proposals sincerely yet for several years stalled upon their application almost entirely – to the Catholic community's considerable disillusionment.

Our St Martin's summer may also be illustrated by the conclusion at Windsor in September 1981 of the Final Report of the Anglican-Roman Catholic International Commission (ARCIC).[23] The eleven years work of the commission, on Eucharist, ministry and authority, was complete. A very carefully laid theological basis now existed for a considerable advance towards full communion between the two churches, at least to some degree of the 'intercommunion' which had been explicitly put forward as an intermediate goal by the Malta Report in 1968. While the commission was international, it is worth noting how very strong was its English representation – no less than eleven of its twenty members: among the Anglicans were Henry Chadwick, Dean of Christ Church and then Regius Professor of Divinity at Cambridge; Julian Charley, a leading Evangelical, and John Moorman, for long Bishop of Ripon; among the Catholics, their chairman Alan Clark, Bishop of East Anglia; Bishop Christopher Butler, and Fr Yarnold of Campion Hall. Perhaps most important for the reality of Church life was the report's stress upon the need to balance conciliarity and primacy within a single communion. Its final words may be quoted as well as any.

> In 1981 it has become abundantly clear that, under the Holy Spirit, our Churches have grown closer together in faith and charity. There are high expectations that significant initiatives will be boldly undertaken to deepen our reconciliation and lead us forward in the quest for the full communion to which we have been committed, in obedience to God, from the beginning of our dialogue.[24]

The following year the Pope came to Britain, the first time in history. It was intended as a pastoral visit. It coincided with the

Falklands War and, as a consequence, the Pope's most striking teaching, in Coventry especially, was upon war and peace. For warmongers he spoke uncomfortably sharply. But by far the most memorable part of the programme was the visit to Canterbury Cathedral.[25] It had not been intended in Rome to be an important part of the tour but, once decided that it should be included, it came inevitably to overshadow everything else. For the Pope to be welcomed solemnly in the mother church of another communion, to join in a public service there, to embrace its bishops and proclaim the Gospel when the Archbishop and primate of that communion had just read the epistle, was to do things, to enter further into Christian fellowship, in a way that was theologically more creative than he may well have intended. Ecclesiology was being enacted here, and it was rather clearly the ecclesiology of ARCIC, rather than that of ultramontanism. The psychological effect of this encounter between pope and archbishop, carried by television into every home in the land, was considerable. Apart from this the papal visit had little effect other than to leave the Church in England with a debt of several million pounds which it could ill afford.

Cardinal Hume was criticized from time to time, especially during his earlier years at Westminster, for actually achieving very little. Always charming, gentle, unassuming, he seemed too good at seeing both sides of every issue ever to take a hard decision when total consensus had not already been reached. Where now did he stand within the contradictions engendered by the double tide of Vatican II, upon the one hand, still flowing inwards across the English Church and English ecumenical relations, and John Paul's Rome, upon the other, driving the Church relentlessly in another direction? In a special article in *The Times*, 3 January 1980, he certainly endeavoured to pour oil on troubled waters, and backed all the right causes, while dodging some of the more awkward questions, but he did prophesy that the ecumenical movement in the next decade would have to go through a 'dark night of the soul'. It was likely to be true. Hume could foresee the strain ahead. He could do little about it. A Benedictine's first duty is obedience and he had himself explained, simply and honestly, as was his wont, that he had accepted the appointment to Westminster for that reason: it was a matter of obedience. But religious obedience can be a dangerous thing. A hundred years earlier John Henry Newman wrote of that excellent Benedictine bishop, William Ullathorne, a true friend of his, as follows: 'Being a monk, he has the instinct of obedience so strong that he would never go against the Pope's private wishes. I think him in his own heart opposed ... but I expect nothing from him.'[26] True of Ullathorne, it might be true of Hume. Yet there can be no hope whatsoever for Christian reunion, if Catholic bishops have not the courage to stand against the pope, even publicly, not so much about doctrine as the manner of papal government, the creeping advance of monarchy over collegiality, the intolerance of ultramontanism. It had been responsible, more than any other factor, both for the schism between East and West and for the sundering break-up of the western Church in the sixteenth century. It had in subsequent centuries steadily narrowed the range of Catholic intellectual and religious experience. Then in the 1960s the Vatican Council had proposed an alternative ecclesiology and pastoral strategy on the basis of which the reunion of Christians could conceivably be achieved. This had nevertheless, owing largely to curial resistance, never begun to be seriously implemented. The result, inevitably, was a great confusion. When John Paul II became pope and set about the business of terminating the confusion by a sustained reassertion of papal monarchy, it would have been hard for anyone to stand in the breach against him. All one can say is that no one would have been more appropriate than Basil Hume, and by the mid-1980s that is what indeed he seemed to be doing, and not too unsuccessfully, at least so far as England was concerned. He was in fact quietly protecting the moderate reformism that had come to develop there from being snuffed out too brutally. He even publicly committed himself, in a major speech at Bruges in June 1985, to supporting the ordination of married men in areas of grave pastoral need. With him the English Catholic hierarchy continued to move quietly forward. The cup at long last could now be given to the laity at all normal masses, and the ARCIC Final Report was fully accepted in May 1985. This acceptance was not hasty; its significance was the greater for that. It was something which could not have happened with the hierarchy of the mid-1970s.

Nevertheless the likelihood of reunion with the Church of England, of 'significant initiatives boldly undertaken', now seemed low, despite the common declarations of popes and archbishops, despite the work of ARCIC, despite the high symbolism of John Paul's presence in Canterbury Cathedral. The historian is no prophet and it would be pointless to speculate here on what the future would in fact bring. All he can point to, a little sadly, is the apparent contrast between the internal momentum of England's Christian experience and the Dictates of Rome.

Theology and Society

The decade of the 1970s received its theology from the 1960s somewhat as the 1920s had taken over Edwardian theology. What was bursting forth, still just a little uncertainly in the earlier phase, has become the accepted wisdom, filling the chairs of divinity in the principal universities, by the latter. These two cycles of liberal theology were not, indeed, so dissimilar. Certainly critics accused the theology dominant between the early 1960s and later 1970s of being a mere revival of the theories of the early years of the century, theories whose popularity was waning by the later thirties. There is some truth in this. Theological history is cyclical to a remarkable extent, its moods as we have seen again and again reflecting with some fidelity those of secular society. Both phases of liberal theology showed themselves at their best in the pursuit of historical truth, a concern which had stood a good deal more lightly to Barthians and Thomists. The middle years of the century had been strong on system and orthodoxy, but rather weak on delving into the relativities and uncertainties of the historical record. The new scholarship, in contrast, was over-prone to appeal to an almost limitless pluralism as the only legitimate conclusion to draw from historical research in both biblical and ecclesiastical history, but it was far better at stressing the complexities of the evidence than at producing thereafter any sort of workable theological synthesis. This was in part because of the ever-increasing scepticism which the leading theologians of the English academic school – Dennis Nineham, Maurice Wiles, John Hick, Geoffrey Lampe and others – were evincing in regard to all the central dogmas most characteristic of Christianity, the incarnation, the Trinity, even for some the very existence of God. It was most in evidence in relation to Christ. 'Is it any longer worthwhile', asked Nineham, the urbane doyen of the school, 'to attempt to trace the Christian's everchanging understanding of his relationship with God directly back to some identifiable element in the life, character and activity of Jesus of Nazareth?'[1] In biblical scholarship the influence of Rudolf Bultmann – with his dismissal of almost any degree of historical reliability in the gospels – was the dominant one. In the wider approach to religious issues a greatly increased recognition of the depth, sincerity and vitality of non-Christian religions (now active on the theologian's very Birmingham doorstep) seemed to lead a little over-easily to a relativist conclusion in regard to any one religion, including Christianity.

The theological writings characteristic of this school, such as the report entitled *Christian Believing*, produced by the Doctrine Commission of the Church of England under the chairmanship of Maurice Wiles, Regius Professor of Divinity at Oxford; Wiles's own *The Remaking of Christian Doctrine* (1974); and – still more – a lively symposium entitled *The Myth of God Incarnate*, edited by John Hick and published in 1978, elicited considerable discussion, even excitement, at the time. They could, none of them, be reasonably described as major works; their argumentation seemed often somewhat hasty, even weak, so that Donald MacKinnon could remark, just a little unkindly, that to turn from them to a critique of their views by Professor Michael Dummett was 'as if a detachment of the Welsh Guards had engaged with "Dad's Army" '.[2] There was furthermore, in *The Myth of God Incarnate*, a rather over-confident note of debunking 'The Incarnation' which rendered this particular exercise in the perennial clerical critique of traditional Christian conviction somewhat unpleasing. Pleasing or displeasing, the consequence of their conclusions could hardly be other than the necessity of winding up historic Christianity, with a minimum of pain to all concerned, as unacceptable to the modern mind. If *The Myth* produced excitement, it was principally the smirking excitement of an agnostic world amused to witness the white flag hoisted so enthusiastically above the long-beleaguered citadel of Christian belief, the stunned excitement of the rank and file of weary defenders on learning that their staff officers had so light-heartedly ratted on them. It was hardly surprising that more than one of the contributors soon after ceased, in even a nominal sense, to be Christian believers or that Don Cupitt, one of the most forceful and publicity minded of the group, published only two years later his commitment to objective atheism: *Taking Leave of God* (1980). The right wing of this movement – and it was one of considerable proportions, extending well beyond the contributors to *The Myth* – tended towards a Christian unitarianism, the middle towards Buddhism, the left wing to atheism.

This theology was undoubtedly 'liberal' in a certain sense of the word but it can hardly claim the name of 'radical', with its note of social significance. It had no social message whatsoever. It might take leave of God but not of well-endowed canonries or deaneries. In this it was oceans away from the truly radical theology of the seventies – that of liberation, with its critique precisely of current academic method, its preoccupation with practice, its committed 'option for the Poor'. The liberation theology of Latin America and other parts of the world tended to be doctrinally fairly conservative but socially and politically radical, at times taking over the categories of Marxism in a pretty simplistic way. It was open to plenty of criticism, fair and unfair, but it was an engaged theology for life in the seventies, an undergirding for commitment to a struggle for justice and peace in a way that the liberal theology of British academe was not, and by the latter half of the decade it was proving increasingly influential even in Britain.

Liberal theology and radical theology were, then, in the seventies – as indeed in the thirties – very different, even antipathetical movements. Yet they were both challenged by the conservative reaction building up by the end of the decade. Here, if the master on the economic side was Milton Friedman, upon the great frontier of thought and society it was Alexander Solzhenitsyn, the prophet to displace William Temple. There was a considerable, if rather mixed, group of thoughtful writers, like David Martin, Mary Douglas, Edward Norman, Paul Johnson, Auberon Waugh, and Christopher Booker, to challenge the certainties of the sixties and spell out a new Christian strategy, anti-liberal, anti-socialist, anti-sixties, appropriate for the age of Margaret Thatcher and John Paul II. In general among English theologians, perhaps only the veteran Eric Mascall should be named in this regard, but on the continent one must think of Hans Urs von Balthasar, as of Cardinal Ratzinger. Two more particular aspects of a revived conservatism, however, require specific mention. One was a change in biblical studies, already noticeable on the Continent in the work of Joachim Jeremias and others by the beginning of the decade, but increasingly evident in the writing of scholars like Martin Hengel, and fresher British biblical work as the years passed. There was, of course, John Robinson's *Redating the New Testament* (1976) with its contention, so extremely uncongenial to liberals, that all the books of the New Testament were written prior to AD 70. Robinson was superbly adroit at riding, doubtless not always quite deliberately, every cultural wave. Perhaps all in all the most intellectually skilful ecclesiastic of his generation, a man of very polished scholarship as well as of considerable faith and much concern for the wide world towards which he would sally out from time to time from the portals of Cambridge, Robinson liked to appear the *enfant terrible*, to whom his colleagues could never quite do justice: the radical liberal of the sixties, the radical conservative of the late seventies. His thesis in this book was an exaggerated one, nevertheless much of the argumentation was sound, and its conclusions could not but call into question a contemporary academic orthodoxy which dismissed the New Testament as highly unreliable evidence. For Robinson the New Testament was something still to be trusted. Much the same conclusion could be drawn from a number of extremely learned works of biblical scholarship emanating from what may be called the Cambridge school of Professor Moule.[3] The impression here is once more, much as it was a generation earlier in the work of Dodd, that the most exacting of modern historical methodology may vindicate, more than it may undermine, the basic reliability of the New Testament witness.[4]

A somewhat comparable development was taking place in the world of philosophy, especially the philosophy of religion. It is worthy of note that three of the principal chairs of philosophy in Oxford and Cambridge were held at the end of our period by Roman Catholics of fairly conservative religious views. How implausible it would have seemed to predict such a thing forty years earlier. A number of important positive studies were now being published, such as those of Richard Swinburne, Professor of Philosophy at Keele, on the intellectual case for the existence of God. This did not, needless to say, mean that there were not many other academic philosophers who were agnostic or atheist, but it did mean that the case for traditional theism was being put in the Britain of the late 1970s with an academic confidence and a methodological sophistication such as had certainly not been the case for a long while.

By the early 1980s the rather facile modernism which had dominated religious thinking, particularly academic theological thinking, for the last twenty years was falling from favour almost as clearly as that of the twenties had disintegrated by the early 1940s. As the general political and social outlook of the world darkened, so did Christian thought move away from the optimistically liberal but also sceptical note which it had adopted since the early sixties. Nevertheless at the point where, perforce, we end this story, the direction of theology remained still rather unsure. We may indeed see much of the significance in the flurry of excitement surrounding David Jenkins, appointed Bishop of Durham in 1984, and his much discussed comments upon both the Empty Tomb and the miners' strike as providing an illustration of the larger quandary of an uncertain direction. There was undoubtedly a challenging missionary note in Dr Jenkins's words, both intellectual and social. Yet did he see himself as a disciple of Nineham or of Gutierrez? The socially conservative and sceptical liberalism of the one could not so easily be harnessed in support of the confident radicalism of the other. If the English churches were now being increasingly drawn within the vortex of third world Christianity, in both practical concerns and inspirational models, their theology – whether conservative or liberal – could not be unaffected. But the process of intellectual realignment was only just beginning.

In December 1978 a 'Christian Marxist' was reported to be organizing pickets to disrupt a Cheshire Home for the Aged called Springwood House. It was the high time of protest and even such a silly little incident can help to explain the reaction of society against socialist (particularly, of course, Trotskyite) thinking, 'industrial action', and the Christian left. There was a built-up irritation behind the support for Edward Norman's Reith Lectures in 1979, *Christianity and the World Order*, in which the dean of Peterhouse endeavoured to rebut the whole line of thinking represented *par excellence* by Bishop Bell's *Christianity and World Order* (1940) and William Temple's *Christianity and Social Order* (1942) – a socialistic moralizing would be replaced by a capitalistic one as the mode allegedly more appropriate for the Christian of the twentieth century.[5] It was not a thesis which was widely found convincing.[6] In fact the most solid achievements of English Christianity in the 1970s were built squarely upon the tradition of Bell and Temple and few of the clergy were prepared to abandon that tradition at the beck of Thatcherism. The Church of England's Board of Social Responsibility, the Catholic Institute for International Relations, the British Council of Churches and Christian Aid were the principal agents here. Some parts of their work were a great deal more effective than others. At the most effective end one may cite the ever increasing millions raised each year by Christian Aid, the 1970 Report on *Man in his Living Environment* of the Board of Social Responsibility – a document well in advance of most ecological discussions at the time – the 1985 Report of a Commission set up by Runcie on 'Faith in the City' much disliked by Government, and the activities of the CIIR in connection with Mozambique, Zimbabwe (then Rhodesia) and Central America. As in previous decades work of this sort was most effective when most professional and most carefully grounded within a homogeneous and recognizably Christian strategy. It was least effective when too obviously amateur and over-ambitious or open to attack as neo-Marxist. Within the political and international field the professionalism of the CIIR was unrivalled.[7] Its standing as international spokesman for 'Justice and Peace Commissions' in many much disturbed parts of the world may be illustrated amusingly by the satirical edition of *Not The Times*, published during that paper's long strike in the summer of 1979. The main centre page article from 'Our Special Correspondent in Nicaragua' was entitled, 'Religion Perverted for Political Ends'. 'Up and down Latin America' one was able to read, 'we find priests and bishops, tenants of the prettily-named "theology of liberation", giving spiritual comfort to terrorism and undermining the handful of enlightened rulers who are still struggling to stem the Communist tide.' It went on to refer to the CIIR as 'perhaps the most successful of all Soviet "front" organisations'. Such notice was praise indeed! It was especially in these circles that English Christianity was in living contact with liberation theology.

To provide some contrast in regard to effectiveness one may recall how in May 1979 the board of Shell was faced at its annual meeting with a resolution condemning the company for breaking oil sanctions against Rhodesia and committing it to obey any future United Nations sanction orders. The resolution was proposed by Harry Morton, General Secretary of the BCC, Mgr Ralph Brown, Vicar-General of the archdiocese of Westminster, Canon James Robertson, secretary of the United Society for the Propagation of the Gospel, and Albert Mosley, General Secretary of the Methodist Church's Overseas Division. The board of Shell urged its shareholders to reject the motion as one with 'political aims'. The motion was rejected. Clearly the action intended here was of a symbolic kind, but in it a large degree of ecclesiastical consensus did appear to be developing, though perhaps not very effectively.

All in all it remains hard to be convinced that in the eighties, the age of Lech Walesa, the Ayatollah Khomeini and Bishop Tutu, religion, even in Britain, was losing – as some sociologists were now arguing – its public significance. In fact it was receiving a good deal more media coverage than had been the case in the past; and not only special events like the visit of the Pope, the Liverpool Pastoral Congress or the utterances of the Bishop of Durham, but the regular work of the Archbishop of Canterbury, the General Synod, and the Archbishop of Westminster too. Certainly the shape of that significance was changing. It is at least arguable that religion as a distinct force of motivation and mobilization was actually more influential than had been the case for many a year, and that this was linked with a weakening of the old links between it and any particular political institution, or class – a weakening which at the same time contributed to its statistical decline. What influence it exercised derived considerably from the freedom with which it was embraced and the cost that embracing might entail. There was in this period a far greater sense than previously of a two-way fellowship between Christians in this country and abroad. The world of the seventies was, increasingly, a world of torture and even martyrdom, and English Christians were no longer in privileged insulation from that fellowship of pain. English Elim missionaries and Jesuits alike were cut down at their stations in Rhodesia. The decade began with Geoffrey Jackson's long incarceration underground in a 'People's Prison' of the Tupamaros, and the first actions of Her Majesty's ambassador, when released, were to make his confession and receive communion.[8] The torturing of Sheila Cassidy in Chile followed a little later.[9] Then came the martyrdom of the Anglican Archbishop Luwum in Uganda. The decade ended in 1980 with the martyrdom of Archbishop Romero in San Salvador as he celebrated mass, just a few hours before the enthronement of Archbishop Runcie in Canterbury Cathedral. Photographs of the two archbishops, one murdered, one enthroned, were on the front pages of the press the next day. 'Nothing but the martyrdom of an archbishop can save the Church of England', Lord Halifax once declared apocalyptically. Could it be done by proxy?

There seemed a fair measure of common mind to be found among English Christians on social and political issues in the mid-seventies. It was expressed to a considerable extent by the British Council of Churches' project, *Britain Today and Tomorrow*, which was inspired by Archbishop Ramsey's final presidential address to the BCC in 1974, taken up by its General Secretary, Harry Morton, and produced by Trevor Beeson, now a canon of Westminster. It represents the benevolent but rather dreary end of a line which began with COPEC and Malvern – commitment to a rather bureaucratic form of 'Social Democracy with a human face', the welfare state plus, 'a good deal of state intervention and a level of national planning not previously experienced in Britain'.[10]

A year later Mrs Thatcher came to power, pledged to move the ship of State in a quite contrary direction, and Edward Norman delivered his Reith lectures to provide the new religious line. The churches, the new radical right was arguing, had got it wrong again: carried away by a facile near-identification of socialism with Christianity, they had pursued equality to the detriment of liberty. And, of course, the see-saw between those two ideals is indeed at the very heart of the enterprise to maintain civilized society. Whatever consensus among Christians the BCC might have discussed in 1978 proved more apparent than real under the mounting strains of the 1980s. It survived, fair enough, when it came to feeding a starving Ethiopia or condemning racial discrimination but it certainly did not exist when it came to defending or dismantling a somewhat ramshackle welfare State or justifying the Falklands War, and still less when it came to condemning or condoning nuclear weapons or abortion. These latter appear as the two most enduring and demanding ethical issues, with major political implications, which society had to face. By 1980 some 140 thousand registered abortions were taking place in Britain every year. The existence of nuclear weapons of ever greater potency and cost had placed all human life in peril and no country in the world had more of them based on its own soil than Britain. The very expense of their production had become one major reason for the economic crisis facing British society.

While the Campaign for Nuclear Disarmament was in no way a specifically Christian movement, its leadership in these years by Mgr Bruce Kent was as important as that of Canon Collins had been twenty years earlier. Kent's essential political moderation and skill in holding people together was a factor of great importance in CND's massive revival. The anti-abortion campaign, while not supported by Church people only, was a far more predominantly Christian movement and one subject to much left-wing abuse. Its strongest support undoubtedly came from the Catholic Church. It is clear that a right wing mentality has tended to be hard on abortion but soft on nuclear weapons while a left wing mentality has tended to be hard on nuclear weapons but soft on abortion: 'It is a pathological feature of the intellectual climate of our time', wrote the Master of Balliol, 'that so few people are consistent in their attitude to the killing of the innocent.'[11] It would be nice to record that there developed a substantial consensus of Christian witness in regard to both – a consensus characteristic, then, of neither left nor right but specifically Christian. But it was not so.

A Church of England working party under John Baker, the bishop of Salisbury, produced a strong anti-nuclear statement, *The Church and the Bomb*, in 1982, and it looked for a moment as if the Established Church might be about to commit itself to a position against government policy over a major issue. General Synod, however, did not accept it. Again, there was a very considerable measure of Christian support for the Corrie Abortion Bill in 1980, which while being a highly reasonable measure by no means went wholly along with the anti-abortion lobby. It did no more than specify that there must be serious reasons for abortion, that it should be illegal after twenty weeks (instead of twenty-eight) and that the financial link between referring agencies and abortion clinics should be broken. But in the end, just as Mgr Bruce Kent and the CND did not get the clear support of middle of the road Christians, neither did the Corrie Bill. The fall-out was mostly from the right over the one, from the left over the other, and both could appeal when it suited them to the sort of view expressed consistently by John Habgood, Bishop of Durham and then Archbishop of York, a vocal opponent (like Lord Soper) of the Corrie Bill, that 'in practice most contentious ethical issues arise in the murky area where principles conflict, facts are ambiguous and differences are largely a question of degree'.[12] There is never, then, a clear moral case for getting too worked up about anything.

Christian leaders might still, nevertheless, deliver an effective witness without consensus and there was probably more mature Christian outspokenness in the field of social affairs in these years than in any era since that of Temple and Bell. It had been made possible by an immense effort of theological reflection on moral issues carried out largely by lay people. The leadership provided by Archbishop Runcie and Cardinal Hume, by Kenneth Greet (secretary of the Methodist Conference and Moderator of the Free Church Federal Council), by Bishop Sheppard and Archbishop Worlock, by Archbishop Huddleston as chairman of Anti-Apartheid, by Mgr Bruce Kent as General Secretary of the Campaign for Nuclear Disarmament, and Kenneth Slack, as director of Christian Aid, certainly compared favourably enough with that provided by politicians or academics.[13]

But the leadership of one person does seem to stand out far beyond all others, and that person was Barbara Ward. One of the founders of the Sword of the Spirit in the Second World War, an outstanding journalist, radio speaker and academic, a founding member (and indeed a principal instigator) of the Pontifical Commission for Justice and Peace in Rome, Schweitzer Professor of International Economic Development in America, and a life peer in Westminster, Barbara Ward seemed everything to everyone. From her early books like *The West at Bay* (1948) to *Progress for a Small Planet* (1979) written at the very end of her life, she was a teacher of genius who could incorporate economics, sociology and history into a single unified vision, intensely humane and far sighted. The 1970s she spent above all working as President of the International Institute for Environment and Development, utterly preoccupied with social justice for the poor nations but also with the protection of the environment, the position of women and the struggle against nuclear weapons. 'The development and betterment of the poorer two-thirds of the world is the most important task before us all in the remainder of this century,' she declared as she lay dying in December 1980, having struggled against cancer through fifteen years. Behind all this she was the most convinced of Catholic Christians, praying the rosary daily, the parable of Dives and Lazarus never far from her mind. She died on 31 May 1981. Her life, personality and achievement might seem to provide as good evidence as any of the continuing effectiveness of Christianity. If there was in truth anything of a deeper Christian consensus in this period it certainly owed most to Barbara Ward. Indeed what Temple was to the first half of the century, Ward was to the second. That is a large claim but a fair one, and it could be made of no one else.

In Which we say Goodbye

Seen in retrospect the 1950s seem almost like a golden age of King
Solomon, the sixties an era of moral prophecy of a fairly Pelagian
sort. The period in which we have now arrived is quite other, an
age of apocalyptic, of doom watch, in which the tragedies of an
anguished world have become just too many to cope with, yet in
which there is the strongest feeling that there may still be worse to
come. The optimism of a Pelagian mood is quite gone. We are
faced instead with an Augustinian predicament. When the Van-
dals are at the gates, there are three possible responses. One is
simply to despair of the kingdom, of any ultimate meaning in the
world or in human history; the second is to withdraw into a
private, sacral sphere, a closed community, monastic or charismatic, abandoning the struggle for the secular state as irremediably corrupt; the third is to imitate Augustine himself, take a very
sombre view but also a very long one, and retain in hope but
without much evidence a Christian concern for the redeemability
of the totality of things. By the 1980s a great many Christians
were succumbing to the first choice, and a great many to the
second, but rather few were making ready for the long haul of the
genuine Augustinian.

English Christianity in the 1980s certainly had a fine past to it,
and we may at this point indulge in a few symbolic leave-takings
in regard to our elders before proceeding to a brief consideration
of the predicament of those remaining on board ship. We might
think first of Robert Selby Taylor as representing that missionary
impetus which had, throughout our period, continued to export
the various strands of English religion, often heroically, across
the globe. In 1984 he retired as Bishop of Central Zambia. He
had gone to Africa in 1935 as a priest of the Universities Mission

to Central Africa, and been consecrated Bishop of Northern Rhodesia on Likoma Island in Lake Malawi in 1941: the very first bishop of the UMCA to be consecrated within Africa. Since then Selby Taylor had been Bishop of Pretoria, of Grahamstown, and for ten years Archbishop of Cape Town. In 1974 he retired from Cape Town but, in old age, heard once more the appeal of part of his former diocese and returned for five years to what was now Zambia. A pastor of vast experience, he had served Africa for fifty years and seen whole dioceses multiply around him. That was one side of twentieth-century English religion: traditional enough yet expansive and quietly confident too.

Dom Sylvester Mooney represented an older tradition still. On the Berkshire Downs, at Douai, in the Abbey of St Edmund, at the very end of our period, the summer of 1985, Dom Sylvester entered his hundredth year, wheeled into the office, the work of God, in the great monastic church he had himself built fifty years earlier, the office which he had attended dutifully for more than eighty years. No medieval monk had practised *stabilitas* better than he. He had been ordained priest for the monastery in 1911 and ruled it as abbot for forty years from 1929 to 1969. As a boy he had been in the school at Douai in France before the monastery moved back to England in 1903, ending three hundred and fifty years of the education of English Catholics in exile in the little town where in the reign of Elizabeth I Cardinal Allen had first established a college. Of all that long line of thousands of young Englishmen who had gone to Douai for schooling and priesting Mooney was the last, a gentle, quiet man, witness to the human fruitfulness of a Benedictine pattern of life, a monastic stability which had well served the community, as it had served him personally, in the pursuit of God.

There were plenty of other old men we may think of, still bent on pursuing God. For instance, a couple of elderly converts, card-carrying agnostics in youth who had, however, for years been preoccupied with religious experience. Malcolm Mugger-idge, a former editor of *Punch* and sharp-eyed commentator across fifty years of the follies of his compatriots, the highly self-conscious clown at the court of King Everyman, was washed up at last in the eighties in the Catholic Church, converted maybe by the one contemporary figure he found it absolutely impossible to be cynical about, Mother Teresa. Philip Toynbee, another brilliant young journalist of the thirties, the only Communist ever to be President of the Oxford Union, also discovered religious faith in old age and was to be found, 'the rosary in my hand', a postcard of the Black Virgin of Chartres above his bed.[1] Finally, Lord Hailsham. Still Lord Chancellor of England in the eighties, he had been a young atheist in the twenties who returned to Christianity in the thirties and became thereafter the quintessential liberal Anglican Tory, a man at the dead centre of the English Establishment. His apologia and autobiography, *The Door Wherein I Went*, may well be judged the most lucid and convincing piece of Christian apologetic writing from the 1970s.

These, and many others, were people of distinction, but of a generation fast passing away. Did Christianity have a future as well as a past? The imponderables of the future are far too many and far too grim for any of us to predict with confidence the future shape of religion or society, or – more profoundly – to have confidence that what does happen will happen for the immediate good of the world. Institutionalized falsehood is just as likely to prevail as what is true and good. The future flourishing of religion is itself proof of neither the one nor the other. Furthermore the historian should not pretend that a reading of the entrails of the past, even the very recent past, can render him a reliable exponent of futurology. Nevertheless, certain things may be said about some of the challenges that English Christianity must most certainly meet if it is to have very much of a future. They relate to its theological message, to its relationship with the State and with society, to the principal form it will take and the schisms which at present still divide it.

Let us, first, consider theology. No church can continue for long without a theology possessing a fair measure of internal coherence, one related organically both to the actual religious practice of believers and to certain basic requirements of credibility or utility posited by contemporary society, though the smaller and more sectlike a church is, the less the final condition applies. By the 1970s the central tradition of English academic theology, particularly Anglican theology as taught at Oxford and Cambridge, was hardly any longer fulfilling these needs. There had long been a notable gap between academic theology and what one may call the theology of the pew, but in previous ages there had remained a sufficient link between them. The theology of Gore, Temple, Ramsey or Farrer was, most certainly, one the Church could live and thrive with. The same cannot be said for that of Nineham, Hick or Cupitt. Scholarship can only be met with scholarship. It is no refutation of their work to say that there is simply no future for a Church which can produce no reasoned expression of its faith stronger than what the dominant theologians of the seventies were able to muster. Maybe there is none. In which case the Church will certainly shrivel rapidly enough, which is of course what many an unbeliever expects to be the case. The Church of England is moreover particularly vulnerable to collapse due to intellectual bankruptcy just because – far more than most – it has long been a thinking Church, finding its very heart in major universities.

It is true that Christianity in England relies greatly on foreign theologians – of late especially Küng, Schillebeeckx, or Moltmann. It is true also that by the mid-eighties there was already a noticeable shift in progress within the English universities in a less sceptical direction. Certainly, the theological battle remains an open one. One cannot reject the scholarly conclusions of able theological thinkers simply because they are too destructive of the core of the tradition of Christian faith and theology. If the destruction is to be avoided the conclusions must be demonstrated to be unconvincing. That may not be easy. But neither the leaders of the Church nor liberal theologians themselves should deceive themselves as to what is at stake. The question mark hanging over the future of theology today hangs directly over the meaningfulness of Christianity in any worthwhile shape or form. That might have been said in 1920 with a little justification; in 1980 with far more so.

Church and State. One summer afternoon in the thirties William Temple and Stanley Baldwin, the Archbishop of York and the Prime Minister, sat chatting on the terrace at Bishopthorpe beside the river Ouse. A barge came drifting by. The bargee looked at them, took the pipe from his mouth and called out: 'Keepin' better company today, I see.' 'I wonder', remarked Baldwin, 'for which of us that pretty compliment was meant.'[2]

The ease, the informality as well as the formalities of an inter-locking relationship at every level between civil and religious authority was what Establishment meant. England's secular establishment was riddled with ecclesiastical woodworm in such a cunning and natural way that it displeased almost no one. A very great deal of this has now gone. Archbishop Fisher was, perhaps, the last true representative of the old order. He was probably also the last senior ecclesiastic to be a Freemason. The Anglican clergy is more clerical than it was, the State and the social establishment which dominates it are a great deal more brazenly secular. Nevertheless, something of England's charac-teristic religious Establishment remains, not only in the rituals of the monarchy, but also in the way that the majority of the English people regard the Church of England and the role the clergy still naturally fills in a good many activities of the local community. Much of this is dwindling fast enough – symbolically, the year our story ends, 1985, was the first since its foundation that Cambridge University had not a single priest among its college heads. Yet the history of the political influence of the churches in modern Britain has certainly not been all decline. The power of the past was a power within bondage. Compare what church leaders had to say about the First World War and what they said about the Falklands War; it would be hard not to prefer the latter.

There are voices raised today, both within and without the Church of England, calling for a final end to Establishment. The arguments given are powerful and attractive ones. It remains, nevertheless, the hesitant conviction of the present writer that they are fallacious. Both Christianity and English society would be further weakened without any real compensating advantage, if what little now remains of the Church's Establishment was cut on principle away. The Church of England would also be re-pudiating too much of its past history and that is never wise to do, especially in a time of admitted weakness. Anglican priests retain very widely a sense of responsibility for the whole of society and all that is in it which goes far beyond what most ministers of other churches feel; it is a sound sense which even in its present practical ineffectualness should not be disparaged. Christians of other traditions might do better to help salvage, rather than dismantle, what survives of the Church of England's 'national' character. *Ecclesia Anglicana* should not go out of business. England would still be vastly impoverished if compelled to adopt the formal secularity of France or America.

Paradoxically, much of the justification for some survival of formal Establishment depends upon the existence of informal religion, what is often called today folk religion. In 1979 a petition was presented to General Synod for the 'continued and loving use' of the Book of Common Prayer and the Authorized Version of the Bible.[3] It was organized by David Martin, Professor of Sociology at the London School of Economics, the author of numerous books on the theme of secularization, an erstwhile Methodist and now an increasingly conservative Anglican priest. Its six hundred signatories included the heads of twenty Oxford and Cambridge colleges; twenty-three cathedral organists; actors, poets, politicians, leaders of the armed services. The press release even made clear that 'some atheists signed with great fervour, holding that it was a national question'. What is one to make of this? The Church has found archaic literature increasingly difficult to use in regular worship, quite apart from the deeper theological deficiencies of the old communion service. But a largely non-worshipping nation – particularly its upper class and aesthetic élite – has felt the cultural loss (but surely for many the sheer religious loss too) as little short of catastrophic. Very much the same thing has happened in the Catholic Church. It is not just a matter of culture, it is a matter of not cutting off the vast subterranean religious roots of the shepherdless multitude of the untheological. In fact in the Church of England a compromise seems in practice to have been reached. Beside the new liturgies '1662' is still used a great deal, particularly in places like cathedrals more likely to be frequented by people who are not regular worshippers.

The underlying issue is how much notice to take of folk or residual religion: the role of a large, well established Church in regard to the millions of people who have no regular connection, and little clear belief, but have nevertheless some personal sense of religious meaning and some openness to one or another aspect – more aesthetic with one, more philanthropic with another – of the Church's work. The Church of England as a regular worshipping community is now a quite small minority of the nation, but it retains a real link of emotion with a vastly much larger proportion. A very great deal of modern Church concern, whether of a Catholic or a Protestant kind, whether it focuses on the Eucharist as the pivot of the local Christian community or on the conversion experience of the 'born-again' Christian, not only ignores but almost of necessity excludes the on-going existence of the Church's wide 'folk' periphery, the millions who are quite unlikely to be drawn in large numbers to communion or believer's baptism. The whole 'Parish and People' type of thinking which stressed the parish communion and turned away from matins, while undoubtedly a great gain from one point of view, in fact tended to alienate the periphery, which could feel at home with the one and feed on it a little, but was far too little committed to relish communion.

The link with the periphery is, as a consequence, little served by the regular worship of ordinary parishes, but it is served very considerably by the more august worship of the great cathedrals – probably the Church of England's most valuable surviving public asset – by royal and national rituals, by bishops when they speak wisely, by the image of countless village churches (even if little used), and by this country's immensely rich heritage of religious culture, much of it accumulated in the present century. There is little which is specifically Protestant in the surviving folk religion of England: personal reading of the Bible in the home, anti-popery, familiarity with *Pilgrim's Progress*, these things have simply faded away. There is, on the other hand, much that is decidedly Catholic, both of a traditional and of a contemporary kind. It is the medieval, rather than the post-Reformation, religious heritage which remains just alive today. 'At the core of all small villages of Anglo-Saxon foundation there is a primal reverence – neither wholly christian, not yet quite pagan – for an inseparable blend of God, antiquity, and the king, which is really the true religion of the people.'[4] This is still just there, watered a little by Betjeman and Eliot, its local symbols a medieval church, a harvest festival, its national symbol the rituals of Westminster Abbey. The service of Nine Lessons and Carols is one of its more successful modern stimulants. Its hero saints of our times are almost all Catholic – Teilhard, Mother Teresa, Pope John. Its principal saint from the past, returned to in our day times without number, was a Speaker of the House of Commons and Lord Chancellor of the realm, Thomas More, perceived as the very model of the English Christian.[5] The most significant Protestant elements remaining in English folk religion are hymn singing (watered by new hymns, the best of which continue to be written by Free Churchmen, and the popularity of the BBC's *Songs of Praise*) an attachment to the Book of Common Prayer and the legal character of the monarchy: the commitment to maintain the Protestant religion as by law established. It is striking how, if the one Englishman of the century of the Reformation to retain a living national religious significance is More, the only Churchman of the 19th century to do so seems to be Newman. No other Victorian religious figure has any comparable surviving importance. More and Newman do together serve to remind us how ambivalent English religion has been in its rejection of Catholicism and of Rome.

The importance of folk religion does, then, lead naturally to the issue of Rome. Hensley Henson, as we saw in Part I, was quite sure at the start of our period that 'the continuing conflict' with Rome remained this country's 'governing ecclesiastical issue'.[6] In 1933 William Temple, in so many other things Henson's antithesis, remarked, 'Some day, no doubt, in a very remote future, the question of union with Rome will become practical. At present I regard it as almost infinitely remote.'[7] That appeared true enough for the time, although Temple himself was probably already beginning to feel that it was less true in his final years with the founding of the Sword of the Spirit. One central theme of this book is when, how and why it ceased to be true: how Roman Catholicism in England was in truth always a great deal more English, even more 'Anglican' – but more Free Church too – than Protestants were able to recognize; but then how English Catholicism was enormously affected over many decades both by the influence upon it of converts from other churches, like Newman, Chesterton, Dawson and Butler, and by the wider ethos of English Christianity in which its laity especially has increasingly shared; and how the Vatican Council then set in motion a vast process which, with qualifications, can, not unreasonably, be seen as the Protestantization of the modern Catholic Church. But our story has equally been of change upon the other side – the rather sad disintegration of traditional English Protestantism, especially its Free Church wing, but also the vast alteration produced within the Church of England by a century of Anglo-Catholic influence, an internal catholicization which has spread to the Free Churches, especially Methodism and what is now the United Reformed Church. Our story has been one of how all these churches were caught up within the ecumenical movement (whose early dynamism came above all from the Free Churches), so that the ideas and forces which were remoulding Protestantism from the 1920s on were from the fifties let loose within Roman Catholicism too.

If Temple could be reasonably convinced in the 1930s that the whole 'ethos of the two communions', Anglican and Roman, was 'radically different', it is not so easy to think so today. Doubtless many a Roman Catholic still finds the Church of England a lot too full of over-liberal bishops and layfolk with the vaguest of beliefs, while many an Anglican still finds the Roman Catholic Church both too authoritarian and too full of people convinced that they have the answer – and a rather too medieval answer – to all the riddles of existence. So it is. Yet many on both sides may now feel that it is more sensible to allow the experience of unity to remedy these defects than to insist upon their being remedied prior to unity. One cannot but ask whether the time is not approaching for a 'historic compromise' – the reacceptance by the Church of England of the papacy within its system, the acceptance by English Roman Catholics of the substantial Christian validity of the Anglican and Protestant experience at the point at which it has now arrived, including – if Anglicans still so prefer – a Church as by law established. If such a union were in the future seriously to be sought, it is vital that it should at least in part include the third historic tradition within English Christianity – the Free Churches. While it would be chimerical to hope that all Christians within the country could, or would, wish to be included within such a Church in the foreseeable future, one would hope that it could somehow embrace both Methodism and the United Reformed Church. It would be the unity of many traditions, reunited but not absorbed, in Dom Beauduin's classic phrase. It sounds Utopian and it may well be so, but it is not quite impossible and it would be well within the on-going logic of the

history we have been reviewing. If the 1964 Nottingham commitment to unity by 1980 has not been realized, there is no compelling reason why a unity larger than Nottingham had in mind
should not be achieved within the lifetime of some of us.

The Church of England has long prided itself upon being a
bridge Church, both Catholic and Protestant. This has always
been as much a hope as a reality. Perhaps a united Church in
England in the future might make of it more of a reality than it has
yet been. A reunited *Ecclesia Anglicana* in full communion with
Rome, as was the case when the Great Charter was written and
signed, would need to remain heir equally to its Reformation
heritage, perpetuating neither the ultramontanism of Rome, nor
the upper-class Erastianism of Anglicanism, nor the narrower
rigidities of the Free Church tradition.

Would it make much difference? There are sociologists who
have argued that ecumenical sentiments are only too clearly an
expression of institutional decline. It is a great over-
simplification, but indeed there is something in it. Good things
are often done in the Church as elsewhere for poor motives. Has
religion, united or divided, the Christian religion especially, any
real place in present or future society? This book has tried to
answer that question, in regard to the immediate past, in a
moderately positive way. There remains, however, a largely
unformulated presupposition to much modern thought, shared
by many a sociologist, historian and even now – it seems –
theologian, which holds that religion really belongs in principle
to the past, that modernity is now in principle religionless, that a
truly modern man must be an atheist, and that history should be
seen in this light as a steady process of secularization, in which
human society moves inexorably from a religious age to total
secularity. It is more a matter of dogma than of evidence though
the statistical decline in church membership is used to buttress it.
The intensely religious condition of the remote past is not easy to
believe in and still harder to prove. Undoubtedly aspects of
religion die as society evolves, but religion has been remarkably
good in the past at finding new and convincing forms and, indeed,
after the initial shock of change adapting both profoundly and
effectively to each new post-revolutionary shape of things. It
seems implausible to declare that it can now do so no more,

especially as our post-industrial age, returning to a kind of pre-industrial existence in which under-employment is rife and life centres more upon the home and the neighbourhood, would seem actually to favour the practice of religion.

Within English history there have been waves of religious enthusiasm, of attempts to convert and truly Christianize a rather nominally Christian England. We see such waves in the tenth century and the thirteenth, the seventeenth and the nineteenth. Hitherto, at least, ours has not been such an age. It is far more like the sixteenth century – one in which, after a period of close integration of the religious and the secular, an integration which left religion rather secularized and society with an over-heavy burden of dated religion weighing on its structures, society thrusts religious things away from its functioning to a quite considerable extent, thus in fact enabling religion itself to stand once more upon its own ground, desecularized. Only when religion has in some way adjusted itself to that expulsion can it effectively resume its missionary task. Our age seems of such a sort, at least so far as the West is concerned. It is one of the secularization of society and the desecularization of religion, one act the more in the ever continuing drama of a wrestling match between the two. Or so at least it appears most probable to the present writer.

Certainly as things stand at present, the business of religion in the West seems perilous enough. The pilgrimage of modern religious man (a very real entity nonetheless, fully modern and fully religious), of late twentieth-century *Homo Religiosus* (to use Eliade's terminology), may seem at times as whimsical as that of Graham Greene's fantasy, Monsignor Quixote.[8] Forbidden by his bishop to celebrate mass, the Monsignor ended his life in a strange journey with a Communist friend. After assaulting an absurd madonna all covered with bank notes, and shot by the police, he found refuge in a friendly monastery. Dying he said a last mass in a sort of dream with imaginary bread and wine and yet, as he did so, revived the faith of his atheist *companero*, the Communist mayor. Religion is a frail and visionary thing. We forget that at our peril, endeavouring to measure its strength with the statistics of sociology, yet may its visible history not well be seen as something of a ceaseless oscillation between the Church of Archdeacon Grantly and that of Monsignor Quixote? The archdeacon was astride his world, sure enough, but what a secularized figure of religious man he was. Monsignor Quixote was a vastly more marginal figure, but he himself was not secularized. He was indeed more potent than the archdeacon in his religiosity, if much less in the ways of this world. The interaction of the religious and the secular goes to and fro between the one type and the other. Neither is final, however much between the monsignor and the archdeacon we may prefer the one or the other.

At present we do not quite belong to either. The world of Lord Hailsham and Mgr Kent lies somewhere between the two. Maybe we are moving steadily enough away from Barsetshire, and towards Quixote. If and when the swing will again begin to change, we cannot say. All we can say with absolute assurance is that if it should prove true that the character of modern culture excludes religion and there thus comes a time when the society of our descendants is indeed religionless, deprived not just of religion in general but of the Christian religion in particular, the religion of George Tyrrell and William Paton, of C. F. Andrews and George Bell, of Barbara Ward and Mother Teresa, yes, of Jesus of Nazareth, then the future deserves of us no less than an infinite pity.

NOTES

CHAPTER 1 (pages 17–29)

[1] C. F. G. Masterman, *England After War* (1922), p. 124.
[2] J. M. Keynes, *The Economic Consequences of the Peace* (1919), p. 131.

CHAPTER 2 (pages 30–48)

[1] J. Bossy, *The English Catholic Community 1570–1850* (1975).
[2] Lord Home, *The Way the Wind Blows* (1976), p. 277.
[3] For Edwardian religion, Owen Chadwick, *The Victorian Church* (2 vols, 1966, 1970), II, is a good opener. Two basic Edwardian works are C. F. G. Masterman, *The Condition of England* (1909), and the massive *Daily News* Survey of London, *The Religious Life of London*, ed. Richard Mudie-Smith (1904); Masterman, 'The Problem of South London', in ibido, is particularly valuable. There are fair discussions of Edwardian religion in R. C. K. Ensor, *England 1870–1914* (1936), pp. 305–10, and Paul Thompson, *The Edwardians* (1975), pp. 203–14. Three important studies are Hugh McLeod, *Class and Religion in the Late Victorian City* (1974); Alan Gilbert, *Religion and Society in Industrial England: Church, Chapel and Social Change 1740–1914* (1976); and Stephen Yeo, *Religion and Voluntary Organisations in Crisis* (1976). This last is principally a close study of the churches in Reading around the turn of the century. See also John Gay, *The Geography of Religion in England* (1971).

[4] C. J. Hammond, *A Fruitful Ministry: a Memoir of the Rev. Robert Henry Hammond* (1908), esp. pp. 98–106.
[5] *Victorian Church*, II, pp. 221–2.
[6] ibid. p. 226; for a Birmingham census, see Roy Peacock, 'The 1892 Birmingham Religious Census', in *Religion in the Birmingham Area*, ed. Alan Bryman (1975), pp. 12–28.
[7] Mudie-Smith, pp. 198–9.
[8] C. Smyth, *Cyril Foster Garbett* (1959), p. 181.
[9] Henry Mess, *Industrial Tyneside* (1928), pp. 131–40.
[10] R. Moore, *Pit-Men, Preachers and Politics* (1974), p. 70.
[11] C. Ward Davis, in *A Social History of the Diocese of Newcastle*, ed. W. S. F. Pickering (1981), p. 207.
[12] *Condition of England*, pp. 14, 268.
[13] Mudie-Smith, p. 151.
[14] *Victorian Church*, II, p. 201.
[15] A. M. Allchin, *The Silent Rebellion: Anglican Religious Communities 1845–1900* (1958).
[16] *Life and Letters of Janet Erskine Stuart 1857–1914* (1922).
[17] F. A. Iremonger, *William Temple* (1948), p. 237.
[18] Alan Wilkinson, *The Church of England and the First World War* (1978); Albert Marrin, *The Last Crusade: the Church of England in the First World War* (1974); Michael Moynihan, *God on Our Side: the British Padre in the First World War* (1983); Stuart Mews, 'Religion and English Society in the First World War', Ph.D. thesis, Univ. Cambridge 1973.
[19] J. G. Lockhart, *Cosmo Gordon Lang* (1949), p. 128.

[20] W. R. Inge, *Diary of a Dean* (1949), p. 56. Henson later called Winnington-Ingram a 'feather headed prelate', Owen Chadwick, *Hensley Henson* (1983), p. 170.

[21] John Oman, *The War and its Issues* (1915), p. 8.

[22] C. Howard Hopkins, *John R. Mott 1865–1955* (1979), p. 433.

[23] See Martin Ceadel, *Pacifism in Britain 1914–1945: the Defining of a Faith* (1980), ch. 4.

[24] But note how fiercely P. T. Forsyth, the leading Congregationalist theologian, rejected their position, in *The Christian Ethic of War* (1916).

[25] Robert Graves, *Goodbye to All That* (1929), pp. 241–3. The evaluation of their wartime ministry by some of the chaplains themselves was far more positive. See, for instance, E. W. Kemp, *The Life and Letters of Kenneth Escott Kirk* (1959), pp. 27–35.

[26] Ronald Blythe, *The Age of Illusion* (1963), pp. 1–14; Moynihan, pp. 46–79.

[27] John G. Vance and J. W. Fortescue, *Adrian Fortescue: a Memoir* (1924), pp. 41–2.

CHAPTER 3 (pages 49–64)

[1] The literature is enormous. There is a long series of twentieth-century Reports by Church Commissions, notably those of 1916 (chaired by Lord Selborne) and 1970 (chaired by Owen Chadwick). David Nicholls, *Church and State in Britain since 1820* (1967), is a useful collection of documents; and Cyril Garbett, *Church and State in England* (1950), is a major work by someone who from every point of view stood in the middle of things.

[2] Lockhart, *Cosmo Gordon Lang*, p. 241.

[3] David L. Edwards, *Leaders of the Church of England 1828–1944* (1971), p. 301.

[4] HL Debates, XIII (1913), p. 1200.

[5] *Report of the Archbishop's Committee on Church and State* (1917), pp. 29–30.

[6] ibid. p. 29.

[7] *Cosmo Gordon Lang*, p. 232.

[8] H. E. Sheen, *Canon Peter Green* (1965), p. 88.

[9] H. H. Asquith, *Memories and Reflections*, 2 vols (1928), I, p. 273.

[10] Leslie Paul, *The Deployment and Payment of the Clergy* (1964), pp. 282–5.

[11] C. A. Alington, *Things Ancient and Modern* (1936), pp. 88–9.

[12] E. N. Bennet, *Problems of Village Life* (1914), pp. 127–8.

[13] Iremonger, *William Temple*, p. 292.

[14] G. K. A. Bell, *Randall Davidson, Archbishop of Canterbury*, 2 vols (1935), pp. 787–9.

[15] ibid. p. 842.

[16] ibid. p. 1229.

[17] See the long introduction to J. Cell, *By Kenya Possessed* (1976).

[18] *Randall Davidson*, p. 1231.

[19] Besides the Lives of Davidson and Temple, see David Thompson, 'The Politics of the Enabling Act of 1919', in D. Baker (ed.), *Church Society and Politics* (1975); and Kenneth A. Thompson, *Bureaucracy and Church Reform: the Organisational Response of the Church of England to Social Change 1800–1965* (1970).

[20] Memorandum of Davidson, 6 February 1921.

[21] H. H. Henson, 'Church and State in England', *Edinburgh Review* (October 1916).

CHAPTER 4 (pages 65–85)

[1] For the history of the Church of England in the twentieth century the best start is Chadwick's major work, *Victorian Church*; adding Roger

Lloyd, *The Church of England 1900–1965* (1966); K. A. Thompson, *Bureaucracy and Church Reform*; E. R. Norman, *Church and Society in England 1700–1970* (1976); Bell, *Randall Davidson*; Lockhart, *Cosmo Gordon Lang*; Iremonger, *William Temple*; and Edwards, *Leaders of the Church of England*.

2 See, for instance, the discussion in David Mole, 'The Victorian Town Parish: rural vision and urban mission', in *The Church in Town and Country*, ed. Derek Baker (1979), pp. 361–71.

3 See, for instance, Lloyd, p. 148.

4 McLeod, *Class and Religion in the Late Victorian City*, p. 27.

5 And the north found difficulty in taking the Church of England quite seriously. See, for instance, J. C. Hardwick's treatment of this theme in *A Professional Christian* (1932).

6 *Modern Churchman* (January 1928). For the problems of a working-class child who was confirmed, see Phyllis Willmott, *A Green Girl* (1983), pp. 39–45, 54–5.

7 H. H. Henson (ed.), *Church Problems: a View of Modern Anglicanism* (1900), p. 21.

8 id. *Letters* (1950), pp. 60–1.

9 The course became in principle at least two years only in 1939. A revealing correspondence between Bishop Headlam of Gloucester and Eric Graham of Cuddesdon about theological education is in R. Holtby, *Eric Graham 1888–1964* (1967), pp. 49–57. At the end of the 1930s Headlam was still quite happy to ordain a man after a single term in a theological college.

10 Alan Paton, *Apartheid and the Archbishop: the Life and Times of Geoffrey Clayton, Archbishop of Cape Town* (1973).

11 J. Leatherbarrow, 'Martley', unpublished typescript n.d., p. 32; cf J. S. Leatherbarrow, 'The Rise and Decline of the Squarson', Ph.D. thesis, Univ. Birmingham 1976, ch. 6, 7.

12 cp Lloyd, p. 343, and J. Leatherbarrow, p. 34.

13 John R. Moorman, *B. K. Cunningham: a Memoir* (1947), p. 10.

14 cf W. M. S. West, *To Be a Pilgrim: a Memoir of Ernest A. Payne* (1983), p. 39.

15 J. W. Robertson Smith, *England's Green and Pleasant Land* (1925), ch. 11. Fictionally the gentleman parson is portrayed at his best by Dorothy L. Sayers, *The Nine Tailors* (1934), and at his worst by George Orwell, *A Clergyman's Daughter* (1935). A new less amateur breed is depicted with the precision of an observant insider by Hardwick, *A Professional Christian*.

16 *Church Times* (18 August 1922), quoted in Sheen, *Canon Peter Green*, p. 95.

17 Fr Kelly, letter to Bishop of Southwell, in Lloyd, p. 187.

18 It, too, had its limitations; cf *Father Joe: the Autobiography of Joseph Williamson of Poplar and Stepney* (1963), pp. 97–101; and *A Professional Christian*, ch. 3.

19 Lloyd, p. 251; *B. K. Cunningham*.

20 See K. E. Kirk, *The Story of the Woodard Schools* (1937).

21 *Annual Report of the Board of Education for 1922–3*, Appendix 4, p. 173.

22 G. Kitson Clark, *The English Inheritance* (1950), p. 143.

23 J. A. Mangan, *Athleticism in the Victorian and Edwardian Public School* (1981).

24 *Randall Davidson*, p. 1242.

25 H. H. Henson, *Retrospect of an Unimportant Life* (1942), I, pp. 156–7.

26 P. Fitzgerald, *The Knox Brothers* (1977), p. 103.

27 Chadwick, *Victorian Church*, II, pp. 385, 387, 393.

[28] ibid. pp. 218–319.

[29] Wilkinson, *The Church of England and the First World War*, p. 178.

[30] G. L. Prestige, *The Life of Charles Gore* (1935), p. 297.

[31] Edmund Knox, *Reminiscences of an Octogenarian* (1935), p. 312.

[32] *Retrospect*, I, p. 54; cf *Letters*, p. 69.

[33] M. Reckitt, *As it Happened* (1941), p. 255.

[34] Quoted in J. G. Lockhart, *Charles Lindley Viscount Halifax*, II (1936), pp. 357–8.

CHAPTER 5 (pages 86–99)

[1] G. Stephenson, *Edward Stuart Talbot* (1936), p. 114. Talbot in fact changed quite a lot in his attitude to the Free Churches, growing considerably more irenic. See J. H. Shakespeare, *The Churches at the Cross-Roads* (1918), pp. 62–3, 206–7.

[2] T. Tatlow, *The Story of the Student Christian Movement* (1933); Eric Fenn, *Learning Wisdom: Fifty Years of the Student Christian Movement* (1939); for a personal impression of the SCM from the late 1920s, see Lesslie Newbigin, *Unfinished Agenda* (1985), pp. 8–38.

[3] Tatlow, p. 384.

[4] ibid. pp. 313–19; E. Jackson, *Red Tape and the Gospel* (1980), pp. 48–52.

[5] *Student Movement*, xxiii (1920), pp. 131–2; see Tatlow, p. 649.

[6] See, for instance, J. C. Pollock, *A Cambridge Movement* (1953).

[7] ibid. p. 195. For a 1920s Cambridge Evangelical with a difference, at home in CICCU but determined to belong to SCM too, see F. W. Dillistone's Life of Max Warren, *Into all the World* (1980), pp. 22–6.

[8] The words are Grubb's, quoted by F. D. Coggan, *Christ and the Colleges* (1934), p. 17.

[9] Norman Grubb, *Once Caught, No Escape* (1969).

[10] cf id. *C. T. Studd, Cricketer and Pioneer* (1970).

[11] D. V. Steere, *God's Irregular: Arthur Shearly Cripps* (1973); Murray Steele, 'With Hope Unconquered and Unconquerable . . . Arthur Shearly Cripps', in *Themes in the Christian History of Central Africa*, ed. T. O. Ranger and John Weller (1975).

[12] Hugh Tinker, *The Ordeal of Love: C. F. Andrews and India* (1979); Daniel O'Connor, *The Testimony of C. F. Andrews* (1974).

[13] For Oldham and Kenya, see Cell, *By Kenya Possessed*.

[14] See C. H. Hopkins, *John R. Mott*.

[15] *Diary of a Dean*, 8 August 1920, 7 February 1921.

[16] Bernard Manning, *Essays in Orthodox Dissent* (1939), p. 144.

[17] Roger Hayden, 'Still at the Cross-roads? Rev. J. H. Shakespeare and Ecumenism', in *Baptists in the Twentieth Century*, ed. K. W. Clements (1983), pp. 31–54.

CHAPTER 6 (pages 100–30)

[1] See, for instance, H. McLachlan, 'Cross Street Chapel in the Life of Manchester', in *Essays and Addresses* (1950), pp. 94–108; G. E. Evans, *Come Wind Come Weather: Chronicle of Tilehouse Street Baptist Church 1669–1969* (1969).

[2] See Ernest Payne, *The Free Church Tradition in the Life of England* (1944); A. C. Underwood, *A History of the English Baptists* (1947); David M. Thompson, *Nonconformity in the Nineteenth Century* (1972); Ernest Payne, *The Baptist Union: a Short History* (1958); *A History of the Methodist Church in Great Britain*, ed. Rupert Davies, A. Raymond George, Gordon Rupp, 3 vols (1965, 1978, 1983); R. E. Davies,

Methodism (1963); R. Tudur Jones, *Congregationalism in England 1662–1962* (1962).

[3] Though Baptists did quite early develop connexional unions of local churches in a way that Congregationalists did not.

[4] See especially Frank Tillyard, 'The Distribution of the Free Churches in England', *Sociological Review*, xxvii (1935), pp. 1–18.

[5] E. Knox, *Reminiscences*, p. 194.

[6] *Christian Century* (April 1925); J. H. Shakespeare, *Churches at the Cross-Roads*, p. 80.

[7] Currie, Gilbert and Horsley, *Churches and Churchgoers* (1977).

[8] Arnold Bennett, *Anna of the Five Towns* (1902).

[9] Contrast Louis Heren, *Growing up Poor in London* (1973), p. 25, and Peter Fletcher, *The Long Sunday* (1958), pp. 41–5.

[10] Paul Rowntree Clifford, *Venture in Faith: the story of the West Ham Central Mission* (1950), p. 29.

[11] Mudie-Smith, pp. 288–9.

[12] Charles Booth, *Life and Labour of the People in London*, 17 vols (1902–3); see Thompson, *Nonconformity*, p. 260.

[13] See *Nonconformity*, pp. 210–12, 227, 238–9.

[14] J. Forsyth, *Rome, Reform and Reaction* (1899), p. 60.

[15] Edmund Gosse, *Father and Son* (repr. 1949), pp. 83–4.

[16] Bernard Lord Manning, 'Some Lapsed Dissenters', *Congregational Quarterly* (April 1951).

[17] Quoted in *The Testing of the Churches*, ed. R. Davies (1982), p. 106.

[18] Chadwick, *Victorian Church*, II, pp. 199–200.

[19] *Contemporary Review* (March 1897); see Thompson, *Nonconformity*, pp. 243–4.

[20] *Rome, Reform and Reaction*, p. 24.

[21] As John Hunter, a Scottish Congregationalist, described it in 1912, Leslie Hunter, *John Hunter, D.D.: a Life* (1921), p. 272.

[22] F. Dillistone, *C. H. Dodd* (1977), p. 36.

[23] Regent's Park, the Baptist college, only moved from London to Oxford in the later 1920s.

[24] Catherine Bramwell-Booth, with Ted Harrison, *Commissioner Catherine* (1983), pp. 58–9.

[25] See A. G. Gardiner, *Life of George Cadbury* (1923); also Richenda Scott, *Elizabeth Cadbury 1828–1931* (1955).

[26] Gardiner, p. 234.

[27] J. L. Hammond, *C. P. Scott of the Manchester Guardian* (1934); H. McLachlan, 'Taylors and Scotts of the *Manchester Guardian*', *Essays and Addresses* (1950), pp. 70–93.

[28] See J. Scott Lidgett, *My Guided Life* (1936); Rupert Davies, ed., *John Scott Lidgett: a Symposium* (1957).

[29] As did the Baptists Robert Rowntree Clifford, his wife and sister, who built up the West Ham Central Mission, an institution as remarkable as Bermondsey; see *Venture in Faith*.

[30] See particularly R. Wearmouth, *The Social and Political Influence of Methodism in the Twentieth Century* (1957); Stephen Koss, *Nonconformity in British Politics* (1975); D. W. Bebbington, *The Nonconformist Conscience: Chapel and Politics 1870–1914* (1982).

[31] Richard Lloyd George, *Lloyd George* (1960), p. 10. For Lloyd George as a religious figure, see, for instance, W. Watkin Davies, *Lloyd George 1863–1914* (1939).

[32] W. L. Bradley, *P. T. Forsyth: the Man and his Work* (1952), p. 43.

[33] *Sunday School Journal* (1906), quoted by Moore, *Pit-Men, Preachers and Politics*, p. 107.

[34] S. D. Waley, *Edwin Montagu* (1964), p. 30.

[35] S. Horne, *Popular History of the*

Free Churches (1903), p. viii.

[36] C. Binsfield, *So Down to Prayers* (1977), p. 200, and see the whole splendid ch. 9, 'No Quest, No Conquest'; also W. B. Selbie, *C. Sylvester Horne* (1920).

[37] *Nonconformity*, p. 272.

[38] *Nonconformist Conscience*, pp. 159–60.

[39] Jack Lawson, *A Man's Life* (1932), p. 69.

[40] H. G. Wood, *Terrot Reaveley Glover* (1953), p. 129.

[41] ibid. p. 67.

[42] 'Who's Who in Methodism 1933', *Methodist Times* (1933).

CHAPTER 7 (pages 131–55)

[1] There is extremely little of a general kind on twentieth-century Roman Catholicism in England: David Mathew, *Catholicism in England* (rev. 1948); Edward Norman, *Roman Catholicism in England* (1985); G. A. Beck, ed., *The English Catholics 1850–1950* (1950); Adrian Hastings, ed., *Bishops and Writers: Aspects of the Evolution of Modern English Catholicism* (1977).

[2] Winston S. Churchill, *Great Contemporaries* (1937), p. 239.

[3] Paul Thompson, *The Edwardians* (1975), p. 104.

[4] The experience of the young Harman Grisewood aged seven, 1913. See *Born Catholics*, ed. F. J. Sheed (1954), pp. 156–7; cf Esther Stokes, in Thea Thompson, *Edwardian Childhoods* (1981), p. 182.

[5] *Letters*, p. 26.

[6] H. Mess, *Industrial Tyneside*, p. 135.

[7] D. G. Jones, *Survey of Merseyside* (1934), p. 337; cp Masterman, in Mudie-Smith, p. 201.

[8] It is not a little revealing that the dedication of the standard history, R. Tudur Jones, *Congregationalism in*

England, is in Welsh.

[9] Garrett Sweeney, *St Edmund's House, Cambridge: the First Eighty Years* (1980), p. 56.

[10] James Sexton, *Sir James Sexton, Agitator* (1936).

[11] See the impression of Ushaw College in Peter Donnelly, *The Yellow Rock* (1950), ch. 4.

[12] *Ushaw Magazine* (1934), p. 179.

[13] F. Sheed, *The Church and I* (1974), p. 83.

[14] See, for instance, Stuart Mews, 'Religion and English Society', pp. 195–6, on the issue of wartime chaplains.

[15] J. Derek Holmes, 'Cardinal Raphael Merry del Val', in *Catholic Historical Review* (1974), pp. 55–64, esp. p. 62.

[16] R. Aubert, *The Church in a Secularised Society* (1978), p. 20; see also M. Larkin, *Church and State in France after Dreyfus* (1974), esp. pp. 118–25, 196–8, for a characterization of Merry del Val.

[17] See John Jay Hughes, *Absolutely Null and Utterly Void* (1968).

[18] J. Derek Holmes, *More Roman than Rome* (1978), pp. 220–1.

[19] ibid. p. 254.

[20] ibid. p. 143, letter to Newman 1870; cf M. Trevor, *A Life of John Henry Newman*, II, *Light in Winter* (1962), p. 481.

[21] Holmes, p. 127.

[22] ibid. pp. 127, 225; see also id. 'English Ultramontanism and Clerical Education', *Clergy Review* (1977), pp. 266–78.

[23] See Michael Williams, *The Venerable English College Rome: a History 1579–1979* (1979).

[24] ibid. p. 161.

[25] For a restrained contemporary discussion of the meaning of ultramontanism by an English Catholic, see F. F. Urquhart's article, in *Encyclopedia of Religion and Ethics*, XII (1921), pp. 505–8.

[26] See Antonia White, *The Hound and the Falcon* (1965).
[27] Fitzgerald, *The Knox Brothers*, p. 140.
[28] M. Ward, *Gilbert Keith Chesterton* (1945), p. 405.
[29] J. J. Kelly, 'On the Fringe of the Modernist Crisis', *Downside Review* (October 1979), pp. 298–9.
[30] N. Abercrombie, *The Life and Work of Edmund Bishop* (1959), p. 406.
[31] *Tablet* (14 February 1925). For von Hügel, see particularly Bernard Holland, ed., *Selected Letters* (1927), and Gwendolen Green, ed., *Letters from Baron von Hügel to a Niece* (1928); also Michael de la Bedoyere, *The Life of Baron von Hügel* (1951); and Lawrence F. Barmann, *Baron Friedrich von Hügel and the Modernist Crisis in England* (1972).
[32] 30 August 1906, *Autobiography and Life of George Tyrrell*, ed. M. D. Petre, 2 vols (1912), II, p. 366.
[33] In the last ten years this has been completely reversed and there is now a spate of publications concerning Tyrrell.
[34] For this Brémond was suspended by Bishop Amigo from exercising his priesthood in the diocese of Southwark. A week later Merry del Val made the suspension universal.
[35] John Root, 'George Tyrrell and the Synthetic Society', *Downside Review* (January 1980), p. 59. For Tyrrell, see esp. *Autobiography and Life*; M. D. Petre, *Von Hügel and Tyrrell* (1937); Ann Louis-David, ed., *Georges Tyrrell: Lettres à Henri Brémond* (Paris, 1971); B. Holland, ed., *Selected Letters*, pp. 165–87; D. G. Schultenover, *George Tyrrell: in Search of Catholicism* (1981). I am much indebted to discussion with Sr Ellen Leonard, and to her *George Tyrrell and the Catholic Tradition* (1982), which she lent me to read prior to publication.

CHAPTER 8 (pages 159–71)

[1] G. K. Chesterton, 'The Ballad of St Barbara' (1922).
[2] J. Galsworthy, *Swan Song* (1928), p. 83.
[3] 27 July 1922; John N. Molony, *The Emergence of Political Catholicism in Italy* (1977), p. 124.
[4] ibid. p. 172.
[5] Quoted in *The Pope is King* by 'Civis Romanus' (1929), pp. 173–4.
[6] *Swan Song*, p. 265.

CHAPTER 9 (pages 172–85)

[1] See, in general, John Oliver, *The Church and Social Order* (1968); Maurice Reckitt, *Maurice to Temple: a Century of the Social Movement in the Church of England* (1947); E. R. Norman, *Church and Society in England*, esp. ch. 7.
[2] Five hundred Anglican priests presented a memorial to Labour MPs in March 1923 congratulating them on forming for the first time the official opposition.
[3] R. Groves, *Conrad Noel and the Thaxted Movement* (1967), p. 252.
[4] H. Maynard-Smith, *Frank: Bishop of Zanzibar* (1926), p. 302.
[5] G. A. Studdert-Kennedy, *Dog-Collar Democracy* (1982).
[6] Remembering that the rail strike of 1913 called forth the 'Song of the Wheels', it is notable that the general strike receives no word of mention in Maisie Ward's biography, an indication of how Chesterton had moved in concern in the meantime.
[7] Edward Norman has certainly endeavoured to make us do so, *Church and Society in England*, esp. pp. 326–36.
[8] Asquith, *Memories and Reflections*, II, p. 232.
[9] E. R. Norman, pp. 335–6.
[10] Adam Fox, *Dean Inge* (1960), p. 203.

[11] J. Oliver, Foreword, p. v.

[12] J. C. W. Reith, *Into the Wind* (1949); Kenneth Wolfe, *The Churches and the British Broadcasting Corporation 1922–1956* (1984). For a critique of Oldham from a Quaker viewpoint, see Cell, *By Kenya Possessed*; and from a Catholic viewpoint (Christopher Dawson's), C. Scott, *A Historian and his World* (1984), p. 133.

[13] Christopher Simon Ford, 'Rev. John Wilcockson 1892–1969: a Case Study on Relations between Church, Politics and Industrial Society', M.Phil. thesis, Univ. Leeds 1985.

[14] Kenneth Ingram, *Basil Jellicoe* (1936).

[15] Lloyd, *Church of England*, p. 325.

[16] R. Speaight, *Hilaire Belloc* (1957), p. 52.

[17] ibid. p. 464.

[18] What a pity the devout could not take at the time as realistic an attitude to Mussolini as can be found in Jack Jones, *My Lively Life* (1928). Jones, a Catholic Labour MP, was not very religious but his judgment on the viciousness of the Duce is in healthy contrast with the pious twaddle of churchmen.

[19] Besides Tawney's major works, see particularly Ross Tervill, *R. H. Tawney and his Times* (1973); John R. Atherton, 'Moral-Theological Aspects of the Work of R. H. Tawney', M.A. thesis, Univ. Manchester 1974.

CHAPTER 10 (pages 186–92)

[1] See, in particular, Bell, *Randall Davidson*.

[2] Besides Oliver and Bell, see Reith's own account, *Into the Wind*, pp. 107–13; and Asa Briggs, *The Birth of Broadcasting* (1961), pp. 378–80.

[3] Ernest Oldmeadow, *Francis Cardinal Bourne* (1944), II, pp. 215–30.

[4] Inge, *Diary of a Dean*, p. 111.

[5] 19 May; Henson, *Retrospect*, II, p. 124. For Henson's personal history across these events, see Chadwick, *Hensley Henson*, ch. 7, 'The Miners'.

[6] *Retrospect*, II, p. 112.

[7] Bishop Auckland had three different Methodist circuits: Wesleyan, United and Primitive.

[8] *Retrospect*, II, pp. 117, 118, 120.

[9] Quoted in George Scott, *The RCs* (1967), p. 85.

[10] D. R. Davies, *In Search of Myself* (1961), p. 87.

[11] Besides Oliver, pp. 88–92, see Iremonger, *William Temple*, pp. 337–44; and A. M. Suggate, 'William Temple's Christian Social Ethics: a Study in Method', D.Phil. thesis, Univ. Durham 1980, pp. 29–37, 302–8.

[12] At the time, of course, the criticism of Temple was that he went too far, not that he did not go far enough; see Suggate, loc. cit.

CHAPTER 11 (pages 193–220)

[1] Holtby, *Eric Graham*, p. 13.

[2] E. Kemp, *Kenneth Escott Kirk*, pp. 51–2.

[3] P. Fitzgerald, *The Knox Brothers*, p. 163.

[4] 5 December 1924; *Letters*, p. 33.

[5] *Reminiscences*, p. 307.

[6] Alan Paton, *Apartheid and the Archbishop*.

[7] It is interesting to note Temple's still rather defensive approach to the cope in 1925; see Iremonger, p. 489.

[8] *Letters*, p. 72.

[9] Lockhart, *Cosmo Gordon Lang*, p. 214.

[10] *Letters*, pp. 96–7.

[11] See, for instance, A. Vidler, *Scenes from a Clerical Life* (1977), p. 31.

[12] Maynard Smith, p. 304.

[13] Bell, *Randall Davidson*, pp. 1250–1.

[14] Henson, *Retrospect*, II, p. 139.
[15] S. Gummer, *The Chavasse Twins* (1963), p. 131.
[16] J. C. Pollock, *A Cambridge Movement*, p. 211.
[17] Douglas Johnson, *Contending for the Faith* (1979), p. 127.
[18] *Retrospect*, II, p. 281.
[19] J. Barnes, *Ahead of his Age* (1979), p. 166.
[20] T. S. Bezzart, 'Bishop Barnes and the Diocese of Birmingham', *Theology* (1945), pp. 14–20.
[21] *Reminiscences*, p. 311.
[22] *Ahead of his Age*, p. 210.
[23] The words of Mervyn Haigh, his chaplain; F. R. Barry, *Mervyn Haigh* (1964), p. 87.
[24] For Henson's position, for once both balanced and constructive, see his 'Open letter to a peer perplexed as to his vote on the Revised Prayer Book', repr. in his *Bishoprick Papers* (1946), pp. 65–75.
[25] *Cosmo Gordon Lang*, p. 305.
[26] Hansard (15 December 1927).
[27] *Reminiscences*, p. 306; *Wake Up England! The Reformation is at Stake*, pamphlet.
[28] *Reminiscences*, p. 323.
[29] It seems that his strangely sudden conversion to disestablishment was in fact prompted in large part by fear of the consequences for the Church of a Labour government; see Chadwick, *Hensley Henson*, pp. 203–6.
[30] See *The Conversations at Malines 1921–1922: Official Documents*, ed. Lord Halifax (1930); Walter Frere, *Recollections of Malines* (1935); Lockhart, *Halifax*; three recent studies are particularly helpful, R. Aubert, 'Cardinal Mercier, Cardinal Bourne and the Malines Conversations', in *One in Christ* (1968), pp. 372–9; R. J. Lahey, 'The Origins and Approach of the Malines Conversations', *Church History* (September 1974), pp. 1–19; id. 'Cardinal Bourne and the Malines

Conversations', in *Bishops and Writers*, ed. A. Hastings (1977), pp. 81–106.
[31] Bede Jarrett would have been the ideal person; not only very irenic, he was also greatly trusted by Cardinal Bourne and English Catholics generally; see Kenneth Wykeham-George, OP, and Gervase Mathew, OP, *Bede Jarrett* (1952).
[32] *Halifax*, p. 327.
[33] *Randall Davidson*, p. 1300.
[34] For a good short account, see J. H. S. Kent, 'The Methodist Union in England, 1932', in Nils Ehrenstrom and Walter Muelder, *Institutionalism and Church Unity* (1963), pp. 195–220; J. M. Turner, 'Methodism in England 1900–1932', in *A History of the Methodist Church in Great Britain*, ed. Davies, III, pp. 309–61.
[35] Robert Currie, *Methodism Divided: a Study in the Sociology of Ecumenicalism* (1968), p. 283.
[36] *Methodist Recorder* (17 January 1929), p. 5, quoted in Currie, p. 299.
[37] *Wesleyan Methodist* (27 November 1924), quoted in Currie, p. 197.
[38] *Methodist Recorder* (26 April 1951).
[39] C. Howard Hopkins, *John R. Mott*.
[40] Tatlow, *Story of SCM*, p. 199.

CHAPTER 12 (pages 221–39)

[1] Darwin was less sure; he was for a time atheist, but by the latter part of his life an agnostic.
[2] Gwen Raverat, *Period Piece* (1952), p. 209.
[3] *The Question of Things Happening: the Letters of Virginia Woolf*, II, *1912–1922* (1976), p. 499.
[4] cf Donald Davie, *A Gathered Church* (1975), p. 6.
[5] See *Studies in the Gospels*, ed. D. E. Nineham (1955), p. viii.

[6] *The Best of Friends: Further Letters to Sydney Carlyle Cockerell*, ed. Viola Meynell (1956), pp. 269–70.

[7] Andrew Boyle, *The Climate of Treason* (1979).

[8] E. R. Dodds, *Missing Persons: an Autobiography* (1977), p. 84.

[9] A. Duff Cooper, *Old Men Forget* (1953), p. oo.

[10] Bertrand Russell, *Autobiography*, I (1967), p. oo.

[11] See J. S. Boys Smith, 'The Interpretation of Christianity in Idealistic Philosophy in Great Britain in the Nineteenth Century', in *Modern Churchman* (1941), pp. 251–73.

[12] See, for instance, G. R. G. Mure, *Idealist Epilogue* (1978).

[13] See James Bradley, 'Hegel in Britain: a Brief History of British Commentary and Attitudes', *Heythrop Journal* (April 1979), pp. 163–82.

[14] Maurice Cowling, *Religion and Public Doctrine in Modern England* (1980), p. 18.

[15] See the discussion in Alan Donagan, *The Later Philosophy of R. G. Collingwood* (1962), pp. 297–307; also John O'Donnell, 'The Impasse of Whitehead's Novel Intuition', *Heythrop Journal* (July 1979), pp. 267–78.

[16] *Modern Churchman*, xi (October 1921), p. 357; cf the discussion in A. M. Ramsey, *From Gore to Temple* (1960). The basic study is now Alan Stephenson, *The Rise and Decline of English Modernism* (1984).

[17] For an extremely penetrating contemporary criticism of the Temple approach, see A. E. Taylor, 'Mens Creatrix', in *Mind* (1918), pp. 208–34; and for an enlightening re-evaluation by the later Temple of his earlier positions, see *Theology* (November 1939), pp. 326–33.

[18] A. S. Dale, *The Outline of Sanity: a Life of G. K. Chesterton* (1982), p. 298.

[19] Prestige, *The Life of Charles Gore*, p. 466.

[20] It was the year that the young Graham Greene, hitherto adhering to 'a dogmatic atheism', was received into the Catholic Church in Nottingham.

[21] C. S. Lewis, *Surprised by Joy* (1950), p. 196.

[22] Bernard Bergonzi, *T. S. Eliot* (1972), p. 112.

[23] To Vanessa Woolf, 11 February 1928; *Letters of Virginia Woolf*, III, *A Change in Perspective, 1923–1928* (1977), pp. 457–8.

[24] *They Stand Together: the Letters of C. S. Lewis to Arthur Greeves (1914–1963)*, ed. Walter Hooper (1979), p. 135.

[25] *Surprised by Joy*, p. 213.

[26] ibid. p. 211.

[27] ibid. p. 215.

[28] Bergonzi, p. 112.

CHAPTER 13 (pages 243–9)

[1] T. Sharp, *A Derelict Area: a Study of the South-West Durham Coalfield* (1935).

[2] Lockhart, *Cosmo Gordon Lang*, p. 405.

[3] *Letters*, p. 99.

CHAPTER 14 (pages 250–61)

[1] Barry, *Mervyn Haigh*, p. 102.

[2] Lockhart, *Cosmo Gordon Lang*, pp. 313, 190.

[3] Described as 'Graceful comments on affairs passing easily from grave to gay', W. R. Matthews, *Memories and Meanings* (1969), p. 387.

[4] *Letters*, pp. 101, 115; Bell's judgment was little less severe, see Lockhart, p. 377.

[5] Ronald Jasper, *Arthur Cayley Headlam: Life and Letters of a Bishop* (1960), p. 357.

[6] Iremonger, p. 37.

[7] ibid. p. 377.
[8] See H. J. Hammerton, *This Turbulent Priest: the Biography of Charles Jenkinson* (1952).
[9] Lloyd, *Church of England*, p. 327.
[10] C. L. Mowat, *Britain between the Wars* (1955), p. 483.
[11] S. A. Quitslund, *Beaudouin: a Prophet Vindicated* (1973).
[12] See the wide-ranging survey of Horton Davies, *Worship and Theology in England: the Ecumenical Century 1900–1965* (1965).
[13] Trevor Beeson, *The Church of England in Crisis* (1973), p. 73.
[14] Michael Ramsey, *The Gospel and the Catholic Church* (1936), p. 175.
[15] See the perceptive analysis by Victor White, 'Doctrine in the Church of England', *Blackfriars* (March 1938), pp. 163–76; (April 1938), pp. 250–63.

CHAPTER 15 (pages 262–72)

[1] See, for instance, Norman Grubb, *Leap of Faith* (1962), pp. 16–18.
[2] T. Leslie Webb, 'The Call to the Ministry in the Methodist Church in Britain', *London Quarterly and Holborn Review* (July 1954), pp. 192–6.
[3] Walter Hollenweger, *The Pentecostals* (1972), pp. 206–17.
[4] For the Elim Pentecostal churches, see Bryan Wilson, *Sects and Society* (1961); also Hollenweger, pp. 197–205.
[5] David Thompson, *Let Sects and Parties Fail: a Short History of the Association of Churches of Christ in Great Britain and Ireland* (1980), p. 127.
[6] E. Payne, *Baptist Union*, pp. 267–8.
[7] F. Tillyard, 'The Distribution of the Free Churches in England', *Sociological Review* (1935), pp. 1–18.

[8] *Minutes of the Methodist Conference 1939*, p. 387.
[9] Davies, *In Search of Myself*, pp. 200–4.
[10] See, for instance, Moore, *Pit-men, Preachers and Politics*, p. 214.
[11] N. Micklem, *Congregationalism Today* (1937), p. 29.
[12] E. L. Allen, 'The Drift to Canterbury', *Congregational Quarterly* (1943), pp. 37–41.
[13] *In Search of Myself*, p. 153.
[14] J. K. Nettlefold, *Unusual Partners* (1956), p. 75.
[15] N. Micklem, *The Box and the Puppets* (1957).
[16] Joost de Blank, *They Became Anglicans*, ed. Dewi Morgan (1959), pp. 30–1.

CHAPTER 16 (pages 273–87)

[1] C. Smyth, *Garbett*, p. 380.
[2] For Hinsley, besides the Life by J. Heenan, see the memoir by Bishop Bell, in *Blackfriars* (May 1943), pp. 165–8; David Mathew, *Catholicism in England*, 2nd edn (1948), new ch.; Thomas Moloney, *Westminster, Whitehall and the Vatican: the Role of Cardinal Hinsley, 1935–43* (1985).
[3] Williams, *The Venerable English College Rome*, pp. 165–6.
[4] M. Derrick, 'The Problem of Vocations in the Roman Catholic Church', *London Quarterly and Holborn Review* (July 1954), pp. 203–7; D. Gwynn, 'Growth of the Catholic Community', in *English Catholics*, ed. G. A. Beck, pp. 410–41.
[5] Gwynn, loc. cit.
[6] C. Smyth, *Garbett*, p. 375.
[7] See A. Hastings, 'Some Reflexions on the English Catholicism of the Late 1930s', in *Bishops and Writers*, pp. 107–25.
[8] M. Ward, *Insurrection versus Resurrection* (1937), p. 546.

[9] *Tablet* (18 December 1937).
[10] Victor Murray, *Congregational Quarterly* (1946), pp. 300–2.
[11] cf C. Smyth, loc. cit.
[12] A. Morey, *David Knowles: a Memoir* (1979), p. 97; see also the review by Eric John, in *New Blackfriars* (1979), pp. 393–5.
[13] Cowling, *Religion and Public Doctrine in Modern England*, p. 155.
[14] See Eric Gill, *Autobiography* (1940); Donald Attwater, *A Cell of Good Living* (1969); R. Speaight, *The Life of Eric Gill* (1966).
[15] R. Hague, *David Jones* (1975), p. 28.

CHAPTER 17 (pages 288–301)

[1] Moorman, *B. K. Cunningham*, p. 161.
[2] ibid. p. 164.
[3] Even so distinguished a Scripture scholar as Streeter at Oxford.
[4] M. Muggeridge, *In a Valley of the Restless Mind* (1938), p. 17.
[5] J. Middleton Murry, in *The Pledge of Peace* (1938), Preface.
[6] *Modern Canterbury Pilgrims*, introd. Stephen Neill (1956), p. 41.
[7] Ian Ramsey, an undergraduate at Christ's (Raven's college 1933–8), was one young exception.
[8] E. L. Allen, in *Religion in Britain since 1900*, ed. G. S. Spinks, James Parkes, and Allen (1952), p. 182.
[9] F. W. Dillistone, *Charles Raven* (1975), p. 275.
[10] See J. D. McCaughey, *Christian Obedience in the University* (1958), pp. 144–5.
[11] Possibly a more significant event than the publication the year before of the heavy, over-prepared, already rather out of date *Report on Doctrine in the Church of England*.
[12] See David Edwards, 'Theology under Dr Vidler', *Theology* (January 1965), pp. 3–14.
[13] A. Vidler, *God's Judgment on Europe* (1940), p. 41; for a Roman Catholic example, see V. White, 'Doctrine in the Church of England', *Blackfriars* (April 1938), pp. 250–63.
[14] See Micklem, *The Box and the Puppets*, pp. 93–9.
[15] *Religion in Britain since 1900*, p. 169.
[16] *Modern Churchman* (June 1939), p. 119.
[17] Arthur Hopkinson, *Pastor's Progress* (1942), p. 187.
[18] McCaughey, p. 124.

CHAPTER 18 (pages 302–8)

[1] R. Rouse and S. C. Neill, *History of the Ecumenical Movement 1517–1948*, 2nd edn (1967).
[2] W. A. Visser 't Hooft, *The Genesis and Formation of the World Council of Churches* (1982), p. 32.
[3] Jackson, *Red Tape and the Gospel*, p. 14.
[4] When Norman Goodall succeeded Paton as secretary of the IMC, a senior member of the Conference of British Missionary Societies thought it wise to take him aside and assure him that he need not assume that 'omnicompetence and omnipotence' were expected of him. N. Goodall, *Second Fiddle* (1979), p. 71.
[5] See, for instance, Visser 't Hooft, 'Dietrich Bonhoeffer and the Self-understanding of the Ecumenical Movement', *Ecumenical Review* (1976), pp. 198–203; id. *The Genesis and Formation of the World Council of Churches*.
[6] See, for instance, Leonard Hodgson's letter to Temple, in *Red Tape and the Gospel*, pp. 232–3.
[7] See Peter Ludlow, 'The International Protestant Community in the Second World War', *Journal of Eccles. History* (1978), pp. 311–62, esp. pp. 335–8, 357–62.

CHAPTER 19 (pages 310–18)

¹ R. Skidelsky, *Oswald Mosley* (1975), p. 359.
² See J. R. C. Wright, *Above Politics* (1974); Richard Gutteridge, *Open Thy Mouth for the Dumb! the German Evangelical Church and the Jews 1879–1950* (1976), ch. 1, 2.
³ A. Rhodes, *The Vatican in the Age of the Dictators 1922–1945* (1973), p. 175.
⁴ As Archbishop Faulhaber remarked just before the concordat was signed, 'Catholics will not understand the Holy Father making a treaty with a Government at a moment when a whole row of Catholic officials are sitting in prison or have been illegally ejected', quoted in Chadwick, 'The Present Stage of the *Kirchenkampf* Enquiry', *Journal of Eccles. History* (1973), p. 38.
⁵ To the Catholic diplomat Ivone Kirkpatrick, quoted by J. S. Conway, 'The Silence of Pope Pius XII', in Charles Delzell, ed., *The Papacy and Totalitarianism between the Two World Wars* (1974), p. 86.
⁶ M. Daphne Hampson, 'The British Response to the German Church Struggle 1933–1939', D.Phil. thesis, Univ. Oxford 1973, p. 30.
⁷ John Stevenson and Chris Cook, *The Slump* (1977), p. 201.
⁸ See Don Sturzo's comment on D. A. Binchy, *Church and State in Fascist Italy*, repr. (1970), Preface, pp. v–vi.
⁹ Rhodes, pp. 74–8.
¹⁰ The figures claimed by the Nationalists after the war: 12 bishops, 5,255 priests, 2,492 monks, 283 nuns, 249 novices.
¹¹ Nathaniel Micklem, *National Socialism and the Roman Catholic Church* (1939).

CHAPTER 20 (pages 319–29)

¹ McCaughey, *Christian Obedience in the University*, p. 70.

² Eric Fenn, *Learning Wisdom*, p. 86.
³ *Christianity and the Social Revolution*, ed. J. Lewis (1935), p. 28.
⁴ See Jasper, *Headlam*, esp. pp. 290–301; and Hampson, 'The British Response to the German Church Struggle'.
⁵ *Guardian* (2 September 1938).
⁶ *Retrospect* II, p. 413.
⁷ See E. C. Hoskyns and Noel Davey, *Crucifixion and Resurrection* (1981), biographical introd. by Gordon Wakefield, pp. 60–7; and James Bentley, 'The Most Irresistible Temptation', *Listener* (16 November 1978), pp. 645–7.
⁸ Robert Erickson, *Theologians under Hitler* (1985).
⁹ Cowling, *Religion and Public Doctrine in Modern England*, p. 73.
¹⁰ Gutteridge, it is to be noted, in due course made very effective amends in 1976 with the publication of his valuable *Open Thy Mouth for the Dumb!*
¹¹ Ulrich Simon, *Sitting in Judgment 1913–1963* (1978), p. 51.
¹² See A. Hastings, 'Some Reflexions on the English Catholicism of the Late 1930s', in *Bishops and Writers*, pp. 107–25; Thomas Moloney, *Westminster, Whitehall and the Vatican*, ch. 2, 'Trial by Fascism'.
¹³ Richard Webster, *Christian Democracy in Italy* (1961), pp. 124–61; see also Gerald Vann, in *Blackfriars* (June 1939), for a contemporary Catholic denunciation of 'the emergence of virulent anti-semitism . . . within the Catholic Church'.
¹⁴ *The Life of Hilaire Belloc*, R. Speaight, p. 464.
¹⁵ Oscar Arnol, 'The Ambivalent Ralliement of La Croix', *Journal of Eccles. History* (1980), pp. 89–106.
¹⁶ C. Hollis, *The Seven Ages* (1974), p. 136.
¹⁷ John Heenan, *Cardinal Hinsley* (1944), p. 56.

[18] J. K. Heydon, *Fascism and Providence* (1937), pp. 153, 142.
[19] Yet the same publishers, Sheed & Ward, could produce the year before a translation of Waldemar Gurion's *Hitler and the Christians* (1938), one of the most important early books on the subject.
[20] Chadwick, *Hensley Henson*, ch. 10, 'The Dictators'.
[21] Constance Babington Smith, *Iulia de Beausobre: a Russian Christian in the West* (1983).

CHAPTER 21 (pages 330–6)

[1] See the authoritative analysis and history of the Pacifist movement, Martin Ceadel, *Pacifism in Britain 1914–1945.*
[2] John S. Conway, 'The Struggle for Peace between the Wars', *Ecumenical Review* (January 1983), pp. 25–40.
[3] A. J. P. Taylor, *English History 1914–1945* (1965), p. 375.
[4] Ceadel, p. 257.
[5] ibid. p. 266.
[6] Jackson, *Red Tape and the Gospel*, p. 76.
[7] F. R. Barry, *Period of My Life* (1970), pp. 127–8.
[8] Ceadel, p. 294.
[9] U. Simon, *Sitting in Judgment*, pp. 70, 74.

CHAPTER 22 (pages 337–45)

[1] The documentation upon this is overwhelming. For an excellent guide, see Victor Conzemius, 'Eglises Chrétiennes et totalitarisme national-socialiste', *Revue d'Histoire Ecclésiastique* (1968), pp. 437–503, 868–948; and Chadwick's more recent survey, 'The Present Stage of the *Kirchenkampf* Enquiry'. The best general books in English are J. S. Conway, *The Nazi Persecution of the Churches 1933–1945* (1968), and Gutteridge, *Open Thy Mouth for the*

Dumb! The latest biography of Niemöller is James Bentley, *Martin Niemöller* (1984). The best books written in England at the time are A. S. Duncan-Jones, *The Struggle for Religious Freedom in Germany* (1938), and Micklem, *National Socialism and the Roman Catholic Church*. Of very great value is Hampson, 'The British Response to the German Church Struggle'.
[2] M. Niemöller, *From U-Boat to Concentration Camp* (1939), p. 281.
[3] See the discussion in Keith Robbins, 'Martin Niemöller: the German Church struggle and English opinion', *Journal of Eccles. History* (1970), pp. 149–70.
[4] See J. R. C. Wright, *Above Parties: the political attitudes of the German Protestant Church leadership 1918–1933* (1947); E. Bethge, *Dietrich Bonhoeffer*, pp. 157, 206 etc.; *Open Thy Mouth for the Dumb!* ch. 2, 3.
[5] A. Frey, *Cross and Swastika*, English edn (1938), Introd., p. 15.
[6] Anon. [Hildebrandt], *Pastor Niemöller and his Creed* (1939), p. 32.
[7] The small movement of Lutheran 'high churchmen' was attempting to remedy this and provided one of the strands in the resistance to Hitler; see J. Bentley, 'British and German High Churchmen in the Struggle against Hitler', *Journal of Eccles. History* (July 1972), pp. 233–49.
[8] Hampson, p. 46.
[9] For Headlam, see esp. Jasper, *Headlam*; for Dorothy Buxton, see Keith Robbins, 'Church and Politics: Dorothy Buxton and the German Church struggle', in *Church Society and Politics*, ed. Baker, pp. 419–33; for both, see Hampson, passim.
[10] Quoted in Hampson, p. 331.
[11] A. J. Sherman, *Island Refuge: Britain and refugees from the Third Reich, 1933–1939* (1973), p. 79; see also Jasper, *George Bell*, pp. 143–4.

[12] P. Ludlow, 'The International Protestant Community in the Second World War', *Journal of Eccles. History* (1978), p. 315.

CHAPTER 23 (pages 346–52)

[1] Hampson, 'The British Response to the German Church Struggle', p. 324.
[2] U. Simon, *Sitting in Judgment*, p. 63.
[3] J. Oliver, *Church and Social Order*, p. 200.
[4] Maurice Bowra's memory was that Hogg 'stood on the simple position that he was for peace and we were for war', *Memories*, p. 353.

CHAPTER 24 (pages 355–63)

[1] C. Babington Smith, *Rose Macaulay* (1972), pp. 156–7; see also pp. 161–70.
[2] See Victor Rothwell, *Britain and the Cold War 1941–1947* (1982).
[3] Gutteridge, *Open Thy Mouth for the Dumb!* p. 227.
[4] W. S. Churchill, *The Second World War*, 6 vols (1948–54), II, p. 567.
[5] 30 October 1940; cf A. J. P. Taylor, *English History 1914–1945*, p. 630.
[6] See Max Hastings, *Bomber Command* (1979), and Freeman Dyson, *Disturbing the Universe* (1979), pp. 19–32.
[7] Alexander McKee, *Dresden 1945* (1982), p. 175.

CHAPTER 25 (pages 364–72)

[1] E. Bethge, *Bonhoeffer*, p. 502.
[2] ibid. p. 648.
[3] G. Zahn, *In Solitary Witness: the Life and Death of Franz Jägerstätter* (1964).
[4] The literature is vast, much of it intensely controversial, stimulated by Rolf Hochhuth's rather unhistorical but unforgettable accusatory drama, *The Deputy* (1963). The basic Vatican documents are published in a number of vols, 1965 on, ed. by the Jesuits, Pierre Blet, Angelo Martini, Burkhart Schneider, and (from vol. III) Robert Graham. The issues are discussed by, among many, Chadwick, 'The Papacy and World War II', *Journal of Eccles. History* (1967), pp. 71–9; V. Conzemius, 'Eglises Chrétiennes . . .'; Guenter Lewy, *The Catholic Church and Nazi Germany* (1964), pp. 295–308; John Conway, 'The Silence of Pope Pius XII', *Review of Politics* (1965), pp. 105–31.
[5] A. C. F. Beales, *The Catholic Church and International Order* (1941), p. 65.
[6] That German protest could be effective is shown very clearly by the remarkable demonstration of six thousand non-Jewish women in Berlin in March 1943, screaming hour after hour for their Jewish husbands; their husbands were spared, see Gutteridge, *Open Thy Mouth for the Dumb!* p. 257.

CHAPTER 26 (pages 373–81)

[1] Moorman, *B. K. Cunningham*, p. 169.
[2] See Peter and Leni Gillman, *Collar the Lot!* (1980), p. 230. It is curious that this well researched book makes no reference whatever to the work of Bell and Paton.
[3] Bell, *Christianity and World Order* (1940), pp. 85, 92.
[4] id. *The Church and Humanity 1939–1946* (1946), p. 56.
[5] See E. Bethge, *Bonhoeffer*, pp. 638–49.
[6] G. Bell, in *Contemporary Review* (October 1945); E. Bethge, *Bonhoeffer*, pp. 661–76.
[7] Jasper, *George Bell*, p. 273.

[8] B. Wasserstein, *Britain and the Jews of Europe 1939–45* (1979); Walter Laqueur, *The Terrible Secret* (1980); Martin Gilbert, *Auschwitz and the Allies* (1981).

[9] Hansard, HL vol. CXXVI, pp. 811–21.

[10] Gilbert, p. 99.

[11] Jasper, p. 276.

[12] Barry, *Mervyn Haigh*, pp. 136–9.

[13] *The Times* (10 February 1944).

[14] Jasper, p. 279.

[15] See A. J. P. Taylor's discussion, *English History 1914–1945*, pp. 648–9, 669–71, 716–18. It is interesting that Taylor avoids any reference to Bell.

[16] U. Simon, *Sitting in Judgment*, pp. 86, 87.

[17] Jasper, p. 284.

[18] Hansard, HL; S. Gummer, *The Chavasse Twins*, p. 159.

[19] Various reports were subsequently produced. First the British Council of Churches, a bland one, ed. by the elderly J. H. Oldham, *The Era of Atomic Power* (1946); then an Anglican one, *The Church and the Atom*, ed. Gordon Selwyn (1948); there was also Ronald Knox, *God and the Atom* (1946).

CHAPTER 27 (pages 382–400)

[1] Graham Greene, *The Lawless Roads* (1939), p. 305.

[2] 8 May 1939 to Dom Bede Griffiths (*Letters of C. S. Lewis*, p. 166).

[3] A. A. Milne, *War with Honour* (1940).

[4] *Hugh Dormer's Diaries* (1947), p. 131.

[5] Keith Robbins, 'Britain, 1940 and Christian Civilization', in *History, Society and the Churches: Essays in Honour of Owen Chadwick*, ed. Derek Beales and Geoffrey Best (1985).

[6] *Letters of C. S. Lewis*, p. 169.

[7] M. Moynihan, ed., *People at War 1939–1945* (1973), p. 52.

[8] Barry, *Mervyn Haigh*, pp. 136–9.

[9] *People at War*, p. 148.

[10] 12 May 1941, *The Letters of Evelyn Underhill*, ed. Charles Williams (1943), p. 308.

[11] *The Light of Experience* (1977), pp. 136–41.

[12] *Two Men of Letters: Correspondence between R. C. Hutchinson and Martyn Skinner, 1957–1974*, ed. Rupert Hart-Davis (1979), p. 43.

[13] J. L. Wilson, 'A Prisoner of the Japanese', *Listener* (24 October 1946), pp. 555–6.

[14] *Hugh Dormer's Diaries*, pp. 139–40, 141, 147, 149.

[15] Alice Cameron, *In Pursuit of Justice: the Story of Hugh Lister and his Friends in Hackney Wick* (1946).

[16] R. Knox, *God and the Atom*, p. 9.

[17] Andrew Boyle, *No Passing Glory* (1955), pp. 254, 259–60.

[18] Nicodemus, *Midnight Hour* (1942), p. 154.

[19] *Born Catholics*, ed. F. J. Sheed, pp. 42–3.

[20] Antonia White, *The Hound and the Falcon*, pp. 151, 162; cf the remarkably similar thoughts of a Frenchwoman writing one month later, 26 May 1942, Simone Weil, *Waiting on God* (1951), p. 58.

[21] *Born Catholics*, p. 38.

[22] E. K. H. Jordan, *Free Church Unity: History of the Free Church Council Movement 1896–1941* (1956).

[23] Mervyn Stockwood, *Chanctonbury Ring* (1982), pp. 50–6.

[24] For Sword of the Spirit, see G. Bell on Cardinal Hinsley, *Blackfriars* (May 1943), pp. 165–8; J. Heenan, *Cardinal Hinsley* (1944), pp. 182–210; Jasper, *George Bell*, pp. 245–55; Christina Scott, *A Historian and his World: a Life of Christopher Dawson* (1984), pp. 137–51; Moloney, *Westminster, Whitehall*

and the Vatican, pp. 186–204; Michael Walsh, *From Sword to Ploughshare: CIIR* (1980), and id. 'Ecumenism in War-Time Britain, the Sword and the Spirit and Religion and Life, 1940–1945', *Heythrop Journal* (1982), pp. 243–58, 377–94.

[25] With Barbara Ward assistant editor, a formidable team.

[26] See page 375.

[27] W. Butterfield, in *Clergy Review* (1942), p. 162; cf pp. 76–9 etc.

[28] M. Walsh, 'Ecumenism in War-Time Britain', pp. 386–91.

[29] C. Smyth, *Garbett*, p. 362.

[30] 27 September 1942, *Chips: the Diaries of Sir Henry Channon*, ed. R. Rhodes James (1967), p. 337.

[31] *Garbett*, p. 293.

[32] See, for instance, Barry, *Mervyn Haigh*, p. 189; G. Hewitt, *Strategist for the Spirit: Leslie Hunter Bishop of Sheffield* (1985), pp. 78–9.

[33] Letter to Cyril Alington, 12 November 1944, *Letters of H. H. Henson*, p. 159.

[34] Lloyd, *Church of England*, p. 460; Edwards, *Leaders of the Church of England*, p. 328.

[35] For a fine tribute by a very distinguished civil servant penned four years later, 'William Temple: a Personal Impression', in John Redcliffe-Maud, *Experiences of an Optimist* (1981), App. II, pp. 171–5.

CHAPTER 28 (pages 403–16)

[1] Kenneth Harris, *Attlee* (1982).

[2] Michael Fogarty, *Christian Democracy in Western Europe 1820–1953* (1957); A. J. Heidenheimer, *Adenauer and the CDU* (1960); R. E. M. Irving, *Christian Democracy in France* (1973); R. Webster, *Christian Democracy in Italy* (1961).

[3] For a stimulating discussion of the 1950s, see *The Age of Affluence*

1951–1964, ed. Vernon Bogdanor and Robert Skidelsky (1970).

CHAPTER 29 (pages 417–35)

[1] Jasper, *Headlam*, p. 331.

[2] 'William Temple and Educational Reform', in R. A. Butler, *The Art of Memory* (1982), pp. 143–63. For a good local Anglican study of the Act and its consequences, see G. W. Hogg, 'The Church and School Education', in *A Social History of the Diocese of Newcastle*, ed. Pickering, pp. 291–312.

[3] The percentage of children in Church of England schools was 22.1 in 1938, 11.8 in 1967; Roman Catholic 7.4 in 1938, 9.3 in 1967. This excludes independent, direct grant, nursery and special schools. Moreover over half the 11.8 per cent were now in 'controlled' schools over which the Church had fairly little say. J. Murphy, *Church, State and Schools in Britain 1800–1970* (1971), p. 125.

[4] C. Smyth, *Garbett*, p. 287.

[5] R. A. Butler, *The Art of the Possible* (1971), p. 124.

[6] ibid. pp. 118–19.

[7] Douglas Thompson, *Donald Soper* (1971), p. 150.

[8] cf E. R. Norman, *Church and Society in England*.

[9] See, for instance, the editorial, 'Church and Statesmanship', *The Times* (28 February 1953), on a speech Garbett made to the United Nations Association in New York; or his speech on the hydrogen bomb (HL 16 March 1955), and *The Times* account of it the next day.

[10] See, for instance, Mervyn Stockwood, *Christianity and Marxism* (1949); or the symposium ed. Donald Mackinnon, *Christian Faith and Communist Faith* (1953).

[11] *The Times* editorial, 28 February 1953.

[12] Daniel Jenkins, *The British, their Identity and their Religion* (1978), p. 74.

[13] Jim Simmons, *Soap-Box Evangelist* (1972), p. 171.

[14] David Bebbington, 'Baptists and Politics since 1914', in *Baptists in the Twentieth Century*, ed. K. W. Clements (1983), pp. 76–95.

[15] Earl of Birkenhead, *Halifax* (1965), p. 589.

[16] L. John Collins, *Faith Under Fire* (1966), pp. 110–13.

[17] See Michael Scott, *A Time to Speak* (1958).

[18] *African Affairs*, xl (April 1950), p. 89.

[19] Besides Collins, *Faith Under Fire*, Scott, *A Time to Speak*, and T. Huddleston, *Naught for Your Comfort* (1956), see J. Peart-Binns, *Ambrose Reeves* (1973); Alan Paton, *Apartheid and the Archbishop*; and A. Hastings, *A History of African Christianity 1950–1975* (1979), pp. 22–8, 103–6, 144–7.

[20] Dillistone, *Into all the World*.

[21] See the obituary notice by Roland Oliver, in *African Affairs* (July 1982), pp. 409–12.

[22] *Faith Under Fire*, pp. 218–21, 187–8.

[23] See 1955 Report upon MRA by the Church Assembly's Social and Industrial Council; together with comments of Maurice Reckitt, one of its authors, in *Theology* (May 1955), pp. 163–6. The Collins/MRA contrast may be observed in John Collins, 'Christianity as a Gospel of Political Action', and Peter Howard (for MRA), 'Christianity as a Gospel of Personal Relationships', both in Victor Gollancz, *Three Views of Christianity* (1962), pp. 11–60, 63–107.

CHAPTER 30 (pages 436–72)

[1] Donald Mackinnon, 'Justice', *Theology* (March 1963), p. 102.

[2] William Purcell, *Fisher of Lambeth* (1969); G. F. Fisher, *The Archbishop Speaks*, ed. E. Carpenter (1958); E. Carpenter, *Cantuar* (1971).

[3] Lloyd, p. 474.

[4] G. F. Townley, 'The Supply and Distribution of Assistant Curates', *Theology* (December 1948), pp. 443–7.

[5] cf C. Smyth, *Garbett*, p. 354; Barry, *Period of My Life*, pp. 184–8.

[6] Beverley Nichols, *A Pilgrim's Progress* (1952), p. 241. By 1958 the vicar of Miss Read's 'Fairacre' was permitted a 'shabby car' despite his stipend being 'very small' (Miss Read, *Storm in the Village* (1958), p. 92).

[7] The Paul Report (1964), p. 23; *Church of England Official Year Book* (1960).

[8] W. Wand, *Changeful Page* (1965).

[9] Paul Welsby, *A History of the Church of England 1945–1980* (1984), pp. 41–4.

[10] E. R. Wickham, *Church and People in an Industrial Society* (1957); Hewitt, *Strategist for the Spirit*.

[11] A. C. Smith, *The South Ormsby Experiment* (1960); id. 'An Experiment in Lincolnshire', *Theology* (February 1960), pp. 63–7.

[12] Though not, perhaps, very successful.

[13] See Mervyn Stockwood, *Chanctonbury Ring*, p. 80. Birley's ambition was to 'have the head of Harwell research station an Old Etonian who learnt Greek at Eton and reads the lesson at Harwell parish church', Anthony Sampson, *Anatomy of Britain Today* (1965), p. 200. For another outstanding headmaster of this period, in this case in fact a priest, Shirley of the King's School, Canterbury, see David L. Edwards, *F. J. Shirley: an Extraordinary Headmaster* (1969).

[14] *Answers to Suicide: presented by the Samaritans to Chad Varah on the occasion of the twenty-fifth anniversary of their founding* (1978).

[15] Peter Jagger, *A History of the Parish and People Movement* (1978).

[16] Eric Mascall was the chief exception. See, for instance, *Corpus Christi*, published opportunely enough in 1955.

[17] *Chanctonbury Ring*, p. 88; cp Joseph McCulloch's ministry at St Mary's, Warwick in the fifties, J. McCulloch, *My Affair with the Church* (1976), ch. 8, 'The Central Altar'.

[18] E. W. Southcott, *The Parish Comes Alive* (1956), p. 132.

[19] 21 January 1946, *Letters*, p. 209; see Basil Willey, *Cambridge and Other Memories 1920–53* (1968).

[20] C. Babington Smith, *Rose Macaulay*, pp. 192–202.

[21] *Official Year Book of the Church of England 1960*, p. 22.

[22] David Paton, ed. *Essays in Anglican Self-Criticism* (1958), p. 131.

[23] Pickering, *A Social History of the Diocese of Newcastle*, p. 122; Jagger, p. 68.

[24] E. R. Wickham, *Church and People in an Industrial Society*, p. 11.

[25] Quoted in *The Paul Report*, p. 68.

[26] See A. A. K. Graham, 'College Chapel 1958–1970', *Worcester College Record* (1983), pp. 24–30.

[27] Oliver Tomkins, *The Life of Edward Woods* (1957).

[28] 'Encyclical Letter to the Faithful in Jesus Christ', *The Lambeth Conference 1958* (1958), 1.17.

[29] Mary Walton, *A History of the Diocese of Sheffield 1914–1977* (1981), pp. 8, 80–1, 144–5.

[30] I wonder whether any other decade could have produced a symposium entitled, *They Became Anglicans* (1959).

[31] One rather odd thing the last two share is the use of the name Imber.

[32] See also Barbara Pym's earlier novel, *Excellent Women* (1952).

[33] *Rose Macaulay*, p. 204.

[34] The number of missionaries sent abroad is a good test of Evangelical fervour. For the seven years 1919–25 Coggan could list only 30 Christian Union men from English universities (21 from Cambridge); for the five years 1929–33 he listed 104 (Cambridge 35, London 44). F. D. Coggan, *Christ and the Colleges* (1934), pp. 216, 227.

[35] Pollock, *A Cambridge Movement*; Arthur Johnston, *The Battle for World Evangelism* (1978); Douglas Johnson, *Contenders for the Faith* (1982).

[36] Frank Colquhoun, *Harringay Story: the Official Record of the Billy Graham Greater London Crusade* (1955), p. 91.

[37] cf F. W. Dillistone's biography, *Into All the World*; as well as Max Warren's own memoirs, *Crowded Canvas* (1974). Dillistone was, like Warren, essentially a 'liberal Evangelical' who tried hard not to lose the movement's confidence by being too liberal. He was Vice-Principal of the London College of Divinity under Donald Coggan in the early fifties, then Dean of Liverpool.

[38] Marley Cole, *Jehovah's Witness* (1956).

[39] *The Times* (4 June 1957), full-page advertisement for Dr Buchman's birthday.

[40] *Baptist Quarterly*, vol. xiii (1951), pp. 92–3.

[41] Kenneth Young, *Chapel* (1972), pp. 208–15.

[42] See, for instance, D. E. Edwards, 'The Villages', *Congregational Quarterly* (1945); and W. G. Latham, 'Truly Rural', ibid. (1956).

[43] Wickham, pp. 167–8.

[44] David Thompson, 'The Older Free Churches', in *The Testing of the Churches*, ed. Rupert Davies.

[45] F. Pagden, 'An Analysis of the Effectiveness of Methodist Churches of varying sizes and types in the Liverpool District', in *Sociological Yearbook of Religion in Britain*, ed. D. Martin (1968), pp. 124–34; Peter Varney, 'Religion in Rural Norfolk', ibid. (1962), pp. 65–77.

[46] Davies, *Methodism*, pp. 142–67.

[47] D. McIllhagga, 'Liturgical Change in the Free Churches', *The Testing of Churches*, ed. R. Davies, pp. 159–74; and Michael Walker, 'Baptist Worship in the Twentieth Century', in *Baptists in the Twentieth Century*, ed. Clements (1983), pp. 21–30.

[48] Douglas Thompson, *Donald Soper* (1971); William Purcell, *Portrait of Soper* (1972).

[49] *Minutes and Yearbook of Methodist Conference 1978*, p. 38.

[50] *Methodist Recorder* (24 July 1960).

[51] W. S. F. Pickering, 'The Present Position of the Anglican and Methodist Churches in the light of available statistics', in *Anglican-Methodist Relations: Some Institutional Factors*, ed. Pickering (1961), p. 31.

[52] For excellent studies of the principal Free Churches in this period, see Thompson, 'The Older Free Churches', and R. Davies, 'Methodism', in *The Testing of the Churches*; and R. Davies, 'Since 1932', in *A History of the Methodist Church*, III, pp. 362–90.

[53] See 1953 Report of Free Church Federal Council, entitled, *The Free Churches and the State*.

[54] Pickering, 'The Present Position'.

[55] C. Driver, *A Future for the Free Churches?* (1962), p. 80.

[56] *Christian World*, one of the most influential Free Church weeklies, ceased publication the next year, 1959. In the 1880s its circulation had been 130 thousand.

[57] For this, see his piece, written jointly with the Catholic layman John Todhunter, 'Full Communion, a tractate towards Church Unity', *Ampleforth Journal*, vol. lxxvii No. 3 (Autumn 1972), pp. 15–26.

[58] *Fisher of Lambeth*, pp. 154–8.

[59] In fact the Church of South India only reunited a minority of Christians in the area, Catholics and the Old Malabar Church being considerably more numerous.

[60] Ian Henderson, *Power Without Glory* (1967), p. 116.

[61] West, *To Be a Pilgrim*.

[62] Goodall, *Second Fiddle*.

[63] *Intercommunion*, ed. Donald Baillie and John Marsh (1952), esp. ch. by Oliver Tomkins, 'Intercommunion in the Ecumenical Movement', pp. 105–37; *Third World Conference on Faith and Order*, ed. Tomkins (1953).

[64] David Paton, *Essays in Anglican Self-Criticism* (1958), p. 13.

[65] By Archbishop Fisher, see Ernest Payne, *Thirty Years of the British Council of Churches 1942–1972* (1972), p. 13.

CHAPTER 31 (pages 473–90)

[1] There is no general study of English Catholicism in this period, except J. Derek Holmes, 'English Catholicism from Hinsley to Heenan', *Clergy Review* (1977), pp. 44–54.

[2] *The Times* (2 November 1942); for a picture of the surviving Catholic poor in the 1950s, see Madeline Kerr, *The People of Ship Street* (1958).

[3] A. E. C. W. Spencer, 'The Demography and Sociography of the Catholic Community in England and Wales', in *The Committed Church*, ed. L. Bright and S. Clements (1966).

[4] Beverley Nichols, *A Pilgrim's Progress*, p. 218.

[5] A. E. C. W. Spencer, 'Demography of Catholicism', *Month* (April 1975), pp. 100–5.

[6] Peter Varney, 'Religion in Rural Norfolk', pp. 65–77.

[7] John Barron Mays, 'New Hope in Newtown', *New Society* (22 August 1963), quoted in *The Paul Report*, pp. 42, 45.

[8] W. Shannon, 'A Geography of Organised Religion in Liverpool', B.A. thesis, Univ. Liverpool 1965; see, in general, Conor Ward, *Priests and People* (1965); Joan Brothers, *Church and School* (1964).

[9] See P. Coman, *Catholics and the Welfare State* (1977).

[10] See Michael Fogarty's highly confident and rather ecumenical assessment of it in 1957, *Christian Democracy in Western Europe 1820–1953*.

[11] For a helpful study of Catholicism in the 1950s, see John Lynch, 'England', in *The Church and the Nations*, ed. Hastings (1959); also the first part of David Lodge, *How Far Can You Go?* (1980).

[12] 'Around a thousand students are now at Oxford and Cambridge, more than three times the figure of twenty years ago', *Tablet* (9 July 1955), p. 29.

[13] *Observer* (16 March 1980).

[14] H. Trevor-Roper, in *New Statesman* (December 1953).

[15] In the judgment of A. J. P. Taylor: 'If future generations want to know what the Second World War was like for English people, they can safely turn to *Sword of Honour*, the greatest work of a great English novelist', *English History 1914–1945*, p. 774.

[16] J. Heenan, *Not the Whole Truth* (1971), pp. 289–304.

[17] F. Sheed, *The Church and I*, p. 305.

[18] It is worth comparing with another book published in England in 1949, which went through six impressions in a year: Monica Baldwin, *I Leap Over the Wall*; the author left a contemplative monastery (Canonesses of St Augustine) in 1941 after twenty-eight years. The experiences of the two authors are quite different, their underlying attitude to the contemplative life almost the same.

[19] cf Monica Furlong, *Merton: a Biography* (1980), paperback (1982), p. 160.

[20] Cecily Hastings, in *Born Catholics*, ed. Frank Sheed, p. 153.

[21] See Andrew Boyle, *No Passing Glory*, ch. 11, 'The Christian'.

[22] For the effect that Spode in the 1950s could have on a Jewish Rabbi, see Lionel Blue, in *The Light of Experience* (1977), pp. 81–6.

[23] 3 July 1956, in *The Letters of Evelyn Waugh*, ed. Mark Amory (1980), p. 473.

[24] Christopher Butler, *Dublin Review*, No. 476 (Summer 1958), pp. 117–18.

[25] Author of *Spiritual Authority in the Church of England* (1953).

[26] Felicitas Corrigan, *Siegfried Sassoon: Poet's Pilgrimage* (1973), p. 180.

[27] Harman Grisewood, in *Born Catholics*, pp. 163–4.

[28] 27 July 1949, in *Letters of Evelyn Waugh*, p. 303.

[29] *Catholicism Today: Letters to the Editor reprinted from The Times* (1949).

[30] Anonymous; it was in fact written by Dom Aelred Graham of Ampleforth.

[31] For much further evidence of such sentiments, see the long correspondence on 'Catholics and Anglicans', *Tablet* (April to September 1955).

[32] There were meetings at Mirfield from 1946 on between Dominicans led by Henry St John and members of the Mirfield community, at Strasbourg in 1950 and London, 1951, between a varied group of theologians including the English Jesuit Maurice Bevenot, and (for

London) George Patrick Dwyer; and in Rome in April 1957, of five Anglican theologians led by Alec Vidler and Richard Hanson, with a Catholic group including Joseph Gill, SJ and Abbot Williams, OSB.

[33] Anthony Kenny, *A Path from Rome* (1985), provides a careful and detailed picture of clerical education and piety in the 1950s.

CHAPTER 32 (pages 491–504)

[1] E. W. Barnes, *Religion and Turmoil* (1949), p. 36.

[2] I might single out a little gem on the Eucharist, the synthesis by a lay theologian of biblical vision, renewed Thomism and the best insights of the liturgical movement, Donald MacKinnon, 'Sacrament and Common Meal', in *Studies in the Gospels* (1955), pp. 201–7.

[3] U. Simon, *Sitting in Judgment*, p. 105.

[4] D. MacKinnon, in *Theology* (January 1962), p. 3.

[5] Sheldon Vanauken, *A Severe Mercy* (paperback edn, 1979), p. 84.

[6] Besides all his own published writing, see the two volumes of correspondence, *Letters*, ed. W. L. Lewis (1966), and *They Stand Together*, ed. Hooper (with important introd. by the ed.); also R. L. Green and W. Hooper, *C. S. Lewis: a Biography* (1974); Humphrey Carpenter, *The Inklings* (1978); Robert Reilly, *Romantic Religion* (1971); Chad Walsh, *C. S. Lewis: Apostle to the Sceptics* (1949); id. *The Literary Legacy of C. S. Lewis* (1979); C. Kilby, *The Christian World of C. S. Lewis* (1965). For a severe criticism both of Lewis's apologetics and of his extensive clientele, see John Beversluis, *C. S. Lewis and the Search for Rational Religion* (1985).

[7] In his inaugural lecture at Cambridge.

[8] See *Religious Broadcasts and the Public* (1955); Kenneth Wolfe, *The Churches and the British Broadcasting Corporation 1922–1956* (1984), pp. 445–54.

[9] Julia Namier, *Lewis Namier* (1971).

[10] E. Evans-Pritchard, *Essays in Social Anthropology* (1962), pp. 29–45.

[11] Barbara Pym catches the change quite well in her novel, *Excellent Women*: the President of the Anthropological Society is a benign old atheist, while the young field worker reading a paper at the meeting he is chairing is a Christian, 'Convert, quite ardent, you know.' Pym was in fact secretary of the International Anthropological Institute.

[12] See, for instance, Professor Meyer Fortes's comments, in *Sacrifice*, ed. M. F. C. Bourdillon and Meyer Fortes (1980), pp. vi–viii.

[13] *New Essays in Philosophical Theology*, p. 35.

[14] J. N. Findlay, *Language, Mind and Value* (1963), p. 206.

[15] Rush Rhees, *Ludwig Wittgenstein: Personal Recollections* (1981), p. 94, quoted in Fergus Kerr, OP, 'Wittgenstein and Theological Studies', *New Blackfriars* (December 1982), pp. 500–8; see also W. Donald Hudson, *Wittgenstein and Religious Belief* (1975); D. Z. Phillips, 'Wittgenstein's Full Stop', in *Perspectives on the Philosophy of Wittgenstein*, ed. Irving Block (1981), pp. 179–200.

[16] See, for instance, R. F. Atkinson's survey of British philosophy, in *The Twentieth Century Mind: 1918–1945*, ed. C. B. Cox and A. E. Dyson (1972), pp. 106–45.

[17] E. Rothenstein, *Stanley Spencer* (1962).

[18] See 'Epstein's Lazarus, preached in

New College Chapel, Oxford', in Austin Farrer, *The End of Man* (1973), pp. 25–9.
[19] *Tablet* (1 March 1980); Robert Melville, *The Imagery of Graham Sutherland*; Douglas Cooper, *The Work of Graham Sutherland* (1962); Edward Sackville-West, *Graham Sutherland* (1945).
[20] As well as a form of the Beatitudes composed by Sir Arthur Bliss.

CHAPTER 33 (pages 507–18)

[1] Frank Parkin, *Middle Class Radicalism* (1968).
[2] Sexual intercourse began
  In nineteen sixty-three,
  Between the end of the Chatterley ban
  and the Beatles' first LP.
    (Philip Larkin)
For a suave, Olympian view of such developments, see C. P. Snow, *The Sleep of Reason* (1968).
[3] In a speech in Birmingham in January 1964.
[4] Quoted in Christopher Booker, *The Neophiliacs* (1969), p. 256.
[5] 'The spontaneity and immediacy of Communitas – as opposed to the jural-political character of structure – can seldom be maintained for very long' (Victor Turner, *The Ritual Process* (1969), p. 132).

CHAPTER 34 (pages 519–31)

[1] Peter Hebblethwaite, *John XXIII* (1984); the best study at the time was E. E. Y. Hales, *Pope John and his Revolution* (1965).
[2] *The Phenomenon of Man*, p. 287.
[3] William Purcell, *Fisher of Lambeth*, p. 271.
[4] Mervyn Stockwood, *Chanctonbury Ring*, pp. 100–1.
[5] C. Smyth, *Garbett*, p. 327.
[6] *Fisher of Lambeth*, p. 273.
[7] ibid. p. 288.

[8] Michael Ramsey, *Canterbury Pilgrim* (1974), p. 174.
[9] J. Moorman, *Vatican Observed; The Second Vatican Council: Studies by Eight Anglican Observers*, ed. B. Pawley (1967).
[10] Bernard and Margaret Pawley, *Rome and Canterbury* (1974), p. 308.
[11] *Documents of Vatican II*, ed. Walter Abbott, SJ (1966), 5 vols, ed. J. Vorgrimler (1969); A. Hastings, *A Concise Guide to the Documents of the Second Vatican Council*, 2 vols (1968, 1969).
[12] *Anglican/Roman Catholic Dialogue*, ed. Alan Clark and Colin Davey (1974), p. 2.

CHAPTER 35 (pages 532–60)

[1] M. Ramsey, *The Christian Priest Today* (1972), p. 100.
[2] Quoted by Trevor Beeson, *The Church of England in Crisis*, (1973), p. 174.
[3] Leslie Paul, *The Training and Deployment of the Clergy*, p. 298; *Church of England Yearbook 1972*.
[4] John Robinson, *Honest to God* (1963); David Edwards, *The Honest to God Debate* (1963).
[5] *Honest to God*, pp. 8, 17–18.
[6] Donald MacKinnon, 'Inter-communion: a comment', *Theology* (February 1962), p. 56.
[7] Peter Jagger, *Parish and People*.
[8] Leslie Paul, *A Church by Daylight* (1973), p. 178.
[9] Nicholas Stacey, *Who Cares?* (1971).
[10] Jagger, p. 107.
[11] For an early expression of a positive English Catholic response, see A. Hastings, 'Intercommunion', *One in Christ* (January 1971), pp. 14–27, and 'Anglican/Roman Catholic Relations and Growth in Intercommunion', ibid. (January 1973), pp. 24–34.

[12] O. Tomkins, *A Time for Unity* (1964), p. 8.

[13] *Unity Begins at Home: a Report from the First British Conference on Faith and Order, Nottingham 1964*, p. 15.

[14] ibid. p. 45; also pp. 77–8.

[15] David Edwards, *Movements into Tomorrow: a Sketch of the British SCM* (1960), Preface.

[16] Janet Lacey, *A Cup of Water* (1970).

[17] Shirley du Boulay, *Cicely Saunders: the Founder of the Modern Hospice Movement* (1984).

[18] Don Cupitt, 'Four Arguments against the Devil', *Theology* (October 1961), pp. 413–15; see also ibid. (January 1962).

[19] A perceptive sociologist observer could remark in 1968: 'the self-liquidation of the theological enterprise is undertaken with an enthusiasm that verges on the bizarre', Peter Berger, *A Rumour of Angels*, p. 25.

[20] Donald MacKinnon, *The Stripping of the Altars* (1969), p. 11; see also his very important 1970 paper, 'Lenin and Theology', and its 1978 Postscript, in id. *Explorations in Theology* No. 5 (1979), pp. 11–29.

[21] Jagger, pp. 116–17.

[22] Douglas Brackenridge, *Eugene Carson Blake* (1978).

[23] Eugene Carson Blake, 'Uppsala and Afterwards', in *The Ecumenical Advance: a History of the Ecumenical Movement*, II, 1948–1968, ed. Harold E. Fey (1970), pp. 413–18.

[24] James Simpson and Edward Story, *The Long Shadows of Lambeth* (1969), pp. 269–70.

[25] Kenneth Slack, *The British Churches Today* (1969 edn), p. xi.

[26] See esp. John M. Turner, *Conflict and Reconciliation: Studies in Methodism and Ecumenism in England 1740–1982* (1985), ch. 10,

'The Walk to the Paradise Garden'.

[27] Ronald Preston, in *The Testing of the Churches*, ed. Davies, p. 83.

[28] The smack in the face was of course delivered equally to Archbishop Ramsey.

[29] Pickering, *A Social History of the Diocese of Newcastle*, p. 108.

[30] *Church of England Yearbook* 1979.

[31] Colin Buchanan, in *Evangelicals Today*, ed. John C. King (1973), p. 61.

[32] James Packer, in ibid., pp. 15–16

[33] For some Evangelicals nevertheless all this was the beginning of disaster; see, for instance, *The Evangelical Succession in the Church of England*, ed. D. N. Samuel (1979), a work sponsored by the Protestant Reformation Society; in particular D. N. Samuel, 'The Challenge of the Twentieth Century'.

[34] *Keele '67: the National Evangelical Anglican Congress Statement*, ed. Philip Crowe (1967), p. 8; see also the preparatory papers, *Guidelines: Anglican Evangelicals Face the Future*, ed. J. I. Packer (1967).

[35] *Keele '67*, p. 35. However ten years later they were less sure of this, see *The Nottingham Statement* (1977), p. 24.

[36] Peter Staples, *The Church of England 1961–1980* (1981).

[37] David Edwards, *Ian Ramsey, Bishop of Durham: a Memoir* (1973).

[38] id. *The British Churches Turn to the Future* (1973).

[39] The best study is Richard Quebedeaux, 'Charismatic Renewal: the origins, development and significance of neo-Pentecostalism as a religious movement in the United States and Great Britain 1901–74', D.Phil. thesis, Univ. Oxford 1975.

[40] Clifford Hall, *West Indian Migrants and the London Churches* (1963); Malcolm Calley, *God's*

People: *West Indian Pentecostal
Sects in England* (1965).
⁴¹ Hollenweger, *The Pentecostals*,
p. 188.
⁴² Roswith Gerloff, 'Black Christian
Communities in Birmingham: the
problem of basic recognition', in
Religion in the Birmingham Area, ed.
Bryman, pp. 61–84.
⁴³ Geoffrey Nelson, 'Religious
Groups in a Changing Social
Environment', in *Religion in the
Birmingham Area*, pp. 45–60.

CHAPTER 36 (pages 561–79)

¹ Spencer, 'Demography of
Catholicism'. For a stimulating and
well documented discussion of
English Catholicism at this period,
see Bernard Sharratt, 'English Roman
Catholicism in the 1960s', in *Bishops
and Writers*, ed. Hastings, pp.
127–58; also John Coventry,
'Roman Catholicism', in *The Testing
of the Churches*, ed. Davies, pp.
3–31; G. Scott, *The RCs*.
² cf a pamphlet issued by the Free
Church Federal Council in 1959,
quoted by James Murphy, *Church,
State and Schools in Britain
1800–1970* (1971), pp. 121–2.
³ *Church, State and Schools*, pp.
121–5.
⁴ John Heenan, *A Crown of Thorns*,
p. 326.
⁵ *Christian Unity: a Catholic View*,
ed. John Heenan (1962). For Heenan
as ecumenist, see esp. Alberic
Stacpoole, OSB, 'Ecumenism on the
Eve of the Council: Anglican/Roman
Catholic Relations', *Clergy Review*
(September 1984), pp. 300–6;
(October 1984), pp. 333–8; and
'Anglican/Roman Catholic Relations
after the Council 1965–1970', ibid.
(February 1985), pp. 55–62; (March
1985), pp. 91–8.
⁶ David Abner Hurn, *Archbishop

Roberts, SJ: his Life and Writings*
(1966), ch. 10.
⁷ Michael de la Bedoyere had been
editor of the *Catholic Herald*
1934–62 when he was edged out as
too progressive. He then founded his
own monthly newsletter, *Search*,
which lasted until July 1968 and
attracted considerable support
among progressive English Catholics.
⁸ Frank Sheed, *The Church and I*,
p. 304.
⁹ But they were, a year later, in David
Lodge's London-based treatment of
much the same themes, *The British
Museum is Falling Down* (1965).
¹⁰ See the 'how to do it' pamphlets on
both subjects (1970–1), with
introductions by Patrick Keegan and
prefaces from Heenan.
¹¹ C. Scott, *A Historian and his
World*, p. 205.
¹² *Daily Telegraph*, 7 November
1964.
¹³ *Letters of Evelyn Waugh*, p. 639;
see also Tolkien writing in 1968, *The
Letters of J. R. R. Tolkien*, ed.
Humphrey Carpenter (1981), p. 393.
¹⁴ Adrian Morey, *David Knowles*,
p. 112.
¹⁵ N. Kokosalakis, 'The Impact of
Ecumenism on Denominationalism:
a sociological study of five Christian
communities in Liverpool', Ph.D.
thesis, Univ. Liverpool 1969, p. 113.
¹⁶ See p. 530.
¹⁷ *Anglican/Roman Catholic
Dialogue*, ed. Clark and Davey; see
also the lengthy analysis of the
Report by H. R. McAdoo, in J. C. H.
Aveling, D. M. Loades and H. R.
McAdoo, *Rome and the Anglicans*
(1982), pp. 211–73; A. Hastings,
'Malta: Ten Years After', *One in
Christ* (1978), pp. 20–9.
¹⁸ Anglican Roman Catholic
International Commission,
established 1969.
¹⁹ The Decree on Ecumenism of the
Council declared (a.13) that among
the communions separated from

Rome the Anglican 'occupies a special place'.

[20] Its distribution to all members of the Lambeth Conference in 1968 was important in this.

[21] T. Eagleton and B. Wicker, ed., *From Culture to Revolution* (1968); p. 3. For *Slant*, see B. Wicker, *First the Political Kingdom* (1967); Donald Nicholl, 'A Layman's Journal', *Clergy Review* (August 1966); John Kent, 'From Temple to *Slant*: aspects of English political theology 1945–70', *Epworth Review* (January 1977), pp. 88–98; Peter J. Gee, ' "Slant" and Christian Radicalism of the 1960s', unpublished paper, Wolfsen College, Oxford, March 1979; Peter McCaffery, 'Catholic Radicalism and Counter-Radicalism: a comparative study of England and the Netherlands', D.Phil. thesis, Univ. Oxford 1980, pp. 47–62.

[22] See p. 392–7.

[23] For first accounts, see the newspapers, such as *The Times* (21 December); including special article by Geoffrey Moorhouse, *Guardian*; there is a full page art. by Davis, in *Observer Review* (1 January 1967). C. Davis, *A Question of Conscience*, was published later in 1967.

[24] From his original press statement, reprinted in *A Question of Conscience*, p. 16.

[25] In the neurotic reaction of ecclesiastical authority, Fr Herbert McCabe, OP was actually suspended from his editorship of *New Blackfriars* (and even briefly from the priesthood) for admitting this in an editorial ably rebutting Davis's real challenge. See S. Clements and M. Lawlor, *The McCabe Affair* (1967).

[26] See, for instance, Geoffrey Moorhouse, 'Catholics at the Crossroads', *Guardian* (29 October 1964); Ivan Yates, 'The Roman Catholic Crisis', *Observer Review* (5 March 1967); and many articles in

Herder Correspondence (1960s).

[27] The same week, *Tablet* published a similar dissenting statement, signed by seventy-five distinguished lay Catholics. Shortly afterwards Burns Oates (hitherto 'Publishers to the Holy See') published a symposium wholly opposed to the encyclical, *On Human Life*, P. Harris and Others (1968). For an even earlier record of dissent, see *The Pope, the Pill and the People*, ed. Brian Murtough (1968).

[28] *Sunday Times*, 6 October 1968.

[29] Anthony Burgess, *The Worm and the Ring* (1961), p. 265. For a fictional picture of the way the post-conciliar climate affected the religious orders, see Rumer Godden, *In This House of Brede* (1969); and also, more fantastically, Muriel Spark, *The Abbess of Crewe* (1974).

[30] *A Crown of Thorns*, p. 389.

[31] ibid. pp. 381–90. A painful example of the quality of Heenan's later leadership is the review he wrote of the symposium, *The Experience of Priesthood*, in *Catholic Herald* (19 July 1968); he denounced the anonymity of contributors while keeping absolutely silent about the Preface written by Archbishop Hurley; he attacked the editor as 'obviously immature', the publisher (Darton, Longman and Todd) as 'irresponsible', one of the contributors as 'mad'. Despite the very positive approach to the priesthood of the majority of writers, and the sheer pain in the accounts of others, Heenan's comments were bitterly scornful. For the more sympathetic Heenan of earlier years, see Anthony Kenny, *A Path from Rome*, ch. 13, 14; and for a pondered statement of what the cardinal thought in his last years, see Heenan, 'Modern Theology and the Care of Souls', *Times Literary Supplement* (22 December 1972), pp. 1551–2.

CHAPTER 37 (pages 580–6)

[1] Spencer, 'Demography of Catholicism'.
[2] *New Cambridge Modern History*, XIII, *Companion Volume* (1979), p. 317.
[3] John Naughton, in *TLS* (21 December 1979), p. 148.

CHAPTER 38 (pages 589–601)

[1] As a matter of fact the prayer in question has nothing to do with St Francis but was the anonymous composition of someone in the twentieth century: it was an extremely popular religious text of the 1960s and 1970s, a verbal symbol of the contemporary spiritual climate.
[2] *Observer*, 28 March 1982.
[3] Anthony Holden, in ibid. (20 July 1980).
[4] Milton Friedman, 'The Myth of Equality', *Listener* (10 April 1980).
[5] *The Times*, 14 March 1980.
[6] Joanna Mack and Stewart Lansley, *Poor Britain* (1985).

CHAPTER 39 (pages 602–29)

[1] For a contemporary survey of English religion in the 1970s, see David Perman, *Change and the Churches: an Anatomy of Religion in Britain* (1977).
[2] The nouns are borrowed from Betjeman.
[3] R. Towler and A. Coxon, *The Fate of the Anglican Clergy* (1979), p. 187. There were however an increasing number of part-time theological training courses for non-stipendiary priests.
[4] See *Minutes and Yearbook of the Methodist Conference*, for various years.
[5] See *Yearbook of the United Reform*

Church, for 1973, 1984–5.
[6] Spencer, 'Demography of Catholicism'.
[7] ibid.; also id. 'Alienation Reconsidered: Catholicism in England and Wales', unpublished paper, BSA Conference on the Sociology of Religion 1979.
[8] *Tablet* (30 July 1983), p. 739; see also Spencer, 'Demography of Catholicism'.
[9] *Tablet* (28 June 1980), p. 638. Nuns were declining the most, priests the least; see annual figures, in *Catholic Directory*.
[10] Lloyd, *Church of England*, p. 148.
[11] Consider also the figures of pupils in maintained schools, January 1976:

	C. of E.	RC
Primary	835,223	470,302
Secondary	138,976	328,658

[12] *UK Christian Handbook 1985/86*, ed. Peter Brierley (1984). The extreme in contrasts is provided by percentages of total Church membership in Dorset and Merseyside:

	C. of E.	RC
Dorset	70%	9%
Merseyside	14%	71%

[13] See, for instance, Christopher Wansey, *The Clockwork Church* (1978), pp. 47–79.
[14] *Church and State: Report of the Archbishop's Commission 1970* (generally known as the Chadwick Report, since the commission's chairman was Owen Chadwick).
[15] Hansard HC.
[16] The case for disestablishment is put in 1980s terms by Tony Benn, Eric James and Bishop Mark Santer, in *The Church and the State*, ed. Donald Reeves (1984), ch. 5, 7, 9; and Peter Cornwell, *Church and Nation* (1983).
[17] John S. Peart-Binns, *Defender of the Church of England: the Life of Bishop R. R. Williams* (1984).
[18] The best book against was probably *Man, Woman and*

Priesthood, ed. Peter Moore (1978).
[19] John Poulton, *Dear Archbishop* (1976); see also the critique by Herbert McCabe, *New Blackfriars* (November 1975), editorial, pp. 482–3.
[20] A. Stacpoole, OSB, 'Intent on Intercommunion', *Ampleforth Journal* (1978), pp. 42–56.
[21] The Bishop of Norwich, a noted Evangelical, had done the same the year before. The voices of Protestant objectors crying, 'Shame on Maurice Wood', were drowned by a great crowd singing, 'Ave Maria'. The Catholic Bishop of East Anglia, Alan Clark, preached the address. *English Churchman* (15 June 1979).
[22] Quoted in J. Bentley, *Cry God for England*, p. 24.
[23] See esp. the study of a rural diocese, Leslie J. Francis, *Rural Anglicanism: a Future for Young Christians?* (1985).
[24] See, for instance, his contributions to Urbana Inter-Varsity Missionary Conventions, 1970, 1973, each attended by several thousand people; John Stott and others, *Christ the Liberator: Urbana 70* (1971); David M. Howard, ed., *Jesus Christ: Lord of the Universe; Hope of the World: Urbana 73* (1974); *Facing the New Challenges: the Message of PACLA* (1978); John Stott, ed., *Gospel and Culture: Papers of the 1978 Consultation on Gospel and Culture* (1979).
[25] Arthur Johnston, *The Battle for World Evangelism* (1978), pp. 299–300.
[26] ibid. pp. 324–32.
[27] Pan African Christian Leadership Assembly.
[28] *Battle for World Evangelism*, p. 301; see John Stott's later major work, *Issues Facing Christians Today* (1985).
[29] John Stott, in *The Nottingham Statement*, Preface; see also 3 vols preliminary papers, Gen. Ed. John

Stott, *Obeying Christ in a Changing World* (1977).
[30] See *Nottingham Statement*, pp. 44–5; and J. Charley, 'The Roman Catholic Church', in *Obeying Christ in a Changing World*, II, pp. 143–59.
[31] For David Watson, an outstanding figure in the renewal movement, at once Evangelical, ecumenical and charismatic, who died of cancer in 1984, see his autobiography, *You Are My God* (1982); and *David Watson: a Portrait by his Friends*, ed. Edward England (1985).
[32] For a remarkable ecumenical study of the relations of Evangelicals, Pentecostals and Catholics, by the English charismatic leader, see Michael Harper, *This is the Day: a Fresh Look at Christian Unity* (1979).
[33] Thus, in Leeds, of twenty-four or twenty-five congregations it affected three: H. Towler and A. Coxon, *The Fate of the Anglican Clergy*, p. 198.
[34] Andrew Walker, *Restoring the Kingdom: the Radical Christianity of the House Church Movement* (1985).
[35] David Clark, *Between Pulpit and Pew* (1981), esp. pp. 81–8.
[36] A good way of studying contemporary Methodism is through the pages of *Epworth Review*, founded 1974, with its strongly practical orientation.
[37] A Raymond George, 'The Changing Face of Methodism: 1. The Methodist Service Book', *Proceedings of Wesley Hist. Soc.* (October 1977), pp. 65–72.
[38] See J. M. Turner, *Conflict and Reconciliation*, pp. 194–232.
[39] Simmons, *Soap-Box Evangelist*, p. 172.
[40] B. Manning, *Essays in Orthodox Dissent*, p. 148.
[41] David L. Edwards, *The British Churches Turn to the Future* (1973).
[42] John Huxtable regarded this as the 'peak moment' of the whole URC, id. 'The First Year in the United

Reformed Church', *Epworth Review*
(1974), pp. 48–51.
[43] David Thompson, *Let Sects and
Parties Fail: a Short History of the
Association of Churches of Christ in
Great Britain and Ireland* (1980).
[44] Kenneth Woollcombe, *The Failure
of the English Covenant* (1983).
[45] Lesslie Newbigin, *Unfinished
Agenda*, pp. 250, 249.
[46] Goodall, *Second Fiddle*, pp.
133–47.
[47] *Tablet* (22 September 1984),
p. 930.
[48] See, for instance, R. T. Beckwith,
G. E. Duffield and J. I. Packer, *Across
the Divide* (1977).
[49] A. Stacpoole, OSB, 'Intent on
Intercommunion', *Ampleforth
Journal* (1978), pp. 42–56.
[50] *Tablet* (7 January 1984).
[51] *Catholic Herald* (7 September
1978).
[52] J. H. Shakespeare, *Churches at the
Cross-Roads*, pp. 200–1.

CHAPTER 40 (pages 630–48)

[1] See, for instance, the story of a
particular parish: John Leslie,
'Religious Ideology in a North
Midlands Parish', unpublished paper,
Sociology of Religious Study Group,
March 1979.
[2] Frank Sheed, *The Church and I*,
p. 103.
[3] cf 'The Predicament of the Catholic
Church Today', in Hastings, *The
Faces of God*, pp. 24–46.
[4] For Catholic schools in this period,
see Michael Hornsby-Smith, *Catholic
Education: the Unobtrusive Partner*
(1978).
[5] See A. Hastings, 'The Priesthood
Today', *Tablet* (8, 15 May 1976); J.
Moore, 'The Catholic Priesthood',
*Sociological Yearbook of Religion in
Britain*, No. 8 (1975), ed. M. Hill,
pp. 30–60.

[6] It was going on world-wide:
between 1967 and 1972 the Jesuits
declined by 11.7; Franciscans 14.3;
Dominicans 16.7; Christian Brothers
18.3 (percentages); cf *New Forms of
Ministry in Christian Communities*
(1974).
[7] The facts (here and elsewhere in this
chapter) are from various edns of
Catholic Directory. In regard to
Friars Minor, it may be noted that
they were having to withdraw from
other parts of the country too; thus in
1978 they closed four important
parishes including the only two
remaining in the archdioceses of
Birmingham and Liverpool: St Mary
of the Angels, Walsall, and St Mary
of the Angels, Fox Street, Liverpool.
See *Tablet* (5 January 1980), p. 22.
[8] At the end of our period Hexham
and Newcastle had 38 priests of
religious orders to 265 thousand
Catholics; Westminster still had 469
to 460 thousand.
[9] A good deal of disintegration was
already in progress, as seen both
from the statistics of decline, and
from the sort of picture David Lodge
provides in the final parts of *How Far
Can You Go?*
[10] Peter McCaffery, 'Catholic
Radicalism and
Counter-Radicalism', D.Phil. thesis,
Univ. Oxford 1981, p. 107, the
source for much in this chapter.
[11] Bill McSweeney, *Roman
Catholicism* (1980), pp. 219–21.
[12] For example, the Faith Association
(chairman Fr Francis Ripley, chief
mover Fr Edward Holloway); Paul
Crane, SJ, ed. *Christian Order*, the
most influential of very right-wing
Catholic journals in Britain; and,
most extreme, *The Keys of Peter*, ed.
Ronald King.
[13] Fr Baker refused for several years
either to use the new mass rite or
leave his presbytery. The case
produced considerable publicity and
conservative Catholics travelled long

distances to attend Fr Baker's
Tridentine mass.

[14] McCaffery, pp. 135–84, analyses
this very well.

[15] See, symbolically, the meeting *Pro
Ecclesia et Pontifice* on 20 February
1982 in Porchester Hall in
preparation for the Pope's visit,
chaired by Sir John Biggs-Davison,
MP, and addressed among others by
Professor Elizabeth Anscombe; the
'Committee of Honour' was
impressive: while the only priests to
be included were Paul Crane and
Michael Clifton, of earls, countesses,
papal dukes, princes, MPs, and some
of the most distinguished names in
recusant history, there were many;
also Auberon Waugh.

[16] For example, Michael Hollings,
Living Priesthood (1977); Michael
Winter, *Mission or Maintenance*
(1973), and *Mission Resumed*
(1979); A. Hastings, *The Faces of
God* (1975), and *In Filial
Disobedience* (1978); also many
editorials of Michael Richards, in
Clergy Review (e.g. May 1980).

[17] Peter Milward, SJ, *Tablet* (18, 25
December 1976).

[18] Richard Quebedeaux,
'Charismatic Renewal', D.Phil.
thesis, Univ. Oxford 1975.

[19] See his monastic reflections:
Cardinal George Basil Hume,
Searching for God (1977).

[20] See the anthology put together in
Edward Yarnold, *They Are in
Earnest: Christian Unity in the
Statements of Paul VI, John Paul I,
John Paul II* (1982).

[21] George Moyser, 'Patterns of Social
Representation in the National
Pastoral Congress', *Month* (March
1980), pp. 95–101; Michael
Hornsby-Smith and Elizabeth
Cordingly, *Catholic Elites: a Study of
the Delegates to the National
Pastoral Congress* (1983); cp
Hornsby-Smith and Raymond Lee,
*Roman Catholic Opinion: a Study of

Roman Catholics in England and
Wales* (1979).

[22] *Liverpool 1980: Official Report of
National Pastoral Congress* (1981);
P. Jennings, 'An Assessment of the
National Pastoral Congress', *Clergy
Review* (July 1980), pp. 233–9;
Michael Gaine, *Month* (December
1979), pp. 413–17; (June 1980), pp.
185–8; (September 1980), pp.
291–3; M. Hornsby-Smith, 'Two
Years After: Reflections on Liverpool
1980', *New Blackfriars* (June 1982),
pp. 252–60.

[23] Anglican–Roman Catholic
International Commission 1981, *The
Final Report* (1982).

[24] ibid. pp. 99–100.

[25] See the documentation, 'Pope John
Paul II in Britain', in *One in Christ*
(1982), pp. 260–77.

[26] J. H. Newman, *Letters and
Diaries*, XXIV (1869), p. 326.

CHAPTER 41 (pages 649–59)

[1] *The Myth of God Incarnate*, ed.
John Hick (1978), p. 202; cp
Professor Maurice Wiles, 'It is not
possible with consistency to ascribe
an absolute authority to a particular
section of experience within the
world, such as the life of Jesus', *The
Remaking of Christian Doctrine*
(1974), p. 48; cf Hick, *God and the
Universe of Faith* (1973); Dennis
Nineham, *The Use and Abuse of the
Bible* (1976); John Kent, *The End of
the Line?* (1978, reissue 1982).

[2] MacKinnon, *Explorations in
Theology*, p. 29.

[3] See, for example, C. F. D. Moule,
The Origin of Christology (1977);
*Suffering and Martyrdom in the New
Testament*, ed. W. Horburt and B.
McNeil (1981); or *Jesus and the
Politics of his Time*, ed. C. Moule
and E. Bammel (1984).

[4] At the level of top NT scholarship,
a comparison between D. Nineham,

Saint Mark (1963), and Martin Hengel, *Studies in the Gospel of Mark* (1985), should make clear the very considerable reversal of seemingly assured anti-conservative positions by the 1980s.
5 See Edward Norman, 'The Denigration of Capitalism', lecture delivered at Shell Centre, May 1978; perhaps the best expression of his thought. See also, besides Reith Lectures, his major study, *Church and Society 1700–1970*.
6 For various replies to Norman, see *Christian Faith and Political Hopes*, ed. H. Willmer (1979); 'A Wreath for Norman', *Christian Action Journal* (Spring 1979); Michael Dummett, *Catholicism and the World Order* (1979); a review, *Tablet* (7 April 1979).
7 Michael Walsh, *From Sword to Ploughshare*.
8 Sir Geoffrey Jackson, *People's Prison* (1973).
9 Sheila Cassidy, *Audacity to Believe* (1977).
10 Trevor Beeson, *Britain Today and Tomorrow* (1978), p. 17.
11 Anthony Kenny, *A Path from Rome*, p. 207.
12 Letter to *The Times* (3 June 1985).

13 See, for instance, Hume's articles in *The Times*: 'Arms and Poverty: the Christian Choice' (3 January 1980); 'Why Warnock is Wrong' (6 June 1985); also David Sheppard, 'The Poverty that Imprisons the Spirit', 1984 Richard Dimbleby Lecture, *Listener* (19 April 1984); David Jenkins, 'The God of Freedom and the Freedom of God', Hibbert Lecture, *Listener* (18 April 1985).

CHAPTER 42 (pages 660–71)

1 Philip Toynbee, *Part of a Journey* (1981), pp. 397–8.
2 Iremonger, *William Temple*, p. 371.
3 Welsby, *A History of the Church of England*, p. 241.
4 Timothy Finn, *Knapworth at War* (1982), p. 46.
5 See, for instance, Lord Gardiner's speech at the unveiling of a plaque to More in Westminster Hall, 13 March 1968; or a leading article in *The Times* (7 February 1978).
6 Henson, *Letters*, p. 26.
7 Iremonger, *William Temple*, p. 419.
8 Graham Greene, *Monsignor Quixote* (1982).

INDEX

INDEX

INDEX